SECOND EDITION

NEW PERSPECTIVES
ON THE AMERICAN PAST

1607–1877

SECOND EDITION

NEW PERSPECTIVES ON THE AMERICAN PAST

VOLUME I: 1607–1877

Edited by STANLEY N. KATZ
The University of Chicago

STANLEY I. KUTLER
The University of Wisconsin

 LITTLE, BROWN AND COMPANY *Boston*

Contents

v

III
TENSION, DISRUPTION, AND
RECONSTRUCTION: 1840–1877   309

Introduction

Historians traditionally have found it difficult to describe their work systematically. Until the late nineteenth century, practically everyone accepted the idea that history was a literary art, subject to aesthetic canons of judgment. But with the work of Leopold von Ranke and the other "scientific" historians who appeared at the end of the last century, new standards for research and writing came into vogue. History was conceived of as subject to precise definition and verification — for the first time, historians became professional men. When examined carefully, however, it is evident that the methodology of the early scientific historians consisted merely of the application of rigid testing to evidence in a manner analogous to the work of linguistic scholars. There was little that was conceptually distinctive in their attack upon the sources, and they were interested primarily in the political and military questions that had always been the substance of the craft.

The German historical school exerted the greatest influence in shaping the work of American historians at the beginning of the twentieth century. Universities throughout the United States adopted the seminar system of teaching and the Germanic method of rigorous research. The result was a tremendous step forward in our understanding of the American past. As doctoral dissertations were produced at Johns Hopkins, Harvard, Wisconsin, and other great universities, a more detailed and dispassionate picture of the development of the United States began to emerge. No longer were pious affirmations of national accomplishments and literary *tours de force* sufficient to command respect. Social and economic institutions, in particular, were analyzed logically and in detail, and most of the chauvinistic myths cultivated by nineteenth-century historians were discarded. Still, for all their descriptive and corrective attempts, historians had not developed many new analytical tools. For the most part, their histories were merely more painstakingly researched and less obviously self-serving.

Coincidentally with the emergence of scientific history, however, were other and more important intellectual events — in particular, the appearance of the social sciences as distinct and legitimate fields of intellectual effort. Psychology, sociology, and economics all date, in their modern garb, from this period. They had in common a desire to account systematically for human behavior, although in doing so they frequently — as in the work of

Freud — resorted to non-rational explanations. As the social sciences became increasingly professionalized and sophisticated, they developed a wide range of techniques, both empirical and intuitive, for investigating human activity. They were also, and this is more important from our point of view, truly scientific in their attitude — they sought to discover the general laws that govern the operation of natural phenomena. For the social scientist, empirical data, however derived, were important only insofar as they enabled him to make statements about individual and group behavior that expressed universal truths.

Until fairly recently — rarely before the Second World War — historians seldom accepted the standards of the social scientists. They prided themselves upon their accuracy, and they occasionally talked about historical laws, but they were not as a rule interested in using historical data in order to establish behavioral generalizations. They were concerned with particular and isolated problems rather than with the rules suggested by repeated problems. History remained, for the most part, a humane and literary discipline provincial in its isolation from other disciplines.

During the past twenty years or so, however, there has appeared a generation of historians who have recognized the importance and application of social science techniques to their own work. They believe that historical data can be employed in the same fashion as experimental data in the establishment of laws of social behavior, and that historians must develop rigorous research methods and standards of proof. This movement toward amalgamation with the social sciences has had an impact upon methodology in three ways. It has evoked an interest in quantification in the search for scientifically measurable historical data. It has, in a somewhat related fashion, led to a behavioral approach at the expense of the study of thought and other less obviously behavioral phenomena. And, finally, social scientific history is characterized by its primary concern with conceptualization, since social historians are less interested in describing isolated historical events than in verifying hypotheses about conduct. In short, where traditional history is primarily descriptive, the new history is oriented toward the establishment of behavioral laws.

Historians have certain obvious liabilities as scientists. They cannot, in any real sense, design and perform experiments. The subjects of their investigation are, for the most part, dead and no longer capable of responding to inquiry. They deal with very limited quantities and types of evidence, and their evidence is frequently not easily adaptable to systematic analysis, quantitative or otherwise.

In spite of these difficulties, historians are increasingly interested in broadening the scope of their effort in the direction of the more rigorous social sciences. Some are becoming extremely adept in the use of quantification and computer techniques, and their work is sufficiently sophisticated so that they call themselves "cliometricians." Economic history has, for obvious reasons, gone farthest down the road of machine analysis. Other historians have begun to "retool" themselves in the techniques of the social sciences. African historians, among others, employ the tools of anthropologists. Social historians are becoming increasingly interested in the possibilities of demographic analysis. The motivational and behavioral discoveries of the psychologist are of obvious interest to anyone who tries to explain why men acted as they did in the past. And, in a more general sense, many historians have become more optimistic about the conceptual possibilities of their craft. They are determined to move beyond description and particularism to the investigation of behavioral — and other — rules. At the very least, the impact of the social sciences has been to make all historians question the character and relevance of their time-honored practices.

Many of the essays in these volumes reflect the new viewpoints, although they are primarily keyed to the traditional topical and chronological subjects of American history. The essays are not chosen to illustrate artificial historiographical debates, but rather to illuminate familiar problems by means of new viewpoints, methodologies, and analyses. As in all collections of readings, a good many subjects are omitted for lack of space or, more important, because of qualitative gaps in the historical literature. Each of the selections is reprinted in its entirety, including all of the footnotes.

History, like most other academic disciplines, is under tremendous pressure to be relevant. The conventional recital of facts, names, dates, and the arbitrary structuring of topics and periods — all fitted into neat, but isolated, compartments — simply lacks meaning for many of today's students. Making history relevant, of course, need not involve history as propaganda or result in a promiscuous use of the past to "prove" the validity of a present viewpoint. Nor are there necessarily great lessons from the past that can be applied to the present or the future. But a comprehension of human behavior at given points and under certain conditions affords insight into similar contemporary experiences. Many of the authors included in these volumes would doubtless be amused or chagrined to discover the common company we have set them in, but we believe that they are all similar in the freshness of their approaches to the ancient problem of understanding man's past. They present a variety of perspectives on the American past, but they share something in their ambition to make it relevant to the present.

Note to the Second Edition

We have been most gratified by the reception of the first edition of this work. We also appreciate very much the kind and generous criticisms and suggestions that we have had from many historians. In the light of those comments, this new edition omits those articles which were thought too difficult for undergraduate instruction and adds essays to cover subject-matter and chronological gaps which existed in the original edition. The resulting emphasis is somewhat less on new kinds of history and more on the kind of discussions and excitement which permeate so much contemporary writing in American history. It has always been true that each generation writes its own history but it is the purpose of this collection to show that real progress has been made in recent years in the interpretation of the American past.

S. N. K.
S. I. K.

SECOND EDITION

NEW PERSPECTIVES
ON THE AMERICAN PAST

1607–1877

I
FROM COLONY TO
REPUBLIC: 1607–1789

The settlement of British colonies in North America created a series of complex problems which had to be solved if the new communities were to survive and prosper. Most basically, settlers had to be transported to the New World, where they required food, clothing, security, shelter, and means of productive employment. In the earliest years, survival itself was a struggle. Secondarily, the settlers had to regularize their relations with their sponsors in England and the royal authorities, and they had to agree upon methods for organizing their own lives in America. The first seventy-five years of settlement were therefore devoted to the establishment of basic institutions, such as governments and churches, and to the discovery of viable modes of economic and social behavior. These experiments were, however, complicated by the dangers (and opportunities) of a wilderness environment, by the need to form new communities only tenuously related to those left behind, and by the uncertainties created by England's internal struggles during the 1640's and 1650's and its failure to assert an effective, coherent imperial policy. Nevertheless, since they were left largely untroubled by outside intervention, the several colonies and multitudinous communities were able to evolve their own ways of life.

The problems of the eighteenth century were quite different. The ten colonies had developed into mature communities with settled forms of behavior and established modes of thought, although the predominantly British population of the continent responded in similar ways to common problems. By 1696 machinery had been perfected to stimulate colonial adherence to the commercial policy of mercantilism, which placed the colonists in an economically subordinate but nevertheless profitable relationship to the mother country. Colonial exports rose from £395,021 in 1700 to £1,151,698 in 1765, while imports increased even more sharply from £344,341 to £1,944,144. The resulting trade imbalance created problems, but they did not seem insuperable.

Thanks largely to their participation in a series of Franco-British wars in the Western Hemisphere, the colonies became accustomed to co-operating with one another and, as intercolonial transportation and communication improved, the beginnings of a national community emerged. At the same time, the colonists modeled themselves increasingly upon a common object of admiration — an idealized notion of contemporary England.

By the middle of the eighteenth century, however, colonial society and its economy had developed to such an extent that the imperial bonds began to chafe. American maturity and self-awareness combined with domestic problems in England so that, under the pressures of the French and Indian Wars, the old values, patterns of behavior, and institutions came under attack from both sides of the Atlantic. Harsh new regulations of the colonial economy and a heightened awareness of the long-term implications of mercantilist trade imbalance combined to make colonists question the value of the imperial system. In a sense, they became disillusioned by what they took to be a decline in the character of English life and government. Simultaneously, colonial society was entering into a period of significant stress. Population was expanding rapidly, faster than territorial settlement, and the economy was thriving, but wealth was distributed ever more unevenly. A combined population of fifty thousand in 1650 rose to 250,000 in 1700, and had reached nearly three million by 1776. After 1750, there appeared for the first time a large group of propertyless, unrooted Americans as well as extraordinarily rich merchants and planters. Becoming aware of common interests, many contended for access to social, economic, and political power.

The American Revolution was the intersection of political-imperial and social change. Independence from Great Britain, though hard won, proved an easy solution to the problem of the imperial relationship. But the final quarter century saw a long-term struggle over the establishment of acceptable domestic institutions and social relationships. The nature of American society was not resolved during the eighteenth century, but the heritage of the colonial and revolutionary experience set the terms within which solutions would be broached. The political settlement symbolized by the Constitution of 1787 was thus only a token of the first stages of national development.

The *Apologia* of Robert Keayne

BERNARD BAILYN

Robert Keayne's portrait might well have served as the frontispiece for Max Weber's The Protestant Ethic and the Spirit of Capitalism. *Keayne was a well-to-do London merchant who came to Massachusetts Bay in 1635, at the height of the "Puritan" migration to the New World. Keayne's merchant enterprises flourished in Massa-*

chusetts, and he soon gained local respect and dignitary rewards. But the strenuousness of his efforts ultimately turned the community against him; he was tried for usury and drunkenness, and he died in the shade of disapproval. As Bernard Bailyn attempts to show, this reversal of public opinion was incomprehensible to Keayne, since it was totally unjustified. Keayne knew himself to be among the elect, and understood that one of the requirements of sanctification was to pursue his calling with unremitting vigor. Religion and commerce were all one for this the prototypical early modern businessman, but somehow the fulfillment of his personal and moral obligations conflicted with the corporate requirements of the community. For the past quarter-century most students of American Puritanism have followed in the footsteps of the late Perry Miller, who devoted his scholarly career to demonstrating that Puritanism was a complex, highly refined system of ideas, the product of "the New England mind." In recent years, however, historians have begun to analyze the social and economic structure of early New England society in such a way as to minimize, or even eliminate, the significance of religious ideas. The new scholarship treats Puritan behavior as typically preindustrial and charcteristically English or Anglo-American. Lost in the process are Miller's notions of the uniquely American quality of Puritanism and of the determining role of ideas in history. Bailyn's discussion of Keayne suggests one of the ways in which Puritan theology can be related to the actual conditions of life in early New England, an approach he also uses in his New England Merchants in the Seventeenth Century *(Cambridge, Mass., 1955). You may still wonder, however, whether there was anything identifiably American about Puritanism. Would Keayne have encountered similar difficulties had he remained a Cornhill merchant?*

"Though I have undergone many censures since I came hither," wrote Robert Keayne of Boston in 1653, "according to mens uncharitable and various apprehentions . . . I have laboured to beare it with patience and to approve my heart and wayes to God that judgeth righteously; yet these things hath made me the more willing to cleare myself in all material things in this my last testamt; though it be somewhat contrary to the nature of a will, yet I am willing to leave this upon publique record as a just defense for myself knowing that a will wilbe read and made knowne and may be p[er]used searched or coppied out by any when other writings wilbe more hid and obscured."[1] Three years later Robert Keayne

Reprinted by permission of the author and the publisher from *William and Mary Quarterly*, 3d Ser., 7 (1950), pp. 568–587.
[1] "THE LAST WILL AND TESTAMENT of me, Robert Keayne all of it written with my owne hands and began by me, Mo: 6: 1: 1653, Comonly called August," *Boston Record Commissioners Report*, X (Boston, 1886), 48 (257). (Hereafter referred to as "Last Will.") The original of this document is missing from the Suffolk County probate

was dead. When his executors came to open this Last Will and Testament they found not only a complicated allocation of his worldly goods but an outpouring of long suppressed indignation, a helter-skelter *apologia pro vita sua* and a reiterated demand that justice be done him even if only in memory. It had taken him five months to write out the document, and when the will was copied into the first volume of the probate records of Suffolk County it filled no less than 158 pages.

Robert Keayne has been remembered because one Goody Sherman insisted that the unpopular merchant had made off with her sow and because the magistrates in the General Court insisted on retaining a negative vote against the more numerous representatives who sided with Mrs. Sherman. The legislature of the Bay Colony thus came to sit in two bodies, and Robert Keayne found a place in American institutional history.[2] Here and there his name crops up in other contexts: as the founder of the Ancient and Honorable Artillery Company,[3] as one of the earliest in the tradition of New England's public benefactors,[4] and as a first generation American businessman.[5] More important, R. H. Tawney pointed out Keayne's condemnation on the charge of usury to illustrate the social controls of Puritanism.[6]

Yet when singled out these characterizations exemplify, as Carl Becker liked to quote from Voltaire, "the tricks we play upon the dead." Keayne was of course ignorant of his future place in the history of bicameralism, and though he took pains to maximize his generosity to town and college it was not his pride in these gifts that kept him adding page after page to his Will but rather the need to explain a series of episodes in his life that had taken place fourteen years earlier. The resulting 51,000 words provide an insight into the workings of a seventeenth-century mind. What he had "here writt out of the greife and trouble of my heart" was an appeal to the Puritan conscience of New England to reconsider its "unchristian, uncharitable and unjust reproaches and slandrs" against him, and raised the hope "that such which have taken liberties to load me with divers reproaches and long to lay me under a darke cloude may have cause to see that they have done amisse and now to be sorry for it though they have not beene so before."[7] By the time Keayne had finished the Will he had received the main incidents in his life, had rewarded the just and punished the evil-doers and had given to history a picture of the man of business twisting in the confines of Puritan ethics.

---

records, but a handwritten copy dated 1892 is in the Suffolk County Court House. Since more than three of the original folio pages are printed on each page of the *Report* I shall place in parentheses after each reference the page numbers as they appeared in the missing volume. Both the *Report* and the Suffolk Court House copy include these original page numbers. The spelling and punctuation throughout is from the *Report*.

[2] Samuel Eliot Morison, *Builders of the Bay Colony* (Boston, 1930), 92–93; for a different interpretation see Charles M. Andrews, *The Colonial Period of American History* (New Haven, 1934), I, 452.

[3] O. A. Roberts, *History of the . . . Ancient and Honorable Artillery Company of Massachusetts* (Boston, 1895), I, 1–21.

[4] Carl Bridenbaugh, *Cities in the Wilderness* (New York, 1938), 81, 131.

[5] N. S. B. Gras and H. M. Larson, *Casebook in American Business History* (New York, 1939), 52–61.

[6] R. H. Tawney, *Religion and the Rise of Capitalism* (New York, 1926), 128–131.

[7] "Last Will," 29 (202), 27 (196), 47 (255).

I

The man who later boasted that he emerged triumphant from financial losses "sufficient to have broken the backe of any one man in the Country," was born the son of a butcher in Windsor, Berkshire County, England, in 1595.[8] He received "no portion from my parents or friends to begin the world withal,"[9] and at the age of ten he was apprenticed for eight years to John Heyfield of Birchin Lane, London.[10] Keayne thus spent his formative years in and around that center of commercial activity, the Cornhill district, remaining there until his departure for New England in 1635. In the atmosphere of trade and competition Keayne flourished, and in his twentieth year he was admitted to the freedom of the Merchant Tailors' company.[11] Two years later he married Anne Mansfield.[12] The marriage was a fortunate one, as it brought Keayne into an established family and linked him with a brother-in-law, the Reverend John Wilson, who was one of the powerful spirits of early Massachusetts.

By 1623 he was being called "gentleman," had attained the freedom of the city, and had capped his social activities by being accepted a member of the Honourable Artillery Company of London.[13] Four children were born to Anne Keayne before 1625, but of these only Benjamin, the eldest, survived infancy.[14]

During the 1620's Keayne first directed his attention to New England. He was one of the adventurers behind the Plymouth Colony and consequently one of the forty-two men listed by Bradford as having been bought out by Isaac Allerton's "bargen" of 1626.[15] That Keayne's interest in the movement was not entirely financial may be gathered from a manuscript volume of sermon notes in his hand dated June, 1627–August, 1628. Two other such volumes, written during his New England years, also attest a constant concern with the church and, if not a deep piety, at least a conscientious attention to what transpired in service and meeting.[16]

By 1634 Keayne had become associated with the Massachusetts Bay Company and had probably invested £100 in the venture. In that year the General Court

[8] *Ibid.*, 16 (162); Roberts, *Artillery Company*, 12.

[9] "Last Will," 47 (255).

[10] Apprentice Book of the Merchant Taylors' Company, quoted in letter of A. A. Folsom to H. F. Waters, *Historical Collections of the Essex Institute*, XXVIII (1891), 84n.

[11] Freeman's Book of the Merchant Taylors' Company, quoted in letter of Folsom to Waters, *Historical Collections of the Essex Institute*, XXVIII, 84n.

[12] *Allegations for Marriage Licenses . . . London*, II (*Publications of the Harleian Society*, XXVI), 51. H. F. Waters, "Genealogical Gleanings," *Historical Collections of the Essex Institute*, XXVIII, 83.

[13] G. Goold Walker, *The Honourable Artillery Company of London* (London, 1926), 42–43; G. A. Raikes, ed., *The Ancient Vellum Book of the . . . Artillery Company* (London, 1890), 35.

[14] Waters, "Genealogical Gleanings," 83n. For the remarkable career of Benjamin's daughter Anna see Edmund S. Morgan "A Boston Heiress and Her Husbands: A True Story," *Publications of the Colonial Society of Massachusetts*, XXXIV (*Transactions, 1937–1942*), 499–513.

[15] W. T. Davis, ed., *Bradford's History of Plymouth Plantation* (New York, 1908), 214–215.

[16] Two of these volumes are in the Massachusetts Historical Society, the third in the Rhode Island Historical Society. See *Proceedings of the Massachusetts Historical Society*, Second Series, IV, 313–314; V, 435; L, 204–207.

appealed to him for further support.[17] He had been consulted in the pricing of certain arms about to be sent to the colony,[18] and about the same time shipped to Boston the sizeable gift of weapons and goods donated to the Puritans by John Wilson's brother Edmund.[19]

Just why the prosperous merchant chose to emigrate to New England in 1635 is not clear. The questionable supposition that Keayne left wholly for religious reasons is given a certain credence by Winthrop's remark that Keayne had "come over for conscience' sake, and for the advancement of the Gospel here."[20] But it is most unlikely that the man who wrote the Last Will and Testament of 1653 could have left England without carefully calculating his economic opportunities.[21] Certainly Keayne was not indifferent to the fact that God would prosper the righteous and industrious in this promised land.

Whatever the immediate cause for their departure, "Robert Keayne 40: Anne Keayne 38: Ben. Keayne 16" embarked on the *Defence* July 17, 1635, having previously been certified by their ministers and justices as to "their Conformitie and ht they are no subsedy man."[22] Once in Boston the merchant quickly settled into the little society. He established himself on the south-west corner of Cornhill (now Washington) and King (now State) streets in the heart of the town. His house was separated by one lot from the First Church and faced the central market square.[23] He had brought over with him "two or 3000 lb in good estate of my owne."[24] A few months after his arrival he was listed by the Boston Town Meeting as having contributed £5 toward building a strong battlement on Fort Hill,[25] and in March of the following year he was officially accepted by the community when he was received into the brotherhood of the First Church.[26]

A reputation for sharp dealing and heartlessness in business had preceded him

---

[17] Frances Rose-Troup, *The Massachusetts Bay Company and Its Predecessors* (New York, 1930), 8, 99, 147.

[18] "Pincheon Papers," *Collections of the Massachusetts Historical Society*, Second Series, VIII, 230.

[19] N. B. Shurtleff, ed., *Records of the Governor and Company of the Massachusetts Bay in New England* (Boston, 1853), I, 128 (hereafter referred to as *Massachusetts Records*). Savage's identification of the donor as William Wilson, John's brother, is incorrect. See James Savage, *Genealogical Dictionary . . . of New England* (Boston, 1862), IV, 584; also *New England Historical and Genealogical Register*, XXXVIII (1884), 306.

[20] J. K. Hosmer, ed., *Winthrop's Journal* (New York, 1908), I, 316.

[21] His investment in the company entitled him to a land grant in New England, which he quickly claimed. Besides his town plot, which he evidently received shortly after his arrival, Keayne was granted 400 acres in 1639. This was the first of a series of land transactions that continued throughout his life. See Mellen Chamberlain, *Documentary History of Chelsea* (Boston, 1908), I, Ch. XIX.

[22] Roberts, *Artillery Company*, I, 12*n*; James Savage, "Gleanings for New England History," *Collections of the Massachusetts Historical Society*, Third Series, VIII, 270.

[23] George Lamb, comp., *Series of Plans of Boston . . .* (supp. to *Boston Record Commissioners Report*, II [Boston, 1905]), plan of 1640. A good indication of the value of this location will be found in *Winthrop's Journal*, I, 318–319, where Winthrop describes the tradesmen's opposition to building the new meeting house elsewhere.

[24] "Last Will," 47 (255–256).

[25] *Boston Town Records* (in *Boston Record Commissioners Report*, II), 8.

[26] Records of the First Church of Boston, 8. Manuscript copy in Massachusetts Historical Society.

to the New World. In 1639 Winthrop wrote that the "corrupt practice of this man . . . was the more observable, because he was wealthy and sold dearer than most other tradesmen, and for that he was of ill report for the like covetous practice in England that incensed the deputies very much against him."[27] Until his death in 1656, however, despite unpopularity and repeated controversies with his fellow citizens, Robert Keayne continued to fill responsible public positions. He held his earliest public office in 1636, when the Boston Town Meeting elected him to a committee charged with the ordering of all land allotments and other business except elections.[28] In the years that followed he was reelected selectman four times, chosen as a representative to the General Court at least seven times and served in innumerable lesser functions such as surveyor of the highways.[29]

Keayne's first activities in New England were colorless enough, but in November, 1639, only three years after his arrival, both church and state struck down the ambitious merchant. This blow to his pride and reputation he felt throughout his life. In drawing up his Will he returned again and again to the events of 1639 as if to ease the pain of that "deepe and sharpe censure that was layd upon me in the Country and carried on with so much bitterness and indignation of some contrary both to law or any foregoing president if I mistake not and I am sure contrary or beyond the quallity and desert of the complaynts that came against me."[30] Keayne had been charged with "taking above six-pence in the shilling profit; in some above eight-pence; and, in some small things, above two for one."[31] The General Court calculated this sin at £200, but the following May the fine was reduced to £80.[32] The Church then took up the matter. The Elders studied "how farr I was guilty of all those claymors and rumors that then I lay under," and after an "exquisite search" into Keayne's defence, they dismissed him with a severe admonition.[33] He was condemned "in the Name of the Church for selling his wares at excessive Rates, to the Dishonor of Gods name, the Offence of the Generall Cort, and the Publique scandall of the Cuntry." Keayne lived under this ban until the seventh of May following, when, "upon his penetentiall acknowledgment thereof this day and prmise of further satisfaction to any that have just offence against him, He is now become Reconciled to the Church."[34]

The merchant protested in his Will, however, that this account, written into the records of state and church and accepted by the community as true, was a

---

[27] *Winthrop's Journal*, I, 316.

[28] *Boston Town Records*, 11.

[29] R. F. Seybolt, *The Town Officials of Colonial Boston* (Cambridge, 1939), 6–15; *Collections of the Massachusetts Historical Society*, Second Series, X, 23–24.

[30] "Last Will," 27 (196).

[31] *Winthrop's Journal*, I, 315.

[32] *Massachusetts Records*, I, 281, 290. Keayne later wrote of the fine, that there were some, who if they "could have had yr wills they would have had the fyne mounted up to 1000 lb yea 500 lb was too little except some corporal punishment was added to it, such as my mans [sic] standing openly one a market day with a Bridle in his mouth or at least aboute his necke, as I was credibly informed. Here was well guided zeale." "Last Will," 34 (216).

[33] "Last Will," 34 (218).

[34] Records of the First Church, 12, 14.

fabric of malicious falsehoods. Instead of a sharp-dealing sinner, Keayne saw himself an honest tradesman who had been savagely libelled by his personal enemies.

> It was the greife of my soule (and I desire it may ever so be in a greater measure) that any act of mine (though not justly but by misconstruction) should be an occasion of scandall to the Gospell and pfession of the Lord Jesus or that my selfe should be looked at as one that had brought any just dishonor to God (which I have endeavored long and according to my weake abilitie desired to prvent) though God hath beene pleased for causes best knowne to himselfe to deny me such a blessing, and if it had beene in my owne power I should rather have chosen to have prished in my cradle than to have lived to such a time.[35]

The truth of the matter, Keayne insisted, was that he had sold a bag of sixpenny nails at the moderate mark-up of two pence, by no means a "haynous sine" or even an unusual practice. But the purchaser[36] (who becomes the devil of this tale), found the nails too small for his use and exchanged them for some of the eight-penny variety. The merchant charged him ten pence a pound and changed the "8" in his account book to "10." For a period of years Keayne continually requested his payment, but finally when the buyer could "for shame keepe the money no longer" he brought Keayne into court on the "quarreling exception and unrighteous complaint" that he had bought only six-penny nails and that Keayne had "corrupted my booke in adding more to the prize than I had set down for them at first delivery."

The buyer was almost successful in sustaining this charge until the messenger who had delivered the second bag of nails testified on Keayne's behalf. But by this time, other busy people were at work, and charges for over-pricing a bridle, "great gold buttons," and a skein of thread were also levelled against him. Keayne wrote that all of these accusations were as false as the first one, but the chief malcontent had won over enough of the court to convict him. The censure was passed, however, "against the desire and judgment of allmost the greatest number of the cheifest and wisest of the Magistrates and Deputies." As for the church conviction, "lesse they could not doe, without some offence, considering what had passed before against me. . . ."[37]

To Keayne's apparent amazement, the accuser next claimed that his father in England had sent him £200 by Keayne which he had never received. The merchant protested the statement as an outright lie: he had returned the sum long before leaving England. But how was one to find proof for this ancient transaction, "it being soe long agoe and things much out of minde and many things passing through my hands in so great a remoovall from on[e] Country to another"?[38] But when it became clear that the fellow not only intended to have

---

[35] "Last Will," 34 (217).
[36] Keayne identifies this person only as one of the magistrates at the time of the trial. One may also conclude from the Will that: (1) he did not leave England before 1634; (2) he probably lived in the London area before that time; (3) he became interested in trade while in New England. From these hints, and especially from the characters of the two men, I would guess Keayne's adversary — assuming that he is not a creation of the merchant's imagination — to have been Richard Bellingham.
[37] "Last Will," 28 (201).
[38] "Last Will," 32 (211).

him severely punished for something he had not done, but also "to make me pay that 200 lb twise over," Keayne applied himself with increased zeal in searching and at last found a full and clear receipt for the money. Backed by this evidence the long-suffering tradesman turned on his accuser and demanded indemnity for slander and injuries. But the Reverend Mr. Cotton advised him to forbear because of his recent troubles, and await a more seasonable time for the counter-suit.

A meeting of some of the most honored citizens was later held at the house of Keayne's friend Captain William Tyng, and Governor Winthrop indicated that he would move the General Court to revoke the original conviction. But since death kept Winthrop from fulfilling his promise, Keayne admonished the overseers of the Will to see that justice was done.

In 1642 the unpopular merchant was again haled through the courts in the famous "sow case."[39] The charges against him were weak, but the controversy over whether or not Keayne had robbed Mrs. Sherman of her sow was soon dwarfed by the refusal of the deputies to abide the "negative voice" of the magistrates.[40] The separation of the houses, in fact, came about when Keayne's countersuit for slander, successful before an inferior tribunal, was appealed to the General Court.

Keayne's public activities in the five years following this episode seem to have reached their zenith. As selectman and representative he served on innumerable committees, was active in several large land deals, became involved in the Lynn iron works, sat in judgment on several petitions and throughout the period carried on his mercantile interests. His son became one of his London agents, and his trade with the West Indies continued.[41]

Yet misfortune continued to nag after him. In the May Court of 1646 he was fined for being absent at the appointed time. To this indignity the merchant replied that "he would pay five pounds as soone as 6d, for which affront he was fined twenty shillings." It was only "upon his acknowledgment of his miscarriage therein" that the Court remitted this second fee.[42] Keayne's son finally went back to England after the "evill carriages"[43] of his wife Sarah Dudley that resulted in her banishment from the Church. Her offence, recorded in the church minutes for October 24, 1647, was not only "Irregular prophecying" but also "falling into odious, lewd, and scandalous uncleane behavior with one Nicholas Hart an Excommunicate pson of Taunton."[44]

It was in 1652 that Keayne came into final and definitive disgrace. The previous year the fifty-six year old tradesman had been elevated to his most important public post. Considering the "great concourse of people and increase of trade" that clogged the Suffolk County court, the colony had created an inferior tribunal

---

[39] Most of the documents bearing on the case are printed in A. P. Rugg, "A Famous Colonial Litigation," *Proceedings of the American Antiquarian Society*, New Series, XXX (1920), 217–250.

[40] Andrews writes, " . . . the weight of the evidence is clearly on Keayne's side." *Colonial Period*, I, 450.

[41] *Aspinwall Notarial Records (Boston Record Commissioners Report*, XXXII [Boston, 1903]), 92; *Winthrop Papers*, (Boston, 1947), V, 185, 224–226.

[42] *Massachusetts Records*, III, 65, 69.

[43] "Last Will," 38 (227).

[44] Records of the First Church, 25.

to try civil cases amounting to less than £10 within the town of Boston. Keayne was one of the seven men appointed to this judicial position.[45] But shortly thereafter, shocking reports reached the ears of the magistrates. By June of 1652 the situation was bad enough to warrant an official inquiry, and the damning evidence was heard before a clerk of the General Court. Two of Keayne's former servants said that they had seen their employer staggering home from Charlestown in the company of one Thomas Lake. They swore that "we saw Captaine Kayne . . . to be full of beere or wyne." The two men, they continued, "led one another for they both fell downe together; and [though?] the weather was frost and snow . . . wee apprehend that hee was full of drink till wee be otherwise satisfied."[46] Joseph Armitage had a similar tale to tell.[47] The testimony of Johana Joy must have been even more convincing. She recalled an evening in a neighbor's house when she saw Keayne "to be much overcome with drink for as he went towards the fyre to take a cole to light a pipe of tobacco he reeled with his head soe forward that she was afraid he would have falne into the fyre." When he finally got the coal "he assayed to take his tobacoe soe unseemly that did plainly declare him to be much in drink." Her husband and a friend concurred in this opinion, and added that "they sawe him butt his head against the james [?] of the chimney as he sate by it and in lighting his pipe he slavered in a beastly or unseemly manner." And, they continued, when Keayne went outside "as he stood upp against the pale he stood nodding his head against the said pales as not being able to stand upright."[48]

The case against the unhappy Keayne was complete, and the Puritan Commonwealth wasted no time in showing him the cost of such miserable "carriages." On May 31, 1652, the General Court pronounced the following sentence:

> Whereas Capt Robt Keayne beinge acused to this Court for drunkenes, the evidences having been perused, and findinge that he is proved to have been three times drunke and to have drunke to excesse two times, for which offenses the Court doth fine him thirty six shillings and eyght pence.[49]

To this was added the fifty-five shillings two pence which the Court had paid in expenses to the witnesses. This time the merchant made no effort to challenge the legislative authority. Instead, he petitioned to resign his place on the Boston tribunal. The members promptly agreed, "as judging him not meet to contynue therein."

II

Keayne's Will would be of interest if it only contained the strange version of the 1639 usury trial. But it is a document of considerable historical value for the picture it supplies of the mind of a Puritan merchant.

The word that expresses best the most basic activity of Keayne's mind is *calculation*. The veil through which he saw the world was not so much colored

[45] *Massachusetts Records*, III, 244–245.
[46] Massachusetts Archives, XXXVIII b, 72 b.
[47] *Ibid.*, 71 b.
[48] Massachusetts Archives, XXXVIII b, 71 c.
[49] *Massachusetts Records*, III, 278.

as calibrated. It was *quantity* that engaged his imagination. The Will shows numerous instances of Keayne's mind working in abstractions or normative judgments and slipping unconsciously into quantitative measurements. After requesting his executors to petition the General Court for a reconsideration of his case, he wrote: "and were it possible for me to know it [his vindication] certainly before I dye (though it be not for love of the money, nor for addition to my estate by it, though it was a considerable sume about Eighty pounds as I remember) it would much ease and refresh my spirit in respect of the equity of it."[50]

Consider the system Keayne worked out to organize his charity. Although one does not expect to find examples of spontaneous self-impoverishment in the records of the seventeenth-century merchants, the calculations implicit in Keayne's "gift to the poore" are striking.

> Now for this 120 lb. before mentioned I am bound to acknowledge and to leave this testimony behinde me concerning it and how I came by it, for I doe not account it properly my owne nor simply my gift to the poore now but theire due and debt as that which for these many years, long before I came out of Old England, I began to gather and devote to God . . . which stocke I have gathered and from weake to weake layd apart by taking one penny out of every shilling which I have gotten by my trade . . . so that when I gayned much in a weeke there hath beene the more layd aside for any good use and when trayding hath beene dead and the gaines lesse there hath beene the lesse layd a syde for this stocke and use . . . by which meanes I have had comonly lyeing by me 50 lb. 60 lb. or 80 lb. ready money especially in old England and some pretty quantity here, till more lately since hath beene so scarce amongst us whereby I have been fayne to borrow out of that stock my selfe for my owne necessary use and occasions when I have wanted money of my owne, and a good comfortable helpe it hath beene to me that way in many pinches but doe still keepe a carefull account what at any time I take out and pay it in againe as money comes to hand.[51]

Besides the sums he gave away, he lent money from this fund to "any poore godly Christian or Minister in neede." Sometimes he had adventured part of it to sea, "that the benefitt of it might redound to the stocke for the poores use."

Consider also the account books he described to his executors. They were first told of an "Inventory booke . . . in which particulars of my whole estate from yeare to yeare, with all that I owe and all debts that are owing to me is breifly set downe under my own hand". Then there was a "Receipt booke of moneyes that I have payd fro time to time," in which he had located the missing receipt of 1639; a "Day booke of what I buy or sell"; a "pocket booke . . . of my dayly or weekely expences and charges for Dyett, Apparell, housekeeping which is sumed up every weeke from yeare to yeare and what ev'y weekes charges amounts to . . . what is payd to bakers, butchers shops, carting of wood, rates and divrs such charges." The overseers of the Will were also to note "2 other bookes bound up in Vellam in my Closet at Boston which I call Number bookes which were

[50] "Last Will," 30 (205).
[51] "Last Will," 12 (149–150).

of use when I kept shop in London and here." Also of importance were his debt books, "of which there is cheifly Three in use, namely one bound in Browne Vellam . . . , the other . . . I call the new Debt booke, the third . . . is called my booke of creditor and Debitor." At his farm the executors would find "a long paper booke bound in parchment . . . which I keepe locked up for my owne use, which is the pticulrs of the charges and profitts that I make of my ffarme ev'y yeare." And since he had at one time the supervision of rents from certain holdings of his London relatives he described a rent book in his possession as well as various out-dated account files, a variety of boxes stuffed with bills and papers, and two cash containers with ennumerated contents.[52]

In this absorption with figuring and cataloguing Keayne was little different from most successful business men of his time. The calculating trait was not restricted to business, however, but found ample expression in his religious life:

> happy yea more happy would it have beene for me if I had beene as carefull and as exact in keeping an account of my sinnes and the debts that I owe to God and of that spirituall estate between God and my owne soule [as he has been in keeping his business accounts] *that I could as easily have made it appeare to others or to my selfe when I gained or when I lost* and to have taken as much paines this way as in the other, which though I cannot truly say I have altogether neglected or omitted, yet comparatively I may justly say I have beene greatly deficient in that one thing necessary.[53]

At one point he declared that his whole life had been recorded in one or another of his accounts "since I was a Prentice . . . [and] now wilbe exposed to the view of others and there censure, when they wilbe p'[er]used after my death."[54] The implication was that righteousness can be measured, catalogued; it took only simple arithmetic to separate the saints from the sinners.

Next to calculation, the attitude most characteristic of Keayne was his timidity before public opinion. Fear of unpopularity is obvious on almost every page of the Will which, it will be recalled, was written to rescue his reputation from the darkness into which it had been cast by the trials of 1639. Keayne examined every possibility of being held in public disrepute. He charged his executors to administer his will most carefully, that there may be no "report that I have given away more than my estate will beare and that I have made a great show of charite, and have nothing or not enough to perform it with."[55] When he left £300 for a water conduit and a town house, he anticipated a charge that he did so to increase the value of his own property.[56] As he listed his bequests to the poor, he explained why he had not made these gifts before.[57] He finally declared his intention to make no great show of charities, "least some should approach me with an affectation and vaine glory."[58]

---

[52] "Last Will," 2 (121), 39–40 (231–233), 41 (236), 39 (231), 41 (236–237), 40 (235), 41–42 (238), 12 (151).
[53] *Ibid.*, 42–43 (240–241). Italics added.
[54] *Ibid.*, 48 (258).
[55] *Ibid.*, 3 (122), 43 (242–243).
[56] *Ibid.*, 9–10 (141 ff). E.g. "now what private ends or advantage can anyone apprehend I can have in that when I am dead?"
[57] *Ibid.*, 15 (160–161).
[58] *Ibid.*, 43–44 (244–245).

Keayne's mind was tenacious and unforgiving. He recalled injuries done him in the past which he had never repaid. For her scandalous behavior his ex-daughter-in-law, Sarah Dudley, was left no inheritance and forbidden to share in her own daughter's portion.[59] His brother-in-law, John Mansfield, he left not a farthing, because this ungrateful relative had plagued him constantly despite all Keayne's generosity.[60] Among the many minor gifts is the following:

> Item I give unto our Brother Renolds shoomaker senior Twenty shillings as a token of my respects to him if he be liveing two yeares after my decease not forgetting a word that he spake publiquely and seasonably in the time of my distresse and other mens vehement opposition against me.[61]

Nor did Keayne's religion desert him in justifying this hardness of heart toward his antagonists. In no less a person than Jesus he found sufficient precedent. "Our Savior remembers his disciples unkind forsaking of him and flying from him in so great a tyme of need," Keayne reminded his readers. Likewise, Jesus "keeps in memory and records the unkind usage of many Citties and Townes and the injuryes that he received of his unthankfull countrymen to his dying day." In fact, "the Scriptures are full of example[s]."[62]

After "renowncing all manner of knowne errors, all Popish and Prelaticall superstitions, all Anabaptisticall inthusiasms and Familisticall delusions, with all other fayned devises, and all Old and New upstart opinions, unsound and blasphemous errors, and other high imaginations," Keayne expressed his personal creed — an unsophisticated statement of certain aspects of Calvinist doctrine. He desired

> from my heart to renownce all confidence and expectation of merritt or desert in any of the best duties or services that ever I shall or can be able to prform acknowledging that all my righteousness, sanctificon and close walking with God if it were or had bin a thousand times more exact than ever I attayned too, is all polluted and corrupt and falls short of comending me to God in point of my justification.

Though he deserved nothing at God's hand "but Hell and Condemnation" he believed his "wayes of holynesse . . . may not be neglected . . . without great Sinne," for they were "ordained of God for me to walke in them carefully," and were to be considered as "good fruites and evidences of justification." His conclusion was, "therefore renowncing though not the Acts yet all confidence in those Acts of holynesse and workes of Sanctification performed by me, I look for my acceptance with God and the Salvation of my soule only from the merritts

---

[59] *Ibid.*, 37–38 (226–227).
[60] *Ibid.*, 25–26 (192–194). Mansfield, it seems, had pursued him "with continuall complaynts to our Eldrs and others seeking to pull a maintenance out of my estate whilst himselfe lived idlie . . . he would have cutt my throate with his false accusations if it had lyen in his power . . . besides he owes me betweene 20 and 30 lb . . . for 16 or 20 lb of which I have his Bond. . . . All my kindnes hath been putt into a broken bagg."
[61] *Ibid.*, 24 (189).
[62] *Ibid.*, 36–37 (222–224).

of righteousness of the Lord Jesus Christ, and from the free bountifull and un-deserved grace and love of God in him."[63]

Such humility before an omnipotent God was, however, difficult for the merchant to maintain. On the next page in the Will he spoke of the hereafter where he should "receive according to the works that I have done in this life according as they have beene good or evill in the sight of God" as well as be rewarded from the "full grace and merits of the Lord Jesus Christ."[64] Protesting his innocence, he expanded the idea of earthly rewards for holy mortals.

> I have and shall still committ my cause and cry to him [God] for right and I have many testemonyes in my spirit that he hath righted me therein, not only in the hearts and judgments of many men that knew and heard of those proceedings, but also in my very outward estate that thought [though?] some intended it for my great hurt, yet God hath beene pleased to turne it to my good so that I have not since fared the worse nor lost by it but hath since carryed me through many and great engagements with comfort.[65]

The merchant saw that God meted out reward or punishment according to his unfathomable intentions, but in the particular case of Robert Keayne God had clearly made known his pleasure. Despite the opinion of the community, the merchant had been provided with sound evidence of his sanctification. Keayne explained how God had helped him through a period of severe reverses. "I begin but now to breathe as it were and through the great mercy and unex-pected support and assistance of my good God to stand upon my owne leggs and doe but now as it were learne to goe alone."[66] This was no God of terror and inscrutable purposes, but one obviously interested in furthering the welfare of Robert Keayne, seeing to it that those who undervalued the righteous merchant were given proper punishment.

> Let such know that if they grow proud and high minded and scorne the kindnes and endeavors of othrs [read: Keayne] that desire to doe more good then themselves God can and it may be will bring such high spiritts into a lower frame and putt them into such a condition that they may stand in need of the helpe of as meane and as much dispised psons as my selfe before they dye.[67]

Toward the leaders of the church Keayne showed the highest respect, even insisting on space in his proposed town house for "a gallery or some other handsome Roome for the Elders to meete in."[68] And he provided a fund made up of the income from "some of my Shops in Boston" to supply the Elders with refreshments and occasional meals at their meetings.[69] But let the reverend min-isters, men of God though they be, tread warily where they had no business. Note the case of Reverend John Eliot: after the merchant had gone to the

[63] *Ibid.*, 1 (118–119).
[64] *Ibid.*, 2 (119).
[65] *Ibid.*, 29 (203).
[66] *Ibid.*, 16 (163).
[67] *Ibid.*, 27 (197).
[68] *Ibid.*, 4 (125).
[69] *Ibid.*, 6 (130).

trouble and expense of surveying and bounding new land which he had bought, and after the General Court had confirmed him in his ownership, the famous missionary had endeavored to reclaim the land for the Indians. Indeed, "he would not be taken off nor psuaded by any nay by none that spake with him about it to surcease his prosecution or endeavor to plucke it out of our hands againe for the Indians." The result of this "unsavory and offencive" conduct was that Keayne reconsidered his original bequest to aid the missionary work and left it to "larger and fuller purses to carry on this great and good worke amongst the Indians." It was at this point that Keayne made clear the boundary between the things of the spirit and those of the world.

> Therefore I would make it my request to the Reverend Eldrs of this Country not to be too stiffe and resolute in accomplishing theire owne wills and wayes but to harken to the advice and counsell of there brethren and to be as easily pswaded to yeeld in civill and earthly respects and things as they expect to prvayl with any of us, when they have a request to make to us for one thing or another, least by too much stiffnes, to have their owne wills and ways, they hinder many good workes that may be pfitable to themselves and to the whole Country.[70]

Though the subtleties of predestination translated themselves for the merchant into a conviction of election, though Christ became remarkably like Keayne in his relentless revenging of old injuries, and though Eliot's efforts to preserve a plot of land for the Indians was seen as at best an "unkinde carriage," nevertheless religion exerted a discipline on Keayne's mind and consequently on his actions. He felt the obligations of the stewardship of wealth, and the public donations in the Will testify that this was not mere verbiage. There was no question in his mind that the accumulation of wealth solely for personal use was sinful; neither, however, must one deny himself to effect the betterment of others. A nice balance should be reached wherein one strove for success in his calling, provided himself and family with a comfortable estate, yet discharged a standing obligation for the good of others.

In several unintentionally humorous sections of the Will Keayne displayed what may justly be called a guilty conscience concerning his money. He frankly set out to dispose of all possible objections to his righteousness that might arise from considerable success in trade. "Ffirst if I value my estate to be worth 4000 lb or thereabouts, how could I get such an estate with a good conscience or without oppression in my calling, seeing it is knowne to some that I had no portion from my parents"? He answered that he had "had good creditt and good esteeme and respect" wherever he had lived; that he had been "industrious and provident" and had not trusted "chapmen" or given "creditts"; that he had between two and three thousand pounds when he landed in America; and lastly he had not, after all, made such a vast fortune as to warrant a suspicion of corruption. "I have not cleared neare 100 lb a yeare above my expenses since I came hither which is not 5 lb. p cent cleare gaines."[71]

Although Keayne said that he was worth £4000, he had a tax rating of only

[70] *Ibid.*, 15 (158).
[71] *Ibid.*, 47–48 (255–256).

£1000, "or sometimes lesse." An explanation of this inconsistency caused Keayne considerable difficulty. He claimed that one need not declare his whole estate and be taxed to the limit "if he can honestly prvent it," and drew examples from common English practice to prove his point. He would injure himself unnecessarily if he declared all, because he would have to include much real estate, cattle and "household stuffe" which "are never valued to the uttermost worth to no man," and because much of the £4000 was in outstanding debts and goods still at sea, "which none can reckon as a sure and safe estate till God brings backe the returnes as wee finde by sad experience and losse."[72]

The world to Keayne was a battlefield where wills were pitted against each other: good against evil, malice against innocence, creditor against debtor. The weak and easily distracted fell to one side as the vigilant triumphed. Good intentions were not sufficient armament for life's battles. The weapon absolutely required for both worldly and spiritual success was effort, constant striving. What was most important for successful living was the grim persistence that refused to relent in the face of adversity. A relaxed enjoyment of life was suspect, and Keayne thus remarked that his many account books would

> testifye to the world on my behalfe that I have not lived an idle, lazie or dronish life nor spent my time wantonly, fruitlessly or in company keeping as some have beene too ready to asperse me or that I have had in my whole time either in Old England or New, many spare houres to spend unprofitably away or to refresh myselfe with recreations, *except reading and writing hath beene a recreation to me which sometimes is mixt with paine and labor enough,* but have rather studied and endeavored to redeem my time as a thing most deare and precyous to me and have often denyed myself in such refreshings that otherwise I might lawfully have made use of.[73]

III

If Keayne had been born a century and a half earlier his career might have been one of those studied by Sylvia Thrupp in her *Merchant Class of Medieval London.* Certain of the traits we find in the Boston merchant were exhibited by his occupational ancestors in London. These medieval businessmen trained their children in the exercise of prudence, and they grew up in an atmosphere of calculation. No less does calculation characterize the teachings of the fifteenth-century Florentine, Leon Battista Alberti.[74] Most successful men of business, whether Renaissance figures or Andrew Carnegies, have had minds that were rooted to external reality, preeminently practical and empirical.[75] Yet there is an important difference between the minds of the medieval and Renaissance merchants and that of Keayne. Miss Thrupp writes, "Although thoughts thus tended to gravi-

---

[72] *Ibid.*, 48 (258–260).
[73] *Ibid.*, 42 (240). Italics added.
[74] Werner Sombart, *The Quintessence of Capitalism,* trans. by M. Epstein (New York, 1915), 104–109.
[75] *Cf.* the excessively lyric preface to Bernhard Groethuysen's *Origines de l'esprit bourgeois en France* (I: *L'Eglise et la Bourgeoisie,* Paris, 1927), vii–xiii.

tate to the making of money the medieval merchant class does not seem to have generated a gospel of hard work. It was probably the practice to keep the apprentices well occupied in waiting upon customers and carrying messages, but there was no great pressure of office work to harass them, nor were they enjoined to spend all their days on earth at labor."[76]

One of the elements that had been added to the merchant's creed in the course of the sixteenth century was the supernatural sanction that rigorized and steeled the personality traits originally engendered by the bourgeois occupations. The prudence that had once been accepted for its utility and stiffened by habit and custom was now further reinforced by revelation. The virtues that Keayne displayed to a hostile community would not have displeased a medieval merchant, but his ancestor might have been surprised at the conviction and self-righteousness with which he buttressed his actions. Moreover, in the cities of the Old World the superior prestige values of gentility and nobility had tended to dilute the attractiveness of purely economic success,[77] but in the New England soil hereditary aristocracy, with its disdain for trade and the shopkeeper's acquisitiveness, found transplantation difficult if not impossible. Thus when we view Keayne's life in a larger perspective we find that the milieu of his society doubly intensified his business drive: by the support of its religion and by its weakening of the superior social values of gentility.

On the other hand, Keayne may also be distinguished from the medieval merchants by his intensified concern with the proper uses of wealth and with the religious limitations of his economic life. English Puritanism was, as Professor M. M. Knappen has pointed out, a movement of organized idealism.[78] The same body of religious precepts that had systematized the virtues making for business success checked their free play in behalf of the community good and the avoidance of the sins of self-indulgence and sensuality. It was to Keayne's intense chagrin that the community reminded him of his moral weakness.

What was demanded of the Puritan merchants, at least as represented in Keayne's career, was character strong enough to maintain its integrity in the face of this simultaneous stimulation and regulation. In a series of incidents from the trials of 1639 to the disgrace of 1652 Keayne showed his inability to keep these burdens in balance. As the possibilities of economic exploitation in the New World became apparent and the religious intensity slackened, the environment of northern society tended to magnify one aspect of the Puritan personality and minimize the other.

It might have been in the very year that Keayne wrote his Last Will and Testament that William Bradford, thumbing through the pages of his *Plymouth Plantation*, fell to musing on the disappointments of his life. When he came to his account of the year 1617 he read again the pledge of the Pilgrims to continue on as they were, "knite togeather as a body in a most stricte and sacred bond

[76] Sylvia L. Thrupp, *The Merchant Class of Medieval London* [1300–1500] (Chicago, 1948), 166–167.

[77] *Ibid.*, Chap. VI, "Trade and Gentility."

[78] M. M. Knappen, *Tudor Puritanism: A Chapter in the History of Idealism* (Chicago, 1939), preface, 341 ff.

and covenant of the Lord . . . straitly tied to all care of each others good, and of the whole by every one and so mutually." On the back of the page the old Pilgrim wrote an epitaph to those noble hopes:

> But (alas) that subtill serpente hath slylie wound in himselfe under faire pretences of necessitie and the like, to untwiste these sacred bonds and tyes, and as it were insensibly by degrees to dissolve, or in a great measure to weaken, the same. I have been happy, in my first times, to see, and with much comforte to injoye, the blessed fruites of this sweet communion, but it is now a parte of my miserie in old age, to find and feele the decay and want thereof (in a great measure), and with greefe and sorrow of hart to lamente and bewaile the same.[79]

The society Bradford had striven for did not anathemize the life of business, but placed it within a structure whose proportions, the Pilgrims were convinced, had been drawn by the hand of God. Looking back to Bradford from an age that celebrated Bruce Barton's *The Man Nobody Knows*, we are apt to find in Robert Keayne if not "that subtill serpente" at least one of the forces that pointed to the future.

Notes on Life in Plymouth Colony

JOHN DEMOS

Historians have pictured local communities in the seventeenth-century New England colonies as pious, hierarchical, and unchanging. They were run, we have been told, by an interlocking elite of religious and political leaders, and they were organized in a tightly controlled patriarchal fashion. Land, like authority, was carefully doled out so as not to diminish either the binding sense of community or the manipulative power of the elite. The social historian John Demos argues that, if Plymouth Colony is at all typical, this traditional conception of the static religious community is quite misleading. In Plymouth, land changed hands rapidly, men frequently moved from one dwelling place to another, and the community very quickly became dispersed and loosely organized. Furthermore, family groups were not dominant in this process of rapid social change; on the contrary, individual activity dominated in an extremely mobile society. Demos uses demographic techniques to demonstrate some of the salient characteristics of the Plymouth population: size of family, life expectancy, patterns of marriage. He

[79] *Bradford's History*, 55n.

shows how it is possible to move from apparently lifeless statistics to novel insights into patterns of courtship and marriage, family structure, and child rearing. Demos's training in sociological technique enables him to re-examine evidence that traditional historians have neglected or misinterpreted, and to exploit new types of historical source material. Demos and other historians currently studying colonial community life are making it possible for us to understand how seventeenth-century New Englanders lived, as well as how they thought and worshipped.

Our traditional picture of the earliest New England communities is essentially a still life. By emphasizing the themes of steadfast piety, the practice of the old-fashioned virtues, measured forms of civil government, and a closely-ordered social life, it suggests a placid, almost static kind of existence. We take for granted the moral and religious aims which inspired the founding of many of these communities; and we accept the assumption of the colonists themselves, that success in these aims depended on maintaining a high degree of compactness and closeness of settlement.

Yet, in the case of the Plymouth Colony at least, this picture is seriously misleading. It has served to obscure certain striking elements of movement and change — indeed, a kind of fluidity that is commonly associated with a much later phase of our national history. Individuals frequently transferred their residence from one house, or one town, to another. Land titles changed hands with astonishing rapidity. Families were rearranged by a wide variety of circumstances.[1]

These tendencies can be traced back to the first years of the settlement at Plymouth. Some of the original townspeople began to take up lots across the river in Duxbury even before 1630; among them were such prominent figures as John Alden, Myles Standish, Jonathan Brewster, and Thomas Prence. The process was accelerated by the arrival to the north of the settlers at Massachusetts Bay. An important new market for cattle and corn was thereby opened up, and the compact town of Plymouth was not large enough to meet the demand for increased production.[2] But the profits to be made from farming were probably not

Reprinted by permission of the author from the *William and Mary Quarterly*, 3d Ser., 22 (1965), pp. 264–286.

[1] Such conclusions, and the observations which follow, are based upon an examination of several sorts of records. Town and church records have been useful for determining certain vital statistics such as dates of birth, marriages, and deaths. Nathaniel B. Shurtleff and David Pulsifer, eds., *Records of the Colony of New Plymouth, in New England* (Boston, 1855–61), offers a broad picture of laws and law-breaking, and, less directly, of deeper social and economic forces at work in 17th-century Plymouth. Numerous genealogical studies provide many relevant dates and places, and are obviously indispensable for establishing family relationships. Land deeds reveal much about the economic and geographic layout of the colony; there are also other deeds relating to such things as marriage and apprenticeship. Finally, of particular importance are the wills, perhaps the prime source of information about family and community organization.

[2] See William Bradford, *Of Plymouth Plantation, 1620–1647*, ed. Samuel E. Morison (New York, 1952), 252–253.

the only, or even the major, stimulus to expansion. The land beckoned because it was empty; the colonists were excited simply by the prospect of ownership for its own sake.

In any case, by the mid-1630's this pattern of geographical expansion had become well established. In 1636 the town of Scituate was officially incorporated and began to send its own representatives to the General Court. Duxbury achieved a similar status the following year; and by 1646 seven other new towns had been established. The direction of the earliest expansion was north and south along the coast; then a westerly thrust began, which led to the founding of such towns as Taunton, Rehoboth, Bridgewater, and Middleborough, all well inland. Still other groups of people pushed onto Cape Cod; indeed, in the early 1640's there was a move to abandon the original settlement at Plymouth altogether and relocate the town on the outer cape. This proposal was finally defeated after much discussion in the meetings of the freemen, but some families went anyway, on their own, and founded the town of Eastham. By 1691, the year that Plymouth ended its independent existence and joined with Massachusetts Bay, it contained no less than twenty-one recognized townships, and many smaller communities as well.[3]

This steady dispersion of settlement caused considerable anxiety to some of the leaders of the colony, and sporadic efforts were made to keep it under control. On several occasions when new land was parceled out, the General Court directed that it be used only for actual settlement by the grantees themselves.[4] Also the Court criticized the unrestrained way in which lands were distributed by the freemen in certain of the newer townships. Grants were no longer confined to upright, religious-minded settlers. Towns accepted, with no questions asked, almost anyone who proposed to move in. Such was the charge leveled against the people of Sandwich, for example, in 1639. A similar situation seems to have prevailed in Yarmouth, for in 1640 the Court specifically directed the town elders there to require of each new arrival a "certificate from the places whence they come . . . of their religious and honest carriage."[5]

William Bradford was one of those to whom the process of dispersion came as a great disappointment; it runs through much of his famous history of Plymouth as a kind of tragic refrain. "This I fear will be the ruin of New Eng-

[3] Plymouth, 1620; Scituate, 1636; Duxbury, 1637; Barnstable, 1639; Sandwich, 1639; Taunton, 1639; Yarmouth, 1639; Marshfield, 1641; Rehoboth, 1645; Eastham, 1646; Bridgewater, 1656; Dartmouth, 1664; Swansea, 1667; Middleborough, 1669; Edgartown, 1671; Tisbury, 1671; Little Compton, 1682; Freetown, 1683; Rochester, 1686; Falmouth, 1686; Nantucket, 1687.

[4] See the terms of the grant to Charles Chauncey, John Atwood, and Thomas Cushman at Mattapoisett, in Plym. Col. Recs., II, 9. Also Bradford, Of Plymouth Plantation, ed. Morison, 253–254, where another kind of attempt to control expansion is described: "Special lands were granted at a place general called Green's Harbor" to "special persons that would promise to live at Plymouth, and likely to be helpful to the church or commonwealth and so [to] tie the lands to Plymouth as farms for the same; and there they might keep their cattle and tillage by some servants and retain their dwellings here." No sooner was the plan put into effect, however, than its beneficiaries demanded permission to move directly onto their new farms. "Alas," concludes Bradford, "this remedy proved worse than the disease."

[5] Plym. Col. Recs., I, 131, 142.

land, at least of the churches of God there," he wrote at one point, "and will provoke the Lord's displeasure against them." When the plan for moving the town to Eastham was debated, Bradford, and others of like mind, discerned the real motive behind the proposal: "Some were still for staying together in this place, alleging men might here live if they would be content with their condition, and that it was not for want or necessity so much that they removed as for the enriching of themselves." Finally, near the end of his work, with more and more of the original stock moving away, Bradford described Plymouth as being "like an ancient mother grown old and forsaken of her children, though not in their affections yet in regard of their bodily presence and personal helpfulness; her ancient members being most of them worn away by death, and these of later time being like children translated into other families, and she like a widow left only to trust in God. Thus, she that had made many rich became herself poor."[6] He could hardly have chosen a better metaphor. It is extremely telling as a literary device, and — more than that — is highly suggestive from a historical standpoint. It describes an experience that must have been quite real, and quite painful, for many Plymouth settlers. The whole process of expansion had as one of its chief effects the scattering of families, to an extent probably inconceivable in the Old World communities from which the colonists had come. This was particularly hard upon elderly people; their anxiety that they should be properly cared for in their old age is readily apparent in the wills they wrote. The flow of men into new areas was inexorable, but it took a profound psychological toll, even among those who were most willingly a part of it.

Nearly every category of person — young and old, rich and poor, immigrant and old settler — was involved in the expansion of the Plymouth community. The careers of the four Winslow brothers who arrived at various times during the early years of the colony may be regarded as more or less typical.[7] Kenelm Winslow came from England to Plymouth in 1629 and moved to Marshfield in 1641; Edward came in 1620 from Leyden and returned to England in 1646; John went from England to Leyden, to Plymouth, and in 1656 to Boston; and Josiah Winslow arrived in Plymouth from England in 1631, moved to Scituate in 1637, and then went from there to Marshfield. Although two of the sons of Kenelm Winslow remained in Marshfield on land that he bequeathed to them, another son moved to Yarmouth and the fourth one moved three times, to Swansea in 1666, to Rochester in 1678, and to Freetown in 1685. And third-generation Winslows could be found scattered among many different towns of Massachusetts and in other colonies as well. Nor did William Bradford's strong convictions on the matter of expansion prevent his own children from leaving Plymouth. His daughter married a Boston man; two sons moved to the neighboring settlement of Kingston; and a third led a large Bradford migration, mostly third generation, to Connecticut.[8]

The movers were often young men, but not invariably so. Indeed there were many who moved in middle age and with a large family. Experience Mitchell

[6] Bradford, *Of Plymouth Plantation*, ed. Morison, 254, 333–334.
[7] See David-Parsons Holton, *Winslow Memorial* . . . , I (New York, 1877).
[8] See Ruth Gardiner Hall, *Descendants of Governor William Bradford* (Ann Arbor, 1951).

and William Bassett, both of whom arrived in the early 1620's, were among the original proprietors — and residents — of three different towns. After several years in Plymouth they resettled in Duxbury (each one, by this time, with a wife and young children), and in the 1650's they went to Bridgewater.

For the most part, removals were arranged and carried out by individuals; they were not affairs of large groups and elaborate organization. Family ties were sometimes a factor, as in the case of the Connecticut Bradfords, but even here the pattern was rather loose. It was usually a matter of one man moving to a new community, and then several other members of his family following, separately and later on.

An obvious concomitant of such general mobility was a rapid rate of turnover in the ownership of land. In this connection the land deeds and proprietary lists that survive from the period become an important source. For example, there are two lists of proprietors for the town of Bridgewater, one made in 1645 at the time of its incorporation, and the other in 1682 when additional grants of land were being debated.[9] Of the fifty-six names on the first list only twelve reappear thirty-seven years later. To the latter group should be added five sons of original proprietors who had died in the meantime, making a grand total of seventeen men who retained their interest in Bridgewater. But this means that thirty-nine relinquished their holdings altogether, fully 70 per cent of the initial group. It is probable that some of them never lived in Bridgewater at all, acquiring rights there only in order to sell.

This pattern of land turnover is further exemplified by the varied transactions of certain individuals, as noted in the *Colony Records*. Samuel Eddy, a good case in point, came to Plymouth in 1630 as a young man of twenty-two. In the next fifty years he was involved in at least eighteen transactions for land and housing.[10] Presumably there were still more, of which no record remains, as in some cases we find him selling lands not previously identified as being in his possession. At least three times he seems to have moved his residence within Plymouth (selling one house in order to buy another, and as an old man he left the town altogether and went to Swansea in the western part of the colony. Two of his sons had already settled there, and he probably wished to be near them. A third son had gone to Martha's Vineyard; and a fourth, who seems to have been particularly restless, moved from Plymouth to Sandwich, to Middleborough, back to Plymouth, back to Middleborough, back to Plymouth, to Taunton, and back once more to Middleborough, over a period of some forty years.

Seven of Samuel Eddy's land transactions seem to have been directly connected with his changes of residence; the rest were for the purpose of enlarging his estate, or for profit. Eddy, incidentally, was a tailor by trade and not a rich man; most of the business in which he engaged was for relatively small amounts of land and money. The profit motive was equally clear in the dealings of many other Plymouth residents. Perhaps one more example will suffice. In June 1639

[9] "A Description of Bridgewater, 1818," in Massachusetts Historical Society, *Collections*, 2d Ser., VII (Boston, 1826), 137–176.

[10] Byron B. Horton, *The Ancestors and Descendants of Zachariah Eddy of Warren, Pa.* (Rutland, Vt., 1930), 29–31.

John Barnes bought four acres of meadowland from John Winslow for eight pounds and a month later resold them to Robert Hicks for nine pounds, fifteen shillings. Soon afterwards he made a similar deal in which he bought a parcel of land for twelve pounds and sold it within a few months for eighteen.[11]

It would be interesting to know more about the lives of these people, and the lives of their ancestors, before their migration to America. Perhaps there was more mobility among inhabitants of the English countryside than is commonly supposed.[12] Perhaps the first colonists at Plymouth were conditioned for change by their prior attempt to establish themselves in Holland. It is hard to say. In any case, the settlers were doubtless predisposed to conceive of wealth in terms of land, and the circumstances of Plymouth, where currency was so scarce and land so plentiful, probably strengthened this instinct. It is clear from the wills they left that their desire to process and to expand was usually satisfied. Even a man of relatively moderate means usually had several plots of land to deed away, and wealthy ones had as many as twelve, fifteen, or even twenty.[13] In some cases these holdings were located in a number of different townships — showing that their owners could not always have thought in terms of actual settlement at the time of acquisition.

It would be interesting to know how many people lived in Plymouth Colony during these years. Three scholars have offered guesses based on varying kinds of evidence.[14] Their findings do not agree, but suggest, when averaged together, that the total number of Plymouth residents was probably around 300 in 1630, and did not exceed 1,000 before the early 1640's. It had passed 3,000 by 1660, 5,000 by 1675, and by the time the colony had merged with Massachusetts probably stood somewhere between 12,000 and 15,000. The rate of growth, if not spectacular, was steady and fairly sharp; the population seems to have doubled about every fifteen years.

This growth was due, in part, to immigration but perhaps even more to certain characteristics of the people within the colony itself. For example, the popular impression today that colonial families were extremely large finds the strongest possible confirmation in the case of Plymouth. A sample of some ninety families about whom there is fairly reliable information, suggests that there was an average of seven to eight children per family who actually grew to adulthood. The number of live births was undoubtedly higher, although exactly how much

---

[11] *Plym. Col. Recs.*, XII, 45, 64–65, 69.

[12] For recent works directed to this point, see E. E. Rich, "The Population of Elizabethan England," *Economic History Review*, 2d Ser., II (1949–50), 247–265; and Peter Laslett and John Harrison, "Clayworth and Coggenhoe," in H. E. Bell and R. L. Ollard, eds., *Historical Essays, 1600–1750, Presented to David Ogg* (London, 1963), 157–184.

[13] See, for example, the wills of Samuel Fuller (Barnstable, 1683) and Thomas Cushman (Plymouth, 1690) in *Mayflower Descendant*, II (1900), 237–241; IV (1902), 37–42.

[14] See Richard LeBaron Bowen, *Early Rehoboth* . . . , I (Rehoboth, 1945), 15–24; Joseph B. Feet, "Population of Plymouth Colony," in American Statistical Association, *Collections*, I, Pt. ii (Boston, 1845), 143–144; and Bradford, *Of Plymouth Plantation*, ed. Morison, xi.

TABLE 1   *Size of Families in Plymouth*

	Average number of children born	Average number lived to age 21
Sixteen first-generation families	7.8	7.2
Forty-seven second-generation families	8.6	7.5
Thirty-three third-generation families	9.3	7.9

higher we cannot be sure because no trace exists today of many who died in infancy and early childhood.[15]

Even allowing for the obvious likelihood that errors in the figures for the number born are somewhat greater than in the figures for those who grow to maturity, the rate of infant mortality in Plymouth seems to have been relatively low. In the case of a few families for which there are unusually complete records, only about one in five children seems to have died before the age of twenty-one. Furthermore, births in the sample come for the most part at roughly two-year intervals [16] with relatively few "gaps" which might indicate a baby who did not survive. All things considered, it appears that the rate of infant and child mortality in Plymouth was no more than 25 per cent [17] — less than half the rate in many parts of the world today.

These figures seem to indicate a surprising standard of health and physical

[15] Various attempts to subject evidence to quantitative analysis have been an important part of my "method," such as it is. It is not possible to achieve anything approaching total accuracy in these computations; the sources simply are not that exact. I have not knowingly employed doubtful figures, but probably a small portion of those that I have used are incorrect. In certain cases I have accepted an approximate date (e.g., 1671, when it might as well be 1670 or 1672), but only where it would not prejudice the over-all result. In general, the numerical data that I shall present should be regarded as suggestive rather than conclusive in any sense. Above all, I have sought to keep my focus on individual lives and to build up my story from there. The people about whom I have assembled information total roughly 2,000. (It is very difficult even to estimate the total number of people who lived in Plymouth Colony between 1620–91, but it was probably between 25,000 and 50,000.) Only a part of these could be employed in the treatment of any particular question, since the data for most individuals are not complete. But a sample of several hundred should still be enough at least to outline certain general patterns.

With respect to the data on family size (Table 1), I have used only families in which both parents lived at least to age 50, or else if one parent died, the other quickly remarried. That is, in all these families there were parents who lived up to, and past, the prime years for childbearing.

[16] This spacing is quite interesting in itself, for it immediately raises questions as to how Plymouth parents avoided having even higher numbers of children. Probably the mothers nursed their babies for at least one year, but — contrary to popular belief — there is no proved biological impediment in this to further conception. Since effective contraceptive methods are a fairly recent development, it seems likely that Plymouth couples simply eschewed sexual contact over long periods of time. In many less advanced cultures of the world today there are taboos on sexual relations between husband and wife for one year or more following the birth of a child. It is just possible that a similar custom prevailed in Plymouth.

[17] It is impossible to estimate what portion of these were infants (less than one year old) and what proportion were young children, for in most cases the records say only "died young."

vigor among Plymouth residents, and a study of their longevity — the average life expectancy in the colony — confirms this impression. The following tables (2 and 3) are based on a sample of more than six hundred people, who lived at least to the age of twenty-one and for whom the age at death was ascertainable.

TABLES 2 AND 3   *Life Expectancy in Plymouth*

TABLE 2   (The figures in the left-hand column are the control points, i.e., a 21-year-old man might expect to live to age 69.2, a 30-year-old to 70.0, and so forth.)

Age	Men	Women
21	69.2	62.4
30	70.0	64.7
40	71.2	69.7
50	73.7	73.4
60	76.3	76.8
70	79.9	80.7
80	85.1	86.7

TABLE 3   (The figures in columns two and three represent the percentages of the men and women in the sample who died between the ages indicated in column one.)

Age group	Men (percentages)	Women (percentages)
22–29	1.6	5.9
30–39	3.6	12.0
40–49	7.8	12.0
50–59	10.2	10.9
60–69	18.0	14.9
70–79	30.5	20.7
80–89	22.4	16.0
90 or over	5.9	7.6

The figures in 2 are really astonishingly high. Indeed, in the case of the men, they compare quite favorably with what obtains in this country today. (The life expectancy of an American male of twenty-one is now a fraction over seventy, and for a female of the same age, is approximately seventy-six.) It is at least possible that some selective bias, built into the data, may have distorted the results. For example, as between two men one of whom died at thirty and the other at ninety, it is more likely that the latter should leave some traces for the genealogist and historian to follow up. Still, I do not believe that this has been a serious problem in the above sample. A good part of the information on longevity has come from a few especially well-preserved graveyards in the Plymouth area, and presumably these offer a fairly random selection of the adults in the community. Moreover, those families for which information is relatively complete — where we know the age at death of all the members — present a picture not very different from that of the total sample. And even if we do allow for a certain inflation of the figures, the outcome is still striking.

The difference in the results for men and women is mainly due to the dangers attendant on childbirth. A young woman's life expectancy was seven years less than a man's, whereas today, with childbirth hazards virtually eliminated by modern medicine, it is six years longer. The second table shows that 30 per cent of the women and only 12 per cent of the men in the sample died between ages twenty and fifty, the normal years of child bearing. If a woman survived these middle years, her prospects for a long life became at least as good as those of a man, and indeed a little better. A majority of those who lived to a really very old age (ninety or more) seem to have been women.

The records which reveal this pattern of growth and dispersion in the colony of Plymouth also provide much information about courtship, marriage, and family life. Courtships were usually initiated by the young people themselves, but as a relationship progressed toward something more permanent, the parents became directly involved. In fact, a requirement of parental consent was written into the colony's laws on marriage: "If any shall make any motion of marriage to any mans daughter . . . not having first obtayned leave and consent of the parents or master so to doe [he] shall be punished either by fine or corporall punishment or both, at the discretion of the bench and according to the nature of the offence."[18] The attitude of parents toward a proposed match depended on a variety of spiritual and material considerations. Speaking very generally, it was desirable that both parties be of good moral and religious character. Beyond that, the couple would hopefully have enough land and possessions, given to them by both sets of parents, to establish a reasonably secure household.

But in a community as fluid as Plymouth it is unlikely that parental control over courtship and marriage could have been fully preserved. A few surviving pieces of evidence suggest that it was possibly quite an issue. In 1692 the widow Abigail Young died without leaving a will. The court moved to settle her estate on the basis of her intentions as revealed in several conversations held before her death. Two sons, Robert and Henry, were the prime candidates for the inheritance. Witnesses testified that "when shee dyed [she said] shee would Leave all the estate that shee had with Henry, if Robart had that gierl that there was a discourse about: but if he had her not I understood that the estate should be devided betwix them." A third son, Nathaniel, confirmed this. "My mother young," he reported, "told me that if Robirt had that gierl which there was a talke about shee would not give him a peny."[19]

---

[18] *Plym. Col. Recs.*, XI, 29, 108, 190. Occasionally there were prosecutions under this statute, the most notorious of which involved Elizabeth Prence, the daughter of a governor of the colony, and Arthur Howland, Jr., who belonged to another of Plymouth's leading families. Many of the Howlands had become Quakers, young Arthur among them; the Governor, on the other hand, was firmly opposed to this new and "foreign" religious movement. Twice he brought Howland before the General Court for having "disorderly and unrighteously endeavored to obtain the affections of Mistress Elizabeth Prence." But the story had a happy ending: after seven long years the Governor relented, and the couple were finally married in the spring of 1668. *Ibid.*, IV, 140, 158–159. For another case of this kind, see *ibid.*, III, 5.

[19] *Mayflower Descendant*, XV (1913), 79–80.

The first official step toward marriage was normally the betrothal or "pre-contract"—a ceremony before two witnesses at which the couple exchanged formal promises to wed in due time. A period of several weeks or months followed, during which these intentions were "published." A betrothed couple was considered to have a special status, not married but no longer unmarried either. They were required to be completely loyal each to the other; the adultery laws treated them no differently from husbands and wives. Sexual contact between them was forbidden; but the penalty for it was only a quarter of what was prescribed for single people.[20] It may be that this actually encouraged premarital relations among betrothed couples because of its implication that fornication was much less reprehensible in their case than otherwise.[21] The Court records show sixty-five convictions for misconduct of this kind, over a forty-five year period. (Note that this total comprises only those who were *caught*, and whose cases were recorded.) In some instances members of the most prominent families were involved: for example, Peregrine White, Thomas Delano, and Thomas Cushman, Jr. Occasionally the basis for conviction was the arrival of a child less than nine months after the wedding ceremony. Perhaps innocent couples were sometimes punished under this system; but the number of "early" babies was, in any event, extremely high.[22]

Once the betrothal was formalized, considerable thought had to be given to the economic future of the couple. In all but the poorest families each child could expect to receive from its parents a "portion"—a certain quantity of property or money with which to make an independent start in life. In most cases this occurred at the time of marriage, and its purpose was everywhere the same. A man was to use it to "be for himself" (in the graphic little phrase of the time); a woman would transfer it to her husband for the greater good of the household which they were starting together. To make special provision for the possibility that he might die while his children were still young, a man usually directed in his will that his "overseers" hold part of his estate intact to be distributed later as portions, at the appropriate time.

There was no set formula governing the actual substance of these portions. More often than not, however, a male child was given land, cattle, tools, and a house or a promise of help in the building of a house; a woman, for her part, usually received movable property, such as furniture or clothing and money. Occasionally the terms of these bequests were officially recorded in a "deed of gift";[23] more often they seem to have been arranged informally. Most parents hoped to have accumulated sufficient property by the time their children came of age to make these gifts without suffering undue hardship. Some had to buy

[20] *Plym. Col. Recs.*, XI, 172.

[21] This point is argued at greater length in George Elliott Howard, *A History of Matrimonial Institutions* . . . , II (Chicago, 1904), 169–200. Howard's discussion of marriage customs in colonial New England is, in general, quite helpful.

[22] For example, a random sampling of fourth-generation Bradfords turned up nine couples whose first child arrived within eight months of their wedding and all but two of these within six months. Also, it appears that Thomas Cushman's first baby was not only conceived, but actually born, before his marriage.

[23] As on the occasion of the marriage of Jacob Cook and Damaris Hopkins in 1646. *Mayflower Descendant*, II, 27–28.

land specifically for this purpose;[24] others petitioned the Court "to accommo-date them for their posterities," i.e., to give them a free grant.[25] It appears that fathers sometimes retained the title to the lands which they gave as portions: there are many Plymouth wills which direct that a son shall inherit "the land wherein he now dwells," or use words to this effect.[26] Perhaps this practice served to maintain some degree of parental authority beyond the years of childhood.

It is widely supposed that people married early in the colonial period. For Plymouth, however — and I suspect for most other communities of that time — this impression cannot be sustained. Indeed, the average age of both men and women at the time of their first marriage was considerably higher then than it is today — and quite possibly has never been exceeded at any subsequent point in our history.

TABLE 4   First Marriages in Plymouth[a]

	Born before 1600	Born 1600–25	Born 1625–50	Born 1650–75	Born 1675–1700
Mean age of men at time of 1st marriage	27.0	27.0	26.1	25.4	24.6
Mean age of women at time of 1st marriage	—[b]	20.6	20.2	21.3	22.3
Percentage of men married at age 23 or over	25%	18%	25%	26%	38%
Percentage of men married at age 30 or over	44%	23%	27%	18%	14%
Percentage of women married at age 25 or over	—[b]	9%	10%	20%	28%

[a] Based on a sample of some 650 men and women.
[b] Insufficient data for women born before 1600.

This table [4] is largely self-explanatory. Only one point requires additional comment: the steady, if unspectacular, narrowing of the age gap between the sexes at the time of marriage. At the start this gap averaged six and one-half years; by the end it was verging on two. Men were marrying earlier and women later. During the early years of the colony there was certainly a shortage of women; spinsters were a rarity, and marriageable girls, of whatever charm and property, must have received plenty of offers. At some point, however, new factors began to come into play, and this imbalance in the sex ratio was gradually corrected. Above all, the process of expansion removed substantial numbers of

[24] In 1653, for instance, John Brown of Rehoboth bought land from Capt. Thomas Willet, which he immediately deeded over to his sons, John and James. Ibid., IV, 84.
[25] Plym. Col. Recs., III, 164.
[26] See, for examples, the wills of John Thompson and Ephraim Tinkham, Mayflower Descendant, IV, 22–29, 122–125.

young men from the areas that had been settled first, and by the end of the century some towns may well have held a surplus of females. Wherever women outnumbered men, there were some who did not find husbands until relatively late and at least a few who never married at all. Conversely, the men had a larger and larger group to choose from and tended to marry somewhat earlier. By 1700 there were occasional marriages in which the woman was older than her husband, and for the first time the number of spinsters had become noticeable. The earliest official count of males and females in Plymouth that still survives comes from a census taken for all Massachusetts in 1765. At that time all of the eastern counties showed a substantial majority of women over men; the reverse was true for the western counties. In the towns which formerly belonged to Plymouth Colony the figures were 53.2 per cent female as against 46.8 per cent male. It is my guess that this surplus began as much as a century earlier.[27]

Marriage was conceived to be the normal estate for adults in colonial New England. When one spouse died, the other usually remarried within a year or two. Most were in their thirties and forties at the time of their remarriage, but some were much older. Robert Cushman, Jr., for instance, took a new wife at eighty! This pattern affected a very considerable portion of the community, as the following table shows.

TABLE 5   *Rates of Remarriage in Plymouth Colony*[a]

Number of marriages	Men		Women	
	Over 50	Over 70	Over 50	Over 70
1	60%	55%	74%	69%
2	34%	36%	25%	30%
3	6%	8%	1%	1%
4	—[b]	.5%	—	—
5	—[b]	.5%	—	—
Total married more than once	40%	45%	26%	31%

[a] The figures for men and women are separate, and in each case there is a percentage for all those who lived to be fifty or more, and another for those who lived to be seventy or more. The sample, comprising over seven hundred people, does not include anyone who died before the age of fifty.
[b] Less than one half of one per cent.

[27] See J. H. Benton, Jr., *Early Census Making in Massachusetts, 1643–1765* . . . (Boston, 1905). The dimensions of the problem, for Plymouth, can be further refined. The findings in the 1765 census are divided into two parts: people under 16, and people 16 and over. The 53.2 to 46.8 ratio, quoted above, is for the 16-and-over group. But, as almost all males remained single until age 21, a more significant ratio would be one for only those males and females who were 21 or over. We can assume, from a breakdown of other parts of the census, that the 16–21 grouping composed about 10 per cent of the total over 16. We also know from the census that the ratio of males under 16 to females under 16 was 51.2 males to 48.8 females. If this ratio of 51.2 to 48.8 is projected to the 16–21 age group for the purpose of eliminating those under 21 from the final ratio, we discover that the ratio of men 21 or older to women 21 or older becomes approximately 53.8 to 46.2. This means that for one out of every seven girls there was no man, at least in her own home area. In a few individual towns the situation was worse — as high as one in four.

Generally speaking, the property of husband and wife was not merged in a second marriage to the extent customary for a first one. The main reason for this, of course, was to preserve the claims of the children by the first marriage to a just inheritance. In fact, wills were always framed with this point in mind. Often the bulk of a man's estate was transmitted at his death directly to his children, or if to his wife, only until she married again. The part that remained to herself alone was usually one third of the estate, and sometimes less. Widows in Plymouth did not control a large amount of property.

When a marriage between a widow and widower was planned it was customary to make an explicit agreement as to terms. The man pledged a certain sum to his (new) wife in the event of his death, but it was often only a token amount, much less than the "thirds" that a first wife might expect. The woman, for her part, retained the right of "sole disposition" of any property she might possess; it never became part of her husband's estate.[28]

A widow's children were placed in a doubtful position when their mother remarried. Sometimes the new husband agreed to take them into his household, but more often they were placed elsewhere. Occasionally the first husband had anticipated this problem before his death. Anthony Besse's will provided that should his widow remarry, "the five bigest [children] to bee put forth and theire Cattle with them according to the Descretion of the overseers." Another father,

> Lawrance Lichfeild lying on his Death bedd sent for John Allin and Ann his wife and Desired to give and bequeath unto them his youngest son Josias Lichfeild if they would accept of him and take him as theire Child; then they Desired to know how long they should have him and the said Lawrance said for ever; but the mother of the child was not willing then; but in a short time after willingly Concented to her husbands will in the thinge; if the said John and Ann would take the Child for theire adopted Child; whereunto they Assented . . . [The boy too] being asked by his owne mother . . . if hee Did Concent and Chuse to live with the said John and Ann as hitherto by the space of about nine yeares hee had Done; Willingly answered yea.

No doubt the boy was deeply attached to the Allens after having lived with them for so long. The agreement, then, imposed no particular hardship on anyone involved; it simply continued, and formalized, a previous arrangement.[29]

If children did remain with their mother after her remarriage, their stepfather was not supposed to exercise normal parental authority over them. Although at the time of his marriage to the widow, Mary Foster, Jonathan Morey contracted to "bring up" her son Benjamin at his own expense, he also agreed not to interfere in any future plans for binding the boy out. A fairly common solu-

[28] See, for example, the agreement between Ephraim Morton and Mary Harlow, widow. *Mayflower Descendant*, XVII (1915), 49. There were, admittedly, some exceptions to the pattern. When William Sherman died in 1680, he left six small children and no will. His widow remarried soon afterwards. When her new husband agreed to provide for the children, the courts ordered Sherman's estate made over to him, because of the obvious expenses he would have to meet. *Ibid.*, IV, 171 ff.

[29] *Ibid.*, XIV (1912), 152; XII (1910), 134.

tion to the problem of stepchildren was to keep them with their mother for a few years and then as they grew older to "put them out." Ultimate responsibility for such children passed to some persons specially designated in their father's will — often to his overseers, occasionally to his own parents. When Jacob Mitchell and his wife were killed by Indians at Rehoboth in 1675, their small children went to live with Mitchell's father in Bridgewater. John Brown of Swansea wrote in his will: "Conserning all my five Children I Doe wholly leave them all to the ordering and Disposeing of my owne father . . . for him to bring them up not once questioning but that his love and Care for them wilbee as it hath bine for my selfe." Brown's wife survived him, and the children probably remained in her day-to-day care, or else were "bound out"; but over-all direction of their lives was henceforth in the hands of their grandfather.[30]

It has been widely assumed that the "extended family" was characteristic of Western society everywhere until at least the eighteenth century, and that the change to our own "nuclear" pattern came only with the Industrial Revolution.[31] The term "extended family" in its strict sense means a household consisting of several couples, related as siblings or cousins, and their children, and perhaps their children's children. This pattern, of course, still prevails in many parts of the world. Its most striking results are a diffusion of affections and authority within the whole, or extended, family, and a sharing of economic responsibilities. The term is also applied, somewhat more loosely, to situations where the various family members do not form one household in the sense of living "under one roof" but still live close together and share loyalties and responsibilities which go beyond their own offspring or parents.

In colonial Plymouth, there were no extended families at all, in the sense of "under one roof." The wills show, beyond any doubt, that married brothers and sisters never lived together in the same house. As soon as a young man became betrothed, plans were made for the building, or purchase, of his own house. For example, when Joseph Buckland of Rehoboth married his father promised "to build the said Joseph a Convenient house for his Comfortable liveing with three score of acrees of land ajoyning to it."[32] Some young men moved out of the family even before marrying, either to join in the expansion toward the interior or simply to "be for themselves" while remaining nearby. Girls stayed with their parents until they found a husband, but never beyond that time. I know of only one case in which there is documentary evidence suggesting that two couples shared a house, and it is truly the exception that proves the rule. The will of Thomas Bliss (Plymouth, 1647) contained this clause: "I give unto my soon Jonathan my house and home lot Conditionally that hee shall give unto my sonninlaw Thomas Willmore his lot which hee now hath and allso the one half of my broken up ground for two yeares and shall healp him to build him an house

---

[30] *Ibid.*, XIV, 15–16; XXI (1919), 185; XVIII (1916), 14–15.

[31] However, a few very recent studies have thrown some doubt on this idea. See Laslett and Harrison, "Clayworth and Coggenhoe," for evidence implying very small families indeed in rural English villages of the late 17th century.

[32] *Mayflower Descendant*, XVI (1914), 82. When Thomas Little of Taunton died leaving two teenage sons, his will directed that £10 be paid to each toward the building of houses "when they shall have occasion." *Ibid.*, IV, 162.

and let him peacably and quietly live in the house with him untell they shall bee able to set up an house for him."[33]

In a true extended family the death of the father, or even of both parents, causes no radical change in living arrangements. The widow or the children, or both, continue their lives much as before, and the functions of the deceased are assumed by other relatives (uncles or cousins or grandparents). When a man died in Plymouth, however, his household usually broke up. If the children were still young, some might remain with their mother, but others were likely to be placed in new families. If the children were adult, the "homestead" was given to a certain designated one of them, who was then obliged to pay to each of his brothers and sisters an amount equivalent to some fair proportion of the property's value.[34]

An unusually wealthy man in Plymouth Colony, and especially one who participated directly in the founding of new towns, could accumulate enough land to provide his sons with lots near or adjoining his own. Wills and land deeds show, for example, that John Washburn divided up his very large estate in Bridgewater with three sons, and that John Turner did the same kind of thing in Scituate.[35] This sort of arrangement comes as close to being an extended family as anything found in and around Plymouth — and it is not very close at all. There is no evidence of shared economic activity, no mention in the wills of profits or crops to be divided up. Moreover, in both the Washburn and the Turner families there were other sons who do not seem to have remained nearby.

Among those who were less wealthy, the drive to expand and to increase their property proved more powerful than the bonds which might have held families together. Children left, when they came of age, to take up new holdings several towns and many miles away. The process of dispersion was, in fact, sometimes encouraged by the very system of portions described earlier. Often a father simply had no land to spare in the immediate vicinity of his own farm. He might, however, own property in one, or two, or three, of the newer townships; and this was what he passed on to his children. The will of William Bradford, Jr., shows that he had sons living in Connecticut (on land which he had given them); and he made additional bequests, to his youngest children, in Plymouth and Duxbury. Similarly, when Benjamin Bartlett died he left his children a wide variety of lots in Duxbury, Middleborough, Little Compton, and Rochester.[36] In some cases the recipients may have sold these gifts soon afterwards, but at least as often they went to make their homes on them.

What we would most like to know is something of the effect of this dispersion on a whole range of more intimate aspects of family life. A court case at Plymouth in 1679 throws some light on such matters. An elderly man named Samuel Ryder had just died and left his whole estate to two sons, Benjamin and John. A third son, Joseph, had been left nothing. What made this especially hard was the fact that Joseph had already built a house on a piece of land belonging to his father and had expected to receive title to it in the father's will. The Court

---

[33] *Ibid.*, VIII (1906), 85.
[34] See, for example, the will of David Linnell (Barnstable, 1688), *ibid.*, X (1908), 100–101.
[35] *Ibid.*, XV, 248–253; V (1903), 41–46.
[36] *Ibid.*, IV, 143–147; VI (1904), 44–49.

approached the problem by taking a number of depositions from friends and family. Elizabeth Mathews was called first and gave the following testimony: "I being att the Raising of Joseph Riyders house; Joseph Ryders Mother Came into the house Joseph then lived in and Cryed and wrong her hands fearing that Joseph would Goe away; Josephs Mother then said that if you would beleive a women beleive mee that youer father saith that you shall never be Molested; and you shall Never be Molested." Samuel Mathews verified this report and supplied additional details: "In the Morning before wee Raised the house old Goodman Ryder Joseph Ryders father Came out and marked out the Ground with his stick; and bid the said Joseph sett his house where it Now stands . . . the occation of the womans Lamenting as above said was fearing her son would Goe away; for shee said if hee went shee would Goe too."[37]

There are several striking things about this episode: the mother's distress at the thought that her son might leave (even to the point of suggesting that she would follow him); the hint of hostility between father and son; the threat to go away used by the son as a means of forcing a gift from his father; and the implication that parents could, and did, use gifts of land to induce their children to stay nearby. Evidence bearing directly on the human dimension of life in Plymouth is extremely hard to come by, but something like the Ryder case does offer a glimpse of the enormous strain that the whole pattern of geographic mobility must have placed upon family ties and sanctions.

Land and property represented one advantage still possessed by most parents when they wished to rearrange their own lives and the lives of their children. They tried to use it in a variety of ways. Bequests to children were often hedged by a requirement of good behavior: "I give [my estate to] my two sonnes Daniell and Samuell [ages 15 and 17] upon this proviso that they bee Obeidient unto theire mother and carrye themselves as they ought . . . but if the one or both live otherwise then they ought and undewtyfully and unquietly with theire Mother . . . then hee that soe carryeth himselfe shall Disinherit himselfe of his parte of this land." Another legacy, this one to a daughter, was made conditional on her "pleas[ing] her mother in her match." In still another case a man left his widow to judge their child's behavior and reward him accordingly from out of his estate. And the reasoning behind this was made explicit: "I would have the boy beholding to my wife; and not my wife to the boy."[38] Sometimes portions were shaped in the same way. One of the rare letters that survives from seventeenth-century Plymouth describes a father bestowing upon his son "the full of his porshon except upon his sons better behaver [he] should desarve more."[39]

It is likely, then, that rewards in the form of property were held out as an inducement to all sorts of "better behavior." But this was especially true in regard to the care of elderly couples and widows. Virtually every man who left

---

[37] *Ibid.*, XI (1909), 50–53. In this context to "molest" means to make trouble about the ownership of something.

[38] Will of Thomas Hicks (Scituate, 1652), will of Samuel Newman (Rehoboth, 1661), and depositions concerning the estate of John Allen (Scituate, 1662), *ibid.*, XI, 160; XV, 234–236; XVII, 218.

[39] Benjamin Brewster to Daniel Wetherell, date not known, *ibid.*, II, 113.

a widow directed in his will that she be looked after by one of their children, and made a large bequest contingent thereupon. Usually the family homestead went to a particular child, with one room or more reserved for the widow. Often the instructions were spelled out in great detail: She would have full rights to the use of the "garden" and "orchard"; yearly payments of a certain specified amount must be made to her, wood must be brought to her door in wintertime, her cows milked, etc.[40]

Some men made arrangements of this kind even before their deaths. John and Deborah Hurd of Barnstable, for example, deeded "all that our hom sted" to their daughter and son-in-law in exchange for "the whole and sole Care and charge of us . . . for and during the tarm of our Natural Lives." And Robert Sprout of Middleborough gave his farm to his sons Ebenezer and James, on condition that they "pay yearly for my support . . . the sum of forty pounds to that child which I live with and provides for me and looks after me."[41] These conditions are nailed down so tightly in so many wills (and similar deeds) that it is tempting to infer some particular anxiety behind them.[42] It clearly was the general custom for aged parents to live with one of their children who would provide the care and support they needed. Probably in the majority of cases this was managed without too much difficulty; but in a society as fluid as Plymouth there must have been some elderly fathers and mothers who were more or less neglected. One recalls Bradford's vivid image of the "ancient mother, grown old and forsaken of her children, though not in their affections, yet in regard of their bodily presence and personal helpfulness."

Although one set of parents with their own children always formed the core of a Plymouth household, this nuclear pattern was, as we have seen, sometimes modified by the inclusion of one or more aged grandparents. It was often further modified by servants and apprentices, who lived in the houses of their masters. Among such people were at least a few Negroes and Indians whose service was normally for life.[43] The vast majority, however, were young boys and girls, "bound out" for a specified term of years. Some of them were orphans but many others had both parents living. Often, in fact, the parents had made all the arrangements and signed a formal contract with the couple whom their child served. In 1660 "An agreement appointed to bee Recorded" stated that "Richard Berry of yarmouth with his wifes Concent; and other frinds; hath given unto Gorge Crispe of Eastham and his; wife theire son Samuell Berry; to bee att the ordering and Disposing of the said Gorge and his wife as if hee were theire owne Child, untill hee shall accomplish the age of twenty one yeares; and in the meane time to provide for the said Samuell in all thinges as theire owne Child; and afterwards if hee live to marry or to goe away from them; to Doe for him

---

[40] See, for examples, the wills of Thomas King, Sr., of Scituate and of Robert Hicks of Plymouth, *ibid.*, XXXI (1933), 101; VIII, 144–146.

[41] *Ibid.*, XVI, 219; VI, 9–10.

[42] One eldest son who inherited his father's homestead complained that the conditions attached to the bequest, especially with regard to his father's widow, were such as to make him virtually "a servant for life." *Ibid.*, XII, 106.

[43] The inventory of the property of John Gorham of Yarmouth in 1675 included the item "1 Negro man." *Ibid.*, IV, 156. For similar treatment of Indian servants, see the wills of Samuel Fuller and Anthony Snow, *ibid.*, II, 237–241; V, 1–5.

as if hee were theire own Child."[44] It is noteworthy that the Crispes took full responsibility for young Samuel — even to the point of promising him a portion. This is, then, a virtual deed of adoption.

No age was indicated for Samuel Berry, but it is clear from other cases that the children involved were often very young. John Smith and his wife gave their four-year-old son to Thomas Whitney "to have the full and sole disposing of him . . . without annoyance or disturbance from the said John Smith or Bennit his wife."[45] Samuel Eddy arranged apprenticeships for three of his sons, at ages six, seven, and nine. Two of them went to the same man, Mr. John Brown of Rehoboth. Upon reaching maturity, they both received property from Brown, and, in addition, were given modest portions by their father. It appears from this that Eddy continued to take a direct interest in his children even after they had left his household.

The most difficult question these arrangements raise is, what purpose lay behind them? No answer that would serve in all cases suggests itself. In some, poverty was obviously a factor. For example, Samuel Eddy, in the apprenticeship papers for his sons, pleaded his "many children" and "many wants." On the other hand, George Soule of Duxbury bound out his daughter to John Winslow, and Soule was a wealthy man. In certain cases, learning a trade was mentioned, but in a perfunctory manner. When young Benjamin Savory was bound out to Jonathan Shaw in 1653, the papers directed that he be taught "whatsoever trad[e] the said Jonathan Shaw can Doe." Something must have gone amiss with this arrangement, because four years later the child was placed with still another family. The terms were only slightly less vague: his new master, Stephen Bryant, was to "teach him in learning that is to say to read and write and to Intruct him in husbandry."[46]

Another possible motive was to improve a child's educational opportunities. Instruction in reading and writing was often included among the conditions of the contract, as in the case of Benjamin Savory above. Finally, Edmund Morgan has suggested in his *The Puritan Family* that "Puritan parents did not trust themselves with their own children . . . and were afraid of spoiling them by too great affection";[47] it was for this reason, he argues, that so many children were placed in families other than their own. It is an interesting thought, but there is simply no explicit proof for it. At least Morgan found none, and I have had no better luck with the materials for Plymouth.

The household of Samuel Fuller seems to have been about as varied as any in Plymouth, and is worth mentioning in this connection. When Fuller died in 1633 it included nine people, six of whom were not of his own immediate family. There were, beside himself, his wife, and his son, a nephew, two servants, a ward, and two "additional children." The last of these had been sent to him for education, from families in Charlestown and Sagos. The ward was the daughter of a close friend who had died some years before. Meanwhile, Fuller's own daughter was living with "goodwife Wallen." Fuller was obliged to leave instruc-

---

[44] *Ibid.*, XV, 34.
[45] *Plym. Col. Recs.*, XII, 181–182.
[46] *Mayflower Descendant*, II, 30; V, 90; XII, 133.
[47] Edmund S. Morgan, *The Puritan Family* . . . (Boston, 1956), 38.

tions about all these people in his will.[48] His daughter was to continue where she was for the time being. The children from Charlestown and Sagos would be returned to their former homes. The ward was committed to his brother-in-law, and passed thereby into her third family. Fuller's son should continue to live in the "homestead" and one day would inherit it; but the same brother-in-law was to take charge of his education. Fuller's wife would have the day-to-day care of the youth until she died or remarried. She would also take charge of the servants for the remainder of their contracted term.

Fuller's household was hardly typical, however. A close reading of hundreds of Plymouth wills has turned up no other family as complicated as this one. In many there were one or two people not of the immediate family — aged grandparents, servants, wards, or additional children — but rarely more. The basic unit remained one set of parents and their children or stepchildren, living apart from all other relatives.

Clearly children in seventeenth-century Plymouth often found themselves growing up in a household other than that of their parents. The records are so scattered that it is impossible to calculate how many this category actually included. It must, however, have been a considerable number; my own guess is somewhere between a third and a half of all the children. This figure does not seem too high when it is remembered that one in three of the parents in the colony married twice or more, and that some children were placed in new homes even when their own father and mother were living.

The impact of these situations on the children cannot be proved — only imagined. But a hint of what they could mean comes to us in the story of a rather sad little episode, which by a lucky chance has been preserved in the *Colony Records*. Christian (Penn) Eaton and Francis Billington, widow and widower, were married in Plymouth in 1635. Christian's son, Benjamin Eaton, was "put forth" into another family immediately thereafter. The couple began to have children of their own: first, Elizabeth, and then, Joseph — both of whom were also placed in other families. But little Joseph apparently did not take to this arrangement very well, for in 1643 the Court was obliged to issue the following order:

> Whereas Joseph, the sonn of Francis Billington . . . was . . . placed with John Cooke the younger, and hath since beene inveagled, and did oft departe his said masters service, the Court, upon longe heareing of all that can be said or alleadged by his parents, doth order and appoynt that the said Joseph shalbe returned to his said master againe immediately, and shall so remaine with him during his terme; and that if either the said Francis, or Christian, his wyfe, do receive him, if he shall againe depart from his said master without his lycence, that the said Francis, and Christian, his wyfe, shalbe sett in the stocks . . . as often as he or shee shall so receive him, untill the Court shall take a further course with them.[49]

Joseph Billington was five years old.

[48] *Mayflower Descendant*, I (1899), 24–28.
[49] *Plym. Col. Recs.*, II, 58–59.

Politics and Social Structure in Virginia

BERNARD BAILYN

Colonial political history has been studied traditionally from an institutional viewpoint. The powers of governors, the role of councils, and the rise of representative assemblies have preoccupied historians who assumed that colonial political systems were sufficient unto themselves, and that their development demonstrated the steady growth of democracy in America. In the following essay, however, the historian Bernard Bailyn defines "politics" very broadly. He argues that there existed in the seventeenth century a correspondence between state and society, and that there was, consequently, a virtual identity between colonial political and social leadership. Bailyn accordingly surveys the history of politics in Virginia to show that patterns of leadership in the highest level of society changed several times in the course of the seventeenth century, and that in response the structure of politics also changed. He suggests that colonial Virginia's major political upheaval, Bacon's Rebellion, was in reality the birthpang of a new ruling elite, the climax to the emergence of a new social structure. The factors that shape the contours of political life thus become, for Bailyn, family structure, provisions for the inheritance of wealth, and the labor system, rather than the prerogatives of the governor and the assembly's power of the purse. It is by means of such fresh sociological points of view that the study of colonial America is being revised, and the understanding of our colonial origins enriched.

By the end of the seventeenth century the American colonists faced an array of disturbing problems in the conduct of public affairs. Settlers from England and Holland, reconstructing familiar institutions on American shores, had become participants in what would appear to have been a wave of civil disobedience. Constituted authority was confronted with repeated challenges. Indeed, a veritable anarchy seems to have prevailed at the center of colonial society, erupting in a series of insurrections that began as early as 1635 with the "thrusting out" of Governor Harvey in Virginia. Culpeper's Rebellion in Carolina, the Protestant Association in Maryland, Bacon's Rebellion in Virginia, Leisler's seizure of power in New York, the resistance to and finally the overthrow of Andros in New England — every colony was affected.

These outbursts were not merely isolated local affairs. Although their imme-

Reprinted by permission of the publisher and the Institute of Early American History and Culture from James M. Smith, ed., *Seventeenth-Century America* (Chapel Hill: University of North Carolina Press, 1959), pp. 90–115.

diate causes were rooted in the particular circumstances of the separate colonies, they nevertheless had common characteristics. They were, in fact, symptomatic of a profound disorganization of European society in its American setting. Seen in a broad view, they reveal a new configuration of forces which shaped the origins of American politics.

In a letter written from Virginia in 1623, George Sandys, the resident treasurer, reported despondently on the character and condition of the leading settlers. Some of the councilors were "no more then Ciphers," he wrote; others were "miserablie poore"; and the few substantial planters lived apart, taking no responsibility for public concerns. There was, in fact, among all those "worthie the mencioninge" only one person deserving of full approval. Lieutenant William Peirce "refuses no labour, nor sticks at anie expences that may aduantage the publique." Indeed, Sandys added, Peirce was "of a Capacitie that is not to bee expected in a man of his breedinge."[1]

The afterthought was penetrating. It cut below the usual complaints of the time that many of the settlers were lazy malcontents hardly to be preferred to the Italian glassworkers, than whom, Sandys wrote, "a more damned crew hell never vomited."[2] What lay behind Sandys' remark was not so much that wretched specimens were arriving in the shipments of servants nor even that the quality of public leadership was declining but that the social foundations of political power were being strangely altered.

All of the settlers in whatever colony presumed a fundamental relationship between social structure and political authority. Drawing on a common medieval heritage, continuing to conceive of society as a hierarchical unit, its parts justly and naturally separated into inferior and superior levels, they assumed that superiority was indivisible; there was not one hierarchy for political matters, another for social purposes. John Winthrop's famous explanation of God's intent that "in all times some must be rich some poore, some highe and eminent in power and dignitie; others meane and in subieccion" could not have been more carefully worded. Riches, dignity, and power were properly placed in apposition; they pertained to the same individuals.[3]

So closely related were social leadership and political leadership that experience if not theory justified an identification between state and society. To the average English colonist the state was not an abstraction existing above men's lives, justifying itself in its own terms, taking occasional human embodiment. However glorified in monarchy, the state in ordinary form was indistinguishable from a more general social authority; it was woven into the texture of everyday life. It was the same squire or manorial lord who in his various capacities collated to the benefice, set the rents, and enforced the statutes of Parliament and the royal decrees. Nothing could have been more alien to the settlers than the idea

---

[1] Sandys to John Ferrar, April 11, 1623, Susan M. Kingsbury, ed., *The Records of the Virginia Company of London* (4 vols.; Washington, D.C., 1906–35), IV, 110–11.

[2] Sandys to "Mr. Farrer," March 1622/23, *ibid.*, 23.

[3] John Winthrop, "Modell of Christian Charity," *Winthrop Papers* (5 vols.; Boston, 1929–47), II, 282.

that competition for political leadership should be open to all levels of society or that obscure social origins or technical skills should be considered valuable qualifications for office. The proper response to new technical demands on public servants was not to give power to the skilled but to give skills to the powerful.[4] The English gentry and landed aristocracy remained politically adaptable and hence politically competent, assuming when necessary new public functions, eliminating the need for a professional state bureaucracy. By their amateur competence they made possible a continuing identification between political and social authority.

In the first years of settlement no one had reason to expect that this characteristic of public life would fail to transfer itself to the colonies. For at least a decade and a half after its founding there had been in the Jamestown settlement a small group of leaders drawn from the higher echelons of English society. Besides well-born soldiers of fortune like George Percy, son of the Earl of Northumberland, there were among them four sons of the West family — children of Lord de la Warr and his wife, a second cousin of Queen Elizabeth. In Virginia the West brothers held appropriately high positions; three of them served as governors.[5] Christopher Davison, the colony's secretary, was the son of Queen Elizabeth's secretary, William Davison, M.P. and Privy Councilor.[6] The troublesome John Martin, of Martin's Brandon, was the son of Sir Richard Martin, twice Lord Mayor of London, and also the brother-in-law of Sir Julius Caesar, Master of the Rolls and Privy Councilor.[7] Sir Francis and Haute Wyatt were sons of substantial Kent gentry and grandsons of the Sir Thomas Wyatt who led the rebellion of 1554 against Queen Mary.[8] George Sandys' father was the Archbishop of York; of his three older brothers, all knights and M.P.'s, two were eminent country gentlemen, and the third, Edwin, of Virginia Company fame, was a man of great influence in the city.[9] George Thorpe was a former M.P. and Gentleman of the Privy Chamber.[10]

More impressive than such positions and relationships was the cultural level represented. For until the very end of the Company period, Virginia remained to the literary and scientific an exotic attraction, its settlement an important moment in Christian history.[11] Its original magnetism for those in touch with intellectual currents affected the early immigration. Of the twenty councilors of 1621, eight had been educated at Oxford, Cambridge, or the Inns of Court. Davison, like Martin trained in the law, was a poet in a family of poets.

[4] Cf. J. H. Hexter, "The Education of the Aristocracy in the Renaissance," *Jour. of Modern Hist.*, 22 (1950), 1–20.

[5] *Dictionary of National Biography*, 1908–9 edn. (New York), XV, 836–37; Annie L. Jester and Martha W. Hiden, comps. and eds., *Adventurers of Purse and Person: Virginia 1607–1625* ([Princeton, N.J.], 1956), 349–50.

[6] D.N.B., V, 632; Richard B. Davis, *George Sandys: Poet-Adventurer* (London, 1955), 112–13n.

[7] Alexander Brown, *Genesis of the United States* (Boston, 1890), II, 943–44.

[8] Jester and Hiden, comps., *Adventurers*, 372; D.N.B., XXI, 1092–93, 1102–4.

[9] Davis, *Sandys*, Chap. I.

[10] Brown, *Genesis*, II, 1031.

[11] Perry Miller, *Errand into the Wilderness* (Cambridge, Mass., 1956), 99–140; Howard Mumford Jones, *The Literature of Virginia in the Seventeenth Century* (*Memoirs of the American Academy of Arts and Sciences*, XIX, Part 2, Boston, 1946), 3–7.

Thorpe was a "student of Indian views on religion and astronomy." Francis Wyatt wrote verses and was something of a student of political theory. Alexander Whitaker, M.A., author of *Good Newes from Virginia*, was the worthy heir "of a good part of the learning of his renowned father," the master of St. John's College and Regius Professor of Divinity at Cambridge. John Pory, known to history mainly as the speaker of the first representative assembly in America, was a Master of Arts, "protege and disciple of Hakluyt," diplomat, scholar, and traveler, whose writings from and about America have a rightful place in literary history. Above all there was George Sandys, "poet, traveller, and scholar," a member of Lord Falkland's literary circle; while in Jamestown he continued as a matter of course to work on his notable translation of Ovid's *Metamorphoses*.[12]

There was, in other words, during the first years of settlement a direct transference to Virginia of the upper levels of the English social hierarchy as well as of the lower. If the great majority of the settlers were recruited from the yeoman class and below, there was nevertheless a reasonable representation from those upper groups acknowledged to be the rightful rulers of society.

It is a fact of some importance, however, that this governing elite did not survive a single generation, at least in its original form. By the thirties their number had declined to insignificance. Percy, for example, left in 1612. Whitaker drowned in 1617. Sandys and Francis Wyatt arrived only in 1621, but their enthusiasm cooled quickly; they were both gone by 1626. Of the Wests, only John was alive and resident in the colony a decade after the collapse of the Company. Davison, who returned to England in 1622 after only a year's stay, was sent back in 1623 but died within a year of his return. Thorpe was one of the six councilors slain in the massacre of 1622. Pory left for England in 1622; his return as investigating commissioner in 1624 was temporary, lasting only a few months. And the cantankerous Martin graced the Virginia scene by his absence after 1625; he is last heard from in the early 1630's petitioning for release from a London debtor's prison.[13]

To be sure, a few representatives of important English families, like John West and Edmund Scarborough, remained. There were also one or two additions from the same social level.[14] But there were few indeed of such individuals, and the basis of their authority had changed. The group of gentlemen and illuminati that had dominated the scene during the Company era had been dispersed. Their disappearance created a political void which was filled soon enough, but from a different area of recruitment, from below, from the toughest and more fortunate

[12] Davis, *Sandys*, especially 190–92; Harry C. Porter, "Alexander Whitaker," *Wm. and Mary Qtly.*, 3rd ser., 14 (1957), 336; Jones, *Literature of Virginia*, 14n, 5–6, 26–28.

[13] Davis, *Sandys*, 195–97, 112–13n; Jester and Hiden, comps., *Adventurers*, 350–51; Brown, *Genesis*, II, 1031, 970; *Va. Mag. of Hist. and Biog.*, 54 (1946), 60–61; Jones, *Literature of Virginia*, 14n.

[14] Scarborough was a well-educated younger son of an armigerous Norfolk family. Among the additions were Charles Harmar (who died in 1640), nephew of the warden of Winchester College and brother of the Greek Reader, later the Greek Professor, at Oxford; and Nathaniel Littleton, whose father was Chief Justice of North Wales, two of whose brothers were Fellows of All Souls and a third Chief Justice of Common Pleas and Lord Keeper of the Great Seal. Susie M. Ames, ed., *County Court Records of Accomack-Northampton, Virginia, 1632–1640* (Washington, D.C., 1954), xxvii, xxix–xxx, xxxv.

of the surviving planters whose eminence by the end of the thirties had very little to do with the transplantation of social status.[15]

The position of the new leaders rested on their ability to wring material gain from the wilderness. Some, like Samuel Mathews, started with large initial advantages,[16] but more typical were George Menefie and John Utie, who began as independent landowners by right of transporting themselves and only one or two servants. Abraham Wood, famous for his explorations and like Menefie and Utie the future possessor of large estates and important offices, appears first as a servant boy on Mathews' plantation. Adam Thoroughgood, the son of a country vicar, also started in Virginia as a servant, aged fourteen. William Spencer is first recorded as a yeoman farmer without servants.[17]

Such men as these — Spencer, Wood, Menefie, Utie, Mathews — were the most important figures in Virginia politics up to the Restoration, engrossing large tracts of land, dominating the Council, unseating Sir John Harvey from the governorship. But in no traditional sense were they a ruling class. They lacked the attributes of social authority, and their political dominance was a continuous achievement. Only with the greatest difficulty, if at all, could distinction be expressed in a genteel style of life, for existence in this generation was necessarily crude. Mathews may have created a flourishing estate and Menefie had splendid fruit gardens, but the great tracts of land such men claimed were almost entirely raw wilderness. They had risen to their positions, with few exceptions, by brute labor and shrewd manipulation; they had personally shared the burdens of settlement. They succeeded not because of, but despite, whatever gentility they may have had. William Claiborne may have been educated at the Middle Temple; Pierce could not sign his name; but what counted was their common capacity to survive and flourish in frontier settle-

[15] The difficulty of maintaining in Virginia the traditional relationship between social and political authority became in 1620 the basis of an attack by a group of "ancient planters," including Francis West, on the newly appointed governor, Sir George Yeardley. Although Yeardley had been knighted two years earlier in an effort to enhance his personal authority, the petitioners argued that his lack of eminence was discouraging settlement. "Great Actions," they wrote, "are carryed wth best successe by such Comanders who haue personall Aucthoritye & greatness answerable to the Action, Sithence itt is nott easye to swaye a vulgar and seruile Nature by vulgar & seruile Spirits." Leadership should devolve on commanders whose "Eminence or Nobillitye" is such that "euerye man subordinate is ready to yeild a willing submission wthowt contempt or repyning." The ordinary settlers, they said, would not obey the same authority "conferrd vpon a meane man . . . no bettar than selected owt of their owne Ranke." If, therefore, the Company hoped to attract and hold colonists, especially of "the bettar sorte," it should select as leaders in Virginia "some eythar Noble or little lesse in Honor or Dower . . . to maintayne & hold vp the dignitye of so Great and good a cawse." Kingsbury, ed., *Records of the Virginia Company*, III, 231–32.

[16] For Mathews' twenty-three servants and his "Denbigh" plantation, described in 1649 as a self-sufficient village, see John C. Hotten, ed., *Original List of Persons of Quality . . .* (London, 1874), 233–34; Jester and Hiden, comps., *Adventurers*, 244–45; *A Perfect Description of Virginia . . .* , in Peter Force, comp., *Tracts and Other Papers Relating Principally to the Origin, Settlement, and Progress of the Colonies in North America* (4 vols., Washington, D.C., 1836–46), II, no. 8, 14–15.

[17] Jester and Hiden, comps., *Adventurers*, 248–49, 321, 329, 339–40; Hotten, ed., *Persons of Quality*, 226, 237, 233, 253, 228; Clarence W. Alvord and Lee Bidgood, *The First Explorations of the Trans-Alleghany Region . . . 1650–1674* (Cleveland, 1912), 34 ff.

ments.[18] They were tough, unsentimental, quick-tempered, crudely ambitious men concerned with profits and increased landholdings, not the grace of life. They roared curses, drank exuberantly, and gambled (at least according to deVries) for their servants when other commodities were lacking.[19] If the worst of Governor Harvey's offenses had been to knock out the teeth of an offending councilor with a cudgel, as he did on one occasion, no one would have questioned his right to the governorship.[20] Rank had its privileges, and these men were the first to claim them, but rank itself was unstable and the lines of class or status were fluid. There was no insulation for even the most elevated from the rude impact of frontier life.

As in style of life so in politics, these leaders of the first permanently settled generation did not re-create the characteristics of a stable gentry. They had had little opportunity to acquire the sense of public responsibility that rests on deep identification with the land and its people. They performed in some manner the duties expected of leaders, but often public office was found simply burdensome. Reports such as Sandys' that Yeardley, the councilor and former governor, was wholly absorbed in his private affairs and scarcely glanced at public matters and that Mathews "will rather hazard the payment of fforfeitures then performe our Injunctions" were echoed by Harvey throughout his tenure of office. Charles Harmar, justice of the peace on the Eastern Shore, attended the court once in eight years, and Claiborne's record was only slightly better. Attendance to public duties had to be specifically enjoined, and privileges were of necessity accorded provincial officeholders. The members of the Council were particularly favored by the gift of tax exemption.[21]

The private interests of this group, which had assumed control of public office by virtue not of inherited status but of newly achieved and strenuously maintained economic eminence, were pursued with little interference from the traditional restraints imposed on a responsible ruling class. Engaged in an effort to establish themselves in the land, they sought as specific ends: autonomous local jurisdiction, an aggressive expansion of settlement and trading enterprises, unrestricted access to land, and, at every stage, the legal endorsement of acquisitions. Most of the major public events for thirty years after the dissolution of the Company — and especially the overthrow of Harvey — were incidents in the pursuit of these goals.

[18] Wm. and Mary Qtly., 2nd ser., 19 (1939), 475n; Davis, Sandys, 158n.

[19] Ames, ed., Accomack-Northampton Recs., xxxiv, xxxix–xl; Susie M. Ames, Studies of the Virginia Eastern Shore in the Seventeenth Century (Richmond, Va., 1940), 181, 183. DeVries wrote of his astonishment at seeing servants gambled away: "I told them that I had never seen such work in Turk or Barbarian, and that it was not becoming Christians." David P. deVries, Short Historical . . . Notes of several Voyages . . . (Hoorn, 1655), reprinted in the New York Hist. Soc., Collections, 2nd ser., 3 (1857), 36, 125.

[20] Harvey readily confessed to the deed, offering as an official justification the fact that it had all taken place outside the Council chamber, and anyhow the fellow had "assailed him with ill language." The Aspinwall Papers, Mass. Hist. Soc., Collections, 4th ser., 9 (1871), 133n.

[21] Kingsbury, ed., Records of the Virginia Company, IV, 110–11; Va. Mag. of Hist. and Biog., 8 (1900–1), 30; Ames, ed., Accomack-Northampton Recs., xxv, xxix; William W. Hening, ed., The Statutes-at-Large . . . of Virginia (1619–1792) (New York, 1823), I, 350, 454; Philip A. Bruce, Institutional History of Virginia in the Seventeenth Century (2 vols.; New York, 1910), II, Chaps. XV, XXIX.

From his first appearance in Virginia, Sir John Harvey threatened the interests of this emerging planter group. While still in England he had identified himself with the faction that had successfully sought the collapse of the Company, and thus his mere presence in Virginia was a threat to the legal basis of land grants made under the Company's charter. His demands for the return as public property of goods that had once belonged to the Company specifically jeopardized the planters' holdings. His insistence that the governorship was more than a mere chairmanship of the Council tended to undermine local autonomy. His conservative Indian policy not only weakened the settlers' hand in what already seemed an irreconcilable enmity with the natives but also restricted the expansion of settlement. His opposition to Claiborne's claim to Kent Island threatened to kill off the lucrative Chesapeake Bay trade, and his attempt to ban the Dutch ships from the colony endangered commerce more generally. His support of the official policy of economic diversification, together with his endorsement of the English schemes of tobacco monopoly, alienated him finally and completely from the Council group.[22]

Within a few months of his assuming the governorship, Harvey wrote home with indignation of the "waywardness and oppositions" of the councilors and condemned them for factiously seeking "rather for their owne endes then either seekinge the generall good or doinge right to particuler men." Before a year was out the antagonisms had become so intense that a formal peace treaty had to be drawn up between Harvey and the Council. But both sides were adamant, and conflict was inescapable. It exploded in 1635 amid comic opera scenes of "extreame coller and passion" complete with dark references to Richard the Third and musketeers "running with their peices presented." The conclusion was Harvey's enraged arrest of George Menefie "of suspicion of Treason to his Majestie"; Utie's response, "And wee the like to you sir"; and the governor's forced return to England.[23]

Behind these richly heroic "passings and repassings to and fro" lies not a victory of democracy or representative institutions or anything of the sort. Democracy, in fact, was identified in the Virginians' minds with the "popular and tumultuary government" that had prevailed in the old Company's quarter courts, and they wanted none of it; the Assembly as a representative institution was neither greatly sought after nor hotly resisted.[24] The victory of 1635 was that of resolute leaders of settlement stubbornly fighting for individual establishment. With the reappointment of Sir Francis Wyatt as governor, their victory was assured and in the Commonwealth period it was completely realized. By 1658, when Mathews was elected governor, effective interference from outside

---

[22] The charges and countercharges are summarized, together with supporting documents, in the profuse footnotes of *Aspinwall Papers*, 131–52.

[23] *Va. Mag. of Hist. and Biog.*, 8 (1900–1), 30, 43–45; 1 (1893–94), 418, 419, 427, 420.

[24] *Ibid.*, 1 (1893–94), 418; Hening, ed., *Va. Stat. at L.*, I, 232–33. For a balanced statement of the importance attached by contemporaries to Virginia's representative Assembly, see Wesley Frank Craven, *Dissolution of the Virginia Company* (New York, 1932), 71 ff., 330 ff. Cf. Charles M. Andrews, *The Colonial Period of American History* (4 vols.; New Haven, Conn., 1934–38), I, 181 ff., and Davis, "'Liberalism' in the Virginia Company and Colony," *Sandys*, Appendix G.

had disappeared and the supreme authority had been assumed by an Assembly which was in effect a league of local magnates secure in their control of county institutions.[25]

One might at that point have projected the situation forward into a picture of dominant county families dating from the 1620's and 1630's, growing in identification with the land and people, ruling with increasing responsibility from increasingly eminent positions. But such a projection would be false. The fact is that with a few notable exceptions like the Scarboroughs and the Wormeleys, these struggling planters of the first generation failed to perpetuate their leadership into the second generation. Such families as the Woods, the Uties, the Mathews, and the Peirces faded from dominant positions of authority after the deaths of their founders. To some extent this was the result of the general insecurity of life that created odds against the physical survival in the male line of any given family. But even if male heirs had remained in these families after the death of the first generation, undisputed eminence would not. For a new emigration had begun in the forties, continuing for close to thirty years, from which was drawn a new ruling group that had greater possibilities for permanent dominance than Harvey's opponents had had. These newcomers absorbed and subordinated the older group, forming the basis of the most celebrated oligarchy in American history.

Most of Virginia's great eighteenth-century names, such as Bland, Burwell, Byrd, Carter, Digges, Ludwell, and Mason, appear in the colony for the first time within ten years either side of 1655. These progenitors of the eighteenth-century aristocracy arrived in remarkably similar circumstances. The most important of these immigrants were younger sons of substantial families well connected in London business and governmental circles and long associated with Virginia; family claims to land in the colony or inherited shares of the original Company stock were now brought forward as a basis for establishment in the New World.

Thus the Bland family interests in Virginia date from a 1618 investment in the Virginia Company by the London merchant John Bland, supplemented in 1622 by another in Martin's Hundred. The merchant never touched foot in America, but three of his sons did come to Virginia in the forties and fifties to exploit these investments. The Burwell fortunes derive from the early subscription to the Company of Edward Burwell, which was inherited in the late forties by his son, Lewis I. The first William Byrd arrived about 1670 to assume the Virginia properties of his mother's family, the Steggs, which dated back to the early days of the Company. The Digges's interests in Virginia stem from the original investments of Sir Dudley Digges and two of his sons in the Company, but it was a third son, Edward, who emigrated in 1650 and established the American branch of the family. Similarly, the Masons had been financially interested in Virginia thirty-two years before 1652, when the first immigrant of that family appeared in the colony. The Culpeper clan, whose private affairs enclose much of the history of the South in the second half of the seventeenth century, was first represented in Virginia by Thomas Culpeper, who arrived in

[25] Wesley Frank Craven, *The Southern Colonies in the Seventeenth Century, 1607–1689* (Baton Rouge, La., 1949), 288–94.

1649; but the family interests in Virginia had been established a full generation earlier: Thomas' father, uncle, and cousin had all been members of the original Virginia Company and their shares had descended in the family. Even Governor Berkeley fits the pattern. There is no mystery about his sudden exchange in 1642 of the life of a dilettante courtier for that of a colonial administrator and estate manager. He was a younger son without prospects, and his family's interests in Virginia, dating from investments in the Company made twenty years earlier, as well as his appointment held out the promise of an independent establishment in America.[26]

Claims on the colony such as these were only one, though the most important, of a variety of forms of capital that might provide the basis for secure family fortunes. One might simply bring over enough of a merchant family's resources to begin immediately building up an imposing estate, as, presumably, did that ambitious draper's son, William Fitzhugh. The benefits that accrued from such advantages were quickly translated into landholdings in the development of which these settlers were favored by the chronology of their arrival. For though they extended the area of cultivation in developing their landholdings, they were not obliged to initiate settlement. They fell heirs to large areas of the tidewater region that had already been brought under cultivation. "Westover" was not the creation of William Byrd; it had originally been part of the De la Warr estate, passing, with improvements, to Captain Thomas Pawlett, thence to Theodorick Bland, and finally to Byrd. Lewis Burwell inherited not only his father's land, but also the developed estate of his stepfather, Wingate. Some of the Carters' lands may be traced back through John Utie to a John Jefferson, who left Virginia as early as 1628. Abraham Wood's entire Fort Henry property ended in the hands of the Jones family. The Blands' estate in Charles City County, which later became the Harrisons' "Berkeley" plantation, was cleared for settlement in 1619 by servants of the "particular" plantation of Berkeley's Hundred.[27]

Favored thus by circumstance, a small group within the second generation migration moved toward setting itself off in a permanent way as a ruling landed gentry. That they succeeded was due not only to their material advantages but also to the force of their motivation. For these individuals were in social origins just close enough to establishment in gentility to feel the pangs of deprivation most acutely. It is not the totally but the partially dispossessed who build up the most propulsive aspirations, and behind the zestful lunging at propriety and status of a William Fitzhugh lay not the narcotic yearnings of the disinherited but the pent-up ambitions of the gentleman *manqué*. These were neither hardhanded pioneers nor dilettante romantics, but ambitious younger sons of

[26] Nell M. Nugent, *Cavaliers and Pioneers* (Richmond, Va., 1934), I, 160; Jester and Hiden, comps., *Adventurers*, 97, 108, 154–55, 288; Louis B. Wright, *The First Gentlemen of Virginia* (San Marino, Calif., 1940), 312–13; *Va. Mag. of Hist. and Biog.*, 35 (1927), 227–28; Helen Hill, *George Mason, Constitutionalist* (Cambridge, Mass., 1938), 3–4; Fairfax Harrison, "A Key Chart of the . . . Culpepers . . . ," *Va. Mag. of Hist. and Biog.*, 33 (1925), f. 113, 339, 344; *D.N.B.*, II, 368; Kingsbury, ed., *Records of the Virginia Company*, II, 75, 90, 391.

[27] Wright, *First Gentlemen*, 155 ff.; Jester and Hiden, comps., *Adventurers*, 98, 108, 339–41, 363–64, 97, 99.

middle-class families who knew well enough what gentility was and sought it as a specific objective.[28]

The establishment of this group was rapid. Within a decade of their arrival they could claim, together with a fortunate few of the first generation, a marked social eminence and full political authority at the county level. But their rise was not uniform. Indeed, by the seventies a new circumstance had introduced an effective principle of social differentiation among the colony's leaders. A hierarchy of position within the newly risen gentry was created by the Restoration government's efforts to extend its control more effectively over its mercantile empire. Demanding of its colonial executives and their advisors closer supervision over the external aspects of the economy, it offered a measure of patronage necessary for enforcement. Public offices dealing with matters that profoundly affected the basis of economic life — tax collection, customs regulation, and the bestowal of land grants — fell within the gift of the governor and tended to form an inner circle of privilege. One can note in Berkeley's administration the growing importance of this barrier of officialdom. Around its privileges there formed the "Green Spring" faction, named after Berkeley's plantation near Jamestown, a group bound to the governor not by royalist sympathies so much as by ties of kinship and patronage.

Thus Colonel Henry Norwood, related to Berkeley by a "near affinity in blood," was given the treasurership of the colony in 1650, which he held for more than two decades. During this time Thomas Ludwell, a cousin and Somerset neighbor of the governor, was secretary of state, in which post he was succeeded in 1678 by his brother Philip, who shortly thereafter married Berkeley's widow. This Lady Berkeley, it should be noted, was the daughter of Thomas Culpeper, the immigrant of 1649 and a cousin of Thomas Lord Culpeper who became governor in 1680. Immediately after her marriage to Berkeley, her brother Alexander requested and received from the governor the nomination to the surveyor-generalship of Virginia, a post he filled for twenty-three years while resident in England, appointing as successive deputies the brothers Ludwell, to whom by 1680 he was twice related by marriage. Lady Berkeley was also related through her mother to William Byrd's wife, a fact that explains much about Byrd's prolific office-holding.[29]

---

[28] Fitzhugh's letters, scattered through the Va. Mag. of Hist. and Biog., I–VI, cannot be equalled as sources for the motivation of this group.

[29] Colonel [Henry] Norwood, A Voyage to Virginia (1649), in Force, ed., Tracts, III, 49, 50; Va. Mag. of Hist. and Biog., 33 (1925), 5, 8; Harrison, "Key Chart," ibid., 351–55, 348; Wm. and Mary Qtly., 1st ser., 19 (1910–11), 209–10. It was after Culpeper's appointment to the governorship that Byrd was elevated to the Council and acquired the auditor- and receiver-generalships. William G. and Mary N. Stanard, comps., The Colonial Virginia Register (Albany, N.Y., 1902), 22–23.

The Berkeley-Norwood connection may be followed out in other directions. Thus the Colonel Francis Moryson mentioned by Norwood as his friend and traveling companion and whom he introduced to the governor was given command of the fort at Point Comfort upon his arrival in 1649, replacing his brother, Major Richard Moryson, whose son Charles was given the same post in the 1660's. Francis, who found the command of the fort "profitable to him," was elevated by Berkeley to the Council and temporarily to the deputy-governorship, "wherein he got a competent estate"; he finally returned to England

The growing distinctiveness of provincial officialdom within the landed gentry may also be traced in the transformation of the Council. Originally, this body had been expected to comprise the entire effective government, central and local; councilors were to serve, individually or in committees, as local magistrates. But the spread of settlement upset this expectation, and at the same time as the local offices were falling into the hands of autonomous local powers representing leading county families, the Council, appointed by the governor and hence associated with official patronage, increasingly realized the separate, lucrative privileges available to it.[30]

As the distinction between local and central authority became clear, the county magistrates sought their own distinct voice in the management of the colony, and they found it in developing the possibilities of burgess representation. In the beginning there was no House of Burgesses; representation from the burghs and hundreds was conceived of not as a branch of government separate from the Council but as a periodic supplement to it.[31] Until the fifties the burgesses, meeting in the Assemblies with the councilors, felt little need to form themselves into a separate house, for until that decade there was little evidence of a conflict of interests between the two groups. But when, after the Restoration, the privileged status of the Council became unmistakable and the county magnates found control of the increasingly important provincial administration pre-empted by this body, the burgess part of the Assembly took on a new meaning in contrast to that of the Council. Burgess representation now became vital to the county leaders if they were to share in any consistent way in affairs larger than those of the counties. They looked to the franchise, hitherto broad not by design but by neglect, introducing qualifications that would ensure their control of the Assembly. Their interest in provincial government could no longer be expressed in the conglomerate Assembly, and at least by 1663 the House of Burgesses began to meet separately as a distinct body voicing interests potentially in conflict with those of the Council.[32]

Thus by the eighth decade the ruling class in Virginia was broadly based on leading county families and dominated at the provincial level by a privileged officialdom. But this social and political structure was too new, too lacking in the sanctions of time and custom, its leaders too close to humbler origins and

---

in the position of colony agent. Norwood, *Voyage*, 50; *Va. Mag. of Hist. and Biog.*, 9 (1900–1), 122–23; Ella Lonn, *The Colonial Agents of the Southern Colonies* (Chapel Hill, 1945), 21 ff.

The inner kinship core of the group enclosed the major provincial positions mentioned above. But the wider reaches of the clique extended over the Council, the collectorships, and the naval offices as well as minor positions within the influence of the governor. On these posts and their holders, see Stanard and Stanard, comps., *Va. Register*, 38–40; Bruce, *Institutional History*, II, Chaps. XXXVIII–XLII. On the limitations of the gubernatorial influence after 1660, see Craven, *Southern Colonies*, 293.

[30] Craven, *Southern Colonies*, 167–69, 270, 288; Bruce, *Institutional History*, II, Chap. XV.

[31] For the Assembly as "the other Counsell," see the "Ordinance and Constitution" of 1621 in Kingsbury, ed., *Records of the Virginia Company*, III, 483–84.

[32] Andrews, *Colonial Period*, I, 184–85; Craven, *Southern Colonies*, 289 ff.

as yet too undistinguished in style of life, to be accepted without a struggle. A period of adjustment was necessary, of which Bacon's Rebellion was the climactic episode.

Bacon's Rebellion began as an unauthorized frontier war against the Indians and ended as an upheaval that threatened the entire basis of social and political authority. Its immediate causes have to do with race relations and settlement policy, but behind these issues lay deeper elements related to resistance against the maturing shape of a new social order. These elements explain the dimensions the conflict reached.

There was, first, resistance by substantial planters to the privileges and policies of the inner provincial clique led by Berkeley and composed of those directly dependent on his patronage. These dissidents, among whom were the leaders of the Rebellion, represented neither the down-trodden masses nor a principle of opposition to privilege as such. Their discontent stemmed to a large extent from their own exclusion from privileges they sought. Most often their grievances were based on personal rebuffs they had received as they reached for entry into provincial officialdom. Thus — to speak of the leaders of the Rebellion — Giles Bland arrived in Virginia in 1671 to take over the agency of his late uncle in the management of his father's extensive landholdings, assuming at the same time the lucrative position of customs collector which he had obtained in London. But, amid angry cries of *"pittyfull fellow, puppy* and *Sonn of a Whore,"* he fell out first with Berkeley's cousin and favorite, Thomas Ludwell, and finally with the governor himself; for his "Barbarous and Insolent Behaviors" Bland was fined, arrested, and finally removed from the collectorship.[33] Of the two "chiefe Incendiarys," William Drummond and Richard Lawrence, the former had been quarreling with Berkeley since 1664, first over land claims in Carolina, then over a contract for building a fort near James City, and repeatedly over lesser issues in the General Court; Lawrence "some Years before . . . had been partially treated at Law, for a considerable Estate on behalfe of a Corrupt favorite." Giles Brent, for his depredations against the Indians in violation of official policy, had not only been severely fined but barred from public office.[34] Bacon himself could not have appeared under more favorable circumstances. A cousin both of Lady Berkeley and of the councilor Nathaniel Bacon, Sr., and by general agreement "a Gent:man of a Liberall education" if of a somewhat tarnished reputation, he had quickly staked out land for himself and had been elevated, for reasons "best known to the Governour," to the Council. But being "of a most imperious and dangerous hidden Pride of heart . . . very ambitious and arrogant," he wanted more, and quickly. His alienation from and violent opposition to Berkeley were wound in among the animosities created by the Indian problem and were further complicated by his own unstable personality; they were related also to the fact that Berkeley finally turned down the

[33] Jester and Hiden, comps., *Adventurers,* 98–99; H. R. McIlwaine, ed., *Minutes of the Council and General Court . . . 1622–1632, 1670–1676* (Richmond, Va., 1924), 399, 423.

[34] Charles M. Andrews, ed., *Narratives of the Insurrections, 1675–1690* (New York, 1915), 96, 27; Wilcomb E. Washburn, "The Humble Petition of Sarah Drummond," *Wm. and Mary Qtly.,* 3rd ser., 13 (1956), 368–69; H. R. McIlwaine, ed., *Journals of the House of Burgesses of Virginia 1659/60–1693* (Richmond, Va., 1914), 14.

secret offer Bacon and Byrd made in 1675 for the purchase from the governor of a monopoly of the Indian trade.[35]

These specific disputes have a more general aspect. It was three decades since Berkeley had assumed the governorship and begun rallying a favored group, and it was over a decade since the Restoration had given this group unconfined sway over the provincial government. In those years much of the choice tidewater land as well as the choice offices had been spoken for, and the tendency of the highly placed was to hold firm. Berkeley's Indian policy — one of stabilizing the borders between Indians and whites and protecting the natives from depredation by land-hungry settlers — although a sincere attempt to deal with an extremely difficult problem, was also conservative, favoring the established. Newcomers like Bacon and Bland and particularly landholders on the frontiers felt victimized by a stabilization of the situation or by a controlled expansion that maintained on an extended basis the existing power structure. They were logically drawn to aggressive positions. In an atmosphere charged with violence, their interests constituted a challenge to provincial authority. Bacon's primary appeal in his "Manifesto" played up the threat of this challenge:

> Let us trace these men in Authority and Favour to whose hands the dispensation of the Countries wealth has been commited; let us observe the sudden Rise of their Estates [compared] with the Quality in wch they first entered this Country. . . . And lett us see wither their extractions and Education have not bin vile, And by what pretence of learning and vertue they could [enter] soe soon into Imployments of so great Trust and consequence, let us . . . see what spounges have suckt up the Publique Treasure and wither it hath not bin privately contrived away by unworthy Favourites and juggling Parasites whose tottering Fortunes have bin repaired and supported at the Publique chardg.

Such a threat to the basis of authority was not lost on Berkeley or his followers. Bacon's merits, a contemporary wrote, "thretned an eclips to there riseing gloryes. . . . (if he should continue in the Governours favour) of Seniours they might become juniours, while there younger Brother . . . might steale away that blessing, which they accounted there owne by birthright."[36]

But these challengers were themselves challenged, for another main element in the upheaval was the discontent among the ordinary settlers at the local privileges of the same newly risen county magnates who assailed the privileges of the Green Spring faction. The specific Charles City County grievances were directed as much at the locally dominant family, the Hills, as they were at

---

[35] Wilcomb E. Washburn, The Governor and the Rebel, A History of Bacon's Rebellion in Virginia (Chapel Hill, 1957), 17–19; Andrews, ed., Narratives, 74, 110. For the offer to buy the monopoly and Berkeley's initial interest in it, see Bacon to Berkeley, September 18, 1675, and William and Frances Berkeley to Bacon, September 21, 1675, Coventry Papers, Longleat Library of the Marquises of Bath, LXXVII, 6, 8 (microfilm copy, Library of Congress); for the refusal, see Aspinwall Papers, 166. Mr. Washburn, who first called attention to these Bacon letters at Longleat, is editing them for publication by the Virginia Historical Society.

[36] Craven, Southern Colonies, 362–73; Va. Mag. of Hist. and Biog., 1 (1893–94), 56–57; Andrews, ed., Narratives, 53.

Berkeley and his clique. Similarly, Surry County complained of its county court's highhanded and secretive manner of levying taxes on "the poore people" and of setting the sheriffs' and clerks' fees; they petitioned for the removal of these abuses and for the right to elect the vestry and to limit the tenure of the sheriffs. At all levels the Rebellion challenged the stability of newly secured authority.[37]

It is this double aspect of discontent behind the violence of the Rebellion that explains the legislation passed in June, 1676, by the so-called "Bacon's Assembly." At first glance these laws seem difficult to interpret because they express disparate if not contradictory interests. But they yield readily to analysis if they are seen not as the reforms of a single group but as efforts to express the desires of two levels of discontent with the way the political and social hierarchy was becoming stabilized. On the one hand, the laws include measures designed by the numerically predominant ordinary settlers throughout the colony as protests against the recently acquired superiority of the leading county families. These were popular protests and they relate not to provincial affairs but to the situation within the local areas of jurisdiction. Thus the statute restricting the franchise to freeholders was repealed; freemen were given the right to elect the parish vestrymen; and the county courts were supplemented by elected freemen to serve with the regularly appointed county magistrates.

On the other hand, there was a large number of measures expressing the dissatisfactions not so much of the ordinary planter but of the local leaders against the prerogatives recently acquired by the provincial elite, prerogatives linked to officialdom and centered in the Council. Thus the law barring office-holding to newcomers of less than three years' residence struck at the arbitrary elevation of the governor's favorites, including Bacon; and the acts forbidding councilors to join the county courts, outlawing the governor's appointment of sheriffs and tax collectors, and nullifying tax exemption for councilors all voiced objections of the local chieftains to privileges enjoyed by others. From both levels there was objection to profiteering in public office.[38]

Thus the wave of rebellion broke and spread. But why did it subside? One might have expected that the momentary flood would have become a steady tide, its rhythms governed by a fixed political constellation. But in fact it did not; stable political alignments did not result. The conclusion to this controversy was characteristic of all the insurrections. The attempted purges and counter-purges by the leaders of the two sides were followed by a rapid submerging of factional identity. Occasional references were later made to the episode, and there were individuals who found an interest in keeping its memory alive. Also, the specific grievances behind certain of the attempted legal reforms of 1676 were later revived. But of stable parties or factions around these issues there were none.

It was not merely that in the late years of the century no more than in the early was there to be found a justification for permanently organized political opposition or party machinery, that persistent, organized dissent was still indistinguishable from sedition; more important was the fact that at the end of

[37] Va. Mag. of Hist. and Biog., 3 (1895–96), 132 ff. (esp. 142–46), 239–52, 341–49; IV, 1–15; II, 172.
[38] Hening, ed., Va. Stat. at L., II, 341–65.

the century as in 1630 there was agreement that some must be "highe and eminent in power and dignitie; others meane and in subieccion."[39] Protests and upheaval had resulted from the discomforts of discovering who was, in fact, which, and what the particular consequences of "power and dignitie" were.

But by the end of the century the most difficult period of adjustment had passed and there was an acceptance of the fact that certain families were distinguished from others in riches, in dignity, and in access to political authority. The establishment of these families marks the emergence of Virginia's colonial aristocracy.

It was a remarkable governing group. Its members were soberly responsible, alive to the implications of power; they performed their public obligations with notable skill.[40] Indeed, the glare of their accomplishments is so bright as occasionally to blind us to the conditions that limited them. As a ruling class the Virginian aristocracy of the eighteenth century was unlike other contemporary nobilities or aristocracies, including the English. The differences, bound up with the special characteristics of the society it ruled, had become clear at the turn of the seventeenth century.

Certain of these characteristics are elusive, difficult to grasp and analyze. The leaders of early eighteenth-century Virginia were, for example, in a particular sense, cultural provincials. They were provincial not in the way of Polish *szlachta* isolated on their estates by poverty and impassable roads, nor in the way of sunken *seigneurs* grown rustic and old-fashioned in lonely Norman chateaux. The Virginians were far from uninformed or unaware of the greater world; they were in fact deeply and continuously involved in the cultural life of the Atlantic community. But they knew themselves to be provincials in the sense that their culture was not self-contained; its sources and superior expressions were to be found elsewhere than in their own land. They must seek it from afar; it must be acquired, and once acquired be maintained according to standards externally imposed, in the creation of which they had not participated. The most cultivated of them read much, purposefully, with a diligence the opposite of that essential requisite of aristocracy, uncontending ease. William Byrd's diary with its daily records of stints of study is a stolid testimonial to the virtues of regularity and effort in maintaining standards of civilization set abroad.[41]

In more evident ways also the Virginia planters were denied an uncontending ease of life. They were not *rentiers*. Tenancy when it appeared late in the colonial period, was useful to the landowners mainly as a cheap way of improving lands held in reserve for future development. The Virginia aristocrat was an

---

[39] Thus the Burgesses, proposing in 1706 that the vestries be made elective, did not dispute the Council's assertion that the "men of Note & Estates" should have authority and assured them that the people would voluntarily elect the "best" men in the parish. H. R. McIlwaine, ed., *Legislative Journals of the Council of Colonial Virginia* (Richmond, Va., 1918–19), I, 468.

[40] Charles S. Sydnor, *Gentlemen Freeholders: Political Practices in Washington's Virginia* (Chapel Hill, 1952), Chaps. I, VI–IX.

[41] Albert Goodwin, ed., *The European Nobility in the Eighteenth Century* (London, 1953), *passim*; John Clive and Bernard Bailyn, "England's Cultural Provinces: Scotland and America," *Wm. and Mary Qtly.*, 3rd ser., 9 (1954), 200–13; Louis B. Wright and Marion Tinling, eds., *The Secret Diary of William Byrd of Westover 1709–1712* (Richmond, Va., 1941).

active manager of his estate, drawn continuously into the most intimate contacts with the soil and its cultivation. This circumstance limited his ease, one might even say bound him to the soil, but it also strengthened his identity with the land and its problems and saved him from the temptation to create of his privileges an artificial world of self-indulgence.[42]

But more important in distinguishing the emerging aristocracy of Virginia from other contemporary social and political elites were two very specific circumstances. The first concerns the relationship between the integrity of the family unit and the descent of real property. "The English political family," Sir Lewis Namier writes with particular reference to the eighteenth-century aristocracy,

> is a compound of "blood," name, and estate, this last . . . being the most important of the three. . . . The name is a weighty symbol, but liable to variations. . . . the estate . . . is, in the long run, the most potent factor in securing continuity through identification. . . . Primogeniture and entails psychically preserve the family in that they tend to fix its position through the successive generations, and thereby favour conscious identification.

The descent of landed estates in eighteenth-century England was controlled by the complicated device known as the strict settlement which provided that the heir at his marriage received the estate as a life tenant, entailing its descent to his unborn eldest son and specifying the limitations of the encumbrances upon the land that might be made in behalf of his daughters and younger sons.[43]

It was the strict settlement, in which in the eighteenth century perhaps half the land of England was bound, that provided continuity over generations for the landed aristocracy. This permanent identification of the family with a specific estate and with the status and offices that pertained to it was achieved at the cost of sacrificing the younger sons. It was a single stem of the family only that retained its superiority; it alone controlled the material basis for political dominance.

This basic condition of aristocratic governance in England was never present in the American colonies, and not for lack of familiarity with legal forms. The economic necessity that had prompted the widespread adoption of the strict settlement in England was absent in the colonies. Land was cheap and easily available, the more so as one rose on the social and political ladder. There was no need to deprive the younger sons or even daughters of landed inheritances in order to keep the original family estate intact. Provision could be made for endowing each of them with plantations, and they in turn could provide similarly for their children. Moreover, to confine the stem family's fortune to a single plot of land, however extensive, was in the Virginia economy to condemn it to swift decline. Since the land was quickly worn out and since it was cheaper to acquire new land than to rejuvenate the worked soil by careful husbandry, geographical mobility, not stability, was the key to prosperity. Finally, since land was only as

---

[42] Willard F. Bliss, "The Rise of Tenancy in Virginia," *Va. Mag. of Hist. and Biog.*, 58 (1950), 427 ff.; Louis B. Wright, *Cultural Life of the American Colonies, 1607–1763* (New York, 1957), 5–11.

[43] Lewis B. Namier, *England in the Age of the American Revolution* (London, 1930), 22–23; H. J. Habakkuk, "Marriage Settlements in the Eighteenth Century," Royal Hist. Soc., *Transactions*, 4th ser., 32 (1950), 15–30.

valuable as the labor available to work it, a great estate was worth passing intact from generation to generation only if it had annexed to it a sufficient population of slaves. Yet this condition imposed severe rigidities in a plantation's economy — for a labor force bound to a particular plot was immobilized — besides creating bewildering confusions in law.

The result, evident before the end of the seventeenth century, was a particular relationship between the family and the descent of property. There was in the beginning no intent on the part of the Virginians to alter the traditional forms; the continued vitality of the ancient statutes specifying primogeniture in certain cases was assumed.[44] The first clear indication of a new trend came in the third quarter of the century, when the leading gentry, rapidly accumulating large estates, faced for the first time the problem of the transfer of property. The result was the subdivision of the great holdings and the multiplication of smaller plots while the net amount of land held by the leading families continued to rise.[45]

This trend continued. Primogeniture neither at the end of the seventeenth century nor after prevailed in Virginia. It was never popular even among the most heavily endowed of the tidewater families. The most common form of bequest was a grant to the eldest son of the undivided home plantation and gifts of other tracts outside the home county to the younger sons and daughters. Thus by his will of 1686 Robert Beverley, Sr., bequeathed to his eldest son, Peter, all his land in Gloucester County lying between "Chiescake" and "Hoccadey's" creeks (an unspecified acreage); to Robert, the second son, another portion of the Gloucester lands amounting to 920 acres; to Harry, 1,600 acres in Rappahannock County; to John, 3,000 acres in the same county; to William, two plantations in Middlesex County; to Thomas, 3,000 acres in Rappahannock and New Kent counties; to his wife, three plantations including those "whereon I now live" for use during her lifetime, after which they were to descend to his daughter Catherine, who was also to receive £200 sterling; to his daughter Mary, £150 sterling; to "the childe that my wife goeth with, be it male or female," all the rest of his real property; and the residue of his personal property was "to be divided and disposed in equall part & portion betwix my wife and children." Among the bequests of Ralph Wormeley, Jr., in 1700 was an estate of 1,500 acres to his daughter Judith as well as separate plantations to his two sons.

Entail proved no more popular than primogeniture. Only a small minority of estates, even in the tidewater region, were ever entailed. In fact, despite the extension of developed land in the course of the eighteenth century, more tidewater estates were docked of entails than were newly entailed.[46]

Every indication points to continuous and increasing difficulty in reproducing

---

[44] Clarence R. Keim, "Influence of Primogeniture and Entail in the Development of Virginia" (unpublished Ph.D. dissertation, University of Chicago, 1926), Chap. I.

[45] E.g., Ames, *Eastern Shore*, 29–32.

[46] Keim, Primogeniture and Entail, 44 ff., 113–14. Keim found that only 1 of a sample of 72 wills in Westmoreland (1653–72) contained provisions for entailing; by 1756–61 the proportions had risen to 14 out of 39, but these entails covered only small parts of the total estates. Typical of his other tidewater samples are Middlesex, 1698–1703, 16 out of 65, and 1759–72, 7 out of 48; Henrico, 1677–87, 2 out of 29, and no increase for the later periods. The piedmont samples show even smaller proportions; *ibid.*, 54–62. The Beverley will is printed in *Va. Mag. of Hist. and Biog.*, 3 (1895–96), 47–51; on Wormeley, see *ibid.*, 36 (1928), 101.

even pale replicas of the strict settlement. In 1705 a law was passed requiring a special act of the Assembly to break an entail; the law stood, but between 1711 and 1776 no fewer than 125 such private acts were passed, and in 1734 estates of under £200 were exempted from the law altogether. The labor problem alone was an insuperable barrier to perpetuating the traditional forms. A statute of 1727, clarifying the confused legislation of earlier years, had attempted to ensure a labor force on entailed land by classifying slaves as real property and permitting them to be bound together with land into bequests. But in 1748 this stipulation had resulted in so many bewildering "doubts, variety of opinions, and confusions" that it was repealed. The repeal was disallowed in London, and in the course of a defense of its action the Assembly made vividly clear the utter impracticality of entailment in Virginia's economy. Slaves, the Assembly explained, were essential to the success of a plantation, but "slaves could not be kept on the lands to which they were annexed without manifest prejudice to the tenant in tail . . . often the tenant was the proprietor of fee simple land much fitter for cultivation than his intailed lands, where he could work his slaves to a much greater advantage." On the other hand, if a plantation owner did send entailed slaves where they might be employed most economically the result was equally disastrous:

> the frequent removing and settling them on other lands in other counties and parts of the colony far distant from the county court where the deeds or wills which annexed them were recorded and the intail lands lay; the confusion occasioned by their mixture with fee simple slaves of the same name and sex and belonging to the same owner; the uncertainty of distinguishing one from another after several generations, no register of their genealogy being kept and none of them having surnames, were great mischiefs to purchasers, strangers, and creditors, who were often unavoidably deceived in their purchases and hindered in the recovery of their just debts. It also lessened the credit of the country; it being dangerous for the merchants of Great Britain to trust possessors of many slaves for fear the slaves might be intailed.[47]

A mobile labor force free from legal entanglements and a rapid turnover of lands, not a permanent hereditary estate, were prerequisites of family prosperity. This condition greatly influenced social and political life. Since younger sons and even daughters inherited extensive landed properties, equal often to those of the eldest son, concentration of authority in the stem family was precluded. Third generation collateral descendants of the original immigrant were as important in their own right as the eldest son's eldest son. Great clans like the Carters and the Lees, though they may have acknowledged a central family seat, were scattered throughout the province on estates of equal influence. The four male Carters of the third generation were identified by contemporaries by the names

---

[47] Hening, ed., Va. Stat. at L., III, 320, IV, 399–400, 222 ff., V, 441–42n (quoted). In 1765 the legal rigors of entailment were permanently relaxed by a law permitting the leasing of entailed land for up to three lives, a move made necessary, the Assembly said, because "many large tracts of entailed lands remain uncultivated, the owners not having slaves to work them. . . ." Ibid., VIII, 183. For a striking example of the difficulties of maintaining entailed lands, see ibid., VI, 297–99; Keim, Primogeniture and Entail, 108.

of their separate estates, and, indistinguishable in style of life, they had an equal access to political power.[48]

Since material wealth was the basis of the status which made one eligible for public office, there was a notable diffusion of political influence throughout a broadening group of leading families. No one son was predestined to represent the family interest in politics, but as many as birth and temperament might provide. In the 1750's there were no fewer than seven Lees of the same generation sitting together in the Virginia Assembly; in the Burgesses they spoke for five separate counties. To the eldest, Philip Ludwell Lee, they conceded a certain social superiority that made it natural for him to sit in the Council. But he did not speak alone for the family; by virtue of inheritance he had no unique authority over his brothers and cousins.

The leveling at the top of the social and political hierarchy, creating an evenness of status and influence, was intensified by continuous intermarriage within the group. The unpruned branches of these flourishing family trees, growing freely, met and intertwined until by the Revolution the aristocracy appeared to be one great tangled cousinry.[49]

As political power became increasingly diffused throughout the upper stratum of society, the Council, still at the end of the seventeenth century a repository of unique privileges, lost its effective superiority. Increasingly through the successive decades its authority had to be exerted through alignments with the Burgesses — alignments made easier as well as more necessary by the criss-crossing network of kinship that united the two houses. Increasingly the Council's distinctions became social and ceremonial.[50]

The contours of Virginia's political hierarchy were also affected by a second main conditioning element, besides the manner of descent of family property. Not only was the structure usually level and broad at the top, but it was incomplete in itself. Its apex, the ultimate source of legal decision and control, lay in the quite different society of England, amid the distant embroilments of London, the court, and Parliament. The levers of control in that realm were for the most part hidden from the planters; yet the powers that ruled this remote region could impose an arbitrary authority directly into the midst of Virginia's affairs.

One consequence was the introduction of instabilities in the tenure and transfer of the highest offices. Tenure could be arbitrarily interrupted, and the transfer to kin of such positions at death or resignation — uncertain in any case because of the diffusion of family authority — could be quite difficult or even impossible. Thus William Byrd II returned from England at the death of his father in 1704 to take over the family properties, but though he was the sole heir he did not automatically or completely succeed to the elder Byrd's provincial offices. He did, indeed, become auditor of Virginia after his father, but only because he had carefully arranged for the succession while still in London; his father's Council seat went to someone else, and it took three years of patient maneuvering

---

[48] Louis Morton, *Robert Carter of Nomini Hall* (Williamsburg, 1941), 11.

[49] Burton J. Hendrick, *The Lees of Virginia* (Boston, 1935), 97.

[50] Percy S. Flippin, *The Royal Government in Virginia, 1624–1775* (New York, 1919), 166–67, 169; Herbert L. Osgood, *The American Colonies in the Eighteenth Century* (4 vols.; New York, 1924–25), IV, 231–32.

through his main London contact, Micajah Perry, to secure another; he never did take over the receivership. Even such a power as "King" Carter, the reputed owner at his death of 300,000 acres and 1,000 slaves was rebuffed by the resident deputy governor and had to deploy forces in England in order to transfer a Virginia naval office post from one of his sons to another. There was family continuity in public office, but at the highest level it was uncertain, the result of place-hunting rather than of the absolute prerogative of birth.[51]

Instability resulted not only from the difficulty of securing and transferring high appointive positions but also and more immediately from the presence in Virginia of total strangers to the scene, particularly governors and their deputies, armed with extensive jurisdiction and powers of enforcement. The dangers of this element in public life became clear only after Berkeley's return to England in 1677, for after thirty-five years of residence in the colony Sir William had become a leader in the land independent of his royal authority. But Howard, Andros, and Nicholson were governors with full legal powers but with at best only slight connections with local society. In them, social leadership and political leadership had ceased to be identical.

In the generation that followed Berkeley's departure, this separation between the two spheres created the bitterest of political controversies. Firmly entrenched behind their control of the colony's government, the leading families battled with every weapon available to reduce the power of the executives and thus to eliminate what appeared to be an external and arbitrary authority. Repeated complaints by the governors of the intractable opposition of a league of local oligarchs marked the Virginians' success. Efforts by the executives to discipline the indigenous leaders could only be mildly successful. Patronage was a useful weapon, but its effectiveness diminished steadily, ground down between a resistant Assembly and an office-hungry bureaucracy in England. The possibility of exploiting divisions among the resident powers also declined as kinship lines bound the leading families closer together and as group interests became clearer with the passage of time. No faction built around the gubernatorial power could survive independently; ultimately its adherents would fall away and it would weaken. It was a clear logic of the situation that led the same individuals who had promoted Nicholson as a replacement for Andros to work against him once he assumed office.[52]

Stability could be reached only by the complete identification of external and internal authority through permanent commitment by the appointees to local interests. Commissary Blair's extraordinary success in Virginia politics was based not only on his excellent connections in England but also on his marriage into the Harrison family, which gave him the support of an influential kinship faction. There was more than hurt pride and thwarted affection behind Nicholson's reported insane rage at being spurned by the highly marriageable Lucy Burwell;

[51] John S. Bassett, ed., *The Writings of "Colonel William Byrd of Westover in Virginia Esqr"* (New York, 1901), xlviii–ix; Morton, *Carter*, 28n.

[52] For the classic outcry against "the party of Malecontents," see Spotswood's letter to the Board of Trade, March 25, 1719, in R. A. Brock, ed., *The Official Letters of Alexander Spotswood* (Richmond, Va., 1882–85), II, 308 ff.; cf. 285. On patronage, see Flippin, *Royal Government*, 208–214; Leonard W. Labaree, *Royal Government in America* (New Haven, Conn., 1930), 102; Worthington C. Ford, "A Sketch of Sir Francis Nicholson," *Mag. of Amer. Hist.*, 29 (1893), 508–12.

and later the astute Spotswood, for all his success in imposing official policy, fully quieted the controversies of his administration only by succumbing completely and joining as a resident Virginia landowner the powers aligned against him.[53]

But there was more involved than instability and conflict in the discontinuity between social and political organization at the topmost level. The state itself had changed its meaning. To a Virginia planter of the early eighteenth century the highest public authority was no longer merely one expression of a general social authority. It had become something abstract, external to his life and society, an ultimate power whose purposes were obscure, whose direction could neither be consistently influenced nor accurately plotted, and whose human embodiments were alien and antagonistic.

The native gentry of the early eighteenth century had neither the need nor the ability to fashion a new political theory to comprehend their experience, but their successors would find in the writings of John Locke on state and society not merely a reasonable theoretical position but a statement of self-evident fact.

I have spoken exclusively of Virginia, but though the histories of each of the colonies in the seventeenth century are different, they exhibit common characteristics. These features one might least have expected to find present in Virginia, and their presence there is, consequently, most worth indicating.

In all of the colonies the original transference of an ordered European society was succeeded by the rise to authority of resident settlers whose influence was rooted in their ability to deal with the problems of life in wilderness settlements. These individuals attempted to stabilize their positions, but in each case they were challenged by others arriving after the initial settlements, seeking to exploit certain advantages of position, wealth, or influence. These newcomers, securing after the Restoration governmental appointments in the colonies and drawn together by personal ties, especially those of kinship and patronage, came to constitute colonial officialdom. This group introduced a new principle of social organization; it also gave rise to new instabilities in a society in which the traditional forms of authority were already being subjected to severe pressures. By the eight decade of the seventeenth century the social basis of public life had become uncertain and insecure, its stability delicate and sensitive to disturbance. Indian warfare, personal quarrels, and particularly the temporary confusion in external control caused by the Glorious Revolution became the occasions for violent challenges to constituted authority.

By the end of the century a degree of harmony had been achieved, but the divergence between political and social leadership at the topmost level created an area of permanent conflict. The political and social structures that emerged were by European standards strangely shaped. Everywhere as the bonds of empire drew tighter the meaning of the state was changing. Herein lay the origins of a new political system.

---

[53] Peter Laslett, "John Locke . . . ," *Wm. and Mary Qtly.*, 3rd ser., 14 (1957), 398; Daniel E. Motley, *Life of Commissary James Blair* . . . (Baltimore, 1901), 10, 43 ff.; William S. Perry, ed., *Historical Collections Relating to the . . . Church* ([Hartford], 1870–78), I, 69, 72–73, 88, 90, 102, 135; Leonidas Dodson, *Alexander Spotswood* (Philadelphia, 1932), 251 ff.

Economic Development and Social Structure in Colonial Boston

JAMES A. HENRETTA

In this essay, James A. Henretta explores the relationship between economic development and the structure of society in prerevolutionary Boston, Massachusetts. Appropriating the economist's concept of "growth," he asks a relatively new historical question: What was the impact of economic growth upon social organization? His response is that economic change steadily transformed Boston from an agricultural, land-based society into a maritime, commercial society — a transformation significantly advanced by the end of the seventeenth century. Using the tax list of 1687 as evidence, Henretta asserts that wealth was fairly evenly distributed in Boston at that time, but that various conditions of social dependency characterized the community. As the economy developed in the eighteenth century, society became more fluid and dependency decreased, but the distribution of wealth fell radically out of balance. As the influence of the propertied classes proliferated, society became more rigidly stratified. Henretta finds, on the basis of the tax list of 1771, that "merchant princes" and "proletarians" were the most notable figures of late eighteenth-century Boston society. Do you think, however, that two sets of tax and property valuation lists are a sufficient basis for such sweeping conclusions?

A distinctly urban social structure developed in Boston in the 150 years between the settlement of the town and the American Revolution. The expansion of trade and industry after 1650 unleashed powerful economic forces which first distorted, then destroyed, the social homogeneity and cohesiveness of the early village community. All aspects of town life were affected by Boston's involvement in the dynamic, competitive world of Atlantic commerce. The disruptive pressure of rapid economic growth, sustained for over a century, made the social appearance of the town more diverse, more complex, more modern — increasingly different from that of the rest of New England. The magnitude of the change in Boston's social composition and structure may be deduced from an analysis and comparison of the tax lists for 1687 and 1771. Containing a wealth of information on property ownership in the community, these lists make it possible to block out, in quantitative terms, variations in the size and influence of economic

Reprinted by permission of the author from the *William and Mary Quarterly*, 3d Ser., 22 (1965), pp. 75–92.

groups and to trace the change in the distribution of the resources of the community among them.[1]

The transformation of Boston from a land-based society to a maritime center was neither sudden nor uniform. In the last decade of the seventeenth century, a large part of the land of its broad peninsula was still cultivated by small farmers. Only a small fraction was laid out in regular streets and even less was densely settled. The north end alone showed considerable change from the middle of the century when almost every house had a large lot and garden. Here, the later-comers — the mariners, craftsmen, and traders who had raised the population to six thousand by 1690 — were crowded together along the waterfront.[2] Here, too, in the series of docks and shipyards which jutted out from the shore line, were tangible manifestations of the commercial activity which had made the small town the largest owner of shipping and the principal port of the English colonies. Over 40 per cent of the carrying capacity of all colonial-owned shipping was in Boston hands.[3]

Dependence on mercantile endeavor rather than agricultural enterprise had by 1690 greatly affected the extent of property ownership. Boston no longer had the universal ownership of real estate characteristic of rural Massachusetts to the end of the colonial period. The tax list for 1687 contained the names of 188 polls, 14 per cent of the adult male population, who were neither owners of taxable property of any kind nor "dependents" in a household assessed for the property tax.[4] Holding no real estate, owning no merchandise or investments which would yield an income, these men constituted the "propertyless" segment of the community and were liable only for the head tax which fell equally upon all men above the age of sixteen.[5] Many in this group were young men, laborers and seamen, attracted by the commercial prosperity of the town and hoping to save enough from their wages to buy or rent a shop, to invest in the tools of an artisan, or to find a start in trade. John Erving, a poor Scotch sailor whose grandson in 1771 was one of the richest men in Boston, was only one propertyless man who rose quickly to a position of wealth and influence.[6]

[1] "Tax List and Schedules — 1687," in *First Report of the Record Commissioners of the City of Boston, 1876* (Boston, 1876), 91–133; "Tax and Valuation Lists — 1771," in Massachusetts Archives, CXXXII, 92–147, State House, Boston.

[2] The tax list for 1687 shows 80 polls with holdings of five acres or more within the town limits. For the size and location of most Boston real estate holdings from 1630 to 1645 see the "Book of Possessions" (and "Appendix"), *The Second Report of the Record Commissioners of the City of Boston*, 2d ed., (Boston, 1881) and also the detailed property maps compiled by George Lamb, *Series of Plans of Boston . . . 1630–1635–1640–1645* (Boston, 1905).

[3] Curtis Nettels, "The Economic Relations of Boston, Philadelphia, and New York, 1680–1715," *Journal of Economic and Business History*, III (1930–31), 185–215.

[4] In 1771, in Concord, Middlesex County, only 26 of 396 polls (6.5 per cent) were without taxable property; in Easton, Bristol County, 26 of 261 (10 per cent); and in Hadley, Hampshire County, 8 of 157 polls (5.1 per cent). Mass. Archives, CXXXII, 199–210, 269–274, 251–254.

[5] William H. Whitmore, ed., *The Colonial Laws of Massachusetts. Reprinted from the Edition of 1672, with the Supplements through 1686* (Boston, 1887), 22–23; Edwin R. A. Seligman, "The Income Tax in the American Colonies and States," *Political Science Quarterly*, X (1895), 221–247.

[6] Clifford K. Shipton, *Sibley's Harvard Graduates*, XII (Boston, 1962), 152–156. For other examples of mercantile success, see Bernard Bailyn, *The New England Merchants in the Seventeenth Century* (Cambridge, Mass., 1955), 192–197.

But many of these 188 men did not acquire either taxable property or an established place in the social order of Boston. Only sixty-four, or 35 per cent, were inhabitants of the town eight years later. By way of contrast, 45 per cent of the polls assessed from two to seven pounds on the tax list, 65 per cent of those with property valued from eight to twenty pounds, and 73 per cent of those with estates in excess of twenty pounds were present in 1695. There was a direct relation between permanence of residence and economic condition. Even in an expanding and diversifying economic environment, the best opportunities for advancement rested with those who could draw upon long-standing connections, upon the credit facilities of friends and neighbors, and upon political influence. It was precisely these personal contacts which were denied to the propertyless.[7]

A second, distinct element in the social order consisted of the dependents of property owners. Though propertyless themselves, these dependents — grown sons living at home, apprentices, and indentured servants — were linked more closely to the town as members of a tax-paying household unit than were the 188 "unattached" men without taxable estates. Two hundred and twelve men, nearly one sixth of the adult male population of Boston, were classified as dependents in 1687. The pervasiveness of the dependency relationship attested not only to the cohesiveness of the family unit but also to the continuing vitality of the apprenticeship and indenture system at the close of the seventeenth century.

Yet even the dependency relationship, traditionally an effective means of alleviating unemployment and preventing the appearance of unattached propertyless laborers, was subjected to severe pressure by the expansion of the economy. An urgent demand for labor, itself the cause of short indentures, prompted servants to strike out on their own as soon as possible. They became the laborers or semiskilled craftsmen of the town, while the sons of the family eventually assumed control of their father's business and a share of the economic resources of the community.[8]

The propertied section of the population of 1687 was composed of 1,036 individuals who were taxed on their real estate or their income from trade. The less-skilled craftsmen, 521 men engaged in the rougher trades of a waterfront society, formed the bottom stratum of the taxable population in this pre-industrial age. These carpenters, shipwrights, blacksmiths, shopkeepers owned only 12 per cent of the taxable wealth of the town.[9] Few of these artisans and laborers had investments in shipping or in merchandise. A small store or house, or a small farm in the south end of Boston, accounted for their assessment of two to seven pounds on the tax list. (Tables 1 and 3, pp. 62 and 64)

---

[7] Mobility and residence data were determined by comparing the names on the tax list of 1687 with those of a list of the inhabitants of Boston in 1695 in the *First Report of the Record Commissioners*, 158–170. While the death rate was higher among the poorer sections of the population, this alone does not explain the variation in permanence of residence. See John B. Blake, *Public Health in the Town of Boston, 1630–1822* (Cambridge, Mass., 1959), chap. 6.

[8] See Samuel McKee, Jr., *Labor in Colonial New York, 1664–1776* (New York, 1935), chaps. 2, 3; also, Richard B. Morris, *Government and Labor in Early America* (New York, 1946), 147–149.

[9] The lower 50 per cent of the property owners is treated as a whole as Tables 1 and 2 and Chart A, below, indicate that the proportion of wealth held by this section of the population is approximately the same in 1687 and 1771.

CHART A   *Lorenz Curves Showing the Distribu-*
            tion of Wealth in Boston in 1687 and
            1771 (Drawn from Data in Tables 1
            and 2)

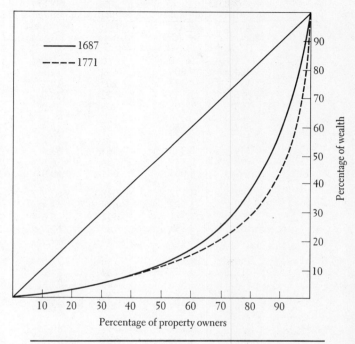

Between these craftsmen and shopkeepers and the traders and merchants who constituted the economic elite of the town was a middle group of 275 property owners with taxable assets valued from eight to twenty pounds. Affluent artisans employing two or three workers, ambitious shopkeepers with investments in commerce, and entrepreneurial-minded sea masters with various maritime interests, bulked large in this center portion of the economic order. Of the 275, 180 owned real estate assessed at seven pounds or less and were boosted into the third quarter of the distribution of wealth by their holdings of merchandise and shares in shipping (Table 3). The remaining ninety-five possessed real estate rated at eight pounds or more and, in addition, held various investments in trade. Making up about 25 per cent of the propertied population, this middle group controlled 22 per cent of the taxable wealth in Boston in 1687. Half as numerous as the lowest group of property owners, these men possessed almost double the amount of taxable assets (Table 1).

Merchants with large investments in English and West Indian trade and individuals engaged in the ancillary industries of shipbuilding and distilling made up the top quarter of the taxable population in 1687. With taxable estates ranging from twenty to 170 pounds, this commercial group controlled 66 per

TABLE 1   *Distribution of Assessed Taxable Wealth in Boston in 1687*[a]

Total value of taxable wealth	Number of taxpayers in each wealth bracket	Total wealth in each wealth bracket	Cumulative total of wealth	Cumulative total of taxpayers	Cumulative percentage of taxpayers	Cumulative percentage of wealth
£ 1	0	£ 0	£ 0	0	0.0%	0.0%
2	152	304	304	152	14.6	1.8
3	51	153	457	203	19.5	2.7
4	169	676	1,133	372	35.9	6.8
5	33	165	1,298	405	39.0	7.8
6	97	582	1,880	502	48.5	11.3
7	19	133	2,013	521	50.2	12.1
8	43	344	2,357	564	54.4	14.2
9	22	198	2,555	586	56.6	15.4
10	45	450	3,005	631	60.9	18.1
11	17	187	3,192	648	62.5	19.2
12	30	360	3,552	678	65.4	21.4
13	13	169	3,721	691	66.6	22.4
14	12	168	3,889	703	67.9	23.4
15	22	330	4,219	725	69.9	25.4
16	21	336	4,555	746	72.0	27.5
17	1	17	4,572	747	72.0	27.6
18	18	324	4,896	765	73.8	29.5
19	1	19	4,915	766	73.9	29.6
20	30	600	5,515	796	76.8	33.2
21–25	41	972	6,487	837	80.7	39.0
26–30	48	1,367	7,854	885	85.4	47.3
31–35	29	971	8,825	914	88.2	53.1
36–40	21	819	9,644	935	90.2	58.1
41–45	19	828	10,472	954	92.1	63.1
46–50	16	781	11,253	970	93.6	67.8
51–60	16	897	12,150	986	95.1	73.2
61–70	19	1,245	13,395	1,005	97.0	80.7
71–80	7	509	13,904	1,012	97.8	83.8
81–90	3	253	14,157	1,015	97.9	85.3
91–100	7	670	14,827	1,022	98.6	89.3
100–	14	1,764	16,591	1,036	100.0	100.0

[a] Money values are those of 1687. Many of the assessments fall at regular five pound intervals and must be considered as an estimate of the economic position of the individual. No attempt was made to compensate for systematic overvaluation or undervaluation inasmuch as the analysis measures relative wealth. The utility of a relative presentation of wealth (or income) is that it can be compared to another relative distribution without regard to absolute monetary values. See Mary Jean Bowman, "A Graphical Analysis of Personal Income Distribution in the United States," *American Economic Review*, XXXV (1944–45), 607–628, and Horst Mendershausen, *Changes in Income Distribution during the Great Depression* (New York, 1946).

TABLE 2 Distribution of Assessed Taxable Wealth in Boston in 1771[a]

Total value of taxable wealth	Number of taxpayers in each wealth bracket	Total wealth in each wealth bracket	Cumulative total of wealth	Cumulative total of taxpayers	Cumulative percentage of taxpayers	Cumulative percentage of wealth
£ 3–30	78	£1,562	£1,562	78	5.0%	0.3%
31–40	86	2,996	4,558	164	10.6	0.9
41–50	112	5,378	9,936	276	17.9	2.2
51–60	74	4,398	14,334	350	22.6	3.5
61–70	33	3,122	17,456	383	24.7	3.8
71–80	165	12,864	30,320	548	35.4	6.5
81–90	24	2,048	32,368	572	36.9	7.0
91–100	142	13,684	46,052	714	46.1	10.0
101–110	14	494	46,546	728	47.1	10.1
111–120	149	17,844	64,390	877	56.7	13.9
121–130	20	2,570	66,960	897	58.0	14.5
131–140	26	4,600	71,560	923	59.7	15.5
141–150	20	2,698	74,258	943	60.9	16.1
151–160	88	14,048	88,306	1,031	66.6	19.1
161–170	11	1,846	90,152	1,042	67.4	19.6
171–180	18	3,128	93,280	1,060	68.6	20.3
181–190	10	1,888	95,168	1,070	69.2	20.7
191–200	47	9,368	104,536	1,117	72.2	22.7
201–300	126	31,097	135,633	1,243	80.4	29.4
301–400	60	21,799	157,432	1,303	84.2	34.1
401–500	58	24,947	182,379	1,361	88.0	39.6
501–600	14	7,841	190,220	1,375	88.9	41.3
601–700	24	15,531	205,751	1,399	90.4	44.6
701–800	26	19,518	225,269	1,425	92.2	48.9
801–900	20	17,020	242,289	1,445	93.4	52.6
901–1,000	16	15,328	257,617	1,461	95.4	55.9
1,001–1,500	41	48,364	305,963	1,502	97.1	66.4
1,501–5,000	37	85,326	391,289	1,539	99.5	84.9
5,001–	7	69,204	460,493	1,546	100.0	100.0

[a] The extant tax list is not complete. In ward 3, there are two pages and 69 polls missing; in ward 7, one page and 24 polls; in ward 12, an unknown number of pages and 225 polls. Only the total number of polls (224) is known for ward 11. The missing entries amount to 558, or 19.3 per cent of the total number of polls on the tax list. Internal evidence (the totals for all wards are known) suggests the absent material is completely random. Nevertheless, it should be remembered that this table represents an 80 per cent sample.

The value of shipping investments and of "servants for life" was not included in the computation of the table as it was impossible to determine the assessor's valuation. For the law regulating the assessment, see The Acts and Resolves, Public and Private, of the Province of the Massachusetts Bay . . . , IV (Boston, 1881), 985–987. Money values are those of 1771.

TABLE 3   *Real Estate Ownership in Boston in 1687 and 1771*[a]

	1687			1771	
Assessed total value of real estate	Number of owners	Cumulative total of owners	Assessed annual worth of real estate	Number of owners	Cumulative total of owners
£ 1	0	0	£ 1	0	0
2	168	168	2	1	1
3	75	243	3	9	10
4	203	446	4	49	59
5	85	531	5	22	81
6	167	698	6	79	160
7	3	701	7	0	160
8	54	755	8	115	275
9	2	757	9	3	278
10	107	864	10	91	369
11	0	864	11	4	373
12	24	888	12	43	416
13	0	888	13	163	579
14	3	891	14	10	589
15	25	916	15	3	592
16	8	924	16	148	740
17	0	924	17	6	746
18	7	930	18	7	753
19	1	931	19	5	758
20	46	932	20	236	994
21–30	25	1,003	21–25	41	1,035
31–40	11	1,014	26–30	163	1,198
41–50	2	1,016	31–35	93	1,291
			36–40	92	1,383
			41–45	5	1,388
			46–50	42	1,430
			51–60	32	1,462
			61–70	10	1,472
			71–80	9	1,481
			81–90	3	1,484
			91–100	3	1,487

[a] The assessed annual worth of real estate in the 1771 valuation must be multiplied by six to give the total property value.

cent of the town's wealth. But economic development had been too rapid, too uneven and incomplete, to allow the emergence of a well-defined merchant class endowed with a common outlook and clearly distinguished from the rest of the society. Only eighty-five of these men, one third of the wealthiest group in the community, owned dwellings valued at as much as twenty pounds. The majority held landed property valued at ten pounds, only a few pounds greater than that of the middle group of property holders.[10] The merchants had not shared equally in the accumulated fund of capital and experience which had accrued after fifty years of maritime activity. Profits had flowed to those whose daring initiative and initial resources had begun the exploitation of the lucrative colonial market. By 1687, the upper 15 per cent of the property owners held 52 per cent of the taxable assets of the town, while the fifty individuals who composed the highest 5 per cent of the taxable population accounted for more than 25 per cent of the wealth (Table 1).

By the end of the seventeenth century widespread involvement in commerce had effected a shift in the locus of social and political respectability in Boston and distinguished it from the surrounding communities. Five of the nine selectmen chosen by the town in 1687 were sea captains.[11] This was more than deference to those accustomed to command. With total estates of £83, £29, £33, £33, and £24, Captains Elisha Hutchinson, John Fairweather, Theophilus Frary, Timothy Prout, and Daniel Turell were among the wealthiest 20 per cent of the population.[12] Still, achievement in trade was not the only index of respectability. Henry Eames, George Cable, Isaac Goose, and Elnathan Lyon, the men appointed by the town to inspect the condition of the streets and roads, had the greater part of their wealth, £105 of £130, invested in land and livestock.[13] And the presence of Deacon Henry Allen among the selectmen provided a tangible indication of the continuing influence of the church.

These legacies of an isolated religious society and a stable agricultural economy disappeared in the wake of the rapid growth which continued unabated until the middle of the eighteenth century. In the fifty years after 1690, the population of the town increased from 6,000 to 16,000. The farms of the south end vanished and the central business district became crowded. In the populous north end, buildings which had once housed seven people suddenly began to hold nine or ten.[14] Accompanying this physical expansion of Boston was a diversification of economic endeavor. By 1742, the town led all the colonial cities in the production of export furniture and shoes, although master craftsmen continued to carry on most industry on a small scale geared to local needs. Prosperity and expansion continued to be rooted, not in the productive capacity or

[10] See Table 3; and Edwin L. Bynner, "Topography and Landmarks of the Provincial Period," in Justin Winsor, ed., *The Memorial History of Boston* . . . , II (Boston, 1881), chap. 17; Bailyn, *New England Merchants*, chaps. 6, 7; Nettels, "Economic Relations," 185–200.

[11] Robert Francis Seybolt, *The Town Officials of Colonial Boston, 1634–1775* (Cambridge, Mass., 1939), 74.

[12] *First Report of the Record Commissioners*, 99, 116, 126, 99, 95; Table 1, above.

[13] Seybolt, *Town Officials*, 74; *First Report of the Record Commissioners*, 98, 109, 127, 109; Bailyn, *New England Merchants*, chaps. 6, 7.

[14] Clifford K. Shipton, "Immigration to New England, 1680–1740," *The Journal of Political Economy*, XLIV (1936), 225–238; Boston's population was 9,000 in 1710; 13,000 in 1730; 16,382 in 1742; 15,731 in 1752; and 15,520 in 1771. Lemuel Shattuck, *Report to the Committee of the City Council Appointed to Obtain the Census of Boston for the Year 1845* (Boston, 1846), 3–5. In 1687 there were 850 houses for 6,000 people or 7.05 persons per house. "Tax Lists and Schedules — 1687." The average number of persons per house in 1742 was 9.53; in 1771, 8.47. Shattuck, *Census of Boston*, 54.

geographic position of the town, but in the ability of the Boston merchants to compete successfully in the highly competitive mercantile world.[15]

After 1750, the economic health of the Massachusetts seaport was jeopardized as New York and Philadelphia merchants, exploiting the rich productive lands at their backs and capitalizing upon their prime geographic position in the West Indian and southern coasting trade, diverted a significant portion of European trade from the New England traders. Without increasing returns from the lucrative "carrying" trade, Boston merchants could no longer subsidize the work of the shopkeepers, craftsmen, and laborers who supplied and maintained the commercial fleet. By 1760, the population of Boston had dropped to 15,000 persons, a level it did not exceed until after the Revolution.[16]

The essential continuity of maritime enterprise in Boston from the late seventeenth to the mid-eighteenth century concealed the emergence of a new type of social system. After a certain point increases in the scale and extent of commercial endeavor produced a new, and more fluid, social order. The development of the economic system subjected the family, the basic social unit, to severe pressures. The fundamental link between one generation and another, the ability of the father to train his offspring for their life's work, was endangered by a process of change which rendered obsolete many of the skills and assumptions of the older, land-oriented generation and opened the prospect of success in new fields and new places. The well-known departure of Benjamin Franklin from his indenture to his brother was but one bright piece in the shifting mosaic of colonial life.

The traditional family unit had lost much of its cohesiveness by the third quarter of the eighteenth century. The Boston tax lists for 1771 indicate that dependents of property owners accounted for only 10 per cent of the adult male population as opposed to 16 per cent eighty-five years earlier. Increasingly children left their homes at an earlier age to seek their own way in the world.

A second factor in the trend away from dependency status was the decline in the availability of indentured servants during the eighteenth century. Fewer than 250 of 2,380 persons entering Boston from 1764 to 1768 were classified as indentured servants.[17] These were scarcely enough to replace those whose indentures expired. More and more, the labor force had to be recruited from the ranks of "unattached" workers who bartered their services for wages in a market economy.[18]

[15] Samuel Eliot Morison, "The Commerce of Boston on the Eve of the Revolution," in American Antiquarian Society, *Proceedings*, New Ser., XXXII (Worcester, 1922), 24–51.
[16] See the table of entries and clearances in 1773 for the major colonial ports, *ibid.*, 28. By 1760 Philadelphia had 23,750 inhabitants and New York 18,000. Carl Bridenbaugh, *Cities in Revolt, Urban Life in America, 1743–1776* (New York, 1955), 5.
[17] Compiled from "Port Arrivals — Immigrants," in Record Commissioners of the City of Boston, *A Volume of Records Relating to the Early History of Boston* (Boston, 1900), 254–312. See, also, Mildred Campbell, "English Emigration on the Eve of the American Revolution," *American Historical Review*, LXI (1955–56), 1–20.
[18] For most of the 18th century, Negro slaves compensated for the lack of white servants. From 150 in 1690, the number of Negroes rose to 1,100 in a population of 13,000 in 1730. In that year, they made up 8.4 per cent of the population; in 1742, 8.4 per cent; in 1752, 9.7 per cent; but only 5.5 per cent in 1765. Computed from data in

This laboring force consisted of the nondependent, propertyless workers of the community, now twice as numerous relative to the rest of the population as they had been a century before. In 1687, 14 per cent of the total number of adult males were without taxable property; by the eve of the Revolution, the propertyless accounted for 29 per cent. The social consequences of this increase were manifold. For every wage earner who competed in the economy as an autonomous entity at the end of the seventeenth century, there were four in 1771; for every man who slept in the back of a shop, in a tavern, or in a rented room in 1687, there were four in the later period. The population of Boston had doubled, but the number of propertyless men had increased fourfold.

The adult males without property, however, did not form a single unified class, a monolithic body of landless proletarians. Rather, the bottom of society consisted of a congeries of social and occupational groups with a highly transient maritime element at one end of the spectrum and a more stable and respected artisan segment at the other. Although they held no taxable property, hardworking and reputable craftsmen who had established a permanent residence in Boston participated in the town meeting and were elected to unpaid minor offices. In March 1771, for instance, John Dyer was selected by the people of the town as "Fence Viewer" for the following year. Yet according to the tax and valuation lists compiled less than six months later, Dyer was without taxable property.[19] At the same town meeting, four carpenters, Joseph Ballard, Joseph Edmunds, Benjamin Page, and Joseph Butler, none of whom was listed as an owner of taxable property on the valuation lists, were chosen as "Measurers of Boards."[20] That propertyless men should be selected for public office indicates that the concept of a "stake in society," which provided the theoretical underpinning for membership in the community of colonial Boston, was interpreted in the widest possible sense. Yet it was this very conception of the social order which was becoming anachronistic under the pressure of economic development. For how could the growing number of propertyless men be integrated into a social order based in the first instance on the principle that only those having a tangible interest in the town or a definite family link to the society would be truly interested in the welfare of the community?[21]

Changes no less significant had taken place within the ranks of the propertied groups. By the third quarter of the eighteenth century, lines of economic division and marks of social status were crystalizing as Boston approached economic maturity. Present to some degree in all aspects of town life, these distinctions

---

Shattuck, Census of Boston, 4–5, 43. The 1771 tax list indicates that only 17 of 318 Negro "servants for life" were held by persons whose property holdings placed them in the lower 50 per cent of the distribution of taxable wealth; 70 by individuals in the third quarter of the economic scale; and 231 or 72.6 per cent by the wealthiest 25 per cent of the population. A somewhat different picture is presented by Robert E. Brown, Middle-Class Democracy and the Revolution in Massachusetts, 1691–1780 (Ithaca, 1955), 19; and McKee, Labor in Colonial New York, 171.

[19] Seybolt, Town Officials, 341; "Tax and Valuation Lists — 1771," ward 1. Dyer apparently paid rent for part of a house assessed at £20.

[20] Seybolt, Town Officials, 340–341; "Tax and Valuation Lists — 1771," wards 1 and 2.

[21] For a different view, see Brown, Middle-Class Democracy, 28–30, 79–95.

were very apparent in dwelling arrangements. In 1687, 85 per cent of Boston real estate holdings had been assessed within a narrow range of two to ten pounds; by the seventh decade of the eighteenth century, the same spectrum ran from twelve to two hundred pounds (Table 3). Gradations in housing were finer in 1771 and had social connotations which were hardly conceivable in the more primitive and more egalitarian society of the seventeenth century. This sense of distinctiveness was reinforced by geographic distribution. Affluent members of the community who had not transferred their residence to Roxbury, Cambridge, or Milton built in the spacious environs of the south and west ends. A strict segregation of the social groups was lacking; yet the milieu of the previous century, the interaction of merchant, trader, artisan, and laborer in a waterfront community, had all but disappeared.[22]

The increasing differences between the social and economic groups within the New England seaport stemmed in part from the fact that craftsmen, laborers, and small shopkeepers had failed to maintain their relative position in the economic order. In the eighty-five years from 1687 to 1771, the share of the taxable wealth of the community controlled by the lower half of the propertied population declined from 12 to 10 per cent (Table 2, p. 63). If these men lived better at the end of the century than at the beginning, it was not because the economic development of Boston had effected a redistribution of wealth in favor of the laboring classes but because the long period of commercial prosperity had raised the purchasing power of every social group.

The decline in the economic distinctiveness of the middle group of property holders, the third quarter of the taxable population in the distribution of wealth, is even more significant. In 1771, these well-to-do artisans, shopkeepers, and traders (rising land values had eliminated the farmers and economic maturity the versatile merchant-sea captain) owned only 12½ per cent of the taxable wealth, a very substantial decrease from the 21 per cent held in 1687. These men lived considerably better than their counterparts in the seventeenth century; many owned homes and possessed furnishings rarely matched by the most elegant dwellings of the earlier period. But in relation to the other parts of the social order, their economic position had deteriorated drastically. This smaller middle group had been assessed for taxable estates twice as large as the bottom 50 per cent in 1687; by 1771 the assets of the two groups were equal.

On the other hand, the wealthiest 25 per cent of the taxable population by 1771 controlled 78 per cent of the assessed wealth of Boston. This represented a gain of 12 per cent from the end of the seventeenth century. An equally important shift had taken place within this elite portion of the population. In 1687, the richest 15 per cent of the taxpayers held 52 per cent of the taxable property, while the top 5 per cent owned 26.8 per cent. Eighty-five years later, the percentages were 65.9 and 44.1 (Tables 1 and 2, and Chart A, pp. 62, 63, 61).

Certain long-term economic developments accounted for the disappearance of a distinct middle group of property owners and the accumulation of wealth among a limited portion of the population. The scarcity of capital in a relatively underdeveloped economic system, one in which barter transactions were often

[22] Walter Muir Whitehill, *Boston, A Topographical History* (Cambridge, Mass., 1959), chaps. 1–3; Bridenbaugh, *Cities in Revolt*, 25.

necessary because of the lack of currency, required that the savings of all members of the society be tapped in the interest of economic expansion. The prospect of rapid commercial success and the high return on capital invested in mercantile activity attracted the small investor. During the first decade of the eighteenth century, nearly one of every three adult males in Boston was involved directly in trade, owning at least part of a vessel. In 1698 alone, 261 people held shares in a seagoing vessel.[23] Trade had become "not so much a way of life as a way of making money; not a social condition but an economic activity."[24] This widespread ownership of mercantile wealth resulted in the creation of a distinct economic "middle class" by the last decades of the seventeenth century.

A reflection of a discrete stage of economic growth, the involvement of disparate occupational and social groups in commerce was fleeting and transitory. It lasted only as long as the economy of the New England seaport remained underdeveloped, without large amounts of available capital. The increase in the wealth and resources of the town during the first half of the eighteenth century prompted a growing specialization of economic function; it was no longer necessary to rely on the investments of the less affluent members of the community for an expansion of commerce. This change was slow, almost imperceptible; but by 1771 the result was obvious. In that year, less than 5 per cent of the taxable population of Boston held shares in shipping of ten tons or more, even though the tonnage owned by the town was almost double that of 1698. Few men had investments of less than fifty tons; the average owner held 112 tons. By way of contrast, the average holding at the end of the seventeenth century had been about twenty-five tons.[25] Moreover, on the eve of the Revolution ownership of shipping was concentrated among the wealthiest men of the community. Ninety per cent of the tonnage of Boston in 1771 was in the hands of those whose other assets placed them in the top quarter of the population.[26] With the increase in the wealth of the town had come a great increase in the number of propertyless men and a bifurcation of the property owners into (1) a large amorphous body of shopkeepers, artisans, and laborers with holdings primarily in real estate and (2) a smaller, somewhat more closely defined segment of the population with extensive commercial investments as well as elegant residences and personal possessions.

A similar trend was evident in other phases of town life. In the transitional decades of the late seventeenth and early eighteenth century, the fluidity inherent in the primitive commercial system had produced a certain vagueness in the connotations of social and economic status. Over 10 per cent of the adult

[23] Bernard and Lotte Bailyn, *Massachusetts Shipping, 1697–1714, A Statistical Study* (Cambridge, Mass., 1959), 56, 79 (Table II).

[24] Bailyn, *New England Merchants*, 194.

[25] In 1771, Bostonians owned 10,396 tons of taxable shipping; the town's tonnage was 6,443 in 1698. See Bailyn and Bailyn, *Massachusetts Shipping*, 79 (Table II).

[26] Only 2.3 per cent of the 8,898 tons of shipping for which the owners are known was held by individuals in the bottom half of the distribution of wealth (estates of £100 or less in Table 2); 5.9 per cent more by those with estates valued from £100 to £200; and an additional 19 per cent by persons with wealth of £200 to £500. 73 per cent of Boston's shipping was held by the wealthiest 12 per cent of the propertied population, those with estates in excess of £500. See Table 2.

males in Boston designated themselves as "merchants" on the shipping registers of the period from 1698 to 1714, indicating not only the decline in the distinctiveness of a title traditionally limited to a carefully defined part of the community but also the feeling that any man could easily ascend the mercantile ladder. Economic opportunity was so evident, so promising, that the social demarcations of the more stable maritime communities of England seemed incongruous.[27] By the sixth decade of the eighteenth century, however, rank and order were supplanting the earlier chaos as successful families tightened their control of trade. The founding in 1763 of a "Merchants Club" with 146 members was a dramatic indication that occupations and titles were regaining some of their traditional distinctiveness and meaning.[28]

An economic profile of the 146 men who composed this self-constituted elite is revealing. Of those whose names appeared on the tax and valuation lists of 1771, only five had estates which placed them in the bottom three quarters of the distribution of wealth. Twenty-one were assessed for taxable property in excess of £1,500 and were thus in the top 1 per cent of the economic scale. The taxable assets of the rest averaged £650, an amount which put them among the wealthiest 15 per cent of the population.

That 146 men, 6½ per cent of the adult male population, were considered eligible for membership in a formal society of merchants indicates, however, that mercantile activity was not dominated by a narrow oligarchy. The range of wealth among the members of the top quarter of the propertied population was so great and the difference of social background so large as to preclude the creation of monolithic class or guild with shared interests and beliefs.

Yet the influence of this segment was pervasive. By the third quarter of the eighteenth century, an integrated economic and political hierarchy based on mercantile wealth had emerged in Boston to replace the lack of social stratification of the early part of the century and the archaic distinctions of power and prestige of the religious community of the seventeenth century. All of the important offices of the town government, those with functions vital to the existence and property of the town, were lodged firmly in the hands of a broad elite, entry into which was conditioned by commercial achievement and family background. The representatives to the General Court and the selectmen were the leaders of the town in economic endeavor as well as in political acumen. John Hancock's taxable wealth totaled £18,000; James Otis was assessed at £2,040, while Colonel Joseph Jackson had property valued at £1,288. Other levels of the administrative system were reserved for those whose business skills or reputation provided the necessary qualifications. Samuel Abbot, John Barrett, Benjamin Dolbeare, John Gore, William Phillips, William White, and William Whitewell, Overseers of the Poor in 1771, had taxable estates of £815, £5,520, £850, £1,747, £5,771, £1,953, and £1,502 respectively. All were among the wealthiest 7 per cent of the property owners; and Barrett and Phillips were two of the most respected merchants of the town. John Scollay, a distiller with an

[27] Bailyn and Bailyn, *Massachusetts Shipping*, 57–58.
[28] "Society for the Encouraging of Trade and Commerce Within the Province of Massachusetts Bay," Ezekiel Price Papers, Massachusetts Historical Society, Boston. See also, Charles M. Andrews, "The Boston Merchants and the Non-Importation Movement," in Colonial Society of Massachusetts, *Publications*, XIX (Boston, 1918), 159–259.

estate of £320, and Captain Benjamin Waldo, a shipmaster assessed at £500, who were among those chosen as "Firewards" in 1771, might in an earlier period have been dominated in town affairs; by the seventh decade of the century, in a mature economic environment, the merchant prince had replaced the man of action at the apex of the social order.

Gradations continued at the bottom of the scale. Different social and occupational levels of the population were tapped as the dignity and responsibility of the position demanded. It was not by accident that the estates of the town assessors, Jonathan Brown, Moses Deshon, and John Kneeland, were £208, £200 and £342. Or that those of the "Cullers of Staves," Henry Lucas, Thomas Knox, and Caleb Hayden, totaled £120, £144, and £156. The assumption of a graded social, economic, and political scale neatly calibrated so as to indicate the relation of each individual to the whole was the basic principle upon which the functioning of town-meeting "democracy" depended. William Crafts, with a taxable estate of £80, was elected "Fence Viewer." Half this amount qualified William Barrett to be "Measurer of Coal Baskets," while Henry Allen and John Bulfinch, "Measurers of Boards," were assessed at £80 and £48. The design was nearly perfect, the correlation between town office and social and economic position almost exact.[29]

As in 1687, the distribution of political power and influence in Boston conformed to the standards and gradations of a wider, more inclusive hierarchy of status, one which purported to include the entire social order within the bounds of its authority. But the lines of force which had emerged on the eve of the American Revolution radiated from different economic and social groups than those of eighty-five years before, and now failed to encompass a significant portion of the population. The weakening of the "extended" family unit and the appearance of a large body of autonomous wage earners, "proletarians" in condition if not in consciousness, had introduced elements of mobility and diversity into the bottom part of society. Equally significant had been the growing inequality of the distribution of wealth among the propertied segment of the community, notably the greater exclusiveness and predominance of a mercantile "elite." Society had become more stratified and unequal. Influential groups, increasingly different from the small property owners who constituted the center portion of the community, had arisen at either end of the spectrum. Creations of the century-long development of a maritime economy in an urban setting, these "merchant princes" and "proletarians" stood out as the salient characteristics of a new social order.

[29] Seybolt, *Town Officials*, 339–343; "Tax and Valuation Lists — 1771."

The American Revolution as a Colonial War for Independence

THOMAS C. BARROW

Professor Barrow argues that much of our difficulty in analyzing the nature of the American Revolution stems from our not understanding what type of revolution it was. It was not, as most American historians have assumed, like the French and Russian revolutions, which sought to destroy decadent and repressive regimes and to replace them with entirely new, broadly based societies. If our revolution had been comparable to those in nineteenth-century France and twentieth-century Russia, it would have been far more violent, chaotic, and productive of fundamental change in government and society. A more appropriate model for comparison, Barrow suggests, is the modern colonial war for independence, in which the major goals are self-determination and the establishment of indigenous national government. Eighteenth-century Americans, viewed from this perspective, found themselves situated similarly to colonial Africans and Asians, and their leaders faced the same sorts of challenges as Nkrumah in Ghana and Sukarno in Indonesia. The major questions for rebellious modern colonial peoples are whether they can gain their independence and whether they can agree upon a common form of national organization. If Barrow is correct in this analysis, historians have much to learn from the recent work on developing societies by economists, sociologists, and political scientists. There is a major difficulty with this approach, however, since it assumes that there was no important social conflict in revolutionary America, and that the progression from Declaration of Independence through Articles of Confederation to Constitution of 1787 represented merely a completion of the partial colonial society. Many historians, both progressives and radicals, vigorously deny that the transition from colony to nation was so orderly. They contend that socioeconomic conflict was the dominant mode of American revolutionary behavior. If they are correct, the French and Russian model is appropriate. There may, however, be a middle ground. Those who find an "internal revolution" have always acknowledged that it occurred simultaneously with the war for independence. What has not been seen so clearly, although Barrow alludes to it, is that the two revolutions may have been interconnecting. Historians have lately discovered the Anglo-American character of colonial politics, the distinctive character of eighteenth-century American provincialism, and they have long recognized the economic interdependence of metropolis and colony. If the several societies of British North America were so complexly interrelated in the im-

perial nexus, it should not be surprising that the pathology of sepa-
ration confused the reordering of internal and external relationships.
Seen from this perspective, however, the significant fact about our
Revolution is that it took place among Englishmen. Does Barrow
convince you that American colonials were analagous to Algerians,
Ghanians, and Indonesians?

The current historiographical controversies over the American Revolution owe
much to Carl Becker. From Becker's day to the present, historians have debated
the question of the existence or non-existence of an "internal revolution" in
American society. Some historians, following Becker's lead, search for traces of
internal social or political turmoil. Others, disagreeing with Becker, stress the
continuity of institutions and traditions during the Revolution. At issue is the
basic question of just "how revolutionary was the American Revolution," and in
the failure of historians to agree on an answer to that question lies the source of
controversy. And so the great debate continues.[1]

Reprinted by permission of the author from the *William and Mary Quarterly*, 25 (July
1968), pp. 452–464.
  [1] The major statements of the Becker-Beard approach are well known: Carl L. Becker,
The History of Political Parties in the Province of New York, 1760–1776 (Madison, 1909);
Charles Beard, *An Economic Interpretation of the Constitution of the United States*
(New York, 1913); J. Franklin Jameson, *The American Revolution Considered as a Social
Movement* (Princeton, 1926). Arthur M. Schlesinger's interpretation is summarized in
his article, "The American Revolution Reconsidered," *Political Science Quarterly*, XXXIV
(1919), 61–78. Jameson's views are re-evaluated in Frederick B. Tolles, "The American
Revolution Considered as a Social Movement: A Re-evaluation," *American Historical
Review*, LX (1954–55), 1–12. The Becker-Beard approach is currently carried on most
sophisticatedly in the work of Merrill Jensen, particularly in *The Articles of Confederation:
An Interpretation of the Social-Constitutional History of the American Revolution, 1774–
1781* (Madison, 1948). For an interesting later review of his earlier position by Jensen
himself see his article, "Democracy and the American Revolution," *Huntington Library
Quarterly*, XX (1956–57), 321–341. Elisha P. Douglass, *Rebels and Democrats: The
Struggle for Equal Political Rights and Majority Rule During the American Revolution*
(Chapel Hill, 1955), summarizes many of the points of controversy and offers his own
arguments for an "abortive" internal revolution. On the other side is Clinton L. Rossiter,
Seedtime of the Republic: The Origin of the American Tradition of Political Liberty
(New York, 1953). See also the treatment of the Revolution in Daniel J. Boorstin, *The
Genius of American Politics* (Chicago, 1953). But the single work which most directly
challenges the Becker-Beard approach is Robert E. Brown, *Middle-Class Democracy and
the Revolution in Massachusetts, 1691–1780* (Ithaca, 1955). A convenient summary
of the "Brown thesis" is in his article, "Democracy in Colonial Massachusetts," *New
England Quarterly*, XXV (1952), 291–313. Bernard Bailyn, "Political Experience and
Enlightenment Ideas in Eighteenth-Century America," *Amer. Hist. Rev.*, LXVII (1962–
63), 339–351, accepts the argument that there was no internal political or social "revolution" but suggests that the true revolution lay in the Americans' intellectual acceptance
of the "revolutionary" implications of their previous experiences concerning government
and society. Some recent publications indicate a renewed emphasis on the radical social
and political aspects of the American Revolution. See, for example, Gordon S. Wood, "A
Note on Mobs in the American Revolution," *William and Mary Quarterly*, 3d Ser., XXIII
(1966), 635–642. Of interest, too, is Wood's effort to graft Bernard Bailyn's "intellectual"
view of the Revolution onto the older socio-economic approach in "Rhetoric and Reality

Unfortunately, there is no adequate definition of a "revolution." The dictionary description of a revolution as a "total or radical change" certainly provides no effective guideline. Since history is the study of change in human society, locating a revolution according to that formula becomes a matter of appraising just how much change is involved in a given event, which inevitably comes down to a question of where one wants to place the emphasis. In any case, precise definitions are somewhat beside the point. When the word *revolution* is used today in connection with a political system, its meaning, if not its precise definition, is abundantly clear. The image called to mind is inescapably that of the French and Russian revolutions, which have provided us with our classic formulas for revolutionary re-structurings of society. A revolution in these terms represents the replacement of an archaic, repressive regime or regimes with something new, something more open, more flexible, more adaptable. In effect, in the interests of "progress," within the political system stability is replaced by instability until some new synthesis is achieved. Only then is stability restored, at which point the revolutionary drama is closed.

For generations now American historians have struggled to fit their "revolution" into this classic mold.[2] The difficulties they have encountered in doing so are reflected in the present historiographical impasse. It is a problem that might have been avoided had we remembered that the American people were, until 1776, colonials. By its very nature, a colonial society must be, in certain vital ways, unstable. Unable to exercise complete political control, subject to continual external intervention and negative interference, a colonial society cannot achieve effective "maturity" — that is, cannot create and control a political system that will be suited to the requirements of the interests indigenous to that society. A colonial society is an "incomplete" society, and consequently an inherently unstable society. This was as true of American society prior to 1776 as it is today of the colonial societies left in our world.[3] And, consequently, if instability is the given fact in American society at the beginning of the imperial crisis, it is hard

---

in the American Revolution," *ibid.*, 3–32. For another approach, see Jackson T. Main, "Government by the People: The American Revolution and the Democratization of the Legislatures," *ibid.*, 391–407; also Staughton Lynd, *Anti-Federalism in Dutchess County, New York* (Chicago, 1962).

[2] The classic statement of the process of "revolution" and its application is Crane Brinton, *The Anatomy of Revolution*, rev. ed. (New York, 1952). See also the formula as worked out in Alfred Meusel, "Revolution and Counter-Revolution," Edwin R. A. Seligman, ed., *Encyclopedia of the Social Sciences* (New York, 1934), XIII, 367–375. But the work that has been most influential in relating the American Revolution to the European revolutionary tradition is Robert R. Palmer, *The Age of the Democratic Revolution: A Political History of Europe and America, 1760–1800*, I (Princeton, 1959).

[3] An example of the relationship between colonial status and instability in colonial America is the Regulator movement in South Carolina. As Richard M. Brown points out in *The South Carolina Regulators* (Cambridge, Mass., 1963), the coastal inhabitants were willing to adjust themselves to the needs of the interior sections but were prevented from doing so by English policy decisions and intervention. The result was social and sectional cleavage and controversy. Another more general example, common to all colonies, is that of the currency problem. Any American attempts to solve the riddle of how to obtain and maintain an adequate currency were frustrated by English intervention, so that the problem remained as a continuous source of friction and instability.

to see how the classic pattern of "stability replaced by instability" can be imposed upon it. The answer, of course, is that it cannot, that in fact colonial wars for independence or "liberation" are generically different from revolutions of the French or Russian variety. And, after all, the American Revolution was just that —a colonial war of liberation. Given the widespread existence of such wars in today's world, it is odd that for so long a time we have overlooked the full implications of this fact.

Colonial wars for independence have an inner logic of their own. The first problem is to achieve self-determination. Once that is accomplished, it then becomes a matter of organization, about which, naturally, there always will be fundamental disagreement. What course this disagreement will take, and how bitter it will be, will be determined by the nature of the particular society. In former colonies which have emerged into nationhood in this century, the determining factor has largely been the heterogeneous nature of their societies; with little internal unity or coherence, these new nations generally have fallen back at first on authoritarian centralism. When this has proved incapable of solving the complex problems confronting the society, it has been replaced usually by some kind of collective leadership, often based on the only effective national organization in existence, the military.[4] It is at this point that many of the emergent nations of today find themselves.

Americans were more fortunate in their escape from colonialism. Thanks to the nature of the First British Empire, with its emphasis on commercial growth rather than on imperial efficiency, its loose organization, and the high degree of self-government allowed to the colonists, Americans had developed effective political units which commanded the allegiance of most inhabitants and served as adequate vehicles for the transition from colonial status to nationhood. Given a common English inheritance and a common struggle against British "tyranny," these states made the transition with a minimum of disagreement and dissension. In effect, by 1760 self-government in America, while still incomplete, had gone far. A tightening of English imperial authority after the last war with France brought about a reaction within the colonies toward complete self-determination, which was achieved finally through military success.

Yet, whatever the difference of the American experience from other colonial wars of liberation, certain elements were of necessity shared in common. Within any colonial society there exists an establishment, a group of men whose interests and situation tie them to the existing structure and whose orientation is towards the preservation of the colonial status. When the issue of independence or self-determination begins to be debated, these men are caught in powerful cross-currents. As natives to the society, they identify to some degree with its problems. At the same time, as beneficiaries of their privileged position within the existing colonial structure, they are not enthusiastic for change. Such men fall back on arguments of moderation, particularly stressing the economic benefits of association with the dominant country and also emphasizing the immaturity of their own society. The gains associated with independence are outweighed

[4] For example, such has been the course of Ghana during and after Nkrumah, of Algiers during and after Ben Bella, and of Indonesia during and after Sukarno.

for them by the prospects of social and political disorganization. So these men cast their lot with their colonial rulers. Such a man was Thomas Hutchinson. So, too, were many of his Tory associates.

And men like Hutchinson found much to disturb them within American society. Actually, not only was American colonial society subjected to the instability normally inherent in colonial status but there were certain peculiar circumstances which complicated matters further. The melting-pot aspects of American society, the diversity of ethnic, religious, and cultural backgrounds to be found within it, created problems of communication.[5] And, of equal importance, American colonial society was, after all, an artificial creation. Unlike most other historic colonial episodes, the American case was not a matter of an indigenous native society being expropriated and exploited by outsiders. In such instances, the pre-existing patterns of such native societies provide a degree of internal continuity and stability. But the English colonies in North America had at their disposal no such pre-existence. They were created specifically and artificially to perform certain functions in relation to the mother country. Most particularly, from the very beginning their economy was geared to production for distant markets over which they had no control and little influence.

At the same time, while there were sizeable non-English elements within the colonial population which created special problems, nevertheless the majority of the colonists were of the same national origin as their "rulers." It was not an instance of a conquered native population forced to bow fatalistically before the superior skills and power of an alien culture. Rather, it was a case in large part of Englishmen being governed and exploited by Englishmen. The result was a high degree of friction between governed and governors — an insistence by the colonists on their rights as Englishmen — that gave a special flavor and complexity to colonial politics.

Thoughtful colonials were well aware of and influenced by these problems. Thomas Hutchinson and John Adams — Tory and Whig — disagreed not so much on the question of the eventual independence of the American colonies as on the question of timing. Hutchinson's toryism sprang in part from his conviction that American society was too immature, too unstable, to stand alone. External force and authority, it seemed to him, would be required for many years to maintain internal order and stability in America. Realistically, he understood that eventually independence was probable: "It is not likely that the American Colonies will remain part of the Dominions of Great Britain another Century."[6] But, Hutchinson added, until then, "as we cannot otherwise subsist I am consulting the best interest of my country when I propose measures for maintain-

---

[5] The best case study of the melting-pot aspect of colonial America is Dietmar Rothermund, *The Layman's Progress* (Philadelphia, 1961). Rothermund's reference to "indirection" as the key to political success is particularly suggestive. *Ibid.*, 93, 134, 140. Interestingly, Rothermund views the Great Awakening as at least partially an effort to use religion to create a bridge, to form a common ground, between the various groups; when religion failed to accomplish this, logically the next development was the use of "patriotism," a "lay religion" acceptable on rational grounds, to fill the same need. *Ibid.*, 59, 62, 134.

[6] Thomas Hutchinson to John Healy Hutchinson, Feb. 14, 1772, Hutchinson Letterbooks (transcripts), XXVII, 296–300, Massachusetts Historical Society, Boston.

ing this subjection [to England]."[7] What particularly disturbed Hutchinson about the changes in English policy after 1760 was that they tended to increase the instability and disorder inherent within American society: "Sieur Montesquieu is right in supposing men good or bad according to the Climate where they live. In less than two centuries Englishmen by change of country are become more barbarous and fierce than the Savages who inhabited the country before they extirpated them, the Indians themselves."[8]

John Adams viewed American development in a different way. Contrasting the New World with the Old, he found the former far superior. The settlement of America had produced men who "knew that government was a plain, simple, intelligible thing, founded in nature and reason, and quite comprehensible by common sense. They detested all the base services and servile dependencies of the feudal system . . . and they thought all such slavish subordinations were equally inconsistent with the constitution of human nature and that religious liberty with which Jesus had made them free."[9] The problem was that this purity of mind and behavior was always threatened by contact with the corruption of the Old World. Specifically, subordination of Americans to a distant Parliament which knew little of their needs and desires was not only frustrating but dangerous to the American experiment: "A legislature that has so often discovered a want of information concerning us and our country; a legislature interested to lay burdens upon us; a legislature, two branches of which, I mean the lords and commons, neither love nor fear us! Every American of fortune and common sense, must look upon his property to be sunk downright one half of its value, the moment such an absolute subjection to parliament is established."[10] Independence was a logical capstone to such reasoning, although it took Adams some time to take that final step.

The differences between Hutchinson and Adams suggest that the divisions in American society between conservatives and radicals on the question of separation from Great Britain were related in part to a disagreement over the means to achieve coherence or stability within American society. For one side, continued tutelage under English authority was a necessity until such a time as maturity was achieved. For the other, it seemed that the major roadblock to maturity, to internal harmony and unity, was that self-same English authority. In effect, it was a disagreement on means, not ends. And disagreements similar to that between Hutchinson and Adams can be found within any society — whether in the eighteenth or twentieth century — which is in the process of tearing itself loose from its colonial ties.

It is possible, too, to suggest certain similarities between American intellectual development in these years and the experience of other colonial peoples. From his study of politics in eighteenth-century America, and particularly from his analysis of the pamphlet literature of the Revolutionary years, Bernard Bailyn has concluded that the "configuration of ideas and attitudes" which comprised the "Revolutionary ideology could be found intact — completely formed — as far

[7] Hutchinson to Richard Jackson, Apr. 21, 1766, *ibid.*, XXVI, 227–228.
[8] Hutchinson to [?], Dec. 30, 1773, *ibid.*, XXVII, 608.
[9] "A Dissertation on the Canon and Feudal Law" (1765), John Adams, *Works of John Adams*, ed. Charles F. Adams (Boston, 1850–56), III, 454.
[10] "Novanglus," *ibid.*, IV, 131.

back as the 1730's" and that these ideas had their origin in the "transmission from England to America of the literature of political opposition that furnished the substance of the ideology of the Revolution."[11] Colonial societies are both fascinated and yet antagonized by the culture of the dominant exploiting nation. They tend to borrow much from their rulers. The English background of a majority of the American colonists in their case made such borrowing a natural and easy process, particularly for those who, for one reason or another, identified themselves with British rule.

However, in colonial societies even many of those who are anxious to assert, or preserve, their native interests or culture cannot resist that fascination exerted by the dominant "mother country." These "patriots" borrow, too, but they are likely to borrow from the dissenting tradition within the dominant culture, from the literature of "opposition," to utilize in their own defense the language and literature of those elements within the ruling society which are critical, or subversive, of the governing traditions. In this way the prestige of the "superior" society can be used against that society itself. On the evidence of Bailyn's research, it seems that the Americans followed just such a line of development, fitting the "opposition" tradition into the framework of their own evolving institutions and traditions—a process which was facilitated by the natural connections between the American religious dissenting traditions and the "opposition" traditions of eighteenth-century English society.

Again, once the movement for independence enters its final phase within a colonial society and becomes an open contest of strength, other divisions tend to become obscured. The most determined supporters of the colonial rule are silenced or forced to rely increasingly on the military strength of their rulers to maintain their position. On the other side, the advocates of independence submerge momentarily whatever differences they may have and present a common front. It is a time of common effort, of mutual support within the forces interested in achieving self-determination. At the same time the "patriot" groups develop special organizations capable of coercing those elements within society, often a majority of the population, which are inclined towards neutrality or moderation. Such were the Sons of Liberty in the American Revolution, and the evidence suggests that they performed their work effectively. Partly because of their efforts, and more generally because of the peculiar character of American colonial society and the nature of the imperial conflict, American society weathered the crisis with relative stability and harmony. As John Adams put it, "The zeal and ardor of the people during the revolutionary war, supplying the place of government, commanded a degree of order, sufficient at least for the temporary preservation of society."[12]

With independence come altered circumstances for a former colonial society. Victorious patriots, confronted with the task of creating a permanent political

[11] Bernard Bailyn, *The Ideological Origins of the American Revolution* (Cambridge, Mass., 1967), xi.

[12] Speech to Congress, Mar. 4, 1797, Adams, *Works*, ed. Adams, IX, 105. During the Revolution itself Adams had written that "there has been more of this tranquillity and contentment, and fewer riots, insurrections, and seditions throughout the whole war, and in the periods of its greatest distress, than there was for seven years before the war broke out." Letter to Mr. Calkoen, Oct. 26, 1780, *ibid.*, VII, 305.

structure, gradually begin to disagree among themselves as to how it can best be done. Since the only effective central direction came previously from the colonial rulers, the problem in each newly independent society is to fit the surviving local units into some coherent national structure. Here the forces of localism and centralism come into conflict. Those men or interests firmly entrenched in their positions at the local level see in increased centralism a threat to their existence and power. On the other hand, those men or interests of a more cosmopolitan nature, geared to extra-local activities and contacts, can see the benefits that would accrue to them through the introduction of the smoother flow of communications and transactions that effective centralization would bring.[13] The disagreement pits the particularism of the entrenched local interests and individuals against the nationalism of the cosmopolitan interests and individuals. In most contemporary emergent societies these latter groups are by far the weaker. Fortunately, in America the cosmopolitan groups were stronger and more effective, partly again because of the unusual origin and nature of American colonial society. From the beginning the English colonies had been geared to production for European markets; it was the reason for their existence. The result was the development of an economy which had geographical variations but a common external orientation. Merchants and large-scale producers of items for export dominated this society. In the period after independence was achieved, these men provided a firm base for the construction of an effective national political system. Their success came with the substitution of the Constitution of 1787 for the Articles of Confederation.

Historians following the Becker-Beard approach put a different interpretation on the period following the achievement of de facto independence. For them, it was the moment of the triumph of radical democratic elements within American society. The wording of the Declaration of Independence, the constitutions of the new state governments, and particularly the drawing up of the Articles of Confederation represent for these historians the influence of a form of "radicalism." Yet, as Elisha Douglass has noted, in the formation of the governments for the new states, rather puzzlingly the one political reorganization that was subjected to the most democratic method of discussion and adoption — that of Massachusetts — turned out to be not only the most conservative of all the state constitutions but more conservative, in fact, than the previous system.[14] Somehow in Massachusetts, at least, an excess of democracy seems to have led to an enthronement of conservatism. And, indeed, the new constitutions or systems adopted in all the states were remarkable generally for their adherence to known and familiar forms and institutions.

[13] The distinguishing characteristics of "cosmopolitan" and "local" elites as developed by Robert K. Merton, Social Theory and Social Structure (Glencoe, 1957), chap. 10, "Patterns of Influence: Local and Cosmopolitan Influentials," are useful. See also, Alvin W. Gouldner, "Cosmopolitans and Locals: Towards an Analysis of Latent Social Roles," Administrative Science Quarterly, II (1957–58), 281–306, 444–480.

[14] "It is paradoxical that the first constitution formed by democratic processes should be one of the most undemocratic of its time. Although drafted by a convention elected by manhood suffrage, it was not only one of the most aristocratic of the Revolutionary period but also more thoroughly ensured government by the upper classes than the constitution of 1778 rejected by the same electorate." Douglass, Rebels and Democrats, 211.

Obviously, given the disruption of the traditional ties to England, the interruption of the natural economic dependence on English markets, the division of American society into opposing Whig and Tory camps, and the presence on American soil of enemy troops (which occupied at different moments the most important commercial centers), some confusion and dissension was inevitable within American society. What is remarkable is how little upheaval and disagreement there actually was. Had American society been ripe for a social upheaval, had it been comprised of oppressing and oppressed classes, no better opportunity could have been offered. The conservative nature of American response suggests that something other than a radical re-structuring of society was what was debated or desired.

Again, some historians have interpreted the decentralized political system created under the Articles of Confederation as a "triumph" of radical democracy. However, if instability, associated with colonial status and with the peculiar character of American colonial society, was a recurrent problem, and if inability to achieve positive control of their own political system was a major irritant, then the decentralization of the Articles was a logical development. In effect, if home rule was the issue and the cure, it was only natural that each local unit should seek as much autonomy within the national framework as possible. Seemingly, decentralization was the best method to bring coherence and stability, or maturity, to American society. Each local unit could look to its own needs, could arrange for the effective solution of its own special problems, could work to create that internal balance and harmony of conflicting interests that are the earmark of stability and maturity.

The problem with the Articles was not an excess of democracy. What brought about an effective opposition to them was their failure to achieve their purpose. The history of the states under the Articles, at least in the eyes of many contemporaries, suggested that decentralization, rather than being a source of stability, was a source of confusion and turmoil. James Madison explained the nature of the mistake in his Tenth Federalist. In spite of independence, under the system created by the Articles, wrote Madison, "complaints are everywhere heard from our most considerate and virtuous citizens . . . that our governments are too unstable." The problem, for Madison, was to control faction within society, and the most dangerous type of faction is that which includes a majority. Unfortunately, the "smaller the society, the fewer probably will be the distinct parties and interests composing it; the fewer the distinct parties and interests, the more frequently will a majority be found of the same party; and the smaller the number of individuals composing a majority, and the smaller the compass within which they are placed, the more easily will they concert and execute their plans of oppression." The solution is to enlarge the sphere, because if "you take in a greater variety of parties and interests," then "you make it less probable that a majority of the whole will have a common motive to invade the rights of other citizens. . . . The influence of factious leaders may kindle a flame within their particular States, but will be unable to spread a general conflagration through the other States."[15]

[15] Jacob E. Cooke, ed., *The Federalist* (Middletown, Conn., 1961), 56–65. Madison considered the question of the appropriate size for political units further in Federalist 14, *ibid.*, 83–89.

Nor was the opposition to the Constitution less concerned than Madison about order and stability within society. Again, disagreement was fundamentally over means, not ends. The anti-Federalists clung to the former ideas of local autonomy. They were, in fact, not more democratic than their opponents but more conservative. They were afraid of change: "If it were not for the stability and attachment which time and habit gives to forms of government, it would be in the power of the enlightened and aspiring few, if they should combine, at any time to destroy the best establishments, and even make the people the instruments of their own subjugation." The trouble was that the system created under the Articles was not yet sanctified by time: "The late revolution having effaced in a great measure all former habits, and the present institutions are so recent, that there exists not that great reluctance to innovation, so remarkable in old communities . . . it is the genius of the common law to resist innovation."[16] George Clinton agreed with Madison on the dangers of faction: "The people, when wearied with their distresses, will in the moment of frenzy, be guilty of the most imprudent and desperate measures. . . . I know the people are too apt to vibrate from one extreme to another. The effects of this disposition are what I wish to guard against."[17] It was on the solution to the problem, not on the nature of the problem, that Clinton differed from Madison. For Clinton, the powerful central government created by the Constitution might too easily become a vehicle for popular tyranny. It was this same sentiment which led eventually to the adoption of the first ten amendments, the Bill of Rights, with their reservations of basic rights and powers to local units and individuals.

It would not do to carry the comparison between the American Revolution and other colonial wars of liberation, particularly those of the twentieth century, too far. But there is enough evidence to suggest certain basic similarities between the American experience and that of other emergent colonial peoples — enough evidence, at least, to suggest that the efforts of historians to impose on the American Revolution the classic pattern of the French and Russian revolutions have led to a distorted view of our national beginnings. A French Revolution is the product of unbearable tensions within a society. The purpose of such a revolution is to destroy society as it exists, or at least to destroy its most objectional aspects, and to replace the old with something new. In contrast, a colonial "revolution" or war of liberation has as its purpose the achievement of self-determination, the "completion" or fulfillment of an existing society, rather than its destruction. A French Revolution is first of all destructive; a colonial revolution, first of all constructive. In either case the process may not be completed. In the instance of the French Revolution, the re-constructed society may contain more of the old than the original revolutionaries desired. And in the case of the colonial revolution, the process of winning independence and the difficulties of organizing an effective national political structure may open the gates to change, may create a radicalism that carries the original society far from its

---

[16] Quoted in Cecelia M. Kenyon, *The Antifederalists* (Indianapolis, 1966), xci–xcii. Miss Kenyon's introduction to this collection is an expansion of her provocative article, "Men of Little Faith: The Anti-Federalists on the Nature of Representative Government," *Wm. and Mary Qtly.*, 3d Ser., XII (1955), 2–43. See also Stanley Elkins and Eric McKitrick, "The Founding Fathers: Young Men of the Revolution," *Pol. Sci. Qtly.*, LXXVI (1961), 200–216.

[17] Quoted in Kenyon, *Antifederalists*, xcii.

former course; the result may be more destruction than was originally envisaged. Yet, the goals of these two revolutions are fundamentally different, and their different goals determine a different process of fulfillment. The unfolding of the revolutionary drama, the "stages" of revolution, will be quite different, if not opposite.

For John Adams, the American Revolution was an epochal event, a moment of wonder for the world to behold and consider. At times his rhetoric carried him beyond the confines of his innate caution, and he sounded like a typical revolutionary: "The progress of society will be accelerated by centuries by this revolution. . . . Light spreads from the dayspring in the west, and may it shine more and more until the perfect day."[18] But, as Edward Handler has noted, "The truth is that if Adams was a revolutionary, he was so in a sense very different than that produced by the other great modern revolutions."[19] Adams did indeed feel that his revolution had a meaning for the world but it was not related to the violent re-structurings of society. Rather its message, for Adams, was that free men can decide voluntarily to limit their freedom in the interests of mutual association, that rational men can devise a system that can at once create order and preserve liberty. The American success was in contrast to the traditional authoritarian systems of the Old World: "Can authority be more amiable or respectable, when it descends from accidents or institutions established in remote antiquity, that when it springs fresh from the hearts and judgments of an honest and enlightened people?"[20]

Most wars of liberation are not so orderly as that of the American Revolution. Most, at least in this century, have led to increasing radicalism and division within the liberated society. National unity has not been easily achieved. That the American emergence from colonialism had a different ending is significant. A firm basis for unity obviously existed within American society, which, naturally, suggests that the reverse, too, was true — that such tensions and divisions as did exist within American society were relatively minor and harmless. It is no wonder that historians determined to find an internal social or political revolution of the French variety within the American Revolution have encountered such difficulties. Nor is it a wonder that the Revolution has become so beclouded with historiographical debates and arguments. The problem has been in our approach. We have been studying, it would seem, the wrong revolution.

[18] Quoted in Edward Handler, *America and Europe in the Political Thought of John Adams* (Cambridge, Mass., 1964), 102.

[19] *Ibid.*, 101. Elsewhere Handler comments that "Adams' experience had nothing in common with the concept of revolution as a total renovation of existing institutions previously condemned as denials and perversions of the natural order" and that "nothing affords more certain indication that the Americans underwent a special kind of revolution than the peculiar breed of revolutionary typified by Adams who carried it through." *Ibid.*, 106–107.

[20] Speech to Congress, Mar. 4, 1797, Adams, *Works*, ed. Adams, IX, 107.

The Nationalists of 1781–1783 and the Economic Interpretation of the Constitution

E. JAMES FERGUSON

E. James Ferguson, a specialist in colonial economic history, believes that the political contest between broad economic groups in American society did not begin at the Constitutional Convention of 1787. The revolutionary process, which shook men free from many of their imperial ties, forced Americans to consider how their interests and ideals would be best served by a new government. Toward the end of the war, it became apparent to many merchants, army officers, and holders of the public debt that a strong central government was essential to the protection of their interests. They also understood that nothing would necessitate a national government as effectively as the creation of a federal debt, for which means of administration and redemption through taxation would have to be provided. These men, the Nationalists of 1781–1783, strove for a combination of political and economic reform against those who preferred the dominance of individual state power as set forth under the Articles of Confederation. The Nationalists failed in 1783, but they succeeded in 1787, and the federal Constitution is in many ways a reflection of their movement. Ferguson thus writes well within the tradition of historical interpretation begun by Charles Beard, Carl Becker, and Arthur Schlesinger. He is careful to point out, however, that the identification of a combination like the Nationalists does not require the historian to attack their motives on moral grounds, as Beard did. The Nationalists were not conspiring to foist a scheme favoring their own petty interests upon an unsuspecting nation, for they were an organic part of the American political process of their era. They were merely the most successful of the many factions who acknowledged the deficiencies of the Confederacy. Ferguson is clearly in line with his Progressive predecessors, however, in arguing that the Nationalists were elitist, and in suggesting that they placed order higher than liberty in their scale of political values. He further suggests that, underlaying the institutional program of the Nationalists was a "group-value system," and it is on this point that a good deal turns. How can historians determine the values of competing social groups, and how can they identify membership within the groups? There are many difficulties in inferring initial values from subsequent political behavior.

In spite of such leaders as George Washington, Alexander Hamilton, James Madison, Robert Morris, and others who were later enrolled among the Founding Fathers, the Nationalist movement of 1781–1783 has not made a distinct impression on historical interpretations of the early national period. Surprisingly, it is seldom brought into disputes over the economic background of the Constitution — a matter to which it is precisely relevant.[1]

It should make a difference to historians that constitutional revision and Hamiltonian funding were first linked together not in 1787, not in 1790, but in the closing years of the Revolution. The movement to reorganize the central government was started by the Nationalists of 1781–1783. They coupled economic with political objectives, formulated a program, and lined up a body of actual and potential supporters for whom such a program had a special appeal. The merger of political and economic goals was organic, and the essential elements of Hamiltonian funding were adopted with the Constitution.

The effort to strengthen Congress began in 1780, in many ways the most discouraging year of the war, when military defeats and the depreciation of paper money seriously undermined patriot morale. Congress, convinced that any further output of Continental currency would destroy what little value it still had, ended emissions late in 1779 — a courageous act, but one that left it without funds. As long as Continental currency had value, Congress enjoyed a freedom of action incommensurate with its constitutional powers under the still unratified Articles of Confederation. The stoppage of emissions disclosed its weakness.[2]

Any political change appealed to some persons more than to others and could be expected to have differential effects upon various groups of the population. In principle, central government was antithetical to liberty, which most Americans associated with local self-rule. Since the war had begun, however, there had been second thoughts on this matter. To the extent that state governments had fallen under "popular" influence, people who had opposed democratic tendencies favored a stronger central authority as the only available check upon abuses of local majorities. This sentiment was most articulated at the time by elite groups in the middle states, but it was a predisposing influence everywhere and certainly an element in the support for political reform.[3]

Reprinted by permission of the Organization of American Historians from *The Journal of American History*, 56 (September 1969), pp. 241–261.

[1] Modern studies that bring out the implications of the Nationalist movement most explicitly are Clarence L. Ver Steeg, *Robert Morris: Revolutionary Financier: With an Analysis of his Earlier Career* (Philadelphia, 1954); Merrill Jensen, *The New Nation: A History of the United States During the Confederation, 1781–1789* (New York, 1950), and E. James Ferguson, *The Power of the Purse: A History of American Public Finance, 1776–1790* (Chapel Hill, 1961). The economic phases of the movement are implicit throughout Robert A. East, *Business Enterprise in the American Revolutionary Era* (New York, 1938); and the political aspects are treated in George Bancroft, *History of the Formation of the Constitution of the United States* (2 vols., New York, 1882).

[2] Worthington C. Ford, ed., *Journals of the Continental Congress, 1774–1789* (34 vols., Washington, 1904–1937), XV, 1019–20. On the constitutional point, see James Madison to Thomas Jefferson, May 6, 1780, Edmund C. Burnett, ed., *Letters of Members of the Continental Congress* (8 vols., Washington, 1921–1936), V, 128–29.

[3] The affinity between central government and political elitism is the central theme of Merrill Jensen, *The Articles of Confederation: An Interpretation of the Social-Constitutional History of the United States* (Madison, 1940). This is made explicit in his con-

The drive for political reform was associated with changes in economic policies. By 1780, the war was supported by massive confiscations; state and federal officers seized what they needed. The people at large were surprisingly patient under these impositions, yet there was widespread resentment against arbitrary acts of government.[4] Other irritants were legal tender laws and economic controls. Such regulations were a general nuisance.[5] Merchants, especially, felt victimized by economic legislation. It could be and was argued that regulations were hopeless, that the answer to high prices and the scarcity of goods was to abolish restraints on trade, and that the solution to governmental fiscal problems was deep taxation and the abandonment of paper money. Such proposals were impractical under the circumstances, but existing policy was so clearly bankrupt that a case could be made for moving in another direction. Although merchants and other businessmen made profits amidst inflation and in the teeth of economic controls, sound money and free trade were better suited to their ethics and presumably to their interests.[6]

A different group of recruits to the cause of stronger government was the officer corps of the Continental army from Washington down. After the capture of General John Burgoyne and the formation of the French alliance, military victory seemed within sight; yet, at this very point, the American war effort faltered. In the winter of 1779–1780, the Continental army suffered as much as at Valley Forge. "We begin to hate the country for its neglect of us," warned Hamilton in 1780.[7] The officers wanted a government that could raise, pay, clothe, feed, and arm enough troops to win the war.

A more direct interest in stronger central government was that of the public creditors. As Congress fell into insolvency, it ceased paying interest on the public

---

cluding statement, pp. 239–45. The same phenomenon in late colonial times is discussed in Edmund S. and Helen M. Morgan, *The Stamp Act Crisis: Prologue to Revolution* (Chapel Hill, 1953), 11–20. With his talent for the pungent and invidious phrase, Gouverneur Morris supposed in 1774 (as paraphrased by his biographer) that an American central government would "restrain the democratic spirit, which the constitutions and local circumstances of the country had so long fostered in the minds of the people." Jared Sparks, *Life of Gouverneur Morris . . . in the Political History of the United States* (3 vols., Boston, 1832), I, 27.

[4] On the magnitude of confiscations, see Ferguson, *Power of the Purse*, 57–64.

[5] Oscar and Mary F. Handlin, "Revolutionary Economic Policy in Massachusetts," *William and Mary Quarterly*, IV (Jan. 1947), 3–26; East, *Business Enterprise*, 195–212. See also Curtis P. Nettels, *The Emergence of a National Economy: 1775–1815* (New York, 1962), 27–29.

[6] East, *Business Enterprise*, 207, describes the repudiation of paper currency in 1781 as a victory for the "rising conservative movement" in which the viewpoint of merchants and lawyers figured prominently. Robert Morris, who frequently expressed himself on this point, looked forward in 1781 to the time when, by the removal of the "detestable tribe" of economic restrictions, people would possess "that freedom for which they are contending." Robert Morris to the Governors of North Carolina, South Carolina, and Georgia, Dec. 19, 1781, Francis Wharton, ed., *The Revolutionary Diplomatic Correspondence of the United States* (6 vols., Washington, 1889), V, 58–59.

[7] Alexander Hamilton to James Duane, Sept. 3, 1780, Harold C. Syrett, ed., Jacob E. Cooke, assoc. ed., *The Papers of Alexander Hamilton* (13 vols., New York, 1961–   ), II, 406.

debt. The creditors, who emerged as a political force in 1780, had reason to urge the establishment of a government capable of paying its debts.[8]

The converging influence of these groups began to affect state and federal policy and to create a disposition toward stronger central government, more "authority," less "liberty" in the conduct of public affairs, and, in the economic sphere, sound money and the abandonment of restraints on trade.[9] The formula appealed primarily to the elite, especially in the middle states, to merchants in general, and to special interest groups such as the army officers and the public creditors. It would be a distortion, however, to attribute the Nationalist impulse wholly to the interest or influence of particular groups. The controlling factor was a national emergency which called for new measures. The degree of support, which the proposal to confer additional powers on Congress eventually received in all the states, shows that leaders at every level were alarmed by the critical state of the war and persuaded that something drastic had to be done about it.

The man who more than anyone else worked out the Nationalist program and gave the movement some degree of organization was Morris. Congress, impressed by the urgent need for reform, appointed him superintendent of finance in 1781. A wealthy Philadelphia merchant, a leader of the conservative anti-constitutionalist party in Pennsylvania, and a security holder, he combined in his own person most of the elements of the Nationalist movement. From long and outstanding service in Congress he had gained an unequalled mastery of congressional administrative and business affairs. He was widely respected, also widely hated, but such duties and powers were soon conferred upon him that he became a virtual prime minister — the real director of congressional policy from the time he took office in the spring of 1781 until the close of the war. Morris proved to be a superb administrator. He was also a statesman, the first in the line of the nation's early financial ministers who tried to steer its institutional development from the treasury.[10]

Associated with Morris were some of the outstanding leaders of the later movement for the Constitution. Madison, who attended Congress from 1780 to 1783, was a strong Nationalist; and he backed Morris' program. In 1782, Hamilton served as Morris' tax receiver, a kind of personal representative, in New York, before moving on to Congress to become one of the most uncompromising advocates of a national system. In the army the foremost influence for Nationalist reform was Washington. Although his military position kept him out of civil administration, he continually urged Congress and the country to give more power to the central government.

The Union was a league of states rather than a national system because Congress lacked the power of taxation. This was not an oversight. In drafting the

[8] "Original Documents: A Hartford Convention in 1780," *Magazine of American History*, VIII (Oct. 1882), 688–89; Bancroft, *History of the . . . Constitution*, I, 14–16; Ferguson, *Power of the Purse*, 149–52.

[9] Jensen, *New Nation*, 45–53; East, *Business Enterprise*, 207–12; Jennings B. Sanders, *Evolution of Executive Departments of the Continental Congress, 1774–1789* (Chapel Hill, 1935), 3–5.

[10] Robert Morris is entitled to a place in the line of succession that includes Hamilton and Albert Gallatin. Although Ver Steeg in his excellent study compares Robert Morris with Hamilton, he does not give Morris enough credit. Ver Steeg, *Robert Morris*, 193–99.

Articles of Confederation, Americans registered their hatred of centralized European systems and their high regard for liberty — which they associated with the supremacy of local government — by denying Congress the power to tax. As Congress needed money to execute its functions, it was in principle dependent on the states at every turn. In practice, it had some leeway, for it could issue paper money and contract loans at home and abroad. By 1780, however, its leeway was pretty well used up. Paper money was failing fast, and neither foreign nor domestic loans were ever large enough to sustain more than a fraction of the expense of fighting the war.[11]

Early in 1781, after a last futile effort to revive Continental currency, Congress struck at the heart of its problem by requesting the states to grant a permanent 5 per cent duty on imports to be collected by federal officers and placed at Congress' disposal. As an amendment to the Articles of Confederation, the impost resolution had to be ratified by every state legislature. Congress at first brought it forward as a war measure, a way of securing an income wholly under federal control and, therefore, acceptable to European nations as security for additional loans then being sought. Within a few months, however, the capture of Cornwallis and signs that Britain was ready to make peace altered its significance. The impost, and whatever federal taxes might later be added to it, were to be a fund for discharging the entire Revolutionary debt.[12]

The impost breached the primary restriction upon congressional authority and was the essential first step in building an effective central government. Of equal importance was federal control of the Revolutionary debt itself. That a federal debt existed at all was inconsistent with the structure of the Union. Congress, it is true, had authority to contract loans, but, since it lacked the taxing power, it could not guarantee repayment. Under the Articles of Confederation, Congress was supposed to get money from requisitions on the states. This system never worked, not entirely because the states were negligent, but because their fiscal systems were geared to local priorities and the use of state currency. With the best of motives, the states could often meet Continental requisitions only with great difficulty, if at all. In a country in which the operative fiscal systems were those of thirteen local and diverse entities, a federal debt was an anomaly.[13]

More compatible with the structure of the Union was the procedure outlined by the Articles of Confederation for dealing with the expenses of the Revolution. Each state was to be assessed according to the value of its landed property. When requisitions proved to be ineffectual, the logical solution — one in harmony with the political system — was to give each state its share of the debt and let each state pay in its own way. In fact, something like this began to happen during the last years of the war. Various states began to settle accounts for debts owed to citizens and soldiers. They absorbed all kinds of claims — not only claims against the state governments but also claims against Congress.

[11] Foreign loans became an important resource for Congress only in 1781 as the fighting drew to a close. Ferguson, *Power of the Purse*, 125–31, 333n.

[12] *Journals*, XVIII, 1033–36, XIX, 110–13; Madison to Edmund Pendleton, May 29, 1781, Burnett, ed., *Letters*, VI, 103–04. The grant of the impost was to be coextensive with the existence of the Revolutionary debt.

[13] Ferguson, *Power of the Purse*, 29–31, 140–41, 221–28.

There was a good chance that the entire mass of unsettled debts would slip into state possession.[14]

Loss of the debt portended disaster to the Nationalist movement. Without a debt there would be little reason to ask for the taxing power, since, when the war was over, paying the debt was about the only thing that Congress would need much money for. Led by Morris, the Nationalists rejected the idea that the states should take over any part of the federal debt. "There is in it," wrote Morris, "a principle of disunion implied which must be ruinous." The debt belonged wholly to Congress. "The creditors trust the Union, and there can be no right to alter the pledge which they have accepted for any other, even for a better one, without their free consent."[15] The obligation to the creditors could be honored only if Congress itself possessed the means of payment. Even if requisitions worked, which they obviously did not, they would not do. Nothing would avail but the impost and other federal taxes. In short, Morris and the Nationalists made payment of the debt contingent upon a revision of the Articles of Confederation to give Congress the taxing power. "The political existence of America," Morris declared, "depends on the accomplishment of this plan."[16]

Morris tried to make sure that unsettled claims against Congress would remain a federal obligation, and at his suggestion Congress resolved in 1782 to send commissioners to all parts of the country to register federal debts due to civilians.[17] The next year Congress declared the large sums owed to the Continental army to be a federal responsibility and refused to allow the states to assume payments of them.[18] Under Morris' guidance the Nationalist Congress clung to the federal debt and enlarged it. At the close of the war, the debt consisted of about $11,000,000 in loan office certificates — the government bonds of the Revolution. By 1786, when the bulk of the unsettled accounts had been examined and new securities issued in recognition of claims against Congress, the debt had risen to more than $28,000,000.[19]

A debt this large was justification enough for the impost, indeed for a whole battery of federal taxes. It was a "bond of union" in the sense of creating a

---

[14] *Ibid.*, 141–44, 180–83, 203–04.

[15] Robert Morris to Governors of Massachusetts, Rhode Island, New York, Delaware, Maryland, and North Carolina, July 27, 1781, Wharton, ed., *Diplomatic Correspondence*, IV, 608.

[16] Robert Morris to Nathaniel Appleton, April 16, 1782, *ibid.*, V, 311. Robert Morris exempted the federal debt from the general expenses of the Revolution which were to be apportioned on the states. Robert Morris to President of Congress, Aug. 28, 1781, *ibid.*, IV, 674–75. At his insistence, Congress refused to allow the states credit for payments they had made to their own lines in the Continental army. Robert Morris to Governor of Rhode Island, June 26, 1782, *ibid.*, V, 524; Robert Morris to Daniel of St. Thomas Jenifer, March 12, 1782; Report on the New Jersey Memorial, Sept. 27, 1782; to Receivers of the several States, Oct. 5, 1782, Official Letterbook C, 97–99, Official Letterbook D, 231–34, 277–78, Robert Morris Papers (Manuscript Division, Library of Congress); *Journals*, XXIII, 629–31. Congress backed down from this position, April 13, 1785. *Ibid.*, XXVIII, 261.

[17] *Journals*, XXII, 82–86.

[18] *Ibid.*, XXIV, 206–10. See Ferguson, *Power of the Purse*, 156–57.

[19] The foreign debt of about $11,000,000 was generally conceded to be a federal obligation and did not affect constitutional issues. On the foreign debt in the postwar era, see Ferguson, *Power of the Purse*, 234–38.

need to confer additional powers upon Congress. It was a bond of union in still another way. The fact was well understood that funding the English national debt had consolidated the Revolution of 1689 by creating a vested interest in the new regime. Irrespective of historical examples, however, the primacy of economic self-interest was a maxim seldom challenged in the eighteenth century. If the federal debt could be funded — that is, the interest regularly paid by means of the import and other federal taxes — security holders throughout the nation could be expected to give their loyalty to the central government. Economic self-interest was that "active principle of the human mind" the Nationalists sought in order to weaken the identification of Americans with their states and generate allegiance to the Union.[20] As Morris phrased it in a report to Congress: a peculiar advantage of domestic loans was that "they give stability to Government by combining together the interests of moneyed men for its support, and consequently in this Country a domestic debt, would greatly contribute to that Union, which seems not to have been sufficiently attended to, or provided for, in forming the national compact."[21]

Up to this point Nationalist objectives were political — to secure federal taxes and to bond the Union with the cement of self-interest. It was the economic program associated with constitutional revision, however, that gave the movement its particular character. The pursuit of political ends by economic means was certain to have economic consequences, some of them integral to and inseparable from the political changes being sought, and others not necessary, perhaps, but closely related to them.

One necessary result was an increase in business capital. That Congress, if fortified by taxation, would fund the debt was certain; otherwise, its improved status could not be actualized, and it must remain a shadow, its powers unexerted. And funding was certain to create domestic capital. After interest payments on the debt ceased in the closing years of the war, the $11,000,000 in loan office certificates, which then comprised the federal debt, had depreciated in market value. If the securities were funded, if regular taxes like the impost were devoted to paying the interest, their market value could be expected to rise, increasing the wealth of the holders.

Morris in 1782 submitted a funding program to Congress remarkably similar to Hamilton's plan in 1790. He recommended a new loan in which old securities could be received at face value in exchange for new securities. After considering a discrimination between original and present holders, he rejected it as detrimental to the public interest. In outlining his plan, he proposed that only the interest be provided for, that payment of the principal be deferred to the indefinite future, and that, in the meantime, a sinking fund be employed to

[20] The quotation is out of context. It is taken from a comment on Hamilton's funding program by Oliver Wolcott, Jr. Hamilton to Oliver Wolcott, Sr., March 27, 1790, George Gibbs, ed., Memoirs of the Administration of Washington and Adams from the Papers of Oliver Wolcott (2 vols., New York, 1846), I, 43.

[21] Robert Morris to President of Congress, Aug. 5, 1782, Journals, XXII, 432. His report was dated July 29, 1782. Robert Morris expected the Bank of North America to create the same kind of unifying appeal. Robert Morris to John Jay, July 13, 1781, Wharton, ed., Diplomatic Correspondence, IV, 563, 568–69; Robert Morris to Benjamin Franklin, July 13, 1781, ibid., IV, 568–69.

purchase and retire outstanding securities. Funding on this basis, he argued, would immediately benefit the nation. Since interest on invested capital in the United States was higher than the interest payments required to support the debt, the new capital created by funding, if properly invested, would bring a net increase in national income. Moreover, since the securities were held by propertied men, the gains from an increase in security values would go to persons in a position to use them not for consumption but for investment. As Morris phrased it, funding would distribute property "into those hands which would render it most productive." He also expected that it would encourage foreign investment in federal securities. He considered the inflow of money a clear gain to the country, since Americans could employ money at rates of return higher than the interest paid to foreign investors. In short, a national debt was an economic as well as a political blessing.[22]

An increase in domestic capital implied, if it did not entail, the founding of commercial banks. Despite a growing need for banks, none had existed in colonial times, and American businessmen had been forced to rely very largely on credit extended by British merchants. But as was demonstrated by the establishment of banks in Philadelphia, New York, and Boston during and after the Revolution, American businessmen were ready to start banking enterprises with money they had made in the war. Funding the debt would provide more capital for such projects. Banking operations, in turn, would multiply the effect of the capital generated by funding, for, as was well understood, banks could expand loans to several times the reserves actually on hand.[23]

Note issues by banks were a prospective substitute for state paper money. In trying to cope with the shortage of coin and dearth of credit facilities — perennial problems of America's economy — colonial governments had employed paper currency, issuing it in public expenditures and in making loans to farmers. It was fiat money, not redeemable in gold or silver, based instead on anticipation of tax receipts and the repayment of loans. In colonial times the paper money system had worked pretty well. Businessmen in most colonies, if not always enthusiastic, were reconciled to it as the only thing possible under the circumstances. What confidence they had in it was destroyed, however, by the depreciation that occurred during the Revolution.[24] In a more democratic age, proper-

[22] Robert Morris' report, dated July 29, 1782, is the fullest theoretical exposition of his views. *Journals*, XXII, 429–46; Wharton, ed., *Diplomatic Correspondence*, V, 619–34. He was thinking not only of the existing loan office debt but also of the enlarged federal debt that would result from the settlement of claims already under way. In his last official communication before he retired from office, he expressed his confidence that the debt would one day be funded and added that it was "a commercial problem which admits of absolute demonstration that the punctual payment of interest on our debts will produce a clear annual gain of more than such interest can possibly amount to." Robert Morris to President of Congress, Sept. 30, 1784, *ibid.*, VI, 822.

[23] Robert Morris to Robert Smith, July 17, 1781, Wharton, ed., *Diplomatic Correspondence*, IV, 582; Alexander Hamilton to James Duane, Sept. 3, 1780, Syrett, ed., *Papers of Alexander Hamilton*, II, 415.

[24] For an appraisal of colonial experience with paper money and a bibliography of the subject up to the date of publication, see E. James Ferguson, "Currency Finance: An Interpretation of Colonial Monetary Practices," *William and Mary Quarterly*, X (April 1953), 153–80. The reorientation of scholarly opinion as to colonial monetary practices

tied men had lost faith in the integrity of legislative bodies; they were afraid that popularly controlled legislatures would deliberately undermine the currency in order to wipe out private and public debts. They wanted to end the paper money system. Because it was unlikely that the country could acquire enough coin or bullion to afford a metallic circulating medium, the only alternative was banks of issue whose notes would serve as a medium of exchange. Funding the Revolutionary debt was a way of solving this problem. The capital created by funding, placed in banks, would provide backing for bank note emissions, which, if on a sufficient scale, would afford a stable currency beyond reach of popular legislatures. The paper money era might well be brought to an end if state governments could be induced to give up paper emissions altogether and conduct their finances by borrowing from banks.[25]

During his term of office, Morris organized the nation's first bank, the Bank of North America, which began operations in 1782.[26] Its capital was only $400,000, not considered a large sum (Morris was able to raise this amount only by buying $254,000 in shares for the government), and it was entirely specie. Morris was aware that he might have employed public securities as part of the bank's capital if the value of securities had been supported by regular interest payments. But, since no interest was being paid, he dared not include them in his venture.[27] In other respects, however, his plans demonstrated how well he

---

has become pretty general. It has been embraced with particular enthusiasm by the new economic historians, who are highly interested in the function of colonial currency and land banks in promoting economic development. See Ralph L. Andreano, ed., *New Views on Economic Development: A Selective Anthology of Recent Work* (Cambridge, Mass., 1965), 41–56. The current reappraisal is judiciously stated by Curtis P. Nettels, who writes that in the middle colonies land banks were prudently managed and "realized the benefits claimed for them," but that serious depreciation took place in Massachusetts, Rhode Island, and South Carolina. (He might have added that the depreciation was at an early date in South Carolina and that for forty-five years before the Revolution the colony's currency was stable.) Nettels concludes by saying that it was the depreciation that occurred during the Revolution that evoked "impassioned opposition" to paper money during the 1780's — the main reason being that creditors no longer trusted the legislatures. Nettels, *Emergence of a National Economy*, 80–81.

[25] For an expression of these ideas, see *Journals*, XVIII, 1157–64, in which a committee report of December 18, 1780, envisages a bank note currency; also, Robert Morris to Franklin, July 13, 1781; Robert Morris to Governors of the States, Sept. 4, 1781, Wharton, ed., *Diplomatic Correspondence*, IV, 562–63, 693; Madison to Pendleton, Feb. 25, 1782, Burnett, ed., *Letters*, VI, 305–06; Hamilton to Robert Morris, April 30, 1781, Syrett, ed., *Papers of Alexander Hamilton*, II, 620, 623–24, 627–30.

[26] *Journals*, XX, 545–48. Wharton, ed., *Diplomatic Correspondence*, IV, 565–68; *Journals*, XXI, 1187–90.

[27] Employing federal securities as bank stock was proposed in Congress, April 12, 1781, *Journals*, XIX, 381. In the plan for a bank which he submitted to Robert Morris, Hamilton suggested that land be accepted as partial payment for shares. Robert Morris replied that he had thought of "interweaving a security" in the bank's capital, but had given up the idea as too risky. Hamilton to Robert Morris, April 30, 1781; Robert Morris to Hamilton, May 26, 1781, Syrett, ed., *Papers of Alexander Hamilton*, II, 621–22, 645–46. See also the plan of a bank Hamilton sent to Duane, Sept. 3, 1780, *ibid.*, II, 400–18. Businessmen already employed securities like money in making payments to one another. In his statement of accounts published in 1785, Robert Morris expressed his continuing faith in the potential economic uses of the public debt, saying: "A due provision for the public debts would at once convert those debts into a real medium of commerce. The possessors of

had defined his goals and the means to reach them. He hoped to expand the bank's capital to the point where it would be "a principal pillar of American credit." He intended, as soon as possible, to bring about a retirement of federal and state paper money and to replace it with bank notes. In fact, he made a start in this direction by floating a mercantile currency consisting of Bank of North America notes and his personal notes. In 1782 and 1783, he had about $1,000,000 of this paper outstanding. It passed at par, or nearly so, in all parts of the country. It was readily accepted by merchants and received as legal tender by most of the states.[28] Morris' larger plans for the bank were too optimistic; certainly they were unrealized. Yet they failed of at least partial accomplishment mainly because they were predicated upon political reforms which did not come to pass.

Owing in no small degree to Morris' leadership, what one might call a mercantile capitalist reorganization of the country's economic institution had become integrated with constitutional revision. Between 1781 and 1783, Morris, as virtual director of congressional policy, set forth a system that fully anticipated the later Federalist program: a government invigorated by taxation; a funded debt whose increase in market value would augment business capital; a national bank that would enhance the effect of capital accumulation, afford commercial credit, and provide a nongovernmental circulating medium beyond reach of state legislatures. Morris in 1783 even proposed the federal assumption of state debts.[29] The measures that constituted this system, and to a large extent the rationale behind them, were communicated to Congress. To what extent they were known to the country at large, or their implications grasped by persons unversed in economic reasoning, can only be conjectured; but the system and the logical relationship of its parts were plainly visible to anyone who was informed about congressional affairs.

The Nationalist movement declined rapidly at the end of the war. Although ratified by all but one state, the impost amendment of 1781 failed; hence, the debt was not funded and the economic reforms contingent upon funding did not materialize. The Bank of North America severed its connection with the government and never became a national institution. Morris lost influence over congressional policy and retired from office with his major goals unaccomplished. Yet the elements which the Nationalists had put together survived and perpetuated a need to execute their program. They had, in effect, created a national

---

certificates, would then become the possessors of money. And of course, there would be no want of it among those who having property wish to borrow provided that the laws and administration are such, as to compel the punctual payment of debts." Robert Morris, *A Statement of the Accounts of the United States of America During the Administration of the Superintendent of Finance* (Philadelphia, 1785), ix.

[28] On the plans, see Robert Morris to Jay, July 13, 1781; Robert Morris to Franklin, July 13, 1781, Wharton, ed., *Diplomatic Correspondence*, IV, 562–65, 568–71. Nettels is perceptive, but no more perceptive than Robert Morris himself, in seeing the implications of the flotation of currency. Nettels, *Emergence of a National Economy*, 32–33. See Robert Morris to Hamilton, Oct. 5, 1782, Syrett, ed., *Papers of Alexander Hamilton*, III, 177–79.

[29] Robert Morris to President of Congress, Aug. 26, 1783, Papers of the Continental Congress, No. 137, III, 33–40 (National Archives); Ferguson, *Power of the Purse*, 209–10.

debt, vested title to it in Congress, and aroused a general expectation that the debt would be paid by means of federal taxes. In 1783, Congress submitted another request for the impost grant to the states, and for several years there was a reasonable chance of its adoption.[30]

In 1786 a new crisis reinvigorated the movement for constitutional reform. Shays' Rebellion, the paper money scandal in Rhode Island, and lesser disturbances in other parts of the country rekindled conservative fear of "unchecked democracy." Perhaps the lowest common denominator of the motives of the Founding Fathers was the desire to impose restraints upon majority rule in order to preserve a republican form of government. But sentiments like this were hardly new in 1786. What gave them peculiar urgency at this time was not entirely the disorders caused by the postwar economic depression; it was the fact that the movement to strengthen the central government had come to a dead end.

After the war, Congress and the states contested for possession of the Revolutionary debt and the consequent exercise of taxing power.[31] As the all-but-unanimous agreement upon the impost amendment showed, there was a general consensus that the Union needed to be "patched together," that Congress should be allowed to fund the debt, and that, for this reason, it should be given a limited power of taxation. Yet, the impost was not unanimously ratified; and, as requisitions on the states did not raise much money, Congress lacked funds to discharge interest on the debt. Congress was in the anomalous position of asserting ownership of the debt, but not being able to pay it.

The states claimed the debt. Responding to appeals from their own citizens who were federal creditors, the states paid interest on the debt with certificates and paper money. States redeemed federal securities by accepting them for taxes and in the sale of land. Some states went further. By 1786, Maryland, Pennsylvania, and New York had carried out a transaction by which they gave their citizens state securities in exchange for federal securities. In this and other ways, various states absorbed more than $8,000,000 in securities — a sum approaching one third of the principal of the federal debt. As other states planned similar action, there was a distinct possibility that most of the debt would soon be absorbed by the states or converted into state debts.

As this unhappy prospect materialized, the impost ran into fatal difficulties. The only state that had not ratified it in one form or another by 1786 was New York. The legislature then approved it, but with stipulations that Congress would not accept. To make matters worse, Congress discovered that the earlier ratifications of Pennsylvania and Delaware were, for quite different reasons, also unacceptable. The Pennsylvania legislature refused to reconsider its position.[32]

That seemed to be just about the end of the impost amendment. In despair, Congress entertained the idea of distributing the debt among the states. The procedure proposed was simple: give each state its share of the total debt and

[30] Jefferson, among others, was hopeful of the impost's adoption. Jefferson to Madison, May 7, 1783, Julian P. Boyd, ed., *The Papers of Thomas Jefferson* (17 vols., Princeton, 1952–　　), VI, 265–67.

[31] The analysis that follows is based on Ferguson, *Power of the Purse*, 220–42.

[32] *Journals*, XXX, 439–44; James Monroe to Madison, Sept. 12, 1786, James Madison Papers (Manuscript Division, Library of Congress).

allow it to pay its share in any way it pleased. Such a step was practical and in accord with the political realities of the Confederation.[33] It signified, however, the complete abandonment of the plan for strengthening the central government. Furthermore, a distribution of the debt was certain to promote disintegrative tendencies in the Union. When the states permanently committed their taxes to the justifiable purpose of paying Congress' creditors, it was not hard to foresee that Congress would be left with attenuated functions, little revenue, and no excuse to ask for more. Self-interest would no longer cement the Union; it would bind the creditors to their states.

The failure of the impost amendment in 1786 had a note of finality, for the absorption of the federal debt by the states destroyed any real hope of securing unanimous ratification in the future. Constitutional revision as heretofore projected had failed; some other way had to be found to achieve it. The Philadelphia Convention took place in this context. The Founders met not only to protect government from the mob but also to save the nation from disunion. It should be added that the crisis was a prospective, not an existent, one. By 1787 the country was recovering from economic depression, and it had no overwhelming problems. The real crisis involved the future of the Union.

The Philadelphia Convention of May 1787 exploited a general consensus favorable to reform and the force of economic interests in stronger central government which had arisen since the war, particularly in the matter of federal regulation of trade.[34] Throwing out the Articles of Confederation altogether, the Convention drafted a plan for a national government with powers exceeding anything the Nationalists of 1781–1783 had dared to imagine. All the delicate questions of state interest upon which the impost foundered were swept aside by the grant of unlimited power of taxation to Congress,[35] a power which George Mason observed "clearly discovers that it is a national government and no longer a Confederation. . . ."[36] Another Nationalist objective was nailed down by prohibiting the states from issuing paper money. So deep was the aversion of the Convention to fiat money that it considered denying the power to issue it even to Congress, but decided in the end to preserve this last resource for emergencies.

[33] Committee report of Aug. 17, 1786, *Journals*, XXXI, 521–23. See John Henry to Governor of Maryland, Aug. 30, 1786, Burnett, ed., *Letters*, VIII, 455–56.

[34] For a discussion of federal regulation of trade, see Nettels, *Emergence of a National Economy*, 66–75.

[35] Duties on exports were excepted. In the struggle over ratification, the Antifederalists tried to limit congressional taxing power. Every state convention that attached amendments to its ratification requested that federal revenues be restricted to indirect taxes in the first instance, that additional sums be raised by requisitions, and that federal collection of taxes within the states be permitted only if the states themselves did not deliver the money. This proposal was considered by the first Congress, along with other amendments, but voted down thirty-nine to nine in the House of Representatives and not included among the amendments sent out to the states for ratification. Jonathan Elliot, ed., *The Debates in the Several State Conventions on the Adoption of the Federal Constitution* (2nd ed., 5 vols., Philadelphia, 1861), I, 175–77, 322–23, 325, 326, 336, II, 545; U. S. Congress, *Annals of Congress: The Debates and Proceedings in the Congress of the United States* (42 vols., Washington, 1834–1856), I, 773–77. See "Luther Martin's Letter on the Federal Convention of 1787," in Elliot, ed., *Debates*, I, 368–69.

[36] Elliot, ed., *Debates*, III, 29.

As the new government was being formed, the Nationalist economic program advanced in mere anticipation of its fulfillment. Federal securities sold in the market before 1787 at ten-to-fifteen cents on the dollar. But because the states paid interest on them or accepted them for land sales, they were a good investment at that price; and speculators bought them up. The evidence indicates that the bulk of the securities changed hands during the mid-1780s. By 1790, at least 80 per cent, and almost certainly an even higher percentage, had been sold by the original holders to people of means who bought them for speculative purposes.[37] After the Constitutional Convention met, the market value of securities rose and continued to go up with every step taken in instituting the new government. At the beginning of 1787, the market value of the entire debt, principal and interest, can be estimated at $7,332,000. Three years later, in December 1789, as Hamilton was about to deliver his report on funding, the market value had shot up to about $16,628,000 — a gain since the beginning of 1787 of about $9,296,000.[38]

[37] This is the market value of "final settlement certificates" issued in satisfaction of military and civilian claims. Loan office certificates, which represented money loaned to the government during the war, were generally higher, about twenty cents on the dollar. On speculation in the public debt, see Ferguson, *Power of the Purse*, 251–86.

[38] These estimates could be refined by exhaustive research without altering them very substantially. The principal and interest have been estimated by collating figures in the following documents: Statement of the Liquidated and Loan Office Debt to Dec. 31, 1786, Papers of the Continental Congress, No. 141, Vol. II (National Archives); Statements of the Financial Affairs of the late Confederated Government, United States, Finance (Manuscript Division, Library of Congress); *American State Papers, Finance: Documents, Legislative and Executive of the United States* (5 vols., Washington, D.C., 1832–1834), I, 12–13, 27, 239; Albert Gallatin, "A Sketch of the Finances of the United States," Henry Adams, ed., *The Writings of Albert Gallatin* (3 vols., Philadelphia, 1879), III, 124–27. Although only $27,569,000 of the debt was settled by December 31, 1786, the amount due in 1789 ($28,344,833) seems a more reliable figure because unsettled claims had value. By December 31, 1789, the principal of the debt was reduced by $960,915 received in payment for public lands; the amount was then $27,383,000. The accumulated interest due on December 31, 1789, has been computed by deducting a year's interest ($1,643,035) from the amount stated in Schedule D of Hamilton's funding report as due on December 31, 1790. *American State Papers: Finance*, I, 27–28.

In the establishment of market values at the beginning of 1787, higher values of up to thirty-seven cents on the dollar in Pennsylvania and forty cents in Maryland were given to principal securities issued in these and other middle states that were funded or otherwise supported by state governments. Higher values were also assigned to loan office as opposed to final settlement certificates issued in adjustment of army and civilian claims. On the market value of securities, see Ferguson, *Power of the Purse*, 253. The market value of indents and unpaid interest has been rated at thirteen cents on the dollar. In the estimates of market values in December 1789, the principal securities have been rated at forty-seven cents on the dollar, indents and accumulated interest at thirty-three cents. These estimates are on the high side, but they reflect what New York speculators were quoting. The market fluctuated violently on the eve of Hamilton's report, prices ranging from forty cents to as high as fifty-two cents. See William Constable to Robert Morris, Dec. 17, 1789; Constable to Garret and Cottringer, Dec. 29, 1789; Constable to Thomas Fitzsimons, Jan. 1, 1790; Constable to John Inglis, Jan. 4, 1790; Constable to Robert Morris, Jan. 4, 1790; Constable to Gouverneur Morris, Jan. 7, 1790, William Constable Letterbook, 1782–1790, Bayard-Campbell-Pearsall Collection (New York Public Library). Lower prices are quoted for Boston but a flurry of speculation raised them to New York levels late in 1789. Joseph Standcliffe Davis, *Essays in the Earlier History of American*

In January 1790, Congress received Hamilton's report on public credit and began to draft a funding act. Many people outside Congress thought that to give one hundred cents on the dollar for securities that had for years sold at no more than one sixth or one eighth of that amount was not only unjust but unnecessary. The alternative was somehow to deal with the debt at its depreciated market value rather than its nominal value, a procedure which Congress and the states had often adopted. One way to accomplish this was to distinguish between original and secondary holders and to pay the full value of securities to original holders but only the market value to secondary purchasers. Since at least 80 per cent of the debt had been transferred and the highest market value at which securities had ever sold had been about fifty cents on the dollar, this plan would have cut the federal debt nearly in half. Hamilton alluded to this idea in his report, but dismissed it as adverse to public credit.[39]

There were only a few repudiationists in Congress. Three or four members of the House of Representatives wanted to revalue the debt. Their proposition never reached the stage of definition, but it had to do with reducing securities to market value.[40] In the Senate, William Maclay pushed a scheme to accomplish the same result by other means. He proposed to fund securities at the low rate of 3 per cent interest and redeem them not in cash but only by receiving them in the sale of western lands.[41] The effect would have been to keep securities nearly at current market levels and enable the government to retire them at their depreciated value as the holders offered them in bidding for western lands.

Repudiation was rejected in both houses. To advocate it was regarded as disgraceful as well as antifederal. To those concerned with implementing the political revolution that had just occurred, it was unthinkable. The proceedings of the first Federalist Congress were dominated by the logic that related sovereignty to taxation and taxation to the payment of the Revolutionary debt. Everywhere in the country congressional action on the debt was awaited as a decisive test of the difference between the new regime and the Confederation. Repudiation would have been a self-denying act, a rejection of the birthright of functions and powers conferred by the Constitution. Moreover, as Hamilton and his supporters argued, it would have undermined public credit. Any substantial scaling down of security values or discrimination between holders would have set a precedent inimical to the right of all future holders of securities to payment in full. Confidence in the government's promises, and in its securities, would have been shaken

---

Corporations (2 vols., Cambridge, Mass., 1917), I, 339. See Andrew Craigie to Leonard Bleecker, Dec. 19, 1789; Craigie to Samuel Rogers, Jan. 11, 1790, Box 3, Andrew Craigie Papers (American Antiquarian Society); Henry Jackson to Henry Knox, Dec. 27, 1789, Henry Knox Papers (Massachusetts Historical Society).

[39] Hamilton, "Report Relative to a Provision for the support of Public Credit [Jan. 9, 1790]," Syrett, ed., Papers of Alexander Hamilton, VI, 73–75. Hamilton added that the idea was "sometimes" suggested of making good the difference to the original possessor, but he did not feel it necessary to discuss this. On repudiationists, see Albert Gallatin's "Sketch of the Finances," Adams, ed., Writings of Gallatin, III, 124, 127, 129, 148.

[40] Annals of Congress, I, 1148–49, 1160–62, II, 1182, 1300.

[41] William Maclay, The Journal of William Maclay, United States Senator from Pennsylvania, 1789–1791 (New York, 1927), 195–96.

right at the beginning.[42] Finally, a repudiation would probably have ruined the valuable credit the United States possessed in Holland. Dutch bankers had invested heavily in American domestic securities at relatively high prices.

The only issue that caused any stir in the House debate over funding was Madison's motion to discriminate between original and secondary holders. His plan called for giving full value to original holders; holders of alienated securities were to get only the highest market value, presumably 50 per cent. However, the remaining 50 per cent was to be restored to the original holders who had sold out at a discount. Madison's proposal had a strong element of justice on its side, but it is important to note that it was not a repudiation. As a Nationalist of long standing and a Virginia gentleman, Madison carefully dissociated himself from the repudiationists and refused to join them. Since his scheme called for funding the debt at its face value and paying 6 per cent interest, it represented fuller payment than Hamilton's plan, which called for an immediate interest rate of about 4.5 per cent. Madison's proposal neither appeased the popular desire for repudiation nor furthered the political and economic objectives of the supporters of the new regime; hence, it had few adherents in Congress.[43] It was voted down in the House thirteen to thirty-six — nine of the minority votes being those of Virginia delegates — and it was never advocated in the Senate.[44] It seems, on the whole, to have been little more than a political maneuver designed, among other things, to make a show of opposition without offering a real alternative and to court favor among Virginians who had sold out to northern speculators.[45]

Congress in the end funded at face value the Revolutionary debt, both principal and interest, in the amount of some $42,000,000. There was no promise ever to pay the principal of the debt, only the interest; however, a sinking fund was created to purchase securities in the market and retire them. This scheme was in outline what Morris had proposed in 1782, but there was one important modification of the earlier Nationalist formula. To insure that Congress would have enough revenue to pay interest on the federal debt and also on the state debts, whose assumption was contemplated, Hamilton proposed that, for a period of ten years, the interest be reduced to about 4.5 per cent. So much he

---

[42] Conceivably, if the debt had been funded on the basis of a repudiation or a discrimination between holders, the credit of the government might have been reestablished afterward by regular payments. But this would have been a work of time.

[43] Maclay fumed against Madison for his refusal to line up with the repudiationists. "Madison's [system] yields no relief as to the burden, but affords some alleviation as to the design the tax will be laid for; and is, perhaps on that account more dangerous, as it will be readier submitted to. . . . He will see Congress in no light than as one party. He seems to prescribe to them to follow laws already made, as if they were an executive body"; whereas, in Maclay's opinion, Congress' duty was to mediate on principles of justice between a few thousand security holders and the mass of the taxpayers. When Madison's motion was defeated, Maclay wrote: "The obstinacy of this man has ruined the opposition." But as Maclay's own remarks show, there was little opposition to Hamilton's proposal respecting the federal debt either in the House or the Senate. Maclay, *Journal*, 194–95, 197.

[44] *Annals of Congress*, II, 1298; Irving Brant, *James Madison, Father of the Constitution, 1787–1800* (New York, 1950), 298–99.

[45] Ferguson, *Power of the Purse*, 297–302.

threw to the repudiationists on the ground of higher necessity, and, notwithstanding the outcries of federal creditors, Congress adopted this provision.[46] Congress saved Hamilton from further ventures into financial unorthodoxy by rejecting, as Morris had once rejected, the idea of offering payment in western lands. Congress struck out all the alternatives except specie payment or the equivalent.[47]

The assumption of state debts was in a different category from the funding of the federal debt. It was not essential to the new political establishment and was, therefore, an arguable proposition. It did, however, bear a visible relationship to national unity, and this consideration was probably foremost in Hamilton's mind. Its purpose was to sidestep divisive issues and reconcile particular states — Massachusetts and South Carolina — to the Union by equalizing the financial burdens left over from the war. For exactly the same reasons, Morris had suggested it in 1783.[48] The matter was more urgent in 1790 because Congress had taken over import duties and deprived indebted states of income. But assumption, which was contrary to the economic interest of several states, ran into heavy opposition, failed once in the House, and passed only as a result of the well-known trade that placed the national capital on the Potomac. Politically, its service to national unity was debatable. It appeased Massachusetts and South Carolina, and this may have been necessary at the time, but it raised lasting resentment in Virginia, North Carolina, and a few other states.[49] Economically, its contribution to Nationalist objectives was more demonstrable. It added $18,300,000 in funded securities to the federal debt, piled up another thick layer of business capital, and converted another body of creditors to national loyalty.

The next year Congress put the finishing touches on the Nationalist economic structure by incorporating the first Bank of the United States. State paper money was prohibited by the Constitution, and banks were now the only source except, possibly, for the federal government, of the paper medium that the country's economy required. The Bank of the United States was to be a truly national institution, with a capital of $10,000,000 and the authority to establish branches about the country. Federal securities, now the "real medium of commerce" that Morris had once envisaged, were directly transformed into bank capital as purchasers of shares were allowed to pay three fourths of their subscription in securities and one fourth in specie.

The demand for securities created by this transaction drove prices up to par. Early in 1792, when securities reached this level, the market value of the federal debt, including principal and accumulated interest, can be estimated at $32,378,000. The market value of federal and state debts combined, according

---

[46] Robert Morris held out in the Senate for 6 per cent. Maclay, *Journal*, 313–15.

[47] The final act departed from Hamilton's original proposals in other details, notably in funding accumulated interest at 3 per cent rather than on equal terms with the principal, by rating old Continental currency at 100 rather than at forty-to-one of specie, and by funding state securities at a slightly lower rate of interest than federal securities. *The Public Statutes at Large* (Boston, 1848), I, 138–44.

[48] See note 29.

[49] Gallatin observed in 1796: "The additional debt laid upon the Union by the assumption, so far from strengthening government, has created more discontent and more uneasiness than any other measure." Adams, ed., *Writings of Gallatin*, III, 131.

to Hamilton, was $43,800,000.[50] Even if the rise in the value of state securities brought about by assumption is disregarded, the appreciation of the federal debt alone since the beginning of 1787 had been a little over $25,000,000. A share of the profits after 1788 went to foreign capitalists, who invested heavily in the domestic debt; and their security purchases brought a voluminous flow of capital into the United States.[51] Within the means available, the economic revolution envisaged by the Nationalists had been accomplished.

What bearing does the Nationalist movement of 1781–1783 have upon the interpretation of the Constitution? First, the economic content of the earlier movement does not necessarily imply that economic motives were primary in the actual process by which the Constitution was drafted and adopted. It does not discount the range of the Constitution's appeal to many elements of the population: to gentlemen fearful of disorder, to frontiersmen desirous of military protection, to merchants and mechanics interested in federal trade regulation, and to all kinds of people who were disgusted by the erratic government of the Confederation or alarmed by the threat of disunion. Such considerations cut across economic, class, and sectional lines; and, in 1787, they fairly well united the country's elite behind the Constitution. For this reason, it is impossible to sustain Charles A. Beard's distinction between realty and personality interests among the gentlemen at the Convention, who, if they were so divided, were doubly united in the determination to erect barriers against popular misrule.

Second, a review of Nationalist antecedents does not tend to maximize the role of crass economic interest in the adoption of the Constitution. Certainly, there were a good many individuals who held stakes in the new government too great to be gainsaid. In 1790, the 280 largest security holders had $7,880,000, nearly two thirds of the federal securities for which ownership can be exactly established from the records. The top 100 holders had $5,000,000.[52] Beneath

[50] *American State Papers, Finance*, I, 149–50. In the computation of the value of the debt, the ratio between the different kinds of securities that were funded was projected over the unfunded debt. The prices Hamilton gave in April, 1792 in purchasing for the sinking fund were used to compute the market value. Hamilton to William Seton, April 4, 1792, Syrett, ed., *Papers of Alexander Hamilton*, XI, 225–26. On the value of the combined debt, see Hamilton to Washington, Aug. 18, 1792, *ibid.*, XII, 232–33. At the time that Hamilton wrote, stocks had risen above par to a value of over $50,000,000.

[51] That funding "created" new capital is of course debatable. Gallatin was perceptive enough to advance in 1796 the argument that it merely redistributed national income. Whatever the process, however, funding generated *effective* capital for investment — a fact which Robert Morris and Hamilton never questioned. It should also be noted that Gallatin differed with Hamilton as to the benefits from foreign investment. See Hamilton's "Report on the Subject of Manufactures," Syrett, ed., *Papers of Alexander Hamilton*, X, 278–79, 295–96, and Gallatin's "Sketch of the Finances," Adams, ed., *Writings of Gallatin*, III, 146–48.

[52] Ferguson, *Power of the Purse*, 284–85. Most of the largest holders were brokers who did not own all the securities registered in their names; hence, the figures might seem to overstate the degree of concentration. However, nearly all the records relative to $18,000,000 (out of a total of about $40,000,000) have been almost completely destroyed. These were of securities registered at the treasury, in which the really great interstate speculators, foreign as well as domestic, tended to invest. If these records were available, the degree of concentration would undoubtedly appear much higher than is suggested by the figures given here.

them was a segment of the propertied class whose holdings were large enough to imply crass economic motive. Yet, if security holders were an influential group, they were only a small fraction of the population; and their motives have to be regarded as mixed. Superimposed upon what might be interpreted as a crass interest was the general allegiance of merchants and businessmen to institutional reforms long sponsored by the Nationalists, a group value system that elevated their endorsement of the Constitution and the Hamiltonian financial program to the level of moral principle.

What can be said with certainty is that the Constitution does have an economic interpretation,[53] one that does not have to be elucidated by doubtful attempts to construct the inner motives of the Founders or depend upon a Beardian or anti-Beardian assessment of the role of security holders. The relationship of economic goals to constitutional revision was neither fabricated nor foisted on the country by interested men; it was organic. If the government was to be strengthened, it had to exercise the taxing power and pay the debt. The profits of speculators were incidental — the price that had to be paid for any degree of centralized authority, even for what most of the Antifederalist leaders were ready to accept in 1787. It is hard to find a prominent man who did not admit the necessity of paying the debt and who, thereby, acquiesced in speculative gains and the advantages to be conferred on the North as opposed to the South.[54] Other Nationalist objectives, such as currency reform and the promotion of banks, were not essential to constitutional reform, yet they were inherent in the funding of the debt and made almost mandatory by the constitutional prohibition of paper money. If the nation wanted a stronger government, it had to accept part or all of the mercantile capitalist formula of economic change.

Thus, an historical necessity existed, which would continue as long as payment of the federal debt impinged upon political reform. If the establishment of a new frame of government had been delayed until circumstances changed — until the debt had disappeared and the nation faced the international crises of the French Revolution — it might well have come in a different guise. In the period immediately after the War of Independence, however, constitutional revision entailed the realization of a mercantile capitalist economic program. The Nationalists of 1781–1783 composed the formula, kept it current after the war by preserving the federal debt, and in some measure committed the nation to an acceptance of at least their basic goals.[55] In 1787 the desire to form a more adequate government had many sources, but in certain fundamental ways the Nationalists had determined under whose auspices and to what ends the reorganization of the Union would take place.

[53] For a powerful summary of the economic effects of the establishment of the national government, see Nettels, *Emergence of a National Economy*, 89–108.

[54] Writing in 1796, Gallatin, leading spokesman of the Republicans on financial matters, said that Republicans had never disputed the necessity of funding the debt, although he suggested mildly that they would have preferred a discrimination between creditors. He himself had no objection to the way the debt was funded. Gallatin, "Sketch of the Finances," Adams, ed., *Writings of Gallatin*, III, 128, 148.

[55] "The situation of our public debts and the very great embarrassments which attended all our concerns on that account, were the *principal* causes, of that revolution which has given us the Constitution." Letter on Hamilton's funding proposals dated New York, Feb. 3, 1790, *Maryland Journal and Baltimore Advertiser*, Feb. 12, 1790.

Rhetoric and Reality in the American Revolution

GORDON S. WOOD

In this essay, Gordon S. Wood attempts to reconcile the apparent contradiction between the socioeconomic and the ideological interpretations of the American Revolution. Are men motivated by the material circumstances of their environment (this Wood terms the behaviorist view of the Becker school) or are they moved to political action by the force of ideas (the idealist view)? Wood notes that the writing of the history of the Revolution was dominated by the behaviorists for most of the first half of the twentieth century, and by the idealists for the last twenty years. He argues that the newer idealist view is as restricted as the behaviorist view, and pleads for a re-examination of the interaction of rhetoric and reality. Commenting that social scientists now accept the view that men respond not merely to objective reality but also to "the meaning they give to that reality," he suggests that we must begin to explore the ways in which men's ideas are rooted in their daily life. If we are not to opt for either the behaviorist or idealist conceptions of the Revolution, and of course there are many versions of each, we must discover the socioeconomic dynamics of ideas. Perhaps the most intriguing question about Wood's interpretation is whether it can be implemented in the present state of historical methodology. Are the psychological and sociological tools at the disposal of historians sufficient to the task? Is there, in point of fact, any practical ground for the marriage of idealism and behaviorism?

If any catch phrase is to characterize the work being done on the American Revolution by this generation of historians, it will probably be "the American Revolution considered as an intellectual movement."[1] For we now seem to be fully involved in a phase of writing about the Revolution in which the thought of the Revolutionaries, rather than their social and economic interests, has become the major focus of research and analysis. This recent emphasis on ideas is not of course new, and indeed right from the beginning it has characterized almost all our attempts to understand the Revolution. The ideas of a period which Samuel Eliot Morison and Harold Laski once described as, next to the English

Reprinted by permission of the author from the *William and Mary Quarterly*, 3d Ser., 23 (1966), pp. 3–32.

[1] This is the title of a recent essay by Edmund S. Morgan in Arthur M. Schlesinger, Jr., and Morton White, eds., *Paths of American Thought* (Boston, 1963), 11–33.

revolutionary decades of the seventeenth century, the most fruitful era in the history of Western political thought could never be completely ignored in any phase of our history writing.[2]

It has not been simply the inherent importance of the Revolutionary ideas, those "great principles of freedom,"[3] that has continually attracted the attention of historians. It has been rather the unusual nature of the Revolution and the constant need to explain what on the face of it seems inexplicable that has compelled almost all interpreters of the Revolution, including the participants themselves, to stress its predominantly intellectual character and hence its uniqueness among Western revolutions. Within the context of Revolutionary historiography the one great effort to disparage the significance of ideas in the Revolution — an effort which dominated our history writing in the first half of the twentieth century — becomes something of an anomaly, a temporary aberration into a deterministic social and economic explanation from which we have been retreating for the past two decades. Since roughly the end of World War II we have witnessed a resumed and increasingly heightened insistence on the primary significance of conscious beliefs, and particularly of constitutional principles, in explaining what once again has become the unique character of the American Revolution. In the hands of idealist-minded historians the thought and principles of the Americans have consequently come to repossess that explanative force which the previous generation of materialist-minded historians had tried to locate in the social structure.

Indeed, our renewed insistence on the importance of ideas in explaining the Revolution has now attained a level of fullness and sophistication never before achieved, with the consequence that the economic and social approach of the previous generation of behaviorist historians has never seemed more anomalous and irrelevant than it does at present. Yet paradoxically it may be that this preoccupation with the explanatory power of the Revolutionary ideas has become so intensive and so refined, assumed such a character, that the apparently discredited social and economic approach of an earlier generation has at the same time never seemed more attractive and relevant. In other words, we may be approaching a crucial juncture in our writing about the Revolution where idealism and behaviorism meet.

I

It was the Revolutionaries themselves who first described the peculiar character of what they had been involved in. The Revolution, as those who took stock at the end of three decades of revolutionary activity noted, was not "one of those events which strikes the public eye in the subversions of laws which have usually attended the revolutions of governments." Because it did not seem to have been a typical revolution, the sources of its force and its momentum appeared strangely unaccountable. "In other revolutions, the sword has been drawn by the arm of offended freedom, under an oppression that threatened the

[2] Samuel E. Morison, ed., "William Manning's *The Key of Libberty*," *William and Mary Quarterly*, 3d Ser., XIII (1956), 208.
[3] Edmund S. Morgan, "The American Revolution: Revisions in Need of Revising," *Wm. and Mary Qtly.*, 3d Ser., XIV (1957), 14.

vital powers of society."[4] But this seemed hardly true of the American Revolution. There was none of the legendary tyranny that had so often driven desperate peoples into revolution. The Americans were not an oppressed people; they had no crushing imperial shackles to throw off. In fact, the Americans knew they were probably freer and less burdened with cumbersome feudal and monarchical restraints than any part of mankind in the eighteenth century. To its victims, the Tories, the Revolution was truly incomprehensible. Never in history, said Daniel Leonard, had there been so much rebellion with so "little real cause." It was, wrote Peter Oliver, "the most wanton and unnatural rebellion that ever existed."[5] The Americans' response was out of all proportion to the stimuli. The objective social reality scarcely seemed capable of explaining a revolution.

Yet no American doubted that there had been a revolution. How then was it to be justified and explained? If the American Revolution, lacking "those mad, tumultuous actions which disgraced many of the great revolutions of antiquity," was not a typical revolution, what kind of revolution was it? If the origin of the American Revolution lay not in the usual passions and interests of men, wherein did it lay? Those Americans who looked back at what they had been through could only marvel at the rationality and moderation, "supported by the energies of well weighed choice," involved in their separation from Britain, a revolution remarkably "without violence or convulsion."[6] It seemed to be peculiarly an affair of the mind. Even two such dissimilar sorts of Whigs as Thomas Paine and John Adams both came to see the Revolution they had done so much to bring about as especially involved with ideas, resulting from "a mental examination," a change in "the minds and hearts of the people."[7] The Americans were fortunate in being born at a time when the principles of government and freedom were better known than at any time in history. The Americans had learned "how to define the rights of nature, — how to search into, to distinguish, and to comprehend, the principles of physical, moral, religious, and civil liberty," how, in short, to discover and resist the forces of tyranny before they could be applied. Never before in history had a people achieved "a revolution by reasoning" alone.[8]

The Americans, "born the heirs of freedom,"[9] revolted not to create but to

[4] [William Vans Murray], *Political Sketches, Inscribed to His Excellency John Adams* (London, 1787), 21, 48.

[5] [Daniel Leonard], *The Origin of the American Contest with Great-Britain . . . [by] Massachusettensis . . .* (New York, 1775), 40; Douglass Adair and John A. Schutz, eds., *Peter Oliver's Origin and Progress of the American Rebellion: A Tory View* (San Marino, 1963), 159.

[6] Simeon Baldwin, *An Oration Pronounced Before the Citizens of New-Haven, July 4th, 1788 . . .* (New Haven, 1788), 10; [Murray], *Political Sketches*, 48; David Ramsay, *The History of the American Revolution* (Philadelphia, 1789), I, 350.

[7] Thomas Paine, *Letter to the Abbé Raynal . . .* (1782), in Philip S. Foner, ed., *The Complete Writings of Thomas Paine* (New York, 1945), II, 243; John Adams to H. Niles, Feb. 13, 1818, in Charles Francis Adams, ed., *The Works of John Adams* (Boston, 1850–56), X, 282.

[8] William Pierce, *An Oration, Delivered at Christ Church, Savannah, on the 4th of July, 1788 . . .* (Providence, [1788]), 6; Enos Hitchcock, *An Oration; Delivered July 4th, 1788 . . .* (Providence, [1788]), 11.

[9] "Petition to the King, Oct. 1774," in Worthington C. Ford, ed., *Journals of the Continental Congress, 1774–1789* (Washington, 1904–37), I, 118.

maintain their freedom. American society had developed differently from that of the Old World. From the time of the first settlements in the seventeenth century, wrote Samuel Williams in 1794, "every thing tended to produce, and to establish the spirit of freedom." While the speculative philosophers of Europe were laboriously searching their minds in an effort to decide the first principles of liberty, the Americans had come to experience vividly that liberty in their everyday lives. The American Revolution, said Williams, joined together these enlightened ideas with America's experience. The Revolution was thus essentially intellectual and declaratory: it "explained the business to the world, and served to confirm what nature and society had before produced." "All was the result of reason. . . ."[10] The Revolution had taken place not in a succession of eruptions that had crumbled the existing social structure, but in a succession of new thoughts and new ideas that had vindicated that social structure.

The same logic that drove the participants to view the Revolution as peculiarly intellectual also compelled Moses Coit Tyler, writing at the end of the nineteenth century, to describe the American Revolution as "preeminently a revolution caused by ideas, and pivoted on ideas." That ideas played a part in all revolutions Tyler readily admitted. But in most revolutions, like that of the French, ideas had been perceived and acted upon only when the social reality had caught up with them, only when the ideas had been given meaning and force by long-experienced "real evils." The American Revolution, said Tyler, had been different: it was directed "not against tyranny inflicted, but only against tyranny anticipated." The Americans revolted not out of actual suffering but out of reasoned principle. "Hence, more than with most other epochs of revolutionary strife, our epoch of revolutionary strife was a strife of ideas: a long warfare of political logic; a succession of annual campaigns in which the marshalling of arguments not only preceded the marshalling of armies, but often exceeded them in impression upon the final result."[11]

II

It is in this historiographical context developed by the end of the nineteenth century, this constant and at times extravagant emphasis on the idealism of the Revolution, that the true radical quality of the Progressive generation's interpretation of the Revolution becomes so vividly apparent. For the work of these Progressive historians was grounded in a social and economic explanation of the Revolutionary era that explicitly rejected the causal importance of ideas. These historians could scarcely have avoided the general intellectual climate of the first part of the twentieth century which regarded ideas as suspect. By absorbing the diffused thinking of Marx and Freud and the assumptions of behaviorist psychology, men had come to conceive of ideas as ideologies or rationalizations, as masks obscuring the underlying interests and drives that actually determined social behavior. For too long, it seemed, philosophers had reified thought, detaching ideas from the material conditions that produced them and investing them

---

[10] Samuel Williams, *The Natural and Civil History of Vermont* . . . (Walpole, New Hamp., 1794), vii, 372–373; Pierce *Oration* . . . *4th July, 1788*, p. 8.

[11] Moses Coit Tyler, *The Literary History of the American Revolution, 1763–1783* (New York, 1897), I, 8–9.

with an independent will that was somehow alone responsible for the determination of events.[12] As Charles Beard pointed out in his introduction to the 1935 edition of *An Economic Interpretation of the Constitution*, previous historians of the Constitution had assumed that ideas were "entities, particularities, or forces, apparently independent of all earthly considerations coming under the head of 'economic.'" It was Beard's aim, as it was the aim of many of his contemporaries, to bring into historical consideration "those realistic features of economic conflict, stress, and strain" which previous interpreters of the Revolution had largely ignored.[13] The product of this aim was a generation or more of historical writing about the Revolutionary period (of which Beard's was but the most famous expression) that sought to explain the Revolution and the formation of the Constitution in terms of socio-economic relationships and interests rather than in terms of ideas.[14]

Curiously, the consequence of this reversal of historical approaches was not the destruction of the old-fashioned conception of the nature of ideas. As Marx had said, he intended only to put Hegel's head in its rightful place; he had no desire to cut it off. Ideas as rationalization, as ideology, remained — still distinct entities set in opposition to interests, now however lacking any deep causal significance, becoming merely a covering superstructure for the underlying and determinative social reality. Ideas therefore could still be the subject of historical investigation, as long as one kept them in their proper place, interesting no doubt in their own right but not actually counting for much in the movement of events.

Even someone as interested in ideas as Carl Becker never seriously considered them to be in any way determinants of what happened. Ideas fascinated Becker, but it was as superstructure that he enjoyed examining them, their consistency, their logic, their clarity, the way men formed and played with them. In his *Declaration of Independence: A Study in the History of Political Ideas* the political theory of the Americans takes on an unreal and even fatuous quality. It was as if ideas were merely refined tools to be used by the colonists in the most adroit manner possible. The entire Declaration of Independence, said Becker, was calculated for effect, designed primarily "to convince a candid world that the colonies had a moral and legal right to separate from Great Britain." The severe indictment of the King did not spring from unfathomable passions but was contrived, conjured up, to justify a rebellion whose sources lay elsewhere. Men to Becker were never the victims of their thought, always the masters of it. Ideas

[12] For a bald description of the assumptions with which this generation of historians worked see Graham Wallas, *Human Nature in Politics*, 3d ed. (New York, 1921), 5, 45, 48–49, 83, 94, 96, 118, 122, 156.

[13] Charles A. Beard, *An Economic Interpretation of the Constitution* (New York, 1935), x, viii.

[14] While the Progressive historians were attempting to absorb and use the latest scientific techniques of the day nonbehaviorists in government departments and others with a traditional approach to political theory — men like Andrew C. McLaughlin, Edwin S. Corwin, William S. Carpenter, Charles M. McIlwain, and Benjamin F. Wright — were writing during this same period of the best work that has ever been done on Revolutionary constitutional and political thought. However, because most of them were not, strictly speaking, historians, they never sought to explain the causes of the Revolution in terms of ideas.

were a kind of legal brief. "Thus step by step, from 1764 to 1776, the colonists modified their theory to suit their needs."[15] The assumptions behind Becker's 1909 behaviorist work on New York politics in the Revolution and his 1922 study of the political ideas in the Declaration of Independence were more alike than they at first might appear.

Bringing to their studies of the Revolution similar assumptions about the nature of ideas, some of Becker's contemporaries went on to expose starkly the implications of those assumptions. When the entire body of Revolutionary thinking was examined, these historians could not avoid being struck by its generally bombastic and overwrought quality. The ideas expressed seemed so inflated, such obvious exaggerations of reality, that they could scarcely be taken seriously. The Tories were all "wretched hirelings, and execrable parricides"; George III, the "tyrant of the earth," a "monster in human form"; the British soldier, "a mercenary, licentious rabble of banditti," intending to "tear the bowels and vitals of their brave but peaceable fellow subjects, and *to wash the ground with a profusion of innocent blood.*"[16] Such extravagant language, it seemed, could be nothing but calculated deception, at best an obvious distortion of fact, designed to incite and mold a revolutionary fervor. "The stigmatizing of British policy as 'tyranny,' 'oppression' and 'slavery,' " wrote Arthur M. Schlesinger, the dean of the Progressive historians, "had little or no objective reality, at least prior to the Intolerable Acts, but ceaseless repetition of the charge kept emotions at fever pitch."[17]

Indeed, so grandiose, so overdrawn, it seemed, were the ideas that the historians were necessarily led to ask not whether such ideas were valid but why men should have expressed them. It was not the content of such ideas but the function that was really interesting. The Revolutionary rhetoric, the profusion of sermons, pamphlets, and articles in the patriotic cause, could best be examined as propaganda, that is, as a concerted and self-conscious effort by agitators to manipulate and shape public opinion. Because of the Progressive historians' view of the Revolution as the movement of class minorities bent on promoting particular social and economic interests, the conception of propaganda was crucial to their explanation of what seemed to be a revolutionary consensus. Through the use of ideas in provoking hatred and influencing opinion and creating at least "an appearance of unity," the influence of a minority of agitators was out of all proportion to their number. The Revolution thus became a display of extraordinary skillfulness in the manipulation of public opinion. In fact, wrote Schlesinger, "no disaffected element in history has ever risen more splendidly to the occasion."[18]

[15] Carl L. Becker, *The Declaration of Independence: A Study in the History of Political Ideas* (New York, 1922), 203, 207, 133.

[16] Quoted in Philip Davidson, *Propaganda and the American Revolution, 1763–1783* (Chapel Hill, 1941), 141, 373, 150.

[17] Arthur M. Schlesinger, *Prelude to Independence: The Newspaper War on Britain, 1764–1776* (New York, 1958), 34. For examples of the scientific work on which the propagandist studies drew, see note one in Sidney I. Pomerantz, "The Patriot Newspaper and the American Revolution," in Richard B. Morris, ed., *The Era of the American Revolution* (New York, 1939), 305.

[18] Davidson, *Propaganda,* 59; Schlesinger, *Prelude to Independence,* 20.

Ideas thus became, as it were, parcels of thought to be distributed and used where they would do the most good. This propaganda was not of course necessarily false, but it was always capable of manipulation. "Whether the suggestions are to be true or false, whether the activities are to be open or concealed," wrote Philip Davidson, "are matters for the propagandist to decide." Apparently ideas could be turned on or off at will, and men controlled their rhetoric in a way they could not control their interests. Whatever the importance of propaganda, its connection with social reality was tenuous. Since ideas were so self-consciously manageable, the Whigs were not actually expressing anything meaningful about themselves but were rather feigning and exaggerating for effect. What the Americans said could not be taken at face value but must be considered as a rhetorical disguise for some hidden interest. The expression of even the classic and well-defined natural rights philosophy became, in Davidson's view, but "the propagandist's rationalization of his desire to protect his vested interests."[19]

With this conception of ideas as weapons shrewdly used by designing propagandists, it was inevitable that the thought of the Revolutionaries should have been denigrated. The Revolutionaries became by implication hypocritical demagogues, "adroitly tailoring their arguments to changing conditions." Their political thinking appeared to possess neither consistency nor significance. "At best," said Schlesinger in an early summary of his interpretation, "an exposition of the political theories of the anti-parliamentary party is an account of their retreat from one strategic position to another." So the Whigs moved, it was strongly suggested, easily if not frivolously from a defense of charter rights, to the rights of Englishmen, and finally to the rights of man, as each position was exposed and became untenable. In short, concluded Schlesinger, the Revolution could never be understood if it were regarded "as a great forensic controversy over abstract governmental rights."[20]

III

It is essentially on this point of intellectual consistency that Edmund S. Morgan has fastened for the past decade and a half in an attempt to bring down the entire interpretive framework of the socio-economic argument. If it could be shown that the thinking of the Revolutionaries was not inconsistent after all, that the Whigs did not actually skip from one constitutional notion to the next, then the imputation of Whig frivolity and hypocrisy would lose its force. This was a central intention of Morgan's study of the political thought surrounding the Stamp Act. As Morgan himself has noted and others have repeated, "In the last analysis the significance of the Stamp Act crisis lies in the emergence, not of leaders and methods and organizations, but of well-defined constitutional principles." As early as 1765 the Whigs "laid down the line on which Americans stood until they cut their connections with England. Consistently from 1765 to 1776 they denied the authority of Parliament to tax them

[19] Davidson, *Propaganda*, xiv, 46.
[20] Schlesinger, *Prelude to Independence*, 44; Arthur M. Schlesinger, *New Viewpoints in American History* (New York, 1923), 179.

externally or internally; consistently they affirmed their willingness to submit to whatever Parliament should enact for the supervision of the empire as a whole."[21] This consistency thus becomes, as one scholar's survey of the current interpretation puts it, "an indication of American devotion to principle."[22]

It seemed clear once again after Morgan's study that the Americans were more sincerely attached to constitutional principles than the behaviorist historians had supposed, and that their ideas could not be viewed as simply manipulated propaganda. Consequently the cogency of the Progressive historians' interpretation was weakened if not unhinged. And as the evidence against viewing the Revolution as rooted in internal class-conflict continued to mount from various directions, it appeared more and more comprehensible to accept the old-fashioned notion that the Revolution was after all the consequence of "a great forensic controversy over abstract governmental rights." There were, it seemed, no deprived and depressed populace yearning for a participation in politics that had long been denied; no coherent merchant class victimizing a mass of insolvent debtors; no seething discontent with the British mercantile system; no privileged aristocracy, protected by law, anxiously and insecurely holding power against a clamoring democracy. There was, in short, no internal class upheaval in the Revolution.[23]

If the Revolution was not to become virtually incomprehensible, it must have been the result of what the American Whigs always contended it was — a dispute between Mother Country and colonies over constitutional liberties. By concentrating on the immediate events of the decade leading up to independence, the historians of the 1950's have necessarily fled from the economic and social determinism of the Progressive historians. And by emphasizing the consistency and devotion with which Americans held their constitutional beliefs they have once again focused on what seems to be the extraordinary intellectuality of the American Revolution and hence its uniqueness among Western revolutions. This interpretation, which, as Jack P. Greene notes, "may appropriately be styled neo-whig," has turned the Revolution into a rationally conservative movement, involving mainly a constitutional defense of existing political liberties against the abrupt and unexpected provocations of the British government after 1760. "The issue then, according to the neo-whigs, was no more and no less than separation from Britain and the preservation of American liberty." The Revolution has therefore become "more political, legalistic, and constitutional than social or economic." Indeed, some of the neo-Whig historians have implied not just that social and economic conditions were less important in bringing on the

---

[21] Edmund S. Morgan, "Colonial Ideas of Parliamentary Power, 1764–1766," *Wm. and Mary Qtly.*, 3d Ser., V (1948), 311, 341; Edmund S. and Helen M. Morgan, *The Stamp Act Crisis: Prologue to Revolution*, rev. ed. (New York, 1963), 369–370; Page Smith, "David Ramsay and the Causes of the American Revolution," *Wm. and Mary Qtly.*, 3d Ser., XVII (1960), 70–71.

[22] Jack P. Greene, "The Flight From Determinism: A Review of Recent Literature on the Coming of the American Revolution," *South Atlantic Quarterly*, LXI (1962), 257.

[23] This revisionist literature of the 1950's is well known. See the listings in Bernard Bailyn, "Political Experience and Enlightenment Ideas in Eighteenth-Century America," *American Historical Review*, LXVII (1961–62), 341n; and in Greene, "Flight From Determinism," 235–259.

Revolution as we once thought, but rather that the social situation in the colonies had little or nothing to do with causing the Revolution. The Whig statements of principle iterated in numerous declarations appear to be the only causal residue after all the supposedly deeper social and economic causes have been washed away. As one scholar who has recently investigated and carefully dismissed the potential social and economic issue in pre-Revolutionary Virginia has concluded, "What remains as the fundamental issue in the coming of the Revolution, then, is nothing more than the contest over constitutional rights."[24]

In a different way Bernard Bailyn in a recent article has clarified and reinforced this revived idealistic interpretation of the Revolution. The accumulative influence of much of the latest historical writing on the character of eighteenth-century American society has led Bailyn to the same insight expressed by Samuel Williams in 1794. What made the Revolution truly revolutionary was not the wholesale disruption of social groups and political institutions, for compared to other revolutions such disruption was slight; rather it was the fundamental alteration in the Americans' structure of values, the way they looked at themselves and their institutions. Bailyn has seized on this basic intellectual shift as a means of explaining the apparent contradiction between the seriousness with which the Americans took their Revolutionary ideas and the absence of radical social and institutional change. The Revolution, argues Bailyn, was not so much the transformation as the realization of American society.

The Americans had been gradually and unwittingly preparing themselves for such a mental revolution since they first came to the New World in the seventeenth century. The substantive changes in American society had taken place in the course of the previous century, slowly, often imperceptibly, as a series of small piecemeal deviations from what was regarded by most Englishmen as the accepted orthodoxy in society, state, and religion. What the Revolution marked, so to speak, was the point when the Americans suddenly blinked and saw their society, its changes, its differences, in a new perspective. Their deviation from European standards, their lack of an established church and a titled aristocracy, their apparent rusticity and general equality, now became desirable, even necessary, elements in the maintenance of their society and politics. The comprehending and justifying, the endowing with high moral purpose, of these confusing and disturbing social and political divergences, Bailyn concludes, was the American Revolution.[25]

Bailyn's more recent investigation of the rich pamphlet literature of the decades before Independence has filled out and refined his idealist interpretation, confirming him in his "rather old-fashioned view that the American Revolution was above all else an ideological-constitutional struggle and not primarily a controversy between social groups undertaken to force changes in the organization of society." While Bailyn's book-length introduction to the first of a multivolumed edition of Revolutionary pamphlets makes no effort to stress the conservative character of the Revolution and indeed emphasizes (in contrast to the

[24] Greene, "Flight From Determinism," 237, 257; Thad W. Tate, "The Coming of the Revolution in Virginia: Britain's Challenge to Virginia's Ruling Class, 1763–1776," *Wm. and Mary Qtly.*, 3d Ser., XIX (1962), 323–343, esp. 340.
[25] Bailyn, "Political Experience and Enlightenment Ideas," 339–351.

earlier article) its radicalism and the dynamic and transforming rather than the rationalizing and declarative quality of Whig thought, it nevertheless represents the culmination of the idealist approach to the history of the Revolution. For "above all else," argues Bailyn, it was the Americans' world-view, the peculiar bundle of notions and beliefs they put together during the imperial debate, "that in the end propelled them into Revolution." Through his study of the Whig pamphlets Bailyn became convinced "that the fear of a comprehensive conspiracy against liberty throughout the English-speaking world — a conspiracy believed to have been nourished in corruption, and of which, it was felt, oppression in America was only the most immediately visible part — lay at the heart of the Revolutionary movement." No one of the various acts and measures of the British government after 1763 could by itself have provoked the extreme and violent response of the American Whigs. But when linked together they formed in the minds of the Americans, imbued with a particular historical understanding of what constituted tyranny, an extensive and frightening program designed to enslave the New World. The Revolution becomes comprehensible only when the mental framework, the Whig world-view into which the Americans fitted the events of the 1760's and 1770's, is known. "It is the development of this view to the point of overwhelming persuasiveness to the majority of American leaders and the meaning this view gave to the events of the time, and not simply an accumulation of grievances," writes Bailyn, "that explains the origins of the American Revolution."[26]

It now seems evident from Bailyn's analysis that it was the Americans' peculiar conception of reality more than anything else that convinced them that tyranny was afoot and that they must fight if their liberty was to survive. By an empathic understanding of a wide range of American thinking Bailyn has been able to offer us a most persuasive argument for the importance of ideas in bringing on the Revolution. Not since Tyler has the intellectual character of the Revolution received such emphasis and never before has it been set out so cogently and completely. It would seem that the idealist explanation of the Revolution has nowhere else to go.[27]

IV

Labeling the recent historical interpretations of the Revolution as "neo-Whig" is indeed appropriate, for, as Page Smith has pointed out, "After a century and a half of progress in historical scholarship, in research techniques, in tools and methods, we have found our way to the interpretation held, substantially, by those historians who themselves participated in or lived through the era of, the Revolution." By describing the Revolution as a conservative, principled defense

---

[26] Bernard Bailyn, ed., assisted by Jane N. Garrett, *Pamphlets of the American Revolution, 1750–1776* (Cambridge, Mass., 1965 —), I, viii, 60, x, 20. The 200-page general introduction is entitled, "The Transforming Radicalism of the American Revolution."

[27] This is not to say, however, that work on the Revolutionary ideas is in any way finished. For examples of the re-examination of traditional problems in Revolutionary political theory see Richard Buel, Jr., "Democracy and the American Revolution: A Frame of Reference," *Wm. and Mary Qtly.*, 3d Ser., XXI (1964), 165–190; and Bailyn's resolution of James Otis's apparent inconsistency in *Revolutionary Pamphlets*, I, 100–103, 106–107, 121–123, 409–417, 546–552.

of American freedom against the provocations of the English government, the neo-Whig historians have come full circle to the position of the Revolutionaries themselves and to the interpretation of the first generation of historians.[28] Indeed, as a consequence of this historical atavism, praise for the contemporary or early historians has become increasingly common.

But to say "that the Whig interpretation of the American Revolution may not be as dead as some historians would have us believe" is perhaps less to commend the work of David Ramsay and George Bancroft than to indict the approach of recent historians.[29] However necessary and rewarding the neo-Whig histories have been, they present us with only a partial perspective on the Revolution. The neo-Whig interpretation is intrinsically polemical; however subtly presented, it aims to justify the Revolution. It therefore cannot accommodate a totally different, an opposing, perspective, a Tory view of the Revolution. It is for this reason that the recent publication of Peter Oliver's "Origin and Progress of the American Rebellion" is of major significance, for it offers us — "by attacking the hallowed traditions of the revolution, challenging the motives of the founding fathers, and depicting revolution as passion, plotting, and violence" — an explanation of what happened quite different from what we have been recently accustomed to.[30] Oliver's vivid portrait of the Revolutionaries with his accent on their vicious emotions and interests seriously disturbs the present Whiggish interpretation of the Revolution. It is not that Oliver's description of, say, John Adams as madly ambitious and consumingly resentful is any more correct than Adams's own description of himself as a virtuous and patriotic defender of liberty against tyranny. Both interpretations of Adams are in a sense right, but neither can comprehend the other because each is preoccupied with seemingly contradictory sets of motives. Indeed, it is really these two interpretations that have divided historians of the Revolution ever since.

Any intellectually satisfying explanation of the Revolution must encompass the Tory perspective as well as the Whig, for if we are compelled to take sides and choose between opposing motives — unconscious or avowed, passion or principle, greed or liberty — we will be endlessly caught up in the polemics of the participants themselves. We must, in other words, eventually dissolve the distinction between conscious and unconscious motives, between the Revolutionaries' stated intentions and their supposedly hidden needs and desires, a dissolution that involves somehow relating beliefs and ideas to the social world in which they operate. If we are to understand the causes of the Revolution we must therefore ultimately transcend this problem of motivation. But this we can never do as long as we attempt to explain the Revolution mainly in terms of the intentions of the participants. It is not that men's motives are unimportant; they indeed make events, including revolutions. But the purposes of men, especially in a revolution, are so numerous, so varied, and so contradictory that their complex interaction produces results that no one intended or could even foresee. It is

[28] Smith, "Ramsay and the American Revolution," 72.
[29] Morgan, "Revisions in Need of Revising," 13.
[30] Adair and Schutz, eds., *Peter Oliver's Origin*, ix. In the present neo-Whig context, Sidney S. Fisher, "The Legendary and Myth-Making Process in Histories of the American Revolution," in American Philosophical Society, *Proceedings* LI (Philadelphia, 1912), 53–75, takes on a renewed relevance.

this interaction and these results that recent historians are referring to when they speak so disparagingly of those "underlying determinants" and "impersonal and inexorable forces" bringing on the Revolution. Historical explanation which does not account for these "forces," which, in other words, relies simply on understanding the conscious intentions of the actors, will thus be limited. This preoccupation with men's purposes was what restricted the perspectives of the contemporaneous Whig and Tory interpretations; and it is still the weakness of the neo-Whig histories, and indeed of any interpretation which attempts to explain the events of the Revolution by discovering the calculations from which individuals supposed themselves to have acted.

No explanation of the American Revolution in terms of the intentions and designs of particular individuals could have been more crudely put than that offered by the Revolutionaries themselves. American Whigs, like men of the eighteenth century generally, were fascinated with what seemed to the age to be the newly appreciated problem of human motivation and causation in the affairs of the world. In the decade before independence the Americans sought endlessly to discover the supposed calculations and purposes of individuals or groups that lay behind the otherwise incomprehensible rush of events. More than anything else perhaps, it was this obsession with motives that led to the prevalence in the eighteenth century of beliefs in conspiracies to account for the confusing happenings in which men found themselves caught up. Bailyn has suggested that this common fear of conspiracy was "deeply rooted in the political awareness of eighteenth-century Britons, involved in the very structure of their political life"; it "reflected so clearly the realities of life in an age in which monarchical autocracy flourished, [and] in which the stability and freedom of England's 'mixed' constitution was a recent and remarkable achievement."[31] Yet it might also be argued that the tendency to see conspiracy behind what happened reflected as well the very enlightenment of the age. To attribute events to the designs and purposes of human agents seemed after all to be an enlightened advance over older beliefs in blind chance, providence, or God's interventions. It was rational and scientific, a product of both the popularization of politics and the secularization of knowledge. It was obvious to Americans that the series of events in the years after 1763, those "unheard of intolerable calamities, spring not of the dust, come not causeless." "Ought not the PEOPLE therefore," asked John Dickinson, "to watch? to observe facts? to search into causes? to investigate designs?"[32] And these causes and designs could be traced to individuals in high places, to ministers, to royal governors, and their lackeys. The belief in conspiracy grew naturally out of the enlightened need to find the human purposes behind the multitude of phenomena, to find the causes for what happened in

---

[31] Bailyn, *Revolutionary Pamphlets*, I, 87, ix.

[32] [Moses Mather], *America's Appeal to the Impartial World* . . . (Hartford, 1775), 59; [John Dickinson], *Letters from a Farmer in Pennsylvania to the Inhabitants of the British Colonies* (1768), in Paul L. Ford, ed., *The Life and Writings of John Dickinson* (Historical Society of Pennsylvania, *Memoirs*, XIV [Philadelphia, 1895]), II, 348. Dickinson hinged his entire argument on the ability of the Americans to decipher the "intention" of parliamentary legislation, whether for revenue or for commercial regulation. *Ibid.*, 348, 364.

the social world just as the natural scientist was discovering the causes for what happened in the physical world.[33] It was a necessary consequence of the search for connections and patterns in events. The various acts of the British government, the Americans knew, should not be "regarded according to the simple force of each, but as parts of a system of oppression."[34] The Whigs' intense search for the human purposes behind events was in fact an example of the beginnings of modern history.

In attempting to rebut those interpretations disparaging the colonists' cause, the present neo-Whig historians have been drawn into writing as partisans of the Revolutionaries. And they have thus found themselves entangled in the same kind of explanation used by the original antagonists, an explanation, despite obvious refinements, still involved with the discovery of motives and its corollary, the assessing of a personal sort of responsibility for what happened. While most of the neo-Whig historians have not gone so far as to see conspiracy in British actions (although some have come close),[35] they have tended to point up the blundering and stupidity of British officials in contrast to "the breadth of vision" that moved the Americans. If George III was in a position of central responsibility in the British government, as English historians have recently said, then, according to Edmund S. Morgan, "he must bear most of the praise or blame for the series of measures that alienated and lost the colonies, and it is hard to see how there can be much praise." By seeking "to define issues, fix responsibilities," and thereby to shift the "burden of proof" onto those who say the Americans were narrow and selfish and the empire was basically just and beneficent, the neo-Whigs have attempted to redress what they felt was an unfair neo-Tory bias of previous explanations of the Revolution;[36] they have not, however, challenged the terms of the argument. They are still obsessed with why men said they acted and with who was right and who was wrong. Viewing the history of the

---

[33] See Herbert Davis, "The Augustan Conception of History," in J. A. Mazzeo, ed., *Reason and the Imagination: Studies in the History of Ideas, 1600–1800* (New York, 1962), 226–228; W. H. Greenleaf, *Order, Empiricism and Politics: Two Traditions of English Political Thought, 1500–1700* (New York, 1964), 166; R. N. Stromberg, "History in the Eighteenth Century," *Journal of the History of Ideas,* XII (1951), 300. It was against this "dominant characteristic of the historical thought of the age," this "tendency to explain events in terms of conscious action by individuals," that the brilliant group of Scottish social scientists writing at the end of the 18th century directed much of their work. Duncan Forbes, " 'Scientific' Whiggism: Adam Smith and John Millar," *Cambridge Journal,* VII (1954), 651, 653–654. While we have had recently several good studies of historical thinking in seventeenth-century England, virtually nothing has been done on the eighteenth century. See, however, J. G. A. Pocock, "Burke and the Ancient Constitution — A Problem in the History of Ideas," *The Historical Journal,* III (1960), 125–143; and Stow Persons, "The Cyclical Theory of History in Eighteenth Century America," *American Quarterly,* VI (1954), 147–163.

[34] [Dickinson], *Letters from a Farmer,* in Ford, ed., *Writings of Dickinson,* 388.

[35] Bailyn has noted that Oliver M. Dickerson, in chap. 7 of his *The Navigation Acts and the American Revolution* (Philadelphia, 1951), "adopts wholesale the contemporary Whig interpretation of the Revolution as the result of a conspiracy of 'King's Friends.' " Bailyn, *Revolutionary Pamphlets,* I, 724.

[36] Morgan, "Revisions in Need of Revising," 7, 13, 8; Greene, "Flight From Determinism," 237.

Revolution in this judicatory manner has therefore restricted the issues over which historians have disagreed to those of motivation and responsibility, the very issues with which the participants themselves were concerned.

The neo-Whig "conviction that the colonists' attachment to principle was genuine"[37] has undoubtedly been refreshing, and indeed necessary, given the Tory slant of earlier twentieth-century interpretations. It now seems clearer that the Progressive historians, with their naive and crude reflex conception of human behavior, had too long treated the ideas of the Revolution superficially if not superciliously. Psychologists and sociologists are now willing to grant a more determining role to beliefs, particularly in revolutionary situations. It is now accepted that men act not simply in response to some kind of objective reality but to the meaning they give to that reality. Since men's beliefs are as much a part of the given stimuli as the objective environment, the beliefs must be understood and taken seriously if men's behavior is to be fully explained. The American Revolutionary ideas were more than cooked up pieces of thought served by an aggressive and interested minority to a gullible and unsuspecting populace. The concept of propaganda permitted the Progressive historians to account for the presence of ideas but it prevented them from recognizing ideas as an important determinant of the Americans' behavior. The weight attributed to ideas and constitutional principles by the neo-Whig historians was thus an essential corrective to the propagandist studies.

Yet in its laudable effort to resurrect the importance of ideas in historical explanation much of the writing of the neo-Whigs has tended to return to the simple nineteenth-century intellectualist assumption that history is the consequence of a rational calculation of ends and means, that what happened was what was consciously desired and planned. By supposing "that individual actions and immediate issues are more important than underlying determinants in explaining particular events," by emphasizing conscious and articulated motives, the neo-Whig historians have selected and presented that evidence which is most directly and clearly expressive of the intentions of the Whigs, that is, the most well-defined, the most constitutional, the most reasonable of the Whig beliefs, those found in their public documents, their several declarations of grievances and causes. It is not surprising that for the neo-Whigs the history of the American Revolution should be more than anything else "the history of the Americans' search for principles."[38] Not only, then, did nothing in the Americans' economic and social structure really determine their behavior, but the colonists in fact acted from the most rational and calculated of motives: they fought, as they said they would, simply to defend their ancient liberties against British provocation.

By implying that certain declared rational purposes are by themselves an adequate explanation for the Americans' revolt, in other words that the Revolution was really nothing more than a contest over constitutional principles, the neo-Whig historians have not only threatened to deny what we have learned of human psychology in the twentieth century, but they have also in fact failed to exploit fully the terms of their own idealist approach by not taking into account all of

---

[37] Edmund S. Morgan, *The Birth of the Republic, 1763–89* (Chicago, 1956), 51.
[38] Greene, "Flight From Determinism," 258; Morgan, *Birth of the Republic*, 3.

what the Americans believed and said. Whatever the deficiencies and misunderstandings of the role of ideas in human behavior present in the propagandist studies of the 1930's, these studies did for the first time attempt to deal with the entirety and complexity of American Revolutionary thought — to explain not only all the well-reasoned notions of law and liberty that were so familiar but, more important, all the irrational and hysterical beliefs that had been so long neglected. Indeed, it was the patent absurdity and implausibility of much of what the Americans said that lent credence and persuasiveness to their mistrustful approach to the ideas. Once this exaggerated and fanatical rhetoric was uncovered by the Progressive historians, it should not have subsequently been ignored — no matter how much it may have impugned the reasonableness of the American response. No widely expressed ideas can be dismissed out of hand by the historian.

In his recent analysis of Revolutionary thinking Bernard Bailyn has avoided the neo-Whig tendency to distort the historical reconstruction of the American mind. By comprehending "the assumptions, beliefs, and ideas that lay behind the manifest events of the time," Bailyn has attempted to get inside the Whigs' mind, and to experience vicariously all of what they thought and felt, both their rational constitutional beliefs and their hysterical and emotional ideas as well. The inflammatory phrases, "slavery," "corruption," "conspiracy," that most historians had either ignored or readily dismissed as propaganda, took on a new significance for Bailyn. He came "to suspect that they meant something very real to both the writers and their readers: that there were real fears, real anxieties, a sense of real danger behind these phrases, and not merely the desire to influence by rhetoric and propaganda the inert minds of an otherwise passive populace."[39] No part of American thinking, Bailyn suggests — not the widespread belief in a ministerial conspiracy, not the hostile and vicious indictments of individuals, not the fear of corruption and the hope for regeneration, not any of the violent seemingly absurd distortions and falsifications of what we now believe to be true, in short, none of the frenzied rhetoric — can be safely ignored by the historian seeking to understand the causes of the Revolution.

Bailyn's study, however, represents something other than a more complete and uncorrupted version of the common idealist interpretations of the Revolution. By viewing from the "interior" the Revolutionary pamphlets, which were "to an unusual degree, *explanatory*," revealing "not merely positions taken but the reasons why positions were taken," Bailyn like any idealist historian has sought to discover the motives the participants themselves gave for their actions, to re-enact their thinking at crucial moments, and thereby to recapture some of the "unpredictable reality" of the Revolution.[40] But for Bailyn the very unpredictability of the reality he has disclosed has undermined the idealist obsession with explaining why, in the participants' own estimation, they acted as they did. Ideas emerge as more than explanatory devices, as more than indicators of motives. They become as well objects for analysis in and for themselves, historical events in their own right to be treated as other historical events are treated. Although Bailyn has examined the Revolutionary ideas subjectively from the inside, he has also

[39] Bailyn, *Revolutionary Pamphlets*, I, vii, ix.
[40] *Ibid.*, vii, viii, 17.

analyzed them objectively from the outside. Thus, in addition to a contemporary Whig perspective, he presents us with a retrospective view of the ideas — their complexity, their development, and their consequences — that the actual participants did not have. In effect his essay represents what has been called "a Namierism of the history of ideas,"[41] a structural analysis of thought that suggests a conclusion about the movement of history not very different from Sir Lewis Namier's, where history becomes something "started in ridiculous beginnings, while small men did things both infinitely smaller and infinitely greater than they knew."[42]

In his *England in the Age of the American Revolution* Namier attacked the Whig tendency to overrate "the importance of the conscious will and purpose in individuals." Above all he urged us "to ascertain and recognize the deeper irrelevancies and incoherence of human actions, which are not so much directed by reason, as invested by it *ex post facto* with the appearances of logic and rationality," to discover the unpredictable reality, where men's motives and intentions were lost in the accumulation and momentum of interacting events. The whole force of Namier's approach tended to squeeze the intellectual content out of what men did. Ideas setting forth principles and purposes for action, said Namier, did not count for much in the movement of history.[43]

In his study of the Revolutionary ideas Bailyn has come to an opposite conclusion: ideas counted for a great deal, not only being responsible for the Revolution but also for transforming the character of American society. Yet in his hands ideas lose that static quality they have commonly had for the Whig historians, the simple statements of intention that so exasperated Namier. For Bailyn the ideas of the Revolutionaries take on an elusive and unmanageable quality, a dynamic self-intensifying character that transcended the intentions and desires of any of the historical participants. By emphasizing how the thought of the colonists was "strangely reshaped, turned in unfamiliar directions," by describing how the Americans "indeliberately, half-knowingly" groped toward "conclusions they could not themselves clearly perceive," by demonstrating how new beliefs and hence new actions were the responses not to desire but to the logic of developing situations, Bailyn has wrested the explanation of the Revolution out of the realm of motivation in which the neo-Whig historians had confined it.

With this kind of approach to ideas, the degree of consistency and devotion to principles become less important, and indeed the major issues of motivation and responsibility over which historians have disagreed become largely irrelevant. Action becomes not the product of rational and conscious calculation but of dimly perceived and rapidly changing thoughts and situations, "where the familiar meaning of ideas and words faded away into confusion, and leaders felt themselves peering into a haze, seeking to bring shifting conceptions somehow into focus." Men become more the victims than the manipulators of their ideas, as their thought unfolds in ways few anticipated, "rapid, irreversible, and irresisti-

---

[41] J. G. A. Pocock, "Machiavelli, Harrington, and English Political Ideologies in the Eighteenth Century," *Wm. and Mary Qtly.*, 3d Ser., XXII (1965), 550.
[42] Sir Lewis Namier, *England in the Age of the American Revolution*, 2d ed. (London, 1961), 131.
[43] *Ibid.*, 129.

ble," creating new problems, new considerations, new ideas, which have their own unforeseen implications. In this kind of atmosphere the Revolution, not at first desired by the Americans, takes on something of an inevitable character, moving through a process of escalation into levels few had intended or perceived. It no longer makes sense to assign motives or responsibility to particular individuals for the totality of what happened. Men were involved in a complicated web of phenomena, ideas, and situations, from which in retrospect escape seems impossible.[44]

By seeking to uncover the motives of the Americans expressed in the Revolutionary pamphlets, Bailyn has ended by demonstrating the autonomy of ideas as phenomena, where the ideas operate, as it were, over the heads of the participants, taking them in directions no one could have foreseen. His discussion of Revolutionary thought thus represents a move back to a deterministic approach to the Revolution, a determinism, however, which is different from that which the neo-Whig historians have so recently and self-consciously abandoned. Yet while the suggested determinism is thoroughly idealist — indeed never before has the force of ideas in bringing on the Revolution been so emphatically put — its implications are not. By helping to purge our writing about the Revolution of its concentration on constitutional principles and its stifling judicial-like preoccupation with motivation and responsibility, the study serves to open the way for new questions and new appraisals. In fact, it is out of the very completeness of his idealist interpretation, out of his exposition of the extraordinary nature — the very dynamism and emotionalism — of the Americans' thought that we have the evidence for an entirely different, a behaviorist, perspective on the causes of the American Revolution. Bailyn's book-length introduction to his edition of Revolutionary pamphlets is therefore not only a point of fulfillment for the idealist approach to the Revolution, it is also a point of departure for a new look at the social sources of the Revolution.

V

It seems clear that historians of eighteenth-century America and the Revolution cannot ignore the force of ideas in history to the extent that Namier and his students have done in their investigations of eighteenth-century English politics. This is not to say, however, that the Namier approach to English politics has been crucially limiting and distorting. Rather it may suggest that the Namier denigration of ideas and principles is inapplicable for American politics because the American social situation in which ideas operated was very different from that of eighteenth-century England. It may be that ideas are less meaningful to a people in a socially stable situation. Only when ideas have become stereotyped reflexes do evasion and hypocrisy and the Namier mistrust of what men believe become significant. Only in a relatively settled society does ideology become a kind of habit, a bundle of widely shared and instinctive conventions, offering

---

[44] Bailyn, *Revolutionary Pamphlets*, I, 90, x, 169, 140. See Hannah Arendt, *On Revolution* (New York, 1963), 173: "American experience had taught the men of the Revolution that action, though it may be started in isolation and decided upon by single individuals for very different motives, can be accomplished only by some joint effort in which the motivation of single individuals . . . no longer counts. . . ."

ready-made explanations for men who are not being compelled to ask any serious questions. Conversely, it is perhaps only in a relatively unsettled, disordered society, where the questions come faster than men's answers, that ideas become truly vital and creative.[45]

Paradoxically it may be the very vitality of the Americans' ideas, then, that suggests the need to examine the circumstances in which they flourished. Since ideas and beliefs are ways of perceiving and explaining the world, the nature of the ideas expressed is determined as much by the character of the world being confronted as by the internal development of inherited and borrowed conceptions. Out of the multitude of inherited and transmitted ideas available in the eighteenth century, Americans selected and emphasized those which seemed to make meaningful what was happening to them. In the colonists' use of classical literature, for example, "their detailed knowledge and engaged interest covered only one era and one small group of writers," Plutarch, Livy, Cicero, Sallust, and Tacitus — those who "had hated and feared the trends of their own time, and in their writing had contrasted the present with a better past, which they endowed with qualities absent from their own, corrupt era."[46] There was always, in Max Weber's term, some sort of elective affinity between the Americans' interests and their beliefs, and without that affinity their ideas would not have possessed the peculiar character and persuasiveness they did. Only the most revolutionary social needs and circumstances could have sustained such revolutionary ideas.[47]

When the ideas of the Americans are examined comprehensively, when all of the Whig rhetoric, irrational as well as rational, is taken into account, one cannot but be struck by the predominant characteristics of fear and frenzy, the exaggerations and the enthusiasm, the general sense of social corruption and disorder out of which would be born a new world of benevolence and harmony where Americans would become the "eminent examples of every divine and social virtue."[48] As Bailyn and the propaganda studies have amply shown, there is simply too much fanatical and millennial thinking even by the best minds that must be explained before we can characterize the Americans' ideas as peculiarly rational and legalistic and thus view the Revolution as merely a conservative defense of constitutional liberties. To isolate refined and nicely-reasoned arguments from the writings of John Adams and Jefferson is not only to disregard the more inflamed expressions of the rest of the Whigs but also to overlook the

[45] See Sir Lewis Namier, *The Structure of Politics at the Accession of George III*, 2d ed. (London, 1961), 16; Sir Lewis Namier, "Human Nature in Politics," in *Personalities and Power: Selected Essays* (New York, 1965), 5–6.

[46] Bailyn, *Revolutionary Pamphlets*, I, 22. The French Revolutionaries were using the same group of classical writings to express their estrangement from the *ancien régime* and their hope for the new order. Harold T. Parker, *The Cult of Antiquity and the French Revolutionaries: A Study in the Development of the Revolutionary Spirit* (Chicago, 1937), 22–23.

[47] The relation of ideas to social structure is one of the most perplexing and intriguing in the social sciences. For an extensive bibliography on the subject see Norman Birnbaum, "The Sociological Study of Ideology (1940–60)," *Current Sociology*, IX (1960).

[48] Jacob Duché, *The American Vine, A Sermon, Preached . . . Before the Honourable Continental Congress, July 20th, 1775 . . .* (Philadelphia, 1775), 29.

enthusiastic extravagance — the paranoiac obsession with a diabolical Crown conspiracy and the dream of a restored Saxon era — in the thinking of Adams and Jefferson themselves.

The ideas of the Americans seem, in fact, to form what can only be called a revolutionary syndrome. If we were to confine ourselves to examining the Revolutionary rhetoric alone, apart from what happened politically or socially, it would be virtually impossible to distinguish the American Revolution from any other revolution in modern Western history. In the kinds of ideas expressed the American Revolution is remarkably similar to the seventeenth-century Puritan Revolution and to the eighteenth-century French Revolution: the same general disgust with a chaotic and corrupt world, the same anxious and angry bombast, the same excited fears of conspiracies by depraved men, the same utopian hopes for the construction of a new and virtuous order.[49] It was not that this syndrome of ideas was simply transmitted from one generation or from one people to another. It was rather perhaps that similar, though hardly identical, social situations called forth within the limitations of inherited and available conceptions similar modes of expression. Although we need to know much more about the sociology of revolutions and collective movements, it does seem possible that particular patterns of thought, particular forms of expression, correspond to certain basic social experiences. There may be, in other words, typical modes of expression, typical kinds of beliefs and values, characterizing a revolutionary situation, at least within roughly similar Western societies. Indeed, the types of ideas manifested may be the best way of identifying a collective movement as a revolution. As one student of revolutions writes, "It is on the basis of a knowledge of men's beliefs that we can distinguish their behaviour from riot, rebellion or insanity."[50]

It is thus the very nature of the Americans' rhetoric — its obsession with corruption and disorder, its hostile and conspiratorial outlook, and its millennial vision of a regenerated society — that reveals as nothing else apparently can the American Revolution as a true revolution with its sources lying deep in the social structure. For this kind of frenzied rhetoric could spring only from the most severe sorts of social strain. The grandiose and feverish language of the Americans was indeed the natural, even the inevitable, expression of a people caught up in a revolutionary situation, deeply alienated from the existing sources of authority and vehemently involved in a basic reconstruction of their political and social order. The hysteria of the Americans' thinking was but a measure of the intensity of their revolutionary passions. Undoubtedly the growing American alienation from British authority contributed greatly to this revolutionary situa-

[49] For recent discussions of French and Puritan revolutionary rhetoric see Peter Gay, "Rhetoric and Politics in the French Revolution," *Amer. Hist. Rev.*, LXVI (1960–61), 664–676; Michael Walzer, "Puritanism as a Revolutionary Ideology," *History and Theory*, III (1963), 59–90. This entire issue of *History and Theory* is devoted to a symposium on the uses of theory in the study of history. In addition to the Walzer article, I have found the papers by Samuel H. Beer, "Causal Explanation and Imaginative Re-enactment," and Charles Tilly, "The Analysis of a Counter-Revolution," very stimulating and helpful.

[50] Bryan A. Wilson, "Millennialism in Comparative Perspective," *Comparative Studies in Society and History*, VI (1963–64), 108. See also Neil J. Smelser, *Theory of Collective Behaviour* (London, 1962), 83, 120, 383.

tion. Yet the very weakness of the British imperial system and the accumulating ferocity of American antagonism to it suggests that other sources of social strain were being fed into the revolutionary movement. It may be that the Progressive historians in their preoccupation with internal social problems were more right than we have recently been willing to grant. It would be repeating their mistake, however, to expect this internal social strain necessarily to take the form of coherent class conflict or overt social disruption. The sources of revolutionary social stress may have been much more subtle but not less severe.

Of all of the colonies in the mid-eighteenth century, Virginia seems the most settled, the most lacking in obvious social tensions. Therefore, as it has been recently argued, since conspicuous social issues were nonexistent, the only plausible remaining explanation for the Virginians' energetic and almost unanimous commitment to the Revolution must have been their devotion to constitutional principles.[51] Yet it may be that we have been looking for the wrong kind of social issues, for organized conflicts, for conscious divisions, within the society. It seems clear that Virginia's difficulties were not the consequence of any obvious sectional or class antagonism, Tidewater versus Piedmont, aristocratic planters versus yeomen farmers. There was apparently no discontent with the political system that went deep into the social structure. But there does seem to have been something of a social crisis within the ruling group itself, which intensely aggravated the Virginians' antagonism to the imperial system. Contrary to the impression of confidence and stability that the Virginia planters have historically acquired, they seemed to have been in very uneasy circumstances in the years before the Revolution. The signs of the eventual nineteenth-century decline of the Virginia gentry were, in other words, already felt if not readily apparent.

The planters' ability to command the acquiescence of the people seems extraordinary compared to the unstable politics of the other colonies. But in the years before independence there were signs of increasing anxiety among the gentry over their representative role. The ambiguities in the relationship between the Burgesses and their constituents erupted into open debate in the 1750's. And men began voicing more and more concern over the mounting costs of elections and growing corruption in the soliciting of votes, especially by "those who have neither natural nor acquired parts to recommend them."[52] By the late sixties and early seventies the newspapers were filled with warnings against electoral influence, bribery, and vote seeking. The freeholders were stridently urged to "strike at the Root of this growing Evil; be influenced by Merit alone," and avoid electing "obscure and inferior persons."[53] It was as if ignoble ambition and demagoguery, one bitter pamphlet remarked, were a "Daemon lately come among us

[51] Tate, "Coming of the Revolution in Virginia," 324–343.

[52] Robert E. and B. Katherine Brown, Virginia, 1707–1786: Democracy or Aristocracy? (East Lansing, Mich., 1964), 236; Alexander White to Richard Henry Lee, 1758, quoted in J. R. Pole, "Representation and Authority in Virginia from the Revolution to Reform," The Journal of Southern History, XXIV (1958), 23.

[53] Purdie and Dixon's Virginia Gazette (Williamsburg), Apr. 11, 1771; Rind's Virginia Gazette, Oct. 31, 1771. See Lester J. Cappon and Stella F. Duff, eds., Virginia Gazette Index, 1736–1780 (Williamsburg, 1950), I, 351, for entries on the astounding increase in essays on corruption and cost of elections in the late 1760's and early 1770's.

to disturb the peace and harmony, which had so long subsisted in this place."[54] In this context Robert Munford's famous play, *The Candidates*, written in 1770, does not so much confirm the planters' confidence as it betrays their uneasiness with electoral developments in the colony, "when coxcombs and jockies can impose themselves upon it for men of learning." Although disinterested virtue eventually wins out, Munford's satire reveals the kinds of threats the established planters faced from ambitious knaves and blockheads who were turning representatives into slaves of the people.[55]

By the eve of the Revolution the planters were voicing a growing sense of impending ruin, whose sources seemed in the minds of many to be linked more and more with the corrupting British connection and the Scottish factors, but for others frighteningly rooted in "our Pride, our Luxury, and Idleness."[56] The public and private writings of Virginians became obsessed with "corruption," "virtue," and "luxury." The increasing defections from the Church of England, even among ministers and vestrymen, and the remarkable growth of dissent in the years before the Revolution, "so much complained of in many parts of the colony," further suggests some sort of social stress. The strange religious conversions of Robert Carter may represent only the most dramatic example of what was taking place less frenziedly elsewhere among the gentry.[57] By the middle of the eighteenth century it was evident that many of the planters were living on the edge of bankruptcy, seriously overextended and spending beyond their means in an almost frantic effort to fulfill the aristocratic image they had created of themselves.[58] Perhaps the importance of the Robinson affair in the 1760's lies not in any constitutional changes that resulted but in the shattering effect the disclosures had on that virtuous image.[59] Some of the planters expressed openly their

---

[54] *The Defence of Injur'd Merit Unmasked; or, the Scurrilous Piece of Philander Dissected and Exposed to Public View. By a Friend to Merit, wherever found* (n.p., 1771), 10. Robert Carter chose to retire to private life in the early 1770's rather than adjust to the "new system of politicks" that had begun "to prevail generally." Quoted in Louis Morton, *Robert Carter of Nomini Hall: A Virginia Tobacco Planter of the Eighteenth Century* (Williamsburg, 1941), 52.

[55] Jay B. Hubbell and Douglass Adair, "Robert Munford's *The Candidates*," *Wm. and Mary Qtly.*, 3d Ser., V (1948), 246, 238. The ambivalence in Munford's attitude toward the representative process is reflected in the different way historians have interpreted his play. Cf. *ibid.*, 223–225, with Brown, *Virginia*, 236–237. Munford's fear of "men who aim at power without merit" was more fully expressed in his later play, *The Patriots*, written in 1775 or 1776. Courtlandt Canby, "Robert Munford's *The Patriots*," *Wm. and Mary Qtly.*, 3d Ser., VI (1949), 437–503, quotation from 450.

[56] [John Randolph], *Considerations on the Present State of Virginia* ([Williamsburg], 1774), in Earl G. Swem, ed., *Virginia and the Revolution: Two Pamphlets, 1774* (New York, 1919), 16; Purdie and Dixon's *Virginia Gazette*, Nov. 25, 1773.

[57] Rind's *Virginia Gazette*, Sept. 8, 1774; Brown, *Virginia*, 252–254; Morton, *Robert Carter*, 231–250.

[58] See George Washington to George Mason, Apr. 5, 1769, in John C. Fitzpatrick, ed., *The Writings of George Washington* (Washington, 1931–44), II, 502; Carl Bridenbaugh, *Myths and Realities: Societies of the Colonial South* (New York, 1963), 5, 10, 14, 16; Emory G. Evans, "Planter Indebtedness and the Coming of the Revolution in Virginia," *Wm. and Mary Qtly.*, 3d Ser., XIX (1962), 518–519.

[59] Rind's *Virginia Gazette*, Aug. 15, 1766. See Carl Bridenbaugh, "Violence and Virtue in Virginia 1766: or The Importance of the Trivial," *Massachusetts Historical Society, Proceedings*, LXXVI (1964), 3–29.

fears for the future, seeing the products of their lives being destroyed in the reckless gambling and drinking of their heirs, who, as London Carter put it, "play away and play it all away."[60]

The Revolution in Virginia, "produced by the wantonness of the Gentleman," as one planter suggested,[61] undoubtedly gained much of its force from this social crisis within the gentry. Certainly more was expected from the Revolution than simply a break from British imperialism, and it was not any crude avoidance of British debts.[62] The Revolutionary reforms, like the abolition of entail and primogeniture, may have signified something other than mere symbolic legal adjustments to an existing reality. In addition to being an attempt to make the older Tidewater plantations more economically competitive with lands farther west, the reforms may have represented a real effort to redirect what was believed to be a dangerous tendency in social and family development within the ruling gentry. The Virginians were not after all aristocrats who could afford having their entailed families' estates in the hands of weak or ineffectual eldest sons. Entail, as the preamble to the 1776 act abolishing it stated, had often done "injury to the morals of youth by rendering them independent of, and disobedient to, their parents."[63] There was too much likelihood, as the Nelson family sadly demonstrated, that a single wayward generation would virtually wipe out what had been so painstakingly built.[64] George Mason bespoke the anxieties of many Virginians when he warned the Philadelphia convention in 1787 that "our own Children will in a short time be among the general mass."[65]

Precisely how the strains within Virginia society contributed to the creation of a revolutionary situation and in what way the planters expected independence and republicanism to alleviate their problems, of course, need to be fully explored. It seems clear, however, from the very nature of the ideas expressed that the sources of the Revolution in Virginia were much more subtle and complicated than a simple antagonism to the British government. Constitutional principles alone do not explain the Virginians' almost unanimous determination to revolt. And if the Revolution in the seemingly stable colony of Virginia possessed internal social roots, it is to be expected that the other colonies were experiencing their own forms of social strain that in a like manner sought mitigation through revolution and republicanism.

[60] Quoted in Bridenbaugh, *Myths and Realities*, 27. See also Morton, *Robert Carter*, 223–225.

[61] John A. Washington to R. H. Lee, June 20, 1778, quoted in Pole, "Representation and Authority in Virginia," 28.

[62] Evans, "Planter Indebtedness," 526–527.

[63] Julian P. Boyd and others, eds., *The Papers of Thomas Jefferson* (Princeton, 1950 —), I, 560. Most of our knowledge of entail and primogeniture in Virginia stems from an unpublished doctoral dissertation, Clarence R. Keim, "Influence of Primogeniture and Entail in the Development of Virginia" (University of Chicago, 1926). Keim's is a very careful and qualified study and conclusions from his evidence — other than the obvious fact that much land was held in fee simple — are by no means easy to make. See particularly pp. 56, 60–62, 110–114, 122, 195–196.

[64] Emory S. Evans, "The Rise and Decline of the Virginia Aristocracy in the Eighteenth Century: The Nelsons," in Darrett B. Rutman, ed., *The Old Dominion: Essays for Thomas Perkins Abernethy* (Charlottesville, 1964), 73–74.

[65] Max Farrand, ed., *The Records of the Federal Convention of 1787* (New Haven, 1911), I, 56; Bridenbaugh, *Myths and Realities*, 14, 16.

It is through the Whigs' ideas, then, that we may be led back to take up where the Progressive historians left off in their investigation of the internal social sources of the Revolution. By working through the ideas — by reading them imaginatively and relating them to the objective social world they both reflected and confronted — we may be able to eliminate the unrewarding distinction between conscious and unconscious motives, and eventually thereby to combine a Whig with a Tory, an idealist with a behaviorist, interpretation. For the ideas, the rhetoric, of the Americans was never obscuring but remarkably revealing of their deepest interests and passions. What they expressed may not have been for the most part factually true, but it was always psychologically true. In this sense their rhetoric was never detached from the social and political reality; and indeed it becomes the best entry into an understanding of that reality. Their repeated overstatements of reality, their incessant talk of "tyranny" when there seems to have been no real oppression, their obsession with "virtue," "luxury," and "corruption," their devotion to "liberty" and "equality" — all these notions were neither manipulated propaganda nor borrowed empty abstractions, but ideas with real personal and social significance for those who used them. Propaganda could never move men to revolution. No popular leader, as John Adams put it, has ever been able "to persuade a large people, for any length of time together, to think themselves wronged, injured, and oppressed, unless they really were, and saw and felt it to be so."[66] The ideas had relevance; the sense of oppression and injury, although often displaced onto the imperial system, was nonetheless real. It was indeed the meaningfulness of the connection between what the Americans said and what they felt that gave the ideas their propulsive force and their overwhelming persuasiveness.

It is precisely the remarkable revolutionary character of the Americans' ideas now being revealed by historians that best indicates that something profoundly unsettling was going on in the society, that raises the question, as it did for the Progressive historians, why the Americans should have expressed such thoughts. With their crude conception of propaganda the Progressive historians at least attempted to grapple with the problem. Since we cannot regard the ideas of the Revolutionaries as simply propaganda, the question still remains to be answered. "When 'ideas' in full cry drive past," wrote Arthur F. Bentley in his classic behavioral study, *The Process of Government*, "the thing to do with them is to accept them as an indication that something is happening; and then search carefully to find out what it really is they stand for, what the factors of the social life are that are expressing themselves through the ideas."[67] Precisely because they sought to understand both the Revolutionary ideas and American society, the behaviorist historians of the Progressive generation, for all of their crude conceptualizations, their obsession with "class" and hidden economic interests, and their treatment of ideas as propaganda, have still offered us an explanation of the Revolutionary era so powerful and so comprehensive that no purely intellectual interpretation will ever replace it.

[66] John Adams, "Novanglus," in Charles F. Adams, ed., *The Works of John Adams* (Boston, 1851), IV, 14.
[67] Arthur F. Bentley, *The Process of Government: A Study of Social Pressures* (Chicago, 1908), 152.

The Founding Fathers: A Reform Caucus in Action

JOHN P. ROCHE

Interpreting the Constitutional Convention of 1787 in Philadelphia has always been a major challenge to students of American history. Some have viewed it as a conservative reaction to the democratic tendencies of the government under the Articles of Confederation. Others have seen it as the embodiment of mature political wisdom, resulting in the creation of a government capable of administering a great nation. Recently, it has been attacked as a body that compromised the egalitarian principles of the Declaration of Independence by acquiescing to the slave system of the Southern states. Interpreters of the Convention have almost always been partisans in the debate over the nature of the American Revolution, and they have been concerned with relating the Constitution to the events of the preceding decade. John P. Roche brings a different perspective to bear upon the study of the Constitutional Convention. As a political scientist (and something of a practical politician), he is impressed with the political artistry of the Founding Fathers. He minimizes the ideological conflicts that have concerned historians and emphasizes the extent to which the framers of the Constitution were devoted single-mindedly to the construction of a practical system of government that would stand a realistic chance of being accepted by the citizens of the several states. He points out that Madison and Hamilton, among others, compromised their principles and even propagandized for a document which in many ways did not express what they felt most deeply about the science of government. The Founding Fathers, for Roche, were politicians first and foremost, and the mark of their success is the fact that they constructed a workable, acceptable frame of government. Roche thus escapes from the traditional controversies about the writing of the Constitution, but one wonders whether his analysis is not weakened by his evident and somewhat uncritical enthusiasm for the work of the Convention.

Over the last century and a half, the work of the Constitutional Convention and the motives of the Founding Fathers have been analyzed under a number of different ideological auspices. To one generation of historians, the hand of God

Reprinted by permission of the American Political Science Association and the author from the *American Political Science Review*, 55 (1961), pp. 799–816.

was moving in the assembly; under a later dispensation, the dialectic (at various levels of philosophical sophistication) replaced the Deity: "relationships of production" moved into the niche previously reserved for Love of Country. Thus in counterpoint to the Zeitgeist, the Framers have undergone miraculous metamorphoses: at one time acclaimed as liberals and bold social engineers, today they appear in the guise of sound Burkean conservatives, men who in our time would subscribe to *Fortune*, look to Walter Lippmann for political theory, and chuckle patronizingly at the antics of Barry Goldwater. The implicit assumption is that if James Madison were among us, he would be President of the Ford Foundation, while Alexander Hamilton would chair the Committee for Economic Development.

The "Fathers" have thus been admitted to our best circles; the revolutionary ferocity which confiscated all Tory property in reach and populated New Brunswick with outlaws has been converted by the "Miltown School" of American historians into a benign dedication to "consensus" and "prescriptive rights." The Daughters of the American Revolution have, through the ministrations of Professors Boorstin, Hartz, and Rossiter, at last found ancestors worthy of their descendants. It is not my purpose here to argue that the "Fathers" were, in fact, radical revolutionaries; that proposition has been brilliantly demonstrated by Robert R. Palmer in his *Age of the Democratic Revolution*. My concern is with the further position that not only were they revolutionaries, but also they were democrats. Indeed, in my view, there is one fundamental truth about the Founding Fathers that *every* generation of Zeitgeisters has done its best to obscure: they were first and foremost superb democratic politicians. I suspect that in a contemporary setting, James Madison would be Speaker of the House of Representatives and Hamilton would be the *éminence grise* dominating (*pace* Theodore Sorensen or Sherman Adams) the Executive Office of the President. They were, with their colleagues, *political men* — not metaphysicians, disembodied conservatives or Agents of History — and as recent research into the nature of American politics in the 1780s confirms,[1] they were committed (perhaps willy-nilly) to working within the democratic framework, within a universe of public approval. Charles Beard *and* the filiopietists to the contrary notwithstanding, the Philadelphia Convention was not a College of Cardinals or a council of Platonic guardians working within a manipulative, pre-democratic framework; it was a *nationalist* reform caucus which had to operate with great delicacy and skill in a political cosmos full of enemies to achieve the one definitive goal — popular approbation.

Perhaps the time has come, to borrow Walton Hamilton's fine phrase, to raise the Framers from immortality to mortality, to give them credit for their magnificent demonstration of the art of democratic politics. The point must be

---

[1] The view that the right to vote in the states was severely circumscribed by property qualifications has been thoroughly discredited in recent years. See Chilton Williamson, *American Suffrage from Property to Democracy, 1760–1860* (Princeton, 1960). The contemporary position is that John Dickinson actually knew what he was talking about when he argued that there would be little opposition to vesting the right of suffrage in freeholders since "The great mass of our Citizens is composed at this time of freeholders, and will be pleased with it." Max Farrand, *Records of the Federal Convention*, Vol. 2, p. 202 (New Haven, 1911). (Henceforth cited as *Farrand*.)

reemphasized; they *made* history and did it within the limits of consensus. There was nothing inevitable about the future in 1787; the *Zeitgeist*, the fine Hegelian technique of begging causal questions, could only be discerned in retrospect. What they did was to hammer out a pragmatic compromise which would both bolster the "National interest" and be acceptable to the people. What inspiration they got came from their collective experience as professional politicians in a democratic society. As John Dickinson put it to his fellow delegates on August 13, "Experience must be our guide. Reason may mislead us."

In this context, let us examine the problems they confronted and the solutions they evolved. The Convention has been described picturesquely as a counterrevolutionary junta and the Constitution as a *coup d'état*,[2] but this has been accomplished by withdrawing the whole history of the movement for constitutional reform from its true context. No doubt the goals of the constitutional elite were "subversive" to the existing political order, but it is overlooked that their subversion could only have succeeded if the people of the United States endorsed it by regularized procedures. Indubitably they were "plotting" to establish a much stronger central government than existed under the Articles, but only in the sense in which one could argue equally well that John F. Kennedy was, from 1956 to 1960, "plotting" to become President. In short, on the fundamental *procedural* level, the Constitutionalists had to work according to the prevailing rules of the game. Whether they liked it or not is a topic for spiritualists —and is irrelevant: one may be quite certain that had Washington agreed to play the De Gaulle (as the Cincinnati once urged), Hamilton would willingly have held his horse, but such fertile speculation in no way alters the actual context in which events took place.

I

When the Constitutionalists went forth to subvert the Confederation, they utilized the mechanisms of political legitimacy. And the roadblocks which confronted them were formidable. At the same time, they were endowed with certain potent political assets. The history of the United States from 1786 to 1790 was largely one of a masterful employment of political expertise by the Constitutionalists as against bumbling, erratic behavior by the opponents of reform. Effectively, the Constitutionalists had to induce the states, by democratic techniques of coercion, to emasculate themselves. To be specific, if New York had refused to join the new Union, the project was doomed; yet before New York was safely in, the reluctant state legislature had *sua sponte* to take the following steps: (1) agree to send delegates to the Philadelphia Convention; (2) provide maintenance for these delegates (these were distinct stages: New Hampshire was early in naming delegates, but did not provide for their maintenance until

---

[2] The classic statement at the *coup d'état* theory is, of course, Charles A. Beard, *An Economic Interpretation of the Constitution of the United States* (New York, 1913), and this theme was echoed by Vernon L. Parrington, Merrill Jensen and others in "populist" historiographical tradition. For a sharp critique of this thesis see Robert E. Brown, *Charles Beard and the Constitution* (Princeton, 1956). See also Forrest McDonald, *We the People* (Chicago, 1958); the trail-blazing work in this genre was Douglass Adair, "The Tenth Federalist Revisited," *William and Mary Quarterly*, Third Series, Vol. VIII (1951), pp. 48–67.

July); (3) set up the special *ad hoc* convention to decide on ratification; and (4) concede to the decision of the *ad hoc* convention that New York should participate. New York admittedly was a tricky state, with a strong interest in a *status quo* which permitted her to exploit New Jersey and Connecticut, but the same legal hurdles existed in every state. And at the risk of becoming boring, it must be reiterated that the *only* weapon in the Constitutionalist arsenal was an effective mobilization of public opinion.

The group which undertook this struggle was an interesting amalgam of a few dedicated nationalists with the self-interested spokesmen of various parochial bailiwicks. The Georgians, for example, wanted a strong central authority to provide military protection for their huge, under-populated state against the Creek Confederacy; Jerseymen and Connecticuters wanted to escape from economic bondage to New York; the Virginians hoped to establish a system which would give that great state its rightful place in the councils of the republic. The dominant figures in the politics of these states therefore cooperated in the call for the Convention.[3] In other states, the thrust towards national reform was taken up by opposition groups who added the "national interest" to their weapons system; in Pennsylvania, for instance, the group fighting to revise the Constitution of 1776 came out four-square behind the Constitutionalists, and in New York, Hamilton and the Schuyler *ambiance* took the same tack against George Clinton.[4] There was, of course, a large element of personality in the affair: there is reason to suspect that Patrick Henry's opposition to the Convention and the Constitution was founded on his conviction that Jefferson was behind both, and a close study of local politics elsewhere would surely reveal that others supported the Constitution for the simple (and politically quite sufficient) reason that the "wrong" people were against it.

To say this is not to suggest that the Constitution rested on a foundation of impure or base motives. It is rather to argue that in politics there are no immaculate conceptions, and that in the drive for a stronger general government, motives of all sorts played a part. Few men in the history of mankind have espoused a view of the "common good" or "public interest" that militated against their private status; even Plato with all his reverence for disembodied reason managed to put philosophers on top of the pile. Thus it is not surprising that a number of diversified private interests joined to push the nationalist public interest; what would have been surprising was the absence of such a pragmatic united front. And the fact remains that, however motivated, these men did demonstrate a willingness to compromise their parochial interests in behalf of an ideal which took shape before their eyes and under their ministrations.

[3] A basic volume, which, like other works by Warren, provides evidence with which one can evaluate the author's own opinions, is Charles Warren, *The Making of the Constitution* (Boston, 1928). The best brief summary of the forces behind the movement for centralization is Chapter 1 of *Warren* (as it will be cited hereafter).
[4] On Pennsylvania see Robert L. Brunhouse, *Counter-Revolution in Pennsylvania* (Harrisburg, 1942) and Charles P. Smith, *James Wilson* (Chapel Hill, 1956), ch. 15; for New York, which needs the same sort of microanalysis Pennsylvania has received, the best study is E. Wilder Spaulding, *New York in the Critical Period, 1783–1789* (New York, 1932).

As Stanley Elkins and Eric McKitrick have suggested in a perceptive essay,[5] what distinguished the leaders of the Constitutionalist caucus from their enemies was a "Continental" approach to political, economic and military issues. To the extent that they shared an institutional base of operations, it was the Continental Congress (thirty-nine of the delegates of the Federal Convention had served in Congress[6]), and this was hardly a locale which inspired respect for the state governments. Robert de Jouvenal observed French politics half a century ago and noted that a revolutionary Deputy had more in common with a non-revolutionary Deputy than he had with a revolutionary non-Deputy;[7] similarly one can surmise that membership in the Congress under the Articles of Confederation worked to establish a continental frame of reference, that a Congressman from Pennsylvania and one from South Carolina would share a universe of discourse which provided them with a conceptual common denominator *vis à vis* their respective state legislatures. This was particularly true with respect to external affairs: the average state legislator was probably about as concerned with foreign policy then as he is today, but Congressmen were constantly forced to take the broad view of American prestige, were compelled to listen to the reports of Secretary John Jay and to the dispatches and pleas from their frustrated envoys in Britain, France and Spain.[8] From considerations such as these, a "Continental" ideology developed which seems to have demanded a revision of our domestic institutions primarily on the ground that only by invigorating our general government could we assume our rightful place in the international arena. Indeed, an argument with great force — particularly since Washington was its reincarnation — urged that our very survival in the Hobbesian jungle of world politics depended upon a reordering and strengthening of our national sovereignty.[9]

Note that I am not endorsing the "Critical Period" thesis; on the contrary, Merrill Jensen seems to me quite sound in his view that for most Americans, engaged as they were in self-sustaining agriculture, the "Critical Period" was not particularly critical.[10] In fact, the great achievement of the Constitutionalists was their ultimate success in convincing the elected representatives of a majority of the white male population that change was imperative. A small group of political leaders with a Continental vision and essentially a consciousness of the United States' *international* impotence, provided the matrix of the movement. To their standard other leaders rallied with their own parallel ambitions. Their

---

[5] Stanley Elkins and Eric McKitrick, "The Founding Fathers: Young Men of the Revolution," *Political Science Quarterly*, Vol. 76, p. 181 (1961).

[6] *Warren*, p. 55.

[7] In *La République des Camarades* (Paris, 1914).

[8] See Frank Monaghan, *John Jay* (New York, 1935), ch. 13.

[9] "[T]he situation of the general government, if it can be called a government, is shaken to its foundation, and liable to be overturned by every blast. In a word, it is at an end; and, unless a remedy is soon applied, anarchy and confusion will inevitably ensue." Washington to Jefferson, May 30, 1787, *Farrand*, III, 31. See also Irving Brant, *James Madison, The Nationalist* (New York, 1948), ch. 25.

[10] Merrill Jensen, *The New Nation* (New York, 1950). Interestingly enough, Prof. Jensen virtually ignores international relations in his laudatory treatment of the government under the Articles of Confederation.

great assets were (1) the presence in their caucus of the one authentic American "father figure," George Washington, whose prestige was enormous;[11] (2) the energy and talent of their leadership (in which one must include the towering intellectuals of the time, John Adams and Thomas Jefferson, despite their absence abroad), and their communications "network," which was far superior to anything on the opposition side;[12] (3) the preemptive skill which made "their" issue The Issue and kept the locally oriented opposition permanently on the defensive; and (4) the subjective consideration that these men were spokesmen of a new and compelling credo: *American* nationalism, that ill-defined but nonetheless potent sense of collective purpose that emerged from the American Revolution.

Despite great institutional handicaps, the Constitutionalists managed in the mid-1780s to mount an offensive which gained momentum as years went by. Their greatest problem was lethargy, and paradoxically, the number of barriers in their path may have proved an advantage in the long run. Beginning with the initial battle to get the Constitutional Convention called and delegates appointed, they could never relax, never let up the pressure. In practical terms, this meant that the local "organizations" created by the Constitutionalists were perpetually in movement building up their cadres for the next fight. (The word organization has to be used with great caution: a political organization in the United States — as in contemporary England[13] — generally consisted of a magnate and his following, or a coalition of magnates. This did not necessarily mean that it was "undemocratic" or "aristocratic," in the Aristotelian sense of the word: while a few magnates such as the Livingstons could draft their followings, most exercised their leadership without coercion on the basis of popular endorsement. The absence of organized opposition did not imply the impossibility of competition any more than low public participation in elections necessarily indicated an undemocratic suffrage.)

The Constitutionalists got the jump on the "opposition" (a collective noun: oppositions would be more correct) at the outset with the demand for a Convention. Their opponents were caught in an old political trap: they were not being asked to approve any specific program of reform, but only to endorse a meeting to discuss and recommend needed reforms. If they took a hard line at the first stage, they were put in the position of glorifying the *status quo* and of denying the need for *any* changes. Moreover, the Constitutionalists could go to the people with a persuasive argument for "fair play" — "How can you condemn reform before you know precisely what is involved?" Since the state legislatures obviously would have the final say on any proposals that might emerge from the Convention, the Constitutionalists were merely reasonable men asking for a chance. Besides, since they did not make any concrete proposals at that

[11] The story of James Madison's cultivation of Washington is told by Brant, *op. cit.*, pp. 394–97.
[12] The "message center" being the Congress; nineteen members of Congress were simultaneously delegates to the Convention. One gets a sense of this coordination of effort from Broadus Mitchell, *Alexander Hamilton, Youth to Maturity* (New York, 1957), ch. 22.
[13] See Sir Lewis Namier, *The Structure of Politics at the Accession of George III*, 2d ed. (New York, 1957); *England in the Age of the American Revolution* (London, 1930).

stage, they were in a position to capitalize on every sort of generalized discontent with the Confederation.

Perhaps because of their poor intelligence system, perhaps because of over-confidence generated by the failure of all previous efforts to alter the Articles,[14] the opposition awoke too late to the dangers that confronted them in 1787. Not only did the Constitutionalists manage to get every state but Rhode Island (where politics was enlivened by a party system reminiscent of the "Blues" and the "Greens" in the Byzantine Empire)[15] to appoint delegates to Philadelphia, but when the results were in, it appeared that they dominated the delegations. Given the apathy of the opposition, this was a natural phenomenon: in an ide-ologically non-polarized political atmosphere those who get appointed to a spe-cial committee are likely to be the men who supported the movement for its creation. Even George Clinton, who seems to have been the first opposition leader to awake to the possibility of trouble, could not prevent the New York legislature from appointing Alexander Hamilton — though he did have the fore-sight to send two of his henchmen to dominate the delegation. Incidentally, much has been made of the fact that the delegates to Philadelphia were not elected by the people: some have adduced this fact as evidence of the "undemo-cratic" character of the gathering. But put in the context of the time, this argu-ment is wholly specious: the central government under the Articles was con-sidered a creature of the component states and in all the states but Rhode Island, Connecticut and New Hampshire, members of the national Congress were chosen by the state legislatures. This was not a consequence of elitism or fear of the mob; it was a logical extension of states'-rights doctrine to guarantee that the national institution did not end-run the state legislatures and make direct con-tact with the people.[16]

II

With delegations safely named, the focus shifted to Philadelphia. While wait-ing for a quorum to assemble, James Madison got busy and drafted the so-called

[14] The Annapolis Convention, called for the previous year, turned into a shambles: only five states sent commissioners, only three states were legally represented, and the instruc-tions to delegates named varied quite widely from state to state. Clinton and others of his persuasion may have thought this disaster would put an end to the drive for reform. See Mitchell, op. cit., pp. 362–67; Brant, op. cit., pp. 375–87.

[15] See Hamilton M. Bishop, Why Rhode Island Opposed the Federal Constitution (Providence, 1950) for a careful analysis of the labyrinthine political course of Rhode Island. For background see David S. Lovejoy, Rhode Island Politics and the American Revolution (Providence, 1958).

[16] The terms "radical" and "conservative" have been bandied about a good deal in connection with the Constitution. This usage is nonsense if it is employed to distinguish between two economic "classes" — e.g., radical debtors versus conservative creditors, radi-cal farmers versus conservative capitalists, etc. — because there was no polarization along this line of division; the same types of people turned up on both sides. And many were hard to place in these terms: does one treat Robert Morris as a debtor or a creditor? or James Wilson? See Brown, op. cit., passim. The one line of division that holds up is between those deeply attached to states'-rights and those who felt that the Confederation was bankrupt. Thus, curiously, some of the most narrow-minded, parochial spokesmen of the time have earned the designation "radical" while those most willing to experiment and alter the status quo have been dubbed "conservative"! See Cecelia Kenyon, "Men of Little Faith," William and Mary Quarterly, Vol. 12, p. 3 (1955).

Randolph or Virginia Plan with the aid of the Virginia delegation. This was a political master-stroke. Its consequence was that once business got underway, the framework of discussion was established on Madison's terms. There was no interminable argument over agenda; instead the delegates took the Virginia Resolutions — "just for purposes of discussion" — as their point of departure. And along with Madison's proposals, many of which were buried in the course of the summer, went his major premise: a new start on a Constitution rather than piecemeal amendment. This was not necessarily revolutionary — a little exegesis could demonstrate that a new Constitution might be formulated as "amendments" to the Articles of Confederation — but Madison's proposal that this "lump sum" amendment go into effect after approval by nine states (the Articles required unanimous state approval for any amendment) was thoroughly subversive.[17]

Standard treatments of the Convention divide the delegates into "nationalists and "states'-righters" with various improvised shadings ("moderate nationalists," etc.), but these are *a posteriori* categories which obfuscate more than they clarify. What is striking to one who analyzes the Convention as a case-study in democratic politics is the lack of clear-cut ideological divisions in the Convention. Indeed, I submit that the evidence — Madison's *Notes*, the correspondence of the delegates, and debates on ratification — indicates that this was a remarkably homogeneous body on the ideological level. Yates and Lansing, Clinton's two chaperones for Hamilton, left in disgust on July 10. (Is there anything more tedious than sitting through endless disputes on matters one deems fundamentally misconceived? It takes an iron will to spend a hot summer as an ideological *agent provocateur*.) Luther Martin, Maryland's bibulous narcissist, left on September 4 in a huff when he discovered that others did not share his self-esteem; others went home for personal reasons. But the hard core of delegates accepted a grinding regimen throughout the attrition of a Philadelphia summer precisely because they shared the Constitutionalist goal.

Basic differences of opinion emerged, of course, but these were not ideological; they were *structural*. If the so-called "states'-rights" group had not accepted the fundamental purposes of the Convention, they could simply have pulled out and by doing so have aborted the whole enterprise. Instead of bolting, they returned day after day to argue and to compromise. An interesting symbol of this basic homogeneity was the initial agreement on secrecy: these professional politicians did not want to become prisoners of publicity; they wanted to retain that freedom of maneuver which is only possible when men are not forced to take public stands in the preliminary stages of negotiation.[18] There was no legal means of binding the tongues of the delegates: at any stage in the game a delegate with basic principled objections to the emerging project could have

---

[17] Yet, there was little objection to this crucial modification from any quarter — there almost seems to have been a gentlemen's agreement that Rhode Island's *liberum veto* had to be destroyed.

[18] See Mason's letter to his son, May 27, 1787, in which he endorsed secrecy as "a proper precaution to prevent mistakes and misrepresentation until the business shall have been completed, when the whole may have a very different complexion from that in which the several crude and indigested parts might in their first shape appear if submitted to the public eye." *Farrand*, III, 28.

taken the stump (as Luther Martin did after his exit) and denounced the convention to the skies. Yet Madison did not even inform Thomas Jefferson in Paris of the course of the deliberations[19] and available correspondence indicates that the delegates generally observed the injunction. Secrecy is certainly uncharacteristic of any assembly marked by strong ideological polarization. This was noted at the time: the New York Daily Advertiser, August 14, 1787, commented that the ". . . profound secrecy hitherto observed by the Convention [we consider] a happy omen, as it demonstrates that the spirit of party on any great and essential point cannot have arisen to any height."[20]

Commentators on the Constitution who have read The Federalist in lieu of reading the actual debates have credited the Fathers with the invention of a sublime concept called "Federalism."[21] Unfortunately The Federalist is probative evidence for only one proposition: that Hamilton and Madison were inspired propagandists with a genius for retrospective symmetry. Federalism, as the theory is generally defined, was an improvisation which was later promoted into a political theory. Experts on "federalism" should take to heart the advice of David Hume, who warned in his Of the Rise and Progress of the Arts and Sciences that ". . . there is no subject in which we must proceed with more caution than in [history], lest we assign causes which never existed and reduce what is merely contingent to stable and universal principles." In any event, the final balance in the Constitution between the states and the nation must have come as a great disappointment to Madison, while Hamilton's unitary views are too well known to need elucidation.

It is indeed astonishing how those who have glibly designated James Madison the "father" of Federalism have overlooked the solid body of fact which indicates that he shared Hamilton's quest for a unitary central government. To be specific, they have avoided examining the clear import of the Madison-Virginia Plan,[22] and have disregarded Madison's dogged inch-by-inch retreat from the bastions of centralization. The Virginia Plan envisioned a unitary national government effectively freed from and dominant over the states. The lower house of the national legislature was to be elected directly by the people of the states with membership proportional to population. The upper house was to be selected by the lower and the two chambers would elect the executive and choose the judges. The national government would be thus cut completely loose from the states.[23]

---

[19] See Madison to Jefferson, June 6, 1787, Farrand, III, 35.

[20] Cited in Warren, p. 138.

[21] See, e.g., Gottfried Dietze, The Federalist, A Classic on Federalism and Free Government (Baltimore, 1960); Richard Hofstadter, The American Political Tradition (New York, 1948); and John P. Roche, "American Liberty," in M. Konvitz and C. Rossiter, eds., Aspects of Liberty (Ithaca, 1958).

[22] "I hold it for a fundamental point, that an individual independence of the states is utterly irreconcilable with the idea of an aggregate sovereignty," Madison to Randolph, cited in Brant, op. cit., p. 416.

[23] The Randolph Plan was presented on May 29, see Farrand, I, 18–23; the state legislatures retained only the power to nominate candidates for the upper chamber. Madison's view of the appropriate position of the states emerged even more strikingly in Yates' record of his speech on June 29: "Some contend that states are sovereign when in fact they are only political societies. There is a gradation of power in all societies, from the lowest

The structure of the general government was freed from state control in a truly radical fashion, but the scope of the authority of the national sovereign as Madison initially formulated it was breathtaking — it was a formulation worthy of the Sage of Malmesbury himself. The national legislature was to be empowered to disallow the acts of state legislatures,[24] and the central government was vested, in addition to the powers of the nation under the Articles of Confederation, with plenary authority wherever ". . . the separate States are incompetent or in which the harmony of the United States may be interrupted by the exercise of individual legislation."[25] Finally, just to lock the door against state intrusion, the national Congress was to be given the power to use military force on recalcitrant states.[26] This was Madison's "model" of an ideal national government, though it later received little publicity in *The Federalist*.

The interesting thing was the reaction of the Convention to this militant program for a strong autonomous central government. Some delegates were startled, some obviously leery of so comprehensive a project of reform,[27] but nobody set off any fireworks and nobody walked out. Moreover, in the two weeks that followed, the Virginia Plan received substantial endorsement *en principe*; the initial temper of the gathering can be deduced from the approval "without debate or dissent," on May 31, of the Sixth Resolution which granted Congress the authority to disallow state legislation ". . . contravening *in its opinion* the Articles of Union." Indeed, an amendment was included to bar states from contravening national treaties.[28]

The Virginia Plan may therefore be considered, in ideological terms, as the delegates' Utopia, but as the discussions continued and became more specific, many of those present began to have second thoughts. After all, they were not residents of Utopia or guardians in Plato's Republic who could simply impose a philosophical ideal on subordinate strata of the population. They were practical politicians in a democratic society, and no matter what their private dreams might be, they had to take home an acceptable package and defend it — and their own political futures — against predictable attack. On June 14 the breaking

---

corporation to the highest sovereign. The states never possessed the essential rights of sovereignty. . . . The states, at present, are only great corporations, having the power of making by-laws, and these are effectual only if they are not contradictory to the general confederation. The states ought to be placed under the control of the general government — at least as much so as they formerly were under the king and British parliament." *Farrand*, I, 471. Forty-six years later, after Yates' "Notes" had been published, Madison tried to explain this statement away as a misinterpretation: he did not flatly deny the authenticity of Yates' record, but attempted a defense that was half justification and half evasion. Madison to W. C. Rivers, Oct. 21, 1833. *Farrand*, III, 521–24.

[24] Resolution 6 gave the National Legislature this power subject to review by the Council of Revision proposed in Resolution 8.

[25] Resolution 6.

[26] *Ibid.*

[27] See the discussions on May 30 and 31. "Mr. Charles Pinkney wished to know of Mr. Randolph whether he meant to abolish the State Governts. altogether . . . Mr. Butler said he had not made up his mind on the subject and was open to the light which discussion might throw on it . . . Genl. Pinkney expressed a doubt . . . Mr. Gerry seemed to entertain the same doubt." *Farrand*, I, 33–34. There were no denunciations — though it should perhaps be added that Luther Martin had not yet arrived.

[28] *Farrand*, I, 54. (Italics added.)

point between dream and reality took place. Apparently realizing that under the Virginia Plan, Massachusetts, Virginia and Pennsylvania could virtually dominate the national government — and probably appreciating that to sell this program to "the folks back home" would be impossible — the delegates from the small states dug in their heels and demanded time for a consideration of alternatives. One gets a graphic sense of the inner politics from John Dickinson's reproach to Madison: "You see the consequences of pushing things too far. Some of the members from the small States wish for two branches in the General Legislature and are friends to a good National Government; but we would sooner submit to a foreign power than . . . be deprived of an equality of suffrage in both branches of the Legislature, and thereby be thrown under the domination of the large States."[29]

The bare outline of the *Journal* entry for Tuesday, June 14, is suggestive to anyone with extensive experience in deliberative bodies. "It was moved by Mr. Patterson [*sic*, Paterson's name was one of those consistently misspelled by Madison and everybody else] seconded by Mr. Randolph that the further consideration of the report from the Committee of the whole House [endorsing the Virginia Plan] be postponed til tomorrow, and before the question for postponement was taken. It was moved by Mr. Randolph seconded by Mr. Patterson that the House adjourn."[30] The House adjourned by obvious prearrangement of the two principals: since the preceding Saturday when Brearley and Paterson of New Jersey had announced their fundamental discontent with the representational features of the Virginia Plan, the informal pressure had certainly been building up to slow down the steamroller. Doubtless there were extended arguments at the Indian Queen between Madison and Paterson, the latter insisting that events were moving rapidly towards a probably disastrous conclusion, towards a political suicide pact. Now the process of accommodation was put into action smoothly — and wisely, given the character and strength of the doubters. Madison had the votes, but this was one of those situations where the enforcement of mechanical majoritarianism could easily have destroyed the objectives of the majority: the Constitutionalists were in quest of a qualitative as well as a quantitative consensus. This was hardly from deference to local Quaker custom; it was a political imperative if they were to attain ratification.

III

According to the standard script, at this point the "states'-rights" group intervened in force behind the New Jersey Plan, which has been characteristically portrayed as a reversion to the *status quo* under the Articles of Confederation with but minor modifications. A careful examination of the evidence indicates that only in a marginal sense is this an accurate description. It is true that the New Jersey Plan put the states back into the institutional picture, but one could argue that to do so was a recognition of political reality rather than an affirmation of states'-rights. A serious case can be made that the advocates of the New Jersey Plan, far from being ideological addicts of states'-rights, intended to substitute

---

[29] *Ibid.*, p. 242. Delaware's delegates had been instructed by their general assembly to maintain in any new system the voting equality of the states. *Farrand*, III, 574.

[30] *Ibid.*, p. 240.

for the Virginia Plan a system which would both retain strong national power and have a chance of adoption in the states. The leading spokesman for the project asserted quite clearly that his views were based more on counsels of expediency than on principle; said Paterson on June 16: "I came here not to speak my own sentiments but the sentiments of those who sent me. Our object is not such a Governmt. as may be best in itself, but such a one as our Constituents have authorized us to prepare, and as they will approve."[31] This is Madison's version; in Yates' transcription, there is a crucial sentence following the remarks above: "I believe that a little practical virtue is to be preferred to the finest theoretical principles, which cannot be carried into effect."[32] In his preliminary speech on June 9, Paterson had started ". . . to the public mind we must accommodate ourselves,"[33] and in his notes for this and his later effort as well, the emphasis is the same. The *structure* of government under the Articles should be retained:

> 2. Because it accords with the Sentiments of the People
>   [Proof:] 1. Coms. [Commissions from state legislatures defining the jurisdiction of the delegates]
>   2. News-papers — Political Barometer. Jersey never would have sent Delegates under the first [Virginia] Plan —
>   Not here to sport Opinions of my own. Wt. [What] can be done. A little practicable Virtue preferable to Theory.[34]

This was a defense of political acumen, not of states'-rights. In fact, Paterson's notes of his speech can easily be construed as an argument for attaining the substantive objectives of the Virginia Plan by a sound political route, i.e., pouring the new wine in the old bottles. With a shrewd eye, Paterson queried:

> Will the Operation and Force of the [central] Govt. depend upon the mode of Representn. — No — it will depend upon the Quantum of Power lodged in the leg. ex. and judy. Departments — Give [the existing] Congress the same Powers that you intend to give the two Branches, [under the Virginia Plan] and I apprehend they will act with as much Propriety and more Energy . . .[35]

In other words, the advocates of the New Jersey Plan concentrated their fire on what they held to be the *political liabilities* of the Virginia Plan — which were matters of institutional structure — rather than on the proposed scope of national authority. Indeed, the Supremacy Clause of the Constitution first saw the light of day in Paterson's Sixth Resolution; the New Jersey Plan contemplated the use of military force to secure compliance with national law; and finally Paterson made clear his view that under either the Virginia or the New Jersey systems, the general government would ". . . act on individuals and not on states."[36]

---

[31] *Ibid.*, p. 250.
[32] *Ibid.*, p. 258.
[33] *Ibid.*, p. 178.
[34] *Ibid.*, p. 274.
[35] *Ibid.*, pp. 275–76.
[36] "But it is said that this national government is to act on individuals and not on states; and cannot a federal government be so framed as to operate in the same way? It surely may." *Ibid.*, pp. 182–183; also *ibid.* at p. 276.

From the states'-rights viewpoint, this was heresy: the fundament of that doctrine was the proposition that any central government had as its constituents the states, not the people, and could only reach the people through the agency of the state government.

Paterson then reopened the agenda of the Convention, but he did so within a distinctly nationalist framework. Paterson's position was one of favoring a strong central government in principle, but opposing one which in fact *put the big states in the saddle*. (The Virginia Plan, for all its abstract merits, did very well by Virginia.) As evidence for this speculation, there is a curious and intriguing proposal among Paterson's preliminary drafts of the New Jersey Plan:

> Whereas it is necessary in Order to form the People of the U.S. of America in to a Nation, that the States should be consolidated, by which means all the Citizens thereof will become equally intitled to and will equally participate in the same Privileges and Rights . . . it is therefore resolved, that all the Lands contained within the Limits of each state individually, and of the U.S. generally be considered as constituting one Body or Mass, and be divided into thirteen or more integral parts.
>
> Resolved, That such Divisions or integral Parts shall be styled Districts.[37]

This makes it sound as though Paterson was prepared to accept a strong unified central government along the lines of the Virginia Plan if the existing states were eliminated. He may have gotten the idea from his New Jersey colleague Judge David Brearley, who on June 9 had commented that the only remedy to the dilemma over representation was ". . . that a map of the U.S. be spread out, that all the existing boundaries be erased, and that a new partition of the whole be made into 13 equal parts."[38] According to Yates, Brearley added at this point, ". . . then a government on the present [Virginia Plan] system will be just."[39]

This proposition was never pushed — it was patently unrealistic — but one can appreciate its purpose: it would have separated the men from the boys in the large-state delegations. How attached would the Virginians have been to their reform principles if Virginia were to disappear as a component geographical unit (the largest) for representational purposes? Up to this point, the Virginians had been in the happy position of supporting high ideals with that inner confidence born of knowledge that the "public interest" they endorsed would nourish their private interest. Worse, they had shown little willingness to compromise. Now the delegates from the small states announced that they were unprepared to be offered up as sacrificial victims to a "national interest" which reflected Virginia's parochial ambition. Caustic Charles Pinckney was not far off when he remarked sardonically that ". . . the whole [conflict] comes to this": "Give N. Jersey an equal vote, and she will dismiss her scruples, and concur in the Natil. system."[40] What he rather unfairly did not add was that the Jersey delegates were not free agents who could adhere to their private convictions; they had to take back, sponsor and risk their reputations on the reforms approved by the Convention — and in New Jersey, not in Virginia.

Paterson spoke on Saturday, and one can surmise that over the weekend there was a good deal of consultation, argument, and caucusing among the delegates. One member at least prepared a full length address: on Monday Alexander Hamilton, previously mute, rose and delivered a six-hour oration.[41] It was a remarkably apolitical speech; the gist of his position was that *both* the Virginia and New Jersey Plans were inadequately centralist, and he detailed a reform program which was reminiscent of the Protectorate under the Cromwellian *Instrument of Government* of 1653. It has been suggested that Hamilton did this in the best political tradition to emphasize the moderate character of the Virginia Plan,[42] to give the cautious delegates something *really* to worry about; but this interpretation seems somehow too clever. Particularly since the sentiments Hamilton expressed happened to be completely consistent with those he privately — and sometimes publicly — expressed throughout his life. He wanted, to take a striking phrase from a letter to George Washington, a "strong well mounted government";[43] in essence, the Hamilton Plan contemplated an elected life monarch, virtually free of public control, on the Hobbesian ground that only in this fashion could strength and stability be achieved. The other alternatives, he argued, would put policy-making at the mercy of the passions of the mob; only if the sovereign was beyond the reach of selfish influence would it be possible to have government in the interests of the whole community.[44]

From all accounts, this was a masterful and compelling speech, but (aside from furnishing John Lansing and Luther Martin with ammunition for later use against the Constitution) it made little impact. Hamilton was simply transmitting on a different wave-length from the rest of the delegates; the latter adjourned after his great effort, admired his rhetoric, and then returned to business.[45] It was rather as if they had taken a day off to attend the opera. Hamilton, never a particularly patient man or much of a negotiator, stayed for another ten days and then left, in considerable disgust, for New York.[46] Although he came back to Philadelphia sporadically and attended the last two weeks of the Convention, Hamilton played no part in the laborious task of hammering out the Constitution. His day came later when he led the New York Constitutionalists into the savage imbroglio over ratification — an arena in which his unmatched talent for dirty political infighting may well have won the day. For instance, in the New York Ratifying Convention, Lansing threw back into Hamilton's teeth the sentiments the latter had expressed in his June 18 oration in the Convention. However, having since retreated to the fine defensive positions immortalized in *The Federalist*, the Colonel flatly denied that he had ever been

[41] J. C. Hamilton, cited *ibid.*, p. 293.

[42] See, e.g., Mitchell, *op. cit.*, p. 381.

[43] Hamilton to Washington, July 3, 1787, *Farrand*, III, 53.

[44] A reconstruction of the Hamilton Plan is found in *Farrand*, III, 617–30.

[45] Said William Samuel Johnson on June 21: "A gentleman from New-York, with boldness and decision, proposed a system totally different from both [Virginia and New Jersey]; and though he has been praised by every body, he has been supported by none." *Farrand* I, 363.

[46] See his letter to Washington cited *supra* note 43.

an enemy of the states, or had believed that conflict between states and nation was inexorable! As Madison's authoritative *Notes* did not appear until 1840, and there had been no press coverage, there was no way to verify his assertions, so in the words of the reporter, ". . . a warm personal altercation between [Lansing and Hamilton] engrossed the remainder of the day [June 28, 1788]."[47]

IV

On Tuesday morning, June 19, the vacation was over. James Madison led off with a long, carefully reasoned speech analyzing the New Jersey Plan which, while intellectually vigorous in its criticisms, was quite conciliatory in mood. "The great difficulty," he observed, "lies in the affair of Representation; and if this could be adjusted, all others would be surmountable."[48] (As events were to demonstrate, this diagnosis was correct.) When he finished, a vote was taken on whether to continue with the Virginia Plan as the nucleus for a new constitution: seven states voted "Yes"; New York, New Jersey, and Delaware voted "No"; and Maryland, whose position often depended on which delegates happened to be on the floor, divided.[49] Paterson, it seems, lost decisively; yet in a fundamental sense he and his allies had achieved their purpose: from that day onward, it could never be forgotten that the state governments loomed ominously in the background and that no verbal incantations could exorcise their power. Moreover, nobody bolted the convention: Paterson and his colleagues took their defeat in stride and set to work to modify the Virginia Plan, particularly with respect to its provisions on representation in the national legislature. Indeed, they won an immediate rhetorical bonus; when Oliver Ellsworth of Connecticut rose to move that the word "national" be expunged from the Third Virginia Resolution ("Resolved that a *national* Government ought to be established consisting of a *supreme* Legislative, Executive and Judiciary"[50]), Randolph agreed and the motion passed unanimously.[51] The process of compromise had begun.

For the next two weeks, the delegates circled around the problem of legislative

[47] *Farrand*, III, 338.
[48] *Farrand*, I, 321.
[49] Maryland's politics in this period were only a bit less intricate than Rhode Island's: the rural gentry, in much the same fashion that Namier described in England, divided up among families — Chases, Carrolls, Pacas, Lloyds, Tilghmans, etc. — and engaged in what seemed, to the outsider, elaborate political Morris dances. See Philip A. Crowl, *Maryland During and After the Revolution* (Baltimore, 1943). The Maryland General Assembly named five delegates to the Convention and provided that "the said Deputies or such of them as shall attend . . . shall have full Power to represent this State," *Farrand*, III, 586. The interesting circumstance was that three of the delegates were Constitutionalists (Carroll, McHenry and Jenifer), while two were opposed (Martin and Mercer); and this led to an *ad hoc* determination of where Maryland would stand when votes were taken. The vote on equality of representation, to be described *infra*, was an important instance of this eccentricity.
[50] This formulation was voted into the Randolph Plan on May 30, 1787, by a vote of six states to none, with one divided. *Farrand*, I, 30.
[51] *Farrand*, I, 335–36. In agreeing, Randolph stipulated his disagreement with Ellsworth's rationale, but said he did not object to merely changing an "expression." Those who subject the Constitution to minute semantic analysis might do well to keep this instance in mind; if Randolph could so concede the deletion of "national," one may wonder if any word changes can be given much weight.

representation. The Connecticut delegation appears to have evolved a possible compromise quite early in the debates, but the Virginians and particularly Madison (unaware that he would later be acclaimed as the prophet of "federalism") fought obdurately against providing for equal representation of states in the second chamber. There was a good deal of acrimony and at one point Benjamin Franklin — of all people — proposed the institution of a daily prayer; practical politicians in the gathering, however, were meditating more on the merits of a good committee than on the utility of Divine intervention. On July 2, the ice began to break when through a number of fortuitous events[52] — and one that seems deliberate[53] — the majority against equality of representation was converted into a dead tie. The Convention had reached the stage where it was "ripe" for a solution (presumably all the therapeutic speeches had been made), and the South Carolinians proposed a committee. Madison and James Wilson wanted none of it, but with only Pennsylvania dissenting, the body voted to establish a working party on the problem of representation.

The members of this committee, one from each state, were elected by the delegates — and a very interesting committee it was. Despite the fact that the Virginia Plan had held majority support up to that date, neither Madison nor Randolph was selected (Mason was the Virginian) and Baldwin of Georgia, whose shift in position had resulted in the tie, was chosen. From the composition, it was clear that this was not to be a "fighting" committee: the emphasis in membership was on what might be described as "second-level political entrepreneurs." On the basis of the discussions up to that time, only Luther Martin of Maryland could be described as a "bitter-ender." Admittedly, some divination enters into this sort of analysis, but one does get a sense of the mood of the delegates from these choices — including the interesting selection of Benjamin Franklin, despite his age and intellectual wobbliness, over the brilliant and incisive Wilson or the sharp, polemical Gouverneur Morris, to represent Pennsylvania. His passion for conciliation was more valuable at this juncture than Wilson's logical genius, or Morris' acerbic wit.

There is a common rumor that the Framers divided their time between philosophical discussions of government and reading the classics in political theory. Perhaps this is as good a time as any to note that their concerns were highly practical, that they spent little time canvassing abstractions. A number of them had some acquaintance with the history of political theory (probably gained from reading John Adams' monumental compilation A *Defense of the Constitutions*

[52] According to Luther Martin, he was alone on the floor and cast Maryland's vote for equality of representation. Shortly thereafter, Jenifer came on the floor and "Mr. King, from Massachusetts, valuing himself on Mr. Jenifer to divide the State of Maryland on this question . . . requested of the President that the question might be put again; however, the motion was too extraordinary in its nature to meet with success." Cited from "The Genuine Information . . ." *Farrand*, III, 188.

[53] Namely Baldwin's vote *for* equality of representation which divided Georgia — with Few absent and Pierce in New York fighting a duel, Houston voted against equality and Baldwin shifted to tie the state. Baldwin was originally from Connecticut and attended and tutored at Yale, facts which have led to much speculation about the pressures the Connecticut delegation may have brought on him to save the day (Georgia was the last state to vote) and open the way to compromise. To employ a good Russian phrase, it was certainly not an accident that Baldwin voted the way he did. See *Warren*, p. 262.

of Government,[54] the first volume of which appeared in 1786), and it was a poor rhetorician indeed who could not cite Locke, Montesquieu, or Harrington *in support* of a desired goal. Yet up to this point in the deliberations, no one had expounded a defense of states'-rights or the "separation of powers" on anything resembling a theoretical basis. It should be reiterated that the Madison model had no room either for the states or for the "separation of powers": effectively *all* governmental power was vested in the national legislature. The merits of Montesquieu did not turn up until *The Federalist*; and although a perverse argument could be made that Madison's ideal was truly in the tradition of John Locke's *Second Treatise of Government*,[55] the Locke whom the American rebels treated as an honorary president was a pluralistic defender of vested rights,[56] not of parliamentary supremacy.

It would be tedious to continue a blow-by-blow analysis of the work of the delegates; the critical fight was over representation of the states and once the Connecticut Compromise was adopted on July 17, the Convention was over the hump. Madison, James Wilson, and Gouverneur Morris of New York (who was there representing Pennsylvania!) fought the compromise all the way in a last-ditch effort to get a unitary state with parliamentary supremacy. But their allies deserted them and they demonstrated after their defeat the essentially opportunist character of their objections — using "opportunist" here in a non-pejorative sense, to indicate a willingness to swallow their objections and get on with the business. Moreover, once the compromise had carried (by five states to four, with one state divided), its advocates threw themselves vigorously into the job of strengthening the general government's substantive powers — as might have been predicted, indeed, from Paterson's early statements. It nourishes an increased respect for Madison's devotion to the art of politics, to realize that this dogged fighter could sit down six months later and prepare essays for *The Federalist* in contradiction to his basic convictions about the true course the Convention should have taken.

[54] For various contemporary comments, see *Warren*, pp. 814–818. On Adams' technique, see Zoltan Haraszti, "The Composition of Adams' *Defense*," in *John Adams and the Prophets of Progress* (Cambridge, 1952), ch. 9. In this connection it is interesting to check the Convention discussions for references to the authority of Locke, Montesquieu and Harrington, the theorists who have been assigned various degrees of paternal responsibility. There are no explicit references to James Harrington; one to John Locke (Luther Martin cited him on the state of nature, *Farrand*, I, 437); and seven to Montesquieu, only one of which related to the "separation of powers" (Madison in an odd speech, which he explained in a footnote was given to help a friend rather than advance his own views, cited Montesquieu on the separation of the executive and legislative branches, *Farrand*, II, 34). This, of course, does not prove that Locke and Co. were without influence; it shifts the burden of proof, however, to those who assert ideological causality. See Benjamin F. Wright, "The Origins of the Separation of Powers in America," *Economica*, Vol. 13 (1933), p. 184.

[55] I share Willmoore Kendall's interpretation of Locke as a supporter of parliamentary supremacy and majoritarianism; see Kendall, *John Locke and the Doctrine of Majority Rule* (Urbana, 1941). Kendall's general position has recently received strong support in the definitive edition and commentary of Peter Laslett, *Locke's Two Treatises of Government* (Cambridge, 1960).

[56] The American Locke is best delineated in Carl Becker, *The Declaration of Independence* (New York, 1948).

V

Two tricky issues will serve to illustrate the later process of accommodation. The first was the institutional position of the Executive. Madison argued for an executive chosen by the National Legislature and on May 29 this had been adopted with a provision that after his seven-year term was concluded, the chief magistrate should not be eligible for reelection. In late July this was reopened and for a week the matter was argued from several different points of view. A good deal of desultory speech-making ensued, but the gist of the problem was the opposition from two sources to election by the legislature. One group felt that the states should have a hand in the process; another small but influential circle urged direct election by the people. There were a number of proposals: election by the people, election by state governors, by electors chosen by state legislatures, by the National Legislature (James Wilson, perhaps ironically, proposed at one point that an Electoral College be chosen by lot from the National Legislature!), and there was some resemblance to three-dimensional chess in the dispute because of the presence of two other variables, length of tenure and re-eligibility. Finally, after opening, reopening, and re-reopening the debate, the thorny problem was consigned to a committee for resolution.

The Brearley Committee on Postponed Matters was a superb aggregation of talent and its compromise on the Executive was a masterpiece of political improvisation. (The Electoral College, its creation, however, had little in its favor as an *institution* — as the delegates well appreciated.) The point of departure for all discussion about the presidency in the Convention was that in immediate terms, the problem was non-existent; in other words, everybody present knew that under any system devised, George Washington would be President. Thus they were dealing in the future tense and to a body of working politicians the merits of the Brearley proposal were obvious: everybody got a piece of cake. (Or to put it more academically, each viewpoint could leave the Convention and argue to its constituents that it had *really* won the day.) First, the state legislatures had the right to determine the mode of selection of the electors; second, the small states received a bonus in the Electoral College in the form of a guaranteed minimum of three votes while the big states got acceptance of the principle of proportional power; third, if the state legislatures agreed (as six did in the first presidential election), the people could be involved directly in the choice of electors; and finally, if no candidate received a majority in the College, the right of decision passed to the National Legislature with each state exercising equal strength. (In the Brearley recommendation, the election went to the Senate, but a motion from the floor substituted the House; this was accepted on the ground that the Senate already had enough authority over the executive in its treaty and appointment powers.)

This compromise was almost too good to be true, and the Framers snapped it up with little debate or controversy. No one seemed to think well of the College as an *institution*; indeed, what evidence there is suggests that there was an assumption that once Washington had finished his tenure as President, the electors would cease to produce majorities and the chief executive would usually be chosen in the House. George Mason observed casually that the selection would be made in the House nineteen times in twenty and no one seriously disputed this point. The vital aspect of the Electoral College was that it got the Convention over the hurdle and protected everybody's interests. The future was left to cope with the problem of what to do with this Rube Goldberg mechanism.

In short, the Framers did not in their wisdom endow the United States with a College of Cardinals — the Electoral College was neither an exercise in applied Platonism nor an experiment in indirect government based on elitist distrust of the masses. It was merely a jerry-rigged improvisation which has subsequently been endowed with a high theoretical content. When an elector from Oklahoma in 1960 refused to cast his vote for Nixon (naming Byrd and Goldwater instead) on the ground that the Founding Fathers intended him to exercise his great independent wisdom, he was indulging in historical fantasy. If one were to indulge in counter-fantasy, he would be tempted to suggest that the Fathers would be startled to find the College still in operation — and perhaps even dismayed at their descendants' lack of judgment or inventiveness.[57]

The second issue on which some substantial practical bargaining took place was slavery. The morality of slavery was, by design, not at issue;[58] but in its other concrete aspects, slavery colored the arguments over taxation, commerce, and representation. The "Three-Fifths Compromise," that three-fifths of the slaves would be counted both for representation and for purposes of direct taxation (which was drawn from the past — it was a formula of Madison's utilized by Congress in 1783 to establish the basis of state contributions to the Confederation treasury) had allayed some Northern fears about Southern over-representation (no one then foresaw the trivial role that direct taxation would play in later federal financial policy), but doubts still remained. The Southerners, on the other hand, were afraid that Congressional control over commerce would lead to the exclusion of slaves or to their excessive taxation as imports. Moreover, the Southerners were disturbed over "navigation acts," i.e., tariffs, or special legislation providing, for example, that exports be carried only in American ships; as a section depending upon exports, they wanted protection from the potential voracity of their commercial brethren of the Eastern states. To achieve this end, Mason and others urged that the Constitution include a proviso that navigation and commercial laws should require a two-thirds vote in Congress.

These problems came to a head in late August and, as usual, were handed to a committee in the hope that, in Gouverneur Morris' words, ". . . these things may form a bargain among the Northern and Southern states."[59] The Committee reported its measures of reconciliation on August 25, and on August 29 the package was wrapped up and delivered. What occurred can best be described in George Mason's dour version (he anticipated Calhoun in his conviction that permitting navigation acts to pass by majority vote would put the South in eco-

---

[57] See John P. Roche, "The Electoral College: A Note on American Political Mythology," *Dissent* (Spring, 1961), pp. 197–99. The relevant debates took place July 19–26, 1787, *Farrand*, II, 50–128, and September 5–6, 1787, *ibid.*, pp. 505–31.

[58] See the discussion on August 22, 1787, *Farrand*, II, 366–375; King seems to have expressed the sense of the Convention when he said, "the subject should be considered in a political light only." *Ibid.* at 373.

[59] *Farrand*, II, 374. Randolph echoed his sentiment in different words.

nomic bondage to the North — it was mainly on this ground that he refused to sign the Constitution):

> The Constitution as agreed to till a fortnight before the Convention rose was such a one as he would have set his hand and heart to. . . . [Until that time] The 3 New England States were constantly with us in all questions . . . so that it was these three States with the 5 Southern ones against Pennsylvania, Jersey and Delaware. With respect to the importation of slaves, [decision-making] was left to Congress. This disturbed the two Southernmost States who knew that Congress would immediately suppress the importation of slaves. Those two States therefore struck up a bargain with the three New England States. If they would join to admit slaves for some years, the two Southern-most States would join in changing the clause which required the ⅔ of the Legislature in any vote [on navigation acts]. It was done.[60]

On the floor of the Convention there was a virtual love-feast on this happy occasion. Charles Pinckney of South Carolina attempted to overturn the committee's decision, when the compromise was reported to the Convention, by insisting that the South needed protection from the imperialism of the Northern states. But his Southern colleagues were not prepared to rock the boat and General C. C. Pinckney arose to spread oil on the suddenly ruffled waters; he admitted that:

> It was in the true interest of the S[outhern] States to have no regulation of commerce; but considering the loss brought on the commerce of the Eastern States by the Revolution, their liberal conduct towards the views of South Carolina [on the regulation of the slave trade] and the interests the weak Southn. States had in being united with the strong Eastern states, he thought it proper that no fetters should be imposed on the power of making commercial regulations; *and that his constituents, though prejudiced against the Eastern States, would be reconciled to this liberality.* He had himself prejudices agst the Eastern States before he came here, but would acknowledge that he had found them as liberal and candid as any men whatever. (Italics added.)[61]

Pierce Butler took the same tack, essentially arguing that he was not too happy about the possible consequences, but that a deal was a deal.[62] Many Southern

---

[60] Mason to Jefferson, cited in *Warren*, p. 584.

[61] August 29, 1787, *Farrand*, II, 449–50.

[62] *Ibid.*, p. 451. The plainest statement of the matter was put by the three North Carolina delegates (Blount, Spaight and Williamson) in their report to Governor Caswell, September 18, 1787. After noting that "no exertions have been wanting on our part to guard and promote the particular interest of North Carolina," they went on to explain the basis of the negotiations in cold-blooded fashion: "While we were taking so much care to guard ourselves against being over reached and to form rules of Taxation that might operate in our favour, it is not to be supposed that our Northern Brethren were Inattentive to their particular Interest. A navigation Act or the power to regulate Commerce in the Hands of the National Government . . . is what the Southern States have given in

leaders were later — in the wake of the "Tariff of Abominations" — to rue this day of reconciliation; Calhoun's *Disquisition on Government* was little more than an extension of the argument in the Convention against permitting a congressional majority to enact navigation acts.[63]

VI

Drawing on their vast collective political experience, utilizing every weapon in the politician's arsenal, looking constantly over their shoulders at their constituents, the delegates put together a Constitution. It was a makeshift affair; some sticky issues (for example, the qualification of voters) they ducked entirely; others they mastered with that ancient instrument of political sagacity, studied ambiguity (for example, citizenship), and some they just overlooked. In this last category, I suspect, fell the matter of the power of the federal courts to determine the constitutionality of acts of Congress. When the judicial article was formulated (Article III of the Constitution), deliberations were still in the stage where the legislature was endowed with broad power under the Randolph formulation, authority which by its own terms was scarcely amenable to judicial review. In essence, courts could hardly determine when ". . . the separate States are incompetent or . . . the harmony of the United States may be interrupted"; the National Legislature, as critics pointed out, was free to define its own jurisdiction. Later the definition of legislative authority was changed into the form we know, a series of stipulated powers, *but the delegates never seriously reexamined the jurisdiction of the judiciary under this new limited formulation.*[64] All arguments on the intention of the Framers in this matter are thus deductive and *a posteriori*, though some obviously make more sense than others.[65]

Exchange for the advantages we Mentioned." They concluded by explaining that while the Constitution did deal with other matters besides taxes — "there are other Considerations of great Magnitude involved in the system" — they would not take up valuable time with boring details! *Farrand*, III, 83–84.

[63] See John C. Calhoun, *A Disquisition on Government* (New York, 1943), pp. 21–25, 38. Calhoun differed from Mason, and others in the Convention who urged the two-thirds requirement, by advocating a functional or interest veto rather than some sort of special majority, i.e., he abandoned the search for quantitative checks in favor of a qualitative solution.

[64] The Committee on Detail altered the general grant of legislative power envisioned by the Virginia Plan into a series of specific grants; these were examined closely between August 16 and August 23. One day only was devoted to the Judicial Article, August 27, and since no one raised the question of judicial review of *Federal* statutes, no light was cast on the matter. A number of random comments on the power of the judiciary were scattered throughout the discussions, but there was another variable which deprives them of much probative value: the proposed Council of Revision which would have joined the Executive with the judges in *legislative* review. Madison and Wilson, for example, favored this technique — which had nothing in common with what we think of as judicial review except that judges were involved in the task.

[65] For what it may be worth, I think that judicial review of congressional acts was logically on all fours with review of state enactments and that it was certainly consistent with the view that the Constitution could not be amended by the Congress and President, or by a two-thirds vote of Congress (overriding a veto), without the agreement of three-quarters of the states. *External* evidence from that time supports this view, see Charles Warren, *Congress, the Constitution, and the Supreme Court* (Boston, 1925), pp. 41–128, but the debates *in* the Convention prove nothing.

The Framers were busy and distinguished men, anxious to get back to their families, their positions, and their constituents, not members of the French Academy devoting a lifetime to a dictionary. They were trying to do an important job, and do it in such a fashion that their handiwork would be acceptable to very diverse constituencies. No one was rhapsodic about the final document, but it was a beginning, a move in the right direction, and one they had reason to believe the people would endorse. In addition, since they had modified the impossible amendment provisions of the Articles (the requirement of unanimity which could always be frustrated by "Rogues Island") to one demanding approval by only three-quarters of the states, they seemed confident that gaps in the fabric which experience would reveal could be rewoven without undue difficulty.

So with a neat phrase introduced by Benjamin Franklin (but devised by Gouverneur Morris)[66] which made their decision sound unanimous, and an inspired benediction by the Old Doctor urging doubters to doubt their own infallibility, the Constitution was accepted and signed. Curiously, Edmund Randolph, who had played so vital a role throughout, refused to sign, as did his fellow Virginian George Mason and Elbridge Gerry of Massachusetts. Randolph's behavior was eccentric, to say the least — his excuses for refusing his signature have a factitious ring even at this late date; the best explanation seems to be that he was afraid that the Constitution would prove to be a liability in Virginia politics, where Patrick Henry was burning up the countryside with impassioned denunciations. Presumably, Randolph wanted to check the temper of the populace before he risked his reputation, and perhaps his job, in a fight with both Henry and Richard Henry Lee.[67] Events lend some justification to this speculation: after much temporizing and use of the conditional subjunctive tense, Randolph endorsed ratification in Virginia and ended up getting the best of both worlds.

Madison, despite his reservations about the Constitution, was the campaign manager in ratification. His first task was to get the Congress in New York to light its own funeral pyre by approving the "amendments" to the Articles and sending them on to the state legislatures. Above all, momentum had to be maintained. The anti-Constitutionalists, now thoroughly alarmed and no novices in politics, realized that their best tactic was attrition rather than direct opposition. Thus they settled on a position expressing qualified approval but calling for a second Convention to remedy various defects (the one with the most demagogic appeal was the lack of a Bill of Rights). Madison knew that to accede to this demand would be equivalent to losing the battle, nor would he agree to condi-

[66] Or so Madison stated, *Farrand*, II, 643. Wilson too may have contributed; he was close to Franklin and delivered the frail old gentleman's speeches for him.

[67] See a very interesting letter, from an unknown source in Philadelphia, to Jefferson, October 11, 1787: "Randolph wishes it well, & it is thought would have signed it, but he wanted to be on a footing with a popular rival." *Farrand*, III, 104. Madison, writing Jefferson a full account on October 24, 1787, put the matter more delicately — he was working hard on Randolph to win him for ratification: "[Randolph] was not inveterate in his opposition, and grounded his refusal to subscribe pretty much on his unwillingness to commit himself, so as not to be at liberty to be governed by further lights on the subject." *Ibid.*, p. 135.

tional approval (despite wavering even by Hamilton). This was an all-or-nothing proposition: national salvation or national impotence with no intermediate positions possible. Unable to get congressional approval, he settled for second best: a unanimous resolution of Congress transmitting the Constitution to the states for whatever action they saw fit to take. The opponents then moved from New York and the Congress, where they had attempted to attach amendments and conditions, to the states for the final battle.[68]

At first the campaign for ratification went beautifully: within eight months after the delegates set their names to the document, eight states had ratified. Only in Massachusetts had the result been close (187–168). Theoretically, a ratification by one more state convention would set the new government in motion, but in fact until Virginia and New York acceded to the new Union, the latter was a fiction. New Hampshire was the next to ratify; Rhode Island was involved in its characteristic political convulsions (the Legislature there sent the Constitution out to the towns for decision by popular vote and it got lost among a series of local issues);[69] North Carolina's convention did not meet until July and then postponed a final decision. This is hardly the place for an extensive analysis of the conventions of New York and Virginia. Suffice it to say that the Constitutionalists clearly outmaneuvered their opponents, forced them into impossible political positions, and won both states narrowly. The Virginia Convention could serve as a classic study in effective floor management: Patrick Henry had to be contained, and a reading of the debates discloses a standard two-stage technique. Henry would give a four- or five-hour speech denouncing some section of the Constitution on every conceivable ground (the federal district, he averred at one point, would become a haven for convicts escaping from state authority!),[70] when Henry subsided, "Mr. Lee of Westmoreland" would rise and literally poleaxe him with sardonic incentive (when Henry complained about the militia power, "Lighthorse Harry" really punched below the belt: observing that while the former Governor had been sitting in Richmond during the Revolution, *he* had been out in the trenches with the troops and thus felt better qualified to discuss military affairs).[71] Then the gentlemanly Constitutionalists (Madison, Pendleton and Marshall) would pick up the matters at issue and examine them in the light of reason.

Indeed, modern Americans who tend to think of James Madison as a rather dessicated character should spend some time with this transcript. Probably Madison put on his most spectacular demonstration of nimble rhetoric in what might be called "The Battle of the Absent Authorities." Patrick Henry in the course

---

[68] See Edward P. Smith, "The Movement Towards a Second Constitutional Convention in 1788," in J. F. Jameson, ed., *Essays in the Constitutional History of the United States* (Boston, 1889), pp. 46–115.

[69] See Bishop, *op. cit., passim.*

[70] See *Elliot's Debates on the Federal Constitution* (Washington, 1836), Vol. 3, pp. 436–438.

[71] This should be quoted to give the full flavor: "Without vanity, I may say I have had different experience of [militia] service from that of [Henry]. It was my fortune to be a soldier of my country. . . . I saw what the honorable gentleman did not see — our men fighting. . . ." *Ibid.*, p. 178.

of one of his harangues alleged that Jefferson was known to be opposed to Virginia's approving the Constitution. This was clever: Henry hated Jefferson, but was prepared to use any weapon that came to hand. Madison's riposte was superb: First, he said that with all due respect to the great reputation of Jefferson, he was not in the country and therefore could not formulate an adequate judgment; second, no one should utilize the reputation of an outsider — the Virginia Convention was there to think for itself; third, if there were to be recourse to outsiders, the opinions of George Washington should certainly be taken into consideration; and finally, he knew from privileged personal communications from Jefferson that in fact the latter *strongly favored* the Constitution.[72] To devise an assault route into this rhetorical fortress was literally impossible.

VII

The fight was over; all that remained now was to establish the new frame of government in the spirit of its Framers. And who were better qualified for this task than the Framers themselves? Thus victory for the Constitution meant simultaneous victory for the Constitutionalists; the anti-Constitutionalists either capitulated or vanished into limbo — soon Patrick Henry would be offered a seat on the Supreme Court[73] and Luther Martin would be known as the Federalist "bull-dog."[74] And irony of ironies, Alexander Hamilton and James Madison would shortly accumulate a reputation as the formulators of what is often alleged to be our political theory, the concept of "federalism." Also, on the other side of the ledger, the arguments would soon appear over what the Framers "really meant"; while these disputes have assumed the proportions of a big scholarly business in the last century, they began almost before the ink on the Constitution was dry. One of the best early ones featured Hamilton versus Madison on the scope of presidential power, and other Framers characteristically assumed positions in this and other disputes on the basis of their political convictions.

Probably our greatest difficulty is that we know so much more about what the Framers *should have meant* than they themselves did. We are intimately acquainted with the problems that their Constitution should have been designed to master; in short, we have read the mystery story backwards. If we are to get the right "feel" for their time and their circumstances, we must in Maitland's phrase, ". . . think ourselves back into a twilight." Obviously, no one can pretend completely to escape from the solipsistic web of his own environment, but if the effort is made, it is possible to appreciate the past roughly on its own terms. The first step in this process is to abandon the academic premise that because we can ask a question, there must be an answer.

Thus we can ask what the Framers meant when they gave Congress the power to regulate interstate and foreign commerce, and we emerge, reluctantly perhaps,

---

[72] *Ibid.*, p. 329.

[73] Washington offered him the Chief Justiceship in 1796, but he declined; Charles Warren, *The Supreme Court in United States History* (Boston, 1947), Vol. 1, p. 139.

[74] He was a zealous prosecutor of seditions in the period 1798–1800; with Justice Samuel Chase, like himself an alleged "radical" at the time of the Constitutional Convention, Martin hunted down Jeffersonian heretics. See James M. Smith, *Freedom's Fetters* (Ithaca, 1956), pp. 342–43.

with the reply that (Professor Crosskey to the contrary notwithstanding)[75] they may not have known what they meant, that there may not have been any semantic consensus. The Convention was not a seminar in analytic philosophy or linguistic analysis. Commerce was *commerce* — and if different interpretations of the word arose, later generations could worry about the problem of definition. The delegates were in a hurry to get a new government established; when definitional arguments arose, they characteristically took refuge in ambiguity. If different men voted for the same proposition for varying reasons, that was politics (and still is); if later generations were unsettled by this lack of precision, that would be their problem.

There was a good deal of definitional pluralism with respect to the problems the delegates did discuss, but when we move to the question of extrapolated intentions, we enter the realm of spiritualism. When men in our time, for instance, launch into elaborate talmudic exegesis to demonstrate that federal aid to parochial schools is (or is not) in accord with the intentions of the men who established the Republic and endorsed the Bill of Rights, they are engaging in historical Extra-Sensory Perception. (If one were to join this E.S.P. contingent for a minute, he might suggest that the hard-boiled politicians who wrote the Constitution and Bill of Rights would chuckle scornfully at such an invocation of authority: obviously a politician would chart his course on the intentions of the living, not of the dead, and count the number of Catholics in his constituency.)

The Constitution, then, was not an apotheosis of "constitutionalism," a triumph of architectonic genius; it was a patch-work sewn together under the pressure of both time and events by a group of extremely talented democratic politicians. They refused to attempt the establishment of a strong, centralized sovereignty on the principle of legislative supremacy for the excellent reason that the people would not accept it. They risked their political fortunes by opposing the established doctrines of state sovereignty because they were convinced that the existing system was leading to national impotence and probably foreign

---

[75] Crosskey in his sprawling *Politics and the Constitution* (Chicago, 1953), 2 vols., has developed with almost unbelievable zeal and intricacy the thesis that the Constitution *was* designed to establish a centralized unitary state, but that the political leadership of the Republic in its formative years betrayed this ideal and sold the pass to states'-rights. While he has unearthed some interesting newspaper articles and other material, it is impossible for me to accept his central proposition. Madison and the other delegates, with the exceptions discussed in the text *supra*, did *want* to diminish the power of the states and create a vigorous national government. But they were not fools, and were, I submit, under no illusions when they departed from Philadelphia that this end had been accomplished. The crux of my argument is that *political realities* forced them to water down their objectives and they settled, like the good politicians they were, for half a loaf. The basic difficulty with Crosskey's thesis is that he knows *too* much — he assumes that the Framers had a perfectly clear idea of the road they were taking; with a semantic machete he cuts blandly through all the confusion on the floor of the meeting to the *real* meanings. Thus, despite all his ornate research apparatus, there is a fundamentally nonempirical quality about Crosskey's work: at crucial points in the argument he falls back on a type of divination which can only be described as Kabbalistic. He may be right, for example, in stating (without any proof) that Richard Henry Lee did *not* write the "Letters from a Federal Farmer," but in this country spectral evidence has not been admissible since the Seventeenth Century.

domination. For two years, they worked to get a convention established. For over three months, in what must have seemed to the faithful participants an endless process of give-and-take, they reasoned, cajoled, threatened, and bargained amongst themselves. The result was a Constitution which the people, in fact, by democratic processes, did accept, and a new and far better national government was established.

Beginning with the inspired propaganda of Hamilton, Madison and Jay, the ideological build-up got under way. *The Federalist* had little impact on the ratification of the Constitution, except perhaps in New York, but this volume had enormous influence on the image of the Constitution in the minds of future generations, particularly on historians and political scientists who have an innate fondness for theoretical symmetry. Yet, while the shades of Locke and Montesquieu *may* have been hovering in the background, and the delegates *may* have been unconscious instruments of a transcendent *telos*, the careful observer of the day-to-day work of the Convention finds no over-arching principles. The "separation of powers" to him seems to be a by-product of suspicion, and "federalism" he views as a *pis aller*, as the farthest point the delegates felt they could go in the destruction of state power without themselves inviting repudiation.

To conclude, the Constitution was neither a victory for abstract theory nor a practical success. Well over a half million men had to die on the battlefields of the Civil War before certain constitutional principles could be defined — a baleful consideration which is somehow overlooked in our customary tributes to the farsighted genius of the Framers and to the supposed American talent for "constitutionalism." The Constitution was, however, a vivid demonstration of effective democratic political action, and of the forging of a national elite which literally persuaded its countrymen to hoist themselves by their own boot straps. American proconsuls would be wise not to translate the Constitution into Japanese, or Swahili, or treat it as a work of semi-Divine origin; but when students of comparative politics examine the process of nation-building in countries newly freed from colonial rule, they may find the American experience instructive as a classic example of the potentialities of a democratic elite.

Novus Ordo Seculorum: Enlightenment Ideas on Diplomacy

FELIX GILBERT

Foreign policy was one of the few aspects of government in which colonial Americans were inexperienced, for though the imperial system had afforded them considerable freedom for domestic self-government, and they had learned a good deal from the conduct of intercolonial relations, the officials in England had always regulated their external affairs. Even during the Revolution, the sole purpose of American foreign policy was simply to further the war for independence from Great Britain. Yet, even before the war had been won, Americans began to consider the terms upon which they should confront the established nations of Europe. On the one hand, they were aware of the need for good trade relations, but, on the other, they feared involvement in the debilitating entanglements of Old World politics. Felix Gilbert, a specialist in European intellectual history of the early modern period, tries to explain how a combination of ideas from the American revolutionary and European Enlightenment periods formed a basis for the development of the first foreign policy of the United States. Perhaps the leading preconception by American leaders was that of American purity in contrast with European corruption, and they therefore hesitated to establish relationships with the retrograde governments of the ancien régime across the Atlantic. They feared "diplomacy," which they conceived to be the outmoded behavior of kings and undemocratic governments. At the same time, though, they felt that the commercial potential of the American continent would permit them to negotiate purely commercial alliances with Europe, free of the dangers of political bonds. Gilbert believes it unfair to characterize the foreign policy of the early republic as isolationist, for he feels that Americans understood the worth of international contact even with its disadvantages. This seems especially plausible in the light of seventeenth-century insistence upon the moral superiority of the American settlements and the contemporary American belief in the international significance of the Revolution. The Declaration of Independence was addressed to the world, both because revolutionary leaders thought in the international, humanistic terms of the Enlightenment and because they understood that a new nation could not survive without friends in the hostile environment of world politics. The Gilbert essay thus clarifies some of the reasons for the apparently contradictory character of our first attempts at foreign policy. It does not attempt, however, to deal with the domestic politics of the formulation of that policy, nor does it take

*into account the conflict of economic interests which have tradi-
tionally influenced our attitudes toward the rest of the world. The
French-Republican, British-Federalist division of the 1790's indicates the extent to which foreign policy soon merged with internal
affairs, and the Ferguson essay suggests one of the ways in which
economic interests affected attitudes toward national policy prior
to 1783. Is Gilbert's intellectual framework compatible with your
conception of politico-economic influences in the formulation of
American foreign policy?*

I

Paine's *Common Sense* was published in January 1776. Throughout the following months, the movement for independence gained increasing momentum. The
final stage in the chain of events which led to the foundation of an independent
United States was reached on June 7, 1776, when the Congress entered upon
the consideration of R. H. Lee's resolution "that these United Colonies are, and
of right ought to be, free and independent States, that they are absolved from
all allegiance to the British crown, and that all political connection between
them and the State of Great Britain is, and ought to be, totally dissolved; that
it is expedient forthwith to take the most effectual measures for forming foreign
Alliances; that a plan of confederation be prepared and transmitted to the respective Colonies for their consideration and approbation."[1]

Confederation, foreign alliances, and independence were presented as inter-
connected measures in this motion; its pivot was the urgent need for foreign
assistance. Because of the difficult economic situation which had developed in
the colonies, Congress had been forced to admit the failure of a policy, the main
weapon of which had been the stoppage of trade between the colonies and the
outside world. Thus on April 6, 1776, the Congress ordered the opening of
American ports to the ships of all nations except Great Britain. Because of the
British supremacy on the seas and the lack of an American navy, the success of
this measure depended on the willingness of foreign powers not only to receive
American trade, but also to protect it. The American leaders were aware, however, that no foreign power could dare to take the risky step of assisting the
American rebels without having a definite guarantee that some stable regime
would be created on the North American continent and that return to British
rule would be made impossible. "Confederation" and "independence" were the
necessary prerequisites for securing "foreign alliances."

But what did the Americans understand by "foreign alliances"? When John
Adams, a few years later, reviewed the events of the summer of 1776, he declared
that in the debates of 1776, on the application to foreign powers he had laid it
down as a first principle that "we should calculate all our measures and foreign

From Felix Gilbert, *To the Farewell Address: Ideas of Early American Foreign Policy*
(copyright © 1961 by Princeton University Press; Princeton Paperback, 1970), pp. 44–75.
Reprinted by permission of Princeton University Press.
[1] *Journals of the Continental Congress*, ed. Worthington Chauncey Ford, vol. V,
Washington 1906, p. 425.

negotiations in such a manner, as to avoid a too great dependence upon any one power of Europe — to avoid all obligations and temptations to take any part in future European wars; that the business of America with Europe was commerce, not politics or war."[2] Yet in 1776, Adams had been a zealous supporter of Lee's resolution which had recommended the conclusion of foreign alliances. At present, the term "alliance" is understood to mean the establishment of cooperation in the political sphere among the contracting parties. If John Adams saw no contradiction between a support of Lee's resolution and an avoidance of political obligations, he must have used the word "alliance" in a sense different from the present-day meaning of a close political bond.

It can probably be said that our identification of "alliance" with political or even political-military commitments derives from the fact that in the modern world, diplomatic instruments which contain political or political-military arrangements are sharply separated from those concerned with regulations of trade, tariffs, and navigation. Yet this separation of political treaties from commercial treaties began only in the eighteenth century. In the Peace of Utrecht of 1713 ending the hostilities of the War of the Spanish Succession between England and France, political and commercial arrangements were dealt with for the first time in separate documents. This new pattern was only slowly adopted; throughout the eighteenth century, one and the same treaty could still contain arrangements about political, commercial, and economic questions. Thus there are many nuances in the seventeenth and eighteenth centuries between the opposite types of the "traité d'alliance offensive et défensive," clearly designating a political-military bond, and the "traité de commerce," exclusively concerned with trade. Such names as "traité d'alliance et de commerce," "traité de paix, de navigation, et de commerce," "traité de navigation et commerce," "traité de marine," suggest the variety of content which could be contained in a single diplomatic document. In the terminology of the eighteenth century, all such treaties established "alliances."

Thus Adams' view that one could have alliances with foreign powers without making political commitments finds its explanation in the usage of the eighteenth century; other Americans used the term "alliance" in the same loose way. In the first six months of the year 1776, before Lee's resolution made the question of foreign alliances an issue of practical politics, the problem had been frequently discussed; and the ambiguity of the term "alliance" had resulted in a great variety of contradictory opinions about the consequences of concluding foreign alliances. They were looked upon with fear, but they were also regarded as the instrument by which America could obtain the necessary assistance without restrictions on her freedom of action. One of the reasons given against the conclusions of alliances with foreign powers was that the bond which had existed between England and the colonies in the past had been an "alliance";[3] Britain

---

[2] John Adams to Secretary Livingston, February 5, 1783, printed in John Adams, *Works*, ed. Charles Francis Adams, vol. VIII, Boston 1853, p. 35.

[3] For instance, Thomas Paine, *Complete Writings*, ed. Philip S. Foner, vol. I, New York 1945, p. 20; John Adams, *Works*, vol. IV, pp. 110, 114; *Letters of Members of the Continental Congress*, ed. Edmund C. Burnett, vol. I, Washington 1921, p. 369; *American Archives*, ed. Peter Force, fourth series, vol. V, Washington 1844, p. 1208; and, most of all, Franklin's "Vindication" of 1775, see Benjamin Franklin, *Works*, ed. Jared Sparks, vol. V, Philadelphia 1840, pp. 83–90.

had provided military protection for the granting of commercial advantages on the part of the colonies. An alliance with a foreign power might lead to the same consequences which the "alliance" with Britain had had; "an expedient of this kind" would lead the colonists into "having their allies, at last, for their masters."[4] It would produce the exchange of domination by one power for domination by another. To avoid this danger, it was suggested that the alliance be restricted to "external assistance";[5] a distinction was to be made between cooperation on land and cooperation at sea. While the French navy should be allowed to play a part in the war, no assistance by a French army should be accepted. In general, Americans were very optimistic about the prospects of receiving the protection of the French navy for American trade without having to make political commitments in return; most Americans believed that the separation of the American colonies from Britain's imperial system and the possibility of trade with the colonies would be regarded by the French as a sufficient attraction. Other Americans were less sanguine. When Franklin wrote about the possibility of exchanging "commerce for friendship,"[6] he seems to have felt that a somewhat more substantial inducement in the form of some monopoly, at least for a definite period, must be offered to France. Thus when the contingency of entering into alliances with foreign powers was debated in the early part of 1776, such a measure comprised a wide range of possibilities: a purely commercial treaty, or a treaty with commercial obligations from the American side and political-military obligations from the French side, or a treaty with reciprocal political commitments. When Lee proposed his resolution on June 7, 1776, the thinking in the colonies had not yet crystallized into a clear conception of the kind of "alliance" America should conclude. Only when the Congress began to deliberate on the treaty to be proposed to France and on the instruction to be given to the American negotiators did the ideas on this problem take a definite form, a form which was striking and novel.

The external story of the further events is clearly established. On June 11, 1776, in consequence of Lee's resolution, a committee was appointed to prepare the model of a treaty to be proposed to the French court. This committee handed in its report on July 18 and the report was discussed in the Continental Congress on August 22, 27, and 29. Then the Congress referred the report back to the committee for amendment and for preparation of instructions to be given to the American agents. On September 17, this final report of the committee was made to the Congress, and the latter's agreement to the prepared instructions was given on September 24. Two days later, Benjamin Franklin, Silas Deane, and Thomas Jefferson were appointed commissioners to France.

The internal story behind these factual events is much more difficult to disentangle. For its reconstruction we have only a few documents — the Model Treaty and the instructions — and brief remarks in the letters and memoirs of the main actors.

John Adams was a member of the committee entrusted with the preparation

---

[4] Cato's "Fifth Letter to the People of Pennsylvania," *American Archives*, fourth series, vol. V, pp. 542–543.

[5] Richard Henry Lee to Landon Carter, June 2, 1776, *Letters of Members of the Continental Congress*, vol. I, p. 469.

[6] Franklin to Joseph Priestley, July 7, 1775, *ibid.*, p. 156.

of the Model Treaty, and he was assigned to draft this document. Adams must be considered as the chief architect of the Model Treaty and its accompanying instructions. He had given much thought to the subject before he entered upon this task. In March 1776, evidently influenced by Paine's *Common Sense*, he had set down on paper his ideas as to the "connection we may safely form" with France and arrived at the following formula: "1. No political connection. Submit to none of her authority, receive no governors or officers from her. 2. No military connection. Receive no troops from her. 3. Only a commercial connection; that is, make a treaty to receive her ships into our ports; let her engage to receive our ships into her ports; furnish us with arms, cannon, saltpetre, powder, duck, steel."[7] How fundamental these ideas were for him can be deduced from the fact that they also appear in letters which he wrote in the spring of 1776. He urged the necessity of sending ambassadors to foreign courts "to form with them, at least with some of them, commercial treaties of friendship and alliance";[8] and when the dangers to American freedom of an alliance with a foreign power were pointed out to him, he stressed that in recommending foreign alliances, he was thinking only of a contractual safeguard of America's trade relations. "I am not for soliciting any political connection, or military assistance, or indeed naval, from France. I wish for nothing but commerce, a mere marine treaty with them."[9]

The Model Treaty was intended to realize the ideas which John Adams had previously developed — namely, that alliance did not imply a political bond and that America's contacts with outside powers should be limited to trade relations. When Adams began to draft the Model Treaty, Franklin put into his hand "a printed volume of treaties" in which he had made some pencil marks beside certain articles. Adams found "some of these judiciously selected, and I took them, with others which I found necessary, into the draught."[10] A comparison of the Model Treaty with earlier documents reveals that Adams relied heavily on two particular treaties: the treaty between James II and Louis XIV of November 16, 1686, concerning the neutrality of the American colonies in case of a conflict between England and France; and the commercial treaty between England and France of 1713. Most of the stipulations of the Model Treaty concerned with the regulation of trade, navigation, and fishing — which is to say, the greater part of the Model Treaty — are taken from these treaties. In other words, agreements which regulated the commercial relations between England and France were used as patterns for the Model Treaty, and, in that, the United States took the place of England. It seems likely that Adams chose the commercial treaty between England and France of 1713 also because its regulations had been of a most liberal character. The liberal spirit which inspired the American draft is reflected particularly in the articles dealing with trade in wartime. The Model Treaty contained a precisely circumscribed and extremely limited list of contraband goods: even foodstuffs and naval stores were excluded from it. Furthermore, neutrals should have the right to trade with

[7] John Adams, *Works*, vol. II, pp. 488–489.
[8] John Adams to William Cushing, June 9, 1776, *Letters of Members of the Continental Congress*, vol. I, p. 478.
[9] John Adams to John Winthrop, June 23, 1776, *ibid.*, p. 502.
[10] John Adams, *Works*, vol. II, p. 516.

belligerents, and the principle was laid down that free ships make free goods. The strongest indication of this tendency towards complete freedom in trade can be found, however, in the first two articles of the Model Treaty, which were concerned with the establishment of basic principles for the future commercial relations between France and America. These articles go beyond anything that Adams could have taken from the treaties between England and France. The Model Treaty suggested that the French should treat the inhabitants of the United States with regard to duties and imports as natives of France and vice versa; moreover, they "shall enjoy all other the Rights, Liberties, Priviledges, Immunities and Exemptions in Trade, Navigation and Commerce, in passing from one port [Part] thereof to another, and in going to and from the same, from and to any Part of the World, which the said Natives, or Companies enjoy."[11] The "instructions" added that only if "his most Christian Majesty shall not consent" to these articles, the commissioners should try to get the French agreement to a most-favored-nation clause.[12] The latter was proposed only as a less attractive alternative if a reciprocity clause could not be obtained. The fundamental concepts behind these proposals are evident and, as far as the practical policy of the period is concerned, striking: in drafting the Model Treaty, the colonists were thinking not only of France but also of other powers. They were, in effect, creating a general pattern for future commercial treaties. Whereas usually commercial conventions were sources of friction and instruments of power politics reinforcing political alliances by commercial preferences, the Americans wanted to establish a commercial system of freedom and equality which would eliminate all cause for tension and political conflicts.

Although John Adams might have wanted to limit the Model Treaty to questions of trade and navigation, a number of political questions had to be taken up. Thus French protection was to replace the former English protection of American ships against the attacks of the Barbary States. Moreover, a number of articles were concerned with the problems which had arisen from the war against the British and had forced the colonists into "their application to foreign powers." It was stipulated that American ships should be protected and convoyed by their allies and that France should give up any claim to territories of the North American continent, while the Americans would not oppose a French conquest of the West Indies.

Since both countries — France and the United States — were moving in a sharply anti-English direction, would it not be desirable that they agree on common action for war and peace and that the conditions of their political cooperation be clearly defined? A treaty with the colonial rebels would unavoidably involve France in a war with England; and for most of the colonial leaders, this was the purpose of an agreement with France. Hence some statement about the reciprocal obligations of the two powers fighting against the same potential enemy was necessary. The manner in which the Model Treaty dealt with this question was surprising, as it revealed the Americans' disinclination to be forced into a political bond with an outside power even under pressure of war. Article 8 stated that in case the alliance with the United States should involve France

---

[11] *Journals of the Continental Congress*, vol. V, p. 769.
[12] *Ibid.*, p. 813.

in war with England, the United States would not assist England in such a war. The promise offered in this article — namely, that America would not use the opportunity of an Anglo-French war for coming to an understanding with England — was little more than a matter of course. What is astounding is how little the Americans were willing to offer. Political and military cooperation with France was to be avoided even if France should enter the war against England.

In the instructions for the American negotiators, it was said that this "article will probably be attended with some Difficulty,"[13] and the article was explained by an unusually long comment. Clearly the article had evoked a heated debate in the committee. A number of members felt that such love of principle defeated its own purpose and that a somewhat more realistic approach was necessary to obtain French participation in the war. Thus they wanted to include in the instructions a paragraph which would have given the American negotiators permission to offer a greater inducement to France: reconquest of the islands in the West Indies which France had ceded to England after the Seven Years' War: "If the Court of France cannot be prevailed on to engage in the War with Great Britain for any consideration already proposed in this Treaty, you are hereby authorized to agree as a further inducement, that these United States will wage the war in union with France, not make peace with Great Britain until the latter France shall gain the possession of those Islands in the West Indies formerly called Nieutral, and which by the Treaty of Paris were ceded to G. Britain: provided France shall make the conquest of these Islands an early object of the War and prosecute the same with sufficient force."[14] However, the majority of Congress was not willing to make commitments about territorial changes, and this paragraph was omitted from the final instructions. Some concessions were made to those who cared more about getting France into the war than about principles of foreign policy. The commissioners were entitled to make some additional offers: the United States was willing to guarantee that it would grant to no other power trading privileges which it had not granted to the French king; furthermore, in case France should become involved in the present war, neither France nor the United States would conclude peace without notifying the other power six months ahead.

The striking thing about the Model Treaty and the accompanying instructions is that, although the Americans were in a desperate situation in which they looked anxiously for foreign help, their leaders insisted on proposals which were entirely alien to the spirit of the diplomatic practice of the time.

II

It was a long journey from the simple brick building of the State House in Philadelphia, with its unpretentious wood paneling, to the palaces of Paris and Versailles, abounding in marble and rosewood, chinoiseries, mirrors, and silk. How did the American leaders have the courage to proffer to the French government, ensconced in eighteenth-century splendor, a treaty which challenged all the diplomatic traditions of which France was the foremost practitioner?

The Americans were convinced of the immense value of the offer which they

[13] *Ibid.,* pp. 814–815.
[14] *Ibid.,* p. 817.

made to France: the ending of the English monopoly of trade with North America. The consequence would be not only to increase French economic prosperity, but also to weaken England, France's old rival. The Americans may have somewhat overestimated the extent to which the opening of the American ports to the ships of all nations would revolutionize the European state system. But in the American view, France would gain such far-reaching advantages that America had a right to determine the nature of the relationship which, in the future, should exist between America and the European powers.

The Model Treaty with which the Americans formulated their concept of this relationship shows the impact of the program which Paine had set forth in *Common Sense*. The Model Treaty and the accompanying instructions were designed to keep America out of European struggles and to secure for her peace and freedom by making all European powers interested partners in American trade. But behind these documents there lay an attitude which leads beyond the image which Paine had given of America's role in foreign policy. Paine's ideas are products of the age in which he was born, of the Enlightenment; but in *Common Sense*, he did not share its optimism. To Paine, the world, with the exception of America, was rotten and lost. "Freedom hath been hunted around the globe. Asia and Africa have long expelled her, Europe regards her like a stranger, and England hath given her warning to depart." America was to be preserved as the last bulwark of liberty, "an asylum for mankind." This censure of Europe corresponded to feelings deeply rooted in America's colonial past and facilitated the acceptance of the ideas of *Common Sense* in America. But American intellectual life was also strongly imbued with the spirit of the Enlightenment. Although most Americans may have agreed with Paine's condemnation of Europe's political and social life as it existed at the time, not all of them shared Paine's gloomy prognostications for Europe's future; many were in accord with the Enlightenment belief in progress and were convinced that a new and better age in the history of the human race was approaching. They believed the American Revolution had started a great experiment; they felt they were setting a pattern which the rest of the world would follow. Thus the Model Treaty had a double face. It was intended, on the one hand, as an instrument to achieve an independent existence for America, secure from the corrupting influence of Europe. On the other hand, by eliminating purely political issues like territorial settlements, by focussing on the regulation of commercial relations, and by placing them on such a liberal basis that the arrangements between France and America could easily be extended to the nations of the whole world, the Americans transformed the Model Treaty into a pattern for all future diplomatic treaties. The Americans entered the European scene as the representatives of the diplomacy of a new era. They did not feel confronted by an entirely hostile world. They might find little sympathy for their ideas with the rulers of France, who thought in terms of traditional diplomacy. But they felt they had many friends: their allies were all the progressive minds of Europe, the writers and thinkers whom we now call "the philosophes."

The philosophes' ideas on foreign policy and diplomacy throw light on the broad background from which the American views on this topic developed. The philosophes confirmed the Americans in their outlook on diplomacy and, for a number of years, were an important factor in determining the course of American foreign policy; finally, they infused a lasting idealistic element into the American attitude toward foreign affairs.

The views of the philosophes both on foreign policy and on domestic policy were based on the conviction that history had reached the end of a long and tortuous development; the contrasts and conflicts of the past would now be resolved in a great synthesis, and a permanent order could be accomplished. The confidence of the philosophes in the near approach of a golden age had its foundation in a peculiar constellation of historical factors.

We have spoken of the change in the political system of Europe signified by the Peace of Utrecht. One of the aspects of this change was the growing awareness of the importance of the non-European parts of the globe. The stipulations of the Treaty of Utrecht covered the entire world and thereby demonstrated to what extent the great European powers, though they remained of central importance, drew their strength from the resources of other continents. This is reflected in Turgot's statement that the trend of the time was to make the boundaries of the political world "become identical with those of the physical world."[15]

This feeling that one civilization now encompassed the whole world was reinforced by the astounding growth of economic interdependence. In the centers of European civilization, people could rely on having a regular supply of goods from all over the world: sugar from the West Indies, tea and china from the Far East, coffee and chocolate from the Americas and Africa. The barriers that existed seemed artificial and ephemeral in comparison with the fine net by which the merchants tied the individuals of the different nations together like "threads of silk."[16] As Sédaine says in his famous comedy *Le philosophe sans le savoir*, the merchants — whether they are English, Dutch, Russian, or Chinese — do not serve a single nation; they serve everyone and are citizens of the whole world. Commerce was believed to bind the nations together and to create not only a community of interests but also a distribution of labor among them — a new comprehensive principle placing the isolated sovereign nations in a higher political unit. In the eighteenth century, writers were likely to say that the various nations belonged to "one society"; it was stated that all states together formed "a family of nations," and the whole globe a "general and unbreakable confederation."[17]

The social force which carried this development was the bourgeoisie. In the eighteenth century, its members became conscious of being a main prop of social life; they felt entitled to have all obstacles to the development of their interests eliminated. The philosophes gave the claims of this class an ideological form. They did for the bourgeoisie what intellectuals usually do when a new and rising class wants to break the restraints which keep it in a subordinate position. Then intellectuals identify the cause of a class with the cause of the human race in

[15] Turgot, *Oeuvres*, ed. Gustave Schelle, vol. I, Paris 1913, p. 263.

[16] Michel-Jean Sédaine, *Le philosophe sans le savoir*, act II, scene 4.

[17] For instance, Mercier de la Rivière, "L'ordre naturel et essentiel des Sociétés Politiques, 1767," in *Collection des Économistes et des Reformateurs Sociaux de la France*, ed. Edgar Depitre, Paris 1910, pp. 242–252; Le Trosne, *De l'Ordre Social*, Paris 1777, pp. 355, 392–393; Gaillard, "Les Avantages de La Paix, 1767," in Gabriel-Henri Gaillard, *Mélanges Académiques, Poétiques, Littéraires, Philologiques*, vol. I, Paris 1806, p. 66.

general and explain that the fight is a fight for freedom against tyranny, rather than for special interests against privileges and suppression by a ruling group. The triumph of the new class is to be a victory of humanity, the final solution of all historical conflicts.

Most of the eighteenth-century philosophes were French. France was the most powerful nation of Europe, the theater in which the issues of the century were fought out. In the economically less advanced countries of Central and Eastern Europe, the power of the feudal and agrarian ruling group could not yet be seriously challenged. In England, as a result of the civil wars and revolutions of the previous century, the commercial classes had gained a steadily increasing influence and were becoming gradually amalgamated with the ruling group. In France, monarchy and nobility were still in exclusive political control, but the bourgeoisie had become a powerful economic and social factor; the forces of the old order and of the new faced each other in almost equal poise. Moreover, although the wars of Louis XIV had brought France to the zenith of power in Europe, they had eventually threatened to carry her beyond that point. The French people had entered the century exhausted and dispirited. The traditional policy of terretorial expansion on the Continent and the drive for European hegemony had lost much of its glamour. Thus the great concern of the philosophes was domestic policy.

If the ideas of the philosophes on foreign policy have been studied less than those on domestic policy, this one-sidedness of modern interests corresponds to the order of value which the philosophes themselves assigned to these two fields of political activity. Their thesis was that the great role which foreign affairs played in the political life of their time was one of the most fundamental evils of the existing political system. D'Argenson has most succinctly formulated this basic attitude of the philosophes with regard to the relationship between domestic and foreign affairs. "The true purpose of the science called politics is to perfect the interior of a state as much as possible. Flatterers assure the princes that the interior is there only to serve foreign policy. Duty tells them the opposite."[18]

The philosophes directed a systematic attack against the view which regarded foreign policy as the center and culmination of political activities. They assailed the entire concept of man which complements this philosophy of power politics that stresses the qualities of physical prowess, honor, and obedience. The high evaluation of military virtues is a "dangerous prejudice, a carry-over from barbarism, a remnant of the former chaos."[19] "True fame consists not in the glory which the stupidity of the people connects with conquests and which the still more stupid historians love to praise to the point of boring the reader";[20] if the right name were to be given to conquests "which for so long have been praised as heroism,"[21] they would be called crimes.

The existing methods of diplomacy were so much geared towards power poli-

[18] D'Argenson, *Considérations sur le Gouvernement Ancient et Présent de la France*, Amsterdam 1764, p. 18.

[19] *Ibid.*, p. 20.

[20] Condillac, "Le Commerce et le Gouvernement, 1776," in Condillac, *Oeuvres Complètes*, vol. IV, Paris 1821, p. 278.

[21] Condorcet, "Discours de Réception à l'Académie Française," in Condorcet, *Oeuvres*, ed. A. C. O'Connor and M. F. Arago, vol. I, Paris 1847–1849, p. 396.

tics and war that they could never serve the opposite purpose — the preservation of peace. The main target of the philosophes was the assumption that the only possibility and guarantee for peace lay in the maintenance of a balance of power among the states. There is hardly a philosophe and reformer who does not inveigh against the idea of balance of power, "this favorite idea of newspapers and coffee-house politicians."[22] This idea, "reducing the whole science of politics to knowledge of a single word, pleases both the ignorance and the laziness of the ministers, of ambassadors and their clerks."[23] In contrast to the ostensible aim of promoting peace, balance of power had, it was said, always done harm to a system of lasting peace and was opposed to it. The reason was that "the system of balance of power is a system of resistance, consequently of disturbance, of shocks and of explosions."[24] With the overthrow of this central concept of eighteenth-century diplomacy, the other concerns of the traditional diplomacy were also reevaluated and shown up in their futility and dangerousness. According to the philosophes, the conclusion of treaties and alliances, the most significant activity of eighteenth-century diplomacy, would not serve to establish friendly relations among states; treaties are nothing but "temporary armistices"[25] and alliances "preparations for treason."[26] Even when they are called defensive alliances, they are "in reality always of an offensive nature."[27] Diplomatic activity, thus being identical with double-dealing and pursuing purposes different from those it openly avows, needs to wrap itself in secrecy and has become an "obscure art which hides itself in the folds of deceit, which fears to let itself be seen and believes it can succeed only in the darkness of mystery."[28] Secrecy, therefore, is not — as the diplomats pretend — necessary for the efficient fulfillment of their functions; it only proves that they are conspirators planning crimes. Diderot, in a satirical piece entitled "Political Principles of Rulers," has summarized the views of the philosophes on the diplomacy of their time. "Make alliances only in order to sow hatred. . . . Incite wars among my neighbors and try to keep it going. . . . Have no ambassadors in other countries, but spies. . . . To be neutral means to profit from the difficulties of others in order to improve one's own situation."[29] Though different writers made different aspects of diplomacy — secrecy or formality of etiquette — the chief butts of their criticism, they were all in agreement that diplomacy could not be reformed by redressing any single abuse. The evil inherent in diplomacy could be removed only by a complete change in the attitude of those who ruled. Foreign affairs showed most clearly the ills of a world not yet ruled by reason. "The blind passions of the

---

[22] [Mirabeau], *L'Ami des Hommes ou Traité de la Population,* nouvelle édition 1759, 3rd part, p. 368.
[23] Mably, *"Principes des Négociations,"* in Abbé de Mably, *Collection Complète des Oeuvres,* vol. V, Paris 1784, p. 66.
[24] Gaillard, *loc. cit.,* pp. 79–80.
[25] Rousseau, "Extrait du Projet de Paix Perpétuelle de M. L'Abbé de Saint Pierre," in J. J. Rousseau, *Political Writings,* ed. C. E. Vaughan, vol. I, Cambridge 1915, p. 369.
[26] Guillaume-Thomas Raynal, *Histoire Philosophique et Politique des Établissements et du Commerce des Européens dans les deux Indes,* vol. VI, Genève 1781, p. 284.
[27] D'Argenson, *op. cit.,* p. 327.
[28] Le Trosne, *op. cit.,* p. 395.
[29] Diderot, "Principes de Politique des Souverains," in Diderot, *Oeuvres Complètes,* ed. J. Assézat, vol. II, Paris 1875, pp. 461–502.

princes"[30] were the cause of wars, conquests, and all the miseries accompanying them. A favorite story of the eighteenth century illustrating the arbitrariness which dominated foreign policy was the story of the palace window: Louvois, fearing disgrace because Louis XIV had expressed displeasure with Louvois' arrangements concerning the construction of the windows of the Trianon, instigated the King to renew the war against the Hapsburgs in order to divert his attention from architectural matters. As long as foreign policy continued to be determined by passions, by whims and arbitrary proclivities, diplomacy could be nothing else but "the art of intrigue."[31]

If one wants to reduce this whole complex of eighteenth-century ideas on diplomacy to a simple formula, it can be summarized as the establishment of a rule of reason. It is the same solution which the philosophes had for the problems of domestic policy. In view of the pre-eminence which they gave domestic over foreign affairs, they considered the introduction of a new and peaceful era in foreign policy dependent on a reorganization of domestic policy. It would even be enough to put the policy of France on a new basis. Since France was the hub in the wheel of European politics, the other nations would quickly follow the French lead; a new period in world history would begin.

Yet how could this change be effected? As much as the eighteenth-century reformers agreed on the basic concepts which we have sketched above, they differed on how their ideas could be realized. Some looked for a solution along conservative, others along radical, democratic lines.

Among those who had a more conservative outlook were the physiocrats. A great number of the philosophes — some in a more, others in a less orthodox way — belonged to the physiocratic school. Although today physiocracy is usually regarded as having propounded an original and important economic doctrine, the significance of physiocratic theories in the eighteenth century seemed to reach far beyond the economic sphere and to range over the entire structure of social and political life. The physiocrats called their political theory "economic policy," not because they were concerned solely with economic questions, but because, to them, economics and politics were identical. They believed that all political problems would be solved if the right economic principles were followed and the right economic measures adopted. The contrast to "economic policy" was the "old policy," the "false policy," or "power politics"; all of these terms were alternately used. "The essence of power politics consists of divergence of interests, that of economic policy of unity of interests — the one leads to war, frustrations, destruction, the other to social integration, co-operation, and free and peaceful sharing of the fruits of work."[32] The physiocrats elaborated this contrast between "the old policy" and "the economic policy," between an "artificial" and a "natural" political situation, with great gusto and especially emphasized that, as a result of the artificiality of the "old policy," dealings had to be shrouded in secrecy and mystery. The diplomats had to be actors — "competitors in

[30] Diderot in article "Paix" in *Dictionnaire Encyclopédique*, in Diderot, *Oeuvres Complètes*, vol. XVI, p. 188.
[31] Mably, *Oeuvres*, vol. V, p. 17.
[32] Baudeau, "Première Introduction à la Philosophie Économique, 1767," in *Physiocrates*, ed. Eugène Daire, vol. II, Paris 1846, p. 742.

grimaces"[33] — and each nation was barricaded behind its own frontiers, intent on making commercial treaties to its own advantage and to the disadvantage of its neighbor. In contrast, the new world in which the "economic policy" was to be realized would have an unrestricted exchange of goods. From mutual interdependence would emerge the realization that increase in one nation's wealth means increased wealth for all other nations, and that the interests of all nations are identical; consequently, there would be no advantage in enlarging one's own territory and combatting one's neighbor. A single measure, namely, the establishment of free trade, would bring about this miraculous change; it was up to the rulers of the states to take this one decisive measure. The physiocrats were favorites of many princes, and their faith in the power of reason was so strong that they believed in the probability of persuading the rulers of the states to make this change. They were no opponents of despotism; on the contrary, they were confident that the new order could be introduced quite easily with and by means of the prince's absolute power.

Other philosophes believed that the physiocrats were deceiving themselves by trusting in princely absolutism. These more radical thinkers saw despotism as an integral part of the old order which had to be overcome. The decisive step in establishing the new order was a change in political leadership; the people themselves had to take over control of political life. These writers were concerned with the problem of how to achieve an effective popular control of foreign policy. Condorcet, who was particularly interested in this question, constructed a mechanism which he considered suitable for this purpose. No convention between nations should be valid without approval of the legislative body. Moreover, as a further safeguard, he demanded that political treaties should be ratified by the single districts of a state. In case of an enemy attack, war might be declared, but only by the legislative; and a declaration of war would have to be followed immediately by new elections, which would give the people the opportunity to express their views on the war. Evidently Condorcet had no doubt that the people would always be peace-loving; the practical issue was to remove all obstacles to a direct expression of the popular will. Condorcet regarded diplomats as such an obstacle, as unnecessary middlemen. He had no use for them, nor for diplomatic arrangements establishing automatic obligations by which the freedom of action of a nation would be bound. "Alliance treaties seem to me so dangerous and so little useful that I think it is better to abolish them entirely in time of peace. They are only means by which the rulers of states precipitate the people into wars from which they benefit either by covering up their mistakes or by carrying out their plots against freedom, and for which the emergency serves as a pretext."[34] The picture which the philosophes envisaged of the relations among nations after the rule of reason had been established was implied in their criticism of the existing foreign policy: the former would be the reverse of the latter. Foreign policy should follow moral laws. There should be no difference between the "moral principles" which rule the relations among individuals and "moral principles" which rule the relations among states. Diplomacy

---

[33] [Mirabeau], *op. cit.*, p. 26.
[34] Condorcet, *Oeuvres*, vol. IX, p. 45; see also pp. 41–46.

should be "frank and open."[35] Formal treaties would be unnecessary; political alliances should be avoided particularly. Commercial conventions should refrain from all detailed regulations establishing individual advantages and privileges; they should limit themselves to general arrangements stating the fundamental rules and customs of trade and navigation. In such a world, the connection among the different states would rest in the hands not of governments but of individuals trading with each other.

If this picture of the foreign policy of the future was not very precise, there was a special reason. Foreign policy and diplomacy were regarded as typical phenomena of the *ancien régime*; they owed their importance to the fact that the rulers followed false ideals and egoistic passions instead of reason. The logical consequence was that in a reformed world, based on reason, foreign policy and diplomacy would become unnecessary, that the new world would be a world without diplomats.

III

The visible symbol of the alliance between the new republic and the philosophes was the meeting of Franklin and Voltaire in a Paris theater, embracing and kissing each other while the public applauded. In our context, an equally significant encounter was that of John Adams with the Abbé de Mably, a philosophe especially interested in the problems of foreign affairs; according to Adams, Mably "spoke with great indignation against the practice of lying, chicaning, and finessing, in negotiations; frankness, candor, and probity, were the only means of gaining confidence."[36]

The American commissioners were regarded in France as representatives of a new diplomacy, and they behaved as such. Silas Deane, whom the Continental Congress had dispatched to France even before independence had been declared, apologized in his first interview with the French Foreign Minister, Count Vergennes, for any violation of form which, inadvertently, he might have committed. "If my commission or the mode of introducing the subject were out of the usual course, I must rely on his goodness to make allowances for a new-formed people, in circumstances altogether unprecedented, and for their agent wholly unacquainted with Courts."[37] But Deane was not so humble as he pretended to be to Vergennes. The same day, he wrote a letter, full of contempt for ceremony and etiquette: "Parade and Pomp have no charms in the eyes of a patriot, or even of a man of common good sense."[38] When Franklin arrived to negotiate the alliance with France, he emphasized by the simplicity of his dress — his shabby brown coat and unpowdered hair — that he was the representative of a new and uncorrupted world; Franklin was probably too much of a skeptic, even about his own enlightened beliefs, to be unaware of the propagandistic value of such an attention-provoking attire. Such subtle irony was entirely alien to John Adams, who followed the others to Europe. With deadly seriousness, Adams lectured

[35] Le Trosne, *op. cit.*, p. 421.
[36] John Adams, *Works*, vol. III, p. 350.
[37] Silas Deane to the Secret Committee of Congress, August 18, 1776, in *New York Historical Society Collections*, vol. XIX: The Deane Papers, vol. I, New York 1887, p. 201.
[38] *Ibid.*, p. 219.

Vergennes, who had advised him to make some adjustment to prevailing diplomatic customs, that "the dignity of North America does not consist in diplomatic ceremonials or any of the subtleties of etiquette; it consists solely in reason, justice, truth, the rights of mankind, and the interests of the nations of Europe."[39]

The diplomatic tasks with which the American agents had to deal could only strengthen their interest in the ideas of the philosophes on foreign policy. The initial concerns of the American diplomats were to conclude an alliance with France and to persuade other Continental powers to an attitude favorable to the American cause. Then they were occupied with the peace negotiations which extended over a long time. When peace with England had finally been concluded, the relations of the newly recognized republic to other powers had to be placed on a permanent footing. As varied as these changing tasks were, one issue was central in all of them: the replacement of the monopolistically arranged bonds between England and America by new regulations of trade and the settlement of the commercial relations which in the future should exist between America and the European powers.

As the Model Treaty, which Congress had adopted in 1776, showed, the problems of trade had two aspects in the American mind: on the one hand, the Americans were anxious to avoid commercial treaties which would make American trade dependent on one power or a bloc of powers and, consequently, draw America into the political rivalries of the European powers. One aim of American policy, therefore, was to make trade as free as possible, because only a complete liberalization of trade could provide full security against the danger that close commercial relations might create a political dependency. On the other hand, the great importance of trade for American economic life made a smooth and uninterrupted flow of commerce urgently desirable; war, in which a strong seapower like England might stop ships and confiscate their goods as contrabrand or declare wide stretches of a coast as blockaded area into which no ships should sail, was the great threat, especially since America had no navy sufficient to protect her merchants. Another aim of American foreign policy, therefore, was to persuade other powers to the acceptance of principles of international law which would mitigate the impact of war on civilian life. America was particularly interested in having the neutral trade secured against interference so that "free ships would make free goods," in reducing the number of articles which could be confiscated as contraband, and in permitting application of the concept of blockade only to ports where the access could be effectively controlled.

Peace and commerce were also the focal ideas in the thinking of the philosophes on foreign policy. As we have seen, they were pacifists, deeply convinced of the usefulness of war and of the necessity to remove war from social life. They saw in commerce a great instrument for bringing about a new age of peace, if nations, instead of trying to further their own commerce at the expense of the commerce of another power, would permit a free flow of goods over the entire globe. Relations between nations would become purely commercial contacts, and the need for a political diplomacy with alliances and balance of power would disappear from the international scene. The ideas with which the Americans en-

---

[39] John Adams to Vergennes, July 18, 1781, in *The Revolutionary Diplomatic Correspondence of the United States*, ed. Francis Wharton, vol. IV, Washington 1889, p. 590.

tered the political theater of Europe were facets of the larger complex of enlightened eighteenth-century thought.

The close connection between the ideas of the philosophes and American foreign policy appeared clearly in the negotiations about commercial treaties which developed after peace with England had been concluded. Even though Americans had tried to hold firm to the principles of the Model Treaty in the preceding years, their foreign policy had naturally been subordinated to the exigencies of the fight for survival and of gaining all possible support against Great Britain. But after the independence of the United States had been internationally recognized, a new and systematic attempt at realization of these principles could be made. Several powers had made feelers towards negotiations about commercial treaties with the United States. Congress was divided about the handling of this question. Some members felt that the main effort should be directed to the re-establishment of commercial relations with Britain; as one member wrote: "The Treaty with Britain presses upon us with much greater weight than with any other nation."[40] But the majority of Congress was not convinced that the gains which the re-establishment of trade with Britain might bring could compensate for the disadvantages involved in making special concessions to England and in abandoning the attempt to establish trade on an entirely general and liberal basis. The report which Congress finally accepted was drafted by Jefferson;[41] it maintained the principles which had first been stated in the Model Treaty of 1776. Great Britain was named as only one among many other states with which the conclusion of treaties of "amity and commerce" would be desirable. The idea of the report was "to form a general system of commerce by treaties with other nations," rejecting special preferences in favor of liberal rules applicable to all nations. Furthermore, the report suggested articles which might limit as far as possible disturbances of trade in wartime. It recommended the appointment of consuls and general consuls, but it stated that it was "inconvenient at present" "to keep ministers resident at the courts of Europe"; this last suggestion, however, was eliminated from the final version of the report. On the basis of this report, Congress issued instructions to its diplomatic agent on May 7, 1784.

The first negotiations to which these new instructions were applied were with Frederick the Great of Prussia. Negotiations with Denmark and Prussia had already been underway when Congress composed its new instructions. Jefferson, who had taken an active part in drafting them, was appointed to serve with Franklin and Adams as American negotiators in Europe. After Jefferson had arrived in Paris and had conferred with Franklin and Adams, he was charged with investigating the changes required to adjust the documents, which had been drafted in the previous negotiations in Europe, to the instructions which Congress had sent. Jefferson decided "to take up the subject as it were anew, to arrange the articles under classes, and while we are reforming the principles to reform also the language of treaties, which history alone and not grammar will justify. The articles may be rendered shorter and more conspicuous, by simplify-

---

[40] Jefferson, *The Papers of Thomas Jefferson*, ed. Julian P. Boyd, vol. VII, Princeton 1953, p. 467.
[41] *Ibid.*, vol. VI, pp. 393–400.

ing their stile and structure."[42] This intention corresponded to a basic feature of Jefferson's mind; to him, style and structure were the external expression of clarity of thought. But one cannot help wondering whether, in simplifying the diplomatic language, Jefferson did not also intend to open the door for a diplomacy which would be divested of its character as a secret science.

Jefferson also drew up the communications which accompanied the revised treaty draft and which explained to the Prussian representative the reasons for the changes in the draft, particularly the insertion of two articles, one providing for the payment of war contraband in case of confiscation, the other protecting civilian life against the ravages of war. The American commissioners wrote that "it is for the interest of humanity in general, that the occasions of war, and the inducements to it should be diminished."[43] Measures to minimize the impact of war were a logical step in the continuing process of improving the law of nations. Since the beginnings of society when "war and extirpation was the punishment of injury," the development of the law of nations had gone forward "humanizing by degrees." Progress had been slow, so that "Ages have intervened between its several steps," but there was no reason why the law of nations should not "go on improving"; it was now a favorable occasion for accelerating this process: "As knowledge of late encreases rapidly, why should not those steps be quickened?" The enlightened belief in progress, coupled with the conviction of being at the threshold of a new age, found expression also in the further correspondence with the Prussian representative. The American commissioners felt that they were leading the way to an "object so valuable to mankind as the total emancipation of commerce and the bringing together all nations for a free intercommunication of happiness."[44] When finally the treaty had been approved by Frederick the Great, John Adams expressed his enthusiasm in words which, although they might indicate some reservation about having these humane measures quickly adopted by the entire world, still suggest that Adams was satisfied with seeing the course of American foreign policy set towards utopia: "I am charmed to find the King do us the Honor to agree to the Platonic Philosophy of some of our Articles, which are at least a good Lesson to Mankind, and will derive more influence from a Treaty ratified by the King of Prussia, than from the writings of Plato, or Sir Thomas More."[45]

The foreign policy of the young republic, with its emphasis on commerce and on avoidance of political connections, has usually been explained as a policy of isolation. Unquestionably, the English background of the ideas which served in the formation of the American outlook on foreign policy contained an isolationist element. However, if we place the ideas which guided early American foreign policy beside those of the European philosophes, it becomes clear that the isolationist interpretation is one-sided and incomplete: American foreign policy was idealistic and internationalist no less than isolationist.

In many minds, these two motives can be found interwoven in such a way that neither of the two elements can be regarded as predominant. This was char-

---

[42] *Ibid.,* vol. VII, pp. 476–477.
[43] *Ibid.,* pp. 491, 492.
[44] *Ibid.,* vol. VIII, p. 28.
[45] *Ibid.,* vol. VII, p. 465.

acteristic of Jefferson. He remained opposed to diplomacy, which he considered as "the pest of the peace of the world, as the workshop in which nearly all the wars of Europe are manufactured."[46] In 1792, when a number of diplomatic nominations had been submitted to the Senate by Washington for approval, Jefferson suggested that diplomatic representatives should be sent by America only to those countries where geographic closeness or interests of commerce demanded a permanent representation; this meant to London, Paris, Madrid, Lisbon, and The Hague. Also, these appointments should be kept "on the lowest grades admissible."[47] Later Jefferson wrote that "Consuls would do all the business we ought to have."[48] Jefferson's inclination towards the adoption of what he called an "a-diplomatic system" sprang from his fear that America might become involved in European politics but, at the same time, he wanted to set an example to the entire world. Jefferson was convinced that the relations between nations in the future would take forms different from those of the diplomacy of the past. His belief in the emergence of a new spirit in international relations is beautifully expressed in a letter to Madison of August 28, 1789. Jefferson pleaded for acknowledging the duties of gratitude in America's relations to France: the often heard view that power and force ruled in the relations between nations "were legitimate principles in the dark ages which intervened between antient and modern civilisation, but exploded and held in just horror in the 18th century. I know but one code of morality for man whether acting singly or collectively."[49]

Thus, although the American outlook on foreign affairs contained two different elements, they could be combined; and then they reinforced each other. But they could also be contradictory. Then those who were concerned with foreign policy suddenly swerved from one extreme to the other. Unexpected resistance or obstacles might turn the utopian hopes for an imminent "reformation, a kind of protestantism, in the commercial system of the world"[50] into its reverse: demand for complete withdrawal from any contact with the outside world. The Americans might have to "recall their Ministers and send no more,"[51] as Adams wrote; or they ought "to stand to Europe precisely on the footing of China,"[52] as Jefferson formulated it. Yet it was immediately argued that this was not possible, because it would mean that the Americans would have to "give up the most of their commerce, and live by their agriculture."[53] It was "theory only."[54] In such moments, the egoistic insistence on isolation appeared no less unrealistic than the altruistic counsels of internationalism.

This dilemma was reflected in an episode which happened at the time of the

[46] Jefferson to William Short, January 23, 1804, "Documents," *American Historical Review*, vol. XXXIII (1927/8), p. 833.

[47] Jefferson to a Committee of the Senate, January 4, 1792, in Thomas Jefferson, *Writings*, ed. Paul Leicester Ford, vol. I, New York 1892, p. 170.

[48] Jefferson to William Short, January 23, 1804, printed *loc. cit.*, p. 833.

[49] Jefferson to James Madison, August 28, 1789, in Jefferson, *Papers*, vol. XV, p. 367.

[50] John Adams, *Works*, vol. VIII, p. 298.

[51] John Adams to John Jay, February 26, 1783, *The Diplomatic Correspondence of the United States of America from 1783 to 1789*, vol. II, Washington 1837, p. 574.

[52] Jefferson, *Papers*, vol. VIII, p. 633.

[53] *The Diplomatic Correspondence of the United States from 1783 to 1789*, vol. II, p. 574.

[54] Jefferson, *Papers*, vol. VIII, p. 633.

end of the War of Independence. Indignation about the brutal way in which England used her seapower had led a number of European states to form a league of "armed neutrality," with the purpose of defending the right of neutrals on the sea. This policy not only corresponded to the general aims of the foreign policy of the United States but also raised the hope of gaining from these powers support in the struggle against Britain. Thus, the United States was anxious to join the league, but, because a belligerent power could hardly become a member of a league of neutrals, the American advances were rebuffed. When, with the signing of the preliminaries of peace, this obstacle was removed and the Netherlands urged America to participate actively in the policy of armed neutrality, Congress took another look at the possible practical consequences of such a policy; it was realized that the league would make the United States a member of a political bloc. Thus Congress, in a resolution[55] which admitted that "the liberal principles on which the said confederacy was established, are conceived to be in general favourable to the interests of nations, and particularly to those of the United States," rejected further negotiations about entry into the league, because "the true interest of these states requires that they should be as little as possible entangled in the politics and controversies of European nations." The principle of avoiding political connections proved to be incompatible with progress toward freeing commerce, which was the great hope for overcoming power politics.

But as contradictory as isolationism and internationalism could sometimes prove themselves to be, these contrasts could be overlooked; and they could be regarded as compatible with each other because there was a common factor between them, though only of a negative character: isolationism existed in a sphere of timelessness; internationalism existed in the future. Neither existed in the world of the present. Thus the attitudes which the young republic had adopted had not yet satisfactorily solved the problem — either practically or theoretically — of how to chart a course in the world as it was.

[55] *Journals of the Continental Congress,* vol. XXIV, p. 394.

II
EXPERIMENT, REFORM, AND THE EMERGENCE OF DEMOCRATIC SOCIETY: 1789–1840

Independence from imperial domination and agreement upon a common constitution were only the merest beginnings of national development. For most Americans, the colonial experience was mainly intracolonial, and modes of national behavior would have to be established if the United States were to thrive. Not least of the national problems was politics, since the Constitution gave few clues as to how political institutions should be implemented. The most dramatic solution was the emergence of national party politics of a type mostly unforeseen in the eighteenth century. During the 1790's, the existence of national politics and a central legislature fostered the creation of two competing parties, and the election of 1800 demonstrated that our political system was capable of successful, peaceful transition from rule by one party to that of another.

Industry and commerce were also forced into new paths, since the heritage of mercantilism was only marginally applicable to the economy of new, quickly growing, and independent nations. America had to fight for her place in the international market, to develop the economic resources of the vast and expanding nation, and to work out ways of nationalizing the economy. The country expanded its production of exportable raw materials and began the process of industrialization, which helped to provide raw and manufactured goods both for its citizens and for the world market. Americans exported $20 million worth of goods in 1790 and $132 million in 1840. Banks and other financial institutions were developed to facilitate national economic life. The labor force grew and diversified, although one should remember that this phenomenon was particularly apparent in the South, where the number of Negro slaves rose from 700,000 in 1790 to more than 2.5 million by 1840. Both the benefits and difficulties of rapid economic expansion were apparent — most Americans prospered, but there were severe national economic setbacks in 1819 and 1837.

Social development was no less rapid. Americans emerged from the Revolution with a confident, evangelistic notion of their social potential. They no longer conceived of society as static, so they shaped their institutions to foster and accommodate change. The period saw dramatic changes

169

in schooling, and the development of prisons, alms houses, and insane asylums. Their goals were largely egalitarian, since the continent seemed to contain material resources sufficient for all, and they devoted a large part of their energy to reform of the social order, since it seemed logical and possible to create a proper world in which to live. Reforms of innumerable kinds were undertaken: temperance, women's rights, and abolition of slavery, to name a few.

The first fifty years of our national history witnessed dramatic territorial expansion—the national domain more than doubled, thanks largely to the Louisiana Purchase. The population grew and diversified as Americans moved westward and as large numbers of Europeans migrated here—commencing especially with the large Irish migration of the 1830's. Between 1790 and 1840 the population rose from just under four million to over seventeen million. New roads and canals began to link the spreading nation, and creative energy in divers fields was released. It was a period of rapid growth and change, characterized by buoyancy of spirit and breathlessness of expectation. The era of Jacksonian democracy seemed the culmination of these trends. There was a price to be paid for the gains of these early years, but in general Americans were not conscious of how soon they would have to pay the piper.

The Meaning of the Jeffersonian Ascendancy

RICHARD E. ELLIS

Although many historians have spoken blithely of the election of Thomas Jefferson as the "Revolution of 1800," they have seldom credited the Jeffersonians with doing more than turning the Federalists out of office. The Jacksonian era is more commonly thought of as the occasion of the democratization of American politics. Richard Ellis believes that we have underestimated the Jeffersonians, however, and contends that it was in the first decade of the nineteenth century that the democratic potential of the American Revolution began to be fulfilled. Ellis bases his analysis on the assertion that the public events of the Jefferson administration were ambiguous because the party itself was deeply divided between a radical-democratic agrarian wing and a much more moderate commercial agrarian wing. It was with the moderates, men such as Jefferson and James Madison, that middle-of-the-road Federalists found it possible to cooperate, and it was only well after 1800 that the moderates

*found themselves in control of the party and Jeffersonianism took on
its mature form. The Jeffersonians were thus not radical Democrats,
but they were deeply committed to the notion of popular sovereignty and to the protection of the agrarian segment of the economy
to which most Americans of the time belonged. The achievement
of the Jeffersonians was to unite the country in favor of democracy and to commit the central government's energy to the protection of the welfare of all Americans, rather than to that of only the
business elite, who were favored by the Federalists. The latent division within survived, however, and resulted later in the parallel
split between the Whigs and the National Republicans, on the one
hand, and between the Old Republicans and the Jacksonian Democrats on the other. Professor Ellis thus does much to restore the
democratic credentials of the Jeffersonians, but does he make it clear
that their notion of "democracy" was the same as that of the Jacksonians? Interestingly, Richard McCormick supports an opposing
theory in the essay following this one and argues that a deep and
fundamental divide separated the two first "democratic" administrations. What do you feel? Is the dominant "economic democracy"
of the moderate Republican-Federalists qualitatively different from
the subordinate "popular democracy" of the radical Jeffersonians?
In explaining the continuity between Adams Federalists and Madison Jeffersonians does Ellis explain too much?*

I

One way of understanding the meaning of Jeffersonian Democracy is to view
it as the final phase of the American Revolution. It is one of the most regrettable
aspects of the highly specialized nature of American historiography that students
of the early national period have tended to consider the years 1789–1815 as an
entity apart from the Revolution. Few historians who have written of the Confederation era take their stories beyond 1788, while those historians writing about
the years immediately following the adoption of the Constitution pay little attention to those years immediately preceding it.[1] Actually there is a great deal of
natural unity to the period 1775–1815. Bounded on both sides by wars with Great

From *The Jeffersonian Crisis: Courts and Politics in the Young Republic* by Richard E.
Ellis. Copyright © 1971 by Oxford University Press, Inc. Reprinted by permission.
    [1] One of the first historians to emphasize the continuity of issues before and after 1788
was Charles A. Beard. See in particular his *Economic Origins of Jeffersonian Democracy*
(New York, 1915). Since the early 1950's an increasing number of scholars has empha-
sized the influence of the Revolution on the period following 1788. For example: John
D. Barnhart, *Valley of Democracy, The Frontier Versus the Plantation in the Ohio Valley,
1775–1815* (Bloomington, 1953); E. James Ferguson, *The Power of the Purse, A History
of American Public Finance, 1776–1790* (Chapel Hill, 1961); Curtis P. Nettels, *The
Emergence of a National Economy, 1775–1815* (New York, 1962); Chilton Williamson,
American Suffrage from Property to Democracy (Princeton, 1960).

Britain, these years in America are marked by an attempt to come to terms with the implications of the Revolution. Most of the political leaders during these years were, in one way or another, involved in the Revolution; and most of the disagreements that occurred among them arose over their inabilities to agree upon the meaning of that event. Writing in 1786, Benjamin Rush noted, "we have only finished the first act of the great drama. We have changed our forms of government, but it remains yet to effect a Revolution in our principles, opinions and manners so as to accommodate them to the forms of government we have adopted."[2] It was this accommodation that dominated the politics of the following decades and was still going on when Jefferson took office as President in 1801.

If there is any consensus among historians about the nature of the American Revolution — and it is by no means clear that there is — it is that the Revolution was democratic in result though not in origin.[3] This was apparent in two separate but related ways. First, as a consequence of independence the king's authority was overthrown, and the structure of politics was altered completely. Prior to 1776 the fact that the great majority of the people had the right to vote had little practical effect on the existing power structure. The career of Thomas Hutchinson of Massachusetts illustrates this. A member of the General Court until 1749, when he made himself unpopular with his constituents by advocating anti-inflationary measures, Hutchinson never won another election, yet the House of Representatives immediately elected him to the upper house of the legislature. During the 1760's he was Lieutenant Governor of Massachusetts, Chief Justice of the Supreme Court, Commander of the Militia, and Probate Judge of Suffolk county; and in 1772 he became governor of the colony, having been appointed to all these positions by the king. Moreover Hutchinson's ability to attain high posts in the government for himself was made even more spectacular as he filled other important offices with friends and relatives. His brother-in-law Andrew Oliver held positions as a member of the Governor's council, Secretary of the Province, and Judge of the Inferior Court of Common Pleas of Essex county. One of his sons sat in the General Court as Salem's representative, and two other relatives, Peter Oliver and Benjamin Lynde, were judges of the Superior Court. A few prominent families dominated the politics of the other colonies in the same manner. In short, colonial America was ruled by a small group of men who, through the royal connection, or what was more typical, through oligarchic domination of the local system, often in opposition to the royal governor and his faction of favorites, controlled the governor's coun-

[2] Benjamin Rush to Richard Price, 25 May 1786, in Lyman Butterfield (ed.), *Letters of Benjamin Rush*, 2 vols. (Princeton, 1951), I, 388.

[3] Scholars who share this point of view, though little else, are: Merrill Jensen, "Democracy and the American Revolution," *Huntington Library Quarterly* XX (August 1957); Cecelia Kenyon, "Republicanism and Radicalism in the American Revolution: An Old Fashioned Interpretation," *William and Mary Quarterly* XIX (April 1962), 153–182; Richard B. Morris, "Class Struggle and the American Revolution," *William and Mary Quarterly* XIX (July 1962), 3–29; Bernard Bailyn (ed.), *Pamphlets of the American Revolution*, 4 vols. (1965–?), I, 169–90. Important exceptions to this point of view are Robert E. Brown, *Middle Class Democracy in Massachusetts* (Ithaca, 1955) and *Virginia 1705–1786: Democracy or Aristocracy* (East Lansing, 1964); also Daniel J. Boorstin, *The Genius of American Politics* (Chicago, 1953), 66–98.

cils, sat on the Superior and county courts, served as justices of the peace and senior militia officers, and also tended to control the election of representatives to colonial assemblies.[4]

This changed with independence, as the elimination of the royal connection and the establishment of republican government made the people the sovereign source of political authority in America. It did not, of course, mean the end of machine politics. But it did mean that in the future political power could be held for long periods of time only with the consent and support of the people. It made elections important, and it ushered in the age of the demagogue. During the 1780's this was most clearly manifested by the activities of John Hancock, George Clinton, and Patrick Henry, who completely changed the tone and style of American politics and who, to varying degrees, achieved positions of enormous power in their respective states by playing upon the hopes and fears of the people.[5]

Second, the constitutional debate with England touched off a genuine intellectual revolution in American political thought. Before 1760 the colonists had generally been too busy making their way in the New World to give much attention to abstract and theoretical questions of the rights of the ruled and their rulers.[6] But England's attempt to tighten up its colonial system during the 1760's, and America's determination to resist it, forced the colonists to think along constitutional and ideological lines. Consequently, as the debate developed over the next decade, Americans began to become aware of and to explore the complicated meanings of such concepts as "sovereignty," "constitution," and "representation."[7] What is especially significant about all this, however, is that innovative political thought did not stop with the Declaration of Independence, but continued and became increasingly radical as Americans debated among themselves about the kinds of political and economic systems under which they wished to live.

[4] Malcolm Freiberg, "How to Become a Colonial Governor: Thomas Hutchinson of Massachusetts," *The Review of Politics* 21 (October 1959), 646–56; Ellen E. Brennan, *Plural Office-Holding in Massachusetts, 1760–1780* (Chapel Hill, 1945), 32–35; Robert J. Taylor, *Western Massachusetts in the Revolution* (Providence, 1954), 11–26; Charles S. Sydnor, *Gentlemen Freeholders* (Chapel Hill, 1952); Jack P. Greene, "Foundations of Political Power in the Virginia House of Burgesses, 1720–1776," *William and Mary Quarterly* XVI (October 1959), 485–506; Oscar Zeichner, *Connecticut's Years of Controversy, 1750–1776* (Chapel Hill, 1949), 3–19; David S. Lovejoy, *Rhode Island Politics and the American Revolution, 1760–1776* (Providence, 1958), 5–31; Leonard W. Labaree, *Conservatism in Early American History* (Ithaca, 1959), 1–31; Frederick B. Tolles, *Meeting House and Counting House* (Chapel Hill, 1948), 109–43; Carl L. Becker, *History of Political Parties in the Province of New York, 1760–1776* (Madison, 1960), 5–22.

[5] Jackson T. Main, "Government by the People, the American Revolution and the Democratization of the Legislatures," *William and Mary Quarterly* XXIII (July 1966), 391–407, and *The Upper House in Revolutionary America 1763–1788* (Madison, 1967). See also Moses Coit Tyler, *Patrick Henry* (Ithaca, 1962), 214–356; E. Wilder Spaulding, *His Excellency George Clinton, Critic of the Constitution* (New York, 1938), 86–183; Herbert S. Allan, *John Hancock: Patriot in Purple* (New York, 1948), 175–296.

[6] Daniel J. Boorstin, *The Americans: The Colonial Experience* (New York, 1958).

[7] Bernard Bailyn (ed.), *Pamphlets of the American Revolution*, I, 90–202; Gordon S. Wood, "Rhetoric and Reality in the American Revolution," *William and Mary Quarterly* XXIII (January 1966), 3–32; Wood, *The Creation of the American Republic, passim*.

It was the interaction of these two developments — the enlarged power of the ballot and the highly politicized nature of society following independence — that was at the heart of the democratic trust of the American Revolution.

Many people were unhappy about the democratic potential of the Revolution and attempted to mitigate its effect. The result was a series of political battles on the state level during the late 1770's and throughout the 1780's involving the writing of state constitutions, the location of state capitals, state fiscal and land policies, the treatment of loyalists, and the confiscation of loyalist estates. Although the political alignments on these questions could be complicated, with personal differences, vested interests, and sundry local considerations playing important, sometimes even dominant, roles, the basic division in most of the states tended to be agrarian democrats versus commercial elitists. The initial outcome of those struggles varied from state to state, but the general direction was clear; for even in such states as Massachusetts and South Carolina where elite-minded groups had emerged from the Revolution in firm control, there was by the middle of the 1780's a real fear of agrarian legislation and social upheaval.[8]

The vulnerability of the state governments to popular control was a principal motive behind the movement for a strong national government.[9] In 1781 a serious attempt, which had even included the possibility of a military takeover, had been made to increase the powers of the Confederation government so that it could act as a check upon the irresponsible actions of democratic state governments.[10] This attempt failed, but the efforts to create a strong national government continued until the Constitution was ratified. To be sure, the struggle over the adoption of the Constitution was a very complicated one, but once local and particularistic interests are accounted for, the underlying division appears again to have been between cosmopolitan, commercial, and elite-minded Americans on the one hand, and provincial, agrarian, and democratic Americans on the other.[11]

The adoption of the Constitution, with its numerous restraints upon the politi-

---

[8] Jackson T. Main, The Anti-Federalists, 21–71; "Sections and Politics in Virginia, 1781–1787," William and Mary Quarterly XII (January 1955), 96–112; "Political Parties in Revolutionary Maryland, 1780–1787," Maryland Historical Magazine 62 (March 1967), 1–27; Robert East, "The Massachusetts Conservatives in the Critical Period," in Richard Morris (ed.), The Era of the American Revolution (New York, 1965), 349–91; Jensen, The New Nation (New York, 1950), 259–326.

[9] For example, see Edmund Randolph's opening speech to the Philadelphia Convention of 1787: He said, "our chief danger arises from the democratic parts of our state constitutions. . . . None of the state constitutions have provided a sufficient check against the democracy." In another place Randolph noted that the evils of the confederation period were to be found "in the turbulence and follies of democracy: that some check therefore was to be sought for against this tendency of our Governments." Elbridge Gerry noted, "The evils we experience flow from the excess of democracy." George Mason complained of "the oppressions and injustice experienced among us from democracy." And Madison: "No agrarian attempts have yet been made in this country, but symptoms of a leveling spirit, as we have understood, have sufficiently appeared in a certain quarter to give notice of the future danger." Max Farrand (ed.), The Records of the Federal Convention of 1787, I, 26–27, 48, 51, 101, 422–23.

[10] E. James Ferguson, The Power of the Purse, 109–76; Jensen, The New Nation, 28–84; Forrest McDonald, We the People (Boston, 1965), 1–32.

[11] Main, The Anti-Federalists, Conclusion; Benson, Turner and Beard, 214–28.

cal and economic activities of the states, was an important victory for the American commercial community. But the Constitution as written and ratified was only a frame of government; actual policies still had to be formulated and implemented. It was at this point that the unity of the American business community began to break down; for while merchants, bankers, artisans, planters and speculators had put up a united front against agrarian groups hostile to their commercial way of life, they were not in agreement about the particular kinds of economic policies which the national government should adopt. An early indication of this disunity was the skirmish which took place between Southern planters and Northern financial interests over Hamilton's proposals to fund the national debt at face value and to assume all the state debts. But the struggle, while intense, was easily compromised and did not create permanent divisions.[12]

Much more serious was the division in the American business community over foreign policy questions, which over the course of the 1790's was to lead to the establishment of political parties.[13] On one side were the great majority of American merchants, who, as a result of experiences during the 1780's, had come to believe that their self-interest, and the future of American economic growth, lay in the establishment and maintenance of close commercial ties with Great Britain. This group, led by Alexander Hamilton, believed that nothing should be done to disrupt or jeopardize America's relation with England, even if it meant compromising America's political independence and allowing economic domination by Great Britain. On the other side were men who were also nationalists, but who were not anglophiles and who had doubts about parts or all of Hamilton's economic program. This group was made up of that very small part of the American mercantile community which did not have close financial ties with England; and commercial farming interests, especially planters, led by James Madison, who were opposed to having the American economy controlled by a single country. The origins of the planters' attitude — and it was this group that dominated the leadership of the Republican party — lay in their experiences during the colonial period and even after independence, when dependence upon English and Scottish merchants forced them to sell their crops cheaply and to pay high prices for services, loans, and manufactured goods, thereby keeping the planters in a condition of perpetual debt. The commercial agricultural community in America wanted to see commerce extended to as many nations other than England as possible, in order to raise prices through competitive bidding for their crops. Madison argued that to do this it would be necessary to build up an American merchant marine and place discriminatory duties on English ships. Only in

---

[12] Ferguson, *Power of the Purse*, 289–326; Whitney Bates, "Northern Speculations and Southern State Debts: 1790," *William and Mary Quarterly*, XIX (January 1962), 30–48; Noble Cunningham, *The Jeffersonian Republicans, The Formation of Party Organization*, 1789–1801 (Chapel Hill, 1957), 3–32.

[13] There appears to be a general consensus among historians of the early national period on this point. See Joseph N. Charles, *The Origins of the American Party System* (New York, 1961), 91–140; William N. Chambers, *Political Parties in a New Nation, The American Experience 1776–1809* (New York, 1963), 34–129; Cunningham, *The Jeffersonian Republicans of Massachusetts*, 74–169; Young, *The Democratic Republicans of New York*, 345–442; Prince, *New Jersey's Jeffersonian Republicans*, 41–69; Harry Ammon, "The Formation of the Republican Party in Virginia, 1789–1796," *Journal of Southern History*, XIX (August 1953), 283–310.

this way, he believed, would it be possible to combat Great Britain, which "has bound us in commercial mannacles, and very nearly defeated the object of our independence."[14]

Although the conflict between Hamilton and Madison over the future course of American economic development began simply as a division within the American commercial community, it was immediately complicated by the outbreak of the French Revolution. At first most Americans hailed the overthrow of the *ancien régime:* the French Declaration of the Rights of Man and the Citizen set forth objectives similar to those of the Declaration of Independence and indicated that an important world power had embarked upon a republican experiment in liberty similar to America's. However, the execution of Louis XVI and the rise of Jacobinism quickly alienated those Americans who had been determined to suppress the radical implications of their own Revolution. But not all Americans were willing to turn their backs on the French Revolution, even after it entered its most radical phase. Extreme democratic-minded Americans continued to support it enthusiastically, their point of view finding expression in many of the Democratic-Republican societies founded to demonstrate America's support of the French Revolution.

The proponents of a radical kind of popularistic democracy, having played an important role in state politics during the 1780's and having formed an essential — even dominant — part of the Anti-Federalist coalition in the struggle over the adoption of the Constitution, did not simply cease to exist after the battle of 1787–88.[15] Despite the fact that they had been defeated in 1788, betrayed by many of their leaders, disappointed by the kinds of amendments that were grafted upon the Constitution, and generally excluded from positions in the new national government, agrarian democrats nevertheless remained a potent political force and added an important dimension to the political battles of the last decade of the eighteenth century.[16]

The continued significance of the agrarian democratic persuasion during the 1790's complicated matters for commercial interests hostile to Hamilton's foreign policy. The essential difference between Hamilton and Madison was that one

[14] *Annals*, 1:1, 238; Paul Varg, *Foreign Policies of the Founding Fathers* (East Lansing, 1963), 70–94; Merrill Peterson, "Thomas Jefferson and Commercial Policy, 1783–1793," *William and Mary Quarterly* XXII (October 1965), 584–610; McDonald, *E Pluribus Unum*, 68–77.

[15] It has recently become fashionable to deny the existence of Anti-Federalist sentiment after the adoption of the Constitution. See the works cited in note 13. Young's book on New York is the only exception.

[16] I do not mean to claim that the Anti-Federalists existed as an organizational entity on the national level, for they did not. Rather I am arguing that their ideas continued to be attractive to a large segment of the electorate. Moreover, on the state level there are some indications that the alignments of the 1780's may have continued on into the early 1790's. Norman Risjord, "The Virginia Federalists," *Journal of Southern History* XXXIII (November 1967), 486–517; Young, *The Democratic-Republicans of New York*, 109–66. The story of what happened to the Anti-Federalists during the 1790's has yet to be told. That their point of view still existed can be seen by examining the rhetoric of the Democratic-Republican societies. On this point see particularly Eugene Link, *Democratic-Republican Societies, 1790–1800* (New York, 1942), esp. chapters III and V. Many of Link's interpretations are questionable, but his is nonetheless an important book because it shows the continued existence of extreme democratic ideas during the 1790's.

was pro-British while the other was anti-British. Yet there were exigencies — the alliance of 1778 with France, the outbreak of war between France and England, and Washington's neutrality proclamation — that forced Madison and his followers to adopt a pro-French position. But they did this only reluctantly and in such a way as to disassociate themselves as much as possible from the more radical, agrarian democratic elements who began to re-enter politics on a large scale in 1793–94: Jefferson, Madison, and their followers either held themselves aloof or tried to control the proceedings of the Democratic-Republican societies, reacted coolly to Citizen Genêt's advances, were unsympathetic to the Whisky Rebellion (though equally critical of the repressive manner in which it was put down), did their best to avoid personal attacks upon President Washington's character, and perhaps most important of all, during the crucial battle over Jay's Treaty backed down rather than support amendments to the Constitution limiting the powers of the executive.[17]

In 1797, when John Adams became President and Thomas Jefferson Vice President, an attempt was made to form a coalition of moderates from both parties by achieving a rapprochement between the two leaders, but it failed.[18] Still, it was only after Hamilton and the High Federalists, with the initial co-operation of Adams, passed the Alien and Sedition Acts and began to place the country on a war footing, that the moderate and commercial Madisonian Republicans, fearing that Hamilton planned to make use of the army to destroy his internal political opposition and put an end to the Republic, entered into an open alliance with the more extreme democratic elements.[19]

Consequently, beginning in the spring of 1798 the Republicans' opposition to Federalist measures took on a new intensity and urgency. They uncompromisingly assaulted and denounced their opponents' centralizing policies, and they increasingly resorted to extremist rhetoric to distinguish themselves from the Federalists. Moreover, through the adoption of the Virginia and especially the Kentucky resolutions, the Republican party appeared to imply that it now favored changes in the Constitution which would restore the balance of power to the states. Often referred to as the "Spirit of 1798," this open and deliberate embracing of the Anti-Federalist point of view by many people who had supported the adoption of the Constitution contributed significantly to Jefferson's election in 1800.

The Republican party at the time of Jefferson's inauguration was not a homogeneous group with a single point of view. It was rather a diverse coalition whose only real bond was opposition to the Federalists. Indeed, two of the most im-

---

[17] Cunningham, The Jeffersonian Republicans, 62–66; Alexander DeConde, Entangling Alliance (Durham, 1958), 283–310; Irving Brant, James Madison, Father of the Constitution, 1787–1800 (Indianapolis, 1950), 416; Stephen G. Kurtz, The Presidency of John Adams (Philadelphia, 1957), 40–45.

[18] Lyman H. Butterfield, "The Dream of Benjamin Rush; the Reconciliation of Jefferson and Adams," Yale Review XL (Winter 1951), 297–319; Kurtz, Presidency of John Adams, 218–38; Dauer, The Adams Federalists, 112–19; Alexander DeConde, The Quasi-War (New York, 1966), 12.

[19] Risjord, The Old Republicans, 11–17; Dumas Malone, Jefferson and the Ordeal of Liberty (Boston, 1962), 359–424.

portant groups in the coalition, commercial farmers and agrarian democrats, had very little in common and were even political enemies on many local issues. Because of this it was by no means clear what Jefferson's victory in 1800 signified. Some Republicans expected it to mean a thorough overhauling of the Constitution and a change in the administration of the national government in a democratic, agrarian, states' rights direction. Others, viewing themselves as protectors of the constitutional settlement of 1788, hoped it would only mean changes in the area of foreign policy and in some of the government's personnel.[20]

It is a mistake, therefore, to argue, as some historians have done, that the true nature of Jeffersonian Democracy is to be found only in the "Spirit of 1798," and that the Republican party, while victorious at the polls, nevertheless failed to implement its program after it came to power in 1800.[21] To many of the more moderate members of the party the "Spirit of 1798" was at best a necessary evil, a means to the end of saving the country from High Federalist extremism. These moderate Republicans never had any intention of implementing many of their campaign promises. For the moderates, the meaning of Jeffersonian democracy is to be found in Jefferson's inaugural address and in his policy of conciliating his political enemies and harmonizing the different interests in the country. There were other Republicans, however, who viewed Jefferson's election as a divinely inspired event and who did wish to see the principles of the "Spirit of 1798" put into practice. Given the fundamental irreconcilability of these two points of view, it is not surprising that the most important political battles of the first decade of the nineteenth century took place between the moderate and radical wings of the Republican party.

II

The rapid, and in some parts of the country almost immediate, demise of the Federalist party after 1800 only served to heighten the differences between radicals and moderates within the Republican party. By 1805, following Jefferson's overwhelming victory in the presidential election of 1804 and the Republican party's rise to power in most of the states, the two wings had begun to fight their battles in full view of the public. An astute Federalist newspaper in an article entitled "Whence so much Third-partyism in States where democracy gains

[20] There is no direct organizational connection between the Federalists and Anti-Federalists of 1787–1788 and the Federalists and Republicans of the 1790's. But impressionistic evidence would seem to indicate strongly that almost all the Federalists of the 1790's had favored the adoption of the Constitution; although not everyone who favored the adoption of the constitution became Federalists, for many, like Madison, went into the Republican party. Likewise, almost all Anti-Federalists, with only a few important exceptions (Patrick Henry, Luther Martin, and Samuel Chase), mostly on the leadership level, became Republicans. So that there would appear to be some connection between political alignments before and after the adoption of the Constitution, though it is not a simple direct and lineal one.

[21] Henry Adams, *History of the United States of America During the Administrations of Thomas Jefferson and James Madison, 1801–1816*, 9 vols. (New York, 1891–96); Richard Hofstadter, "Thomas Jefferson: The Aristocrat as Democrat," in *The American Political Tradition* (New York, 1957), 18–44. It is also the standard interpretation found in most college textbooks.

the ascendancy?" described the difficulties of the moderate and eventually dominant wing of the Republican party in this manner:

> There are among the leaders of the democrats, many men who have sense enough to know that the principles they advance, in opposition to federalism, tend to the subversion of order and the destruction of society. They sin against light, knowingly and willfully. — But as there is no other way of putting down federalism and putting them selves up, they ostensibly unite with the real jacobins, and make with them a common cause. When they succeed, they well know that adherence to their declared opinions would ruin society and whelm themselves in the general destruction. Hence they are disposed to attempt some restraint, upon the very vice and passions they have cherished. They begin to adopt many of the salutary maxims of the federalists, but the floodgates they have opened are not easily shut. They find their pupils in violence and insubordination unmanageable, and are in turn denounced by them as tyrants, aristocrats and oppressors.[22]

The struggle between radicals and moderates for control of the Republican party took place on the national level during Jefferson's first administration. Battles were fought not only over how patronage should be dispensed and what to do about the Federalist-controlled judiciary, but also over other issues. On fiscal policy the radicals wished to indict the previous administrations for corruption, scale down and perhaps even repudiate part of the national debt, and abolish the first Bank of the United States. The moderates, on the other hand, wished only to reduce government spending, pay off the national debt as quickly as possible, and neutralize the political activities of the national bank.[23] The radicals wished to change the Constitution in order to make its wording more precise, the judiciary and senate more amenable to popular control, and the states more powerful. Most moderates really did not want to see any changes made in the Constitution, if only because they feared that once they started to make changes they would not be able to control the kinds of changes made. "I confess I do not like tampering with established systems or forms of Government," wrote Thomas McKean, "and would rather submit to small real injuries under them, than set everything afloat. I never desire to see any more Revolutions, and pant after tranquility, peace and sociability."[24] Such thinking made many moderates reluctant to even support the seemingly harmless and necessary Twelfth Amendment.[25] The two wings of the party also split over the kind of

[22] *The Repertory*, (Boston), 11 October 1805.

[23] Adams, *History of the United States, 1801–1816*, I, 237–43; Risjord, *The Old Republicans*, 37–38; Raymond Walters, *Albert Gallatin*, 143–54; 170–84; Alexander Balinky, *Albert Gallatin, Fiscal Theories and Policies* (New Brunswick, 1958), 17–127; Bray Hammond, *Banks and Politics in America from the Revolution to the Civil War* (Princeton, 1957), 114–43, 197–226. Jeffersonian fiscal policy is a subject much in need of further research.

[24] Thomas McKean to Uriah Tracy, 14 January 1804, McKean Papers, HSP.

[25] Jacob Crowinshield to George W. Prescott, 15 November 1803, Alexander C. Washburn Collection, MHS; Samuel Smith to Timothy Pickering, 29 December 1803, Pickering Papers, MHS; Lolabel House, *A Study of the Twelfth Amendment of the Constitution of the United States* (Philadelphia, 1901).

reception to be given the aged but still popular Tom Paine, who returned to America in 1804. The radicals wanted him to be given a hero's welcome and did so in many of the newspapers under their control; but Jefferson and the moderate-controlled national administration did not pay him a great deal of attention and even went so far as to have Sam Adams and William Duane request him to stop writing controversial newspaper articles on religious subjects.[26]

Radicals and moderates also battled on the state level. The timing and intensity of these struggles varied from state to state and depended most importantly upon the relative strength of the Federalists and the ability of agrarians and radicals to organize and articulate their demands. In Kentucky and Georgia, where the Federalists were weak and agrarians active, the divisions in the Republican party had already become apparent during the 1790's, thus foreshadowing the struggles that were to take place in most of the other states after 1800. The rise to power of the Jeffersonians coincided with a new wave of constitution writing and numerous unsuccessful attempts to rewrite older constitutions, which forced radicals and moderates to declare themselves on just how democratic they wanted the fundamental law of their state to be.

Banking was another issue. For all their hostility to banks during the 1790's, the Jeffersonians, once in power, established more state banks than the Federalists had ever thought of creating.[27] Much of this was deliberate on the part of the moderates and bitterly opposed by the radicals. True, it still remains to be proved that the alignments on the banking issue were the same or similar to those on judicial and legal reform, but there is strong impressionistic evidence to indicate that they were. For example, commenting on an electoral campaign in Virginia, where there was no real judiciary struggle but where there was a bitter fight over the establishment of a bank, Samuel Smith wrote in 1805, "It is a struggle . . . between those who would carry Democracy to lengths dangerous to civil society . . . and those whose good sense, talents, and abilities, produce the present state of things and wish to proceed no further in reform."[28]

This mixed picture makes it impossible to explain the significance of Jeffersonian Democracy simply in terms of Jefferson's election in 1800. A series of full-scale political battles had to be fought within the Republican party during the first decade of the nineteenth century before the meaning of Jefferson's election became clear. The real meaning of Jeffersonian Democracy, it would seem, is to be found in the political triumph of the moderate Republicans and their eventual amalgamation with the moderate wing of the Federalist party. This represented a victory of moderation over the extremism of the ultra-nationalist, neo-mercantile wing of the Federalist party on the one hand, and the particu-

[26] Tom Paine to the Editor of the National Intelligencer, 1 January 1803, Foner (ed.), *Complete Writings of Tom Paine*, 1432–33; Tom Paine to Samuel Adams, 1 January 1803, ibid., 1434–38; Tom Paine to Thomas Jefferson, 12 January 1803, ibid., 1439; Gideon Granger to William Eustis, 18 November 1802, William Eustis Papers, LC; William Duane to Thomas Jefferson, 27 November 1802, Jefferson Papers, LC; Levi Lincoln to Thomas Jefferson, 6 December 1802, ibid.; Alfred Owen Aldridge, *Man of Reason* (Philadelphia, 1959), 273–79.

[27] Hammond, *Banks and Politics*, 144–96; Goodman, *The Democratic-Republicans of Massachusetts*, 170–81; Gilpatrick, *Jeffersonian Democracy in North Carolina*, 149–52; Prince, *New Jersey's Jeffersonian Republicans*, 151, 158, 165–67, 172–73, 252.

[28] Samuel Smith to ?, 14 December 1805, Samuel Smith Papers, LC.

laristic, Anti-Federalist–Old Republican wing of the Democratic-Republican party on the other. It meant, as one moderate wrote, that a successful defense had been made against all attacks upon the true principles and institutions of the American Revolution whether "under the mask of Federalism, artfully employed to disguise monarchy; or in the garb of Democracy, unworthily employed as a cover for anarchy."[29] For the over-all development of American democracy it meant the preservation of a government that was to be responsive but not directly and immediately controlled by the people.

There is a remarkable unity to the period 1776–1815. The constitutional struggles of the 1780's were over the question of how powerful the legislature should be, those of the 1790's involved the executive branch primarily, and so it was, in a way, natural for the final phase of the constitutional struggle to center on the judiciary. As John Adams noted in 1815, "the last twenty years of the last century, and first fifteen years of this may be called the age of Revolutions and Constitutions."[30]

III

It yet remains to explore the significance of the triumph of the moderate Republicans after 1800. Did it simply ensure the preservation of the constitutional settlement of 1788 and pave the way for the adoption of Federalist policies under Republican control? Or did Republican policies represent something different from those of the Federalists and help establish a new set of political and economic forces on the American scene? The answer is very much the latter; for to argue, as so many historians have done, that all the Republicans in power did was to out-federalize the Federalists is to fundamentally misunderstand the significance of the years of the Jeffersonian ascendancy.

Politically, the Jeffersonian ascendancy meant that for the first time since the country had embarked upon its "experiment in liberty" the official sources of power were completely under the control of people who were unqualifiedly committed to a republican form of government. While it is true that the overwhelming majority of the Federalists had shared this commitment, a small and powerful group in the Federalist party had shown a decided willingness to make use, among other things, of the army to thwart majority rule when circumstances warranted. Centered around Robert Morris during the early 1780's and around Alexander Hamilton during the 1790's, these High Federalists were probably the most influential and dynamic minority that America has ever known. They had no counterpart in the Republican party. In short, the Jeffersonian triumph of 1800 probably secured the liberal tradition in America.[31]

In like manner the Republican party also contained a point of view that was not to be found in the Federalist party. For agrarian democrats invariably be-

[29] *Freeman's Journal* (Philadelphia), 25 March 1805.
[30] Quoted in Peter Gay, "The Enlightenment," in C. Vann Woodward (ed.), *The Comparative Approach to American History* (New York, 1968), 42. For a penetrating study of the coming of the War of 1812 as a crisis in republicanism see Roger H. Brown, *The Republic in Peril: 1812* (New York, 1964).
[31] It seems to me that Louis Hartz, in *The Liberal Tradition in America*, a truly brilliant book, has greatly underestimated the threat of a military takeover that existed in America during the last two decades of the eighteenth century.

came Jeffersonians. They may not have been very important politically during Washington's administrations, but their influence increased sharply between 1798 and 1800, and they played an important role in the political battles of the first decade of the nineteenth century. The fact that the Federalists were no longer politically very important after 1800 allowed the moderate and radical Republicans to become the dominant political forces in the country, and, as a result, the tone, style and content of American politics shifted in a decidedly democratic direction.

Another important difference between the Federalists and moderate Republicans was in their attitudes toward massive popular participation in politics. Neither group thought it a good thing to appeal to the passions and prejudices of the public. But the moderate Republicans, never willing to publicly denounce the concept of majority rule, were prepared for and capable of playing the game of democratic politics when circumstances required. The Federalists, on the other hand, publicly denied the ability of the people to govern themselves, stressed the need for elitist guidance, and never were able to successfully practice the art of popular politics. This is an important point because it helps explain why, as moderate and radical Republicans battled each other during the first decade of the nineteenth century, voter participation reached new highs in most states. It also helps explain why political democracy was an established fact of life, on a theoretical if not always a practical level, well before the Jacksonians came to power.[32]

Even though the moderate Republicans were more willing than the Federalists to play upon the hopes and fears of the electorate in order to obtain and maintain power, they nonetheless shared with the Federalists the prevalent eighteenth-century view that party politics was a bad thing. Madison had pointed out in *The Federalist* No. 10 that any kind of faction could be dangerous to the life of the republic, and that a majority faction was the most dangerous faction of all. Jefferson put it differently in his first inaugural address when he claimed, "We are all republicans — we are all federalists," but he meant much the same thing. The most important part of the moderate Jeffersonian political program, therefore, was that of putting an end to the first American party system, which had developed during the 1790's. And in 1817, as James Monroe's first administration ushered in the "Era of Good Feelings," it appeared as if they had succeeded.

There were also important differences between the economic policy of the Federalists and that of the moderate Republicans. The economic policies of the Federalist party when it was in power spoke to the needs of the American mercantile community and its English connections. Because this group represented at best only a small percentage (10 per cent would be a very liberal estimate) of the American population, Federalist policies, by necessity, became tied to maintaining an elite-directed political order. The moderate Republicans, on the other hand, placed special emphasis upon the agricultural sector of the economy as the base from which the country was to undergo its economic growth; and because such a large portion of the population was involved in agricultural pursuits,

[32] For a different interpretation, which, in my opinion, greatly overemphasizes the importance of the Federalist Party after 1800, see Fischer, *The Revolution of American Conservatism*, 182–99.

the moderate Republicans were able to operate successfully, though not always happily, within a democratic framework of politics.

Closely related to all this were the attitudes of the two groups towards the settlement and economic development of the west. The Federalists had never been happy about the flood of settlers that began to move across the mountains after the Revolution. Indeed, they feared its consequences, for as new states entered the union they overwhelmingly supported the Republican party. While in power, therefore, the Federalists did their best to retard the settlement of the west: they only sold land in large lots and charged high prices; they attempted, in one of those happy conjunctions of interest and humanity, to do justice to Indian claims; and they only reluctantly, in deference to political necessity, put pressure on Spain to open the Mississippi to American navigation. In contrast, the moderate Republicans encouraged the growth and development of the west: they reduced the size of tracts of land needed for a minimum purchase, and, until 1820, sold much of the national domain to settlers on credit; they treated the Indians in the old northwest and southwest very harshly, and eventually removed those who remained to the Missouri river; and they adopted a very aggressive stance toward the New World possessions of France and Spain, which led first to the Louisiana Purchase and then to the acquisition of Florida.[33]

Moderate Republicans also were aware that real dangers existed in the too rapid settlement of the west. For if settlement were allowed to take place in an indiscriminate and haphazard fashion, the number of people outside the market economy would increase. Many people in post-Revolutionary America recognized that this could be dangerous, because there existed a great gulf, one that could be harmful to the very fabric of society, between those who were and those who were not part of the cash nexus. To offset this danger, Jeffersonian land policy attempted, though unsuccessfully, to bring about a controlled and orderly settlement of the west, and harshly treated the large number of squatters who settled on the unsurveyed part of the public domain.[34]

To ensure the commercialization of the west, moderate Republicans also favored a system of internal improvements. One demonstration of this was the provision made at the time of Ohio's admission as a state, that part of the proceeds from the sale of its public lands be used to help build the national road. Another was Jefferson's call, in his second inaugural address, for an amendment to the constitution which would allow the Federal government to apply the surplus revenue *"in time of peace* to rivers, canals, roads, arts, manufactures, education and other great objects within each state." He repeated this request even more strongly in his sixth annual address to Congress. In 1808 Gallatin presented an elaborate plan for a national system of internal improvements which provided for a complex of roads and canals to link the country together, North to South, and East to West. A series of circumstances prevented Gallatin's plan from being brought to fruition by the Federal government, but it nevertheless represented one of the greatest hopes of moderate Republicans and was

[33] Payson Jackson Treat, *The National Land System, 1785–1820* (New York, 1967); Reginald Horsman, *Expansion and American Indian Policy, 1783–1812* (East Lansing, 1967).
[34] Treat, *National Land System*, 101–43; Benjamin Horace Hibbard, A *History of the Public Land Policies* (Madison, 1965), 144–51.

eventually implemented through an alliance of public and private enterprise at the state and national level. Nor was it entirely fortuitous that the steamboat, which was to do so much to spread the market economy through the west, was first effectively developed in America by Robert Fulton, under the sponsorship of Robert R. Livingston, an important agricultural-minded moderate Republican from New York.[35]

Although moderate Republicans placed primary emphasis upon the development of commercial agriculture, they were neither antagonistic nor indifferent to the other sectors of the economy.[36] "You may be assured not a man in the administration is an enemy to commerce," wrote Jacob Crowninshield, an important merchant and moderate Republican from Massachusetts. "I will not say so much of their opposers. The Govt. may mistake what is the real interest of Commerce, but surely Mr. Jefferson has done enough to show that he has no hostile views to the Commercial interest."[37] The main thrust of the moderate Republican economic policy was to make the United States as self-sufficient as possible. To this end the administration was generally sympathetic to what it believed were the proper needs of the American mercantile community. "It is material," Jefferson asserted, "to the safety of Republicanism to detach the mercantile interest from its enemies and incorporate them into the body of its friends. A merchant is naturally a Republican, and can be otherwise only from a vitiated state of things."[38] The economic hopes of moderate Republicans came to partial fulfillment during the closing year of Madison's second administration, when a protective tariff was passed, the second Bank of the United States was established, and the Bonus Bill of 1817 was approved by both Houses, only to be vetoed by Madison for constitutional, not policy reasons.

Here then was another important difference between the moderate Republicans and the Federalists. The latter believed that American economic growth was dependent upon close ties with England, while the former stressed American self-sufficiency through the development of an internal market. What is especially important about this is that American economic growth between 1800 and 1828 generally took place in the way moderate Republicans envisioned it would: American agricultural staples brought in foreign capital; American industries, fostered by a protective tariff, gradually provided cheap manufactured

[35] See especially Joseph H. Harrison. "The Internal Improvement Issue in the Politics of the Union, 1783–1825." (Unpublished doctoral dissertation, University of Virginia, 1954), 135–200. See also Carter Goodrich, "National Planning of Internal Improvements," Political Science Quarterly, LXIII (March 1948), 16–44.

[36] Much too much has been made of Jefferson's agrarianism. It only lasted for a short time and does not seem to be very important during the years he was President. As for Madison, he never appears to have been an agrarian. William D. Grampp, "A Re-examination of Jeffersonian Economics," The Southern Economic Journal, XII (January 1946), 263–82; Joseph J. Spengler, "The Political Economy of Jefferson, Madison, and Adams," in David Kelly Jackson (ed.), American Studies in Honor of William Kenneth Boyd (Durham, 1940), 3–59; Joseph Dorfman, The Economic Mind in American Civilization, 1606–1865, I, 433–46.

[37] Jacob Crowninshield to Captain Nathaniel Silsbee, 13 January 1805, Crowninshield Papers, PM.

[38] Thomas Jefferson to Albert Gallatin, 12 July 1803, Ford (ed.), Works of Jefferson, X, 15–16.

goods and a domestic market for agricultural surpluses; the economic system thus generated was made possible by a series of roads and canals; and the domestic economy was regulated and a stable currency maintained by the second Bank of the United States.[39]

The moderate Jeffersonians, during the years of their ascendancy, created a new political and economic synthesis from the old dichotomies of the Revolution. For in the years immediately following independence most people generally believed that business enterprise and democracy were incompatible; what the moderate Jeffersonians did was to democratize business enterprise.

IV

During the years 1816 to 1819 an incomplete but nonetheless genuine fulfillment of the Jeffersonian belief in the harmony of interests took place as most Americans evinced an unbounded faith in the country's economic prosperity and a general lack of concern with politics. This came to an end with the Panic of 1819, when America underwent its first major national depression. The psychological shock was enormous, and what followed was a resurgence of radical and Old Republican principles, a decade of political strife and tension culminating in the election of 1828, and the re-establishment of a two-party system of politics.

Attempting to find the origins of the party divisions that took place between 1828 and 1848, some historians have argued that they can be traced back to the Federalist-Jeffersonian struggles of the 1790's.[40] Other historians have denied the existence of any connection between the first and second American party systems.[41] What has not been adequately appreciated, however, is the extent of the continuity between the moderate Republicans and the National Republicans and Whigs, on the one hand, and the agrarian democratic, radical, Old Republican wing of the Republican party and Jacksonian Democrats on the other.

One indication of the continuity between radical Jeffersonians and Jacksonians and between moderate Republicans and Whigs is to be found in the similarity of the categories of thought used in the various debates over judicial reform and in the debates over banking reform, which was the key issue on both the national and state levels during the 1830's. Advocates of a moderate kind of judicial reform and defenders of a stable and well-regulated currency argued primarily in terms of political economy, whereas the advocates of a radical kind of judicial reform and hard money proponents argued mainly in political and moral terms.

Also, while the continuity between the two sets of groups took place most clearly on an ideological level, there also exists a kind of tenuous connection between the personnel involved. Many of the most prominent Whigs — Henry

[39] Douglass C. North, *The Economic Growth of the United States, 1790–1860* (Englewood Cliffs, 1961).

[40] For example see: Arthur M. Schlesinger, Jr., *The Age of Jackson* (Boston, 1950), 267–82; Louis Hartz, *The Liberal Tradition in America*, 89–113.

[41] Lee Benson, *The Concept of Jacksonian Democracy, New York as a Test Case* (Princeton, 1961), 4–11; Richard P. McCormick, *The Second American Party System* (Chapel Hill, 1966), 3–16.

Clay, Nicholas Biddle, and John Quincy Adams — had at one time been moderate Republicans, while most surviving radicals and Old Republicans — William Duane, Felix Grundy, and John Randolph — tended to espouse the Jacksonian cause.

Recognizing that a real and definite, though imperfect, connection existed between the bi-factional party battles of the first decade of the nineteenth century and the two-party battles of the 1830's helps explain some of the paradoxes of the Jackson era. In particular, it helps explain why Whigs and Democrats could both claim to be good Jeffersonians; and why the party battles of the 1830's involved democracy but did not pose a threat to democracy. For what was involved was a contest between the positive state economic democracy of the moderate-Republican-sponsored American system and the negative popularistic political democracy of the agrarian, radical, and Old Republican wing of the Jeffersonian party.[42]

Political Development and the Second Party System

RICHARD P. MC CORMICK

Political scientists have been concerned with discovering how the growth of parties relates to the development of new nations: the integration of local parts into a political whole, economic growth, the creation of cosmopolitan social groupings. Richard McCormick, like Thomas Barrow in his essay on the Revolution, recognizes similarities between contemporary postcolonial nations and early America, and he wants to learn what part political organization played in the development of the United States. McCormick is impressed by the apparent discontinuity of party development in the period before the Civil War. He finds the party behavior of the Federalists and Jeffersonian Republicans to be primitive, insofar as the parties never took root in state politics and failed to have truly national impact. Thus the Federalists became exclusively a New Eng-

---

[42] Marvin Meyers in *The Jacksonian Persuasion* (Stanford, 1960), 13, describes the party battles of the 1820–1840 period as between the Whigs, who spoke to the "explicit hopes of Americans," and Jacksonians, who "addressed their diffuse fears and resentments." Lee Benson, *Concept of Jacksonian Democracy*, 104–9, says much the same thing when he claims the Whigs advocated a positive liberal state while the Jacksonians wanted a negative liberal state. For an interpretation somewhat similar to mine, though with much less stress on ideological factors, see Lynn Marshall, "The Strange Stillbirth of the Whig Party," *American Historical Review* LXXII (January 1967), 445–68. Finally, see the perceptive treatment in Peterson, *The Jefferson Image*, 17–111.

land party after 1800, and they had so little hope of electoral
victory by 1814 that they opted out of traditional politics altogether. In contrast, the second party system, which emerged out
of the elections of 1824 and 1828, made possible two-party competition throughout the expanding nation. Furthermore, the Demo-
crat-Whig system encouraged widespread and deep popular
participation through the use of party nominating conventions and
new styles of campaigning.] Why should there have been such a
dramatic difference in American party systems before and after
the election of 1824? McCormick suggests, very briefly, that the
answer lies in the increasing similarity of state political and constitutional arrangements, the shift to popular election of presidential
electors, the transportation revolution, rising economic expectations,
and the dramatic social transformation of the period. He also speaks
of the "increasingly egalitarian flavor of American society," to
which the parties responded by projecting "the same democratic
image." In short, the popularization of the parties was a response
to the change and democratization of American life. The advantage
of McCormick's approach to the study of politics is that he can
readily find relationships between politics and economic and social
change. Clearly some of the reasons for the decline of the Federalist-Jeffersonian parties and the rise of the Whigs and Democrats
have to do only with changes within the operation of the political
system. But our experience of contemporary life ought to suggest
the profound interconnections between politics and other aspects
of our lives: economic interests, racial, cultural, and geographical
affiliations, local and national custom.

Historians engaged in the study of political parties in the United States have
commonly focused their attention on individual parties as distinctive entities or
on the contests between parties. Studies of particular parties abound, both at the
state level and in larger contexts, and much of our political history is written in
terms of the clashing rivalry of Jeffersonian Republicans and Federalists, Whigs
and Democrats, or Democrats and Republicans. This approach has tended to
emphasize the differences between parties, especially in terms of their ideologies
and their constituencies. Worthy, rewarding, and time-honored as this usual
type of inquiry may be, there is an alternative — or complementary — approach
that can be expected to yield important insights into American political development. We can view the parties in existence at any given time as comprising a
party system; and with the party system, rather than individual parties, as the
phenomenon under scrutiny, we can proceed to new categories of questions and
hypotheses.

In studying individual political parties, for example, we may properly direct our attention to certain activities in which parties engage, such as nominating candidates, conducting campaigns, aggregating interests, formulating ideological positions, and managing governmental power. We may also be concerned with the structure, or pattern of organized relationships between leaders and identifiers, of a particular party. If on the other hand the party system is the object of our concern, we may endeavor to formulate understandings of how and under what circumstances party systems emerge, define the character of the party system in terms of various proposed typologies, and evaluate the contribution of the party system — as an element in the larger political system — to the handling of certain "problems" or the meeting of specified "crises." To the degree that we are able to develop suitable and meaningful concepts of broad applicability, we can engage in the comparative analysis of successive party systems within our own nation over a period of time as well as of party systems in different nations. By engaging in such comparative studies, we may hope to formulate and test hypotheses regarding the role of party systems in our culture.[1]

[Proceeding within this frame of reference, we can say that in the period between the establishment of a new government under the federal Constitution in 1789 and the disruption of the Union in 1860, two party systems rose and declined and a third was in the process of being formed as the nation confronted the crisis of disunion. The first party system, properly recognized as the first modern party system in any nation, was formed in the 1790's, deteriorated after 1815, and in a loose sense came to an end in 1824. The second party system had its origins in the presidential contest of 1824, acquired its full dimensions by 1840, and began to disintegrate in the early 1850's. By 1856, with the sudden rise of the Republican party to national prominence, there were signs that a third party system was emerging, although the disunited condition of the opposition parties down through 1860 and the cataclysmic effects of the Civil War and the subsequent era of Reconstruction left the eventual outlines of this party system in doubt until the 1870's.[2]]

These three party systems shared many attributes. They were all, for example, two-party systems. But they differed in the circumstances surrounding their origins — and in the cases of the first and second party systems in the circumstances associated with their disintegration — as well as in such important re-

---

[1] My own interest in the comparative study of party systems has been influenced in various ways by Gabriel A. Almond and James S. Coleman (eds.), *The Politics of the Developing Areas* (Princeton, 1960); Maurice Duverger, *Political Parties: Their Organization and Activity in the Modern State* (New York, 1954); Seymour Martin Lipset, *The First New Nation* (New York, 1963); Sigmund Neumann (ed.), *Modern Political Parties* (Chicago, 1956); and Joseph LaPalombara and Myron Weiner (eds.), *Political Parties and Political Development* (Princeton, 1966). For an admirable and full bibliography, see the last work, pp. 439–64. William N. Chambers has broken new ground with his brilliant conceptualization of American party systems in *Political Parties in a New Nation: The American Experience, 1776–1809* (New York, 1963); and in "Party Development and Party Action: The American Origins," *History and Theory*, III (1963), 111–17. I have found many of his formulations suggestive.

[2] Two useful but outdated standard histories of American parties are Wilfred E. Binkley, *American Political Parties: Their Natural History* (New York, 1962); and Edgar E. Robinson, *The Evolution of American Political Parties* (New York, 1924).

spects as the character of their sectional alignments, the comprehensiveness of their appeal to potential participants, and their apparent capacity for resolving conflicts. They are, however, comparable, and when sufficient descriptive studies become available, it should be fruitful to engage in a comparative analysis of all three. Then it may be possible to identify similarities and differences and advance hypotheses to explain them.

II

This brief introduction will suffice to establish the general conceptual framework within which my particular subject — the second American party system — is presented. My main concern will be to offer a descriptive account of the formation of this party system and its growth to maturity in the 1840's.[3] In order to place the subject in proper perspective, I shall deal briefly with some aspects of party development before 1824 and after 1840 and suggest some comparisons among the party systems under consideration.

By way of background, it is relevant to offer some very general observations on the conduct of politics before the emergence of the first party system. Unlike most nations of the world, the United States had considerable experience in operating representative institutions long before the advent of parties. Passing over the colonial period, which, as current research has demonstrated, was marked by a lively brand of politics inspired by an ideology that came to assume an increasingly democratic thrust, it should be recognized that even after 1776 republican governments functioned without political parties. In all of the states leaders were recruited, substantial proportions of the adult males were involved in the electoral process, stability was maintained, the legitimacy of governmental authority was recognized, and important conflicts were resolved. In this era of popular or semipopular non-party politics, independence was secured, grievous postwar problems were met, a new Constitution was adopted, and the federal government was established. Many of the obvious pre-conditions for the rise of parties existed in many of the states — elected legislatures, broad suffrage provisions, open competition for offices, a society of differentiated interests sharing common goals — but there was no semblance of a national party system, and, with two or three interesting but questionable exceptions, no party formation at the state level. Politics remained essentially local in scope and factional in character, and was therefore readily managed through informal structures.

Any general approach to the comparative study of American party systems must surely include some analysis of this pre-party era, for only through such an analysis can we test adequately any hypotheses that may be advanced to explain the emergence of parties shortly after 1789. Similarly, by comparing how certain functions conventionally ascribed to parties were actually performed in the pre-party period and after the advent of parties, we may be able to obtain valid understanding of what parties have contributed to our political system. Or, to put the matter differently, what obvious deficiencies existed in the political system before the 1790's that were rectified by the formation of parties? These questions can only be raised at this point; not until we have available well-

---

[3] Much of the material in this essay is drawn from my study, *The Second American Party System: Party Formation in the Jacksonian Era* (Chapel Hill, 1966).

conceived studies of colonial and state politics before 1789 can they be answered with any assurance.

National parties did not form during the Confederation period, but within a few years after the establishment of the new federal government; and surely by 1795, there were clear signs that party formation was well under way at all levels of government.[4] The origins of these parties can be detected first in cleavages that developed within the highest level of the national administration. Next, comparable factions formed within Congress. The emergence of these congressional factions encouraged the formation of parties at the state level. Finally, successive contests for the presidency in 1796 and 1800 provided an additional stimulant and served to focus and reinforce party feelings.

In endeavoring to account for the creation of parties at this particular time, we are obliged to ask what new conditions arose in the 1790's that seemingly created an environment more favorable to the formation of national parties than had maintained a decade earlier. It is my view that the critical new factor was the creation of a national political arena as the result of the adoption of the federal Constitution. Politics assumed an entirely new dimension — a national dimension — and the informal techniques of political management that had sufficed previously were replaced by party techniques. In particular, the constitutional arrangements for electing a President encouraged co-operation among political leaders throughout the nation in behalf of particular candidates. In quite a different way, the election of members of the House of Representatives by popular vote served to relate state and national politics. As parties were delineated on this national basis, the same alignments became operative in contests for state and even local offices.

1ST
system
*

Overly simple as this formulation may appear, it is not without its complications. It would seem that down to 1796, at least, we are confronted with a fairly clear case of parties whose origins were of the "interior" type, or "internally created" parties, to employ Maurice Duverger's typology.[5] That is, parties were formed first within the Congress and then were extended to the electorate. The complication arises because almost at once — in 1796 — quite a different influence entered the scene; namely, the contest for the presidency. The rivalry between John Adams and Thomas Jefferson in 1796 and again in 1800 served not only to dramatize and polarize the emerging partisan cleavage: it also enlarged party strife beyond the bounds of congressional districts, bringing it to embrace entire states and, by extension, the whole nation. Without pausing to develop this admittedly crucial point, I would contend that it was the contest for the

---

[4] In addition to Chambers's *Political Parties in a New Nation*, which provides the best summary account of early party formation, two outstanding works are Joseph Charles, *The Origins of the American Party System* (Williamsburg, Va., 1956); and Noble E. Cunningham, Jr., *The Jeffersonian Republicans: The Formation of Party Organizations, 1789–1801* (Chapel Hill, 1957); see also Manning J. Dauer, *The Adams Federalists* (Baltimore, 1953). I share many of the understandings that Paul Goodman has set forth in his essay on "The First American Party System," in this volume. In particular, I agree with his insistence that the creation of a national political arena and its particular character was the crucial factor in the array of preconditions for the formation of national parties.

[5] Duverger, *Political Parties*, xxiii–xxxvii.

presidency that was to exert the determining influence on the structure of the American party system.

The first party system, launched with such enterprise and vigor in the 1790's, soon entered upon what might be termed a stage of arrested development. It did not become established in the newer states that entered the Union after 1796; it soon languished in the Southern states; and in some other areas it succumbed to factional discord. By 1824 the remnants of the first party system possessed some vitality in only five states — Maine, Massachusetts, New Jersey, Delaware, and Maryland — although there were numerous isolated instances elsewhere of Federalists still offering challenges to their Republican adversaries.[6] Vestiges of old party organizations survived in some cases and party identities lingered on, but elections were rarely contested within the framework of the party system.

The first party system, then, can be seen in terms of failure as well as success. It failed to achieve truly national dimensions and, quite obviously, it failed to survive; and it also came perilously close to recording an even more serious failing. As the party system matured it became increasingly unbalanced. That is, the Republicans achieved such a lopsided superiority on a national basis that their Federalist opponents could scarcely hope to compete. What rendered this situation especially ominous was that the Federalist strength was sectionally concentrated, chiefly in New England, and that strength could now scarcely be effective in national politics. In consequence, the Federalists experienced a keen sense of political frustration, amounting to a sense of loss of their political efficacy. Much of New England's disaffection during the War of 1812 can be related to this factor, and the Hartford Convention, with its demands for revision of the constitutional "rules of the game," and even its implied threat of a division of the Union, brought the tensions to a crisis. What the ultimate result might have been had Andrew Jackson's victory at New Orleans in 1815 not transformed popular reactions to the war and to the record of the national administration must remain problematical. It can at least be suggested that the first party system as of 1814 was failing lamentably in achieving national integration and was even bringing the very legitimacy of the government into question. In other terms, the first party system was a failure because the parties became excessively unbalanced and took on a sectional alignment to the point where one sectionally oriented party, feeling that it could not compete, would no longer play the game according to the recognized rules.

In sequel, the first party system in its latter years — after 1815 — can be held responsible for a peculiar example of a "crisis of participation." Having failed to secure a revision of the rules, and having lost any prospect of electoral success, the Federalists in many states simply withdrew entirely from the arena of politics. In New Hampshire, for example, where the Federalists ceased to contest for state offices after 1817, voter participation declined from a high of slightly more than 80 per cent of those eligible in the gubernatorial election of 1814 to a low

---

[6] Contrary to some understandings, the Federalist party did not experience an abrupt demise in 1815. Indeed, it was still amazingly vigorous as late as 1826 in Delaware — see John A. Munroe, *Federalist Delaware, 1775–1815* (New Brunswick, N.J., 1954). Two of the best studies on the Federalists are David Hackett Fischer, *The Revolution of American Conservatism: The Federalist Party in the Era of Jeffersonian Democracy* (New York, 1965); and Shaw Livermore, *The Twilight of Federalism* (Princeton, 1962).

of 44 per cent by 1822. In Connecticut, for similar reasons, voter participation dropped from 45 per cent in 1819 to 22 per cent by 1822; in Vermont there was a comparable decline from 66 per cent in 1818 to 25 per cent by 1821; and in Rhode Island there was an abrupt falloff from nearly 50 per cent in 1818 to 15 per cent in 1819.[7] In other states, as party competition languished, voter participation generally sank to a low level.

Why did the first party system disintegrate? If we could answer this question with complete authority we should no doubt possess an important key to understanding the nature of the system. Without attempting to offer a comprehensive explanation for the breakdown of the parties, we could propose the simple proposition that the failure of the Federalists to extend, or even maintain, the bases of support they held in 1800 brought about a condition of extreme party imbalance. At this point the Federalists confronted the alternatives of rebelling against the system or withdrawing from it. After experiencing failure with the first alternative, they adopted the second in most states. No longer confronted by a formidable opposition, the Republicans in most areas succumbed to internal factionalism.

Approaching the problem from even a narrower perspective, we could advance the hypothesis that the first party system disintegrated because the chief purpose for which it had been formed had lost its urgency. That is, the fact that the contest for the presidency subsided after 1800 deprived the party system of the main source of its vitality and even the reason for its existence. The fortuitous availability of the members of the "Virginia Dynasty," the succession of Jefferson, Madison, and Monroe, and the failure of the Federalists as politicians to grasp the full significance of the importance of the presidential contest, together with certain impediments that inhered in the existing constitutional and social environment, all combined to reduce and ultimately eliminate the contest for the presidency as the stimulus to party action. This hypothesis — that the contest for the presidency provided the first party system with its crucial function — would obviously require extensive testing. Here it can only be noted that in the absence of a contest for the presidency there was little tendency for parties to form within individual states for the purpose of competing for state and local offices. Moreover, there is no evidence to suggest that cleavages within the Congress, even after 1815, could provide the basis for the rehabilitation or reconstruction of the party system. Finally, the revival of the contest for the presidency after 1824 had the immediate effect of stimulating the formation of a new party system.

As the national party system disintegrated, especially after 1815, it is noteworthy that there was not much of a tendency toward the formation of state-oriented parties, that is, parties organized solely for the purpose of contesting offices at the state level. The obvious exceptions to this generalization were New York, with its Bucktail and Clintonian parties; Georgia, with its peculiar Troup-Clark alignments; and Kentucky, where Old Court and New Court parties carried on a brief struggle.[8] It is also significant, I believe, that divisions did not

---

[7] For the sources of these, and other voting data cited, see my Second American Party System, 373–9.

[8] Although I recognize that some may contend that the formations in New York, Georgia, and Kentucky were not parties, I believe that they are entitled to this designation. The point to be emphasized, however, is that these formations were exceptional and that in the absence of the stimulus of the contest for the presidency, parties did not form around state issues or group cleavages within states.

form within Congress to provide the basis for a new party alignment even when such crises as those attendant upon the economic depression of 1819 or the furore over the admission of Missouri to statehood agitated public feelings.

III

It would seem to be quite clear that the stimulus for the formation of the second party system was supplied by the revival of the contest for the presidency in 1824. With the expiration of Monroe's second term there was no notable Virginian to take his place; the weak and discredited Republican congressional caucus was unable to produce a disciplined solution to the problem of succession; and soon there were four candidates — all self-styled Republicans — contending for the presidency. Except in New England, where John Quincy Adams had virtually no opposition, the contest was extremely confused and did not at once produce new party alignments. Because it was so chaotic, and also because in many states one or another of the candidates enjoyed overwhelming support from local political leaders, voter participation was remarkably low.

The most important consequence of 1824, in terms of party formation, was that it projected Andrew Jackson to the fore as the rival to Adams. Looking ahead to 1828, rival political leaders from state to state began to calculate their courses of action with respect to what was termed the "presidential question." Obviously, many considerations entered into their appraisals, but the fact that loomed largest, no doubt, was the highly sectional nature of the appeal of the two candidates.

This sectional bias was clearly revealed in the election of 1828. Adams swept New England, securing majorities of three-to-one or better in four of the six states. Jackson was equally impressive in the South, and won commanding majorities in most of the newer states of the West. Having no sectional candidate of their own in the race, the Middle States provided the major battleground of the election, and — except in Pennsylvania — the vote was extremely close. The party alignments that formed in the Middle States by 1828 tended to be durable, as Table 1 shows,[9] although in both New York and Pennsylvania the anti-Jackson forces lacked cohesion and were distracted by Antimasonry. With these important exceptions, we could say that a new two-party system had emerged in the Middle States by 1828 and that it had been given definition by the presidential contest. In New England, because of the overwhelming loyalty to the sectional favorite, the opposition Jacksonian parties were able to make little headway until after Adams had been defeated. But by 1829 the political balance had altered considerably, and the Jacksonians rapidly moved into a competitive position in most states. In the South and West — except for the very special case of Kentucky — the election of 1828 stimulated the temporary formation of parties. Once the election was over, however, the alignments did not persist and politics continued to be conducted in what was essentially an unstructured fashion.

Despite the large issues that presumably were involved, the election of 1832 had remarkably little effect on party formation. In the South and West there

---

[9] See Table 1 for an index of the balance — or imbalance — of parties in each state for the presidential elections from 1828 through 1844. It will be observed that the average differential between the total vote obtained by the presidential candidates in 1828 was 36 points, which would mean an average percentage of 68 for the victor and 32 for the defeated candidate.

TABLE 1   *Differential between Percentages of Total Vote Obtained by Major Presidential Candidates, 1828–44*

State	1828	1832	1836	1840	1844
Maine	20	10	20	1	13
New Hampshire	7	13	50	11	19
Vermont	50	10	20	29	18
Massachusetts	66	30	9	16	12
Rhode Island	50	14	6	23	20
Connecticut	50	20	1	11	5
New York	2	4	9	4	1
New Jersey	4	1	1	4	1
Pennsylvania	33	16	4	1	2
Delaware	—	2	6	10	3
Maryland	2	1	7	8	5
Virginia	38	50	13	1	6
North Carolina	47	70	6	15	5
Georgia	94	100	4	12	4
Kentucky	1	9	6	29	8
Tennessee	90	90	16	11	1
Louisiana	6	38	3	19	3
Alabama	80	100	11	9	18
Mississippi	60	77	2	7	13
Ohio	3	3	4	9	2
Indiana	13	34	12	12	2
Illinois	34	37	10	2	12
Missouri	41	32	21	14	17
Arkansas	—	—	28	13	26
Michigan	—	—	9	4	6
Average Differential	36	36	11	11	9

were feeble efforts to organize support for Henry Clay, but in most states he fared even less well than had Adams in 1828. In the Middle States, the close balance that had become evident in 1828 persisted. The most striking shift occurred in New England, where in every state the Jacksonians made tremendous gains and captured Maine and New Hampshire. Perhaps this remarkable upheaval can be attributed to the popularity of Jackson's policies regarding the bank, tariff, and internal improvements. Yet I am inclined to believe that the explanation is to be found quite simply in the fact that Clay lacked the strong sectional appeal that Adams had possessed.

How well developed, then, was the new party system by the end of 1832? In broad terms, it was well established in New England and the Middle States, despite the complications of Antimasonry. In every state the Jacksonians had acquired recognized leaders, constructed an elaborate party apparatus, and enlisted in their ranks multitudes of voters who identified with the Jackson party. The opposition, plagued by the lack of a persistent standard bearer, nevertheless managed to maintain a competitive position, whether under the Adams, National Republican, or Antimasonic label. The South, except for Kentucky, could best be described as politically monolithic. Where nearly all political leaders and candidates were nominally, at least, of the Jacksonian persuasion, there could scarcely be a functioning two-party system. In certain of the newer states of the West what can only be described as a dual party system existed. There were temporary party formations in 1828 and 1832 for the purpose of contesting the presidential election, but in state and congressional elections the contests were either conducted on a non-party basis or, in some instances, on the basis of alignments quite different from those that obtained in the presidential elections. It is common, in describing American politics in this era, to assert that by 1828 or by 1832 a functioning party system existed; but it would be my contention that in many states the crucial stage of party formation had not yet been reached.

Slight as was the effect of the election of 1832 on party formation, it did reveal an undercurrent that was soon to assume the proportions of a tidal wave. Although Jackson retained, and even increased, his huge majorities throughout the South, there were strong manifestations of dissatisfaction with his running mate and heir-apparent, Martin Van Buren of New York. In Virginia, North Carolina, Georgia, and Alabama, factions that professed loyalty to Jackson also launched organized efforts to oppose Van Buren's candidacy for the vice-presidency, and there were similar signs of restiveness in other Southern states as well. Some of these early anti-Van Burenites were admirers of John C. Calhoun, and others were appalled at the prospect of having to support a Northerner for the presidency. Still others, no doubt, were calculating how they might exploit anti-Van Buren sentiment to advance their political fortunes within their particular states.

What can best be characterized as a political explosion rocked the South from Virginia to Mississippi in 1834 and 1835. With Jackson nearing the end of his tenure, the political consensus that seemingly had prevailed was abruptly replaced by a sharp cleavage in almost every state. Those who remained loyal to the Jackson party found themselves confronted with a virulent opposition that shared a common antagonism to Martin Van Buren. While some of those "antis" continued to profess their undying loyalty to Old Hickory and his policies, others declaimed against executive usurpation, the removal of bank deposits, and the tariff, or sounded the changes on states' rights. The new sides were drawn in the state and congressional elections of 1834 and 1835, and by 1836 the Southern opposition parties — often bearing the name Whig — had found their standard bearer in Hugh Lawson White of Tennessee.

In the Western states, too, the approach of the election of 1836 spurred the slow process of party formation. More-or-less well-organized Van Buren-Democratic parties faced bitter struggles with opposition parties pledged variously to a local here — William Henry Harrison of Indiana — or to mixed White-Harrison tickets. In part because of the unprecedented personal campaign waged by Harrison, the election aroused considerable interest. The alignments that emerged in this election persisted, even though state elections in Illinois, Indiana, and Missouri continued for a few years to bear only a vague resemblance to party contests.

The least studied of all our presidential elections, the election of 1836, was of crucial importance in determining the ultimate outlines of the second party system. In marked contrast to the situation that had existed in 1832, there were now two parties contesting elections in every state, and — no less significantly —

in the large majority of the states the parties were competitive. Although Van Buren eked out a victory in the 1836 election, the party that he headed had very different dimensions from the one that had twice swept Jackson into office. In the South, where Jackson had encountered little more than token opposition, Van Buren polled slightly less than 50 per cent of the popular vote. Jackson had won 100 per cent of the votes in Georgia and 95 per cent of the votes in Tennessee in 1832; Van Buren lost both of these states in 1836. In the West, too, Van Buren's strength was far less than that of Jackson. Only in New England did Van Buren enhance the strength of the Democratic party. In the evenly balanced Middle States there was no large shift.

In brief, the effect of Van Buren's candidacy was to end the monolithic character of Southern politics and delineate and strengthen alignments in the West, thereby giving a truly national dimension to the second party system. While in 1832 the victorious candidate had secured a two-to-one margin in eleven states, only one state remained in that category in 1836: New Hampshire, which Van Buren carried by a three-to-one margin. Fittingly enough, the state in which Van Buren found his weakest support was Vermont. Here, indeed, is a conundrum for political analysts.

The anti-Van Buren or Whig parties that had formed in the several states between 1834 and 1836, together with those in New England and the Middle States that had originated earlier, had yet to develop national cohesion and leadership. Such an achievement would be essential if they were to contest successfully for the presidency. Meeting at Harrisburg in December 1839, in one of the most astutely contrived conventions ever held, they performed the difficult feat by agreeing to unite on the best available hero, Old Tippecanoe Harrison, and by sedulously avoiding any semblance of a party platform. Thus effectively mobilized, the Whigs proceeded to put on a spectacular campaign that was to fix a new style in American political drama.[10] The exciting contest, waged furiously now in every state, stimulated an unprecedented outpouring of voters and sent Van Buren down to a crushing defeat in the electoral college, although the popular vote was far less lopsided.

The campaign of 1840 brought the second American party system at last to fruition. In every region of the country, and indeed in every state, politics was conducted within the framework of a two-party system, and in all but a handful of states the parties were so closely balanced as to be competitive.[11] In broad terms, it was the contest for the presidency that shaped this party system and defined its essential purpose. The same party system, however, was to be utilized as the framework within which competition for office at all other levels of government would be conducted. The two parties were similar in structure, employed similar campaign techniques, and performed similar functions. Although in specific features the parties remained somewhat differentiated from state to state, there had in fact occurred a nationalization of institutional forms and po-

[10] The story of this memorable campaign is ably detailed in Robert G. Gunderson, *The Log Cabin Campaign* (Lexington, Ky., 1957).

[11] See Table 1. In twenty of the states in 1840 the margin between the two parties was 15 points or less and the average differential was only 11 points. Note the contrast between 1832 and 1840.

litical styles. There was also a nationalization of political identities. Voters
everywhere would respond to candidates and issues as Whigs or Democrats.]

IV

With this brief and even partial synopsis of party development in mind, it becomes possible to attempt some analyses of what it all signifies. We can approach this question by attempting some broad comparisons between the first
and second party systems. But before engaging in this exercise, we might well
pause to consider how politics was conducted in the absence of parties, for only
with some understanding of this phase of our political history can we measure
and evaluate the effects of parties.

Even after the appearance of the first party system, many states continued to
conduct politics on a non-party basis. An example is Tennessee, which did so
for roughly forty years.[12] With no vestige of political parties, the Tennessee
brand of politics featured hard-fought contests for seats in the legislature and
in Congress that not uncommonly brought over 70 per cent of the electorate to
the polls. In the process, the state produced a host of outstanding political
figures, including not only Andrew Jackson but James K. Polk, Hugh Lawson
White, John Bell, and Felix Grundy as well. Reference could readily be made
to a dozen other states where as late as the 1820's, or even 1830's, political
parties were nonexistent. Leaving aside the intriguing question of why parties
were not formed, at least for the purpose of conducting state politics, it would
no doubt be illuminating if we could answer the question of what functions
usually ascribed to political parties were not being performed in some manner
in Tennessee and other non-party states. Probably none of us would insist that
representative government was inconceivable without political parties, but we
may readily err in attributing to parties a larger and more comprehensive role
in the American political process than they in fact deserve. Unfortunately, we
know even less about pre-party politics in the United States than we do about
party politics, with the result that as yet we are not well prepared to make reliable comparisons between the two systems.

We are on slightly firmer ground when we endeavor to compare the first and
the second party systems, although admittedly our knowledge of both is inadequate and the conceptual framework within which we structure our comparisons
is incomplete. For the purposes of this essay, the comparative analysis must
necessarily be kept within brief limits and deal only with large and readily visible
attributes.

The first and second American party systems did not have precisely the same
origins. It would seem that cleavages within Congress preceded and even forecast the formation of parties in the 1790's. In theoretical terms, it would be
extremely important to be able to affirm that the first party system represented
an "internally created" or "interior" type of party formation. Unfortunately, we
cannot be sure how far this interior process of party formation might have pro-

---

[12] Tennessee might be called a "one-party" state in the sense that nearly all public
figures, as well as voters, identified themselves as Jeffersonian Republicans, or — after 1824
— as Jacksonians. But there was no formal party structure, and vigorously contested elections were conducted without relevance to parties.

ceeded, for superimposed on the impulse supplied by the congressional parties was the mobilization for the presidential contests in 1796 and 1800. It is my view that these contests for the presidency supplied a greater stimulus to party formation than did the congressional groupings. Nevertheless, the early existence of congressional alignments in the 1790's has no counterpart in the 1820's. Moreover, the parties of the 1790's possessed at the outset an issue-orientation that can hardly be discerned in 1824 or 1828. Finally, the first party system had a relatively rapid emergence, whereas the second was formed in stages over a period of roughly sixteen years.

Both party systems, the second more clearly than the first, were oriented toward contesting presidential elections. This orientation presents a striking contrast to the situation in other Western political systems, where parties have been oriented toward securing as large a representation as possible in the national legislature (although it must be noted that in most cases it has been the legislature that names the functioning executive in such systems). It is this peculiarity, among others, that makes it so difficult to conceptualize American party systems in terms that would be relevant to other nations. In organizational terms, the congressional district has presented awkward problems for our parties, quite unlike the parliamentary constituencies in Europe. Why should the executive rather than the legislative branch have been the focal point for the party system, especially in the first half of the nineteenth century? No doubt an extended answer to this question could tell us much about the special character of American parties.

There were pronounced differences in the organizational structures of parties in the first and second party systems. The caucus reflected in part the prominent role taken by legislators — national and state — in guiding early party development, and it was extensively employed as a management device under the first party system.[13] In most states, as well as at the national level, party members within the legislature, often joined by non-legislators, performed extensive nominating functions and — usually through such agencies as central committees — directed party affairs generally. In many states, conspicuously in New England and Virginia, the caucus and its agencies operated a highly centralized party apparatus, although in time local party units increasingly employed delegate conventions to nominate candidates for lesser offices. Two states, New Jersey and Delaware, were exceptional in that they instituted the state convention. Because of the great variations in constitutional structures from state to state, the precise forms of party organization and even the functions performed by the caucus differed widely; but in its most highly developed form — notably in Massachusetts — the caucus structure was highly integrated and extremely efficient. At the national level, party management was relatively weak. The Republican congressional caucus was a promising institution, which under slightly altered circumstances might have exerted a lasting influence on the structure of American parties, but for reasons that must be passed over it failed to develop and main-

[13] For interesting material on the caucus-style party organization under the first party system, see Cunningham, *Jeffersonian Republicans*, 162–6; Cunningham, *The Jeffersonian Republicans in Power: Party Operations 1801–1809* (Chapel Hill, 1963), 111–12, 127, 133, 137, 142, 145–6; and Fischer, *Revolution of American Conservatism*, 60–90 *passim*.

tain its authority and grew increasingly ineffective, especially after 1816. The Federalists, with their small and geographically unrepresentative delegation in Congress, could scarcely use the caucus as an authoritative national agency, and they had little success in developing the convention as an alternative.

Under the second party system, the caucus was almost completely replaced by the convention as the characteristic device for party management. The change-over, which has not yet been studied thoroughly, had great theoretical significance. In addition to reflecting demands for popular participation in party affairs the convention also represented a highly practical solution to problems facing party leaders at a time when party identities in legislative bodies were extremely confused, or when incipient parties had too few legislative representatives to organize a respectable caucus. Much might be made of the fact that the Anti-masonic party, the first clear example of what Maurice Duverger calls an "externally created" or "exterior" type of party in the United States, was especially zealous in developing the convention technique and, as we know, held the first national party convention. Whether the extralegislative origins of the Jackson and Adams parties in most — but not all — states would justify our describing them as "exterior" parties could lead to considerable debate. What would seem to be indisputable is that the shift from caucus to convention implied a loss in the political authority of legislative bodies. While they were suffering this loss, they were also experiencing general curtailment of their elective functions, as evidenced by the trend toward the popular choice of electors, governors, and other state officials. Again, one would like to be able to understand fully why this downgrading of the legislative branch occurred and what implications it had for our system of politics.

The widespread adoption of the convention system in the 1830's, with its hierarchy of delegate conventions and party committees extending from the smallest electoral unit up to the national conventions, made for an exceedingly elaborate and complex organizational structure. Because candidates had to be nominated at so very many different levels of government, elections were held so frequently, and the party system embraced the entire range of offices, the organizations that had evolved in most states by the 1840's were marvels of ingenuity and intricacy and required enormous manpower to staff them. In contrast to the diversity of organizational forms under the first party system, there was now a high degree of uniformity throughout the nation and in both major parties.

It is possible that the shift from the caucus to the convention may have tended greatly to emphasize the purely electoral functions of the party apparatus. The members of a caucus, in their dual capacity as legislators and party managers, may have been more concerned with matters of program and policy than were the members of conventions. It would also appear that in its most centralized form, the caucus structure imposed a much higher degree of discipline than was to prevail under the convention system. Despite their elaborate organization, the new parties of the second party system were actually decentralized structures. The party apparatus at each level of government, or within each type of constituency, possessed considerable autonomy. Party mechanisms were better designed for achieving agreement on nominations than for formulating policies. Perhaps the very complexity and magnitude of the formal organizational structure contributed to the rise of the professional party manager and the informal leader, or boss.

In discussing any formal party structures, whether of the caucus or convention type, the problem inevitably arises as to whether the formal structure reflected the actual locus of power or influence. Superficially, the delegate convention system of the 1830's and 1840's resulted in the "democratization" of parties, but we have yet to determine the degree to which conventions were genuine decision-making bodies. Perhaps they were, but they must also be viewed as having what might be termed a cosmetic function; that is, they gave a democratic appearance to what might in fact have been decisions determined by a party oligarchy. Indeed, Ostrogorski used the term "democratic formalism" to describe the convention structure.

The two party systems could also be compared with respect to participation. The installation of the convention party structure unquestionably multiplied opportunities for party followers to assume roles as activists. This development was especially prominent in those states where previously there had been little or no formal party organization, but its effects could be noted everywhere. Moreover, intense inter-party competition stimulated unprecedented levels of voter participation, not uncommonly rising to 80 per cent of the electorate, whereas prior to 1824 in a very large number of states it was exceptional for half of the eligible voters to participate regularly in elections.[14] Both in the comprehensiveness of their structures and in the universality of their appeal, then, the new parties could truly be characterized as mass parties.

One may properly speculate as to whether the measurable increase in voter participation had a direct influence on party programs and governmental actions. To put the question differently, when vast numbers of men who had formerly lacked the franchise or who had been apathetic entered the electoral arena, were there discernable shifts in party attitudes or public policy? Did the parties and the governments become more "democratic"? This would be an extremely difficult question to answer, but I have the impression that the "new" voters tended to divide between the two parties in much the same proportion as the "old" voters.[15] We might conclude that both parties accommodated the new voters by modifying their appeals and their programs. An alternative conclusion could be that because the new voters did not enter predominantly into one party and make it the instrument for achieving their political goals, they had no great effect on the parties. Any sure evaluation of the effects of enlarged participation

[14] See my "New Perspectives on Jacksonian Politics," *American Historical Review*, LXV (1960), 288–301, for illustrative data on the increase in voter participation. In those states where the parties were competitive after 1800, it was not uncommon for 70 per cent or more of the adult white males to vote, and on occasion higher levels were reached. But in states where the parties were unbalanced, or where elections were not contested on a party basis, participation would usually be under 50 per cent. There are, however, curious exceptions to these generalizations. Alabama recorded the suspiciously high figure of 97 per cent in a gubernatorial election in 1819, and Tennessee reached 80 per cent in the gubernatorial election of 1817. These, and other data that could be cited, suggest that high participation could be achieved in the absence of parties, and even in the absence of the stimulus of a presidential contest.

[15] See my "Suffrage Classes and Party Alignments: A Study in Voter Behavior, *Mississippi Valley Historical Review*, XLVI (1959), 397–410.

must depend on further studies, but at least we might agree that the mass participation that we associate with the second party system did affect the style of politics.

The extended form of participation in politics in the era of the second party system can scarcely be comprehended in purely political terms — that is, only in terms of rivalry between opposing power elites or interest groups for dominance in the state and for control over public policy. It would be difficult to account for all the phenomena of the system within these limited concepts, and the varieties of experiences that parties in this era afforded to the electorate went beyond the political sphere.[16] Those tens of thousands of men and women who attended the mammoth Whig festival at Nashville in 1840; those untold millions who carried torches, donned uniforms, chanted slogans, or cheered themselves hoarse at innumerable parades and rallies; those puffed-up canvassers of wards, servers of rum, and distributors of largesse; and all those simple folk who whipped themselves into a fury of excitement and anxiety as each election day approached, were thrilling to a grand dramatic experience, even a cathartic experience. There was no spectacle, no contest, in America that could match an election campaign, and all could identify with and participate in it.

Innumerable foreign observers saw clearly this amazing dimension of American politics. As Michael Chevalier perceived it, the political campaign and all its attendant pageantry and exaltation meant to Americans what religious festivals had meant to the peoples of Catholic Europe. Witnessing a post-election celebration of New York City Democrats, he was struck by the resemblance.

> The procession was nearly a mile long; the democrats marched in good order to the glare of torches; the banners were more numerous than I had ever seen them in any religious festival; all were in transparency, on account of the darkness. On some were inscribed the names of the democratic societies or sections, . . . others bore imprecations against the Bank of the United States; *Nick Biddle* and *Old Nick* here figured largely and formed the pendant of our *libera nos a malo*. Then came portraits of General Jackson afoot and on horseback . . . Those of Washington and Jefferson, surrounded with democratic mottoes, were mingled in all tastes and of all colors. Among these figured an eagle, not a painting, but a real live eagle, tied by the legs, surrounded by a wreath of leaves, and hoisted upon a pole, after the manner of the Roman standards. The imperial bird was carried by a stout sailor, more pleased than ever was a sergeant permitted to hold one of the strings of the canopy, in a Catholic ceremony. From further than the eye could reach, came marching on the democrats. I was struck with the resemblance of their air to the train that escorts the *viaticum* in Mexico or Puebla. . . . The democratic procession, also, like the Catholic procession, had its halting places; it stopped before the house of the Jackson men to fill the air with cheers, and halted at the doors of the leaders of the Opposition, to give three, six, or nine groans.

[16] M. Ostrogorski, among other foreign observers, has some extremely perceptive comments on the "ritual character" of American parties in *Democracy and the Party System in the United States* (New York, 1910), 408–12.

. . . If these scenes were to find a painter, they would be admired at a distance, not less than the triumphs and sacrificial pomps, which the ancients have left us delineated in marble and brass; for they are not mere grotesques after the manner of Rembrandt, they belong to history, they partake of the grand; they are the episodes of a wondrous epic which will bequeath a lasting memory to posterity, that of the coming of democracy.[17]

Finally, the first and second party systems exhibited pronounced differences in their extent and their alignment. The parties of the 1790's had never really been extended to more than fifteen states, and in several of those they scarcely became rooted. The second party system comprehended every state, although there might well be some reservations about South Carolina. The first party system was, from one point of view, very badly aligned. Early in its history the New England states were heavily inclined toward the Federalist party, while in the South the Republicans possessed a lopsided supremacy. Although New England in time achieved a brief balance of parties, the South became virtually a one-party region. The second party system was extraordinary in that the two parties were fairly evenly balanced in every region.[18] Between 1836 and 1852, as in no other period in our history, each of the parties was truly national in its extent.

V

It would be possible and even profitable to explain why the two party systems differed in so many attributes, but such a disquisition would probably have to be very lengthy if it were to be at all persuasive. Within the limited compass of this essay it is appropriate to attempt no more than a brief reference to the most salient factors.

Of foremost importance in affecting the structures of parties as well as the specific tasks that elements within the party organization had to perform were certain fundamental changes in the constitutional and legal environment.[19] To put the matter simply, the rules under which the political game was to be played changed greatly between 1800 and 1840. The most obvious development was a trend from diversity to uniformity in governmental structures and electoral procedures from state to state. The magnitude and significance of this quiet revolution in the electoral environment has generally been ignored, except for a curious preoccupation with modifications in suffrage qualifications.[20] We have

[17] Michael Chevalier, *Society, Manners and Politics in the United States* (Boston, 1839), 318–19.
[18] See Table 1.
[19] Constitutions and electoral laws, as demonstrated by the studies of Duverger and others, strongly conditioned the nature of party systems. This is not to maintain that all attributes of parties are explainable in these terms, and in seeking to account for cleavages between parties, political styles, or the characteristics of political elites, for example, relevant social factors must be considered. But I would agree with Lipset that "electoral laws determine the nature of the party system as much as any other structural variable." See Lipset, *The First New Nation*, 293.
[20] There have been scarcely any comparative studies of constitutional change at the state level, although this field offers rich opportunities for scholars. For a pioneering study, which still stands alone, see Fletcher M. Green, *Constitutional Development in the South Atlantic States, 1776–1860* (Chapel Hill, 1930).

yet to assess adequately the relevance to our party system of the movements toward the popular, at-large election of presidential electors, the choice of congressmen by districts, the popular election of governors, and the multiplication in numbers of locally elected officials. In a related realm, the adoption of printed ballots, the creation of small voting districts, and the consolidation of elections on a single day had enormous consequences for political parties.

One general effect of this quiet revolution was to complicate the tasks of the parties. In a situation where, for example, members of a legislature were elected from the county as a unit and where the legislature in turn appointed the governor, presidential electors, and county officials, parties would have very limited tasks, as contrasted with a situation where members of each house of the legislature were chosen from different constituencies, and presidential electors, the governor, and county officials were popularly elected. Compelled to elaborate an intricate organization capable of making nominations and conducting campaigns within a bewildering variety of constituencies, and obliged at the same time to appeal for the broadest possible base of support, the new parties confronted a staggering challenge, especially when they might be called upon to engage in electoral combat two or three times within a single year. It is no wonder that they were reduced to little more than electoral machines.

If one change in the electoral environment loomed larger than all the rest it was the shift to the popular, at-large election of presidential electors. This development gave a popular dimension to the contest for the presidency, reduced the political authority of the state legislatures, called forth elaborate and intensive campaign efforts, facilitated the building of national parties, reduced the effectiveness of third parties, and made the presidential election the focal point of the party system — to suggest but a few consequences. How and through what influences this transformation of the process of choosing electors was brought about has yet to be studied, but a complete understanding of its implications might well be crucial to any conceptualization of the American party system.

The political environment was profoundly influenced not only by these constitutional and legal developments, but also by fairly obvious technological, economic, and social changes. Revolutionary improvements in means of transportation and communication made it feasible, for example, for parties to hold state and even national conventions and conduct nationwide campaigns. Rising economic expectations associated with the transformation and expansion of the economy gave new energy to democratic dogmas and spurred mass participation in politics. The entrance of new states into the union broadened the spatial dimensions of the party system, and the growth of urban areas and the sharp rise in immigration created new challenges. Above all, the increasingly egalitarian flavor of American society, now given voice in an incontestable rhetoric, compelled both parties to project the same democratic image.

These briefly enumerated changes in the constitutional and cultural environment may account for certain fairly obvious differences in organization and style between the first and second party systems. But they do not fully explain what was most distinctive about the latter, namely, its lack of sectional bias. As the second party system reached maturity in the 1840's, it scarcely reflected the fact that the basic cleavage within the nation, transcending all others, was that which may be vaguely defined as North-South sectionalism. The first party system had mirrored this tension to the degree that after 1800 the Federalists were very largely a Northern party. The third party system as it finally became aligned in the 1870's also contained a decided sectional bias, with its solidly Democratic South and its Northern-oriented Republican party. In attempting to explain how the second party system produced not sectional parties but parties that were remarkably well balanced throughout the nation, we are confronted with a paradox. In the successive contests for the presidency between 1824 and 1836 strong sectional loyalties shaped the responses of political leaders and voters in each region to the opposing candidates. But by 1836 the end result of the series of realignments was a sectionally balanced party system. In brief, the explanation for the paradoxical character of the second party system is to be found in the peculiar circumstances associated with the contests for the presidency.

To recapitulate, the second party system did not emerge suddenly; it developed in a series of stages, and at each stage it was shaped by the sectional identifications of the candidates. With Andrew Jackson and John Quincy Adams as the candidates in 1828, a highly sectionalized vote resulted; New England went almost as overwhelmingly for Adams as the South did for Jackson; only the Middle States were evenly divided. When Henry Clay was substituted for Adams, New England was no longer held together by its loyalty to a sectional favorite, and parties throughout the North came into balance. When Martin Van Buren was substituted for Jackson — and opposed by White and Harrison — the South and much of the new West ceased to be politically monolithic, as anti-Van Buren parties quickly mobilized. These sectional responses to the presidential candidates were crucial at the time of party formation. Once the parties had been formed and identities had been acquired by the voters, alignments tended to remain relatively firm. Thus highly sectional responses in a series of presidential elections resulted in the formation of non-sectional parties.

Merely to emphasize their distinctiveness, I have chosen to call these national parties "artificial" because their ultimate alignments bore no direct relationship to the realities of sectional antagonism. At maturity, each party sought to aggregate interests that were national in scope; and within each party almost equally powerful Northern and Southern wings contested for supremacy. Intraparty tensions were greater than the tensions between the two parties. The federalized character of our constitutional structure and the inability of any national party agency to exercise firm discipline made it all but impossible to restrain the intra-party tensions. Responsible leaders of both parties understood that such parties could be destroyed by issues that were sectional in character. The parties could indulge themselves in furious controversies over the "Monster Bank," but they might be rent asunder by such issues as expansionism or the status of slavery in the territories.

The second American party system was truly a wondrous creation. Emerging over a period of sixteen years from the circumstances associated with the successive contests for the presidency, it elaborated a complex organizational structure within which there could be orderly competition for offices at all levels of government. It also provided maximal opportunities for mass participation and produced a political style that took on the aspects of a democratic religion. It could perform a wide range of electoral functions, and it could resolve conflicts that were not highly charged with sectional antagonisms. But, like the first party system, it, too, met with failure.

Apparently it was still in a healthy condition down to about 1850. Then, under the strain of the sectional issues confronting the nation, it began to crumble. The first sign was the collapse of the Whig party in the lower South, and by 1856 the already altered Democratic party was confronted by the newly marshalled Republican party and, in some areas, by the short-lived American, or "Know-Nothing," party as well. At last, in 1860, the Democrats succumbed to a fateful division and the Civil War followed. Although in the North a viable new party system operated, it was not until the 1870's, with the nation reunited and the South released from the abnormal years of Reconstruction, that the third party system assumed national dimensions.

Why did the second party system fail? One answer could be that it was inadequate to cope with conflicts that arrayed section against section. The first party system had come perilously close to foundering on this rock in 1814; but the second party system, for the reason that its parties were truly national in scope and lacked a pronounced sectional bias, was presumably better designed to manage divisive pluralism. Here we face a dilemma. If in a democratic two-party system the parties became so aligned as to reflect crucial ideological, class, social, or sectional cleavages, and they therefore present the electorate with drastic alternatives, the strain on the political system as a whole, and particularly at the level of government, may be disruptive. If, on the other hand, each party is expected to mediate conflicting interests by aggregating the broad spectrum of those interests, the strain on the political system at the level of the parties may be disruptive. I have no solution to propose to this dilemma, other than to suggest that a party system that is *too* comprehensive — as was the second party system — may be potentially as explosive as a party system that is polarized around drastic alternatives — as was the third party system in its formative years.[21] Perhaps this is to say that threatening problems or the strains of crises must be shared between the party system and the government.

VI

In conclusion, some crude assessments of the contributions of the party systems to American political development down to 1860 might be attempted. Such an appraisal must be extremely tentative because the concept of political development, as formulated by LaPalombara and Weiner or others, is awkwardly elusive.[22] And even if one accepts the notion that such problems as national

[21] For an interesting discussion of the conditions under which a two-party system may be less able to resolve conflict than a multi-party system, see Lipset, *The First New Nation*, 308–12.

[22] The discussion that follows draws upon some of the concepts advanced by LaPalombara and Weiner in *Political Parties and Political Development*, 399–435. Similar concepts have been perceptively applied to an analysis of American party development by William N. Chambers in an extremely important essay in the same volume, "Parties and Nation Building in America," 79–106. For a contrasting view, which minimizes the effects of parties as independent variables, see Morton Grodzins's essay, "Political Parties and the Crisis of Succession in the United States: The Case of 1800," in the same volume, 303–27. I would suggest that the election of 1824 is an even better illustration of Grodzins's point.

integration, political participation, distribution, legitimacy, and management of conflict are relevant to political development, it is all but impossible to measure the specific contributions of party systems to the solution of those problems. Consequently, what follows must be regarded as impressionistic and even subjective.

We must begin with the understanding that the United States in the 1790's did not confront crises of the same kind and magnitude as those facing the newly emergent nations of today. An extensive experience with the operation of representative institutions that dated back to early in the seventeenth century gave the new nation a politically skilled leadership corps, a broad and alert electorate, and an informed respect for constitutional order. In addition to possessing a common language, a cultural heritage that stemmed largely from British origins, and a relatively homogeneous Protestant religious background, the former colonies had strengthened their sense of national identity through their struggle for independence and had reaffirmed their unity by adopting the federal Constitution. The legitimacy of the new government was not challenged by a party of disaffection, nor was it threatened with subversion by a hereditary elite, an entrenched bureaucracy, or a powerful military establishment. The economy seemed to be capable of gratifying the expectations of the citizens. In relative terms, a high degree of literacy existed; and a flourishing, free press sustained political communication. Not least of all, if we accept the persuasive formulation of Louis Hartz concerning the flowering of a liberal tradition in America, there was consensual agreement on basic national values.[23]

The new American republic was designed as a federal republic, however, in recognition of the sovereign authority held by the several states, and the powers assigned to the national government were explicitly limited. This intricate, carefully adjusted political system was decidely experimental, and by its very nature it placed restraints on national integration and even permitted the possibility of contests over legitimacy between state and national authorities. Given the complex of factors that conditioned the formation of the national union, we can appreciate the virtues of these arrangements, but they were to occasion very special problems for American party systems. These problems were to become especially formidable as the nation expanded in size and — most ominously — as sectional interests diverged and took precedence over other cleavages.

In gross terms I would take the view that the first and second American party systems were not confronted with serious crises of participation, nor with major crises of distribution. Neither were they required to meet challenges to the legitimacy of the constitutional regime, unless we choose to regard the menace of secession as a threat to legitimacy rather than to national integration. The two areas in which the party systems might be expected to contribute to political development were in advancing national integration and in managing conflicts

We know, of course, that internal conflicts were not successfully managed in the 1850's and that the nation disintegrated in 1860–61, after having somewhat fortuitously averted a similar crisis in 1814. Now two possible courses of argument are open to us. We might adduce evidence to sustain the position that the first two party systems, despite their defects, held the nation together and

[23] Louis Hartz, *The Liberated Tradition in America* (New York, 1955).

resolved a number of conflicts over a period of sixty years, only to fail when confronted by irreconcilable cleavages. Or we might defend the position that the party systems, perhaps because of the difficulties inherent in the federal system, were ill-adapted to resolving conflicts that were sectional in character and that in 1814 and again in 1860 they were malintegrative in their effects.

Whichever position seems to us most plausible, one conclusion is inescapable: the early American party systems are no less notable for their failures than for their successes. We may properly hail the ingenuity of the political architects who constructed the first modern party system in history, but we must record that that party system fell victim to a kind of entropy after 1815. We can marvel at the comprehensiveness and popularity of the second party system, and at the incredible technical proficiency of its professional corps of managers, but that system collapsed within a generation. And as the third party system began to form, the nation divided. Whatever the contributions of the party systems to American political development, they were not after all adequate to avert the disaster of civil war.

The Age of Mercantilism: An Interpretation of the American Political Economy, 1763 to 1828

WILLIAM APPLEMAN WILLIAMS

William Appleman Williams, a diplomatic historian, argues that the Revolutionary War did not liberate the new American nation from the prevailing European notion of political economy. He believes that Americans accepted the tenets of mercantilism even before they declared independence, and persisted in utilizing them until the Jacksonians popularized laissez-faire capitalism. Interpreting mercantilism as an economic theory requiring domestic self-sufficiency and a favorable balance of foreign trade, Williams sees internal economic integration and expansionism as the critical points in the mercantilist program. This unusual perspective leads him to describe James Madison as a leading mercantilist, and to dismiss Alexander Hamilton, generally credited with being a mercantilist, as a man who merely paid lip service to the theory. John Quincy Adams is the hero of the essay, the true originator of the American empire, who desired, correctly, an empire only large enough to sustain a balanced domestic economy. If Williams is right, we must reject the older view that the liberal, free trade views of Adam Smith represented the philosophy of the infant United

States, and we must revise the traditional acceptance of Hamiltonian centralism as the origin of the modern American state. Does Williams convincingly state the case for a necessary connection between the foreign policy of expansionism and a domestic policy of publicly stimulated economic growth? Does Madison, for instance, fit gracefully into the outfit Williams has tailored for him?

Based upon the suggestion by Curtis P. Nettels that one of the consequences of British mercantilism was the creation "of a new mercantilist state on this side of the Atlantic," and upon recent re-evaluations of mercantilism by William D. Grampp, Gunnar Myrdal, Jacob Viner, Charles Wilson, and others, this essay advances the hypothesis that the central characteristic of American history from 1763 to 1828 was in fact the development and maturation of an American mercantilism.[1] Let it be emphasized that the interpretation is offered as a hypothesis and no more — as an idea to be examined and tested, then accepted, modified, or rejected on the basis of its relevance and validity. There is no intention, furthermore, even to imply that the approach as here stated offers final answers to all the vexing problems connected with understanding early American society. It is merely proposed that a re-examination of the era from this angle may lead to new insights, and hence contribute to a broader interpretation of the period.[2]

At the outset, for example, the use of the concept of mercantilism restores to its properly central place the fact that Americans thought of themselves as an empire at the very beginning of their national existence — as part of their assertive self-consciousness which culminated in the American Revolution. Though

Reprinted by permission of the author from the *William and Mary Quarterly*, 3d Ser., 15 (1958), pp. 419–437.

[1] Curtis P. Nettels, "British Mercantilism and the Economic Development of the Thirteen Colonies," *Journal of Economic History*, XII (Spring, 1952), 105–114; William D. Grampp, "A Re-examination of Jeffersonian Economics," *Southern Economic Journal*, XII (Jan. 1946), 263–282; "On the Politics of the Classical Economists," *Quarterly Journal of Economics*, LXII (Nov. 1948), 714–747; and "The Liberal Elements in English Mercantilism," *ibid.*, LXVI (Nov. 1952), 465–501; Gunnar Myrdal, *The Political Element in the Development of Economic Theory* (London, 1953); Jacob Viner, "Power versus Plenty as Objectives of Foreign Policy in the Seventeenth and Eighteenth Centuries," *World Politics*, I (Oct. 1948), 1–29; Charles Wilson, " 'Mercantilism': Some Vicissitudes of an Idea," *Economic History Review*, 2d Ser., X (Dec. 1957), 181–188. This essay owes an equal debt to the extensive publications of Merrill Jensen and to his generous and helpful interests in this approach to the era. His keen criticisms and perceptive suggestions were invaluable. It also benefited from the interest and intelligence of James Cooper, Lloyd Gardner, Kent Kreuter, Thomas J. McCormick, Walter La Feber, and Martin Sklar. This article is a foreshortened statement of the first section of a longer three-part essay dealing with the characterization and periodization of American history. Together with the other two portions, "The Age of Laissez Moi Faire, 1828–1896," and "The Age of Corporate Capitalism, 1896–1958," it [was] published as *The Contours of American History* by the World Publishing Company [in 1961].

[2] Some readers may feel that the vigor of the subsequent presentation contradicts these caveats. Perhaps they will be reassured by remembering that any tool has to be sharp, though later it may be laid aside out of preference for another.

it may seem surprising, especially when contrasted with the image of isolationism which has been accepted so long, in reality this early predominance of a pattern of empire thought is neither very strange nor very difficult to explain. Having matured in an age of empires as part of an empire, the colonists naturally saw themselves in the same light once they joined issue with the mother country.

Revolutionary leaders were confident of their ability "not only to take territory by the sword, but to hold and govern it under a colonial status."[3] Long before the break with England, for example, Benjamin Franklin was a leader of those who entertained a "burning interest in westward expansion." At the threshold of the revolution he visualized an American Empire including Canada, the Spanish Floridas, the West Indies, and perhaps even Ireland.[4] George Washington, John Adams, John Livingston, and Thomas Lee were among those who shared such conceptions of an American Empire.[5] By the end of the war, such men as Silas Deane looked forward to the time when "Great Britain, America and Russia united will command not barely Europe, but the whole world united."[6] And in 1789, after remarking that "it is well known that empire has been travelling from east to west," Congregational minister and geographer Jedidiah Morse concluded that "probably her last and broadest seat will be America . . . the largest empire that ever existed."[7]

While the vigor, even cockiness, of such statements may be explained by the consciousness of having whipped the champion, the underlying emphasis on expansion and empire was an integral part of the general outlook of mercantilism, a conception of the world shared by most of the revolutionary generation. Though they revolted against British mercantilism, there is considerable evidence to suggest that early American leaders do not, as so often is assumed, rebel against the ideal and practice of mercantilism itself. In stressing the role of natural-rights philosophy in the thinking of the leaders of the revolution, the traditional view of the American Revolution has slighted this key point.

An acceptance of natural law is not incompatible with mercantilism, as is indicated by John Locke's vigorous espousal of both systems. Much of the talk in America about natural rights, moreover, concerned what Thomas Paine called

---

[3] Albert Bushnell Hart, *The Foundations of American Foreign Policy* (New York, 1901), pp. 174–175. The best published study of the early empire outlook is Arthur B. Darling, *Our Rising Empire, 1763–1803* (New Haven, 1940).

[4] Gerald Stourzh, *Benjamin Franklin and American Foreign Policy* (Chicago, 1954), p. 54.

[5] On Washington see, among others, Charles H. Ambler, *George Washington and the West* (Chapel Hill, 1936), and Curtis P. Nettels, *George Washington and American Independence* (Boston, 1951). Also consult *Letters of Members of the Continental Congress*, ed. Edmund C. Burnett (Washington, 1921), III, 476; Malbone W. Graham, *American Diplomacy in the International Community* (Baltimore, 1948), pp. 9–24; and Max Savelle, "The Appearance of An American Attitude Toward External Affairs, 1770–1775," *American Historical Review*, LII (July 1947), 655–666.

[6] *The Revolutionary Diplomatic Correspondence of the United States*, ed. Francis Wharton (Washington, 1889), II, 332.

[7] Jedidiah Morse, *The American Geography; or A View of the Present Situation of the United States of America* (Elizabeth Town, 1789), pp. 468–469, quoted in Richard W. Van Alstyne, "American Conceptions of Empire," a lecture delivered at the University of Chicago, May 5, 1953, copies available from the author.

the "natural right" to one's own empire.[8] And though they were willing to use Adam Smith's polemic in behalf of laissez faire as a weapon against British mercantilism (and against their domestic opponents), most Americans adhered firmly in their own practice to the principle that the state had to intervene in economic affairs. America's romance with Smith's laissez faire came later and was of relatively short duration. Hence it would appear that a better understanding of early American history depends in considerable measure upon a grasp of nature and practice of American mercantilism as it developed between 1763 and 1825.

Traditionally thought of as little more than a narrow and selfish point of view held by the trading interest, mercantilism was in fact a broad definition and explanation of the world shared by most of Western Europe in the seventeenth and eighteenth centuries.[9] In this sense it was the basic outlook of those who labored to build a dynamic balanced economy of agriculture and business organized on a capitalistic basis within a nationalistic framework. Depending upon their specific function and power at any given stage in the process, mercantilists argued among themselves over the best means to achieve and maintain such a system — and differed in their estimates of whether or not it had been established — but they agreed on the objective and upon the need to use the state as a tool.

Whether agrarian or urban, therefore, mercantilists were essentially nationalists who strove for self-sufficiency through increased domestic production and a favorable balance (and terms) of trade. Their emphasis on production and the control of export markets and sources of raw materials, rather than on consumption and economic interdependence, led them to fear surpluses as a sign of crisis and failure. Thus they dropped the old feudal restrictions on exports and replaced them with taxes on imports. Their greatest fear was a surplus of goods. In this respect, furthermore, mercantilism was reinforced — albeit in a back-handed and even unintentional way — by the broad ethical outlook of Puritanism (which frowned on luxury), even though mercantilism itself was a secular and almost amoral system. Likewise, the concept of a chosen people, so strong in Puritanism, also strengthened the secular and economic nationalism of mercantilism. Thus mercantilists constantly labored to build a tightly organized and protected national market and to increase their share of the world market. The key points in their program were integration at home and expansion abroad.

---

[8] See Léon Dion, "Natural Law and Manifest Destiny in the Era of the American Revolution," *Canadian Journal of Economics and Political Science*, XXIII (May 1957), 227–247, as a supplement to Albert K. Weinberg, *Manifest Destiny* (Baltimore, 1935).

[9] Of the immense literature on mercantilism, the following items proved most stimulating: Max Beer, *Early British Economics from the Thirteenth Century to the Middle of the Eighteenth Century* (London, 1938); Philip W. Buck, *The Politics of Mercantilism* (New York, 1942); Edgar S. Furniss, *The Position of the Laborer in a System of Nationalism* (Boston, 1920); E. F. Heckscher, *Mercantilism*, rev. ed., ed. E. F. Soderlund (London, 1955), esp. Vol. II; E. A. J. Johnson, *American Economic Thought in the Seventeenth Century* (London, 1932), and *Predecessors of Adam Smith* (New York, 1937); Ephraim Lipson, *The Economic History of England* (London, 1948–49); Gustav F. von Schmoller, *The Mercantile System and Its Historical Significance* (New York, 1931); and the items cited in note 1.

In the exuberant confidence of their victory over Britain, Americans tended to assume that each new state could survive and thrive as a mercantile empire unto itself. That attitude was not too surprising, for each of the new states appeared to enjoy the raw materials, labor supply, and trading facilities for a balanced economy. That estimate of the situation was supported and reinforced by the conviction, itself part of traditional therapy, that a state could remain democratic in political and social life only if it were small and integrated, and by the experiences of the colonies in dealing with Great Britain's imperial policy after 1763. Yet the political outlook and faith contradicted certain basic tenets of mercantilism, which Americans also entertained, or assumed.

The first attempt to reconcile the conflict produced the Articles of Confederation. That instrument of government stressed the independence of the states as self-contained units of mercantilism and democratic republicanism, yet also established a central government for the purposes of war and, as in the case of Canada, future expansion. But specific postwar developments, such as the serious recession, the expansionist conflicts between the states, and the difficulties in dealing with other countries in economic affairs, combined to disillusion many Americans with their experiment in particularistic mercantilism.

Broadly speaking, the resulting movement toward a stronger central government grew out of internal and international economic difficulties analyzed and explained with the ideas of mercantilism. By 1785, for example, most of the states, including agrarian ones, were switching from tariffs for revenue to tariffs for international retaliation and protection. Merchants demanded American navigation acts, artisans agitated for protection of their labor, and agricultural interests wanted help in balancing their political economy.[10] Various groups of Americans who concerned themselves directly with the problem of strengthening the central government — and there were many who were preoccupied with local and immediate difficulties or opportunities — offered several proposals for handling the problem. Centered in New England, the smallest group favored establishing an aristocratic society at home and rejoining the British Empire as a contractual junior partner. Such men were not willing to return to colonial status, but they did favor economic and social reintegration. Most Americans opposed that solution, favoring instead either the delegation of more power to the central government under the Articles of Confederation or the substitution of an entirely new instrument of government.

A letter from James Madison to Thomas Jefferson in the spring of 1786 not only indicates that the agrarian as well as the urban interests favored one or the other of those last two approaches, but dramatizes the fundamental mercantilism of the entire movement. "A continuance of the present anarchy of our commerce," Madison explained, "will be a continuance of the unfavorable

[10] Here see Oliver M. Dickerson, *The Navigation Acts and the American Revolution* (Philadelphia, 1951), on the attitude of the colonists toward the Navigation Acts per se. Then consult Oscar and Mary F. Handlin, *Commonwealth: A Study of the Role of Government in the American Economy: Massachusetts, 1774–1861* (New York, 1947); Louis Hartz, *Economy Policy and Democratic Thought: Pennsylvania, 1776–1860* (Cambridge, Mass., 1948); and Merrill Jensen, *The New Nation: A History of the United States During the Confederation, 1781–1789* (New York, 1950), on the development of an American mercantilism at the state level.

balance on it, which by draining us of our metals . . . [will bring our ruin]. In fact, most of our political evils may be traced up to our commercial ones, and most of our moral way to our political."[11]

Against this background, the Constitution appears as an instrument of centralized national government framed in the classic manner by men thinking within the framework of mercantilism and blessed with the physical and human resources for a balanced economy. It provided the foundation for a national system of economics and politics and organized American strength for the struggle with other mercantile empires and for the conquest of less powerful peoples. The latter considerations were essential, for the Founding Fathers resolved the contradiction between the stress on expansion in mercantilism and the emphasis on a small state in existing democratic political theory by developing a theory of their own which held that democratic republicanism could be sustained by just such expansion. James Madison, often called the Father of the Constitution, provided the most striking formulation of this proposition, but Thomas Jefferson, John Adams and other early leaders either shared or adopted it in one form or another within a reasonably short time.

Taking his cue from David Hume, the Englishman who attacked Montesquieu's argument that democracy was a system that could work only in small states, Madison asserted that a large state offered a much better foundation for republicanism.[12] Institutional checks and balances could help, and were therefore necessary, but they were not enough in and of themselves. "Extend the sphere," he argued, "and you take in a greater variety of parties and interests; you make it less probable that a majority of the whole will have a common motive to invade the rights of other citizens; or if such a common motive exists, it will be more difficult for all who feel it to discover their own strength, and to act in unison with each other. . . ."[13]

While it is possible to conclude from Madison's remarks that he had in mind a static conception of such a large state, three considerations would appear to weaken that reading of his thesis. First, Madison used the verb "extend" in its active, unlimited sense. Second, he was stating a general theory, not making an argument in behalf of a given territorial settlement. And third, he advocated and vigorously supported the continued expansion of the United States. It seems more probable, therefore, that Madison was proposing, as a guide to policy and action in his own time, the same kind of an argument that Frederick Jackson Turner formulated a century later, when he advanced his frontier thesis which explained America's democracy and prosperity as the result of such expansion.

Madison's theory became the key to an American mercantilism. Merchants and manufacturers who wanted their own empire found it convincing and convenient. And Jefferson's thesis that democracy and prosperity depended upon a society of landholding freemen was a drastically simplified version of the same

---

[11] Madison to Jefferson, Mar. 18, 1786, *Letters and Other Writings of James Madison. Published by order of Congress* (New York, 1884), I, 226–227.

[12] Robert L. Ketchum, "Notes on James Madison's Sources for the Tenth Federalist Paper," *Midwest Journal of Political Science*, I (May, 1957), 20–25; Douglass Adair, " 'That Politics May be Reduced to a Science': David Hume, James Madison, and the Tenth *Federalist*," *Huntington Library Quarterly*, XX (Aug. 1957), 343–360.

[13] Madison, Federalist No. 10, *The Federalist*, ed. Henry Cabot Lodge (New York, 1900), pp. 58–60.

idea. Edward Everett of Massachusetts captured the essence of the interpretation in his judgment that expansion was the *"principle* of our institutions."[14] Additional support for this interpretation is offered by Madison's later prophecy (in 1828–29) that a major crisis would occur in about a century, when the continent was filled up and an industrial system had deprived most people of any truly productive property. In the event, Madison's fears proved true sooner than he anticipated. For in the crisis of the 1890's, when Americans *thought* that the frontier was gone, they advanced and accepted the argument that new expansion was the best — if not the only — way to sustain their freedom and prosperity.[15]

Madison's original statement of the expansionist thesis was important for two reasons. First, it provided the theoretical basis for an American mercantilism combining commercial and territorial expansion with political democracy. Second, by thus re-emphasizing the idea of empire, and proposing expansion as the key to national welfare, Madison opened the way for a discussion of the basic questions facing American mercantilism. Those issues concerned domestic economic affairs, the kind of expansion that was necessary and desirable, and the means to accomplish such gains while the nation was young and weak.

Washington's Farewell Address formulated a bipartisan answer to the problem of basic strategy. The solution was to build a commercial empire (which included markets for agricultural surpluses) by avoiding political involvement in the European system, meanwhile retaining complete freedom of action to secure and develop a continental empire in the Western Hemisphere. Washington's proposition was classically simple: play from the strength provided by America's basic economic wealth and geographic location in order to survive immediate weakness and emerge as *the* world power. "If we remain one people, under an efficient government," he promised, "the period is not far off when we may defy material injury from external annoyance . . . when we may choose peace or war, as our interest, guided by justice, shall counsel." Sharing that objective, and quite in agreement with the strategy, Thomas Jefferson summed it all up a bit later in one famous axiom: "entangling alliances with none." And with the enunciation of the Monroe Doctrine, freedom of action became the avowed and central bipartisan theme of American foreign policy.

As a condition of that pervasive agreement, however, several serious conflicts had to be resolved. Perhaps they can be discussed most clearly by defining and considering them within the framework of the gradual defeat and amalgamation of the pro-British and pro-French minorities by a growing consensus in favor of an American mercantilism. Such an approach has the additional value of making it possible to organize the analysis around familiar personalities as symbols

[14] Edward Everett, *Orations and Speeches on Various Occasions* (Boston, 1850–68), I, 210.
[15] Here see Charles S. Campbell, Jr., "American Business Interests and the Open Door in China," *Far Eastern Quarterly*, I (Nov. 1941), 43–58; Nancy L. O'Connor, "The Foreign Policy of the Farmers' Movements, 1890–1900," unpubl. masters thesis, University of Oregon, 1957; William A. Williams, "The Frontier Thesis and American Foreign Policy," *Pacific Historical Review*, XXIV (Nov. 1955), 379–395, and "The Large Corporation and the Political Economy of American Foreign Policy: 1890–1958," paper read at the State University of Iowa Conference on Social Sciences, May 1958.

of certain ideas, functional groups, and special interests. Let it be posited, there-fore, that the following men are key figures in the evolution of an American mercantilism: Timothy Pickering, John Adams, and John Quincy Adams of Massachusetts; Alexander Hamilton of New York; and James Madison, Thomas Jefferson, and John Taylor of Virginia.

In many respects, at any rate, Pickering and Taylor represented the nether fringes of American mercantilism. Pickering trod the trail from reluctant revo-lutionary to threatening secessionist in the name of a domestic merchant aris-tocracy functioning as a quasi-independent contractual member of the British Empire. His ideal was a central government charged with the responsibility (and armed with the power and authority) to establish and sustain a politically and socially stratified society and to provide the economic assistance (especially funded credit) that was necessary for the rationalized operations of overseas cor-respondents of British mercantilism and for domestic speculative ventures. Though Pickering and his supporters fit the traditional stereotype of mercantilists, they were in fact and function no more than the agents of British mercantilism. They were very successful agents, to be sure, but they did not view or define America in terms of its own mercantilism. Rather did they visualize it as a self-governing commonwealth of the British Empire. Hence it was only very late and with great reluctance, if at all, that they supported the measures necessary for a mercantilist state in America.

At the other extreme, John Taylor developed his program as a variation on a theme first stated by the French physiocrats. He emphasized the primacy of agriculture as narrowly as Pickering stressed the virtue and necessity of the merchant-trader-speculator. Taylor's tirades against funded debts and bank stock, and his soliloquies in praise of the noble farmer, seem alike in their total opposition to the principles of mercantilism. But in other respects his ideas were not so untainted by mercantilism as his rhetoric indicated. As with most other planters, for example, his theory of labor coincided at all essential points with the view held by British mercantilists.[16] So, too, did his conception of the role of western lands in the economy of the seaboard "mother country."

With respect to foreign trade, moreover, Taylor was trapped by the weakness of the physiocrats in that area of economics.[17] Ostensibly free traders, the physi-ocrats did not favor the navy essential to such a program. Taylor and other American imbibers of the physiocratic elixir awoke to discover that their vision did not correspond to reality. Taylor himself was not very adaptive, and ended his career in attacks on Jefferson and other agrarians who did develop an Ameri-can mercantilism. But Taylor's position does dramatize the dilemma faced by the agrarians.[18] The contradiction between theory and actuality confronted them with a rather apparent choice: either they could content themselves with slow

[16]Though independently worked out, this analysis is supported by Charles R. Haygood, "Mercantilism and Colonial Slave Labor, 1700–1763," *Journal of Southern History*, XXIII (Nov. 1957), 454–464.

[17] Arthur I. Bloomfield, "The Foreign-Trade Doctrines of the Physiocrats," *American Economic Review*, XXVIII (Dec. 1938), 716–735.

[18] William D. Grampp, "John Taylor: Economist of Southern Agrarians," *Southern Economic Journal*, XI (Jan. 1945), 255–268, esp. pp. 258, 263, on Taylor's developing opposition to Jefferson.

economic stagnation or they could build an American maritime system, accept dependence upon a foreign naval power, or support an American industry. In that choice lies a key aspect of the rise of a mature American mercantilism; for it developed most consciously and was ultimately practiced most rigorously by the Southern agrarians who are often assumed to have been most rabidly anti-mercantilist. If nothing else, the weakness of their ideal program drove them into mercantilism.

It is particularly important to keep that fact in mind when considering Hamilton, about whom the discussion of American mercantilism has billowed for so long. Joseph Charles was essentially correct in his view that "the standard works on Hamilton evade the main issues which his career raises," and his judgment remains relevant despite the plethora of centennial essays and biographies.[19] The entire question of Hamilton's mercantilism has to be decided with reference to three points: the meaning and significance of the *Report on Manufactures*, his role in the Jay Treaty episode, and his plans to join in the further expansion of the British Empire in the Western Hemisphere. However difficult it may be to pin him down with an alternate characterization, Hamilton simply cannot be considered the fountainhead of American mercantilism unless those aspects of his career can be interpreted within the framework of mercantilist thought and action.

Since the *Report on Manufactures* is often accepted as proof, as well as evidence, of Hamilton's mercantilism, it is convenient to give first consideration to that document. In doing so, it seems wise to recall the chronology of his three state papers on economic affairs. Hamilton was commissioned as Secretary of the Treasury on September 11, 1789; and there followed the manifesto on public credit in January 1790, the report on a central bank in December 1790, and the paper on manufacturing in December 1791. Even the most cursory review of those dates catches the two-year delay between the reports on credit and manufacturers. That interval becomes even more striking when viewed in the context of other events.

It was Madison rather than Hamilton, for example, who gave more attention to protective duties on manufactures during the Constitutional Convention. That is still more illuminating since associations for the promotion of American manufactures had appeared in New York, Boston, Providence, and Baltimore as early as 1785; and resolutions for domestic goods had followed the next year from such additional and widely separated localities as Hartford, Germantown, Richmond, and Halifax (South Carolina). By 1789, furthermore, not only had the anti-Federalists picked up political support from such groups in New England, New

[19] Joseph Charles, *The Origins of the American Party System* (Williamsburg, 1956), pp. 11–12. Also see John C. Livingston, "Alexander Hamilton and the American Tradition," *Midwest Journal of Political Science*, I (Nov. 1957), 209–224; Arnold A. Rogow, "Edmund Burke and the American Liberal Tradition," *Antioch Review*, XVII (June 1957), 255–265; James O. Wettereau, "Letters from Two Business Men to Alexander Hamilton on Federal Fiscal Policy, November, 1789," *Journal of Economic and Business History*, III (Aug. 1931), 667–686; Samuel Rezneck, "The Rise and Early Development of Industrial Consciousness in the United States, 1760–1830," *ibid.*, IV (Aug. 1932), 784–811. This approach to Hamilton had been worked out in all essentials prior to the publication of the most recent biographies, and for that reason it was deemed wise to present it in the form in which it was originally cast.

York, and Pennsylvania, but the special session of Congress received numerous requests and petitions from various manufacturing societies.[20]

Having passed an emergency revenue bill in the form of tariff legislation, the Congress than *ordered* Hamilton, on January 15, 1790, to prepare a specific report on manufactures. That makes his delay even more noticeable, whatever allowances may be granted for his other duties and the thoroughness of his research. As late as October 1791, moreover, the administration saw no need to increase the tariff of 1789. In matters of chronology, urgency, and emphasis, therefore, it seems clear that Hamilton gave priority to funding the debt and establishing the bank. Those operations represented precisely the needs and objectives of the merchants who were semiautonomous correspondents of British mercantilism, and who were fundamentally opposed to a strong American industry. Their economic, political, and social position would be threatened by a vigorous program of industrialization; for at the very least they would have to make drastic changes in their outlook and actions. Since Hamilton's personal and political position was based on his rapport with that group, it seems relevant to consider whether Hamilton's mercantilism was as thoroughgoing as historians have assumed it was.

In Hamilton's behalf, it can be argued with considerable validity that domestic industry had to have a sound credit system as a cornerstone. But that approach only raises the question of why Hamilton did not present his funding and bank programs as the means to achieve an independent balanced economy. Since he did not, the most relevant explanation would seem to be that Hamilton was in fact a mercantilist who was hamstrung by his political dependence upon the Federalists around Pickering. His association with Tench Coxe would serve to strengthen that analysis.[21] The same argument could then be used to explain why Hamilton delayed his paper on manufactures for almost two years after the Congress had asked for it in January 1790.

The weakest point in that interpretation concerns Hamilton's response to Madison's resolution of January 3, 1794, that "the interests of the United States would be promoted by further restrictions and higher duties in certain cases on the manufactures and navigation of foreign nations employed in the commerce of the United States." Working through William Smith of South Carolina, Hamilton killed Madison's entire program which was designed to promote commercial and industrial independence. Instead, Hamilton's committee in the House reported in favor of more borrowing and further domestic taxes. For that matter, neither Hamilton nor the Federalist party acted to increase protection after 1792.[22]

[20] This section draws heavily on Charles, *Origins of the American Party System*, and on Vols. I and II of Irving Brant, *James Madison* (Indianapolis and New York, 1941 — in progress). A more detailed account of these early episodes can be found in Vol. I of Edward Stanwood, *American Tariff Controversies in the Nineteenth Century* (Boston, 1903).

[21] Here see Rezneck, "The Rise and Early Development of Industrial Consciousness in the United States, 1760–1830"; and Joseph Dorfman, *The Economic Mind in American Civilization, 1606–1865* (New York, 1946), I, 253–256, 290–293.

[22] Stanwood, *American Tariff Controversies*, I, 108–110, 120–121; and for considerable insight into the role of Smith of South Carolina, consult Joseph Ernst, "Growth of the South Carolina Commons House of Assembly, 1761–1775," unpubl. masters thesis, University of Wisconsin, 1958.

The explanation of Hamilton's action which does the most to sustain his reputation as an American mercantilist is not as generous to his standing as a reformed monarchist. For given the broad and vigorous agitation from manufacturing societies for greater protection, Madison's resolutions offered Hamilton a striking opportunity to widen the base of the Federalist party. That would have strengthened his hand against the pro-British group within the party and have enabled him to give substance to the *Report on Manufactures*. If it be said that Hamilton favored domestic excise taxes in preference to domestic manufacturing, then his mercantilism appears even more questionable. A strong argument could be made by reference to Hamilton's known reservations about democracy, which would account for his refusal to court the manufacturers as a counterweight to the merchants around Pickering.

It may be, however, that Hamilton's vigorous opposition to Madison's resolutions of 1794 derived in considerable part from the fact that Madison's program was aimed at Great Britain. Not only was that true in the immediate, particular sense, but it also was the case in that Madison's proposals pointed toward general economic independence. That approach to the question of Hamilton's mercantilism has the virtue of having considerable relevance to his role in Jay's Treaty. An American mercantilist could explain and defend Hamilton's basic attitude and maneuvers behind Jay's back by one or both of two arguments. First, England had to be courted while the United States built a navy. Second, Hamilton stressed the political side of mercantilism.

Neither of those explanations is very convincing: Hamilton always favored the Army over the Navy, and political mercantilism is such a contradiction in terms that it begs the entire issue. That interpretation becomes even less convincing when asked to account for the fact that at the end of his career Hamilton turned not toward manufacturing but in the direction of becoming a partner in Britain's imperial adventures in Latin America. Indeed, Hamilton's foreign policy does less to settle the question of his mercantilism than to recall the report in 1793 that "the English considered Hamilton, [Rufus] King, and [William] Smith, of South Carolina, as main supports of British interest in America. Hamilton, not Hammond, was their effective minister."[23] Perhaps the most to be said of Hamilton's mercantilism is that it was latent and limited, for his actions belied his rhetoric.

As in many other contexts, it is Madison who emerges as the central figure in the development of an American mercantilism. While there are many illustrations, perhaps his resolutions of January 1794 provide the most illuminating evidence. Once again Charles points the way: "The program with which Madison began the first strategic moves against the Federalists was not one which could be called anti-Federalist, particularist, or States' rights."[24] His plan was to combine landed expansion to the west with support for domestic manufacturing and an independent American commercial policy. Considered at the practical political level, it represented a bid to the growing numbers of dissident Federalists who opposed a one-way relationship with Britain. Some of those men eyed a bull market for domestic manufactures. Others thought of an expansionist for-

[23] Eugene P. Link, *Democratic-Republican Societies, 1790–1800* (New York, 1942), n. 16, p. 49.
[24] Charles, *Origins of the American Party System*, p. 97.

eign policy with the established states cast in the role of "mother country." Madison saw such groups as allies for the anti-Federalists, as well as the building blocks of an American mercantilism.

Madison's conception of an American mercantilism was possibly too comprehensive as well as too premature politically to be adopted by Congress in 1794, though it was extensively debated before being sidetracked by Hamilton and Smith. But it did serve as a keen analysis and program for the growing consensus among anti-Federalists. That drive toward economic independence manifested itself in the Non-Intercourse Bill introduced in the summer of 1794, a move which was defeated only by the vote of Vice-President John Adams. Equally significant is the fact that it was backed by congressmen from Pennsylvania and Delaware as well as by those from southern states. Madison's mercantilism picked up new allies very rapidly, and two subsequent events served as catalysts in the process. Considered in the order of their importance, they were Jay's Treaty and the last stage in the defection of John Adams from High Federalism.

Following so closely upon the narrow defeat of the Non-Intercourse Bill, Jay's Treaty added injury to frustration. The great majority of Americans reacted bitterly and vigorously. Already weakened by deep fissures, the Federalist party cracked open under the ensuing attack. It cost them key leaders in such states as New Hampshire and Pennsylvania and alienated unknown numbers of voters south of the Potomac. As one who had cast the deciding vote against the Non-Intercourse Bill only with great reluctance, John Adams provided temporary leadership for such Federalist dissidents.

Adams strengthened his position even more by refusing to go quietly along to war with France at the bidding of the High Federalists. The differences between Hamilton and Adams were numerous, but perhaps none is so important to an appreciation of the maturing American mercantilism as the contrast between Hamilton's passion for a large army and Adams' emphasis on an American navy. Hamilton's military policy was that of the British nabob in North America, while that of Adams represented American mercantilism. Against that background, and in the context of his deciding vote on the Non-Intercourse Bill of 1794, it is possible to appreciate the full impact of Jay's Treaty on Adams. He made peace with France and forced Pickering out of the cabinet.

Little wonder, then, that Jefferson was willing to give way in favor of Adams. But thanks to Madison, who had been organizing a party as well as projecting a theory and a program, Jefferson became President. Once in power, Jefferson and his supporters were prodded by necessity and spurred by their own visions of empire toward the full development of an American mercantilism. There are several explanations for this phenomenon. Among the most important, one might list the following: the foreign-trade dilemma inherent in physiocratic theory (which was intensified by the wars stemming from the French Revolution); the creative leadership provided by such men as Madison and Albert Gallatin (who made his own *Report on Manufactures* in 1810); the political necessities and expediences of unifying and sustaining a national party; and the maturing thought of Jefferson himself. But wherever one chooses to place the emphasis, the fact remains that the Jeffersonians in action were far more mercantilistic than the Federalists had been — even in theory and rhetoric.

As early as 1791, for that matter, Jefferson began to shift away from the physiocratic dogma of free trade. And by 1793 he concluded his *Report on Commercial Policy* with a series of retaliatory proposals that were as mercantilistic as any he criticized. Perhaps even more significant was his early ambivalence toward manufacturing, which he never condemned outright once and for all. Jefferson disliked cities and the factory system for what he judged their negative impact on politics and morals, and for the conditions and style of life they imposed on human beings, but he never discounted the importance of home manufacturing and commerce. He could not afford to, either as the leader of agrarians beginning to produce surpluses for sale, or as one who sought and accepted support from the increasing number of urban groups of all classes who preferred an empire of their own to rejoining the British system. Even if Jefferson had not caught the intellectual flaw in physiocratic trade theory, its practical consequences were something he could not avoid. In substance, therefore, the Jeffersonians based their strength and their policies on the mercantilistic program of a balanced economy at home and a foreign policy of expansion.

Their strategy was to exploit the policy of neutrality initiated by Washington and continued by John Adams. To do so, Jefferson ultimately resorted to the intensely mercantilistic policies of the embargo and non-importation against Britain and France. It was with obvious pride that he remarked, in 1809, that those policies "hastened the day when an equilibrium between the occupations of agriculture, manufactures, and commerce, shall simplify our foreign concerns to the exchange only of that surplus which we cannot consume [in return] for those articles of reasonable comfort or convenience which we cannot produce."[25] Not even Madison ever provided a more classic statement of American mercantilism.

Quite in line with Jefferson's recommendations of the 1790's, and his actions between 1800 and 1809, his successors acted vigorously against such weaker opponents as the Barbary Pirates who threatened American trade. On a more general level, Jefferson's argument that American democracy depended upon a surplus of land was but another, even more overtly formulated, version of Madison's theory that extending the sphere was the key to controlling factions. Hence he and his followers initiated and encouraged such expansion wherever they could, as in Florida and to the West; and it was precisely Jefferson's general expansionist outlook which overrode his concern that the Louisiana Purchase was unconstitutional.

The Louisiana Purchase opened the way to apply the tenets of American mercantilism to the entire hemisphere. It also encouraged an explicit American formulation of the expansionist philosophy of history that was implicit in mercantilism. Americans began to call openly and militantly for further expansion whenever and wherever they encountered domestic or foreign difficulties. Indians and Spaniards had to be pushed out of the way or destroyed. Interference with exports had to be stopped, by war if necessary. Canada offered the solution to other domestic economic problems, and should be taken forthwith.

After 1807, when economic troubles appeared at home, that expansionist outlook and program focused on Great Britain as the chief offender against the American Empire. Growing out of an alliance of business and agrarian interests

[25] Quoted in Grampp, "A Re-examination of Jeffersonian Economics," p. 279.

which favored war to relieve immediate difficulties and forestall future crises, the War of 1812 was a classic mercantilist conflict for trade and colonies.[26] The Jeffersonians' earlier economic and maritime warfare, which almost secured the immediate objectives, and which had appeared capable of clearing the way for a general advance, was just as mercantilistic in nature. Though in many ways it failed to attain its avowed objectives, the War of 1812 was in no sense a strategic defeat for American mercantilism. If only in turning Americans to the west and the south, it focused the general spirit of expansion in a new and powerful manner. Perhaps even more significant, the stalemate strengthened the idea of an American System as opposed to the rest of the world. It was in the wake of the War of 1812, after all, that the vapors of Manifest Destiny gathered themselves for an explosion westward to the Pacific.

John Quincy Adams formulated his own concept of Manifest Destiny as early as 1796, when he assured President Washington that the American System would "infallibly triumph over the European system. . . ."[27] Fifteen years later he defined America as "a nation, coextensive with the North American Continent, destined by God and nature to be the most populous and most powerful people ever combined under one social compact."[28] He pushed overseas economic expansion just as vigorously. Even his harshest critics, the High Federalists of New England who wanted to re-enter the British Empire in some form or another, recognized his mercantilism. They called him one of the species of "amphibious politicians, who live on both land and water. . . ."[29]

Both before and after he served as Secretary of State under President James Monroe, Adams devoted his energies to building such an American Empire. His rational program for a dynamic balanced economy at home was too demanding for his countrymen. They grew ever more enamored of a philosophy that assured them that expansion was the way to ease their dilemmas and realize their dreams. Hence they paid little heed to his proposals for domestic development or to his warning that America should go "not abroad in search of monsters to destroy." But to the extent that Adams wanted an empire big enough to sustain such a balanced economy, and to the degree that he partook of the expansionist elixir, he won support and influence. And, indeed, his very presence in the cabinet of Monroe was a symbol of the maturity of American mercantilism. Having broken with the old pro-British party to vote for the Louisiana Purchase and the measures of economic warfare against Europe, Adams became the leader of those business interests which supported territorial as well as commercial expansion.

In timing, authorship, and content, the Monroe Doctrine was the classic statement of mature American mercantilism. Seizing the opportunity presented by the decay of the Spanish Empire, Monroe and Adams moved quickly, decisively, and independently to give substance to Henry Clay's fervent exhortation to "be-

[26] On eastern urban votes for war see Warren H. Goodman, "The Origins of the War of 1812: A Survey of Changing Interpretations," reprinted in *The Shaping of American Diplomacy*, ed. William A. Williams (Chicago, 1956), p. 122.

[27] Quoted in Samuel F. Bemis, *John Quincy Adams and the Foundations of American Foreign Policy* (New York, 1949), p. 64.

[28] *Ibid.*, p. 180.

[29] *Ibid.*, p. 148.

come real and true Americans and place ourselves at the head of the American System."[30] Adams caught the tone and meaning of the doctrine in his famous remark that it was time for America to stop bobbing along as a cock-boat in the wake of the British Empire. Acting in that spirit, he spurned Secretary George Canning's not-so-subtle suggestion that America join England in a joint guarantee of Latin American independence and pledge against their own expansion in the region. Canning claimed high honors for having brought in the New World to redress the balance of the Old, but one would like to think that Adams enjoyed a hearty chuckle over such ability to put a rhetorical gloss on a policy defeat. For what Canning had done was to block the old empires only to be confronted by the challenge of a mature American mercantilism.

In the negative sense, the Monroe Doctrine was designed to check further European colonization in the Western Hemisphere. But Americans were quite aware of the positive implications of the strategy: it left the United States as the most powerful nation on the scene. America's ultimate territorial and commercial expansion in the New World would be limited only by its energies and its preferences — just as Washington had argued.[31] The negative side of the Monroe Doctrine is the least significant feature about it: the crucial point is that it was, in the minds of its authors, in its language, and in its reception by Americans, the manifesto of an American Empire.

[The Monroe Doctrine was the capstone of a system destined to succumb to its own success. For in broad historical perspective, the classic function of mercantilism was to build a system strong enough to survive the application of the principles of Adam Smith. Without an American mercantilism there could have been no Age of Jacksonian Laissez Moi Faire. Perhaps, indeed, the greatest tribute to the leaders of American mercantilism lies in the fact that their handiwork withstood the trauma of a civil war and the sustained shock of unrestrained and irrational exploitation for some seventy years — until it became necessary in the Crisis of the 1890's to undertake the building of a new corporate system.]

---

[30] *Ibid.*, p. 352; but cf. pp. 364, 127.

[31] The traditional neglect of commercial interests and pressures in connection with the formulation and enunciation of the Monroe Doctrine, an approach symbolized in Dexter Perkins, *Monroe Doctrine, 1823–1826* (Baltimore, 1929), is somewhat corrected by Charles L. Chandler, "United States Commerce with Latin America at the Promulgation of the Monroe Doctrine," *Quarterly Journal of Economics*, XXXVIII (May 1924), 466–486. Even more illuminating are Dorothy B. Goebel, "British-American Rivalry in the Chilean Trade, 1817–1820," *Journal of Economic History*, II (Nov. 1942), 190–202; Charles C. Griffin, *The United States and the Disruption of the Spanish Empire, 1810–1822* (New York, 1937); and Arthur Preston Whitaker, *The United States and the Independence of Latin America, 1800–1830* (Baltimore, 1941).

The Working Classes of the Pre-Industrial American City, 1780–1830

DAVID MONTGOMERY

We are accustomed to thinking of nineteenth-century America as an era of general and increasing prosperity, especially in the decades immediately preceding the democratic Jacksonian period. One imagines an America composed of prosperous farms, thriving infant industries, and a vigorous frontier in the first third of the century. The tribulations of the conflict with Great Britain and the trauma of the Panic of 1819 strike a more somber note, but they seem exceptions to the norm. Historians of the colonial period, such as James Henretta, have begun to reveal the less happy aspects of national development in their findings of the considerable numbers of propertyless Americans within the mainly prosperous society. These men, women, and children tended to live in the urban areas of the northern United States: in Boston, New York, Philadelphia, and Baltimore. We know very little about who they were and how they lived, since in every society the well-to-do leave better records, but we are now conscious of the need to know more about the non-elite members of American society. David Montgomery points out that we have tended to inquire into the character of the working classes mainly in the period of industrial expansion following 1870, but he argues that there is an equal need to investigate the working class history of the pre-industrial cities of the late-eighteenth and early-nineteenth centuries. In this exploratory essay he surmises that the period was one of favorable conditions for artisans, the category comprising the most highly skilled workmen, whose wages were higher than those of their English counterparts even though the paternalistic relations between master and apprentice of an earlier era were doubtless fast disappearing. Laborers, the unskilled workers, were also probably better off than their fellows in Great Britain; they were occupationally more versatile, working generally in transportation and commerce and moving freely between jobs and cities. In fact, he adds, the working classes of the period spanned a wide spectrum of economic and social strata, ranging from the self-conscious role the artisans played in politics and business to the frequently impoverished conditions of woman and child workers. Moreover, Montgomery demonstrates the existence of a pre-industrial working class and suggests some of the reasons for more intensive study of the early history of American working people. Labor history, when seen in such a broad perspective, touches on the concerns of economics, politics, social organization, and the history of ideas. It presupposes that one cannot understand our na-

tional history fully by studying only the relatively few individuals who control wealth, social and political power, for we must have knowledge of, and sympathy for, all its members in order to understand the society fully.

In the years since Raymond W. Goldsmith submitted to Congress his statistical findings on the rise of per capita incomes in the United States many economic historians have come to date the beginnings of sustained industrial growth at some time during the 1830s.[1] This chronology has provided historians of the working class with a significant bench-mark to guide their own research and analysis. Among other things it raises questions concerning the sources, size, and character of the labor supply which was at hand before the acceleration of economic growth and the ideological baggage (attitudes, customs institutions) which the available workers carried with them when they entered the industrial era. The objective of this article is to suggest some parameters for both sets of questions derived from an examination of the working classes in the young nation's four northern cities: Boston, New York, Philadelphia, and Baltimore.

During the five decades before 1830 these cities were essentially depots for trans-oceanic shipping, and their labor force was largely tied to maritime commerce. Surrounding each of them was "a vast scene of household manufacturing" where, wrote Alexander Hamilton, country folk produced clothing, shoes, and other necessities, "in many instances, to an extent not only sufficient for the supply of the families in which they are made, but for sale, and even, in some cases, for exportation."[2] Such a countryside Albert Gallatin found twenty years later in New Hampshire, where the average farmer's house had at least one spinning wheel, and every second house boasted a loom on which from 100 to 600 yards of saleable cloth were woven annually (at a time when journeymen weavers in their homes averaged only 829 yards per year and factory looms, 1,111 yards).[3] Most manufacturing, in other words, was carried on outside of the major cities. By 1820 some 12 percent of the nation's labor force was engaged in

Reprinted by permission of the publisher from *Labor History*, 9 (1968), pp. 3–22.

[1] U.S. Congress, Joint Economic Committee, *Hearings [on] Employment, Growth and Price Levels,* "Part 2 — Historical and Comparative Rates of Production, Productivity, and Prices," 86th Cong., 1st Sess., 1959, 230–279; George Rogers Taylor, "The National Economy Before and After the Civil War," in *Economic Change in the Civil War Era,* edited by David T. Gilchrist and W. David Lewis (Greenville, Del., 1965), 1–22; Douglass C. North, *Growth and Welfare in the American Past* (Englewood Cliffs, N.J., 1966), 15–17, 75–89; Robert Gallman, "Commodity Output, 1839–1899," in *Trends in the American Economy in the Nineteenth Century, National Bureau of Economic Research Studies in Income and Wealth Volume Twenty-Four* (Princeton, N.J., 1960), 13–67. Stuart Bruchey finds indices of significant industrial growth before the 1830s, *The Roots of American Economic Growth, 1607–1861, An Essay in Social Causation* (New York, 1965), 76–91.

[2] Alexander Hamilton, "Report on Manufactures," in Hamilton, *Papers on Public Credit, Commerce, and Finance,* edited by Samuel McKee, Jr. (Indianapolis and New York, 1957), 222.

[3] Albert Gallatin, "Manufactures," *American State Papers,* Finance, II, 434–435.

manufacturing and construction, and 28 percent in all non-agricultural occupations, but at that time the residents of these cities and their contiguous suburbs totalled only 356,452, or 3.7 percent of the American people.[4]

The merchant elite of these communities, furthermore, was concerned not so much with hiring labor as with vending the produce of labor, both agricultural and mechanical. Mathew Carey went so far as to accuse the merchants of hostility toward manufacturing interests, of striving "to impress upon the public mind, that the national prosperity depended almost altogether on commerce; that the protection of manufactures by duties on imports was impolitic and unjust."[5] Understandably the broadsides of Carey, Gallatin, Tench Coxe, and other promoters of manufacturing bore the aspect of appeals to the dominant agricultural and commercial interests of the land to pay some heed to the needs of industry and to believe that the growth of domestic manufactures could take place without depriving farmers and merchants of either manpower or customers.

But Carey's conception of the merchant as industry's relentless foe slighted the encouragement offered manufacturing by the commercial city itself. The concentration of population in seaports required by a growing flow of commerce prevented urban residents from producing their own necessities in the fashion of farm families. It generated a social division of labor within the city itself and hence a need for sedentary artisans. The accumulation of merchant fortunes, furthermore, created a demand for luxury goods and thus for expert craftsmen: for silversmiths, goldbeaters, clockmakers, wig and peruke makers, printers of books and journals, tailors, and cordwainers familiar with European fashions and capable of reproducing them. By the end of the eighteenth century, moreover, seaboard merchants had opened a substantial oceanic trade in shoes, clothing, barrels, and ironwares with the regions of slave plantations. This trade encouraged the development of both the putting-out system and the early efforts toward factory organization of production.

Although most manufacturing was carried on outside the great urban centers, the seaport itself, therefore, generated a demand for labor in production as well as trade. In the eighteenth century most manufacture had been performed in the workshops of mechanics who, with the aid of family, apprentices, and occasional journeymen, made the wares they vended themselves.[6] The printer, for example, was usually a bookseller and a journalist as well, in the manner of Mathew Carey, who in the 1790s composed his own editorials in type and then hawked the paper about Philadelphia. Only after 1810 did urban newspapers gravitate into the hands of publishers who were not printers but, in the language

[4] Figures on distribution of labor force are calculated from U.S. Department of Commerce, Bureau of the Census, *Historical Statistics of the United States, 1789–1945* (Washington, D.C., 1949), 29. Population figures for city and suburban areas are taken from those presented by Professor Everett S. Lee at the 1966 Eleutherian Mills-Hagley Foundation Conference on the Growth of Seaport Cities, 1790–1825.

[5] Mathew Carey, *Autobiography* (Research Classics, Number One, Brooklyn, 1942), 95.

[6] See Carl Bridenbaugh, *Colonial Craftsman* (New York, 1950); Richard B. Morris, *Government and Labor in Early America* (New York, 1946); Staughton Lynd and Alfred Young, "After Carl Becker: The Mechanics and New York City Politics, 1774–1801," *Labor History*, V (Fall, 1964), 215–224.

of the journeymen, "speculators on the labor of printers" who installed "hireling editors" to write the columns printers now set in type.[7]

The colonial conception of a journeyman as tomorrow's master mechanic was neither dead nor fully obsolete by 1820, for vertical mobility was still remarkable. Among the early members of the Franklin Typographical Association of New York, a trade society of journeymen founded in 1799, were David Bruce, the future owner of the city's largest printing shop and a pioneer typefounder; Thurlow Weed, a future boss of state politics; Samuel Woodworth, the poet of "Old Oaken Bucket" fame; and Peter Force, America's most eminent historical archivist.[8] Two of the master shoemakers who testified against the cordwainers union in Philadelphia's 1805 conspiracy trial were former journeymen and union members, as were two of the employers at the similar Pittsburgh trial ten years later.[9] But by the first two decades of the nineteenth century the emergence of distinct societies of journeymen and of masters among printers, tailors, shoemakers, carpenters, stone cutters, and other trades in every seaport indicated a new awareness of distinct class interests. The seventeen benevolent societies of Philadelphia carpenters, ship masters, stone cutters, and other trades listed by James Mease in 1811 were clearly organizations of master mechanics. Their initiation fees ranging from $10 up and their annual dues of four or five dollars contrast remarkably with the one dollar initiation and the 25 cents monthly dues (waived after ten years' membership) charged by that city's printers union.[10] Societies of journeymen that sought to combine benevolent functions with the enforcement of union wage scales ultimately found it necessary to either expel members who had risen to the rank of employers, or to succumb to the urgings of "alimoners" in their midst and abandon the effort to regulate trade conditions. Thus the printers' organizations in Philadelphia and Boston during the 1820s converted themselves into friendly societies open to employers and workmen alike, while the New York society, bent on controlling wages and aware that the "interests of the journeymen are separate and in some respects opposite to those of the employers," resolved in 1817 "that when any member of this society shall become an employing printer he shall be considered without the limits of this society."[11]

The myth of harmonious personal relationships among masters, journeymen, and apprentices in a setting of domestic paternalism may be quite anachronistic when applied to post-Revolutionary decades. Ian Quimby's study of apprentice contracts in eighteenth century Philadelphia revealed a persistent erosion of filial duties and loyalties by the emerging ethos of commercialism. The mutual

[7] Carey, Autobiography, 11–25; Ethelbert Stewart, "Documentary History of the Early Organization of Printers," in U.S. Department of Commerce and Labor, Bulletin of the Bureau of Labor, No. 61 (Washington, D.C., 1905), 912.

[8] George A. Stevens, New York Typographical Union No. 6 (Albany, 1913), 38, 81–102.

[9] Commonwealth v. Pullis, in John R. Commons, et al., Documentary History of American Industrial Society (10 vols., Cleveland, 1910), III, 59–248; Commonwealth v. Morrow, in ibid., IV, 15–88.

[10] Thomas Wilson, Picture of Philadelphia, for 1824, Containing the "Picture of Philadelphia, for 1811, by James Mease, M.D." with All Its Improvements since that Period (Philadelphia, 1823), 267–276; Stewart, 943.

[11] Stevens, op. cit., 76.

moral obligations of apprentices and masters in such matters as work expected of the boy, and the education and clothing due him were converted over the course of the century into money values and specified in ever-increasing detail in the contracts.[12] The experience of cabinetmakers, furthermore, suggests that journeymen seldom remained long enough with any master to develop a sense of personal attachment. The journeymen of Samuel Ashton's Philadelphia cabinet shop between 1795 and 1803 averaged scarcely six months in his employ. So rapid was the turnover of craftsmen that, though Ashton rarely needed more than five workmen at a time, forty-nine different men worked for him during those eight years.[13] Under such circumstances class antagonisms based on chronic disputes over wages could be quite consistent with a high level of upward social mobility.

By the 1820s, therefore, the urban working classes comprised recognizable and self-conscious elements of urban society. The "classes . . . who are wholly dependent upon wages," wrote Reverend Joseph Tuckerman, "are very numerous" and, he continued:

> would, indeed, be numerous, if we looked for them among only those who have no trade, and who are generally distinguished alone, as labouring men. This large division includes shop, market, and other porters; carmen; those who are employed in lading, and unlading vessels; wood-sawyers; hod carriers; house servants; those employed by mechanics in a single branch of their business; and multitudes, who are men and women of any work, occasionally required in families, as washing, scouring, etc.; or on the wharves, or in the streets of the city. Besides these, the number is great of those, who are journeymen, and many of whom will never be anything but journeymen, in the various mechanic arts; and considerable number are also employed in the different departments of large manufactories, who possess no capital; and who know, and will continue to know, little or nothing in any other department of these establishments, except that in which they are themselves employed. All these, in the strictest sense, and in the common acceptation of the term, are dependent on the wages which they obtain for their services.[14]

Tuckerman's definition of the wage earning classes suggests that journeymen, mechanics, casual laborers, and factory operatives must be analyzed separately. Even though many mechanics would "never be anything but journeymen," they enjoyed the highest incomes and status of any wage earners and were psychologically the most firmly wedded to the social values and practices of the traditional artisan. Apprenticeship was the historic route of access to "the art and mysteries" of any trade, and the journeymen of this period strove to bar any

[12] Ian M. G. Quimby, "Apprenticeship in Colonial Philadelphia," (unpublished Master's Thesis, University of Delaware, 1963), 60–63.

[13] Morrison H. Heckscher, "The Organization and Practice of Philadelphia Cabinetmaking Establishments, 1790–1820," (unpublished Master's Thesis, University of Delaware, 1964), 22–25.

[14] Joseph Tuckerman, An Essay on the Wages Paid to Females for Their Labour . . . (Philadelphia, 1830), 8.

other avenue of entry. The Philadelphia Typographical Society, which sought with occasional success to reserve all printing positions in town for its own members, excluded from membership anyone "who shall not have served an apprenticeship satisfactory to the board of directors" of the union, and subsequently tried to keep from the presses anyone who had "broken into the trade" after he was twenty-one years old.[15] Both the income and the honor associated with the printer's art were thus to be reserved to those who elected to ply it when they first attained the age of productive manhood at fifteen or sixteen years old. Altogether Philadelphia's complete records of apprentices bound between October 1771 and October 1773 revealed 1,075 youths apprenticed to sixty-eight trades (including many girls indentured to learn "housewifery"). Ten percent of them were to learn the cordwainer's art, and the trades of tailor, mariner, carpenter, and cooper followed shoemaking in order of preference.[16]

Sons of mechanics apprenticed to trades were supplemented by those of farmers who, for example, constituted the bulk of Massachusetts' supply of shoemakers,[17] and in Baltimore by young slaves. The emancipation of northern slaves meant the eclipse of Negro apprenticeship in most urban trades elsewhere. Because the training of slave craftsmen had rarely been complete, freed Negro artisans, who faced intense animosity from white craftsmen and had lost the protection of their masters, rarely survived in positions where they could train apprentices of their own race, and even fewer whites would engage black youth for training.[18] The influx of white farm boys to urban trades, on the other hand, was inhibited by that "desire of being an independent proprietor of land" which Alexander Hamilton believed would always keep small the numbers of those "who would be diverted from it towards manufacturers."[19] Youths who did elect urban trades, furthermore, often fled their apprenticeships after only a year or two of service and, to the great distress of established journeymen, easily found employment as half-trained workmen at substandard wages. The supply of labor was thus rapidly increased at the expense of its quality. The founding of mechanics' institutes (vocational schools) in every major northern city in the 1820s bears witness to the breakdown of traditional apprenticeship training.[20]

The fact remains that residents of rural areas in the Northeast were being lured toward the city, just as others were migrating westward, and frequently such migrants had been craftsmen, rather than (or as well as) farmers. In every decade between 1790 and 1840, the population of all four cities under review grew at a rate substantially above the 33 percent to 36 percent growth for the nation as a whole, with two exceptions: both Philadelphia and New York grew at less than the national rate between 1810 and 1820, and Baltimore's increase after

[15] Stewart, *op. cit.*, 877, 943.

[16] Quimby, *op. cit.*, 30.

[17] Blanche Evans Hazard, *Organization of the Boot and Shoe Industry in Massachusetts before 1875* (Cambridge, Mass., 1921), 322–323.

[18] Leonard Price Stavisky, "The Negro Artisan in the South Atlantic States, 1800–1860: A Study of Status and Economic Opportunity with Special Reference to Charleston" (unpublished Ph.D. dissertation, Columbia University, 1958), 16–22; Morris, *op. cit.*, 182–188; Leon Litwack, *North of Slavery: The Negro in the Free States, 1790–1860* (Chicago, 1961), 153–162.

[19] Hamilton, *op. cit.*, 203.

[20] See Bruchey, *op. cit.*, 188–189.

1820 was chronically below the national pace.[21] This urbanization of native Americans was supplemented by the arrival of European immigrants, but the extent of the trans-oceanic contribution to the growth of these seaports is difficult to measure. Although newcomers to America totalled 400,000 between 1790 and 1830, with 1801–1807, 1816, and 1828–1830 being the years of greatest influx, the bulk of them came not to the American seaport but through it.[22] It was the demand for farm laborers in the hinterland which produced, for example, the large scale trafficking in redemptioners Frances Wright witnessed in the Philadelphia of 1818.[23]

Among the immigrants who tarried in the city, however, were many skilled mechanics. British emigrants and British trade union practices (complete to the oaths sworn over union scales and the trappings of secrecy necessitated in the old country by the Combination Acts but retained here as a matter of custom) showed up in every conspiracy trial of union journeymen. When the prosecutor charged Philadelphia cordwainers in 1805 with "crimes" committed by union members a decade earlier, the defense replied with only slight exaggeration that none of the journeymen on trial had been in America when those acts were committed.[24] Stocking weavers in Germantown and Kensington outside of Philadelphia had almost all learned their trade in Leicester or Nottingham or the Rhineland. Linen weavers had poured out of northern Ireland in the early 1770s and again at the close of the American Revolution, many of them coming to the new republic. In 1784 alone 11,000 passengers embarked from Dublin, most of them emigrants of this type.[25]

An extreme case of immigrants' providing an industry with its skilled labor was offered by the thousand or so carpet weavers in the country in the early 1830s, at least nine-tenths of whom were Scots, largely from Kilmarnock and Ayr. So well did these mechanics know each other that when sixty-three of them struck the Thompsonville Carpet Manufacturing Company in Connecticut, they quickly assembled, compiled from memory a list of the eleven other principal carpet manufactories in the nation, wrote personal letters to friends in each of them explaining the dispute, notified the Blue Bonnet Tavern in New York City,

---

[21] Everett S. Lee, figures on urban population growth presented at the 1966 Eleutherian Mills-Hagley Foundation Conference on the Growth of Seaport Cities, 1790–1825. See also D. B. Warden, *Statistical, Political, and Historical Account of the United States of North America* (3 vols., Edinburgh, 1819), I, xlii. Between 1775 and 1790 the growth rates of these cities had fallen well behind the national rate. George Rogers Taylor, "American Economic Growth before 1840: An Exploratory Essay," *Journal of Economic History*, XXIV (Dec., 1964), 439.

[22] *Historical Statistics of the United States*, 34; Curtis P. Nettels, *Emergence of a National Economy, 1775–1815* (New York, 1962), 133; Marcus Lee Hansen, *Atlantic Migration, 1607–1860* (Harper Torchbook edition, New York, 1961), 84; E. P. Thompson, *Making of the English Working Class* (New York, 1966), 430–432.

[23] Frances Wright, *Views of Society and Manners in America*, edited by Paul R. Baker (Cambridge, Mass., 1963), 240–241. Compare the observations of Johann David Schoepf in Baltimore in 1783. *Travels in the Confederation*, translated and edited by Alfred J. Morrison (2 vols., Philadelphia, 1911), I, 339–340.

[24] Commons, *Documentary History*, III, 108.

[25] Edwin T. Freedley, *Philadelphia and Its Manufactures* (Philadelphia, 1858), 241–242; Arthur Redford, *Labour Migration in England 1800–1850*, edited and revised by W. H. Chaloner (Manchester, 1964), 166–167.

which served as the country's hiring hall for carpet weavers, to divert men from the struck plant, and dispatched an appeal to the *Old Countryman* in that city to warn off any Scots not reached by the other methods.[26]

Such incidents suggest the hypothesis that America was then a land of opportunity for handicraftsmen whose skills were being undermined by the industrial revolution in England but still in high demand in the more backward American economy. True, the number of handloom weavers and stockingers working in England continued to grow rapidly down to 1820 and perhaps beyond, despite the unmistakeable deterioration of income and status in those trades. Many older craftsmen, Arthur Redford found, moved to manufacturing cities in England, there continuing to ply their obsolete trades while depending increasingly on the earnings of their factory-employed children.[27] The Scottish carpet weavers brought to trial in Connecticult for their strike, however, were remarkably young men, twenty-two years of age or less. The presumption is that the craftsman-immigrant tended to be neither the daring innovator nor the veteran artisan who could not quit his obsolescent trade, but the mobile youth who spurned Briton's factory for the possibility of plying the (to him) preferable family trade in a new location.

This hypothesis is consistent with Hamilton's belief that "the disparity" between the "dearness of labor" in America and that in England was "much less in regard to artificers and manufacturers, than in regard to country labourers," a belief recently concurred in by H. J. Habakkuk and Stuart Bruchey.[28] During the first two decades of the nineteenth century skilled tradesmen in England engaged in "hounourable work" (a high quality work not yet subjected to a division of labor and deterioration of apprenticeship standards) looked upon 30s. weekly ($7.50) as an expected income, while some earned £3 and over. Such a 30s. standard fell below the $8.25 of an American shoemaker or the $9 a more seasonal carpenter might ordinarily have expected when working at union standards by precisely the differential of 12 percent–20 percent in America's favor which J. Leander Bishop found for glass workers.[29] True, American workmen paid considerably fewer taxes than their English counterparts, and as D. B. Warden observed of Philadelphia, "Smiths, shoemakers, weavers, and tailors have generally one or two acres of land, which afford pasture for a cow, fuel, and esculent plants."[30] But such bucolic benefits were by no means unknown to English weavers, croppers, and shoemakers, most of whom still worked in their cottages in rural villages.

Far more extreme was the contrast between the American municipal or canal laborer's expectation of some $4.50 a week (often paid partly in board) and the

---

[26] *Thompsonville Carpet Manufacturing Compnay vs. William Taylor . . .* , in Commons, *Documentary History*, IV — Supplement, 16–125.

[27] Thompson, *op. cit.*, 279–296; Redford, *op. cit.*, 186.

[28] Hamilton, *op. cit.*, 208; H. J. Habakkuk, *American and British Technology in the Nineteenth Century: The Search for Labour-Saving Inventions* (Cambridge, 1962), 21–43; Bruchey, *op. cit.*, 162–164.

[29] J. Leander Bishop, *History of American Manufactures from 1680–1860* (2 vols., Philadelphia, 1864), I, 242. For a description of "honourable work" in England see Thompson, 234–268.

[30] Warden, *op. cit.*, II, 107.

earnings of the English casual laborer, which then ranged from perhaps 11s. weekly in cotton factories to 1s. a day for wheelbarrow men in Birmingham. Taking 10s. (i.e., $2.50) as good weekly pay for such laborers in the second decade of the century, the unskilled American enjoyed a premium of 80 percent over his British counterpart.[31] That the wage differential was less rather than greater for the artisan than for casual labor is thus evident even without investigation of the real values of money wages in the two countries. Yet British craftsmen did migrate, spurred by the deteriorating conditions in their trades at home and lured, as one emigrant manual declared, by the openings in American trades left by "the strong emulation of the *cute* native Yankee to elevate himself above the common labour class."[32]

Whether graduates of American or British apprenticeships, urban tradesmen were both geographically mobile enough and sufficiently well informed about the state of the labor market elsewhere to maintain rather uniform wage standards throughout the northeastern cities. When Philadelphia shoemakers demanded a schedule of prices based on $4 a pair for back strap boots in October 1805, they were aware that the New York union had established precisely that scale in March. Similarly, when Pittsburgh shoemakers unionized at the end of that decade, they quickly drove up their prices from 75 cents below the Philadelphia wage to parity with it — but when they sought a scale higher than Philadelphia's, they were roundly defeated by their masters.[33] Both the New York and Washington societies of printers undertook — by correspondence with their counterparts in Philadelphia, Baltimore, Boston, and Albany — to establish uniform scales, and all these societies exchanged "rat lists" with each other, so that typographers who violated union rules and standards could not find refuge in other communities.[34] At times employers cooperated with these efforts of the journeymen, as did master printers in New York in 1815, or, more dramatically, the master weavers of Baltimore, who in 1829 did everything in their power to ostracize a fellow employer for slashing his journeymen's wages below the city norm.[35]

Although the mechanic was ranked by Tuckerman within the wage-earning classes, there is little evidence that prior to the 1830s he either identified himself with "the poor" or felt in any way alienated from the existing social order. Despite the absence from common American parlance of the rigid British distinction between "honourable" and "dishonourable" work, only the scale of the New York shoemakers out of all the union price lists which have been preserved

---

[31] For data on wages of unskilled labor see Mathew Carey, *Appeal to the Wealthy of the Land* . . . (Philadelphia, 1833), 17; Warden, II, 85; Christopher Roberts, *The Middlesex Canal* (Cambridge, Mass., 1938), 78–82. For comparable wages in England see Thompson, 310, 313; Redford, 39.

[32] Patrick Matthew, *Emigration Fields: North America, The Cape, Australia, and New Zealand* (Edinburgh and London, 1839), 40.

[33] Commons, *Documentary History*, III, 106, 368–369; *ibid.*, IV, 34.

[34] Stewart, *op. cit.*, 866, 871–872, 877, 881, 886, 888. Compare the efforts of Philadelphia's union curriers, Leonard Bernstein, "The Working People of Philadelphia from Colonial Times to the General Strike of 1835," *Pennsylvania Magazine of History and Biography*, LXXIV (July, 1950), 325.

[35] Stewart, *op. cit.*, 877; "Report of the Trial of the Journeymen Weavers in Baltimore City Court," in Commons, *Documentary History*, IV, 269–272.

from that period (mainly those of printers, shoemakers, tailors, and weavers) included a specified wage for coarse work, partially completed work, or the work of helpers. While the Pittsburgh shoemakers union did explicitly deem coarse work "out of society" and posed no objection to non-members performing such tasks, there is no such clear evidence from any of the seaport cities. It is remarkable, however, that the prosecutor in the New York shoemakers' trial, while conceding that many journeymen were not members, insisted that "all the best workmen were of the society." Similarly Philadelphia shoemakers considered themselves fully unionized between 1798 and 1804, when their society had 100 to 150 members, while the city directory for 1798 listed 292 shoemakers and cordwainers.[36] A plausible inference is that cheap shoes for slaves and for auction sale, which did not appear in the union's scale of prices, were deliberately relegated to inferior workmen whom the society made no effort to recruit.

The mechanics proudly preserved an ideological heritage blended of Ben Franklin's maxims and Tom Paine's "rights of man." The best local legal talent defended their societies in the several conspiracy trials to which they were subjected, as witness Philadelphia's shoemakers enlisting Caesar Rodney, whom President Jefferson was soon to appoint Attorney General of the United States. When seventeen years earlier that city's mechanics had paraded with their masters in joyous celebration of the ratification of the federal constitution, they had borne such emblems as "the weavers' flag, a rampant lion in a green field, holding a shuttle in his dexter paw — motto — '*may the government* protect us,'" the boat builders' flag (atop the thirty-three foot schooner *Federal Union* drawn down Market Street for the occasion) being "an axe and an adze crossing each other — motto, 'by these we live,'" or the bricklayers' flag, with "the federal city rising out of a forest, workmen building it, and the sun illuminating it," motto, "'*both buildings and rulers are the works of our hands.*'" At the close of the procession, bakers distributed bread to the poor, victuallers slew their "two stately oxen" and gave away the meat, and millers provided the needy with flour.[37] The best the printers could do was to read the destitute a poem, but clearly the citizen craftsmen were dispensers, not recipients, of charity.

Very different was the outlook of the impoverished residents of the Rittenhouse Square vicinity, who petitioned the Philadelphia city council in 1830 to halt the dumping in the square of offal swept from neighboring streets, "which being in heaps, occasions numerous ponds of stagnant and putrescent water in the immediate spots, which in summer sent forth pestilential vapours wafted by every breeze to the dwellings of your petitioners, whose only comfort, health, is thus destroyed." These poor argued that "being of the working class, their whole time is indispensably employed in various labour to maintain their families," so that sickness is "a scourge the most severe."[38] Here was a group whose annual incomes ranged far closer to $200 than to $400 or $425 expected by craftsmen,

[36] *Ibid.*, III, 368–370; *ibid.*, III, 72–81, 84–85; *ibid.*, IV, 28–40; Cornelius Wm. Stafford, *Philadelphia City Directory for 1798.*
[37] *American Museum*, IV, (July, 1788), 57–78.
[38] Samuel Hazard, ed., *Register of Pennsylvania*, V (Feb. 20, 1830), 124. Rittenhouse Square became a wealthy neighborhood only after 1850. See Nathaniel Burt, *The Perennial Philadelphians: The Anatomy of an American Aristocracy* (Boston and Toronto, 1963), 531.

a group who Reverend Tuckerman feared "have lived, and to a great extent are living, as a *caste* — cut off from those in more favoured circumstances; and doomed to find their pleasures, and sympathy in their suffering, alone among themselves."[39]

The seaport poor were by no means a new phenomenon at the end of the 1820s. James Henretta has clearly traced their emergence in eighteenth-century Boston as a function of the growth of overseas commerce. He discovered from the Boston tax rolls of 1687 that only 14 percent of the adult male population of the city, that is, 188 men, were neither "dependent" nor owners of property. In contrast to them stood the 17 percent of the adult males who as servants, apprentices, or participants in family home enterprise were classified as dependent. The propertied classes numbered 1,036 (69 percent of the adult males) and included 521 poor craftsmen, 275 artisans of the "middling sort" with two or three journeymen apiece, and the wealthier tradesmen, professionals, and merchants. By 1771 only 10 percent of the adult males were dependent in the traditional sense, while 29 percent were neither dependent nor propertied. These were wage earners in the full meaning of the term, and while the city's population had doubled between the two counts, their number had increased fourfold. They ranged in occupation from seamen and longshoremen at one end of the scale to journeymen at the other, but, while the latter ranked close to the small property-holding mechanic, the division of wealth between the upper and lower halves of property owners was far sharper than had been the case in the seventeenth century.[40]

Most day laborers participated directly in transportation and commerce. It was the demand for seamen, longshoremen, carters, and domestic servants which absorbed unskilled wage earners already in the eighteenth century. By the early nineteenth century, construction work, wood cutting, and road building employed many, while thousands of Philadelphia's poor, Mathew Carey found, "travel hundreds of miles in quest of employments on canals at 62½, 75 and 87½ cents per day, paying a dollar and a half or two dollars per week for their board, leaving families behind, depending on them for support."[41] By 1830 Carey estimated "labourers, hodmen, seamstresses, families of workmen on canals and rail-roads" at 40 percent of the working classes and 25 percent of the total population of Philadelphia.[42]

Many laborers reached the city from the farm by way of the sea. The merchant fleet of Massachusetts, wrote Samuel Eliot Morison, "was manned by successive waves of adventure-seeking boys, and officered by such of them as determined to make the sea their calling." The great majority on the crew lists professed "to be native-born Yankees, and probably were."[43] Seamen would register

[39] Tuckerman, *op. cit.*, 25.
[40] James A. Henretta, "Economic Development and Social Structure in Colonial Boston," *William and Mary Quarterly*, Third Series, XXII (Jan., 1965), 75–92. See also Jackson Turner Main, *Social Structure of Revolutionary America* (Princeton, 1965), 37–40.
[41] Carey, *Appeal*, II. On canal laborers see William A. Sullivan, *Industrial Worker in Pennsylvania 1800–1840* (Harrisburg, 1955), 71–73.
[42] Carey, *Appeal*, 7.
[43] Samuel Eliot Morison, *The Maritime History of Massachusetts 1783–1860* (Sentry Edition, Boston, 1961), 106, 108.

with federal revenue agents after 1796 and receive, for a fee of 25 cents, papers certifying their United States citizenship. Between that year and 1812, 106,757 seamen collected their papers, and of them only 1,530, or 1.4 percent were naturalized citizens. The registrations reported for the years after 1808 were certainly still incomplete, for district revenue collectors were very tardy in submitting their reports to Washington. The fact that registration was heaviest in years such as 1797 and 1805, when the danger of British impressment was most severe, indicates that enrollment was never very thorough.[44] These figures, nevertheless, can suggest the large number of native Americans who took to the sea.

So high were the rates of promotion, death, and desertion that the man who spent more than twelve years before the mast was rare indeed. No other occupation offered an unskilled farmboy so great an opportunity to rise quickly in wealth and standing — or to topple from yardarm into the cold Atlantic. Few seamen dwelt long in any port, but while ashore they augmented the local casual labor supply significantly. Illustrative of their role was young Charles Erskine, whose mother moved to Boston in the early 1820s after his father (a currier) had deserted her. Playing about the docks, Erskine heard the tales of sailors and through them was lured to sea. Between voyages he and his mates earned their keep ashore by whatever employment was available wherever they happened to be. He once helped construct an aqueduct in Washington and at another time worked in a Philadelphia hook and eye factory.[45]

In marked contrast to the artisan's tendency to ply for life the trade he had learned in his adolescence, the laborer was the epitome of versatility. To move from sea to canal digging to hod carrying to factory work was well within the realm of possibility. Many of the half-trained journeymen and "botches" who bedevilled mechanics' efforts to retain high quality and wage standards were of this sort. New England's first factory to use cotton spinning machinery, founded in Beverly, Massachusetts, in 1787, wasted precious quantities of material in training its workmen, then was driven close to ruin when it had to raise wages to prevent its partly-taught employees from deserting to rival firms. Mercifully, perhaps, the factory burned down in 1808.[46] A happier experience with such labor was reported by a cotton mill near Providence, which employed fifty-three workers in the factory and 125 on putting-out by 1810. The owners, reported Albert Gallatin, at first suffered "in being put to much expense by English workmen, who pretended to much more knowledge in the business than they really possessed." But the phony Samuel Slaters were discharged, "and Americans, as apprentices, &c. are getting the art very fast," though the company did not anticipate dividends "for a considerable time."[47]

The fact that machine operatives could be trained made the "factory controversy" of this period focus not on the fate of the workers, as was to be the case in the 1830s and 1840s, but on the potential impact of manufacturing upon the nation's supply of farm labor. Wages of farm hands, Henry Carey reported, were

[44] *American State Papers*, Commerce & Navigation, I, 955, 968; Act of May 28, 1796, *Public Statutes at Large of the United States of America* (17 vols., Boston, 1850), I, 477.

[45] See J. Grey Jewell, *Among Our Sailors* (New York, 1874), 1–50; Charles Erskine, *Twenty Years before the Mast* (Philadelphia, 1896), 2–9, 272.

[46] Bishop, *op. cit.*, I, 399–401.

[47] Gallatin, *op. cit.*, 434.

higher in the vicinity of the cities than in more rustic settings.[48] Whether this differential in money wages was a sign of competition from urban employments or simply an indication that the market economy was more mature near the cities (that a smaller portion of the farm laborer's income was paid in kind and more in cash than was the case to the West) is not clear. Whichever it meant, advocates of governmental aid to manufactures from Coxe though Carey felt obliged to echo Hamilton's famous assurance that manufacturing would not attract able-bodied men away from the land, that it would rather "afford occasional and extra employment to industrious individuals and families," through which farmers could profit by the home produce of their wives and daughters, and provide steady employment for "persons who would otherwise be idle, and in many cases a burthen on the community," and render women and children "more useful, and the latter more early useful . . . than they should otherwise be."[49]

At this period, therefore, it was impossible to speak of the factory labor force without directing attention to women, children, and charitable institutions. This was the case long before the mills of Lowell arose. Philadelphia's first large-scale use of spinning jennies was undertaken by the United Company of Philadelphia for Promoting American Manufactures, founded by patriotic subscriptions in 1775. By the late 1780s it employed 400 women, most of them recruited from the city's poor rolls. Despite the pride with which the Society displayed a jenny of eighty spindles in the Federal Procession of 1788, and boasted that the woman operating it was "a native of and instructed in this city," the company's building was destroyed by an arsonist only two years later.[50] Newly-inaugurated President Washington found a similar labor force when he visited a Boston sail duck factory. Here pairs of little girls spun and wove flax from eight in the morning until six at night, but their demeanor favorably impressed the President, who described them as "daughters of decayed families" and "girls of character — none others are admitted."[51]

Two decades later the Secretary of the Treasury reported that eighty-seven cotton mills then in operation or about to commence operations in the United States needed a labor force of about 500 men and 3,500 women and children.[52] Such a work force was for Gallatin proof positive that manufacturing need not lure men from the farm. Tench Coxe agreed:

> Female aid in manufactures, which prevents the diversion of men and boys from agriculture, has greatly increased. Children are employed, as well as the infirm and the crippled. The assylums of the poor and unfortunate, and the penitentiaries of indiscretion and immorality are improved and aided by the employment and profits of manufactures.[53]

---

[48] Henry C. Carey, *Essay on the Rate of Wages: with an Examination of the Causes of the Differences in the Conditions of the Labouring Population throughout the World* (Philadelphia, 1835), 91.

[49] Hamilton, *op. cit.*, 193.

[50] Bishop, *op. cit.*, I, 384–387; *American Museum*, V (July, 1788), 60.

[51] Edward Everett, *Mount Vernon Papers* (New York, 1860), 112.

[52] Gallatin, *op. cit.*, 427.

[53] Tench Coxe, *Statement of the Arts and Manufactures of the United States of America, for the Year 1810* . . . (Philadelphia, 1814), xiv.

The markets of seamstresses were especially crowded with unmarried and widowed women, not to speak of those whose husbands were "travelling" — in the informal divorce procedure of the day. When such women bid on sewing work, they competed with both married women trying to supplement their own families' meager incomes and recipients of work relief. While female operatives in Philadelphia factories earned two or three dollars a week in the 1820s, seamstresses rarely surpassed $1.25, and the city's home relief system helped keep those earnings low. In slack seasons so many women applied to the Provident Society and other charities for work to tide them over that the scale offered by almshouses became, during the 1820s, the standard price offered by private firms. Thus the U.S. War Department offered seamstresses 12½ cents a shirt, the very wage given by the Provident Society. In reply to a plea that such a price reduced the seamstresses "to the degradation of pauperism," the Secretary of War termed the subject "of such delicacy, and so intimately connected with the manufacturing interests, and the general prices of this kind of labour in the city of Philadelphia" that he dared not change his Department's practice.[54]

While the seamstress stood with one foot in the poor house, this was not the case with the weaver, for in the urban areas most cloth was still put out to families with handlooms. The city and county of Philadelphia in 1809 produced 65,326 yards of cloth in its six factories on both hand and power looms, but its home production amounted to 233,232 yards.[55] Furthermore, the spinning mills, while they continued to be staffed primarily by women and children, tended to free themselves by the second decade of the century from dependence on public charities. The reason is that unmarried women, widows, and orphaned families gravitated toward them by free choice.

Especially was this the case in New England, where the textile mill became a means of emancipation for the "maiden aunts" who lived with so many of the region's families. In Massachusetts the 1810 male population under the age of sixteen outnumbered females of the same age in the ratio of 104 to 100. Between the ages of sixteen and forty-five, however, the proportions were reversed. During the marrying season (ages sixteen through twenty-five) there were 103 women for every 100 men, but in the post twenty-six age of the spinster, women outnumbered men by a ratio of 107 to 100. And Massachusetts had 3,335 more women of that age than it had men.[56] Theirs was the choice, at best, of boarding with parents, or a married sister, or entering a mill. Since the loss of males was a result of the westward movement, it would seem that, as far as New England's early textile industry is concerned, the famous "safety-valve" worked in reverse. The migration of men to the West created a surplus of female labor in the East.

Neither New York State nor Pennsylvania exhibited such an imbalance of the sexes, for both were receiving substantial immigration, and considerable west-

[54] Exchange of correspondence with the Secretary of War, printed in Mathew Carey, *Appeal to Common Sense and Common Justice* (Philadelphia, 1822), xii–xiii. On the role of charities in fixing urban wage levels see Mathew Carey, *Essays on the Public Charities of Philadelphia* . . . (Philadelphia, 1829), 18–19; Benjamin J. Klebaner, "The Home Relief Controversy in Philadelphia, 1782–1861," *Pennsylvania Magazine of History and Biography*, LXXIVII (Oct., 1954), 420.

[55] Coxe, *op. cit.*, 44.

[56] Warden, *op. cit.*, I, 200.

ward movement still occurred within their boundaries. But within the cities of New York and Philadelphia free white women between the ages of sixteen and twenty-five sharply outnumbered the men of the same age. The New York ratio in 1820, for example, was 119 women to 100 men in that age bracket, while in Philadelphia women of this marriageable age outnumbered men 122 to 100. Similarly, the Boston ratio was 127 to 100, and that of Baltimore 108 to 100.[57] Although the terrible toll of childbirth, among other hazards, more than corrected the balance of the sexes in all four cities after the age of twenty-six, each of the seaports was naturally provided with a sizeable force of women for whom there was no prospect of marriage and for whom entry into the labor market was a necessity.

Each of these groups of city workers of the pre-industrial epoch (journeymen mechanics, male laborers, and women) merits careful historical study. Little new work has been done in this area since David J. Saposs contributed his chapters to John R. Commons' *History of Labour in the United States* in 1917, and because of this deficiency the labor historian's view of this period has fallen seriously out of phase with that of the economic historian. For example, Saposs' contention that "the wages of the unskilled were going up while those of the skilled were kept down by the merchant-capitalist" in the century's first two decades finds no support in the wage data of this article or in recent economic studies.[58]

The problem assumes considerable significance in the light of George Rogers Taylor's hypothesis that per capita income in America declined rather steadily between 1807 and the early 1830s.[59] The impact of such a trend could logically have been different for mechanics, for factory operatives, for casual laborers, and for women sewing in their rented rooms. Only specific studies of particular groups of workers can yield conclusive data on the standard of living. Jackson Turner Main and James Henretta have shown that enough evidence exists in tax rolls, judicial records, and the press of the eighteenth century to enable the historian to reconstruct patterns of property and income distribution quite clearly.[60] Their work challenges other historians to trace the evolution of these patterns in early nineteenth century city life and to reduce their reliance on impressionistic evidence.

Still greater is the need for research into the cultural and intellectual life of the working classes of this period. We need to know what the urban poor expected of life, how they reacted to the commercial ethos of their cities, and how they conceived their relationship to the government merchant elites. Were they, as some historians have recently portrayed the poor of Naples or London, simultaneously devoted to the traditional social order, aware of their power as a mob, confident the city would care for them in times of want, and, profoundly

[57] The ratios are calculated from statistics presented by Everett S. Lee at the 1966 Eleutherian Mills-Hagley Foundation Conference on the Growth of Seaport Cities, 1790–1825.

[58] John R. Commons, *et al., History of Labour in the United States* (4 vols., New York, 1918–1935), I, 105. *Cf.*, Sullivan, *op. cit.*, 31, 72–73.

[59] Taylor, "American Economic Growth before 1840," 437.

[60] See note 40.

hostile toward the emerging impersonal and amoral market economy?[61] Was it such a mentality which made some 200 assembled New York sailors, idled by the embargo, respond obediently when Mayor Marinus Willet commanded them to disperse, with assurances that the embargo was "the *Captain's Orders*," and that the city would "do everything possible for your relief"?[62] Such questions cannot yet be answered because a fixation on the clash of "agrarian" and "industrial" values has distracted us from exploring pre-industrial urban values and customs.

Similarly American historians have yet to probe the culture of the American mechanic as, say, E. P. Thompson did for his British counterpart. Our concern has been either with the journeyman's economic circumstances (where there is still much to be learned) or with whether he voted for Andrew Jackson (and may we be spared that debate for a while). Because the mechanics were frequently organized and far more articulate than the urban poor, research into the mind of the journeyman should prove relatively easy. The ideas suggested in this article need careful testing, to begin with, and beyond them lie several major issues for research. How open was economic mobility for the journeymen, and what changes did the post-Revolutionary generation experience in this regard? Why did this class provide most of the country's early nineteenth century adherents to deism, and just how widespread and significant was infidelity among them?[63] What new circumstances made craftsmen in every major city between 1827 and 1837 expand the horizons of their concern beyond the limits of their own trades, create city Trades' Unions as new institutions to fuse the efforts of the several crafts, undertake unprecedented united actions with the unskilled laborers, giving rise to something worthy of the name labor movement?

These problems suggest that we have rushed ahead to evaluate labor's response to industrialism without first ascertaining labor's pre-industrial behavior and attitudes. In exploring the shock of change after the Civil War our attention has been directed half a century too late, and our concern with the fate of agrarian values has led us to ignore the impact of the spreading factory system on the cultural heritage of urban America's lower orders.

[61] See E.J. Hobsbawm, *Primitive Rebels. Studies in Archaic Forms of Social Movement in the 19th and 20th Centuries* (New York, 1965), 108–125; Thompson, 55–76.

[62] George Daitsman, "Labor and the Welfare State in Early New York," *Labor History*, IV (Fall, 1963), 250.

[63] See Herbert M. Morais, *Deism in Eighteenth Century America* (New York, 1934); Albert Post, *Popular Freethought in America, 1825–1850* (New York, 1943); Lewis Masquerier, *Sociology: Or, The Reconstruction of Society . . .* (New York, 1877).

The Challenge of Crime

DAVID J. ROTHMAN

This selection is drawn from David Rothman's book The Discovery of the Asylum, *a study of "social order and disorder" in America before the Civil War. Professor Rothman is struck by the apparently contradictory moods of the new republic: on the one hand, confidence in the future of the republican experiment and its ability to cope with the problems of an expanding nation, but, on the other hand, fear of the challenges, and uncertainties of an all too rapidly and unforseeably changing society. Colonial Americans had been confident of the divinely sanctioned, hierarchical, and stable character of their lives. Bred in the Calvinist tradition, they were not surprised when the inadequacies of human nature led to crime, and they treated criminals with a mixture of charity and firmness, sure that social deviancy could never be totally eradicated. Postrevolutionary Americans met abnormal behavior with an optimism derived from their belief that they could devise remedies to eliminate socially undesirable habits permanently. Dealing with the problem of crime, their first instinct was to think that harsh colonial criminal statutes were the cause of crime, since punishments were so harsh as to be unenforceable and ineffective. If criminal laws were reasonable and easily understood, they would be enforced and obeyed. But their statutory reforms did not eliminate crime, and the increasing social ferment and disorder seemed to demand more reliable solutions. Americans of the Jacksonian period, convinced of the basic innocence of human nature, turned their attention instead to the deteriorated conditions of family life and the prevalence of vice, which they thought responsible for the corruption of potentially good citizens. They began to think in terms of the reform of the family and of the removal of criminals from society through their incarceration in prisons, among other reforms, in order to remove corrupting influences from the lives of young Americans. The environment was at fault, and a better, more orderly society would be attainable through the actions of the state and of private groups. A darker realization underlay their efforts, however, for the urge to reform was spurred by a profound sense that the symmetrical and predictable society envisioned by their colonial forebearers was threatened by a volatile community which seemed day by day more difficult to bring under control. Rothman's theme of the interplay of social order and disorder and his discussion of social control is drawn from sociology. It suggests the extent to which historians have been restricted by the conceptual conservatism of traditional American history, for the study of crime in an historical context requires a systematic examination of the interplay of social, eco-*

nomic, and political forces. Rothman uses unusual source materials, such as the reports of prison inspectors, in an attempt to understand why men acted as they said they did. Do you believe that his assumptions about the motivations of Americans in responding to the challenge of crime was well founded? Are they historically demonstrable? More immediately, does his analysis of the threat of crime help you to understand the problem in its twentieth-century setting?

Eighteenth-century notions of dependency and deviancy did not survive for very long into the nineteenth, nor did its methods of dispensing charity and correction. The social, intellectual, and economic changes that differentiated the states of the new republic from the several colonies prompted a critical reappraisal and revision of the ideas and techniques of social control. Americans felt compelled to rethink inherited procedures and devise new methods to replace old ones. They devoted extraordinary attention to this issue, hoping to establish quickly and effectively alternatives to the colonial system.

Between 1790 and 1830, the nation's population greatly increased and so did the number and density of cities. Even gross figures reveal the dimensions of the change. In these forty years, the population of Massachusetts almost doubled, in Pennsylvania it tripled, and in New York it increased five times; border and midwestern states, practically empty in 1790, now held over three million people. At Washington's inauguration, only two hundred thousand Americans lived in towns with more than twenty-five hundred people; by Jackson's accession, the number exceeded one million. In 1790, no American city had more than fifty thousand residents. By 1830, almost half a million people lived in urban centers larger than that.[1] During these same years factories began to dot the New England and mid-Atlantic rivers. The decade of the 1830's witnessed the first accelerated growth of manufacturing in the nation.[2] At the same time, Enlightenment ideas challenged Calvinist doctrines; the prospect of boundless improve-

    [1] U.S. Bureau of the Census, Historical Statistics of the United States, Colonial Times to 1957 (Washington, D.C., 1960), 12–14; George Rogers Taylor, The Transportation Revolution, 1815–1860 (New York, 1951), 6–10, 141–144. The sophisticated studies of geographic mobility take their starting point with 1870, so we have no precise figures for the earlier period. However, gross numbers tell a good deal, and the very transportation revolution that Taylor writes about is another indication of the opportunity for mobility and the frequent use of the facilities. In 1790, the urban population was 5.1 percent of the nation; it rose to 7.3 percent in 1810, declined slightly to 7.1 percent in 1820, and thereafter increased steadily to 1860, reaching 19.8 percent. Some new and important efforts to examine migration patterns in this period may be found in Stephan Thernstrom and Richard Sennett, eds., Nineteenth-Century Cities (New Haven, 1969).
    [2] Douglass North, The Economic Growth of the United States, 1790–1860 (New York, 1961), 167, 189 ff.; George Rogers Taylor, Transportation Revolution, chs. 10–11.

ment confronted a grim determinism.[3] But these general trends are not sufficient to explain the very specific reactions to the issue of deviant and dependent behavior. To them must be added Americans' understanding of these changes. Under the influence of demographic, economic and intellectual developments, they perceived that the traditional mechanisms of social control were obsolete. The premises upon which the colonial system had been based were no longer valid.

Each change encouraged Americans to question inherited practices and to devise new ones. Inspired by the ideals of the Enlightenment, they considered older punishments to be barbaric and traditional assumptions on the origins of deviant behavior to be misdirected. Movement to cities, in and out of territories, and up and down the social ladder, made it difficult for them to believe that a sense of hierarchy or localism could now stabilize society. When men no longer knew their place or station, self-policing communities seemed a thing of the past. Expanding political loyalties also made colonial mechanisms appear obsolete. Citizens' attachment to state governments promoted a broader definition of responsibility, so that a sentence of banishment seemed a parochial response. The welfare of the commonwealth demanded that towns no longer solve their problems in such narrow and exclusive ways.

This awareness provoked at least as much anxiety as celebration. Americans in the Jacksonian period could not believe that geographic and social mobility would promote or allow order and stability. Despite their marked impatience and dissatisfaction with colonial procedures, they had no ready vision of how to order society. They were still trapped in many ways in the rigidities of eighteenth-century social thinking. They knew well that the old system was passing, but not what ought to replace it. What in their day was to prevent society from bursting apart? From where would the elements of cohesion come? More specifically, would the poor now corrupt the society? Would criminals roam out of control? Would chaos be so acute as to drive Americans mad?[4] All of these questions became part of a full, intense, and revealing investigation of the origins of deviant and dependent behavior. To understand why men turned criminal or became insane or were poor would enable reformers to strengthen the social order. To comprehend and control abnormal behavior promised to be the first step in establishing a new system for stabilizing the community, for binding citizens together. In this effort, one finds the clearest indications of how large-scale social changes affected thinking and actions of Americans in the Jacksonian

---

[3] A good starting point for the intellectual history of this period is Perry Miller, *The Life of the Mind in America: From the Revolution to the Civil War* (New York, 1965). See too Charles I. Foster, *An Errand of Mercy* (Chapel Hill, N.C., 1960), for a discussion of the Protestant response to these changing conditions, how they equated movement with a return to barbarism.

[4] One of the best accounts of the tensions that social change created in post-1820 America is Marvin Meyers's *The Jacksonian Persuasion* (Stanford, 1957). Meyers, however, seems to locate all the tensions within the Jackson camp. . . . The anxieties were far more broadly spread through the society. Another account, not as finely drawn as Meyers's, but sensitive to the darker side of the Jackson years is Fred Somkin, *Unquiet Eagle: Memory and Desire in the Idea of American Freedom, 1815–1860* (Ithaca, N.Y., 1967). For an incisive examination of these themes in the world of art see Neil Harris, *The Artist in American Society* (New York, 1966).

period. And here one also finds the crucial elements that led to the discovery of the asylum.

In the immediate aftermath of independence and nationhood, Americans believed that they had uncovered both the prime cause of criminality in their country and an altogether effective antidote. Armed with patriotic fervor, sharing a repugnance for things British and a new familiarity with and faith in Enlightenment doctrines, they posited that the origins and persistence of deviant behavior would be found in the nature of the colonial criminal codes. Established in the days of oppression and ignorance, the laws reflected British insistence on severe and cruel punishments. The case of William Penn seemed typical. He had attempted to introduce mild and humane legislation into his province, drawing up the Great Law of 1682, but the crown, in the person of Queen Anne, had callously disallowed it. "The mild voice of reason and humanity," explained New York Quaker Thomas Eddy, "reached not the thrones of princes or the halls of legislators." The mother country had stifled the colonists' benevolent instincts, compelling them to emulate the crude customs of the old world. The result was the predominance of archaic and punitive laws that only served to perpetuate crime.[5]

A reading of the Enlightenment tract of Cesare Beccaria verified for Americans in the 1790's the link between barbaric laws and deviant behavior. The treatise, On Crimes and Punishments, first appeared in 1764, was quickly translated, and was already being quoted by John Adams as early as 1770 in defense of the British soldiers implicated in the Boston Massacre. Beccaria insisted, and American experience seemed to confirm, that "if we glance at the pages of history, we will find that laws, which surely are, or ought to be, compacts of free men, have been, for the most part, a mere tool of the passions of some." They were all too often not only inhumane but self-defeating. "The severity of punishment of itself emboldens men to commit the very wrongs it is supposed to prevent," Beccaria announced. "They are driven to commit additional crimes to avoid the punishment for a single one. The countries and times most notorious for severity of penalties have always been those in which the bloodiest and most inhumane of deeds were committed." Punishment, to be effective, had to be unavoidable. "The certainty of a punishment, even if it be moderate, will always make a stronger impression than the fear of another which is more terrible but combined with the hope of impunity." Beccaria's summary advice was succinct and his program straightforward: "Do you want to prevent crimes? See to it that the laws are clear and simple and that the entire force of a nation is united in their defense."[6]

The young republic quickly took this message to heart, for it fit well with its own history and revolutionary ideals. Americans fully appreciated that the laws could be a tool of the passions of a handful of men. Did this not explain almost

[5] Thomas Eddy, An Account of the State Prison or Penitentiary House, in the City of New-York (New York, 1801), 5; this same argument is put forth by William Bradford, An Enquiry how far the Punishment of Death is Necessary in Pennsylvania (Philadelphia, 1793), 14–20.

[6] See the translation of Henry Paolucci (Indianapolis, 1963), 8, 43–44, 58, 94, for the several quotations.

every piece of British colonial legislation after 1763? They believed that they had also witnessed the self-defeating quality of cruel punishments. Had not colonial juries often let a prisoner go free rather than condemn him to the gallows for a petty theft? In this way, criminals had escaped all discipline, and the community had allowed, even encouraged, them to persist in their ways. But independence in this new world made the time and place right for reform. The rhetoric of the Revolution had prepared Americans to fulfill a grand mission, and now they would demonstrate how to uplift one part of mankind, the criminal class. With the Revolution, declared Eddy, fitting Beccaria's doctrine into an American context, "the spirit of reform revived . . . strengthened by the general principles of freedom." The criminal codes of New York had to be revised, for the state could not tolerate laws of "barbarous usages, corrupt society, and monarchical principles . . . [so] imperfectly adopted to a new country, simple manners, and a popular form of government."[7]

Independence made citizens increasingly appreciative of conditions in the new world. They were not Englishmen, and their setting was not England's either. In 1793, William Bradford of Philadelphia explained in a widely read pamphlet, *An Enquiry how far the Punishment of Death is Necessary in Pennsylvania*, that the new nation was the ideal place for enacting Beccaria's principles. "It is from ignorance, wretchedness or corrupted manners of a people that crime proceeds," declared Bradford. "In a country where these do not prevail moderate punishments strictly enforced, will be a curb as effectual as the greatest severity." America, a New York reform society declared, was "a land where the theatre of experiment is boundless. The relations of civil society were few and simple, and the complex abuses of long existing systems, in social order, were unknown." Southern states heard the same message. One Virginia legislator urged his colleagues to revise and moderate the criminal laws to make punishments "comport with the principles of our government."[8] And Robert Turnbull, returning from a visit north, counseled the readers of the *Charleston Daily Gazette* that more lenient laws helped to prevent crime, especially here, when "the mind of man is once more accessible to the mild influence of reason and humanity."[9]

These conceptions had an immediate and widespread appeal. The reform seemed worthy of the new republic, and feasible, so that by the second decade of the nineteenth century, most of the states had amended their criminal codes.

[7] Thomas Eddy, *An Account of the State Prison*, 9. Eddy was very familiar with the writings of Beccaria. See too the Philadelphia Society for Alleviating the Miseries of Public Prisons, *Extracts and Remarks on the Subject of Punishment and Reformation of Criminals* (Philadelphia, 1790), 3–4.

[8] William Bradford, *An Enquiry*, 43. The Society for the Prevention of Pauperism in the City of New-York, *Report on the Penitentiary System in the United States* (New York, 1822), 12; for the influence upon them of Beccaria, see 9, 33. To appreciate how widespread these notions were, see E. Bruce Thompson, "Reforms in the Penal System of Tennessee, 1820–1850," *Tennessee Historical Quarterly*, I (1942), 293.

[9] George K. Taylor, *Substance of a Speech . . . on the Bill to Amend the Penal Laws of this Commonwealth* (Richmond, Va., 1796), 23. Robert James Turnbull, *A Visit to the Philadelphia Prison* (Philadelphia, 1796), 3. The Philadelphia pamphlet was a reprint of a newspaper article. See 75–76 for the argument that certainty of punishment was the most critical element in criminal law.

The death sentence was either abolished for all offenses save first-degree murder or strictly limited to a handful of the most serious crimes. Instead, the statutes called for incarceration, the offender to serve a term in prison. Construction kept apace with legal stipulations.[10] Pennsylvania led the way, turning the old Philadelphia jail at Walnut Street into a state prison. In 1796, the New York legislature approved funds for building such institutions, and soon opened the Newgate state prison in Greenwich Village. The New Jersey penitentiary was completed in 1797, and so were others in Virginia and Kentucky in 1800. That same year, the Massachusetts legislature made appropriations for a prison at Charlestown, and in short order Vermont, New Hampshire, and Maryland followed suit. Within twenty years of Washington's inaugural, the states had taken the first steps to alter the traditional system of punishment.[11]

In this first burst of enthusiasm, Americans expected that a rational system of correction, which made punishment certain but humane, would dissuade all but a few offenders from a life in crime. They located the roots of deviancy not in the criminal, but in the legal system. Just as colonial codes had encouraged deviant behavior, republican ones would now curtail, or even eliminate it. To pass the proper laws would end the problem. This perspective drew attention away from the prisons themselves. They were necessary adjuncts to the reform, the substitutes for capital punishment, but intrinsically of little interest or importance. A repulsion from the gallows rather than any faith in the penitentiary spurred the late-eighteenth century construction. Few people had any clear idea what these structures should look like or how they should be administered — or even addressed themselves seriously to these questions. To reformers, the advantages of the institutions were external, and they hardly imagined that life inside the prison might rehabilitate the criminal. Incarceration seemed more humane than hanging and less brutal than whipping. Prisons matched punishment to crime precisely: the more heinous the offense, the longer the sentence. Juries, fully understanding these advantages, would never hesitate to convict the guilty, so that correction would be certain. The fact of imprisonment, not its internal routine, was of chief importance.

By the 1820's, however, these ideas had lost persuasiveness. The focus shifted to the deviant and the penitentiary, away from the legal system. Men intently scrutinized the life history of the criminal and methodically arranged the institution to house him. Part of the cause for this change was the obvious failure of the first campaign. The faith of the 1790's now seemed misplaced; more rational codes had not decreased crime. The roots of deviancy went deeper than the cer-

[10] Raymond T. Bye, *Capital Punishment in the United States* (Philadelphia, 1919), 4–9. Ohio, in 1788, was the first to limit the death penalty to murder; Pennsylvania followed suit in 1794. Few states abolished the death penalty altogether; by 1900, only six had done so. See too David B. Davis, "The Movement to Abolish Capital Punishment in America, 1787–1861," *American Historical Review*, 63 (1957), 23–46. A classic nineteenth-century statement is Edward Livingston, *On the Abolition of the Punishment of Death* (Philadelphia, 1831), originally a report to the Louisiana legislature in March 1822.

[11] The first prison structures in the United States are discussed in Orlando F. Lewis, *The Development of American Prisons and Prison Customs, 1776–1845* (Albany, N.Y., 1922), chs. 1–8; less detailed is Blake McKelvey, *American Prisons: A Study in American Social History Prior to 1915* (Chicago, 1936), ch. 1.

tainty of a punishment. Nor were the institutions fulfilling the elementary task of protecting society, since escapes and riots were commonplace occurrences.[12] More important, the second generation of Americans confronted new challenges and shared fresh ideas. Communities had undergone many critical changes between 1790 and 1830, and so had men's thinking. Citizens found cause for deep despair and yet incredible optimism. The safety and security of their social order seemed to them in far greater danger than that of their fathers, yet they hoped to eradicate crime from the new world. The old structure was crumbling, but perhaps they could draw the blueprints for building a far better one.

Americans in the pre–Civil War era intently pondered the origins of deviant behavior. Philanthropists organized themselves into societies to investigate the question, hoping to devise an effective method of punishment. Legislators, no less interested in a theory for crime, prepared to amend the statutes and appropriate the funds for a new system. To judge by the numerous periodical articles, laymen were also concerned with a subject that had a direct and obvious bearing on their daily lives. Traditional answers were no longer satisfactory.[13]

One of the best examples of their effort appeared in the early reports of the inspectors of New York's Auburn penitentiary. These officials, charged with the management of the prison, attempted to understand the causes of deviancy by collecting and appending to their 1829 and 1830 reports to the state legislature biographical sketches of inmates about to be discharged. The purpose of these brief ten- to twenty-line vignettes, the inspectors explained, was to exhibit "facts which must be interesting, as well to the legislator as to the philanthropist and the Christian." Here, in the life stories of several hundred convicts, they could discover the origins of crime. Impatient with theology and disappointed in the

---

[12] The disillusionment with the first experiments appears in many pamphlets; see Thomas Eddy, An Account of the State Prison, 15–16, on the disappointment of "many citizens . . . [who] sometimes express a regret at the change . . . and returning to a system of accumulated severity and terror." Other expressions may be found in the Philadelphia Society for Alleviating the Miseries of Public Prisons, A Statistical View of the Penal Code of Pennsylvania (Philadelphia, 1817), 35; Stephan White, Sherman Leland, Bradford Sumner, Report on . . . the State Prison at Charlestown [Massachusetts], (Boston, 1827), 1. William Tudor, "The Penitentiary System," North American Review, 13 (1821), 417–420. Gershom Powers, A Brief Account of the Construction, Management, and Discipline . . . of the New York State Prison at Auburn (Auburn, N.Y., 1826), 64–69.

[13] Jacksonian theories on deviancy have received little attention, but see David Brion Davis, Homicide in American Fiction, 1798–1860 (Ithaca, N.Y., 1957). Davis's analysis is close to mine, but his interests are more in the literary expression of the problem than in the social origins of the ideas and their influence on social policy. There is also a discussion in W. David Lewis, From Newgate to Dannemora: The Rise of the Penitentiary in New York, 1796–1848 (Ithaca, N.Y., 1965). Lewis argues that 1840 was a turning point, that after that date an environmental concern came to the fore; he finds the influence of phrenology vital to the story. There is, however, . . . much evidence of these ideas in the 1820's, and even more in the 1830's; furthermore, it was not phrenology that accounted for them, I believe, but a peculiar view of American society. For a concise survey of current theories of deviant behavior, see Richard A. Cloward and Lloyd E. Ohlin, Delinquency and Opportunity (New York, 1960), chs. 2–4.

law, they turned to the careers of offenders for the information they wanted.[14]

At first glance, these accounts are curiously naïve. Officials obtained the facts, we are told, in interviews with the convicts just before their release, and obviously made no effort to check the accuracy of the statements. When the sketches recount the events that led up to the prisoner's conviction, each convict emerges as the innocent victim of some misunderstanding. He sold goods he did not know were stolen, or passed bills he did not recognize were counterfeit, or took a horse he did not realize belonged to a neighbor. The investigators, however, did not contradict these assertions or declare their own skepticism. They were not trying to prove that the courts of justice always convicted the right man, that the legal system was infallible. Clearly their concern was different. No record survives of how interrogators conducted the interviews or how they phrased their questions, what kinds of suggestions they openly or covertly made to the convicts. But the finished products follow so set a pattern, and officials were so eager to publicize them, that undoubtedly they heard what they wished to hear, learned what they wished to learn. Their interest was not in the process of conviction, they were quite certain that a collection of criminals stood before them. No, they were preoccupied with the convicts' early years, their growing up in the family, their actions in the community. And of the reliability and pertinence of this information they were certain.

In their search for the roots of deviant behavior, investigators concentrated on the convicts' upbringing, devoting the most space to it in almost every one of these biographies. They focused their questions on the criminals' childhood, recording what they wanted legislators and philanthropists to learn. No matter at what age the deviant committed an offense, the cause could be traced back to his childhood. Prisoner number 315, discharged in 1829, had been convicted for forgery at the age of fifty-five. Until then, he had apparently "maintained a respectable standing in the society." Why had a man of property with no previous record been guilty of such an act? His history provided the answer:

> No. 315.—A. N., born in Massachusetts; father was killed at Quebec when he was very young; family soon after scattered, and he was bound out to a farmer, with whom he lived till of age; was a wild, rude boy, and early addicted to some bad habits, drinking, swearing, etc.

In the early years, if you looked carefully, were the origins of deviancy.

And look carefully they did. The 1829 and 1830 reports of the Auburn penitentiary contained 173 biographies, and in fully two-thirds of them, the supervisors selected and presented the data to prove that childhood made the man. Almost always a failure of upbringing — specifically, the collapse of family control — caused deviant behavior. In these sketches, one of three circumstances

---

[14] "Abstract of Brief Biographical Sketches as Taken From Convicts When Discharged from this Prison," "Annual Report of the Inspectors of the State Prison at Auburn," N.Y. *Senate and Assembly Documents*, 1830, I, no. 38, pp. 37–54. The second group of biographies is found in "Annual Report of Auburn Prison," N.Y. *Senate Docs.*, 1831, I, no. 15, pp. 32–63. All the cases below come from these pages and are identified by their number in sequence. The quotation is from the 1930 report, p. 5.

characterized the failure. First, the children duplicated the parents' corrupt behavior. Prisoner 339 was typical: "Brought up . . . under the influence of a bad example; says his father has been in the New York prison." Or case 317: "Father a very intemperate man, and brought him up to it." Second, the family disintegrated because of death or divorce or desertion, turning an undisciplined child loose on the community. Inevitably, the results were disastrous. H. L., "born in Vermont; after his father's death, when he was a mere boy, worked out for a living and had his own way." And M. R. R.: "His father went off before his remembrance, and never returned . . . his mother married again . . . to a very intemperate bad man, who drove his stepchildren off, and told them he would kill them if they ever came home again." And J. L.: "Parents separated when he was seven on account of his father's going after other women; was then bound out to a farmer . . . ran away from him." Third, the child, through no obvious fault of the parents, left home. M. H., a girl born in Massachusetts, "ran away from her parents at thirteen years of age, and went into Rensselaer county . . . where she . . . soon became a common prostitute."[15]

Investigators had no need to question the truth of these facts. The very presence of the convict at the interview made them self-confirming. They did not doubt that the common whore had run off from her family, that the father of a thief was a drunkard, that a counterfeiter had been on his own from an early age. The moral was clear to them and could not be lost on their readers: deviancy began with the family.

Officials had no difficulty in tracing criminal behavior directly to circumstances of family life. They were certain that children lacking discipline quickly fell victim to the influence of vice at loose in the community. Inadequately prepared to withstand the temptations, they descended into crime. To document this idea, investigators inquired into and reported upon convicts' drinking habits, and those of their companions, and tried to discover other corruptions to which they had succumbed. Once again, they assembled the right facts for the story. In these sketches, the vices permeating the society made the family's failure decisive.

The undisciplined youth typically began to frequent taverns, soon became intemperate, and then turned to crime to support his vice. J. A., a French Canadian, "lost his parents when young, and was thrown friendless upon the world; had troubles which led him to excessive drinking. . . . Convicted of grand larceny." J. T., who had the misfortune to serve an apprenticeship under a drunken master, also "fell into the habit of drinking too much himself; it was in a grocery where he had been drinking too freely, that he committed the crime [theft] that brought him to prison." The temptation of liquor was so great that occasionally those properly raised succumbed to it in time of crisis. J. M. "was a steady young man and continued so till after his wife died . . . when he broke up housekeeping and went about from place to place; soon got to drinking too freely, became very intemperate, and at length took to stealing." R. R., "a steady industrious and

[15] H. L. was case 433; M. R. R., 440; J. L., 319; M. H., 303. Of the 173 cases, 99 were explained directly in terms of parental failures. In 26, the parents set a bad example; in 27, they were absent by reason of death or desertion; in 32 cases, the child left home very young, in 11 he went to an apprentice. Two were at home but "wild," and one was in a "very poor" household.

moral young man . . . has been worth $3000; on account of domestic trouble took to drinking, and followed it up till he came to prison." If the best of sorts might yield to vice, those without rigorous moral training were certain victims.[16]

Persons outside family government often began to wander, falling in with bad company and acquiring the worst habits. Some first became intemperate and then committed crimes, others went directly to theft and burglary. Predictably, M. S., having run away from his apprenticeship at age fourteen, then roamed "about the country, with no other business than stealing." In another common variation, those lacking family counsel took up an occupation that was almost certain to lead to vice and crime. Enlistment in the army was one such step. The authors of these sketches were convinced that military service was a "school for vice." T. L., in their estimation, had proved himself an "apt scholar": while serving with the British forces in Canada, he "gave himself up to drinking, stealing, etc. and was ripe for crime when he came into this state." The American situation was no different: J. L., born in Albany, New York, enlisted after running away from a local farmer. "Had previously been a sober, industrious boy but in the army became very intemperate and vicious; after his discharge, strolled about the country, drinking more and more till he came to prison." Soldiers suffered from too little supervision once they left the barracks. The trouble with the military was that it was not military enough.

The sailor's life also offered an education in immorality. At sea, J. H. "became excessively intemperate, and addicted to all sorts of vice; had no sense of moral obligation; lived without God in the world. When he quit the seas, came into this state . . . through intemperance was led to the commission of a crime." Officials believed it axiomatic that anyone who "has been in almost every seaport in the world," would be "addicted to every bad habit in the world." Some civilian occupations were equally dangerous — for example, digging New York's new canal. J. P., typical of those leaving home without parental consent, "came to work on the [Erie] canal; fell into vicious company, and consequently vicious habits; became intemperate." Soon the courts convicted him for passing counterfeit money. G. J. "had previously been sober and industrious." But on the canal, "he soon got into many bad habits, drinking, gambling, stealing, etc.," till he arrived at the Auburn penitentiary.[17]

These carefully designed, really contrived biographies, undoubtedly strike the modern reader as crude and simplistic versions of later, more sophisticated analyses. Yet when looked at from the vantage point of the eighteenth century, they are in many ways important and different. For one thing, they are highly secular documents. Officials were interested in crime, not sin, and had no inclination to view legal offenses as Lucifer's handiwork or the retributive judgment of an angry God. The accounting system of the colonial period — where crime rates reflected both the community's religiosity and divine judgment on it — was out-

---

[16] J. A. was case 443; J. T., 444; J. M., 493; R. R., 352. Of the 99 cases which defined parental problems as critical, 27 children, according to the biographies, went directly into a life of crime; 13 first succumbed to a vice; 17 wandered and then began committing crimes. Twenty-one followed a corrupting occupation, such as sailor or canal-worker, and 20 ran away or had a bad apprenticeship. One suffered a series of misfortunes.

[17] M. S. was case 492; T. L., 480; J. L., 419; J. H., 326; J. P. was case 399; G. J., 340.

dated. Officials, in fact, gave surprisingly little attention to the convicts' religious history. Occasionally they noted if someone was raised without family prayer or had never regularly attended church. But even then religious training was an indicator of the quality of his upbringing, and without intrinsic importance. It revealed in one more way how the family had failed to educate and discipline the child.

Nor did these vignettes show the Revolutionary War generation's concern for legal reform. Officials now looked to the life of the criminal, not to the statutes, in attempting to grasp the origins of deviancy. They presented biographical sketches, not analyses of existing codes. They did not bother to gather information about or report upon convicts' previous encounters with the law, what kinds of punishments they had received, or their feelings about them. Such questions were for the 1790's, not the 1820's and '30's.

In a still more crucial way the concept of deviant behavior implicit in these sketches signaled a new departure. Although the colonists had blamed inadequate parental and religious training for crime, they were preoccupied with the sinner himself. Convinced that the corrupt nature of man was ultimately at fault, they did not extensively analyze the role of the criminal's family or the church or the general society. Furthermore, they shared a clear understanding of what the well-ordered community *ought to* look like, and this too stifled any inclination to question or scrutinize existing arrangements. Their religious and social certainty covered the discrepancies between ideas and realities, obviating new approaches and theories. Americans in the Jacksonian period stood in a very different position. They learned that men were born innocent, not depraved, that the sources of corruption were external, not internal, to the human condition. Encouraged by such doctrines to examine their society with acute suspicion, they quickly discovered great cause for apprehension and criticism.

But why did they become so anxious in their concern? Why did they so easily discover corruption? They were, it is true, predisposed to this finding, yet it is puzzling that they located all that they looked for. Communities were not overrun with thieves and drunkards, prostitutes and gamblers; the rate of crime, for example, probably did not increase over these years.[18] Rather, Americans conducted this examination with grandiose expectations. Assuming that deviant behavior was symptomatic of a failing in society, they expected to ferret out corruption and eliminate crime. With the stakes so high, they could ignore no possible malfeasance.

Another consideration expanded their list of social evils. Many Americans in the Jacksonian period judged their society with eighteenth-century criteria in mind. As a result, they defined as corrupting the fluidity and mobility that they saw. Thinking that an orderly society had to be a fixed one, they judged the discrepancies between traditional postulates and present reality as promoting deviant behavior. Not having evolved an alternative to the colonial vision of society, they looked back both with envy and discomfort. They were embarrassed

[18] Roger Lane, "Crime and Criminal Statistics in Nineteenth-Century Massachusetts," *Journal of Social History*, 2 (1968), 156–163. See also William Nelson, "Emerging Notions of Modern Criminal Law," *New York University Law Quarterly* (1967), 461–462; prosecutions for morality practically disappeared in Massachusetts after the Revolution.

about the cruelty and shortsightedness of earlier punishments, and hoped to be humanitarian innovators. Yet they also believed that their predecessors, fixed in their communities and ranks, had enjoyed social order. But how were they now to maintain cohesion in so fluid and open a society? This ambivalence gave a very odd quality to their thinking. On the one hand, they aimed at the heights, about to eliminate crime and corruption. On the other, they doubted the society's survival, fearing it might succumb to chaos. They confronted, it seemed, unprecedented opportunity, and unprecedented peril.

Holding such a position, American students of deviant behavior moved family and community to the center of their analysis. New York officials accumulated and published biographies because this technique allowed them to demonstrate to legislators and philanthropists the crucial role of social organizations. Accordingly, almost every sketch opened with a vivid description of an inadequate family life and then traced the effects of the corruptions in the community. While many a convict may possibly have come from a broken home or been prone to drink, no one ought to take the inspectors' findings as straight facts. They had a prior commitment to gathering and publicizing this type of information to explain the origins of crime. Interviewers probably induced the convicts to describe, whether accurately or not, their early life in grim terms. Sympathetic questioners, letting the criminal know that they thought that much of the blame for his fate rested with his parents, would soon hear him recount his father's drinking habits and the attraction of the tavern around the corner. These sketches reflected the ideas of the questioner, not some objective truth about the criminal. The doctrine was clear: parents who sent their children into the society without a rigorous training in discipline and obedience would find them someday in the prison. The case of W. S. can summarize both the approach and the message: "Lived with his parents who indulged him too much for his good; was a very wild unsteady boy; fond of company and amusements; when he could not get his parents' consent, would go without it." The result? "Convicted of an attempt to rape . . . and sentenced to three years."[19]

The pessimism and fear underlying this outlook pointed to the difficulty Americans had in fitting their perception of nineteenth-century society as mobile and fluid into an eighteenth-century definition of a well-ordered community. Their first reaction was not to disregard the inherited concept but to condemn present conditions. Hence, in these biographies a dismal picture emerged of a society filled with a myriad of temptations. It was almost as if the town, in a nightmarish image, was made up of a number of households, frail and huddled together, facing the sturdy and wide doors of the tavern, the gaudy opening into a house of prostitution or theater filled with dissipated customers; all the while, thieves and drunkards milled the streets, introducing the unwary youngster to vice and corruption. Every family was under siege, surrounded by enemies ready to take advantage of any misstep. The honest citizen was like a vigilant soldier, well trained to guard against temptation. Should he relax for a moment, the re-

[19] W. S. was case 301. Note too that poverty as a direct cause of crime did not enter into this story very often. Others . . . made the link; but here it was a predisposing cause and not in itself a sufficient explanation for deviancy.

sults would be disastrous. Once, observers believed, neighbors had disciplined neighbors. Now it seemed that rowdies corrupted rowdies.

Yet for all the desperation in this image, Americans shared an incredible optimism. Since deviant behavior was a product of the environment, the predictable result of readily observable situations, it was not inevitable. Crime was not inherent in the nature of man, as Calvinists had asserted; no theological devils insisted on its perpetuation. Implicit in this outlook was an impulse to reform. If one could alter the conditions breeding crime, then one could reduce it to manageable proportions and bring a new security to society.

One tactic was to advise and warn the family to fulfill its tasks well. By giving advice and demonstrating the awful consequences of an absence of discipline critics would inspire the family to a better performance. (The biographical sketches, then, were not only investigations but correctives to the problem.) One might also organize societies to shut taverns and houses of prostitution, an effort that was frequently made in the Jacksonian period. But such measures, while important, were slow-working, and by themselves seemed insufficient to meet the pressing needs of this generation. Another alternative then became not only feasible but essential: to construct a special setting for the deviant. Remove him from the family and community and place him in an artificially created and therefore corruption-free environment. Here he could learn all the vital lessons that others had ignored, while protected from the temptations of vice. A model and small-scale society could solve the immediate problem and point the way to broader reforms.

Almost everyone who wrote about deviancy during the Jacksonian era echoed the findings of Auburn's inspectors and many emulated their methodology. Officials at other prisons conducted similar surveys among convicts, validating the general conclusions reached in New York. Interested laymen, organized into such benevolent societies as the New York Prison Association and the Boston Prison Discipline Society, made their own investigations and then helped to publicize the same ideas among a still broader portion of the population. Well-known reformers, like Dorothea Dix, Francis Lieber, and Samuel Gridley Howe, concerned with a spectrum of causes, paid great attention to the problem of crime and its correction and further popularized the concepts. Family disorganization and community corruption, an extreme definition of the powers of vice and an acute sense of the threat of disorder were the standard elements in the discussions. A wide consensus formed on the origins of crime.

Prison officials everywhere informed state legislators of the crucial role of the family and community in causing deviant behavior. "The mass of criminals," explained the inspectors of Pennsylvania's Eastern State Penitentiary, "is composed of persons whose childhood and youth were spent in the uncontrolled exercise of vicious instincts." The warden of the Ohio penitentiary listed the breakdown of the household among the leading causes of crime. "Unhappy orphanage," he lamented, "leaves the susceptible youth without those restraints and safeguards which conduct to a life of probity."[20] To buttress this argument one

---

[20] Inspectors of the Eastern State Penitentiary of Pennsylvania, *Seventeenth Annual Report* (Philadelphia, 1846), 58. *Annual Report of the Ohio Penitentiary for 1850* (Columbus, Ohio, 1851), 12–13.

official calculated that of the 235 men committed to the prison in one year, 86 were under twenty-five years of age, a sure sign that the failure of the family was at the root of the problem. Another appropriately conducted interviews and compiled case histories. His most important finding, he believed, was that 221 convicts from a sample of 350 had been "thrown out from under parental influence and restraint," before reaching the age of twenty-one; in fact, 89 of them were without guardians by the time they were twelve. They had "never learned to submit to proper authority," or to understand that "their own safety and happiness are secured by such obedience."

All observers agreed that the forces at work in the community aggravated the family's errors. The future convict, concluded the Pennsylvania group, "social to a fault," took his cues from his surroundings; predictably, "the vices of social life have heralded the ruin of his fortunes and his hopes." Ohio's officials shared this view: "Without the refining and elevating influences of the home, without parental restraint and example, they were thrown upon a cold and selfish world, and often wronged. . . . They have done as might have been expected."[21]

An identical interpretation appeared in the opening pages of the first annual report (1844) of the New York Prison Association. According to one of its founders, the Unitarian minister William H. Channing, the association was formed to aid persons awaiting trial, to help reform convicts, and to assist released prisoners. This commitment, he explained, was not only testimony to a Christian desire to have good triumph over evil and to avoid "the vindictive spirit," but also reflected the community's ultimate responsibility, because of its "neglect and bad usages," for "the sins of its children." The first part of this formulation needed little clarification, but the second did, and so he elaborated on the role of the family and community in the origins of crime.[22]

"The first and most obvious cause," began Channing, "is an evil organization derived from evil parents. Bad germs bear bad fruit." Although his language suggested that a biological process was at work, he did not consider heredity anything more than a predisposing force that could be "cleansed away by a healthful moral influence." A properly organized social system would "purify away what is bad," and shield its members "from the temptations beneath which they are peculiarly liable to fall." The existence of crime pointed to the community's inability to fulfill its task, not the influence of heredity. Channing went on to link the failure of family training directly to deviant behavior. Of the 156 inmates recently admitted to Pennsylvania's Eastern State Penitentiary, he reported, fourteen had been orphaned by age twelve, thirty-six were missing one parent or another soon thereafter, 143 had received no religious instruction, and 144 never attended Sabbath school. "Such statistics," affirmed the minister, "tell at a glance that early neglect was certainly, in part, probably in great part, the cause of after crime."[23]

Channing too believed that the corruptions pervading the community made

---

[21] *Annual Report of the Ohio Penitentiary for 1852* (Columbus, Ohio, 1853), 35; *Annual Report of the Ohio Penitentiary for 1858* (Columbus, Ohio, 1859), 40–41. Inspectors of the Eastern State Penitentiary, *First and Second Annual Report* (Philadelphia, 1831), 10.

[22] New York Prison Association, *First Annual Report* (New York, 1845), 30–31. (Hereafter abbreviated N.Y.P.A.)

[23] *Ibid.*, 31–33.

early parental neglect so injurious; in fact, he was surprised that the power of vice did not debilitate still more people. "We seldom appreciate," he declared, "how easily, if left alone, unsustained by worthy example . . . we might become lawless and perverse. . . . Slight deviations, uncorrected, hurry the transgressor into a rapid downward course. . . . Tempters ensnare the inexperienced. . . . The spirit of mere adventure entangles the careless into a web of vile associations, from which there is no after escape. . . . How many a young man . . . took, almost without a thought, the first step in that path which ended in the gambler's hell, the plausible deceits of the forger and counterfeiter." Well-baited traps were so pervasive that the slightest miscalculation brought terrible consequences. "The sight of evil, as by contagion, awakens the desire to commit evil." Yet, for all his anxiety about society, Channing, like other Americans in the Jacksonian period, did not succumb to despair. "The study of the *causes* of the crime," he concluded, "may lead us to its *cure*." His environmental theory encouraged rather than stifled action.[24]

Succeeding reports of the New York Prison Association repeated these themes. Continuously stressing the critical role of the family, they reminded parents of the "importance of exercising careful supervision and wholesome discipline." Otherwise, the contagion of vice would be irresistible. Intemperance was "the giant whose mighty arm prostrates the greatest numbers, involving them in sin and shame and crime and ruin." And behind it, "never let it be forgotten, lies the want of early parental restraint and instruction." Readers even learned that "the loss of the father more frequently than that of the mother leads to criminal conduct on the part of the children"; for "mothers, as a general thing, are less able than fathers to restrain their sons."

The catalogue of seductions that led hapless youngsters to the penitentiary did not become thinner with time.[25] The 1855 association report devoted a lengthy appendix to the sources of crime, first paying due regard to the position of the family as the "bulwark against temptation," and then spelling out the social evils rampant in the community. There was the tavern and the brothel house — appropriately joined with a quote from Hosea, "whoredom and wine . . . taketh away the heart"; the theaters and the gambling houses were menaces, and so were the men who sold licentious books and pictures at the railroad station and boat landings. Still, no matter how lengthy the list, the organization assured its followers that "energetic and enlightened action of the people in . . . social and individual capacities" would effectively combat crime.[26]

A rival and perhaps more famous association, the Boston Prison Discipline Society, differed on many substantive issues with its New York counterpart, but both agreed on the sources of deviant behavior. Founded in 1825 by Louis Dwight, a onetime agent of the American Bible Society, the Boston group set down a very familiar creed. "This society," announced one of its early reports,

---

[24] *Ibid.*, 34–35.
[25] See, for example, N.Y.P.A., *Nineteenth Annual Report* (New York, 1864), 352. By that date, such views were no longer as popular as they had been in the 1830's, but were still expressed.
[26] N.Y.P.A., *Tenth Annual Report* (Albany, N.Y., 1855), Appendix A., by James S. Gould, 61–117. Quotations are on pp. 61, 73, 93–94, 108–109, 116–117.

"shows the importance of family government. . . . It is the confession of many convicts at Auburn [New York] and Wethersfield [Connecticut] that the course of vice, which brought them to the prison, commenced in disobedience to their parents, or in their parents' neglect." No one was probably surprised to learn that "youth, when unrestrained and neglected by their parents, find their way to the tavern and the grog shop."[27] This was the meaning of member Samuel Gridley Howe's pronouncement: "Thousands of convicts are made so in consequence of a faulty organization of society. . . . They are thrown upon society as a sacred charge; and that society is false to its trust, if it neglects any means for their reformation."[28] Those to blame for this state of affairs had the duty, and seemingly the power to effect reform.

Two of the most important figures in the New York and Boston organizations, Channing and Dwight, had first followed religious careers — the former was actually a minister, the latter had studied for it and then worked for the Bible Society. But one must define very carefully the religious influence in reform societies. The changes in Protestant thinking from the eighteenth to the nineteenth century had certainly increased the clergy's concern and attention to social reform, and because of their insistence that men were to do good by improving the common weal, many Americans participated in benevolent activities. Nevertheless, the prescriptions of what was right action, the definition of the policy that men of goodwill were to enact, revealed more of a secular than a religious foundation. Channing and Dwight echoed prevailing social anxieties; they did not make a uniquely religious perspective relevant. Their vision of the well-ordered society did not indicate the influence of their special training. In this sense, they, unlike their predecessors, followed the pack rather than heading it.[29]

Noted reformers and pamphleteers in pre–Civil War America were keenly interested in the predicament of the criminal. Francis Lieber was distressed by the treatment of offenders as well as of slaves. "The history of by far the greatest majority of criminals," insisted Lieber, "shows the afflicting fact, that they were led to crime by the bad example of their parents." From this first cause flowed a sequence of events, "a gradual progress in vice, for which society often offers but too many temptations." No effort to assist the deviant should be spared, he argued, for "society takes upon itself an awful responsibility, by exposing a criminal to such moral contagion, that, according to the necessary course of

[27] Boston Prison Discipline Society, Fourth Annual Report (Boston, 1829), 64. (Hereafter abbreviated B.P.D.S.); B.P.D.S., Eleventh Annual Report (Boston, 1835), 35. On Dwight, see William Jenks, A Memoir of the Reverend Louis Dwight (Boston, 1856).

[28] Samuel Gridley Howe, An Essay on Separate and Congregate Systems of Prison Discipline (Boston, 1846), 79.

[29] John L. Thomas, "Romantic Reform in America, 1815–1865," American Quarterly, 17 (1965), 656–681, notes a malaise but attempts to account for it as a crisis in church affairs; the argument here sees the crisis as far broader, touching all the society. So, too, I differ with the stress in Timothy L. Smith, Revivalism and Social Reform in Mid-Nineteenth Century America (Nashville, Tenn., 1957). Indeed, the evidence Smith brings forward on the actual social welfare work done by religious organizations, as apart from Bible distribution, is not very great.

things, he cannot escape its effects."[30] A more celebrated contemporary, Dorothea Dix, wrote about the convict as well as the insane, publishing an important pamphlet, *Remarks on Prisons and Prison Discipline in the United States*. "It is to the defects of our social organization," declared Dix, "to the multiplied and multiplying temptations to crime that we chiefly owe the increase of evil doers."[31] And like Lieber, she too announced that the community had the responsibility and the resources to confront and eliminate the problem.

The Jacksonians' conception of the causes of crime had an obvious and precise relevance for understanding juvenile delinquency. The child offender, no less than the adult one, was a casualty of his upbringing. The importance of family discipline in a community pervaded with vice characterized practically every statement of philanthropists and reformers on delinquency. Both mature and immature offenders were victims of similar conditions. Not that Americans, insensitive to an idea of childhood, unthinkingly made children into adults. Quite the reverse. They stripped the years away from adults, and turned everyone into a child.

The custodians of juvenile delinquents asked the same questions and drew the same conclusions as wardens in state prisons. No sooner did New York, for reasons we shall soon explore, establish a house of refuge in 1824 to incarcerate minors guilty of criminal offenses, than its managers collected and published case histories. Their inquiries, following a set form, indicated a common perspective on deviant behavior. How long had the youngster been under family government? How often, and how long, had he served as an apprentice? What was the moral character of his parents and his masters? Did the delinquent drink? Or have other vices? What about his companions? What was his first illegal act? His second and his third? The very thoroughness of the examination reflected how much the interrogators valued the information.

Refuge managers located in parental neglect the primary cause of deviant behavior. In typical instances: J. C., at fourteen, ran away from an inattentive and corrupt father. He soon returned, to steal six watches; his father helped to sell the loot. R. W., whose parents were intemperate, roamed the streets, and stayed away from home for weeks on end; he pilfered or begged his daily subsistence until arrested. J. L., another inmate caught stealing, recounted that after his father's death, his mother began drinking, "and then we all went to destruction, mother, brothers, sisters, all."[32] Each case was proof that the child who became "his own boss and went in the way that was right in his own eyes," was a prison convict in the making.

The sketches demonstrated the dire consequences of even minor acts of disobedience. The delinquent moved inexorably from petty to major crimes. W. O.

---

[30] Lieber's remarks appear in his translator's preface, reprinted in Gustave de Beaumont and Alexis de Tocqueville, *On the Penitentiary System in the United States* (Carbondale, Ill., 1964), 14–15. See too his *Remarks on the Relation between Education and Crime* (Philadelphia, 1835), 13.

[31] (2nd ed., Philadelphia, 1845), 25.

[32] Records of the New York House of Refuge, Syracuse University Library; for these biographies, see *Case Histories*, nos. 78 (December 10, 1825), 800 (September 30, 1830), 2657 (February 24, 1841).

first stole one shilling from his father, then some items of clothing from a stranger, later robbed a watch and some broadcloth from a shop, and finally wrecked, burned, and looted a house. E. M. began his career by pilfering small change from drunkards and graduated to highway robbery. J. R. went from pennies to dollars, and C. B. from fruits and cakes in the kitchen cupboard to cash in store registers.[33] What a careless parent dismissed as a comparatively harmless prank was a crucial event. A few pennies and some sweets, as these biographies revealed, were the first symptoms of a criminal life.

The vices at loose in the community invariably brought the unwary and untrained child to the prison gates. Delinquents' careers demonstrated the debilitating influences of the tavern, where they first began to drink, and the noxious quality of theaters and the houses of prostitution, where they learned other corruptions. Temptations seemed so omnipresent that when dedicating a new building at the New York refuge, the presiding minister reminded his audience that, had their parents been less vigorous or their training less thorough, they too might have become delinquent. "Who of us dare to say," he asked, "that if he had been exposed to the same influences, he would have preserved his integrity and come out of the fiery ordeal unscathed? The sight of such a group of children . . . in yonder gallery should fill us with humility and teach us lessons of mercy!"[34]

Thus, Jacksonians located both the origins of crime and delinquency within the society, with the inadequacies of the family and the unchecked spread of vice through the community. The situation appeared bleak, almost desperate. What elements would now stabilize the community? What kind of social order would keep deviancy within bounds? But if the dangers were immense, so were the possibilities. Convinced that crime was the fault of the environment, not a permanent or inevitable phenomenon, and eager to demonstrate the social blessings of republican political arrangements to the world, Americans set out to protect the safety of the society and to achieve unprecedented success in eradicating deviancy. Their analysis of the origin of crime became a rallying cry to action.

[33] Case no. 11 (January 1, 1825), case 55 (January 15, 1825), 1602 (July 30, 1835), 803 (October 8, 1830). To sample the many volumes of inmates' records, I examined the first 30 cases in the record book volume I, 1824–25, then the first 15 cases in vols. II (1825–27), V (1830–32), VIII (1835–36), XII (1841–42), XX (1851–52).

[34] New York House of Refuge, *Thirtieth Annual Report* (New York, 1855), 55.

Patent-Office Models of the Good Society: Some Relationships Between Social Reform and Westward Expansion

ARTHUR E. BESTOR, JR.

Ever since Frederick Jackson Turner proposed his famous "frontier thesis" in the 1890's, American historians have considered westward expansion as a significant factor in the development of the nation. In this essay Arthur E. Bestor, Jr., examines the relationship of nineteenth-century communitarian experiments to the westward movement in an effort to discover what is distinctive about American social reform. He concludes that communitarianism was not so much caused by the frontier as it was, in Turner's words, one of the "traits called out elsewhere because of the existence of the frontier." It was a response to the challenge existing in a new and expanding country to build social institutions from the ground up, and an opportunity to use actual experimentation to demonstrate the correctness of one's social principles. In Bestor's eyes, the model communities were distinctly not utopian, for the most basic intention of their originators was to put their ideas into practice. Communitarianism is thus a peculiar branch of social reform, aimed at creating models for behavior rather than at altering existing social institutions. In constructing his argument, Bestor makes important assumptions about the dynamics of social change, the impact of ideas on human motivation, and the significance of the immensity of American territorial resources. He implies that there was a distinctive style of ante-bellum reform, although he never defines it precisely. How does Bestor's interpretation compare with John L. Thomas's view in the essay following this one?

In the mechanical realm, nineteenth-century American inventiveness left as its most characteristic record not a written description of a drawing but a working model, such as the Patent Office then required. In somewhat similar fashion, the societal inventiveness of the first half of the nineteenth century embodied itself in a hundred or so co-operative colonies, where various types of improved social machinery were hopefully demonstrated. Patent-office models of the good society we may call them.[1]

Reprinted by permission of the author from the *American Historical Review*, 58 (1952), pp. 505–526.
[1] This paper was read before the Mississippi Valley Historical Association in Cincinnati, April 19, 1951.

To build a working model is not the same thing as to draw a picture. Hence it is necessary, at the outset, to distinguish between communitarianism, or the impulse which constructed these hundred model communities, and utopianism, or the impulse to picture in literary form the characteristics of an ideal but imaginary society. The distinction is more than verbal. A piece of utopian writing pictures a social order superior to the present, and it does so, of course, in the hope of inspiring men to alter their institutions accordingly. But a utopian work (unless it happens also to be a communitarian one) does *not* suggest that the proper way of going about such a reform is to construct a small-scale model of the desired society. Edward Bellamy's *Looking Backward*, for example, was a utopian novel, but definitely *not* a piece of communitarian propaganda, because the social transformation that Bellamy was talking about could not possibly be inaugurated by a small-scale experiment; it could come about only through a great collective effort by all the citizens of the state.

The communitarian, on the other hand, was by definition the apostle of small-scale social experiment. He believed that the indispensable first step in reform was the construction of what the twentieth century would call a pilot plant. The communitarian was not necessarily a utopian; few of the religious communities, for example, attempted to visualize an ideal future society this side of heaven. When the communitarian did indulge in utopian visions, the characteristic fact about them was that they always pictured the future as something to be realized through a small-scale experiment indefinitely reduplicated. The communitarian conceived of his experimental community not as a mere blueprint of the future but as an actual, complete, functioning unit of the new social order. As the American communitarian Albert Brisbane wrote:

> The whole question of effecting a Social Reform may be reduced to the establishment of one Association, which will serve as a model for, and induce the rapid establishment of others. . . . Now if we can, with a knowledge of true architectural principles, build one house rightly, conveniently and elegantly, we can, by taking it for a model and building others like it, make a perfect and beautiful city: in the same manner, if we can, with a knowledge of true social principles, organize one township rightly, we can, by organizing others like it, and by spreading and rendering them universal, establish a true Social and Political Order.[2]

This is a fair summary of the communitarian program.

Historically speaking, the idea of undertaking social reform in this particular way — by constructing a patent-office model or a pilot plant — is not a common idea but a distinctly uncommon one. No other period comes close to matching the record of the first half of the nineteenth century, which saw a hundred communitarian experiments attempted in the United States alone. The vogue of communitarianism can be delimited even more sharply than this. During a period of precisely fifty years, beginning in 1805, when the first communitarian colony was planted in the Old Northwest, at least ninety-nine different experiments were

---

[2] Albert Brisbane, *A Concise Exposition of the Doctrine of Association* (2d ed., New York, 1843), pp. 73–74.

actually commenced in the United States.[3] Nearly half of these — forty-five to be exact — were located in the Old Northwest, strictly defined.[4] Another twenty-eight were in areas which belonged to the same general cultural region — that is, western New York, the parts of the Ohio River valley outside the Old Northwest, and certain adjoining areas on the other side of the upper Mississippi.[5] A total of seventy-three communities — roughly three quarters of the total — thus belonged to what can be described, without undue geographical laxness, as the Middle West.

Such a clear-cut localization of communitarian ideas in time and place can hardly be fortuitous. It is the kind of fact that cries aloud for explanation in terms of historical relationships. What, then, were the unique elements in the historical situation of the Old Northwest that help to explain why communitarianism should have reached its peak there during the first half of the nineteenth century?

Twenty years ago an answer would have been forthcoming at once, and would probably have gone unchallenged: *the frontier.* If, however, the frontier is given anything like a satisfactorily limited definition — if, in other words, the term is taken to signify primarily that "outer margin of the 'settled area'" which figured in Frederick Jackson Turner's original essay — then a close relationship between the frontier and communitarianism is hard to find.

In the first place, communitarian ideas cannot be said to have arisen spontaneously among any groups living in actual frontier zones. The leading communitarian philosophies, in point of fact, were elaborated in Europe — not only those of Robert Owen, Charles Fourier, and Étienne Cabet but also those of most of the religious sects. The Moravians in the eighteenth century found their "general economy" well adapted to new settlements, but its principles were ones the sect had worked out and partially practiced before they came to America. The Shakers faced frontier conditions when they first arrived in America, but they worked out their communistic polity later. It was, in fact, their way of settling down after the frontier stage had passed. The nonreligious communitarianism of the nineteenth century drew its ideas from sources even more obviously unconnected with the frontier. Robert Owen's plan was a response to conditions which the factory system had created in Britain, and it made no significant impression in America until Owen himself brought it to this country. Americans did take the initiative in importing certain communitarian theories, but here again frontier motivation was absent. Albert Brisbane, though the son of a pioneer settler in western New York, became aware of social problems gradually, first in

[3] The statistical evidence incorporated in this and subsequent paragraphs is tabulated in a "Checklist of Communitarian Experiments Initiated in the United States before 1860," appended to Arthur E. Bestor, Jr., *Backwoods Utopias* (Philadelphia, 1950), pp. 231–43. Communities numbered 8–11, 24–30, 34–79, 82–109, 113–20, and 123–28 in the "Checklist" are the ones founded between 1805 and 1854, inclusive. Accounts of the individual communities established before 1829 will be found in the text of the work cited; later ones will be treated in a sequel (nearing completion), tentatively entitled *Phalanxes of Social Reform: The Fourierist Phase of Communitarian Socialism in America.*
[4] That is, twenty-one in Ohio, eleven in Indiana, eight in Wisconsin, four in Illinois, and one in Michigan.
[5] That is, eleven in western New York, seven in western Pennsylvania, one in what is now West Virginia, two in Kentucky, two in Missouri, and five in Iowa.

New York City, then in the ancient but impoverished realms of eastern Europe. He finally brought back from the Continent the most sophisticated social theory of the period, Fourierism, and made it the leading American communitarian system of the 1840's, by dint of propaganda directly largely from New York and Boston.[6]

If the ideas of the communitarians did not arise on the frontier, neither did the impulse to put them in practice. The handful of communities that were actually located in or near the true frontier zones were all planted there by groups from farther east or from Europe.[7] They were not established there with the hope or expectation of gaining recruits from among the frontiersmen; on the contrary, communitarian leaders were often warned against accepting local settlers.[8] Finally, communitarians were misled if they expected greater toleration of their social nonconformity in the West than in the East. The mobs who attacked the Shakers in Ohio, at any rate, were indistinguishable from those who attacked them in Massachusetts.[9]

Nothing created by the frontier contributed positively to the growth of communitarianism. Only as a passive force — as an area of relatively cheap land or relatively few restrictions — could the frontier be said to have had anything to do with the communitarian movement. These passive advantages of the frontier were, as a matter of fact, almost wholly delusive. The Shakers afforded an excellent test case, for their villages were to be found in regions of various types. The most successful were in long-settled areas, reasonably close to cities. The one Shaker settlement on the actual frontier — at Busro on the Wabash River above Vincennes — had a dismal history of discontent, hostility, and failure, from the time of its founding in 1810, through its evacuation at the time of the War of

[6] See Arthur E. Bestor, Jr., "Albert Brisbane — Propagandist for Socialism in the 1840's," *New York History*, XXVIII (April, 1947), 128–58.

[7] The following communities of the period were closest to the actual western frontier: (i) communities of immigrants from Europe: Equality (no. 84 in Bestor, "'Checklist'"), Icaria, Tex. (no. 126); (ii) communities founded close to the frontier by European theorists: New Harmony (no. 35), Nashoba (no. 49); (iii) communities that migrated from the East: Harmonie, Ind. (no. 9), Iowa Pioneer Phalanx (no. 72); (iv) frontier branches of eastern communities: West Union or Busro (no. 28), Union Grove (no. 111); (v) communities established on the frontier by groups from cities or settled areas of the West: Wisconsin Phalanx (no. 71).

[8] Just before the establishment of the New Harmony Community, for example, Robert Owen received the following advice from his son, who had been visiting the neighboring frontier settlements in Indiana and Illinois: "Although I do not perceive opposition to your plans in any quarter & although there is often an appearance of interest excited for a time, yet the character of the people is so little enthusiastic & all parties have been so long accustomed to be dilatory in business & to be thinking only of overreaching others & acting an insincere part, that an entire change must be effected in order to make them valuable members. . . . I have seen only one or two persons, who *as they are*, I should consider desirable associates. I certainly look forward with more favorable expectations to those, who come from Europe." William Owen, Vincennes, Ind., to Robert Owen, Washington, D.C., Feb. 7, 1825, MS in Robert Owen Papers, no. 58, in Co-operative Union, Manchester, England.

[9] Cf. Clara Endicott Sears, *Gleanings from Old Shaker Journals* (Boston, 1916), chaps. xi, xiv, xvii; and J. P. MacLean, "Mobbing the Shakers of Union Village," in his *Shakers of Ohio* (Columbus, 1907), pp. 362–87.

1812, until its abandonment in 1827.[10] The withdrawal of the Rappites from their westernmost outpost — in the very same region and at the very same time — may be taken as evidence that they too felt the frontier to be basically unfavorable to communitarianism. Thomas Hunt, a British Owenite who led a colony to Wisconsin in the 1840's, had to admit that whatever physical advantages the frontier might offer could "be secured, not only by bodies of men, but by private individuals." This fact was quickly discovered by members of co-operative communities which moved to the frontier. "On their arrival here," Hunt observed, "they . . . find many opportunities of employing their labour *out of the society they are connected with.*" Though Hunt saw advantages for communitarianism in the cheaper lands of the frontier, he saw none in the state of mind which the frontier engendered. Among the factors prejudicial to success, he listed, with emphasizing italics, "the *influence which the circumstances of this country may exert over their minds, in drawing them again into the vortex of competition.*"[11]

Hunt was probably wrong in regarding even the cheap lands of the frontier as a real economic boon to communitarianism. They proved to be the exact opposite, according to the shrewdest of all the nineteenth-century historians of the movement. This was John Humphrey Noyes, himself founder of the successful Oneida Community (located, incidentally, far from the frontier), who reached the following conclusions after carefully analyzing the history — particularly the record of landholdings — of communitarian ventures contemporaneous with his own:

> Judging by our own experience we incline to think that this fondness for land, which has been the habit of Socialists, had much to do with their failures. Farming is . . . the kind of labor in which there is . . . the largest chance for disputes and discords in such complex bodies as Associations. Moreover the lust for land leads off into the wilderness, "out west," or into by-places, far away from railroads and markets; whereas Socialism, if it is really ahead of civilization, ought to keep near the centers of business, and at the front of the general march of improvement. . . . Almost any kind of a factory would be better than a farm for a Community nursery. . . . Considering how much they must have run in debt for land, and how little profit they got from it, we may say of them almost literally, that they were "wrecked by running aground."[12]

The frontier, then, did not generate communitarianism. It did not inspire its inhabitants to join communitarian ventures. It did not show itself particularly hospitable to communitarian ideas. It did not even offer conditions that could contribute substantially to communitarian success. Communitarianism in other words, cannot be explained as an outgrowth of the conditions of frontier life. In point of fact, communitarianism developed in a fairly normal environment

---

[10] See the vivid contemporary record in MacLean, pp. 281–346.

[11] Thomas Hunt, "The Past and Present of the Colony of 'Equality,' " *The New Moral World*, XIII (Aug. 2, 1845), 472, a communication dated Equality, Spring Lake, Mukwonago [Wisconsin Territory], June 2, 1845.

[12] John Humphrey Noyes, *History of American Socialisms* (Philadelphia, 1870), pp. 19–20.

of settled agricultural and commercial life. The foreign-language sectarian communities, it is true, were not indigenous to the localities in which they were established. The Rappites, for example, were conducted as a body from Germany to Harmonie, Pennsylvania, then to Harmonie, Indiana, and finally back to Economy, Pennsylvania. None of the original members had any previous connection with these places, and the number of members recruited in the neighborhood was negligible. The same could be said of communities like Zoar, Ebenezer, and Amana. In the history of the communitarian movement as a whole, however, this pattern was the exception rather than the rule. The Shakers illustrated a more typical development. Each village of theirs was "gathered" (the phrase was a favorite one with them) from among the converts in a given locality, and was established upon a farm owned by one of the group or purchased with their combined resources. When communitarianism assumed a secular character, beginning in the 1820's, this local pattern became even more characteristic of the movement.

Of the thirty-six Owenite and Fourierist communities established in the United States during the half century under consideration,[13] only one — Hunt's colony in Wisconsin — represented an immigrant group comparable to the Rappites or Zoarites. Only ten others involved any substantial migration of members, and in many of these the recruits from the immediate vicinity clearly outnumbered those drawn from a distance.[14] At least two thirds of the Owenite and Fourierist communities were experiments indigenous to the neighborhood in which they were located. Sometimes groups in a small village or on adjoining farms threw their lands together or traded them for a larger tract nearby.[15] Sometimes groups in a larger town moved to a domain which they acquired a few miles out in the country.[16] It is difficult to distinguish between the two processes, and unnecessary. In neither case did the moving about of men and women constitute anything like a true migration to a new environment. Clearly enough, communi-

[13] The thirty-six are those named in Bestor, "Checklist," nos. 35–41, 54–79, and 82–84. The Owenite and Fourierist experiments, rather than the entire group of communities, have been selected for analysis because their characteristics can be more accurately determined. They constituted the most important and representative group of secular experiments during the half century.

[14] Three communities only were clear-cut examples of migration to the western frontier: Wisconsin Phalanx (no. 71), Iowa Pioneer Phalanx (no. 72), and Hunt's colony (no. 84). Two communities migrated from the East to unite with an already existing western (but hardly frontier) experiment: Forestville Community (no. 38) and Integral Phalanx (no. 76). Though most of its population probably came from the surrounding neighborhood, New Harmony (no. 35) did include substantial groups of members who migrated from eastern centers. Five communities migrated from cities to unsettled mountainous areas in the East: Social Reform Unity (no. 55), Sylvania Phalanx (no. 57), Morehouse Union (no. 58), Society of One-Mentians (no. 82), and Goose Pond Community (no. 83).

[15] For example, the Owenite communities of Kendal (no. 39) and Blue Spring (no. 41), and the Fourierist phalanxes of LaGrange (no. 60), Alphadelphia (no. 65), and Trumbull (no. 70).

[16] For example, the Owenite communities of Yellow Springs (no. 36), Franklin (no. 37), and Valley Forge (no. 40); Brook Farm (no. 54); the Clermont Phalanx (no. 69); and the various Fourierist communities that radiated from Rochester, N.Y.: Clarkson (no. 61), Bloomfield (no. 62), Sodus Bay (no. 66), Mixville (no. 67), and Ontario (no. 68).

tarianism as a secular doctrine of social reform made its impact in already settled areas and it inspired its adherents to act in their own neighborhoods far more frequently than it led them to seek the frontier.

Yet the fact remains that the great outburst of communitarian activity occurred during the period when the frontier of agricultural settlement was pushing ahead most rapidly, and it tended to concentrate in the area lying in the wake of that forward thrust. Some connection obviously existed between the idea and the situation. The true nature of that relationship must be explored.

In his original statement of the so-called frontier thesis, Frederick Jackson Turner enumerated certain ideas and habits of mind that he deemed characteristically American. "These," he exclaimed, "are traits of the frontier, or traits called out elsewhere because of the existence of the frontier."[17] The latter half of the sentence has a rather off-hand air about it, suggesting that Turner did not fully recognize how radically different were the two types of causation he was bracketing together.[18] Indeed, if the implications of the second part of the statement had been followed out fully and carefully by Turner and his disciples, the frontier thesis itself might have been saved by much of the one-sidedness that present-day critics discover in it.[19] Be that as it may, the second part of the

[17] Frederick Jackson Turner, "The Significance of the Frontier in American History" (1893), as reprinted in his *The Frontier in American History* (New York, 1920), p. 37. Turner's most explicit discussion of communitarianism and its relation to the frontier is in his "Contributions of the West to American Democracy" (1963), *ibid.*, pp. 261–63.

[18] Turner's actual illustrations were such traits as the "practical, inventive turn of mind," the "masterful grasp of material things," and the "restless, nervous energy," which he believed were engendered by conditions of life on the actual frontier. If these traits were, as he believed, transmitted directly to other areas and to later generations, and if they constitued the dominant features of American thought as a whole, then no one could deny his thesis "that to the frontier the American intellect owes its striking characteristics." But then there would be no need for the saving clause, "traits called out elsewhere because of the existence of the frontier." This afterthought constitutes, in effect, a confession of weakness so far as the central thesis is concerned, for it introduces a totally different causal explanation. The traits that induced men to go to the frontier become, in this way of thinking, valid examples of frontier influence. To argue that the frontier was a creative force in such circumstances is a little like saying that the cheese created the mouse because it lured him into the trap.

[19] By failing to take seriously the ideas "called out elsewhere" — that is, by failing to reckon with these ideas as potent historical facts in their own right — the frontier school was trapped into its most notorious blunder: the acceptance of the "safety-valve" doctrine as an objective fact of economic history. The exposure of this error by recent scholarship has dealt a more serious blow to the frontier thesis than is sometimes realized. Turner shared very largely the nineteenth-century positivistic aim of explaining ideas as the products of external physical and material conditions of life. The frontier thesis must be understood partly in this light. By implication it denied (or at least played down) the importance not merely of ideas imported from Europe but of ideas generally, as creative, causative factors in history. The safety-valve doctrine served as a crucial test-case of the adequacy of this positivistic approach. If the frontier actually operated as a safety valve drawing off discontent from settled areas, then here was a clear-cut example of materialistic events or forces generating ideas directly and at a distance. But it turns out that the safety-valve doctrine was a preconception about the frontier, not a generalization from actual occurrences there. It was so powerful a preconception, moreover, that it actually generated action (in the form of homestead legislation, etc.) which directly affected the current of events in the West itself. By destroying the historicity of the safety-valve doctrine, scholarship did more than correct a mere detail of the frontier interpretation; it

quoted sentence does describe the kind of relationship that existed between westward expansion and the vogue of such an idea as communitarianism. The latter was one of the "traits called out elsewhere because of the existence of the frontier."

This paper purposes to explore the process through which communitarianism — and, by extension, a variety of other social ideas — were "called out" by the mere existence of the frontier. The statement we are using is, in part, a figurative one. For the sake of precision it ought to be restated at the outset in completely liberal terms. Three points require brief preliminary discussion. In the first place, ideas are not produced by the mere existence of something. They result from reflection upon that something, reflection induced either by direct observation or by knowledge derived at second hand. We are, by definition, interested in the reflections of men and women who did not participate in, and did not directly observe, the frontier process. In the second place, ideas rarely, if ever, spring into existence fresh and new. Reflection upon a new occurrence does not produce a set of new ideas. It exercises a selective influence upon old ones. It represses some of these. It encourages others. It promotes new combinations. And it may infuse the whole with deeper emotional feeling. The resulting complex of ideas and attitudes may be new, but the newness lies in the pattern, not in the separate elements. Finally, though we have adopted Turner's phrase, and with it his use of the word "frontier," we will find that it was really the westward movement as a whole, and not the events at its frontier fringe, that the men and women "elsewhere" were meditating upon.[20]

With these three considerations in mind, we are ready to restate the subject of our inquiry in distinct, if prosaic, terms. The rephrasing will be clearer if cast in the form of a series of questions, although these will not have to be taken up in order or answered separately in the discussion that follows. How, then, did the expansion of population into unsettled areas, and the planting of civilized

---

stood the whole theory on its head. Today the intellectual historian who would deal with "frontier" ideas is forced to take as a starting-point, not the conditions of life at the edge of settlement and the traits supposedly born out of that life, but rather the body of preexisting ideas concerning the West and the significance thereof for mankind. One may even argue that the frontier thesis itself was less an induction from historical data than a restatement, with historical illustrations, of a time-honored set of intellectual assumptions concerning American westward expansion.

[20] Turner's central theme, likewise, was really not the frontier, but something larger: the westward movement, the West which it created, and the influence of both on American life. With something of the instinct of a poet, Turner seized upon one special aspect, the frontier, to serve as a symbol of the whole. But in the end, it seems to me, he was led astray by his own symbolism. The frontier was a picturesque part, but only a part, of the larger theme he was exploring. Instead of dropping the symbol, however, when it became obviously inapplicable to the other matters under discussion, he stuck to the word "frontier" until gradually its value as a denotative term was destroyed. Worst of all, vices of language are apt to become vices of thought. Having grown accustomed to speak of the influence or the significance of the frontier, rather than of the westward movement, Turner and his disciples tended to look for crucial factors solely among the events and ideas that occurred along the very margins of settlement, and then to assume that the intellectual life of the entire West (and, through it, the entire nation) derived from this pioneer thinking.

institutions there, strike the imaginations of those who took no direct part in the process? What ideas of theirs about the nature of social institutions were confirmed and amplified by their reflections upon this continuing event? Which of their hopes were encouraged, which desires rendered more certain of fulfillment, by what they conceived to be taking place? And how did this new pattern of ideas and aspirations correspond to the pattern embodied in a doctrine of social reform like communitarianism?

Now, communitarianism involved, as we have seen, certain very definite convictions about the way social institutions are actually created. It assumed the possibility of shaping the whole society of the future by deliberately laying the appropriate foundations in the present. And it called upon men to take advantage of this possibility by starting at once to construct the first units of a new and better world.

In this set of beliefs we can not immediately detect certain of the ideas that took shape in the minds of men as they contemplated — from near or far — the upbuilding of a new society in the American West?

First among these ideas, certainly, was the sense of rapid growth and vast potentiality. No theme was so trite in American oratory and American writing; quotations of a general sort are not needed to prove the point. But one particular aspect of this belief in the future greatness of the United States requires special notice. The point in question was enshrined in a couplet which was composed in New England in 1791 and which quickly became one of the most hackneyed in the whole of American verse:

> Large streams from little fountains flow;
> Tall oaks from little acorns grow.[21]

American civilization, to spell out the interpretation which hearers instinctively gave to these lines, was destined for greatness, but this greatness was growing, and would grow, out of beginnings that were small indeed.

The converse of this idea formed a second important element in the reflections which the westward movement induced. The habit of tracing greatness back to its tiny source, led easily to the conception that every beginning, however casual and small, held within it the germ of something vastly greater. In a stable society, small happenings might have no consequences. But to men who pondered the expansion going on in the West, there came a sense that no event was so insignificant that it might not affect the future character of an entire region — perhaps for evil (if men lacked vigilance), but more probably for good.

A third idea, closely linked to these others, provided the most distinctive element in the entire pattern. Human choice could play its part in determining the character of the small beginnings from which great institutions would in future infallibly grow. But — and this is the uniquely important point — an organized effort to shape them would be effective only during the limited period of time that institutions remained in embryo. This concept is not, of course, the obvious and quite unremarkable idea that what one does today will affect what happens

[21] David Everett (1770–1813), lines beginning "You'd scarce expect one of my age," written in 1791 and first published in 1797. See Francis E. Blake, *David Everett* (n. p., n. d.), p. 7.

tomorrow. On the contrary, it assumed that there was something extraordinary about the moment then present, that the opportunity of influencing the future which it proffered was a unique opportunity, never to be repeated so fully again.

The corollary to all this — the fourth element in the complex of ideas — was a moral imperative. Men and women were duty-bound to seize, while it still existed, the chance of building their highest ideals into the very structure of the future world. When men spoke of "the mission of America," it was this particular idea, more than any other, that imparted to their words a sense of urgency. This moral imperative applied to the transplanting of old institutions as well as the establishment of new. The link between reformer and conservative was their common belief that institutions required positively to be planted in the new areas. Naturally the *best* institutions were the ones that should be so planted. For most men and women this meant the most familiar institutions, or at least the most respected among the familiar ones. Consequently the greater part of the effort which this concept inspired went into reproducing old institutions in the new West. A few men and women, however, always sought these best institutions not among those that already existed but among those that might exist. Hence the concept gave scope for reform as well as conservation.

Even when it assumed a reformist character, however, this concept must not be equated with reform in general. That it is to say, it was not identical with the sense of duty that urges men to remedy social injustices and to remake faulty institutions wherever they find them. The present concept was much narrower. Without necessarily overlooking abuses hoary with age, those who thought in this particular way concentrated their attention upon institutions at the rudimentary stage, believing that the proper shaping of these offered the greatest promise of ultimate social reformation.

The group of four concepts we have been considering formed an altruistic counterpart to the idea of the West as a land of opportunity for the individual. The dreams of wealth, of higher social station, and of greater freedom were doubtless the most influential ideas which the West generated in the minds of those who reflected upon its growth. The action which such dreams inspired was participation in the westward movement. But all men who thought about the West did not move to it. There were also dreams which men who remained in the East might share, and there were actions appropriate to such dreams. Throughout the world, as men reflected upon the westward movement, they grew more confident that success would crown every well-intended effort to create a freer and better society for themselves and their fellows. And many of them felt that the proper way to create it was to copy the process of expansion itself, by planting the tiny seeds of new institutions in the wilderness.

What men thought about the West might or might not conform to reality. But in the fourfold concept we have analyzed, there was much that did correspond with developments actually taking place in America. At the beginning of the nineteenth century the vast area beyond the Appalachians was in process of active settlement, yet its future social pattern was still far from irrevocably determined. Different ways of living existed within its borders: aboriginal, French, English, Spanish, Southern, Yankee, the ways of the fur trader and the ways of the settled farmer. The pressures from outside that were reinforcing one or another of these patterns of life were vastly unequal in strength, and this fact portended ultimate victory to some tendencies and defeat to others. But the victory of no one of the contending social systems had yet been decisively won. And the modifications which any system would inevitably undergo as it spread across the region and encountered new conditions were beyond anyone's predicting. Half a century later this indeterminateness was no longer characteristic of the West. Many of the fundamental features of its society had been determined with such definiteness as to diminish drastically the range of future possibilities. Just as the surveyors had already laid down the township and section lines which fixed certain patterns irrevocably upon the land, so the men and women of the region, in subtler but no less certain fashion, had by the middle of the nineteenth century traced and fixed for the future many of the principal lines in the fundamental ground-plan of their emergent society.

The consciousness that they were doing this was stronger in the minds of Americans during the first fifty years of the nineteenth century than ever before or since. The idea had found expression earlier, of course, but never had it been validated by so fast a process of institutional construction as was taking place in the Mississippi Valley. The idea might linger on after the middle of the nineteenth century, but every year it corresponded less with the realities of the American scene, where social institutions were being elaborated or painfully reconstructed rather than created fresh and new. The first half of the nineteenth century was the period when it was most natural for Americans to assert and to act upon the belief that the new society of the West could and should be shaped in embryo by the deliberate, self-conscious efforts of individuals and groups.

This conviction received clearest expression in the pulpit and in the publications devoted to missions. An eastern clergyman, addressing the American Home Missionary Society in 1829, called upon the imagination of his hearers, asking that they place themselves "on the top of the Allegheny, survey the immense valley beyond it, and consider that the character of its eighty or one hundred million inhabitants, a century hence, will depend on the direction and impulse given it now, in its forming state." "The ruler of this country," he warned, "is growing up in the great valley: leave him without the gospel, and he will be a ruffian giant, who will regard neither the decencies of civilization, nor the charities of religion."[22]

The tone of urgency increased rather than diminished as the great valley filled up and men sensed the approaching end of the time during which its institutions might be expected to remain pliant. "The next census," wrote the editor of *The Home Missionary* in 1843, "may show, that the majority of votes in our national legislature will belong to the West." The myriads there, in other words, "are soon to give laws to us all." The conclusion was obvious: "*Now is the time when the West can be saved; soon it will be too late!*"

> Friends of our Country — followers of the Saviour — [the editor continued] . . . surely the TIME HAS COME . . . when the evangelical churches must occupy the West, or the enemy will. . . . The way is open — society in the West is in a plastic state, worldly enterprise is held in check, the people are ready to receive the Gospel. . . .

[22] J. Van Vecten, "Address," *The Home Missionary*, II (June 1, 1829), 21.

When the present generation of American Christians have it in their power, instrumentally, to determine not only their own destiny and that of their children, but also to direct the future course of their country's history, and her influence on all mankind, they *must* not be — we hope they *will not be* — false to their trust![23]

If one is tempted to regard this as the attitude only of easterners seeking to influence western society from outside, listen for a moment to a sermon preached before the legislature of Wisconsin Territory in 1843:

It will not answer for you to fold your hands in indolence and say "Let the East take care of the West. . . ." The West must take care of itself — the West *must* and *will* form its own character — it must and will originate or perpetuate its own institutions, whatever be their nature. . . . Much as our brethren in the East have done, or can do for us, the principal part of the task of enlightening and evangelizing this land is *ours;* if good institutions and virtuous principles prevail, it must be mainly through our own instrumentality. . . . In the Providence of God, you have been sent to spy out and to take possession of this goodly land. To *you* God has committed the solemn responsibility of impressing upon it your own image: the likeness of your own moral character — a likeness which . . . it will, in all probability, bear through all succeeding time. Am I not right then in saying that you . . . occupy a position, both in time and place, of an exceedingly important nature?[24]

The same evangelical fervor began to infuse the writings of educational reformers in the second quarter of the nineteenth century, and the same arguments appeared. When Horace Mann bade his "official Farewell" to the school system of Massachusetts, he too spoke in terms of "a futurity rapidly hastening upon us." For the moment this was "a futurity, now fluid, — ready, as clay in the hands of the potter, to be moulded into every form of beauty and excellence." But, he reminded his fellow citizens, "so soon as it receives the impress of our plastic touch, whether this touch be for good or for evil, it is to be struck into . . . adamant." "Into whose form and likeness," he asked, "shall we fashion this flowing futurity?" The West was explicitly in his mind. In settlements already planted, the lack of educational provision posed problems of peculiar exigency, for "a different mental and moral culture must come speedily, or it will come too late." Nor was this all.

Beyond our western frontier [he continued], another and a wider realm spreads out, as yet unorganized into governments, and uninhabited by civilized man. . . . Yet soon will every rood of its surface be explored. . . . Shall this new empire . . . be reclaimed to humanity, to a Christian life, and a Christian history; or shall it be a receptacle where the avarice . . . of a corrupt civilization shall . . . breed its monsters? If it is ever to be saved from such a perdition, the Mother

[23] "Important Position of Home Missionary Affairs," *ibid.,* XVI (September, 1843), 97–99, italics and capitals as in the original.

[24] J. M. Clark, "The West Summoned to the Work," *ibid.,* XVI (August, 1843), 75–76.

States of this Union, — those States where the institutions of learning and religion are now honored and cherished, must send out their
hallowing influences to redeem it. And if . . . the tree of Paradise
is ever to be planted and to flourish in this new realm; . . . will not
the heart of every true son of Massachusetts palpitate with desire . . .
that her name may be engraved upon its youthful trunk, there to
deepen and expand with its immortal growth?[25]

Religious and educational ideals were not the only ones which Americans
cherished and whose future they were unwilling to leave to chance. In establishing their political institutions, they were weighed down with thoughts of posterity, and of a posterity that would occupy lands as yet almost unexplored.
At the Constitutional Convention James Wilson of Pennsylvania spoke to the
following effect: "When he considered the amazing extent of country — the
immense population which is to fill it, the influence which the Govt. we are to
form will have, not only on the present generation of our people & their multiplied posterity, but on the whole Globe, he was lost in the magnitude of the
object."[26]

Such ideas as these found embodiment in the great series of documents which
provided for the extension of government into the American West. Usually the
purpose was so self-evident as to require no explicit statement. The Northwest
Ordinance of 1787, for example, was without a preamble. It proceeded directly
to the task of providing frames of government for the Northwest Territory,
through all the stages up to statehood, and it concluded by setting forth certain
"articles of compact" which were to "forever remain unalterable" and whose
manifest purpose was to determine irrevocably for the future certain institutional
patterns of the region. The framers of this and similar constitutional documents
were proclaiming, by actions rather than words, their adherence to the set of
beliefs under discussion here, namely, that the shape of western society was being
determined in their own day, and that they possessed both the opportunity and
the responsibility of helping to direct the process. "I am truly Sensible of the
Importance of the Trust," said General Arthur St. Clair in 1788 when he accepted the first governorship of the Northwest Territory. He was aware, he continued, of "how much depends upon the due Execution of it — to you Gentlemen, over whom it is to be immediately exercised — to your Posterity! perhaps
to the whole Community of America!"[27]

Economic and social patterns, Americans believed, could also be determined
for all future time during a few crucial years at the outset. Nothing was of
greater concern to most inhabitants of the United States than the pattern of land-

[25] Horace Mann, "Twelfth Annual Report of the Secretary of the Board of Education,"
dated Nov. 24, 1848, in Massachusetts, Board of Education, *Twelfth Annual Report*
(Boston, 1849), pp. 141–44.

[26] Max Farrand, ed., *Records of the Federal Convention of 1787* (New Haven, 1911),
I, 405 (Mon., June 25, 1787, notes of James Madison). Robert Yates recorded in his
notes of Wilson's speech the following additional sentence: "When we are laying the
foundation of a building, which is to last for ages, and in which millions are interested,
it ought to be well laid." *Ibid.*, p. 413.

[27] Address at Marietta, July 9, 1788, in Clarence E. Carter, ed., *Territorial Papers of
the United States*, III (Washington, 1934), 264.

ownership which was likely to arise as a consequence of the disposal of the public domain. In this as in other matters, the present interests of the persons involved were naturally more compelling than the prospective interests of unborn generations. Nevertheless, concern for the latter was never pushed very far into the background. "Vote yourself a farm" was doubtless the most influential slogan of the land reformers. But not far behind in persuasiveness were arguments that dwelt upon the kind of future society which a particular present policy would inevitably produce. The argument was often put in negative form; propagandists warned of the evils that would inescapably follow from a wrong choice made during the crucial formative period.

> The evil of permitting speculators to monopolize the public lands [said a report of the land reformers in 1844], is already severely felt in the new states. . . . But what is this evil compared with the distress and misery that is in store for our children should we permit the evil of land monopoly to take firm root in this Republic? . . .
>
> Time rolls on — and in the lapse of a few ages all those boundless fields which now invite us to their bosom, become the settled property of individuals. Our descendants wish to raise themselves from the condition of hirelings, but they wish it in vain . . . and each succeeding age their condition becomes more and more hopeless. They read the history of their country; they learn that there was a time when their fathers could have preserved those domains, and transmitted them, free and unincumbered, to their children.

If once lost, the opportunity could never be regained. But if seized upon "by one bold step," the report continued, "our descendants will be in possession of an independence that cannot fail so long as God hangs his bow in the clouds."[28] Certain aspects even of the slavery controversy grow clearer when examined in the light of this characteristic American belief. One central paradox, at least, becomes much more understandable. "The whole controversy over the Territories," so a contemporary put it, "related to an imaginary negro in an impossible place."[29] This was in large measure true. Even the admission of new slave states or of new free ones — and such admissions were occurring regularly — aroused no such controversy as raged about the exclusion of slavery from, or its extension to, unsettled areas where no one could predict the possible economic utility of the institution or its ability to survive. The violence of this controversy becomes explicable only if one grasps how important in the climate of opinion of the day was the belief that the society of the future was being uniquely determined by the small-scale institutional beginnings of the present. From the Missouri crisis of 1819–21 onwards, practically every major battle in the long-continued contest was fought over the question of whether slavery should go into, or be excluded from, territories whose social institutions had not

---

[28] *Working Man's Advocate* (New York), July 6, 1844, as printed in *A Documentary History of American Industrial Society*, ed. John R. Commons and others, VII (Cleveland, 1910), 299, 302.

[29] James G. Blaine, *Twenty Years of Congress* (2 vols., Norwich, Conn., 1884), I, 272, quoting an unnamed "representative from the South."

yet crystallized. So long as both sides could rest assured that the existence or non-existence of slavery was settled for every inch of territory in the United States, then the slavery controversy in politics merely smoldered. Such a salutary situation resulted from the Missouri Compromise, which drew a geographical dividing line across the territories. But when the Mexican War opened the prospect of new territorial acquisitions, the controversy burst into flame again with the Wilmot Proviso, which aimed to nip in the bud the possibility that slavery might ever become an institution in the new areas. The Compromise of 1850 composed the dispute with less definitiveness than had been achieved thirty years before, for the question of slavery in New Mexico and Utah was left open until those territories should be ripe for statehood. Though the Compromise was, for this reason, intrinsically less stable than the earlier one, the uncertainties that it left were in areas which settlement was hardly likely to reach in the near future. Comparative calm thus ensued until the Kansas-Nebraska Act of 1854. By opening to slavery the territories north of the old Missouri Compromise line, this measure threw back into uncertainty the character of the future social order of an area now on the verge of rapid settlement. Bleeding Kansas resulted from the effort to settle by force what could no longer be settled by law, namely, the kind of social institutions that should be allowed to take root in the new territory and thus determine its future for untold ages to come.

Abraham Lincoln in his speech at Peoria on October 16, 1854, made perfectly clear his reasons for opposing the doctrine of popular sovereignty embodied in the new act:

> Another important objection to this application of the right of self-government, is that it enables the first FEW, to deprive the succeeding MANY, of a free exercise of the right of self-government. The first few may get slavery IN, and the subsequent many cannot easily get it OUT. How common is the remark now in the slave States — "If we were only clear of our slaves, how much better it would be for us." They are actually deprived of the privilege of govering themselves as they would, by the action of a very few, in the beginning.[30]

Four years later Lincoln restated the argument in a letter to an old-time Whig associate in Illinois. His point of departure was a statement of Henry Clay's. "If a state of nature existed, and we were about to lay the foundations of society, no man would be more strongly opposed than I should to incorporate the institution of slavery among it's elements," Clay was quoted as saying. "Exactly so," was Lincoln's comment.

> In our new free ter[r]itories, a state of nature does exist. In them Congress lays the foundations of society; and, in laying those foundations, I say, with Mr. Clay, it is desirable that the declaration of the equality of all men shall be kept in view, as a great fundamental principle; and that Congress, which lays the foundations of society, should, like Mr. Clay, be strongly opposed to the incorporation of slavery among it's [sic] elements.[31]

[30] Roy P. Basler, ed., *Abraham Lincoln: His Speeches and Writings* (Cleveland, 1946), p. 306.
[31] Lincoln to J. N. Brown, Springfield, Oct. 18, 1858, *ibid.*, p. 479.

These statements come as close as any to explaining the true nature of the issue which neither side was willing to compromise in 1860–61. In the midst of the crisis, it will be remembered, Congress passed and transmitted to the states for ratification a proposed constitutional amendment forever prohibiting any alteration of the Constitution that would permit Congress to interfere with slavery in the states.[32] This provision was acceptable to Lincoln and the Republicans even though they were refusing to concede a single inch to slavery in the territories. On the other hand, the complete guarantee of slavery where it actually existed was insufficient to satisfy the Southern leaders, so long as permission to extend slavery into new areas was withheld. For both sides the issue was drawn over potentialities. But this does not mean that it involved unrealities. In the mid-nineteenth-century climate of opinion, potentialities were among the most real of all things. The issue of slavery in the territories was an emotionally potent one because it involved a postulate concerning the creation and development of social institutions, and a corresponding ethical imperative, both of which were woven into the very texture of American thought.

How communitarianism fitted into this tradition should now be clear. The communitarian point of view, in simplest terms, was the idea of commencing a wholesale social reorganization by first establishing and demonstrating its principles completely on a small scale in an experimental community. Such an approach to social reform could command widespread support only if it seemed natural and plausible. And it was plausible only if one made certain definite assumptions about the nature of society and of social change. These assumptions turn out to be precisely the ones whose pervasive influence on American thought this paper has been examining.

A belief in the plasticity of social institutions was prerequisite, for communitarians never thought in terms of a revolutionary assault upon a stiffly defended established order. To men and women elsewhere, the West seemed living proof that institutions were indeed flexible. If they failed to find them so at home, their hopes turned westward. As Fourierism declined in the later 1840's, its leaders talked more and more of a "model phalanx" in the West. George Ripley, founder of Brook Farm in Massachusetts, defended this shift, though it belied his earlier hopes for success in the East:

> There is so much more pliability of habits and customs in a new country, than in one long settled, that an impression could far more easily be produced and a new direction far more easily given in the one than in the other. An Association which would create but little sensation in the East, might produce an immense effect in the West.[33]

But it was more than pliancy which communitarians had to believe in. Their doctrine assumed that institutions of world-wide scope might grow from tiny seeds deliberately planted. Such an assumption would be hard to make in most periods of history. The great organism of society must usually be taken for granted — a growth of untold centuries, from origins wrapped in obscurity. Rarely

---

[32] It passed the House on Feb. 28, 1861, by a vote of 133 to 65; the Senate on March 2, by 24 to 12.

[33] [George Ripley], "Model Phalanx," *The Harbinger*, IV (Jan. 16, 1847), 94.

does experience suggest that the little projects of the present day are likely to develop into the controlling institutions of the morrow. Rarely has society been so open and free as to make plausible a belief that new institutions might be planted, might mature, and might reproduce themselves without being cramped and strangled by old ones. In America in the early nineteenth century, however, men and women believed that they could observe new institutions in the making, and they were confident that these would develop without check and almost without limit. Large numbers of Americans could be attracted to communitarianism because so many of its postulates were things they already believed.

Large numbers of Americans *were* attracted to communitarianism. If the experimental communities of the Middle West had been exclusively colonies of immigrants, attracted to vacant lands, then communitarianism would have had little significance for American intellectual history. But for the most part, as we have seen, communitarian colonies were made up of residents of the region. Though such experiments did not arise spontaneously on the frontier itself, they did arise with great frequency and spontaneity in the settled areas behind it. There men possessed a powerful sense of the plasticity of American institutions but were at the same time in contact with the social ideas circulating throughout the North Atlantic world. One strain of thought fertilized the other. In a typical communitarian experiment of the Middle West, men might pay lip service to Owen or Fourier, but their central idea was the conviction that a better society could grow out of the patent-office model they were intent on building.

On the whole, the fact that communitarianism stood in such a well-defined relationship to a central concept in American thought is perhaps the most important thing which the intellectual historian can seize upon in attempting to assess the significance of the communitarian movement. This movement has been looked at from many different points of view: as part of the history of socialism or communism, as a phase of religious history, as one manifestation of a somewhat vaguely defined "ferment" of democratic ideas. Communitarianism was relevant to these different categories, of course, but its true nature is hardly made clear by considering it within the limits of any one of these classifications. The only context broad enough to reveal the true significance of the communitarian point of view was the context provided by the early nineteenth-century American way of thinking about social change.

This way of thinking was summed up and applied in the manifesto with which Victor Considerant launched his ambitious but ill-fated colony of French Fourierites in Texas in 1854:

> If the nucleus of the new society be implanted upon these soils, to-day a wilderness, and which to-morrow will be flooded with population, thousands of analogous organizations will rapidly arise without obstacle and as if by enchantment around the first specimens. . . .
>
> It is not the desertion of society that is proposed to you, but the solution of the great social problem on which depends the actual salvation of the world.[34]

[34] Victor Considerant, *The Great West: A New Social and Industrial Life in Its Fertile Regions* (New York, 1854), p. 58.

The last sentence stated an essential part of the true communitarian faith. A remaking of society, not an escape from its problems, was the aim of communitarian social reform during the period when it exerted a real influence upon American social thought. The dwindling of the ideal into mere escapism was the surest symptom of its decline. Such decline was unmistakable in the latter half of the nineteenth century. By 1875 a genuinely sympathetic observer could sum up in the following modest terms the role which he believed communitarian colonies might usefully play in American life:

> That communistic societies will rapidly increase in this or any other country, I do not believe. . . . But that men and women can, if they *will*, live pleasantly and prosperously in a communal society is, I think, proved beyond a doubt; and thus we have a right to count this another way by which the dissatisfied laborer may, if he chooses, better his condition.[35]

In the late nineteenth century, it is true, numerous communitarian experiments were talked about and even commenced, and their prospectuses echoed the brave old words about planting seeds of a future universal social order. But such promises had ceased to be credible to any large number of Americans. Industrialism had passed beyond the stage at which a community of twenty-five hundred persons could maintain, as Owen believed they could, a full-scale manufacturing establishment at current levels of technological complexity and efficiency. Before the end of the nineteenth century, even communitarian sects like the Rappites and Shakers were in visible decline. The impulse to reform had not grown less, but it had found what it believed were more promising methods of achieving its ends. Men and women who were seriously interested in reform now thought in terms of legislation, or collective bargaining, or organized effort for particular goals, or even revolutionary seizure of power. Rarely did they consider, as so many in the first half of the century instinctively did, the scheme of embodying their complete ideal in a small-scale experimental model. When they did so, it was almost always a temporary move, a way of carrying on in the face of some setback, or a way of organizing forces for a future effort of a quite different sort.[36] Such revivals of the communitarian program were apt to be sternly denounced as escapism by the majority of up-to-date socialists.[37] In America, as in the world

---

[35] Charles Nordhoff, *The Communistic Societies of the United States* (New York, 1875), p. 418. In his "Introduction" Nordhoff expressed clearly his hope that through communitarian colonies laboring men might escape from the growing sense of economic dependence that was fostering "Trades-Unions and International Clubs," which wielded, he believed, "a power almost entirely for evil" (p. 13).

[36] On the episodic and tangential character of certain late nineteenth-century communitarian plans sponsored by individuals and groups whose main efforts took quite a different direction, see Morris Hillquit, *History of Socialism in the United States* (4th ed., New York, 1906), pp. 331–32; and Howard H. Quint, "Julius A. Wayland, Pioneer Socialist Propagandist," *Mississippi Valley Historical Review*, XXXV (March, 1949), 585–606, especially pp. 592–93, 605.

[37] Thus Charles H. Kerr, head of the principal firm issuing socialist books, published a history of the Ruskin community written by one of the participants, but inserted his own cautionary preface explaining that the experiment was "a scheme which sought to build a new social order without regard to the essential facts familiar to all socialists . . . , an

at large, communitarianism had become a minor eddy in the stream of socialism, whose main channel had once been defined by the communitarian writings of Robert Owen, William Thompson, Charles Fourier, Albert Brisbane, Victor Considerant, and Etienne Cabet.

The decline of communitarian confidence and influence paralleled the decline of the cluster of beliefs or postulates which this paper has been exploring. These intellectual assumptions faded out, not because the so-called free land was exhausted nor because the frontier line had disappeared from maps of population density but simply because social patterns had become so well defined over the whole area of the United States that the possibility no longer existed of affecting the character of the social order merely by planting the seeds of new institutions in the wilderness.[38]

How quickly and completely the old set of beliefs vanished from the American mind was revealed by certain observations of James Bryce in 1888. In a speech to a western legislature Bryce reminded his hearers of "the fact that they were the founders of new commonwealths, and responsible to posterity for the foundations they laid." To his immense surprise, he discovered that this point of view — "trite and obvious to a European visitor," so he believed — had not entered the minds of these American legislators.[39] In this instance it was not Bryce but his hearers who showed the greater perception. The idea he expressed had once been held with tenacity. In the end, however, it had grown not trite but anachronistic. No longer did it state a profound reality, as it might have done half a century before. By the 1880's there was no point in talking about laying the foundations of new commonwealths within the United States. The reforms in American life which Bryce thought necessary were not to be achieved that way. Serious social reformers in the later nineteenth century were faced with the task of altering institutions already firmly established. Henry George and Edward Bellamy recognized this in their writings; Grangers and trade unionists in their organizations; opponents of monopoly in the legislative approach they adopted. For most American reformers in an industrialized age, communitarianism was a tool that had lost its edge, probably for ever.

---

attempt on the part of a group of people to escape from capitalism and establish co-operation." Isaac Broome, *The Last Days of the Ruskin Co-operative Association* (Chicago, 1902), "Publisher's Preface," p. 4.

[38] The most significant revival of communitarianism in recent times has been in Israel, precisely the spot in the modern world where the idea of planting a radically new society rather than transforming an old one has been most clearly put and most strongly supported. For a recent study of these co-operative colonies see C. W. Efroymson, "Collective Agriculture in Israel," *Journal of Political Economy*, LVIII (February, 1950), 30–46.

[39] James Bryce, *The American Commonwealth* (3d ed., 2 vols., New York, 1894), II, 838.

Romantic Reform in America, 1815–1865

JOHN L. THOMAS

The historian John L. Thomas finds the roots of ante-bellum reform in the emergence of a distinctive, religious concept of human nature, one that viewed the moral capabilities of the individual in a very optimistic light and held out the hope of the perfectibility of humanity. The reformers, who were romantic in their emphasis upon the primacy and potentiality of the individual, rejected social institutions and politics as hopelessly corrupt. They placed their faith in efforts to stimulate the regeneration of each man, and to communicate the example of individual moral achievement. Although they were revolted by the society in which they lived, Thomas argues, they nevertheless entertained the notion of an ideal society in which human beings would be free to fulfill their moral potential. Proceeding on this line of reasoning, some perfectionist reformers became communitarians, determined to construct an experimental model of the good society in order to demonstrate the possibilities for moral social behavior. Thomas thus arrives at an internal and intellectual explanation of the communitarian movement in its relation to social reform, for he sees it as the ultimate embodiment of the reformers' conception of human perfectibility. Bestor, on the other hand, seems to place more emphasis on the external pressures of expansionism and social change than on the ideas of the reformers. Do you suppose that Thomas and Bestor, beginning from quite different conceptualizations of the problem, reach basically similar conclusions? One test might be to compare their respective judgments of the impact of the Civil War upon the reform movement.

Confronted by the bewildering variety of projects for regenerating American society, Emerson concluded his survey of humanitarian reform in 1844 with the observation that "the Church, or religious party, is falling away from the Church nominal, and . . . appearing in temperance and nonresistance societies; in movements of abolitionists and of socialists . . . of seekers, of all the soul of the soldiery of dissent." Common to all these planners and prophets, he noted, was the conviction of an "infinite worthiness" in man and the belief that reform simply meant removing "impediments" to natural perfection.[1]

Emerson was defining, both as participant and observer, a romantic revolution

Reprinted by permission of the author and publisher from *American Quarterly*, 17 (1965), pp. 656–681. Copyright, 1965, by Trustees of the University of Pennsylvania.

[1] Ralph Waldo Emerson, "The New England Reformers," *Works* (Centenary ed.), III, 251; "Man the Reformer," *Works*, I, 248–49.

which T. E. Hulme once described as "spilt religion."[2] A romantic faith in perfectibility, originally confined by religious institutions, overflows these barriers and spreads across the surface of society, seeping into politics and culture. Perfectibility — the essentially religious notion of the individual as a "reservoir" of possibilities — fosters a revolutionary assurance "that if you can so rearrange society by the destruction of oppressive order then these possibilities will have a chance and you will get Progress." Hulme had in mind the destructive forces of the French Revolution, but his phrase is also a particularly accurate description of the surge of social reform which swept across Emerson's America in the three decades before the Civil War. Out of a seemingly conservative religious revival there flowed a spate of perfectionist ideas for the improvement and rearrangement of American society. Rising rapidly in the years after 1830, the flood of social reform reached its crest at midcentury only to be checked by political crisis and the counterforces of the Civil War. Reform after the Civil War, though still concerned with individual perfectibility, proceeded from new and different assumptions as to the nature of individualism and its preservation in an urban industrial society. Romantic reform ended with the Civil War and an intellectual counter-revolution which discredited the concept of the irreducible self and eventually redirected reform energies.

Romantic reform in America traced its origins to a religious impulse which was both politically and socially conservative. With the consolidation of independence and the arrival of democratic politics the new nineteenth-century generation of American churchmen faced a seeming crisis. Egalitarianism and rising demands for church disestablishment suddenly appeared to threaten an inherited Christian order and along with it the preferred status of the clergy. Lyman Beecher spoke the fears of more than one of the clerical party when he warned that Americans were fast becoming "another people." When the attempted alliance between sound religion and correct politics failed to prevent disestablishment or improve waning Federalist fortunes at the polls, the evangelicals, assuming a defensive posture, organized voluntary benevolent associations to strengthen the Christian character of Americans and save the country from infidelity and ruin. Between 1815 and 1830 nearly a dozen moral reform societies were established to counter the threats to social equilibrium posed by irreligious democrats. Their intense religious concern could be read in the titles of the benevolent societies which the evangelicals founded: the American Bible Society, the American Sunday School Union, the American Home Missionary Society, the American Tract Society. By the time of the election of Andrew Jackson the benevolent associations formed a vast if loosely coordinated network of conservative reform enterprises staffed with clergy and wealthy laymen who served as self-appointed guardians of American morals.[3]

---

[2] T. E. Hulme, "Romanticism and Classicism," *Speculations: Essay on Humanism and the Philosophy of Art*, ed. Herbert Read (London, 1924), reprinted in *Critiques and Essays in Criticism, 1920–1948*, ed. Robert Wooster Stallman (New York, 1949), pp. 3–16.

[3] For discussions of evangelical reform see John R. Bodo, *The Protestant Clergy and Public Issues, 1812–1848* (Princeton, 1954) and Clifford S. Griffin, *Their Brothers' Keepers* (New Brunswick, N.J., 1960).

The clerical diagnosticians had little difficulty in identifying the symptoms of democratic disease. Infidelity flourished on the frontier and licentiousness bred openly in seaboard cities; intemperance sapped the strength of American workingmen and the saving word was denied their children. Soon atheism would destroy the vital organs of the republic unless drastic moral therapy prevented. The evangelicals' prescription followed logically from their diagnosis: large doses of morality injected into the body politic under the supervision of Christian stewards. No more Sunday mails or pleasure excursions, no more grog-shops or profane pleasures, no family without a Bible and no community without a minister of the gospel. Accepting for the moment their political liabilities, the moral reformers relied on the homeopathic strategy of fighting democratic excess with democratic remedies. The Tract Society set up three separate printing presses which cranked out hundreds of thousands of pamphlets for mass distribution. The Home Missionary Society subsidized seminarians in carrying religion into the backcountry. The Temperance Union staged popular conventions; the Peace Society sponsored public debates; the Bible Society hired hundreds of agents to spread its propaganda.

The initial thrust of religious reform, then, was moral rather than social, preventive rather than curative. Nominally rejecting politics and parties, the evangelicals looked to a general reformation of the American character achieved through a revival of piety and morals in the individual. By probing his conscience, by convincing him of his sinful ways and converting him to right conduct they hoped to engineer a Christian revolution which would leave the foundations of the social order undisturbed. The realization of their dream of a nonpolitical "Christian party" in America would ensure a one-party system open to moral talent and the natural superiority of Christian leadership. Until their work was completed, the evangelicals stood ready as servants of the Lord to manage their huge reformational apparatus in behalf of order and sobriety.

But the moral reformers inherited a theological revolution which in undermining their conservative defenses completely reversed their expectations for a Christian America. The transformation of American theology in the first quarter of the nineteenth century released the very forces of romantic perfectionism that conservatives most feared. This religious revolution advanced along three major fronts: first, the concentrated anti-theocratic assault of Robert Owen and his secular utopian followers, attacks purportedly atheistic and environmentalist but in reality Christian in spirit and perfectionist in method; second, the revolt of liberal theology beginning with Unitarianism and culminating in transcendentalism; third, the containment operation of the "new divinity" in adapting orthodoxy to the criticism of liberal dissent. The central fact in the romantic reorientation of American theology was the rejection of determinism. Salvation, however variously defined, lay open to everyone. Sin was voluntary: men were not helpless and depraved by nature but free agents and potential powers for good. Sin could be reduced to the selfish preferences of individuals, and social evils, in turn, to collective sins which, once acknowledged, could be rooted out. Perfectionism spread rapidly across the whole spectrum of American Protestantism as different denominations and sects elaborated their own versions of salvation. If man was a truly free agent, then his improvement became a matter of immediate consequence. The progress of the country suddenly seemed to depend upon the regeneration of the individual and the contagion of example.

As it spread, perfectionism swept across denominational barriers and penetrated even secular thought. Perfection was presented as Christian striving for holiness in the "new heart" sermons of Charles Grandison Finney and as an immediately attainable goal in the come-outer prophecies of John Humphrey Noyes. It was described as an escape from outworn dogma by Robert Owen and as the final union of the soul with nature by Emerson. The important fact for most Americans in the first half of the nineteenth century was that it was readily available. A romantic religious faith had changed an Enlightenment doctrine of progress into a dynamic principle of reform.

For the Founding Fathers' belief in perfectibility had been wholly compatible with a pessimistic appraisal of the present state of mankind. Progress, in the view of John Adams or James Madison, resulted from the planned operation of mechanical checks within the framework of government which balanced conflicting selfish interests and neutralized private passions. Thus a properly constructed governmental machine might achieve by artifact what men, left to their own devices, could not — gradual improvement of social institutions and a measure of progress. Perfectionism, on the contrary, as an optative mood demanded total commitment and immediate action. A latent revolutionary force lay in its demand for immediate reform and its promise to release the new American from the restraints of institutions and precedent. In appealing to the liberated individual, perfectionism reinforced the Jacksonian attack on institutions, whether a "Monster Bank" or a secret Masonic order, entrenched monopolies or the Catholic Church. But in emphasizing the unfettered will as the proper vehicle for reform it provided a millenarian alternative to Jacksonian politics. Since social evils were simply individual acts of selfishness compounded, and since Americans could attempt the perfect society any time they were so inclined, it followed that the duty of the true reformer consisted in educating them and making them models of good behavior. As the sum of individual sins social wrong would disappear when enough people had been converted and rededicated to right conduct. Deep and lasting reform, therefore, meant an educational crusade based on the assumption that when a sufficient number of individual Americans had seen the light, they would automatically solve the country's social problems. Thus formulated, perfectionist reform offered a program of mass conversion achieved through educational rather than political means. In the opinion of the romantic reformers the regeneration of American society began, not in legislative enactments or political manipulation, but in a calculated appeal to the American urge for individual self-improvement.

Perfectionism radically altered the moral reform movement by shattering the benevolent societies themselves. Typical of these organizations was the American Peace Society founded in 1828 as a forum for clerical discussions of the gospel of peace. Its founders, hoping to turn American attention from the pursuit of wealth to the prevention of war, debated the question of defensive war, constructed hypothetical leagues of amity, and in a general way sought to direct American foreign policy into pacific channels. Perfectionism, however, soon split the Peace Society into warring factions as radical nonresistants, led by the Christian perfectionist Henry C. Wright, denounced all use of force and demanded the instant creation of an American society modeled on the precepts of Jesus. Not only war but all governmental coercion fell under the ban of the nonresistants who refused military service and political office along with the right to vote. After a series of skirmishes the nonresistants seceded in 1838 to form their own New England Non-Resistant Society; and by 1840 the institutional strength of the peace movement had been completely broken.

The same power of perfectionism disrupted the temperance movement. The founders of the temperance crusade had considered their reform an integral part of the program of moral stewardship and had directed their campaign against "ardent spirits" which could be banished "by a correct and efficient public sentiment." Until 1833 there was no general agreement on a pledge of total abstinence: some local societies required it, others did not. At the first national convention held in that year, however, the radical advocates of temperance, following their perfectionist proclivities, demanded a pledge of total abstinence and hurried on to denounce the liquor traffic as "morally wrong." Soon both the national society and local and state auxiliaries were split between moderates content to preach to the consumer and radicals bent on extending moral suasion to public pressure on the seller. After 1836 the national movement disintegrated into scattered local societies which attempted with no uniform program and no permanent success to establish a cold-water America.

By far the most profound change wrought by perfectionism was the sudden emergence of abolition. The American Colonization Society, founded in 1817 as another key agency in the moral reform complex, aimed at strengthening republican institutions by deporting an inferior and therefore undesirable Negro population. The cooperation of Southerners hoping to strengthen the institution of slavery gave Northern colonizationists pause, but they succeeded in repressing their doubts until a perfectionist ethic totally discredited their program. The abolitionist pioneers were former colonizationists who took sin and redemption seriously and insisted that slavery constituted a flat denial of perfectibility to both Negroes and whites. They found in immediate emancipation a perfectionist formula for casting off the guilt of slavery and bringing the Negro to Christian freedom. Destroying slavery, the abolitionists argued, depended first of all on recognizing it as sin; and to this recognition they bent their efforts. Their method was direct and intensely personal. Slave holding they considered a deliberate flouting of the divine will for which there was no remedy but repentance. Since slavery was sustained by a system of interlocking personal sins, their task was to teach Americans to stop sinning. "We shall send forth agents to lift up the voice of remonstrance, of warning, of entreaty, and of rebuke," the Declaration of Sentiments of the American Anti-Slavery Society announced. Agents, tracts, petitions and conventions — all the techniques of the moral reformers — were brought to bear on the consciences of Americans to convince them of their sin.

From the beginning, then, the abolitionists mounted a moral crusade rather than an engine of limited reform. For seven years, from 1833 to 1840, their society functioned as a loosely coordinated enterprise — a national directory of antislavery opinion. Perfectionist individualism made effective organization difficult and often impossible. Antislavery delegates from state and local societies gathered at annual conventions to frame denunciatory resolutions, listen to endless rounds of speeches and go through the motions of electing officers. Nominal leadership but very little power was vested in a self-perpetuating executive committee. Until its disruption in 1840 the national society was riddled with controversy as moderates, disillusioned by the failure of moral suasion, gradually turned to politics, and ultras, equally disenchanted by public hostility, abandoned American institutions altogether. Faced with the resistance of Northern churches and state legislatures, the perfectionists, led by William Lloyd Garrison, deserted politics for the principle of secession. The come-outer abolitionists, who eventually took for their motto "No Union with Slaveholders," sought an alternative to politics in the command to cast off church and state for a holy fraternity which would convert the nation by the power of example. The American Anti-Slavery Society quickly succumbed to the strain of conflicting philosophies and warring personalities. In 1840 the Garrisonians seized control of the society and drove their moderate opponents out. Thereafter neither ultras nor moderates were able to maintain an effective national organization.

Thus romantic perfectionism altered the course of the reform enterprise by appealing directly to the individual conscience. Its power stemmed from a millennial expectation which proved too powerful a moral explosive for the reform agencies. In one way or another almost all of the benevolent societies felt the force of perfectionism. Moderates, attempting political solutions, scored temporary gains only to receive sharp setbacks. Local option laws passed one year were repealed the next. Despite repeated attempts the Sunday School Union failed to secure permanent adoption of its texts in the public schools. The Liberty Party succeeded only in electing a Democratic president in 1844. Generally, direct political action failed to furnish reformers with the moral leverage they believed necessary to perfect American society. The conviction spread accordingly that politicians and legislators, as Albert Brisbane put it, were engaged in "superficial controversies and quarrels, which lead to no practical results."[4] Political results, a growing number of social reformers were convinced, would be forthcoming only when the reformation of society at large had been accomplished through education and example.

The immediate effects of perfectionism, therefore, were felt outside politics in humanitarian reforms. With its confidence in the liberated individual perfectionism tended to be anti-institutional and exclusivist; but at the same time it posited an ideal society in which this same individual could discover his power for good and exploit it. Such a society would tolerate neither poverty nor suffering; it would contain no condemned classes or deprived citizens, no criminals or forgotten men. Impressed with the necessity for saving these neglected elements of American society, the humanitarian reformers in the years after 1830 undertook a huge rescue operation.

Almost to a man the humanitarians came from moral reform backgrounds. Samuel Gridley Howe was a product of Old Colony religious zeal and a Baptist education at Brown; Thomas Gallaudet a graduate of Andover and an ordained minister; Dorothea Dix a daughter of an itinerant Methodist minister, school mistress and Sunday school teacher-turned-reformer; E. M. P. Wells, founder

---

[4] Arthur Brisbane, *Social Destiny of Man: or, Association and Reorganization of Industry* (Philadelphia, 1840), introduction, p. vi.

of the reform school, a pastor of a Congregational church in Boston. Louis Dwight, the prison reformer, had been trained for the ministry at Yale and began his reform career as a traveling agent for the American Tract Society. Robert Hartley, for thirty years the secretary of the New York Association for Improving the Condition of the Poor, started as a tract distributor and temperance lecturer. Charles Loring Brace served as a missionary on Blackwell's Island before founding the Children's Aid Society.

In each of these cases of conversion to humanitarian reform there was a dramatic disclosure of deprivation and suffering which did not tally with preconceived notions of perfectibility — Dorothea Dix's discovery of the conditions in the Charlestown reformatory, Robert Hartley's inspection of contaminated milk in New York slums, Samuel Gridley Howe's chance conversation with Dr. Fisher in Boston. Something very much like a conversion experience seems to have forged the decisions of the humanitarians to take up their causes, a kind of revelation which furnished them with a ready-made role outside politics and opened a new career with which they could become completely identified. With the sudden transference of a vague perfectionist faith in self-improvement to urgent social problems there emerged a new type of professional reformer whose whole life became identified with the reform process.

Such, for example, was the conversion of Dorothea Dix from a lonely and afflicted schoolteacher who composed meditational studies of the life of Jesus into "D. L. Dix," the militant advocate of the helpless and forgotten. In a very real sense Miss Dix's crusade for better treatment of the insane and the criminal was one long self-imposed subjection to suffering. Her reports, which recorded cases of unbelievable mistreatment, completed a kind of purgative rite in which she assumed the burden of innocent suffering and passed it on as guilt to the American people. The source of her extraordinary energy lay in just this repeated submission of herself to human misery until she felt qualified to speak out against it. Both an exhausting schedule and the almost daily renewal of scenes of suffering seemed to give her new energies for playing her romantic reform role in an effective and intensely personal way. Intense but not flexible: there was little room for exchange and growth in the mood of atonement with which she approached her work. Nor was her peculiarly personal identification with the victims of American indifference easily matched in reform circles. Where other reformers like the abolitionists often made abstract pleas for "bleeding humanity" and "suffering millions," hers was the real thing — a perfectionist fervor which strengthened her will at the cost of psychological isolation. Throughout her career she preferred to work alone, deploring the tendency to multiply reform agencies and ignoring those that existed either because she disagreed with their principles, as in the case of Louis Dwight's Boston Prison Discipline Society, or because she chose the more direct method of personal appeal. In all her work, even the unhappy and frustrating last years as superintendent of nurses in the Union Army she saw herself as a solitary spokesman for the deprived and personal healer of the suffering.

Another reform role supplied by perfectionism was Bronson Alcott's educator-prophet, the "true reformer" who "studied man as he is from the hand of the Creator, and not as he is made by the errors of the world." Convinced that the self sprang from divine origins in nature, Alcott naturally concluded that children were more susceptible to good than people imagined and set out to develop a method for uncovering that goodness. With the power to shape personality the teacher, Alcott was sure, held the key to illimitable progress and the eventual regeneration of the world. The teacher might literally make society over by teaching men as children to discover their own divine natures. Thus true education for Alcott consisted of the process of self-discovery guided by the educator-prophet. He sharply criticized his contemporaries for their fatal mistake of imposing partial and therefore false standards on their charges. Shades of the prison house obscured the child's search for perfection, and character was lost forever. "Instead of following it in the path pointed out by its Maker, instead of learning by observation, and guiding it in that path, we unthinkingly attempt to shape its course to our particular wishes. . . ."[5]

To help children avoid the traps set by their elders Alcott based his whole system on the cultivation of self-awareness through self-examination. His pupils kept journals in which they scrutinized their behavior and analyzed their motives. Ethical problems were the subject of frequent and earnest debate at the Temple School as the children were urged to discover the hidden springs of perfectibility in themselves. No mechanical methods of rote learning could bring on the moment of revelation; each child was unique and would find himself in his own way. The real meaning of education as reform, Alcott realized, came with an increased social sense that resulted from individual self-discovery. As the creator of social personality Alcott's teacher was bound by no external rules of pedagogy: as the primary social reformer he had to cast off "the shackles of form, of mode, and ceremony," in order to play the required roles in the educational process.

Alcott's modernity lay principally in his concept of the interchangeability of roles — both teacher and pupils acquired self-knowledge in an exciting give-and-take. Thus defined, education became a way of life, a continuing process through which individuals learned to obey the laws of their own natures and in so doing to discover the laws of the good society. This identification of individual development with true social unity was crucial for Alcott, as for the other perfectionist communitarians, because it provided the bridge over which they passed from self to society. The keystone in Alcott's construction was supplied by the individual conscience which connected with the "common conscience" of mankind. This fundamental identity, he was convinced, could be demonstrated by the learning process itself which he defined as "sympathy and imitation, the moral action of the teacher upon the children, of the children upon him, and each other." He saw in the school, therefore, a model of the good community where self-discovery led to a social exchange culminating in the recognition of universal dependency and brotherhood. The ideal society — the society he hoped to create — was one in which individuals could be totally free to follow their own natures because such pursuit would inevitably end in social harmony. For Alcott the community was the product rather than the creator of the good life.

Fruitlands, Alcott's attempt to apply the lessons of the Temple School on a larger scale, was designed to prove that perfectionist educational reform affected

[5] For a careful analysis of Alcott's educational theories see Dorothy McCuskey, *Bronson Alcott, Teacher* (New York, 1940), particularly pp. 25–40 from which these quotations are taken.

the "economies of life." In this realization lay the real import of Alcott's reform ideas; for education, seen as a way of life, meant the communitarian experiment as an educative model. Pushed to its limits, the perfectionist assault on institutions logically ended in the attempt to make new and better societies as examples for Americans to follow. Communitarianism, as Alcott envisioned it, was the social extension of his perfectionist belief in education as an alternative to politics.

In the case of other humanitarian reformers like Samuel Gridley Howe perfectionism determined even more precisely both the role and intellectual content of their proposals. Howe's ideal of the good society seems to have derived from his experiences in Greece where, during his last year, he promoted a communitarian plan for resettling exiles on the Gulf of Corinth. With government support he established his colony, "Washingtonia," on two thousand acres of arable land, selected the colonists himself, bought cattle and tools, managed its business affairs, and supervised a Lancastrian school. By his own admission these were the happiest days of his life: "I laboured here day & night in season & out; & was governor, legislator, clerk, constable, & everything but patriarch."[6] When the government withdrew its support and brigands overran the colony, Howe was forced to abandon the project and return home. Still, the idea of an entire community under the care of a "patriarch" shouldering its collective burden and absorbing all its dependents in a cooperative life continued to dominate the "Doctor's" reform thinking and to determine his methods.

The ethical imperatives in Howe's philosophy of reform remained constant. "Humanity demands that every creature in human shape should command our respect; we should recognise as a brother every being upon whom God has stamped the human impress." Progress he likened to the American road, Christian individualism required that each man walk separately and at his own pace, but "the rear should not be left too far behind . . . none should be allowed to perish in their helplessness . . . the strong should help the weak, so that the whole should advance as a band of brethren." It was the duty of society itself to care for its disabled or mentally deficient members rather than to shut them up in asylums which were "offsprings of a low order of feeling." "The more I reflect upon the subject the more I see objections in principle and practice to asylums," he once wrote to a fellow-reformer. "What right have we to pack off the poor, the old, the blind into asylums? They are of us, our brothers, our sisters — they belong in families. . . ."[7]

In Howe's ideal society, then, the handicapped, criminals and defectives would not be walled off but accepted as part of the community and perfected by constant contact with it. Two years of experimenting with education for the feeble-minded convinced him that even "idiots" could be redeemed from what he called spiritual death. "How far they can be elevated, and to what extent they may be educated, can only be shown by the experience of the future," he admitted in his report to the Massachusetts legislature but predicted confidently that "each succeeding year will show even more progress than any preceding

[6] Letter from Howe to Horace Mann, 1857, quoted in Harold Schwartz, *Samuel Gridley Howe* (Cambridge, 1956), p. 37.

[7] Letter from Howe to William Chapin, 1857, quoted in Laura E. Richards, *Letters and Journals of Samuel Gridley Howe* (2 vols.; New York, 1909), II, 48.

one."[8] He always acted on his conviction that "we shall avail ourselves of special institutions less and the common schools more" and never stopped hoping that eventually all blind children after proper training might be returned to families and public schools for their real education. He also opposed the establishment of reformatories with the argument that they only collected the refractory and vicious and made them worse. Nature mingled the defective in common families, he insisted, and any departure from her standards stunted moral growth. He took as his model for reform the Belgian town of Geel where mentally ill patients were boarded at public expense with private families and allowed maximum freedom. As soon as the building funds were available he introduced the cottage system at Perkins, a plan he also wanted to apply to reformatories. No artificial and unnatural institution could replace the family which Howe considered the primary agency in the perfection of the individual.

Howe shared his bias against institutions and a preference for the family unit with other humanitarian reformers like Robert Hartley and Charles Loring Brace. Hartley's "friendly visitors" were dispatched to New York's poor with instructions to bring the gospel of self-help home to every member of the family. Agents of the AICP dispensed advice and improving literature along with the coal and groceries. Only gradually did the organization incorporate "incidental labors" — legislative programs for housing reform, health regulations and child labor — into its system of reform. Hartley's real hope for the new urban poor lay in their removal to the country where a bootstrap operation might lift them to sufficiency and selfhood. "Escape then from the city," he told them, " — for escape is your only recourse against the terrible ills of beggary; and the further you go, the better."[9] In Hartley's formula the perfectionist doctrine of the salvation of the individual combined with the conservative appeal of the safety-valve.

A pronounced hostility to cities also marked the program of Charles Loring Brace's Children's Aid Society, the central feature of which was the plan for relocating children of the "squalid poor" on upstate New York farms for "moral disinfection." The Society's placement service resettled thousands of slum children in the years before the Civil War in the belief that a proper family environment and a rural setting would release the naturally good tendencies in young people so that under the supervision of independent and hard-working farmers they would save themselves.[10]

There was thus a high nostalgic content in the plans of humanitarians who emphasized pastoral virtues and the perfectionist values inherent in country living. Their celebration of the restorative powers of nature followed logically from their assumption that the perfected individual — the truly free American — could be created only by the reunification of mental and physical labor. The rural life, it was assumed, could revive and sustain the unified sensibility threatened by

[8] Second Report of the Commissioners on Idiocy to the Massachusetts Legislature (1849), quoted in Richards, *Howe*, II, 214.
[9] New York A.I.C.P., *The Mistake* (New York, 1850), p. 4, quoted in Robert H. Bremner, *From the Depths: the Discovery of Poverty in the United States* (New York, 1956), p. 38.
[10] Brace's views are set forth in his *The Dangerous Classes of New York and Twenty Years Among Them* (New York, 1872). For a brief treatment of his relation to the moral reform movement see Bremner, *From the Depths*, chap. iii.

the city. A second assumption concerned the importance of the family as the primary unit in the reconstruction of society. As the great debate among social reformers proceeded it centered on the question of the limits to which the natural family could be extended. Could an entire society, as the more radical communitarians argued, be reorganized as one huge family? Or were there natural boundaries necessary for preserving order and morality? On the whole, the more conservative humanitarians agreed with Howe in rejecting those communal plans which, like Fourier's, stemmed from too high an estimate of "the capacity of mankind for family affections."[11]

That intensive education held the key to illimitable progress, however, few humanitarian reformers denied. They were strengthened in their certainty by the absolutes inherited from moral reform. Thus Howe, for example, considered his work a "new field" of "practical religion." The mental defective, he was convinced, was the product of sin — both the sin of the parents and the sin of society in allowing the offspring to languish in mental and moral darkness. Yet the social evils incident to sin were not inevitable; they were not "inherent in the very constitution of man" but the "chastisements sent by a loving Father to bring his children to obedience to his beneficent laws."[12] These laws — infinite perfectibility and social responsibility — reinforced each other in the truly progressive society. The present condition of the dependent classes in America was proof of "the immense space through which society has yet to advance before it even approaches the perfection of civilization which is attainable."[13] Education, both the thorough training of the deprived and the larger education of American society to its obligations, would meet the moral challenge.

The perfectionist uses of education as an alternative to political reform were most thoroughly explored by Horace Mann. Mann's initial investment in public school education was dictated by his fear that American democracy, lacking institutional checks and restraints, was fast degenerating into "the spectacle of gladiatorial contests" conducted at the expense of the people. Could laws save American society? Mann thought not.

> With us, the very idea of legislation is reversed. Once, the law prescribed the actions and shaped the wills of the multitude; here the wills of the multitude prescribe and shape the law . . . now when the law is weak, the passions of the multitude have gathered irresistible strength, it is fallacious and insane to look for security in the moral force of law. Government and law . . . will here be moulded into the similitude of the public mind. . . .[14]

In offering public school education as the only effective countervailing force in a democracy Mann seemingly was giving vent to a conservative dread of unregulated change in a society where, as he admitted, the momentum of hereditary opinion was spent. Where there was no "surgical code of laws" reason, con-

---

[11] Letter from Howe to Charles Sumner, Apr. 8, 1847, quoted in Richards, *Howe*, II, 255–56.

[12] First Report of the Commissioners on Idiocy (1848), quoted in Richards, *Howe*, II, 210–11.

[13] *Ibid.*, pp. 210–11.

[14] Horace Mann, "The Necessity of Education in a Republican Government," *Lectures on Education* (Boston, 1845), pp. 152, 158.

science and benevolence would have to be provided by education. "The whole mass of mind must be instructed in regard to its comprehensive and enduring interests." In a republican government, however, compulsion was theoretically undesirable and practically unavailable. People could not be driven up a "dark avenue" even though it were the right one. Mann, like his evangelical predecessors, found his solution in an educational crusade.

> Let the intelligent visit the ignorant, day by day, as the oculist visits the blind man, and detaches the scales from his eyes, until the living sense leaps to light. . . . Let the love of beautiful reason, the admonitions of conscience, the sense of religious responsibility, be plied, in mingled tenderness and earnestness, until the obdurate and dark mass of avarice and ignorance and prejudice shall be dissipated by their blended light and heat.[15]

Here in Mann's rhetorical recasting was what appeared to be the old evangelical prescription for tempering democratic excess. The chief problem admittedly was avoiding the "disturbing forces of party and sect and faction and clan." To make sure that education remained nonpartisan the common schools should teach on the *"exhibitory"* method, "by an actual exhibition of the principle we would inculcate."

Insofar as the exhibitory method operated to regulate or direct public opinion, it was conservative. But implicit in Mann's theory was a commitment to perfectionism which gradually altered his aims until in the twelfth and final report education emerges as a near-utopian device for making American politics simple, clean and, eventually, superfluous. In the Twelfth Report Mann noted that although a public school system might someday guarantee "sufficiency, comfort, competence" to every American, as yet "imperfect practice" had not matched "perfect theory." Then in an extended analysis of social trends which foreshadowed Henry George's classification he singled out "poverty" and "profusion" as the two most disturbing facts in American development. "With every generation, fortunes increase on the one hand, and some new privation is added to poverty on the other. We are verging toward those extremes of opulence and penury, each of which unhumanizes the mind."[16] A new feudalism threatened; and unless a drastic remedy was discovered, the "hideous evils" of unequal distribution of wealth would cause class war.

Mann's alternative to class conflict proved to be nothing less than universal education based on the exhibitory model of the common school. Diffusion of education, he pointed out, meant wiping out class lines and with them the possibility of conflict. As the great equalizer of condition it would supply the balance-wheel in the society of the future. Lest his readers confuse his suggestions with

[15] "An Historical View of Education; Showing Its Dignity and Its Degradation," *Lectures on Education,* pp. 260, 262.

[16] This quotation and the ones from Mann that follow are taken from the central section of the *Twelfth Report* entitled "Intellectual Education as a Means of Removing Poverty, and Securing Abundance," Mary Peabody Mann, *Life of Horace Mann* (4 vols.; Boston, 1891), IV, 245–68. See also the perceptive comments on Mann in Rush Welter, *Popular Education and Democratic Thought in America* (New York, 1962), pp. 97–102, from which I have drawn.

the fantasies of communitarians Mann hastened to point out that education would perfect society through the individual by creating new private resources. Given full play in a democracy, education gave each man the "independence and the means by which he can resist the selfishness of other men."

Once Mann had established education as an alternative to political action, it remained to uncover its utopian possibilities. By enlarging the "cultivated class" it would widen the area of social feelings — "if this education should be universal and complete, it would do more than all things else to obliterate factitious distinctions in society." Political reformers and revolutionaries based their schemes on the false assumption that the amount of wealth in America was fixed by fraud and force, and that the few were rich because the many were poor. By demanding a redistribution of wealth by legislative fiat they overlooked the power of education to obviate political action through the creation of new and immense sources of wealth.

Thus in Mann's theory as in the programs of the other humanitarians the perfection of the individual through education guaranteed illimitable progress. The constantly expanding powers of the free individual ensured the steady improvement of society until the educative process finally achieved a harmonious, self-regulating community. "And will not the community that gains its wealth in this way . . . be a model and a pattern for nations, a type of excellence to be admired and followed by the world?" The fate of free society, Mann concluded, depended upon the conversion of individuals from puppets and automatons to thinking men who were aware of the strength of the irreducible self and determined to foster it in others.

As romantic perfectionism spread across Jacksonian society it acquired an unofficial and only partly acceptable philosophy in the "systematic subjectivism" of transcendental theory.[17] Transcendentalism, as its official historian noted, claimed for all men what a more restrictive Christian perfectionism extended only to the redeemed. Seen in this light, self-culture — Emerson's "perfect unfolding of our individual nature" — appeared as a secular amplification of the doctrine of personal holiness. In the transcendentalist definition, true reform proceeded from the individual and worked outward through the family, the neighborhood and ultimately into the social and political life of the community. The transcendentalist, Frothingham noted in retrospect, "was less a reformer of human circumstances than a regenerator of the human spirit. . . . With movements that did not start from this primary assumption of individual dignity, and come back to that as their goal, he had nothing to do."[18] Emerson's followers, like the moral reformers and the humanitarians, looked to individuals rather than to institutions, to "high heroic example" rather than to political programs. The Brook-Farmer John Sullivan Dwight summed up their position when he protested that "men are anterior to systems. Great doctrines are not the origins, but the product of great lives."[19]

[17] The phrase is Santayana's in "The Genteel Tradition in American Philosophy." For an analysis of the anti-institutional aspects of transcendentalism and reform see Stanley Elkins, *Slavery* (Chicago, 1959), chap. iii.

[18] Octavius Brooks Frothingham, *Transcendentalism in New England* (Harper Torchbooks ed.: New York, 1959), p. 155.

[19] John Sullivan Dwight as quoted in Frothingham, *Transcendentalism*, p. 147.

Accordingly the transcendentalists considered institutions — parties, churches, organizations — so many arbitrarily constructed barriers on the road to self-culture. They were lonely men, Emerson admitted, who repelled influences. "They are not good citizens; not good members of society. . . ."[20] A longing for solitude led them out of society, Emerson to the woods where he found no Jacksonian placards on the trees. Thoreau to his reclusive leadership of a majority of one. Accepting for the most part Emerson's dictum that one man was a counterpoise to a city, the transcendentalists turned inward to examine the divine self and find there the material with which to rebuild society. They wanted to avoid at all costs the mistake of their Jacksonian contemporaries who in order to be useful accommodated themselves to institutions without realizing the resultant loss of power and integrity.

The most immediate effect of perfectionism on the transcendentalists, as on the humanitarians, was the development of a set of concepts which, in stressing reform by example, opened up new roles for the alienated intellectual. In the first place, self-culture accounted for their ambivalence toward reform politics. It was not simply Emerson's reluctance to raise the siege on his hencoop that kept him apart, but a genuine confusion as to the proper role for the reformer. If government was simply a "job" and American society the senseless competition of the marketplace, how could the transcendentalist accept either as working premises? The transcendentalist difficulty in coming to terms with democratic politics could be read in Emerson's confused remark that of the two parties contending for the presidency in 1840 one had the better principles, the other the better men. Driven by their profound distaste for manipulation and chicanery, many of Emerson's followers took on the role of a prophet standing aloof from elections, campaigns and party caucuses and dispensing wisdom (often in oblique Emersonian terminology) out of the vast private resources of the self. In this sense transcendentalism, like Christian perfectionism, represented a distinct break with the prevailing Jacksonian views of democratic leadership and the politics of compromise and adjustment.

One of the more appealing versions of the transcendental role was the hero or genius to whom everything was permitted, as Emerson said, because "genius is the character of illimitable freedom." The heroes of the world, Margaret Fuller announced, were the true theocratic kings: "The hearts of men make music at their approach; the mind of the age is like the historian of their passing; and only men of density like themselves shall be permitted to write their eulogies, or fill their vacancies."[21] Margaret Fuller herself spent her transcendentalist years stalking the American hero, which she somehow confused with Emerson, before she joined the Roman Revolution in 1849 and discovered the authentic article in the mystic nationalist Mazzini.

Carlyle complained to Emerson of the "perilous altitudes" to which the transcendentalists' search for the hero led them. Despite his own penchant for hero-worship he came away from reading the *Dial* "with a kind of shudder." In their pursuit of the self-contained hero they seemed to separate themselves from "this

[20] "The Transcendentalist," *Works*, I, 347–48.
[21] Such was her description of Lamennais and Beranger as quoted in Mason Wade, *Margaret Fuller* (New York, 1940), 195.

same cotton-spinning, dollar-hunting, canting and shrieking, very wretched generation of ours."[22] The transcendentalists, however, were not trying to escape the Jacksonian world of fact, only to find a foothold for their perfectionist individualism in it. They sought a way of implementing their ideas of self-culture without corrupting them with the false values of materialism. They saw a day coming when parties and politicians would be obsolescent. By the 1850s Walt Whitman thought that day had already arrived and that America had outgrown parties.

> What right has any one political party, no matter which, to wield the American government? No right at all . . . and every American young man must have sense enough to comprehend this. I have said the old parties are defunct; but there remains of them empty flesh, putrid mouths, mumbling and speaking the tones of these conventions, the politicians standing back in shadow, telling lies, trying to delude and frighten the people. . . .[23]

Whitman's romantic alternative was a "love of comrades" cementing an American brotherhood and upholding a redeemer president.

A somewhat similar faith in the mystical fraternity informed Theodore Parker's plan for spiritual revolution. Like the other perfectionists, Parker began by reducing society to its basic components — individuals, the "monads" or "primitive atoms" of the social order — and judged it by its tendency to promote or inhibit individualism. "Destroy the individuality of those atoms, . . . all is gone. To mar the atoms is to mar the mass. To preserve itself, therefore, society is to preserve the individuality of the individual."[24] In Parker's theology perfectionist Christianity and transcendental method merged to form a loving brotherhood united by the capacity to apprehend primary truths directly. A shared sense of the divinity of individual man held society together; without it no true community was possible. Looking around him at ante-bellum America, Parker found only the wrong kind of individualism, the kind that said, "I am as good as you, so get out of my way." The right kind, the individualism whose motto was "You are as good as I, and let us help one another,"[25] was to be the work of Parker's spiritual revolution. He explained the method of revolution as one of "*intellectual, moral* and *religious* education — everywhere and for all men." Until universal education had done its work Parker had little hope for political stability in the United States. He called instead for a new "party" to be formed in society at large, a party built on the idea that "God still inspires men as much as ever; that he is immanent in spirit as in space." Such a party required no church, tradition or scripture. "It believes God is near the soul as matter to the sense. . . . It calls

[22] Quoted in Wade, *Margaret Fuller*, pp. 88–89.
[23] Walt Whitman, "The Eighteenth Presidency," an essay unpublished in Whitman's lifetime, in *Walt Whitman's Workshop*, ed. Clifton Joseph Furness (Cambridge, 1928), pp. 104–5.
[24] Quoted in Daniel Aaron, *Men of Good Hope* (Oxford paperback ed.: New York, 1961), p. 35.
[25] Theodore Parker, "The Political Destination of America and the Signs of the Times" (1848) excerpted in *The Transcendentalists*, ed. Perry Miller (Anchor ed.: Garden City, N.Y., 1957), p. 357.

God father and mother, not king; Jesus, brother, not redeemer, heaven home, religion nature."[26]

Parker believed that this "philosophical party in politics," as he called it, was already at work in the 1850's on a code of universal laws from which to deduce specific legislation "so that each statute in the code shall represent a fact in the universe, a point of thought in God; so . . . that legislation shall be divine in the same sense that a true system of astronomy be divine." Parker's holy band represented the full fruition of the perfectionist idea of a "Christian party" in America, a party of no strict political or sectarian definition, but a true reform movement, apostolic in its beginnings but growing with the truths it preached until it encompassed all Americans in a huge brotherhood of divine average men. Party members, unlike time-serving Whigs and Democrats, followed ideas and intuitions rather than prejudice and precedent, and these ideas led them to question authority, oppose legal injustice and tear down rotten institutions. The philosophical party was not to be bound by accepted notions of political conduct or traditional attitudes toward law. When unjust laws interpose barriers to progress, reformers must demolish them.

So Parker himself reasoned when he organized the Vigilance Committee in Boston to defeat the Fugitive Slave Law. His reasoning epitomized perfectionist logic: every man may safely trust his conscience, properly informed, because it is the repository for divine truth. When men learn to trust their consciences and act on them, they naturally encourage others to do the same with the certainty that they will reach the same conclusions. Individual conscience thus creates a social conscience and a collective will to right action. Concerted right action means moral revolution. The fact that moral revolution, in its turn, might mean political revolt was a risk Parker and his perfectionist followers were willing to take.

Both transcendentalism and perfectionist moral reform, then, were marked by an individualist fervor that was disruptive of American institutions. Both made heavy moral demands on church and state; and when neither proved equal to the task of supporting their intensely personal demands, the transcendentalists and the moral reformers became increasingly alienated. The perfectionist temperament bred a come-outer spirit. An insistence on individual moral accountability and direct appeal to the irreducible self, the faith in self-reliance and distrust of compromise, and a substitution of universal education for partial reform measures, all meant that normal political and institutional reform channels were closed to the perfectionists. Alternate routes to the millennium had to be found. One of these was discovered by a new leadership which made reform a branch of prophecy. Another was opened by the idea of a universal reawakening of the great god self. But there was a third possibility, also deeply involved with the educational process, an attempt to build the experimental community as a reform model. With an increasing number of reformers after 1840 perfectionist anti-institutionalism led to heavy investments in the communitarian movement.

The attraction that drew the perfectionists to communitarianism came from their conviction that the good society should be simple. Since American society was both complicated and corrupt, it was necessary to come out from it; but at

[26] Quoted in R. W. B. Lewis, *The American Adam* (Chicago, 1955), p. 182.

the same time the challenge of the simple life had to be met. Once the true principles of social life had been discovered they had to be applied, some way found to harness individual perfectibility to a social engine. This urge to form the good community, as John Humphrey Noyes experienced it himself and perceived it in other reformers, provided the connection between perfectionism and communitarianism, or, as Noyes put it, between "Revivalism" and "Socialism." Perfectionist energies directed initially against institutions were diverted to the creation of small self-contained communities as educational models. In New England two come-outer abolitionists, Adin Ballou and George Benson, founded cooperative societies at Hopedale and Northampton, while a third Garrisonian lieutenant, John Collins, settled his followers on a farm in Skaneateles, New York. Brook Farm, Fruitlands and the North American Phalanx at Redbank acquired notoriety in their own day; but equally significant, both in terms of origins and personnel, were the experiments at Raritan Bay under the guidance of Marcus Spring, the Marlboro Association in Ohio, the Prairie Home Community of former Hicksite Quakers, and the Swedenborgian Brocton Community. In these and other experimental communities could be seen the various guises of perfectionism.

Communitarianism promised drastic social reform without violence. Artificiality and corruption could not be wiped out by partial improvements and piecemeal measures but demanded a total change which, as Robert Owen once explained, "could make an immediate, and almost instantaneous, revolution in the minds and manners of society in which it shall be introduced." Communitarians agreed in rejecting class struggle which set interest against interest instead of uniting them through association. "Whoever will examine the question of social ameliorations," Albert Brisbane argued in support of Fourier, "must be convinced that *the gradual perfecting of Civilization* is useless as a remedy for present social evils, and that the only effectual means of doing away with indigence, idleness and the dislike for labor is to do away with civilization itself, and organize Association . . . in its place."[27] Like the redemptive moment in conversion or the experience of self-discovery in transcendentalist thought, the communitarian ideal pointed to a sharp break with existing society and a commitment to root-and-branch reform. On the other hand, the community was seen as a controlled experiment in which profound but peaceful change might be effected without disturbing the larger social order. Massive change, according to communitarian theory, could also be gradual and harmonious if determined by the model.

Perfectionist religious and moral reform shaded into communitarianism, in the case of a number of social reformers, with the recognition that the conversion of the individual was a necessary preparation for and logically required communal experimentation. Such was John Humphrey Noyes' observation that in the years after 1815 "the line of socialistic excitement lies parallel with the line of religious Revivals. . . . The Revivalists had for their one great idea the regeneration of the soul. The great idea of the Socialists was the regeneration of society, which is the soul's environment. These ideas belong together and are the complements

<hr/>

[27] Albert Brisbane, *Social Destiny of Man*, p. 286, quoted in Arthur Eugene Bestor, *Backwoods Utopias: The Sectarian and Owenite Phases of Communitarian Socialism in America: 1663–1829* (Philadelphia, 1950), p. 9.

of each other."[28] So it seemed to Noyes' colleagues in the communitarian movement. The course from extreme individualism to communitarianism can be traced to George Ripley's decision to found Brook Farm. Trying to win Emerson to his new cause, he explained that his own personal tastes and habits would have led him away from plans and projects. "I have a passion for being independent of the world, and of every man in it. This I could do easily on the estate which is now offered. . . . I should have a city of God, on a small scale of my own. . . . But I feel bound to sacrifice this private feeling, in the hope of the great social good." That good Ripley had no difficulty in defining in perfectionist terms:

> . . . to insure a more natural union between intellectual and manual
> labor than now exists; to combine the thinker and the worker, as far
> as possible, in the same individual; to guarantee the highest mental
> freedom, by providing all with labor, adapted to their tastes and
> talents, and securing to them the fruits of their industry; to do away
> with the necessity of menial services, by opening the benefits of
> education and the profits of labor to all; and thus to prepare a
> society of liberal, intelligent, and cultivated persons, whose relations
> with each other would permit a more simple and wholesome life,
> than can be led amidst the pressure of our competitive institutions.[29]

However varied their actual experiences with social planning, all the communitarians echoed Ripley's call for translating perfectionism into concerted action and adapting the ethics of individualism to larger social units. Just as the moral reformers appealed to right conduct and conscience in individuals the communitarians sought to erect models of a collective conscience to educate Americans. Seen in this light, the communitarian faith in the model was simply an extension of the belief in individual perfectibility. Even the sense of urgency characterizing moral reform was carried over into the communities where a millennial expectation flourished. The time to launch their projects, the social planners believed, was the immediate present when habits and attitudes were still fluid, before entrenched institutions had hardened the American heart and closed the American mind. To wait for a full quota of useful members or an adequate supply of funds might be to miss the single chance to make the country perfect. The whole future of America seemed to them to hinge on the fate of their enterprises.

Some of the projects were joint-stock corporations betraying a middle-class origin; others were strictly communistic. Some, like the Shaker communities, were pietistic and rigid; others, like Oneida and Hopedale, open and frankly experimental. Communitarians took a lively interest in each others' projects and often joined one or another of them for a season before moving on to try utopia on their own. The division between religious and secular attempts was by no means absolute: both types of communities advertised an essentially religious brand of perfectionism. Nor was economic organization always an accurate means of distinguishing the various experiments, most of which were subjected to periodic constitutional overhauling and frequent readjustment, now in the direction

[28] John Humphrey Noyes, *History of American Socialism* (Philadelphia, 1870), p. 26.
[29] Letter from Ripley to Ralph Waldo Emerson, Nov. 9, 1840, in *Autobiography of Brook Farm*, ed. Henry W. Sams (Englewood Cliffs, N.J., 1958), pp. 5–8.

of social controls and now toward relaxation of those controls in favor of individual initiative.

The most striking characteristic of the communitarian movement was not its apparent diversity but the fundamental similarity of educational purpose. The common denominator or "main idea" Noyes correctly identified as *the enlargement of home — the extension of family union beyond the little man-and-wife circle to large corporations.*[30] Communities as different as Fruitlands and Hopedale, Brook Farm and Northampton, Owenite villages and Fourier phalanstaeries were all, in one way or another, attempting to expand and apply self-culture to groups. Thus the problem for radical communitarians was to solve the conflict between the family and society. In commenting on the failure of the Brook Farmers to achieve a real community, Charles Lane, Alcott's associate at Fruitlands, identified what he considered the basic social question of the day — "whether the existence of the marital family is compatible with that of the universal family, which the term 'Community' signifies."[31] A few of the communitarians, recognizing this conflict, attempted to solve it by changing or destroying the institution of marriage. For the most part, the perfectionist communitarians shied away from any such radical alteration of the family structure and instead sought a law of association by which the apparently antagonistic claims of private and universal love could be harmonized. Once this law was known and explained, they believed, then the perfect society was possible — a self-adjusting mechanism constructed in accordance with their recently discovered law of human nature.

Inevitably communitarianism developed a "science of society," either the elaborate social mathematics of Fourier or the constitutional mechanics of native American perfectionists. The appeal of the blueprint grew overwhelming: in one way or another almost all the communitarians succumbed to the myth of the mathematically precise arrangement, searching for the perfect number or the exact size, plotting the precise disposition of working forces and living space, and combining these estimates in a formula which would ensure perfect concord. The appeal of Fourierism stemmed from its promise to reconcile productive industry with "passional attractions." "Could this be done," John Sullivan Dwight announced, "the word 'necessity' would acquire an altogether new and pleasanter meaning; the outward necessity and the inward prompting for every human being would be one and identical, and his life a living harmony."[32] Association fostered true individuality which, in turn, guaranteed collective accord. In an intricate calculation involving ascending and descending wings and a central point of social balance where attractions equalled destinies the converts to Fourierism contrived a utopian alternative to politics. The phalanx represented a self-perpetuating system for neutralizing conflict and ensuring perfection. The power factor — politics — had been dropped out; attraction alone provided the stimulants necessary to production and progress. Here in the mathematical model was

---

[30] Noyes, *American Socialism,* p. 23.

[31] Charles Lane, "Brook Farm," *Dial,* IV (Jan. 1844), 351–57, reprinted in Sams, *Brook Farm,* pp. 87–92.

[32] John Sullivan Dwight, "Association in its Connection with Education," a lecture delivered before the New England Fourier Society, in Boston, Feb. 29, 1844. Excerpted in Sams, *Brook Farm,* pp. 104–5.

the culmination of the "peaceful revolution" which was to transform America.

The communitarian experiments in effect were anti-institutional institutions. In abandoning political and religious institutions the communitarians were driven to create perfect societies of their own which conformed to their perfectionist definition of the free individual. Their communities veered erratically between the poles of anarchism and collectivism as they hunted feverishly for a way of eliminating friction without employing coercion, sure that once they had found it, they could apply it in a federation of model societies throughout the country. In a limited sense, perhaps, their plans constituted an escape from urban complexity and the loneliness of alienation. But beneath the nostalgia there lay a vital reform impulse and a driving determination to make American society over through the power of education.

The immediate causes of the collapse of the communities ranged from loss of funds and mismanagement to declining interest and disillusionment with imperfect human material. Behind these apparent reasons, however, stood the real cause in the person of the perfectionist self, Margaret Fuller's "mountainous me," that proved too powerful a disruptive force for even the anti-institutional institutions it had created. It was the perfectionist ego which allowed the communitarian reformers to be almost wholly nonselective in recruiting their membership and to put their trust in the operation of an atomistic general will. Constitution-making and paper bonds, as it turned out, were not enough to unite divine egoists in a satisfactory system for the free expression of the personality. Perfectionist individualism did not make the consociate family. The result by the 1850's was a profound disillusionment with the principle of association which, significantly, coincided with the political crisis over slavery. Adin Ballou, his experiment at Hopedale in shambles, summarized the perfectionist mood of despair when he added that "few people are near enough right in heart, head and habits to live in close social intimacy."[33] Another way would have to be found to carry divine principles into social arrangements, one that took proper account of the individual.

The collapse of the communitarian movement in the 1850's left a vacuum in social reform which was filled by the slavery crisis. At first their failure to consolidate alternative social and educational institutions threw the reformers back on their old perfectionist individualism for support. It was hardly fortuitous that Garrison, Mann, Thoreau, Howe, Parker, Channing, Ripley, and Emerson himself responded to John Brown's raid with a defense of the liberated conscience. But slavery, as a denial of freedom and individual responsibility, had to be destroyed by institutional forces which could be made to sustain these values. The antislavery cause during the secession crises and throughout the Civil War offered reformers an escape from alienation by providing a new identity with the very political institutions which they had so vigorously assailed.

The effects of the Civil War as an intellectual counterrevolution were felt both in a revival of institutions and a renewal of an organic theory of society. The war brought with it a widespread reaction against the seeming sentimentality and illusions of perfectionism. It saw the establishment of new organizations

[33] Letter from Ballou to Theodore Weld, Dec. 23, 1856, quoted in Benjamin P. Thomas, *Theodore Weld: Crusader for Freedom* (New Brunswick, N.J., 1950), p. 229.

like the Sanitary and the Christian Commissions run on principles of efficiency and professionalism totally alien to perfectionist methods. Accompanying the wartime revival of institutions was a theological reorientation directed by Horace Bushnell and other conservative churchmen whose longstanding opposition to perfectionism seemed justified by the war. The extreme individualism of the ante-bellum reformers was swallowed up in a Northern war effort that made private conscience less important than saving the Union. Some of the abolitionists actually substituted national unity for freedom for the slave as the primary war aim. Those reformers who contributed to the war effort through the Sanitary Commission or the Christian Commission found a new sense of order and efficiency indispensable. Older perfectionists, like Dorothea Dix, unable to adjust to new demands, found their usefulness drastically confined. Young Emersonians returned from combat convinced that professionalism, discipline and subordination, dubious virtues by perfectionist standards, were essential in a healthy society. A new emphasis on leadership and performance was replacing the benevolent amateurism of the perfectionists.

Popular education and ethical agitation continued to hold the post-war stage, but the setting for them had changed. The three principal theorists of social reform in post-war industrial America — Henry George, Henry Demarest Lloyd, and Edward Bellamy — denounced class conflict, minimized the importance of purely local reform, and, like their perfectionist precursors, called for moral revolution. The moral revolution which they demanded, however, was not the work of individuals in whom social responsibility developed as a by-product of self-discovery but the ethical revival of an entire society made possible by the natural development of social forces. Their organic view of society required new theories of personality and new concepts of role-playing, definitions which appeared variously in George's law of integration, Lloyd's religion of love, and Bellamy's economy of happiness. And whereas Nemesis in the perfectionist imagination had assumed the shape of personal guilt and estrangement from a pre-established divine order, for the post-war reformers it took on the social dimensions of a terrifying relapse into barbarism. Finally, the attitudes of the reformers toward individualism itself began to change as Darwinism with the aid of a false analogy twisted the pre-war doctrine of self-reliance into a weapon against reform. It was to protest against a Darwinian psychology of individual isolation that Lloyd wrote his final chapter of *Wealth Against Commonwealth*, declaring that the regeneration of the individual was only a half-truth and that "the reorganization of the society which he makes and which makes him is the other half."

> We can become individual only by submitting to be bound to others. We extend our freedom only by finding new laws to obey. . . . The isolated man is a mere rudiment of an individual. But he who has become citizen, neighbor, friend, brother, son, husband, father, fellow-member, in one is just so many times individualized.[34]

Lloyd's plea for a new individualism could also be read as an obituary for perfectionist romantic reform.

[34] Henry Demarest Lloyd, *Wealth Against Commonwealth* (Spectrum paperback ed.: Englewood Cliffs, N.J., 1963), pp. 174, 178.

American Continentalism: An Idea of Expansion, 1845–1910

CHARLES VEVIER

Nineteenth-century American foreign policy is difficult to charac-
terize. There were of course certain notable events, such as the
War of 1812 and the Mexican-American War as well as such mani-
festations of policy as the Monroe Doctrine, but these have all
seemed easier to explain as products of essentially domestic devel-
opments. The single conception which comprehends most of what
is considered foreign policy is "manifest destiny," but even this
idea seems better suited to explaining American continental expan-
sion than American attitudes toward Europe, Latin America, and
Asia. Charles Vevier attempts to show how American attitudes
toward the conquest of the home continent were intimately con-
nected with American desires for international expansionism. He
describes the prevalence of a geopolitical theory in the mid-nine-
teenth century which saw the United States as occupying a geo-
graphically central position in world political economy. Our coun-
try, the theorists asserted, lay in a geographical position to stem
the European mercantile thrust toward Asia by maintaining su-
periority in Latin America, building and controlling a Central
American channel linking the Atlantic and Pacific, and providing
effective transportation and communication across the North
American continent. The last point was the most important, for
without control and exploitation of our own continent we would
not be in a position to assert our rightful economic superiority in
the undeveloped market of the Pacific. For these early expansion-
ists, continentalism implied imperialism. Interpreted in this way,
then, the imperialism of the 1890's, inspired by Theodore Roosevelt
and Alfred Thayer Mahan, was not a new foreign policy; it merely
fulfilled implications of the ideas of William Seward and his
predecessors. Vevier thus argues that the United States has had
ideas of world expansionism and commercial imperialism from
virtually the earliest years of her existence. If you think back to
Felix Gilbert's emphasis on revolutionary American fears of in-
volvement in world politics you may wonder how the aggressiveness
described by Vevier came into existence. Or are the two interpre-
tations incompatible? The essay by William A. Williams suggested
that an era of American mercantilism extended from the 1760's
until the age of Jackson, you may perhaps conclude that Gilbert
underestimated the force of American commercial pretensions.
There is another possibility, however, which involves the ideological
impact of continental expansion upon the expansionists themselves.
Historians have argued that the War of 1812 was the product of

expansionist forces, and there is no doubt that the idea of expansionism manifested itself very early in our history, but it may well have gained in depth and changed in character as the implications of control of the whole of the majestic continent came clear to Americans later in the ante-bellum period. In any event, Gilbert, Williams, and Vevier are united in agreement that protection of commerce was the dominant theme of early American foreign policy. If they are correct, it is not hard to imagine how the formulation of foreign policy was, indeed, an aspect of domestic politico-economic development.

Ideology is the means by which a nation bridges the gap between its domestic achievement and its international aspiration. American continentalism, as the term is used here, provided just such an order of ideology and national values. It consisted of two related ideas. First, it regarded the United States as possessing identical "national and imperial boundaries." These were located within the physical framework of a "remarkably coherent geographic unit of continental extent." Second, it viewed much of North America as a stage displaying the evolving drama of a unique political society, distinct from that of Europe and glowing in the white light of manifest destiny.[1] This attitude sharpened the practice of American foreign policy. Encountering the opposition of Europe's powers, it asserted that the United States was engaged in a domestic and therefore inevitable policy of territorial extension across the continent. American diplomacy in the nineteenth century thus appeared to demonstrate national political and social worth rather than acknowledge its active involvement in international affairs. Relying on its separation from the Old World, the United States redefined the conventional terms of foreign relations by domesticating its foreign policy.

But sharp and immediate disengagements in history are rare. Professor Norman Graebner has argued persuasively that the acquisition of Oregon and California — conventionally set within the background of territorial expansion to the west and guaranteed by manifest destiny — was due predominantly to maritime influence and executed by a President whose party represented the agrarian expansionsim of Jefferson.[2] In spite of its apparent territorial insularity, American

Reprinted by permission of the author from *American Historical Review*, 65 (January 1960), pp. 323–335.
  [1] Bernard De Voto, *The Course of Empire* (Boston, 1952), xiii and Albert K. Weinberg, *Manifest Destiny* (Baltimore, Md., 1935), 1–2, 8. For an over-all definition of continentalism, see Charles A. Beard, *A Foreign Policy for America* (New York, 1940), 12–35. The argument presented in this paper is not in support or opposition to Beard as such; in fact, I have derived a considerable portion of the argument by reversing the order of Beard's term continental Americanism, in order to demonstrate that his insulationist outlook is also subject to an expansionist interpretation. See Max Lerner, *America as a Civilization* (New York, 1957), 887–88, who raises this issue in a mild way without intending to pursue it further.
  [2] Norman Graebner, *Empire on the Pacific* (New York, 1955), 3, 218; Robert G. Cleland, "Asiatic Trade and American Occupation of the Pacific Coast," *Annual Report, American Historical Association, 1914* (2 vols., Washington, D.C., 1916), I, 283, *passim.*

continentalism was bound to an older doctrine that had been overshadowed by the record of land acquisition of the 1840's. In these years, and in the 1850's as well, there were some men who were affected by the outlook of American continentalism and who adapted for their own ends the great objective of European expansion that dated from the age of Columbus and the Elizabethans. They sought to deepen commercial contact with Asia, an ambition that added a maritime dimension to the era of territorial expansion preceding the Civil War.

Students of American Far Eastern policy have already pointed out the rough coincidence of the westward movement across the continent with the rising activity of American interest in the Pacific Ocean and trade in China."[3] By the early 1840's, Hawaii had already shifted into the continental orbit.[4] Exploration of the Pacific Ocean had been undertaken by the government beginning with the Wilkes expedition in 1838 and concluding with the Ringgold voyages to the northern Pacific in 1853–1859.[5] The Cushing Treaty with China in 1844 and the opening of Japan by Perry a decade later reflected the attraction of Far Eastern trade markets to American merchants on the Atlantic seaboard. The gold strike of 1849 stimulated railroad passage across the Isthmus of Panama, encouraged shipping operations between New York and California,[6] and suggested continuation of this traffic to the Orient. The wider commercial possibilities implied by these forces meshed with an older American interest in the Caribbean, particularly in Cuba and the picket line of West Indian islands that ran down to Latin America. In an age of the clipper ship and the steady reduction of the tariff at the behest of agrarian elements, these developments drew taut the strand of national mercantile expansionist ambition that seemingly had lain slack while the territorial lines of American continentalism were cast westward across North America. This added tension suggested to some that the United States was linked to the historic expansionism of Europe westward to Asia, that it was the fulfillment of the long search for a "passage to India," and that a great mercantile empire could be developed on the basis of Asian commerce.[7]

Historians have been prone to examine American expansionism in terms of conflicting mercantile and agrarian interests.[8] They have overlooked the presence

---

[3] Eldon Griffin, *Clippers and Consuls* (Ann Arbor, Mich., 1938), 9–12 and Tyler Dennett, *Americans in Eastern Asia* (New York, 1922), 175–76, 178.

[4] Harold Whitman Bradley, "Hawaii and the American Penetration of the Northeastern Pacific 1800–1845," *Pacific Historical Review*, XII (Sept. 1943), 286–87.

[5] Allan B. Cole, "The Ringgold-Rodgers-Brooke Expedition to Japan and the North Pacific, 1853–1859," *ibid.*, XVI (May 1947), 152 ff.

[6] John Haskell Kemble, "The Panama Route to the Pacific Coast, 1848–1869," *ibid.*, VII (Feb. 1938), 1 ff.

[7] Henry Nash Smith, *Virgin Land: The American West as Symbol and Myth* (Cambridge, Mass., 1950), 3–51. Smith's work has been very helpful in this study.

[8] In his book *The Idea of National Interest* (New York, 1934), 50, Beard states: *"For the sake of convenience in tracing the application of the national interest conception* in the external relations of the United States, those relations may be divided into territorial and commercial, *although in practice the two are seldom, if ever, divorced."* My point here in citing Beard is not to raise the issue of the over-all validity of the approach to the problem that he employed. His is a great work that attempted to lay out a theoretical framework for the study of American foreign policy. In this instance, I am more interested in the agreement of belief enforced by ideology and the considerations included in it rather than

of a unifying view of American world geographical centralism that was grounded
in a "geopolitical" interpretation of American continentalism and its place in
the history of Europe's expansion to Asia. What emerged was a combination of
two deterministic patterns of thought reflected in the outlook of such men as
William Gilpin, Asa Whitney, Matthew Fontaine Maury, and Perry McDonough
Collins. These men shaped an expectation of commercial empire as an end in
itself as well as a means of developing the internal continental empire. Today,
after the bitter experiences of its practice in the 1930's, geopolitics deservedly
has an unsavory reputation. Although it did not exist in any organized form or
established theory before the Civil War, it was, nevertheless, a conceptual instrument whose economic implications projected American continentalism onto the
world scene and anticipated in some respects its greater use by the expansionists
of 1898.

William Gilpin, "America's first Geopolitician,"[9] declared that the unifying
geographical features of the North American continent, particularly the Mississippi Valley, contrasted favorably with Europe and Asia. A summary of his views
in the period 1846–1849 reveals his belief that the physical environment of
America promised the growth of an area equal in population and resources to
that of the entire world. A Jeffersonian democrat and a devotee of the writings
of Alexander von Humboldt, he believed in the inevitable westward march of
an agrarian civilization to the Pacific Ocean. He also associated westward expansion with American commerce and whaling enterprise already established there.
During the Oregon crisis in 1846, Gilpin advised congressmen, as he may have
suggested to President James Polk, that settlers moving into Oregon from the
Mississippi Valley, the geographically favored heart of the continent, would
make the mouth of the Columbia River an outlet for the export of American
farm produce to Asia. Since agriculture sought through commerce an "infinite
market of consumption" in the Far East, Oregon became the "maritime wing
of the Mississippi Valley upon the Pacific, as New England was on the Atlantic."[10] A strong bid for Asian trade, therefore, depended on the construction of
a transcontinental railroad from the Mississippi to the Columbia River that
would link the agricultural heart of the North American continent with the

---

in the differences fostered by economic interest and their political expression. By italicizing
Beard's own qualifications above I have tried to indicate my own use of them in approaching the problem. See also footnote one.

[9] Bernard De Voto, "Geopolitics with the Dew on It," *Harper's Magazine*, CLXXXVIII
(Mar. 1944), 315. De Voto's piece is brilliantly suggestive and should be read in conjunction with Smith, *Virgin Land*, 35–44. See also Maurice O. Georges, "A Suggested Revision
of the Role of a Pioneer Political Scientist," *Frances Greenburg Armitage Prize Winning
Essays: Armitage Competition in Oregon Pioneer History, Reed College* (2 vols., Portland,
Ore., 1945–46), and James C. Malin, *The Grassland of North America* (Lawrence, Kan.,
1947), 177–92.

[10] Gilpin to James Semple, Mar. 17, 1846, in *Report* (*Senate Executive Document*, 29
Cong., 1 sess., V, No. 306), 21, 44, 23, 30; "Speech on the Pacific Railroad," Nov. 5,
1849, in William Gilpin, *The Central Gold Region: The Grain, Pastoral and Gold Regions
of North America* (Philadelphia and St. Louis, 1860), 20–21; Gilpin to David R. Atchison, Jan. 23, 1846, in *Report* (*Senate Executive Document*, 29 Cong., 1 sess., IV, No.
178), 4.

Pacific Ocean. By developing the interior, thereby gaining access to the coast, the United States might become the center of a new world traffic pattern. America's "intermediate geographical position between Asia and Europe . . . invests her with the powers and duties of arbiter between them," he wrote in 1860. "Our continent is at once a barrier which separates the other two, yet fuses and harmonizes their intercourse in all relations from which force is absent."[11]

The Pacific railroad, in fact, was closely identified with the career of Asa Whitney, who had returned from China after a successful career as a merchant and who had campaigned from 1845 onward for the construction of a railroad from the upper portion of the Mississippi Valley to Oregon. It was Whitney's project that dominated for five years the great American debate over this vital internal transportation scheme.[12] Unless Oregon was bound to the rest of the country by a transcontinental railroad, Whitney warned, the nation would be forced to engage in a balance-of-power diplomacy in the European manner, an eventuality that he thought would destroy the continental homogeneity of America. In presenting his Pacific railway scheme, he proposed to connect Oregon with the rest of the country, open oriental trade marts to American commerce and agriculture, particularly if the railroad was tied to a Pacific Ocean shipping line, and provide an instrument for the internal development of the nation-continent that would serve as "the means, and only means, by which the vast wilderness between civilization and Oregon can be settled." Thus he exalted the continental potential of producing "the most necessary and important products of the earth — bread stuffs and meat," and stressed the value of an international "commerce of reciprocity — an exchange of commodities." The railroad, he insisted, would "revolutionize the entire commerce of the world; placing us directly in the centre of all, . . . all must be tributary to us, and, in a moral point of view, it will be the means of civilizing and Christianizing all mankind."[13]

Matthew Fontaine Maury, hydrographer of the United States Navy and adviser on railroad and international commercial problems to southern businessmen and politicians, was also interested in the relationship of the Pacific railroad issue to the old dream of the "passage to India."[14] But he formulated a wider geo-

[11] De Voto, "Geopolitics," 319; Gilpin to Atchison, Jan. 23, 1846, *Report* (*Senate Executive Document*, 29 Cong., 1 sess., IV, No. 178), 6, 7; Gilpin to Semple, Mar. 17, 1846, *ibid.*, V, No. 306, 25, 30; Gilpin, *Central Gold Region*, vi.

[12] Margaret L. Brown, "Asa Whitney and His Pacific Railroad Publicity Campaign," *Mississippi Valley Historical Review*, XX (Sept. 1933), 209–24; George L. Albright, *Official Explorations for Pacific Railroads 1853–1855* (Berkeley, Calif., 1921), 10–18.

[13] Cole, "Ringgold-Rodgers-Brooke," 152; *Memorial of Asa Whitney*, Feb. 24, 1846 (*Senate Executive Document*, 29 Cong., 1 sess., IV, No. 161), 8–9, 1, 6, 2, 5.

[14] Cole, "Ringgold-Rodgers-Brooke," 153; Smith, *Virgin Land*, 153–54; Henry F. Graff, *Bluejackets with Perry in Japan* (New York, 1952), 45; Merle Curti, *The Growth of American Thought* (New York, 1943), 321, for mention of Maury's religiosity. See R. S. Cotterill, "Memphis Railroad Convention, 1849," *Tennessee Magazine of History*, IV (June 1918), 83 ff., for an account of the South's view of the Pacific railroad issue. Maury was also elected a vice-president of the National Railroad Convention that met in St. Louis before the opening of the Memphis convention. He represented the Board of Directors of the Virginia and Tennessee Railroad. *Proceedings of the National Railroad Convention which Assembled in the City of St. Louis on the Fifteenth of October, 1849* (St. Louis, 1850).

political conception of the North American continent by linking it with Latin America as well as with Asia. He agreed that a Pacific railroad was needed to develop the continental interior as a means of raising land values, encouraging settlement of the western lands, and providing for the continental defense of the nation. He, too, shared the conviction of the importance of the Asian trade and, faithful to the interests of the South, he pressed for the construction of a transcontinental railroad from Memphis to Monterey.[15]

Maury, however, was influenced by an old geographical-historical idea that river valley civilizations were the most enduring and fruitful forms of society. In his view, the basins of the Mississippi and the Amazon Rivers were united in a vast continental-maritime complex that depended upon American supremacy of the Gulf of Mexico and the Caribbean Sea, the "American Mediterranean" as he called it. Aware of the potential of an age of steam, he believed that conventional ideas of geographical relationships had to change. Maury urged Americans to think of ocean navigation around the globe in terms of great circle travel rather than of routes laid out on the Mercator projection. This placed his Memphis-Monterey transcontinental railroad project that was to service the Mississippi Valley close to the great circle running from Central America to Shanghai at a point off the coast of California. Cut a canal through the Isthmus of Panama that would link the Pacific Ocean with the "American Mediterranean" and the shortened route to Asia would force European commerce to use a passageway that Maury insisted should never be under the control of a foreign power since it violated traditional American policy to allow foreign interference in the Western Hemisphere. "I regard the Pacific railroad and a commercial thoroughfare across the Isthmus as links in the same chain, parts of the great whole which . . . is to effect a revolution in the course of trade. . . . Those two works . . . are not only necessary fully to develop the immense resources of the Mississippi valley . . . but . . . their completion would place the United States on the summit level of commerce. . . ." In effect, Maury extended the line of American continental interest south from the Mississippi in order to command the same degree of geographic centralism that had marked the ideas of Gilpin and Whitney. The canal, taken in conjunction with the Pacific railroad, demonstrated his ambition for the United States to overcome the "barrier that separates us from the markets of six hundred millions of people — three-fourths of the population of the earth. Break it down . . . and this country is placed midway between Europe and Asia; this sea [Gulf of Mexico and the Caribbean] becomes the centre of the world and the focus of the world's commerce."[16]

---

[15] Maury to John C. Calhoun, Mar. 29, 1848, in J. D. B. De Bow, ed., *The Industrial Resources, etc., of the Southern and Western States* . . . (3 vols., New Orleans, 1852–53), I, 257, 259; Maury to T. Butler King, Jan. 10, 1847, in *Steam Communication with China, and the Sandwich Islands* (*House of Representatives Reports of Committees*, 30 Cong., 1 sess., III, No. 596), 23 ff.

[16] Maury to Calhoun, Mar. 29, 1848, De Bow, *Industrial Resources*, 365, 373, 369, 370; Maury to King, Jan. 10, 1847, *Steam Communication* (*Report, House of Representatives*, 30 Cong., 1 sess., III, No. 596), 20, 23; William L. Herndon and Lardner Gibbon, *Exploration of the Valley of the Amazon* (*Senate Executive Document*, 32 Cong., 2 sess., VI, No. 36), 190, 191, 193, testifying to Maury's influence in urging this expedition and

This doctrine of geopolitical centralism was reflected in the activity of Perry McDonough Collins, whose career had been shaped by the westward movement, experience with steamship operations on the Mississippi, and the California gold rush. Living on the West Coast in the 1850's, he not only absorbed the impact of the nation's new geographical position on the Pacific but also read about Russia's explorations of the northern Pacific Ocean and its expansion into eastern Siberia. Quickly he "fixed upon the river Amoor in Eastern Siberia as the destined channel by which American commercial enterprise was to penetrate the obscure depths of Northern Asia."[17]

Supported by President Franklin Pierce and Secretary of State William Marcy, Collins traveled throughout Siberia in 1856 and saw there elements of the American West. He felt himself to be a "pioneer in these wilds in the shape of a live Yankee," encountering many of the "difficulties that all western men who have blazed the first trail in a new country know by experience." Russian expansion in this region he interpreted as similar in objective and spirit to that of American continental expansion. Russia, he predicted, would move into Manchuria just as the United States had gone into Louisiana. The Amur River in eastern Siberia he likened to the Mississippi in North America. In his mind the spirit of the American frontier had international and historical significance: the emergence of the United States in North America was the first vital step in linking Europe and Asia. "The problem of a North Western passage to India . . . , which has occupied the great minds of Europe for some centuries, has been solved by the continuous and onward march of American civilization to the West . . . the commerce of the world will find its path across this continent. . . ."[18]

Collins inspired Western Union's project for the construction of an international overland telegraph system through British Columbia, Alaska, and Siberia in 1865 which was to be linked with Russia's own network to Europe. Basic to the whole scheme was the anticipation that the transcontinental telegraph line to the Pacific built by Western Union in 1860–1861 would be in the center of the vast enterprise. "Consequently," ran one of the company's circulars, "when the extension line of this company shall be completed the commerce of the

---

in coloring the conclusions regarding the linkage of the Amazon and the Mississippi Valleys; T. Butler King, Jan. 16, 1849, *Railroad Across the Isthmus of Panama* (*House of Representatives Reports of Committees*, 30 Cong., 2 sess., I, No. 26), 2–3, citing Maury on the importance of an isthmian railroad to link the Caribbean Sea and the Pacific Ocean; F. P. Stanton, *Railroad to the Pacific* (*House of Representatives Reports of Committees*, 31 Cong., 1 sess., III, No. 439), 32, 14, 27.

[17] I have drawn upon my article "The Collins Overland Line and American Continentalism" in the *Pacific Historical Review*, XXVIII (Aug. 1959), 237–53. The quotation is in Perry McDonough Collins, *A Voyage Down the Amoor* (New York, 1860), 1. A valuable contribution to knowledge of Collins' career and activities has been made by Vilhjalmur Stefansson in his book *Northwest to Fortune* (New York, 1958), 243–53.

[18] Perry McDonough Collins, Feb. 28, 1857, *Extract from Notes* (*House of Representatives Executive Document*, 35 Cong., 1 sess., XII, No. 98), 50; Collins to Marcy, Jan. 31, 1857, *ibid.*, 16–17, 19–20; Perry McDonough Collins, "Overland Telegraphic via Behring Strait and Across Asiatic Russia to Europe," in Western Union, *Statement of the Origin, Organization and Progress of the Russian-American Western Union Extension, Collins Overland Line* (Rochester, N.Y., 1866), 164.

whole of Europe, Asia, and North America, radiating from their great commercial centers will be tributary to it."[19]

The outlook formulated by these various opinions suggests the existence of two related American worlds. The first was the nation-continent created through the interaction of foreign policy and territorial expansion that resulted in the acquisition of contiguous territory in North America. In turn, it projected the concept of the second American world, the continental domain that was fated to extend its influence over the entire world through the expansion of commerce and control of international communications. The relations of both worlds were reciprocal. All this, however, depended upon realizing the economic implications of the central position conferred upon the United States through its expansion in North America and the significance of this event in the general expansionist history of the European world.

By the middle of the 1850's, aspects of this informal system of geopolitical thought had made its impression upon public discussion, affecting debates over internal communication and transportation as well as foreign policy.[20] It is true, however, that the notion of an American "empire" based on the idea of the United States as the great land bridge to Asia had given way to the growing tension of the sectional debates over federal policy dealing with the development of the continental interior.[21] Nevertheless, the fund of ideas that had projected American continentalism onto the world scene were restated and maintained by William Henry Seward, an expansionist, a worshipper of the continental tradition established and exemplified earlier by John Quincy Adams, and a man whose outlook[22] matched the geopolitical determinism exhibited by Gilpin, Whitney, Maury, and Collins.

[19] Western Union, *Statement of the Collins Overland Line*, 15. The company also hoped to run extensions from Russia's trunk system to China and Japan. This explains the grandiose vision of telegraphic supremacy in Asia. In addition, Collins began negotiations with Latin American governments to unite their lines with the American trunk system. In this sense, one should read "Western Hemisphere" for "North America" in the passage quoted in the company's prospectus.

[20] The standard work dealing with this phase is Robert R. Russel, *Improvement of Communication with the Pacific Coast as an Issue in American Politics, 1783–1864* (Cedar Rapids, Iowa, 1948), 18–19, who asserts that from the 1850's onward the emphasis shifted to discussion of internal affairs and development. Smith, *Virgin Land*, 282, note 28; James C. Malin, "The Nebraska Question: A Ten Year Record, 1844–1855," *Nebraska History*, XXXV (Mar. 1954), 14, for an interesting discussion of the global perspective of Stephen Douglas; Richard W. Van Alstyne, "Anglo-American Relations, 1853–1857," *American Historical Review*, XLII (Apr. 1937), 493, for an incisive critique by John F. Crampton of American ambition in a letter to Lord Clarendon; James G. Swan, *The Northwest Coast* (New York, 1857), 403, linking affairs in China and Russia with the Washington territory, and his article "Explorations of the Amoor River: And Its Importance on the Future Great Inter-Oceanic Trade Across the American Continent," *Hunt's Merchant's Magazine*, XXXIX (Aug. 1858), 176–82.

[21] Smith, *Virgin Land*, 29.

[22] "Neither politicians nor statesmen control events. They can moderate them and accommodate their ambitions to them, but they can do no more." Seward to Charles Francis Adams, Nov. 4, 1862, *Papers Relating to Foreign Affairs of the United States* (Washington, D.C., 1862), 231; Seward to Thurlow Weed, Apr. 4, 1847, Thurlow Weed Papers, University of Rochester, for a sample of Seward's veneration of John Quincy Adams.

Ten years before Seward became Secretary of State, he advocated the construction of a Pacific railroad and telegraph in the debates over the admission of California to the Union. Americans who understood the benign future of the American continent, Seward argued, had to prevent a division between the North and the South in order to overcome the more portentous split between East and West caused by the expansion of the United States. Centralized political unity, the economic welfare of the continental empire, and mastery of the seas that bounded the great land mass between two worlds—these were required if the United States was to take effective advantage of its geographical position to direct commerce with Europe and "intercept" trade with the Far East. He charged the South with obstruction of the American primacy on the world stage that was promised by its domestic development. "This nation is a globe," he cried, "still accumulating upon accumulation, not a dissolving sphere."[23] "Even the discovery of this continent [North America] and its islands, and the organization of society and government upon them," Seward stated, "grand and important as these events have been were but conditional, preliminary, and ancillary" to the great goal of European expansion for four hundred years, the attainment of the seat of all civilization—Asia.[24] The revolts of 1848 and the strain of maintaining the "crazy balance of power" forecast the destruction of Europe, and it fell to the United States to seize the torch and light the way. Because the United States was writ large on the sphere of world geography and history, it had the obligation to extend by means of its institutions the "civilization of the world westward . . . across the continent of America," across the Pacific to Asia, on through Europe until it reached "the other side, the shores of the Atlantic Ocean."[25]

This rhetoric was not separated from the realities that Seward encountered as Secretary of State. The continent under American dominion, he reported, "like every other structure of large proportions," required "outward buttresses" that were strategically favorable to the United States. Thus the policy of attempting to buy naval installations in the Caribbean after the Civil War reflected his conviction at the outbreak of the conflict that Spanish intrusion in the region partially justified the launching of a propaganda counterattack throughout Latin America as well as war against Spain. In 1864, he insisted that commerce and communication in North America were centralized in the United States and had to be extended as a means of uniting domestic and foreign commerce and encouraging the development of American "agricultural, forest, mineral, and marine resources." It was Seward who wrote the vital provisions of the Burlingame Treaty of 1868 with China that provided for the importation of Chinese coolies to work on the transcontinental railroad and western mining undertakings. He also contributed to the continental basis of the argument used by Senator Charles Sumner, who supported the purchase of Alaska by pointing out that the new territory rounded off the continental domain and permitted contact with Far Eastern markets by the shortest possible sea route from the

[23] The Works of William H. Seward, ed. George E. Baker (5 vols., New York, 1853–84), I, 91.
[24] Ibid., 247–49.
[25] Ibid., IV, 124; Cong. Globe, 36 Cong., 2 sess., 251 (Jan. 5, 1861).

West Coast. Later Seward made his meaning more clear to Canadians when he implied that the Alaskan purchase was a portent of "commercial and political forces" that made "permanent political separation of British Columbia from Alaska and the Washington territory impossible."[26] And, it was Seward's system of roughhewn continental geopolitics and beliefs cut out of the American grain that gives depth to the vigor with which he pursued American interests in the Far East. Much of his ambitious program, however, was not fulfilled because, as he said, "no new national policy deliberately undertaken upon considerations of future advantages ever finds universal favor when first announced."[27] But Alfred Thayer Mahan countered this argument when he remarked in 1902 that "all history is the aggressive advance of the future upon the past, the field of collision being the present."[28]

Mahan might well have added, however, that it was his geopolitics as well as that of Brooks Adams that defined the "field of collision." For the serious domestic crisis in the United States occurring in the 1890's within the context of a global economy and an international transportation revolution forecast a pessimistic future. Each, in his own way, attempted to swamp it with a conception of the past that he carried with him. Both Mahan's quest for a new mercantilism and Adams' propaganda for a new empire illustrate a retreat into history for a model that might avert disaster. One theme emerged — the extension of the nation's economic power from the line of the West Indies, Panama, and Hawaii to Asia. Here, the expansionist projection of the American continental experience that was developed in the pre-Civil War period acquired some relevance in the outlook of Brooks Adams. Viewing the expansion of Europe and of the United States as complementary developments, he turned to geopolitics to explain the nature of the problem.[29]

The Germans and the Russians appeared ready to march to the East. This move would reverse the historical westward trend of the exchanges that formed the basis of world power. Obsessed by the belief that control over Asia and its resources was the issue between the Russo-German bloc and what he believed to be a weakened England, Adams called for an Anglo-American rapprochement. This would allow the geographical center of the exchanges to "cross the Atlantic and aggrandize America." The result? "Probably," Adams suggested, "human society would then be absolutely dominated by a vast combination of peoples whose right wing would rest upon the British Isles, whose left would overhang

---

[26] Charles C. Tansill, *The United States and Santo Domingo, 1798–1863* (Baltimore, Md., 1938), 227; Frederick W. Seward, comp., *William Henry Seward: An Autobiography* (3 vols., New York, 1891), II, 535; Seward to Chandler, May 14, 1864, Western Union, *Statement of the Collins Overland Line*, 51; Dennett, *Americans in Eastern Asia*, 530; James Alton James, *The First Scientific Exploration of Russian America and the Purchase of Alaska* (Evanston and Chicago, 1942), 19, 35, 27; for Sumner's argument advocating the purchase, see *Charles Sumner, His Complete Works*, ed. George F. Hoar (20 vols., Boston, 1900), XV, 36 ff.; Baker, *Seward*, V, 574.

[27] Seward to Yeaman, Jan. 29, 1868, in Seward Papers.

[28] Alfred Thayer Mahan, "Subordination in Historical Treatment," in *Naval Administration and Warfare* (Boston, 1908), 269.

[29] I have drawn upon my article "Brooks Adams and the Ambivalence of American Foreign Policy," *World Affairs Quarterly*, XXX (Apr. 1959), 3–18.

the middle province of China, whose centre would approach the Pacific, and who encompass the Indian Ocean as though it were a lake, much as the Romans encompassed the Mediterranean."[30] Specifically, Adams, Mahan, and the imperial expansionists who clustered around Theodore Roosevelt urged upon the United States the "large policy of 1898," which revived the Caribbean-Panama-Pacific Ocean relationship that had been sketched out in the 1840's and 1850's and publicized by Seward.[31] But by 1909, the outer edges of this grandiose empire were frayed by abrasive realities in Asia. The failure of the open door in China, the knowledge that the Philippines could not be defended, the growing tension with Japan over Manchuria — all this was complicated by the existence of the ideological *Realpolitik* of Theodore Roosevelt, who claimed American manipulative power over affairs in Asia but who was cautious enough to realize that he did not have it. Roosevelt's refusal to carry out completely Adams' program drove Adams back to examine his own nationalist assumptions in a biography of his grandfather that he never completed.[32]

At this point in his quest, the traditional elements of American continentalism received a full statement — geographical determinism, political and social separation from Europe, and independent action in foreign affairs. Nevertheless, Adams, like Mahan, continued to interpret the history of American continentalism as an expression of eighteenth-century mercantilist imperialism. Just as Asia appeared in his own time to be the principal objective that would guarantee survival through expansion, so North America had appeared to the European powers. "Men believed that he who won America might aspire to that universal empire which had been an ideal since the dawn of civilization."[33] Franklin, Washington, and John Quincy Adams had understood the need for a consolidated, unified, and expansionist state strong enough to establish itself in North America. In 1823, the Monroe Doctrine confirmed what the American Revolution had already demonstrated: the leadership of the westward march of the exchanges would pass from a divided Europe to a unified America. "It was the first impressive manifestation of that momentous social movement which has recently culminated in the migration of the centre of the equilibrium of human society across the Atlantic."[34] Here the nationalist met the imperialist when the expansionist projection of continentalism made clear that America, the prize of empire in the eighteenth century, had to become an empire in the twentieth century.

[30] Brooks Adams, *America's Economic Supremacy* (New York, 1900), 196, 13, 190, 12, 25.

[31] Julius Pratt, "The Large Policy of 1898," *Mississippi Valley Historical Review*, XIX (Aug. 1932), 233, 229–30, for Albert Shaw's agreement with Bryan on this as well as the statement by Senator William E. Chandler; Alfred Thayer Mahan, *The Interest of America in Sea Power* (Boston, 1897), 260, and *The Problem of Asia* (Boston, 1900), 7–9, for his remarks on the preparation for imperialist expansion that had occurred earlier in American history on the basis on this geographical outlook.

[32] Arthur Beringause, *Brooks Adams* (New York, 1955), 304 ff.; Brooks Adams, "Unpublished Biography of John Quincy Adams" in the Massachusetts Historical Society (microfilm copy by courtesy of Mr. Lyman Butterfield and the Massachusetts Historical Society).

[33] Adams, "Unpublished Biography of John Quincy Adams," 130.

[34] *Ibid.*, 299.

Contemporary students of the United States foreign policy that developed at the turn of the century are confronted with a problem of perspective. From the standpoint of the expansionist projection of American continentalism revealed in the pre–Civil War era, the imperialism of McKinley and Roosevelt was not a new departure in American history. It was not an "aberration" of national behavior which has been loosely defined as the emergence of the United States to world power. The geopolitical suggestions of Mahan and Brooks Adams helped American statesmen to install the United States as such a power. It was also a startling demonstration of the adjustment of the new ideological justifications of the 1890's to an older nationalistic expansionist base formulated by men of an earlier generation.[35] Gilpin, Whitney, Maury, and Collins had sensed the meaning of the new technology, its effect upon geographical relationships, and the interrelations between aspects of the economic system at home, and these men were captured by a desire to assume the leadership of an entire Western civilization in order to make a lasting impression upon Asia.

Historians who are sensitive to the relationship of foreign and domestic affairs as well as to the play of ideas upon foreign policy might do well to reexamine and explore the concept of American continentalism as an ideology of overseas expansion. Conventionally employed to explain the separatist and isolationist quality of the American outlook on world affairs in the nineteenth century, American continentalism also possessed a geopolitical character — natively derived in large measure — that was contrary to its own spirit. The only virtue of geopolitics is that it draws attention to the facts of political geography; its greatest vice is that it lends itself to almost mystical judgments of national purpose in international affairs. Seemingly dealing with reality, it becomes a refuge for unclear and unfulfilled aspirations. Geographers long ago learned this bitter lesson. Historians of American foreign policy might profit by investigating further the active presence in nineteenth-century America of this aspect of thought, not as a justification for foreign policy but as an important stimulus of nationalist expansionism.

[35] Julius Pratt, "The Ideology of American Expansion," in *Essays in Honor of William E. Dodd*, ed. Avery Craven (Chicago, 1935), 347, for a comment that stresses manifest destiny rather than American continentalism as employed in this essay. See also the judgment of Seward's biographer regarding the continuity of the expansionist impulse in Frederic Bancroft, "Seward's Ideas of Territorial Expansion," *North American Review*, CLXVII (July 1898), 79 ff.

III

TENSION, DISRUPTION, AND
RECONSTRUCTION: 1840–1877

If the first half-century represented the youth of American life — characterized by rapid growth, confidence of power, ceaseless activity — the next forty years constituted a painful transition into adulthood. Most economic and social growth carried over from the early years, since the development of the nation was, in general, continuous, but problems became ever more apparent. Although national population reached twenty-three million in 1850, thirty-one million in 1860, and forty-seven million in 1877, the composition of the population was more significant, since by 1860 it included rapidly increasing numbers of European immigrants and over four million black Americans, the vast majority of them slaves. Industry continued to expand, diversify, and thrive, and the beginnings of large-scale railroad construction in the 1850's marked the inauguration of a truly national economy. Meanwhile the Mexican-American War pushed the frontier further into the southwest and the discovery of gold stimulated the development of California. By the time of the Civil War, the domestic demands of Manifest Destiny had been fulfilled.

Americans gradually came to realize how difficult it was to manage a nation of such immense territorial dimensions. The federal system provided a formal answer to the problem of governing a continent, but the Constitution nowhere explained how large-scale regional disagreements could be accommodated. Formal political compromises did not reach to the root of most sectional antagonisms, and the dual problem of southern regionalism and the institution of slavery proved especially intractable. However one looked at it, slavery posed an insoluble dilemma: many Southerners believed it to be necessary to their social system, a good many non-Southerners thought it a moral monstrosity, and still others found it an essentially socioeconomic ill.

The Civil War ended slavery and confirmed national sovereignty, but it did little to eliminate the basic national brittleness. The political system proved incapable of arriving at a graceful and generally acceptable plan of reconstructing the national fabric, and Negroes achieved only the most elementary sort of freedom. Regional distinctions survived, as did much of Southern leadership and many Southern values. A new nation failed to rise from the ashes of the old, although some important changes had taken place. From the standpoint of the long-term development of the United States, the Civil War was epiphenomenal and hardly central to national growth.

There is another sense, however, in which the turbulence of the 1840's and 1850's and of the war itself represents a highly significant period of our history. Well before the war Americans were aware of the potential for disorder, violence, and destruction which underlay the rapid pace of social change. They hoped to control these bad effects through the manipulation of social control, but they understood that the risk was great. The Civil War was only one indication among many that a nation with great ambitions and potential could destroy itself.

Social Disorganization
and Economic Policy

OSCAR HANDLIN AND MARY F. HANDLIN

In their history of Massachusetts from the Revolution until the Civil War, Commonwealth: A Study of the Role of Government in the American Economy, Oscar and Mary Handlin try to show the impact of economic change upon the lives of the people of a single state. The Handlins start with the assumption that the communal experience of state building from 1774 to 1780 had left the inhabitants of Massachusetts with a tangible sense of "commonwealth." In a commonwealth the state has an identity separate from those of the individuals and groups within it, and it has an interest which transcends those of its constituents. By the second decade of the nineteenth century, however, the conditions of life in Massachusetts had begun to change so dramatically that the concept of commonality was severely tested. The underlying changes were those in the economy of Massachusetts itself and of the larger nation. Essentially, the commercial capitalism of the eighteenth century began to give way to industrialism within the state at the same time as the economic development of the West (and transportation to it from the Atlantic coast) placed the traditional economy of mercantile Massachusetts under severe strain. The result was the rechanneling of economic opportunity in Massachusetts with a consequent tightening of social boundaries for such groups as the merchants and the destruction of traditional roles for others now less fortunately placed in the society. The revolutionary inte-

gration of the community shattered under the impact of economic change, to the accompaniment of increasingly intense demands for social reform. No longer did the citizens of Massachusetts take it for granted that the benefits of their society would accrue to the common good, and they looked to political means to enforce their individual rights. The state, people came to think, must regulate behavior for the common good, although state action must be tempered by common agreement upon the values of liberal humanism. Unlike contemporary Europe, rigid notions of laissez faire had little attraction in Massachusetts. Writing in highly abstract terms, the Handlins display an organic view of the nature of historical change. Although their ostensible focus is on the economy, they perceive necessary relationships between economic and social change, the growth of ideas, and the development of politics. What emerges most clearly from this discussion of Massachusetts is the highly transitional character of the United States in the first half of the nineteenth century. Industrialism, immigration and population growth, urbanization, western expansion, sectional conflict, and the transformation of basic social institutions (schools and the family, for instance) combined to change the early republic into a more powerful and fluid, less coherent and stably balanced nation. Many historians have come to believe that the contours of contemporary America found their basic orientation in the formative era of the decades before the Civil War.

The transformation in the character of the corporation came within a context of precipitous social change that upset the structure of the old economy, tore apart traditional modes of action and of thought, and drove deep fissures into the community. By the time the Civil War intervened with its own conditioning impact, both the means and end of government action had taken on a strange aspect.

The War of 1812 had stimulated household industry to a high level of efficiency. The setback consequent upon peace and the revival of British imports did not seriously retard home manufactures.[1] Many still looked hopefully to such enterprises as a patriotic activity and as a spur to agricultural prosperity.[2] But

Reprinted by permission of the publishers from *Commonwealth: A Study of the Role of Government in the American Economy, Massachusetts, 1774–1861* by Oscar Handlin and Mary Flug Handlin. Cambridge, Mass.: The Belknap Press of Harvard University Press. Copyright, 1947, 1969, by the President and Fellows of Harvard College.

[1] See, e.g., J. G. Holland, *History of Western Massachusetts* (Springfield, 1855), I, 397, 398; J. E. A. Smith, *The History of Pittsfield . . . 1800 to . . . 1876* (Springfield, 1876), p. 464; G. B. Perry, *Discourse Delivered in the East Parish in Bradford* (Haverhill, 1821), p. 10; A. H. Cole, *American Wool Manufacture* (Cambridge, Mass., 1926), I, 183.

[2] *Boston Commercial Gazette*, Jan. 23, June 12, 1817. See also *Commonwealth History of Massachusetts*, ed. A. B. Hart (New York, 1927–1930), IV, 363 ff.

this source failed to satisfy the ever widening native market protected by the adoption of the American system in the tariff of 1816. An adjunct to farming, dependent for low costs on spare-time labor, it lacked the capacity for growing indefinitely in the face of continued emigration of husbandmen.

If household industry would not supply the demand, another system, controlled by other people, would. The period was one of great mental activity in industry; inventions revamped the methods of fabrication for many articles and opened fabulous opportunities to the imaginative and venturesome.[3] The local capitalists, merchants and shopkeepers, often distributors for neighborhood products, gradually acquired control of numerous mills and mill sites, grasping the promise of new markets and new methods. Family groups like the Pomeroys and the Bordens sought out and made fresh openings, applying capital and skill to one activity after another, wool and shoes, iron and paper, power and transportation, and in the process transformed many fields of production.[4]

The tempestuous commercial policy of the decade before 1815 had also turned the attention of some merchants to the possibilities of American industry. Few regarded Jefferson's embargo with the equanimity of William Gray and John Bromfield, who found solace in the thought that the "good to the community at large" would outweigh immediate injuries.[5] Most were bitter, particularly after the failures of 1807 reduced traders brought up in affluence to "the cold courtesy of creditors."[6] Worst of all, the War of 1812 suspended some branches of overseas business; William Appleton, for instance, closed his doors for the duration. Yet, despite losses reflected in acrimonious divisions over policies, accumulated surpluses remained in the hands of enough mercantile families to constitute a problem of investment.[7]

After the war new factors continued to drive commercial capital into industry. Movement of the great American market across the Alleghenies deepened Boston's disadvantages as an entrepôt. Again, as in 1789, the merchants turned to manufacturing to offset their weakened condition. But unlike the Beverly factory, the new enterprises held forth the prospect of direct profits. The success of the Waltham Company showed investors the advantage of complete factory organization. The corporate form permitted traders who acted as selling agents to participate without assuming the identity of the project and to earn dividends and commissions from the same venture.[8]

---

[3] See D. A. Wells to Sumner, Jan. 24, 1853, Charles Sumner, "Letters Received, 1830–74" (MSS, Houghton Library, Harvard University), XXI, 21.

[4] See R. K. Lamb, "Development of Entrepreneurship in Fall River: 1813–1859" (unpub. diss. Harvard University, 1935, University Archives); History of Bristol County, ed. D. H. Hurd (Philadelphia, 1883), pp. 314 ff, 370 ff, 393 ff, 411; W. R. Bagnall, Sketches of Manufacturing Establishments in New York City (Washington, D.C., 1908), II, 1066–1071; Cole, American Wool Manufacture, I, 225, 229; H. H. Earl, Centennial History of Fall River (New York, 1877), pp. 8, 12 ff.

[5] Hill to Quincy, Feb. 11, 1808, Jan. 3, 1809, Willard Phillips Papers, 1769–1836 (MSS, MHS); K. W. Porter, Jacksons and the Lees (Cambridge, Mass., 1937), II, 829 ff.

[6] William Willis, Journals of the Rev. Thomas Smith and the Rev. Samuel Deane (Portland, 1849), p. 407; also pp. 387 ff, 406.

[7] See "Memoir of Hon. William Appleton," Mass. Hist. Soc. Proceedings, VI (1863), 436.

[8] Cole, American Wool Manufacture, I, 210 ff, 289 ff.

Between 1822 and 1826 men like Henry Lee and Harrison Gray Otis, without other outlets for investment, began to put into manufacturing corporations large sums released by a contracting public debt. Buying up existing concerns and establishing new ones, they developed the Boston-office factories, owned partly in the Hub by merchants and partly locally by managers. The famous Lowell plants, the Boston & Springfield Manufacturing Company, and the Greenfield Manufacturing Company early illustrated the process.[9]

New developments in transportation completed this stage of evolution. Canals, railroads, and a growing volume of coastal shipping extended markets and permitted conversion from water power to steam by lowering the price of coal. Busy factories mushroomed along the route of the Blackstone and of the successive strands in the railroad web. Low interest rates extended by numerous financial institutions further stimulated manufacturing. Finally, a new supply of immigrant labor, eager to work at any price, facilitated further expansion in these industries after 1845.[10]

The growth of factory production affected every element in Massachusetts. Although merchants were the chief beneficiaries, finding in the mills rich dividends as stockholders and even richer profits as selling agents, the rise of industry was at first a source of dissension among them. Economically the interests of investors in manufacturing clashed with those who regarded the tariff as an attempt "to enact the country into riches."[11] The decline of the East India piece-goods trade as a result of domestic competition fortified the complaint that protection would "drive capital out of commercial investments."[12]

That division was transient only. At the very start, Henry Lee perspicaciously noted that the tariff drew heavy support from the merchants, "that Class of People who are the greatest Sufferers."[13] Throughout the period, defense of the tariff policy in terms of commercial interest minimized the splintering effect of the issue. The system of protection, it was argued, was an instrument for securing concessions from England through reciprocity and an essential ingredient of triangular traffic.[14] Although the conception of limited duties, low on iron,

[9] See [A. H. Everett], "American System," *North Amer. Rev.*, 32 (1831), 127 ff; Otis to Harrison, Mar. 21, 1823, S. E. Morison, *Life and Letters of Harrison Gray Otis* (Boston, 1913), II, 289; Porter, *Jacksons and the Lees*, I, 470; Cole, *American Wool Manufacture*, I, 227; Justin Winsor, *Memorial History of Boston* (Boston, 1880–1881), IV, 103 ff.

[10] See Israel Plummer, "History of the Blackstone Canal," *Colls. Worc. Soc.*, I (1888), 47; Barbara Vatter, "Industrial Borrowing by New England Textile Mills," *Jour. of Econ. Hist.*, 21 (1961), 216 ff; Oscar Handlin, *Boston's Immigrants, 1790–1865* (Cambridge, Mass., 1959), pp. 74 ff.

[11] See [Edward Everett], "Debate in Congress," *North Amer. Rev.*, 19 (1824), 232 ff, 252; Morison, *Harrison Gray Otis*, II, 242; *Hunt's Merchants' Mag.*, 16 (1847), 362.

[12] See "The Prospect Before Us," *North Amer. Rev.*, 17 (1823), 191; J. T. Austin, "Proposed New Tariff," *ibid.*, 12 (1821), 61 ff; [Joseph Story], "Daniel Webster," *The New-England Magazine*, 7 (1834), 101 ff.

[13] Lee to Palmer, Oct. 26, 1817, Porter, *Jacksons and the Lees*, II, 1295.

[14] See Oscar Handlin, "Laissez Faire Thought in Massachusetts, 1790–1880," *Tasks of Economic History* (December 1943), pp. 57, 58; *Report of the Committee of the Boston Board of Trade Appointed to Make a Thorough Investigation of the Recent Monetary Difficulties* (Boston, 1858), pp. 4 ff; *Boston Daily Advertiser*, June 7, 29, July 1, 7, 1843.

wool, and tallow, high on woolens, gave way to a recognition that "the only security is in the union of all the friends of the protective system," the question
was not disruptive. The merchants and their industries thrived whether rates
went up or down, and that took the edge off the argument.[15]

Ultimate consonance of opinion on the tariff reflected a growing cohesion
among the traders, or, more properly, among the trading families. In these
years the great Boston merchants ceased to act merely as individuals drawn together from time to time by combinations of interests arising out of a common
occupation. By now not all maintained activities in commerce; some concerned
themselves with a stake in manufacturing and others lived on incomes that permitted indulgence in the learned, the legal, or the political professions. Common origins in foreign trade nevertheless became the wellspring of unity from
which developed an esprit de corps that tied these people together with a coherence and solidarity transcending questions of immediate benefit. Their far-
flung and diversified ventures in other fields became more important in practice
but remained peripheral in their thinking. As late as 1858 William Appleton
sadly recorded that he was losing money, noting that a year's mercantile business
had netted a loss, and then added parenthetically that incidental investments
had returned a profit of one hundred thousand dollars.[16] The absence of commercial opportunities warded off newcomers and accentuated the consciousness
of homogeneity. With a measure of exclusiveness came pride of ancestry; the
Adamses now shunned reminders that the father of the second president had
been a shoemaker.[17]

Among the members of the first generation, among those who had made their
mark in the half-century after the Boston Port Act, awareness of recent rise in
status never wore off completely. Men like Edward Everett, whose brothers were
debtors and farmers, did not completely put aside their origin; they maintained
substantial if primarily sentimental connections with the hinterland.[18] But the
sons of the merchants no longer had roots in the soil. They lacked the personal
and family associations of their fathers with the back country, revolted against

[15] See Mason to Webster, May 27, 1832, [G. S. Hillard], *Memoir and Correspondence
of Jeremiah Mason* (Cambridge, Mass., 1873), pp. 337 ff; Everett to Holland, Sept. 25,
1848, Edward Everett Papers (MSS, MHS), LXXXVI, 3. For the attitude to the tariff of
1846 see *Boston Daily Advertiser*, Jan. 13, 1847; *Senate Docs.*, 1846, no. 65. See also
Daniel Webster, *Works* (Boston, 1853), I, lxxxv ff; J. Q. Adams, *Memoirs*, ed. C. F.
Adams (Philadelphia, 1874–1877), VIII, 437–443, IX, 318; Edward Everett, "American
Manufactures," *Orations and Speeches on Various Occasions* (Boston, 1853–1868), II,
68 ff; *Boston Commercial Gazette*, Dec. 18, 1823; E. Everett to Perkins, Lawrence, and
A. Everett, Jan. 20, Dec. 23, 1827, June 28, 1828, Everett Papers, LX, 20, LXII, 193,
LXIII, 18; *Bowen's Boston News-Letter*, Dec. 2, 1826; *Senate Docs.*, 1846, no. 2, p. 8.

[16] William Appleton, *Selections from the Diaries of William Appleton, 1786–1862*
(Boston, 1922), p. 214.

[17] See Everett to Blunt, Apr. 25, 1827, Everett Papers, LX, 77; also G. M. Elsey, "First
Education of Henry Adams," *New England Quarterly*, 14 (1941), 683.

[18] See, e.g., E. to A. Everett and to Clay, Sept. 29, 1825, Oct. 12, 1826, Everett Papers,
LVI, 56, LVIII, 31; T. L. Nichols, *Forty Years of American Life, 1821–1861* (New York,
1937), pp. 83, 84.

leveling traditions that forced them into the common schools, and toiled to master the accomplishments of gentlemen.[19]

The interests the merchants' families shared with the rest of the state waned. Trade had only a slight connection with the base in Massachusetts. Many firms shifted their activities to New York; by 1830 a good share of the China business, even when carried on ships owned in Boston, had moved to the port on the Hudson. Investments in railroads were more likely to be in the Midwest than in the Bay State. The industries also lost their ties with the countryside. The new mills, unlike the old, had little contact with the surrounding agricultural areas, drawing their raw materials from distant sources and working them up entirely within the factory. Meanwhile, immigration developed a distinctive proletariat that stood completely apart.[20]

Divorce from the community strengthened the consciousness of the merchants' identity as a group. By the end of the period, Theodore Parker spoke of an "organized Trading Power" controlling all things, "amenable only to the almighty dollar" and allied with the organized ecclesiastical and literary guilds which kaleidoscopically diffused the coalescent opinions of those they served. Then Holmes's Brahmin, with two generations of gentlemen behind him, was ready to step onto the Boston scene.[21]

Other groups also found their places in the community altered. While the growth of cities increased farmers' markets a little, the negative effects were more serious. The agricultural products of the fresh lands in New York and the West, brought into competition with those of the Bay State by improvements in transportation, pushed native wheat and other grains out of their accustomed selling places. By 1833 a legislative committee complained "that a farm in the vicinity of Buffalo is worth more by the acre, to raise anything for the Boston market . . . than the same quality of land on the Connecticut River."[22] The building of the Western made matters worse; flour shipped from Albany to Boston on the road more than doubled in volume between 1842 and 1846.[23] Attempts to compensate by introducing new products like silk in Northampton and Dighton were notably unsuccessful.[24] The few branches which remained prosperous through improved methods, beef fattening, sheep raising, dairying, and lumber-

---

[19] See C. F. Adams, 1835–1915: An Autobiography (Boston, 1916), pp. 21 ff; also Edward Everett's letters to his son at Cambridge University, Everett Papers, CXIII, 28, 129, 161, 175.

[20] S. E. Morison, Maritime History of Massachusetts, 1783–1860 (Boston, 1921), p. 275; Winsor, Boston, IV, 143 ff; J. T. Morse, Memoir of Colonel Henry Lee (Boston, 1905), p. 17.

[21] See Theodore Parker, Experience as a Minister (Boston, 1859), pp. 92, 93.

[22] Senate Docs. 1833, no. 29, p. 20. See also P. W. Bidwell, "Agricultural Revolution in New England," Amer. Hist. Rev., 26 (1921), 684 ff.

[23] Hunt's Merchants' Mag., 16 (1847), 325.

[24] See Henry Colman, "Third Report of the Agriculture of Massachusetts," Senate Docs., 1840, no. 36, pp. 97 ff, 104, 154 ff; J. R. Trumbull, Recollections (Northampton, 1898–1902), pp. 156, 157; also Whalemen's Shipping List and Merchants' Transcript (New Bedford), June 22, 1858; Elizabeth Ramsey, History of Tobacco Production in the Connecticut Valley (Northampton, 1930), pp. 133–146.

ing, generally required substantial investments of capital and offered no easy relief to the husbandmen.[25]

The growth of factories further weakened the position of rural Massachusetts by taking away an important source of income, the domestic system. Under the impact of the new method of production, household fabrication inevitably decayed; by the 1850's even the familiar clothing industries had disappeared from the farms and moved to the cities.[26] Deprived of extra cash from these sources, the farmers found themselves without a buffer against the shocks of contracting markets. With a few fortunate exceptions, their position was economically weak and unstable. Emigration accelerated, drawing away many discontented with diminishing earnings and increasing hard work.[27] Those who remained resisted stubbornly each additional challenge to their calling. Waging a losing battle, they fought emigration to the West or to the city that sapped away their youth. Suspicious of all enticement, they condemned the academies that led boys to "quit the plough, attend . . . a few months, and become too inflated with a very little learning to return to their labors of the field."[28] Resentment of the cities and of those who lived in them mounted steadily and on occasion burst forth in angry movements of protest.[29]

The large and hitherto prosperous groups of artisans, the "workingmen," also suffered. Trade and transportation, burgeoning with the new energies of an expanding economy, brought the products of distant shops and mills into competition with those of Massachusetts. Widening markets provide a dubious boon, for they reduced producers to dependence upon mercantile middlemen. And everywhere calamitous machines seemed to put to nought the craftsman's cunning. Unable to compete in the new industrial system, many independent skilled laborers soon faced the disagreeable choice between emigration and new employment at home. Not a few ultimately adjusted well, often in managerial positions, but uncertainty and insecurity of economic status engendered continuing bitterness.[30]

Social divisions did not turn about a contrast in fortune alone. Other prospering groups could no more find a bond of interest with the merchants than could the depressed. Lesser traders in the outlying towns and in the Hub itself, and the new manufacturers not connected with commerce but often wealthy and powerful, discovered a wall, real and usually insurmountable, between themselves and the Boston great merchants. Differences of interest set apart aggressive outsiders, struggling with varying degrees of success for a foothold, from the

[25] Figures for the decade 1840–1850 may be found in the "First Annual Report of the Board of Agriculture," Senate Docs., 1854, no. 7, pp. 20, 24, 31–38, 81–90.
[26] Bidwell, "Agricultural Revolution in New England," Amer. Hist. Rev., 26 (1921), 693–696; Cole, American Wool Manufacture, I, 279 ff.
[27] See Boston Daily Herald, Nov. 25, 1836.
[28] Boston Commercial Gazette, Feb. 5, 1816. See also Albert Mordell, Quaker Militant, John Greenleaf Whittier (Boston, 1933), p. 12; Springfield Gazette, July 9, 1841.
[29] See Boston Daily Herald, Dec. 7, 1836.
[30] See O. A. Brownson, "The Laboring Classes," Boston Quarterly Review, 3 (1840), 472 ff; O. A. Brownson, "Address of the Workingmen of Charlestown," ibid., 4 (1841), 121; Robert Rantoul, Jr., Memoirs (Boston, 1854), pp. 222 ff; Springfield Gazette, Dec. 18, 1844.

long-arrived, already entrenched behind the barriers of economic power and the prestige of social position.

In an economy battered by the impact of radical innovations and disrupted by unforeseen changes in status, social fragmentation snapped communal ties and often cast individuals free but adrift. Attenuation of old responsibilities and weakening of old controls at every level, from state to family, left men to cope alone with increasingly complicated problems arising from industrialization, growth of cities, and integration into broader markets. The displaced artisan and marginal farmer frequently suffered, aggressive new manufacturers and struggling traders sometimes profited, and the great merchants usually managed to retain their wealth if not their equanimity. But whatever the experience of any group, friction at every level was a concomitant of disintegration in the community.

The contrast between these actual conditions and the society's fundamental articles of faith gave rise to the conviction that the "selfish dissocial system . . . must give way to Christianity."[31] There was still no doubt that man was naturally good and naturally progressing toward perfectibility. The social evils, poverty, crime, intemperance, and the rest, arose not from his own nature or from uncontrollable forces like excess population, but from defective human institutions capable of correction.[32] Partly this feeling sprang from a rising appreciation of the dignity of man, partly from democratic egalitarianism in a country where "the distinction of the One, the Few & the Many has no existence."[33] The revival, among some elements of the population, of evangelical Protestantism with the hopes of quick conversion and imminent millennial regeneration, and the spread among others of an optimistic and rational humanitarianism associated with Unitarianism lent the impulse of urgency to these benevolent reveries. But whatever the source, the essential truth seemed to be that "the chief end of the social state is the elevation of all its members as intelligent and moral beings." All looked forward to a "great approaching modification of society . . . under which every man will be expected to contribute to this object according to his ability."[34]

There was faith that the democratic state would play a part in the movement to assure to each human being the opportunity for fullest development of his capacities, turning its energies to save men from the consequences of poverty, to fit them by education for the problems of citizenship and the economy, and to guard them against the temptations of dissipation, gambling, liquor, and crime.[35]

But the same aspiration for social progress through improvement of the individual subtly called the government into service in another guise. In numberless

---

[31] W. E. Channing, *Memoir* (Boston, 1848), III, 38.

[32] See Francis Bowen, *Principles of Political Economy* (Boston, 1856), p. 172, and the general argument against Malthus, *ibid.*, pp. 155 ff. See also *Woburn Journal*, Dec. 13, 1851; John Pierce, *Brookline Jubilee* (Boston, 1847), pp. 31 ff; M. P. Braman, *Discourse on the Annual Election January 1, 1845*, (Boston, 1845), pp. 12 ff.

[33] Everett to Kirkland, Oct. 23, 1826, Everett Papers, LVIII, 50.

[34] Channing, *Memoir*, III, 38; see also Dickinson to Bancroft, Jan. 27, 1835, George Bancroft Papers (MSS, MHS); Theodore Sedgwick, *Public and Private Economy* (New York, 1839), I, 196.

[35] See . . . Chapter 10 [in the book from which this selection is taken].

day-to-day relations the old codes of propriety decayed. The conventions of a trade, of commercial negotiations, of family behavior, of simple neighborliness grew less binding as radical change undermined the presumptions on which they rested. Faced by new circumstances, lacking the assurance of traditional ways of action, and deprived of alternative modes of redress, those who felt the need for the intercession of a superior power turned more frequently to the services of the state as an arbiter to render tempered judgments assuring equitable conditions for all. Government was thus to render impartial judgments as well as to stimulate individual improvement. Through both channels, the urge to retain the elements of human dignity and decency in an impersonalized and decentralized society broadened the conception of what the community owed its members who were unable to protect themselves.

Threads of this reform spirit ran through the patterns of thought of almost every sector of the community. This was the common heritage of a common social environment. But the application to politics, and through politics to the economic structure of Massachusetts, raised consequential differences among voters and officials.

Certainty of progress had a millennial quality. The pervasive impression of imminence produced a generation of enthusiasts who expected through rational examination to recast existing institutions. For them immediate action was necessary and inevitable; delay or compromise needlessly put off the moment of final redemption. Zealots supplied the leadership for the endlessly sprouting causes; their following came from the fund of discontent built up by new circumstances.

The luckless farmers and handicraftsmen found solace, sometimes confidence, in the faith in a new dispensation. And for them reform had a further mission — to enable men to compete with one another on an equal footing by leveling all artificial barriers erected by the government. Each new road to the West that cut into the Massachusetts market for Berkshire wheat, each new mechanical device that lured customers away from the artisan's shop to the corporation's factory, steadily, incessantly, eroded the belief in the common interest on which had rested the old Commonwealth concept. The gradual disappearance of economic integration that had made understandable special grants to some for the benefit of all brought into question the social justification of the privileges through which the state acted. Without a common interest to cherish and defend, the General Court merely legislated for the select few, forbidding one man "to do what he has a natural right to do" and authorizing another "to do what he has not a natural right to do . . . counting itself the real owner and sovereign disposer of the individual . . . disfranchising all individuals, and then pretending to redistribute individual rights, according to its own caprice, interests, or necessities."[36] People from all strata had attempted and would continue to attempt to put government to their own service. Yet in practice each specific favor raised the protest by those adversely affected that it served the

---

[36] *Boston Quarterly Review*, 1 (1838), 71, 72; O. A. Brownson, "Constitutional Government," *ibid.*, 5 (1842), 31.

welfare only of its holders.[37] "Fanatics in freedom," indiscriminately battling "tolls, taxes, turnpikes, banks, hierarchies, governors, yea laws," meshed together the struggle for reform and the struggle against privilege.[38] The concrete concern in ending pernicious favors reinforced the longing for regeneration, which in turn supplied the intellectual framework for an attack upon special advantages.

The merchants shared the abstract outlook on reform. They were in agreement on the evils of slavery, on the need for temperance. They were impressed by the movement for better treatment of criminals, of the insane, and of the diseased. And they used the identical arguments based on progress and the need for revising old institutions when they fought for changes in their own interest. Furthermore, these men, though prosperous, daily faced problems involving their own status that sensitized them to reform tendencies. Those who stood apart in a democracy but who still wished to maintain a governing position needed an effective technique, grounded in the spirit of the times, for relations with other groups.[39]

Long practice had taught the merchants how thus to operate within the democratic framework. They were aware of the close correlation between power and wealth. The final abolition of property qualifications in the state, however, reduced the formal weight of their influence and accentuated their dependence upon the cooperation of other elements in the state. Shaky in their political position, they sought sympathetic contacts to compensate for growing social and economic isolation.[40]

Generous with charity for the unfortunate and the destitute, accepting the fact that the poor would always be with them, the merchants yet perceived the danger of the existence of a class of perpetual paupers. Consequently, high wages played an important part in economic thought. Wages which reflected "the actual state of the whole community" reduced the burden of relief and preserved a measure, but only a measure, of social mobility. If the poor man is bound to his class, "himself and his heirs for ever," he "must regard the . . . society, which holds him in this condition, as an inhabitant of a conquered

[37] *Boston Quarterly Review*, 1 (1838), 200–206; George Bancroft, *Address at Hartford before the Delegates to the Democratic Convention of the Young Men of Connecticut, on the Evening of February 18, 1840* (n.p., n.d.), p. 1.

[38] R. W. Emerson, "Life and Letters in New England," *Lectures and Biographical Sketches* (Boston, 1884), p. 309; Theodore Sedgwick to Theodore Sedgwick, Mar. 21, 1833, Theodore Sedgwick Papers, 1768–1858 (MSS, MHS), 2 ser., IX. For the general intellectual background see Russel B. Nye, *William Lloyd Garrison and the Humanitarian Reformers* (Boston, 1955); Arthur M. Schlesinger, Jr., *Age of Jackson* (Boston, 1945), pp. 132–176, 267 ff.

[39] See, e.g., Morse, *Henry Lee*, p. 119; Winsor, *Boston*, IV, 641 ff.

[40] See *Journal of Debates and Proceedings in the Convention to Revise the Constitution of Massachusetts, 1820* (Boston, 1853), pp. 309 ff; Webster, "First Settlement of New England," *Works*, I, 36, 39; Francis Bowen, "Distribution of Property," *North Amer. Rev.*, 67 (1848), 126 ff; *House Docs.*, 1840, no. 9, p. 38; Henry Farnam to J. P. Bigelow, Dec. 10, 1850, J. P. Bigelow Papers (MSS, Houghton Library, Harvard University); E. Everett to Milmay, Jan. 26, 1851, Everett Papers, XCIX, 61 ff; O. A. Brownson, "Constitutional Government," *Boston Quarterly Review*, 5 (1842), 33; Chilton Williamson, *American Suffrage from Property to Democracy* (Princeton, 1860), pp. 190 ff.

territory looks upon a citadel of the conquerors. He is naturally, and . . . almost . . . justifiably, an enemy of the government" as long as the state merely guarantees "an existence of no value."[41] Revolution and the most violent measures were then justified. On the other hand, an equitable distribution of landed property through proper inheritance laws and the preservation of economic opportunity would destroy both the need and the justification for revolt.[42] That very mobility would undermine the validity of the English fund and natural-rate theories of wages. Since the Malthusian argument was invalid in America, high wages were compatible with an essential to high profits, which in the last analysis depended on the country's resources.[43]

The merchants also set education to serving their purpose. Through their thinking ran the wistful hope that schooling would develop a respect for private rights, restrain the "predominant influence of mere numbers, check the tendency of popular government . . . to radicalism & anarchy," and advance "the interests of the whole people" as distinct from those of any special group.[44] In the face of deepening divisions, they sought to teach that there need be no conflict among all the elements in society. Borrowing from the commonwealth idea, they reiterated the concept that all but the idle were "workingmen," and all "inseparably bound together in a community of interest."[45] The connection of schooling with the vestigial doctrine of common interests led such men as Edward Everett to oppose Orestes Brownson's project for industrial training, fighting the idea "that there are different classes of our youth requiring different kinds of education."[46] With a body of voters trained to believe that "agriculture, manufactures, and commerce, are intimately blended and mutually dependent, and each equally connected with the permanent welfare of the community," there would be no fear of democracy or the tyranny of the majority. Universal

[41] Willard Phillips, Manual of Political Economy (Boston, 1828), pp. 149–152; Rantoul, Memoirs, pp. 248 ff; Lawrence to Sumner, Nov. 2, 1848, Charles Sumner, "Letters Received," XII, 148; Sedgwick, Public and Private Economy, III, 29 ff.

[42] See Bowen, "Distribution of Property," North Amer. Rev., 67 (1848), 126 ff, 137 ff, 151 ff; Bowen, Political Economy, pp. 493 ff; Rantoul, Memoirs, pp. 135 ff; Webster, Works, I, lxiii, 34 ff; Sedgwick, Public and Private Economy, I, 237, III, 68 ff.

[43] Bowen, Political Economy, pp. 131 ff, 193 ff, 201, 237 ff; Phillips, Manual of Political Economy, p. 159. See also J. J. Spengler, "An American Opponent of Malthus," New England Quarterly, 12 (1936), 97 ff. On wages and the tariff see Springfield Gazette, Feb. 16, 1842. For a hostile view of the wage position see Amaziah Bumpus (pseud.), A Series of Letters to Gov. John Davis (Dedham, 1842), pp. 15–17.

[44] Governor Briggs, Boston Daily Advertiser, Jan. 13, 1847; Bowen, Political Economy, p. 18; Rantoul, Memoirs, pp. 238 ff; Everett to Bates, Oct. 25, 1852, Everett Papers, CII, 43; Phillips, Manual of Political Economy, pp. 153, 154; "A Plea for the Laboring Classes," The New England Magazine, 9 (1835), 429 ff; Webster, Works, I, 41 ff; Sedgwick, Public and Private Economy, I, 238.

[45] Edward Everett, "The Workingmen's Party," Orations and Speeches, I, 283 ff; Edward Everett, "Accumulation, Property, Capital, Credit," ibid., II, 289 ff; Sedgwick, Public and Private Economy, I, 232; Francis Bowen, "Phillips on Protection," North Amer. Rev., 72 (1851), 415.

[46] Everett to Brownson, May 16, 1836, Everett Papers, LXVII, 87; Rantoul, Memoirs, p. 138.

suffrage and free elections were "in reality great conservative principles"; revolutions came from withholding those rights.[47]

Sympathizing with reform, the merchants nevertheless feared the consequences of allowing radicals to set the pace and determine the scope. An impassioned striving for newness seemed dangerous to those who knew that the gentlest current of change could suddenly debouch into an uncontrollable flood. "State Street had an instinct that" reform "invalidated contracts and threatened the stability of stocks."[48] The urge to precipitate legislation, particularly when linked to the attack upon privilege, often was heedless of the rights of property and thus antagonized the wealthy, fearful of the implications for their own holdings.

Furthermore, attacks upon special state patronage frequently became attacks upon the select group, the constant prosperity of which invited the belief that its share in privilege was excessive. Criticism of banks easily turned into fulminations against a "financial aristocracy" which lacked "fixed opinions of a moral nature." Locofocos and debt repudiators who seized control on other states, Dorrites who launched an armed rebellion, raised a terrifying specter for this minority: to weaken privilege at any point would be an entering wedge that would ultimately leave all wealth entirely at the mercy of every future legislature.[49] "Public necessity," Webster thought, under these circumstances "is apt to be public feeling, and on this rock we are in danger of making ship wreck of the bill of rights."[50] To set the proper limits for action generated by the surging reform impulse called for an autonomous body of rights founded on the principles of natural law, "rules of conduct . . . coeval with society"; indeed many saw the fundamental problem of the period in terms of a conflict between liberty and law.[51]

Few Massachusetts men questioned the inviolability of private property and of contract. Property held "a higher and stronger title than any which society can confer"; without it "all other rights became worthless and visionary," and it alone made progress possible.[52] A compact rested upon a "principle of policy . . . essential to all tolerable governments . . . the absolute security of property."

[47] Phillips, *Political Economy*, pp. 125, 126; Everett to Peel, Holland, and Hallam, Mar. 23, 29, 1837, July 25, 1848, Everett Papers, LXVII, 155, 157, LXXXIV, 157, LXXXV, 221. However, Everett significantly denied the need for the secret ballot (to Denison, April 1853, *ibid.*, CII, 84).

[48] Emerson, "Life and Letters in New England," *Lectures*, p. 325.

[49] *Boston Commercial Gazette*, Jan. 25, 1838.

[50] *Charles River Bridge* v. *Warren Bridge* (1829), 7 Pickering 441.

[51] L. S. Cushing, *Introduction to the Study of Roman Law* (Boston, 1854), pp. 8, 17; Rufus Choate, "American Bar as an Element of Conservatism," *Addresses and Orations* (Boston, 1878), pp. 143–150; A. H. Everett, *Defense of the Character and Principles of Mr. Jefferson* (Boston, 1836), pp. 27, 29.

[52] Bowen, "Distribution of Property," *North Amer. Rev.*, 67 (1848), 121; Bowen, "Phillips on Protection," *ibid.*, 82 (1851), 416; [B. R. Curtis], "Debts of the States," *ibid.*, 58 (1844), 145 ff; Cary, "Dependence of Fine Arts on Security of Property," *Boston Daily Advertiser*, Nov. 18, 1844; Joseph Story, *Discourse Pronounced upon the Inauguration as Dane Professor of Law in Harvard University* (Boston, 1829), pp. 24 ff; Sedgwick, *Public and Private Economy*, I, 14ff, II, 85 ff; John Adams, *Works*, ed. C. F. Adams (Boston, 1850–1856), VI, 8 ff; Bancroft to Barre Committee, July 10, 1840, Bancroft Papers.

Its binding force "depends upon a law which neither kings nor people enacted or can repeal. It comes from the awful Being who created and fashioned us . . . and the united will of the whole human race cannot influence it."[53] In the most famous test of the contractual relation in this period, all parties recognized its sanctity. Even Judge Marcus Morton, a reform democrat anxious to circumscribe the application of the idea, admitted that "a contract is deemed sacred, and the constitution nowhere allows the violation of its obligations . . . for any exigency or upon making compensation. . . . Any legislative act . . . having this effect, is a nullity."[54] If the radicals could put the idea of contract to the service of their own extreme proposals, that only emphasized further Chief Justice Parker's assumption that the principles themselves were no longer disputable.[55]

There was no agreement, however, about the extent to which commitments hobbled a government prompted by supplications in the name of reform to venture into unfamiliar paths. The defenders of privilege attempted to broaden the conception of property and contract to protect previous grants from adverse legislative action, seeking to prevent the General Court from becoming sole judge of exigency in disputes to which it was a party, a role inconsistent "with all sound and just notions of private right."[56] The franchise, they reasoned, was, like other property, beyond state control. The individual owner of a licensed bridge which seriously obstructed navigation claimed successfully that there was no authority capable of forcing him to remove or alter his structure.[57]

But the failure to secure the same vantage point for the corporation left privilege teetering at the edge of disaster. The test came with the claim in 1829 of the proprietors of the Charles River Bridge that their act of incorporation was a contract by which they acquired "an incorporeal hereditament; being a valuable property, consisting in the franchise of being a corporation." The charter to the competing Warren Bridge, cheek by jowl with their own structure, was, they contended, unconstitutional as a violation of contract and as confiscation of property.[58] They vigorously asserted that their rights covered the whole line of travel between Charlestown and Boston and included the essential power "to put down injurious competition"; for, "where a thing is granted, all that is necessary to the enjoyment of it goes with it." And if the government could create as many bridges as it pleased without regard to the prosperity of the existent ones, then the splendid security of the original act of incorporation was of no value. The franchise would remain intact on the statute books but would

[53] [Curtis], "Debts of the States," *North Amer. Rev.*, 58 (1844), 142, 145; *New York Review*, 2 (1838), 372 ff; *Boston Daily Advertiser*, Nov. 16, 22, 23, 24, 27, 1843.

[54] *Charles River Bridge* v. *Warren Bridge* (1829), 7 Pickering 453, 459.

[55] *Charles River Bridge* v. *Warren Bridge* (1829), 7 Pickering 506 ff. See also Governor Morton's address, *House Docs.*, 1840, no. 9, p. 5; *Proceedings of the Democratic Legislative Convention Held in Boston, March 1840* (Boston, 1840), p. 4.

[56] See *Charles River Bridge* v. *Warren Bridge* (1829), 7 Pickering 399, 405, 427, 438; also C. G. Loring, *Argument on Behalf of the Eastern Railroad Company* (Boston, 1845), pp. 3, 6 ff.

[57] *Commonwealth* v. *Breed* (1827), 3 Pickering 460.

[58] *Charles River Bridge* v. *Warren Bridge* (1829), 7 Pickering 354, 355, 356, 395, 396, 427, 436, 440. See also "Solemn Protest," *Senate Docs.*, 1836, no. 83, pp. 1, 10 ff; *Charles River Bridge, in Equity* v. *Warren Bridge* (1828), 6 Pickering 376.

rot away beneath an insidious attack against which the Chinese wall of contract would offer no defense.[59]

The contrary argument of the Warren Bridge that the act of incorporation referred only to the immediate termini, that there was "no contract by the commonwealth, that no new charter shall be granted, which shall interfere with the business or profits of the old" drew the support of half the Massachusetts court.[60] More disconcerting was the decision of the chief justice. Parker could not reconcile what seemed valid in both positions. He saw merit in Webster's conception of an implicit guarantee, in the grant of a bridge, that there would be crossers; otherwise the franchise would have little value. But he was not certain: "This appears to me a very reasonable doctrine; but I confess I am not able to adduce any authorities in support of it. I ground it on the principles of our government and constitution, and on the immutable principles of justice." On the other hand, indirect loss by government action was a risk inherent in the possession of all private property. In opening new roads, for instance, "it will often happen, that estates upon old roads are diminished in value; the seat of business may be transferred . . . inns and stores . . . may become deserted . . . but the proprietors would have no claim . . . for redress, for it is necessarily one of the contingencies on which property is . . . held, that it is liable to be impaired by future events of this kind." The chief justice was therefore unwilling to rule.[61] Divided, the state court refused to act and threw the whole question into the federal judiciary. In Washington, Justice Story labored mightily to protect the corporation, but Taney's court, heavy-weighted with Jacksonians, turned the balance against privilege. Corporations could not count on safety in the contract idea.[62]

Other decisions further reduced the margin of security. The courts refused to hold unconstitutional those reservations in corporate charters that permitted the legislature to alter or repeal, judging that these were not judicial acts and therefore not contrary to the separation-of-powers clause in the Bill of Rights.[63] Eventually the bench laid down the broad maxim that "the whole of a franchise might be taken by the legislature for public uses . . . on payment of a full compensation, without violating the clause in the constitution of the United States, against any law which impairs the obligation of contracts."[64]

This line of decisions had not sprung full-grown from the specific issues of the cases involved. Its period of gestation reached back to the moment, decades earlier, when the Commonwealth yielded to demands for the extension of privilege. But the cumulative effect, the unmistakable trend, coinciding with the fragmentation of society and the mounting intensity of humanitarian reform,

---

[59] 7 Pickering 432, 433, 483, 494.

[60] 7 Pickering 407, 412, 417, 424, 425, 454–475.

[61] 7 Pickering 522, 512, 514, 519 ff, 524 ff.

[62] *Charles River Bridge* v. *Warren Bridge* (1837), 11 Peters 420. See also Story to Mason, Dec. 23, 1831, [Hillard], *Jeremiah Mason*, pp. 336 ff; *Senate Docs.*, 1833, no. 52, p. 8.

[63] St. 1830, ch. 81; *Creese* v. *Babcock* (1839), 23 Pickering 334; Francis Hilliard, *Supplement Being a Digest of Pickering's and Metcalf's Reports* (Boston, 1843), p. 132. Cf., however, *Charles River Bridge* v. *Warren Bridge* (1829), 7 Pickering 520.

[64] *Boston Water &c.* v. *Boston and Worcester &c.* (1839), 23 Pickering 360; Hilliard, *Supplement*, pp. 90, 91; *House Docs.*, 1843, no. 176.

shook the merchants' faith in the judiciary as defender of vested rights. Harrison Gray Otis perceived at once that the Charles River Bridge case exposed the whole realm of private property to legislative interference.[65] The like-minded gradually withdrew into a stubborn opposition, holding with the elder Dana: "The whole modern system seems to me to be grounded on a false view of man — in his power of self-restoration & self-elevation, &, in reality, as acknowledging no God, nor the need of any . . . there is a spirit of self-confidence in it which, left to its natural tendencies, will inevitably bring a deeper & wider woe upon man than earth has ever yet known. It is my sincere belief that we are preparing for ourselves an awful rebuke to our pride. The 19th century spirit is anything rather than a hopeful one to me."[66] Broody over the turn of events, they fell in with the position of old Nathan Appleton, who pointedly lectured an ambitious young lawyer, "I believe in the law of *force* — . . . and that human nature . . . can be governed by no other — . . . I should be very unwilling to rely on simple abstract justice — without force to back it."[67]

But not many merchants drew the same intransigent conclusions or felt it necessary to choose flatly between the law of force and abstract justice. Most still looked to the General Court for measures in their own interest and found it impossible to reject the idea of state action as such. Acknowledging, in any case, the ultimate justness of reform, they temporized, hoping by private benevolence to forestall the need for government intervention and, when action came, to moderate its effects upon their own concerns and upon property in general.

Litigation now became more engrossed with questions of what constituted public use and full compensation. Bickering over whether exigencies existed and haggling over the size of indemnities further strengthened the professional and technical character of the law. By 1830 the accretion of precedents and the elaboration of rules of procedure had erased any danger of interference by laymen.[68] Investigations of Roman, Continental, and English jurisprudence, heavy sales of learned treatises and journals, and the establishment of law schools were marks of rapid formalization.[69] The widening of equity powers after 1815 made it easier than before to avoid trial by jury and hastened the curtailment of lay influence.[70] Popular agitation against these tendencies met fierce resistance.[71] Proposals to codify the common law were "deemed to smack of radicalism," and Rantoul's insistence that all jurisprudence be reduced to "a positive and unbending text" to minimize the discretion of judges produced only innocuous re-

[65] Morison, *Harrison Gray Otis*, II, 286. See also *New York Review*, 2 (1838), 385–398; [C. S. Davies], "Constitutional Law," *North Amer. Rev.*, 46 (1838), 135.

[66] To Sumner, Aug. 16, 1853, Sumner, "Letters Received," XXII, 12. See also Choate, "American Bar as an Element of Conservatism," *Address and Orations*, p. 143.

[67] Sumner, "Letters Received," IX, 60.

[68] Story, *Discourse*, pp. 18 ff; Everett to Denison, Jan. 13, 1851, Everett Papers, XCV, 139.

[69] See Everett to Denison, Oct. 11, 1845, Everett Papers, LXXVII, 8; Cushing, *Roman Law*, pp. 179 ff.

[70] See *Boston Commercial Gazette*, Feb. 1, 1816; *Boston Daily Advertiser*, Mar. 1, 5, 1844; st. 1857, ch. 214; 7 Pickering 354, 358, 364, 369.

[71] See *American Monthly Magazine*, 1 (1829), 369 ff, 469 ff; Theodore Sedgwick to Theodore Sedgwick, Feb. 6, 1833, Sedgwick Papers, 2 ser., IX.

visions of the statutes in 1835 and 1857.[72] Dependence upon the independent judiciary as the last bulwark of life, liberty, and property quickly restored the salaries of judges when those were reduced for partisan motives.[73] The link between the law and private rights was clearly in the mind of the contemporary who wrote, on the occasion of the appointment of Chancellor Kent to the Harvard Law School, "If anything can *retard* (*stop it* you can not) the jacobinical torrent which is sweeping past and undermining the foundations of . . . our institutions, the barrier of sound law and conservative influences which the Harvard Law School is building up, will do it."[74]

Further to secure property, the merchants sought an alliance of all those concerned with the preservation of worldy goods and offered farmers, manufacturers, traders, and even artisans a program of change within the limits of vested rights. No opposing combination of forces held together until well into the 1850's. The artisans, as Brownson realized, could count on neither the capitalists nor the agriculturists but served merely to "swell the forces of one or the other."[75] The "poor — of whom I think more than of the rich — seem to have no hope," wrote Channing sadly. At critical moments "the middle classes will foresake them. They have no helpers."[76]

With every other element in society chaotically uncertain, the merchants found a ready tool for control in the swiftly changing party system. Among the Whigs, merchant influence was always weighty. And although Bancroft and Morton for a time harnessed the Democratic organization to "radical democracy, . . . hostility to monopolies, and [the] . . . desire to promote the intellectual and moral improvement of the whole people," their success in doing so was qualified and short-lived.[77] The merchants, manufacturers, and traders who generally guided the Democrats viewed change in the same light as other men of wealth. Moreover, the inability of the party, tied to a southern platform, to take a forthright position on the slavery issue, and the growing weight of its conservative Irish constituents cast suspicion on its devotion to reform.[78]

---

[72] Everett to Thacher and Grennell, Jan. 20, Mar. 5, 1836, Everett Papers, LXVII, 30, 40; Rantoul, *Memoirs*, pp. 48, 277. See also *Report of the Commissioners on the Revision of the Statutes, 1858* (Boston, 1858), pp. iii–vii; *Senate Docs.*, 1855, no. 10, pp. 4–10; Governor Gardner's address, *Senate Docs.*, 1857, no. 3, pp. 39 ff; *Senate Docs.*, 1859, no. 202, pp. 5 ff; W. W. Story, *Life and Letters of Joseph Story* (Boston, 1851), II, 241–248.

[73] Governor Washburn's address, *Senate Docs.*, 1854, no. 3, p. 12. For the question of salaries see *Address of the Democratic Members of the Legislature of Massachusetts . . . 1843* (Boston, 1843), pp. 9, 10; *Commonwealth History*, ed. Hart, IV, 59–67; *Boston Daily Advertiser*, Oct. 7, 9, Nov. 7, 1843, Feb. 9, 1844; Story to Webster, Jan. 10, 1824, Story, *Joseph Story*, I, 438; *Senate Docs.*, 1853, no. 5, p. 22.

[74] Silliman to Sumner, June 29, 1846, Sumner, "Letters Received," X, 70. See also *American Jurist and Law Magazine*, 1 (1829), 26 ff, 378; *ibid.*, 2 (1829), 192.

[75] *Boston Quarterly Review*, 3, (1840), 475.

[76] Channing, *Memoir*, III, 294.

[77] Morton to Bancroft, Sept. 9, 1835, Marcus Morton, "Letters, 1818–1864" (MSS, MHS), I; Morton to Henshaw, Calhoun, and Van Buren, Feb. 1, 1830, Feb. 13, 1834, Mar. 27, 1837, *ibid.*, I; Bancroft, *Address*, pp. 9 ff.

[78] For Morton's personal difficulties and his opinion that his program had failed, see, e.g., his letters to Niles, Bancroft, and Hildreth, Feb. 12, 1846, Mar. 24, 1848, May 11, 1849, Morton, "Letters," III, 107, 318, IV, 18. See also Orestes Brownson, "The Policy to be Pursued," *Boston Quarterly Review*, 4 (1841), 74 ff, 124–126; Jeremiah G. Harris to Bancroft, 1838, Bancroft Papers.

Neither party was radical, but both compromised and allied with extremists. The system of general ticket representation, which gave a bare majority possession of the entire slate in a town, deprived minorities of any voice in the legislature.[79] For every group the only alternative to permanent subordination was a program of enough compromise to command wide popular support. A Whig governor pointed out to an English prime minister, "Little is . . . gained by resisting popular reforms; . . . everything is gained by measures of conciliation, which keep the great majority in good humor."[80] With his usual insight Theodore Parker saw all the politicians as a single group, "the Parties in office, or seeking to become so. This [group] makes the statutes, but is commonly controlled by the trading power, and has all of its faults . . . yet it seems amenable to the instincts of the People, who, on great occasions, sometimes interfere and change the traders' rule."[81]

The two national political parties passed through a long chain of permutations. Every few years between 1820 and 1860, observers noted hopefully or despondently that public events were getting into new channels, that new lines were about to be traced and the old ones forever effaced. This instability of political organizations derived to a considerable measure from the impact of a succession of short-lived but significant minor parties that mirrored all the vicissitudes of social and economic maladjustment.

In the 1820's such groups as the "middling interest," composed of "men of property and men of substance," developed out of transient local incidents.[82] But after 1830 new parties, each dedicated to a single issue, became the vehicles of visionaries who aspired to lead the state toward "Reform, Improvement, Liberty." These causes gathered support from the discontented and often exerted considerable influence through combination with the older organizations. Inexorably, the challenge of aggressive platforms drove both Democrats and Whigs along the road to reform.[83]

From time to time between 1830 and 1845 the balance of power fell into the hands of the Workingmen's party, the Locofocos, the Anti-Masonic party, and various nativist and abolitionist factions all resting heavily on the votes of the rural population and of the urban mechanics.[84] But after 1845 the splintering effects of the slavery issue on both old parties offered those primarily interested

[79] See Alvord to Sumner, Aug. 21, 1849, Sumner, "Letters Received," XIII, 92.

[80] Everett to Peel, Jan. 8, 1850, Everett Papers, XCI, 251. For complaints by an old Whig against compromises see Phelps to Bigelow, Dec. 26, 1842, Bigelow Papers.

[81] Parker, *Experience as a Minister*, pp. 92, 93. See also Channing, *Memoir*, III, 262.

[82] See *An Exposition of the Principles and Views of the Middling Interest in the City of Boston, May, 1822* (Boston, 1822), p. 5; *Defence of the Exposition of the Middling Interest on the Right of Constituents to Give Instructions to Their Representatives and the Obligation of These to Obey Them* (Boston, 1822); Morison, *Harrison Gray Otis*, II, 238–241.

[83] A. H. Everett, speech quoted in *Boston Daily Advocate*, Nov. 14, 1835; Braman, *Annual Election*, p. 79. For the relation of reform to the major and minor parties see Edward Everett to Denison, Delavan, April, Sept. 30, 1853, Everett Papers, CII, 84, CIII, 71.

[84] See Morton to Simpson, Pearce, Harrington, and Henshaw, Feb. 17, 20, 1834, Jan. 9, June 1, 6, 1836, Morton, "Letters," I; Everett to Shattuck, Hallett, Dec. 24, 1832, Oct. 5, 1835, Everett Papers, LXVI, 186, 291; *Springfield Gazette*, Sept. 14, 1842; A. B. Darling, "Workingmen's Party in Massachusetts," *Amer. Hist. Rev.*, 29 (1923), 81 ff, 84–86; J. Q. Adams, *Memoirs*, IX, 33 ff.

in reform the opportunity finally to seize the state government.[85] The Free-Soilers attempted to capture the Whig party in 1848 and urged the conservative, Edward Everett, to accept an independent nomination for the vice-presidency. Although they failed in both efforts, the outcome of the election that year encouraged many disillusioned rank-and-file Whigs to turn their backs upon their old party.[86]

After 1850 the reformers dominated the state, first in a coalition of Free-Soilers and Democrats and then marshaled under a nativist banner after defeat of the radical constitution of 1853 by the Irish vote. The Know-Nothings reigned until their mantle fell upon the new Republican party in 1858.[87] This culmination of the shifting political alliances steadily strengthened reform influence and threw conservatives into confusion.[88] After years of half-satisfaction through paltry concessions by the old parties, the radicals held sway without substantial restraint. The program of reform and the battle against privilege, shackled for so long, approached fulfillment. Worked up from the materials brought to hand by the experience of the past, and following the broad outlines sketched in the resolution of numerous specific issues for many years earlier, the new structure of state action took finished form in the final decade before the Civil War.[89]

The Significance of the Slave Plantation
for Southern Economic Development

EUGENE D. GENOVESE

Economists and historians have long debated the question of the profitability of slavery. If the slave system was uneconomic, the argument goes, then the Civil War was unnecessary, for slavery would have died a natural death. If, on the other hand, slavery was profitable for the plantation owners, then only a war could have done away with the South's peculiar institution. Eugene D.

[85] Everett to Aberdeen, Nov. 14, 1845, Everett Papers, LXXVII, 90.

[86] E. to A. H. Everett, Oct. 30, 1846, Everett Papers, LXXX, 32. See also Everett to Winthrop, Kent, Hallam, Sumner, Bancroft, and Peel, Apr. 25, June 22, July 25, Aug. 4, Oct. 31, Dec. 23, 1848, *ibid.*, LXXXIV, 270, LXXXV, 226, 227, LXXXVI, 39, LXXXVII, 30, 204.

[87] See Everett to Green and Clay, Nov. 5, Dec. 3, 1851, Everett Papers, XCIX, 28, 79; "S" and Stone to Sumner, Feb. 15, 1853, Mar. 15, Dec. 29, 1854, Sumner, "Letters Received," XXI, 48, XXIII, 118, XXV, 148; Everett to Fillmore, Cushing, Dec. 16, 1854, Nov. 11, 1855, Everett Papers, CIV, 55, CV, 7.

[88] Everett to Capen, Nov. 6, 1858, Everett Papers, CIX, 104.

[89] See Handlin, *Boston's Immigrants*, pp. 191 ff; *Commonwealth History*, ed. Hart, IV, 74–82.

Genovese defends what amounts to the old unprofitability position — but from the broader perspective of economic development. He contends that the neglected area in the study of the Southern economy is demand, and the following essay attempts to estimate the nature of Southern economic demand and its effects. The key point, according to Genovese, is that the very nature of plantation slavery limited the purchasing power of the Southern population so drastically that the economy could not sustain the development of domestic industry. Without industry there could be little urbanization, and without urbanization there could be little diversification of agriculture. Thus slavery was the fundamental cause of economic retardation in the South, and of the consequent economic bondage of the South to the North. Genovese's conclusions are based upon extensive work in the records of Southern plantations, and his observations about the character of the plantation system carry conviction. Is his economic theory, however, equally compelling? Genovese stresses the dysfunctional nature of the Southern one-crop system, and the question arises whether it was slavery or King Cotton (or a combination of the two) that retarded Southern economic growth before the Civil War.

Historians are no longer sure that plantation slavery was responsible for the economic woes of the Old South. The revisionist doubts rest on two propositions of dubious relevance. The first is that slave labor could have been applied successfully to pursuits other than the raising of plantation staples; the second is that slave agriculture was possibly as profitable as were alternative industries and can not be held responsible for the unwillingness of Southerners to use their profits more wisely.[1] The first confuses slave labor and its direct effects with the slave system and its total effects; it is the latter that is at issue, and the versatility of slave labor is a secondary consideration. The second rests on the assumption that the master-slave relationship was purely economic and not essentially different from an employer-worker relationship. Yet, when confronted with the issue direct, who could deny that slavery gave rise to a distinct politics, ideology, and pattern of social behavior and that these had immense economic consequences?

We need not examine at the moment the precise relationship between slavery and the plantation. Certainly, plantation economies presuppose considerable

Reprinted by permission of the Managing Editor from the *Journal of Southern History*, 28 (November 1962), pp. 422–437.

[1] See, for example, the well known writings of R. R. Russel, including his "The General Effects of Slavery upon Southern Economic Progress," *Journal of Southern History*, IV (February 1938), 34–54, or the more recent statement of Alfred H. Conrad and John R. Meyer, "The Economics of Slavery in the Ante-Bellum South," *Journal of Political Economy*, LXVI (April 1958), 95–130.

compulsion, if only of the *de facto* type now prevalent in Latin America. The historical fact of an ante bellum plantation-based slave economy is our immediate concern, although, undoubtedly, post bellum developments preserved some of the retardative effects of ante bellum slavery.

Those retardative effects were too many even to be summarized here. A low level of capital accumulation, the planters' high propensity to consume luxuries, the shortage of liquid capital aggravated by the steady drain of funds out of the region, the low productivity of slave labor, the need to concentrate on a few staples, the anti-industrial, anti-urban ideology of the dominant planters, the reduction of Southern banking, industry, and commerce to the position of auxiliaries of the planatation economy — all these are familiar and yet need restudy in the light of the important work being done on the economics of underdeveloped countries. For the present let us focus on another factor, which in itself provides an adequate explanation of the slave South's inability to industrialize: the retardation of the home market for both industrial and agricultural commodities.

Thirty years ago Elizabeth W. Gilboy complained that economic historians studying the process of industrialization were too much concerned with supply and insufficiently concerned with demand.[2] Her complaint was justified despite brilliant work on the problem of markets by a few outstanding men from Karl Marx to R. H. Tawney and Paul Mantoux. Since then, demand has received much more attention, although possibly not so much as it deserves. Important essays by Maurice Dobb, Simon Kuznets, H. J. Habakkuk, and Gunnar Myrdal, among others, have helped to correct the imbalance,[3] as has new research on European industrialization and the economics of underdeveloped countries. If there is one lesson to be learned from the experience of both developed and underdeveloped countries it is that industrialization is unthinkable without an agrarian revolution which shatters the old regime of the countryside. While the peasantry is tied to the land, burdened with debt, and limited to minimal purchasing power, the labor recruitment and market pre-conditions for extensive manufacturing are missing. "Land reform" — i.e., an agrarian revolution — is the essential first step in the creation of an urban working class, the reorganization of agriculture to feed growing cities, and the development of a home market.

There are several ways in which agricultural reorganization can provide markets for manufactures; for our immediate purposes we may consider two. First, when the laborers are separated from the land, as they were during the English enclosures, they necessarily increase the demand for clothing and other essentials formerly produced at home. Paradoxically, this expansion of the market is com-

---

[2] Elizabeth W. Gilboy, "Demand As a Factor in the Industrial Revolution" in *Facts and Factors in Economic History; Articles by the Former Students of Edwin F. Gay* (Cambridge, Mass., 1932), 620–39.

[3] Maurice Dobb, *Studies in the Development of Capitalism* (New York, 1947), 6 ff, 87 ff, 98 ff, 290–96; Simon Kuznets, "Toward a Theory of Economic Growth" in Robert Lekachman (ed.), *National Policy for Economic Welfare at Home and Abroad* (New York, 1955), 12–77; H. J. Habakkuk, "The Historical Experience on the Basic Conditions of Economic Progress" in L. H. Dupriez (ed.), *Economic Progress* (Louvain, Belgium, 1955), 149–69; Gunnar Myrdal, *Rich Lands and Poor* (New York, 1957), *passim*, 23–38 especially.

patible with a marked reduction in the laborers' standard of living. Second, the farmers left on the countryside to produce for growing urban markets provide an increased demand for textiles, agricultural equipment, and so forth.

The rapid extension of the rural market was the way of the North, but the slave plantations dominated the South until such time as reorganization was imposed from without by a predatory foe interested primarily in a new system of rural exploitation. An adequate home market could not arise in the ante bellum South and has only evolved slowly and painfully during the last century.

In 1860 about 75 per cent of the Southern cotton crop was exported; during no ante bellum year did the grain exports of the United States exceed 5 per cent of the grain crop. No doubt, cotton profits were an important element in the financing of America's economic growth. The question is, were the profits syphoned off to build up the Northern economy? We know that the credit mechanisms alone, to a considerable extent, did just that. The South's dependence on the export trade, in contradistinction to the North's primary reliance on its home market, indicates not merely a social division of labor but the economic exploitation of the exporting South.

Robert G. Albion, in his excellent examination of the colonial bondage of the South to the North, concludes that the South's lack of direct trade with Europe constituted an irrational arrangement secured by the impudence of New York's aggressive entrepreneurs. We can agree that, had the South imported from abroad as much as the North and West, there could have been no sensible reason to route through New York either the South's cotton or its share of European goods; but Albion's assumption of a rough equality of imports, an assumption shared by contemporaries like George McDuffie and T. P. Kettell, can not be substantiated. The slave South's total market for manufactured goods was small relative to that of the free states; and even though the South depended upon Europe as well as the North for manufactured goods, its imports from Europe were smaller in value than imports into the North and West and smaller in bulk than the staples it exported. If the ships carrying cotton had sailed from Southern ports direct to Europe and back, they would have had to return in ballast.[4] New York's domination of the South's export trade was, therefore, not accidental. Furthermore, if the South's share in American imports had

---

[4] See Robert Greenhalgh Albion, The Rise of New York Port, 1815–1860 (New York, 1939) and Albion, Square-Riggers on Schedule; the New York Sailing Packets to England, France, and the Cotton Ports (Princeton, 1938). For similar arguments presented by contemporaries, see James E. B. De Bow (ed.), The Industrial Resources, etc., of the Southern and Western States . . . (3 vols., New Orleans, 1852–1853), 125, 365; and De Bow's Review, IV (1847), 208–25, 339, 351. For a perceptive Northern reply, see the anonymous pamphlet, The Effects of Secession upon the Commercial Relations Between the North and South and upon Each Section (New York, 1861), 15. For the weakness of the Southern import trade, see George Rogers Taylor, The Transportation Revolution, 1815–1860 (New York, 1951), 198; Philip S. Foner, Business & Slavery; the New York Merchants & the Irrepressible Conflict (Chapel Hill, 1941), 6–7; and Samuel Eliot Morison, The Maritime History of Massachusetts, 1783–1860 (Boston, 1921), 298–99. Many of the lines carrying cotton from Northern ports were deeply involved in bringing immigrants to the United States, which was one of the reasons why their ships did not have to return from Europe in ballast. John G. B. Hutchins, The American Maritime Industries and Public Policy, 1789–1914; an Economic History (Cambridge, Mass., 1941), 262–63.

been as Albion suggests, and if the coastal trade had been as large as he implies, the greater part of the goods sent from New Orleans to the plantation areas would have originated in Europe and been reshipped through New York rather than being — as is known — of Western origin.[5]

Albion's acceptance of the assumption of nearly equal imports is the more surprising in view of the evidence of restricted Southern demand. The Southern cotton, iron, paper, wool, and railroad industries — to mention a few — struggled with indifferent results against a low level of Southern patronage. Antislavery leaders like Henry Ruffner and Cassius M. Clay made slavery's effects on the home market a cardinal point in their indictment. Thoughtful proslavery Southerners also commented frequently on the market problem. The opinion of the editor of the *Southern Agriculturalist* in 1828 that the South lacked sufficient customers to sustain a high level of manufacturing was echoed throughout the ante bellum period. The speech of Col. Andrew P. Calhoun to the Pendleton, South Carolina, Farmers' Society in 1855, for example, was strikingly similar in tone and content. On the other side, someone like Beverley Tucker would occasionally argue that Northerners would never risk a war "which, while it lasted, would shut them out from the best market in the world."[6] It is difficult to imagine that many, even those who adopted such arguments for political purposes, took seriously a proposition so palpably false.

Alfred Glaze Smith, Jr., and Douglass C. North have traced the low level of Southern demand, in part, to plantation self-sufficiency. This view is not borne out by the data in the manuscript census returns from the cotton belt, which reveal only trivial amounts of home manufactures on even the largest plantations and which bear out the judgments of Rolla M. Tryon and Mary Elizabeth Massey on the weakness of Southern household industry.[7] In De Soto and Marshall counties, Mississippi, the big planters (those with thirty-one or more slaves) averaged only seventy-six dollars worth of home manufactures in 1860, and farmers and small planters averaged much less. In Dougherty and Thomas counties, Georgia, the small planters (those with from twenty-one to thirty slaves) led other groups of slaveholders with one hundred and twenty-seven dollars, and the big planters produced only about half as much. Most of the planters in both clusters of counties recorded no home manufactures at all.[8]

---

[5] Emory R. Johnson and others, *History of the Domestic and Foreign Commerce of the United States* (2 vols., Washington, 1915), I, 242; R. B. Way, "The Commerce of the Lower Mississippi in the Period 1830–1860," *Mississippi Valley Historical Association, Proceedings*, X (1918–1919), 62; Louis Bernard Schmidt, "The Internal Grain Trade of the United States, 1850–1860," *Iowa Journal of History and Politics*, XVIII (January 1920), 110–11.

[6] *Southern Agriculturalist* (Charleston), I (September 1828), 404; *Farmer and Planter*, VI (December 1855), 270–71; *Southern Quarterly Review*, XVIII (September 1850), 218.

[7] Alfred G. Smith, *Economic Readjustment of an Old Cotton State: South Carolina, 1820–1860* (Columbia, S.C., 1958), 134; Douglass C. North, *The Economic Growth of the United States, 1790–1860* (Englewood Cliffs, N.J., 1961), 132–33; Rolla M. Tryon, *Household Manufacturers in the United States, 1640–1860; a Study in Industrial History* (Chicago, 1917); Mary Elizabeth Massey, *Ersatz in the Confederacy* (Columbia, 1952), 80, 98.

[8] From the five Mississippi and the five Georgia cotton belt counties regarded as typical by Lewis C. Gray in his *History of Agriculture in the Southern United States to 1860* (2 vols.,

Sample studies from Virginia's tobacco area, wheat area, and tide-water reveal the same situation. Plantation manuscripts show surprisingly frequent, and often quite large, expenditures for artisans' services and suggest that plantations were much less self-sufficient and exhibited much less division of labor than is generally appreciated.[9] The root of the insufficient demand must be sought in the poverty of the rural majority composed of slaves, subsistence farmers, and poor whites.

In nineteenth-century America as a whole both capital and labor were in short supply. Industrial development was spurred by farmers who provided a large market for goods and tools, and manufacturing arose on the foundation of this immense rural demand. Eastern manufacturers gradually awoke to their dependence on this rural market and by 1854 were supporting homestead legislation not only to gain support for higher tariffs and for purposes of speculation but to expand the market for their goods. Farmers in New England saw their futures linked with industrial development, and their hostility toward commercial middlemen was not usually transferred to the manufacturers.[10] The same was true in

---

Washington, 1933), I, 334–35, II, 918–21, I have analyzed for each state the two that come closest to the mode in the only variable for which there is clear evidence, the size of slaveholdings. A review of the economic and natural conditions of the South reveals nothing to suggest that the four counties so chosen are not roughly typical of the cotton belt. I have used the four counties primarily for an investigation of purchasing power — to gain clues to the general structure of the market — and the insignificant expenditures recorded indicate that even with due allowance for the possibility of a wide, say 50%, deviation in other counties and for incorrect reporting in the census returns, the results could not conceivably be substantially different.

As a random sample, I selected the first ten names on each page of U.S. Census, 1860, Georgia, Schedule 4, Productions of Agriculture, Dougherty and Thomas counties (Library, Duke University, Durham, North Carolina) and U.S. Census, 1860, Mississippi, Schedule 4, De Soto and Marshall counties (Mississippi State Archives, Jackson). From the U.S. Census, 1860, Georgia, Schedule 2, Slave Inhabitants, Dougherty and Thomas counties, and U.S. Census, 1860, Mississippi, Schedule 2, De Soto and Marshall counties (National Archives, Washington), I determined the number of slaves held by each agriculturist in my sample. Where Schedule 4 gave the amount of produce but not its monetary value, I used a specially prepared price schedule in order to translate the amounts into dollar values. See Eugene D. Genovese, "The Limits of Agrarian Reform in the Slave South" (unpublished Ph.D. thesis, Columbia University, 1959), appendixes.

[9] These expenditures were for blacksmiths' services, road building, cabin building, and even for such trivial tasks as the erection of door frames. The accounts often run into hundreds of dollars. See, for example, Moses St. John R. Liddell and Family Papers (Library, Louisiana State University, Baton Rouge), Haller Nutt Papers (Library, Duke University, Durham, N.C.), Everard Green Baker Papers (Southern Historical Collection, University of North Carolina, Chapel Hill), I, 139; Killona Plantation Journals (Mississippi State Department of Archives and History, Jackson), I, 60 ff.

[10] Roy M. Robbins, *Our Landed Heritage; the Public Domain, 1776–1936* (New York, 1950), 177; Joseph Brennan, *Social Conditions in Industrial Rhode Island, 1820–1860* (Washington, 1940), 18; Samuel Rezneck, "The Rise and Early Development of Industrial Consciousness in the United States, 1760–1830," *Journal of Economic and Business History*, IV (1932), 784–811; Isaac Lippincott, *A History of Manufactures in the Ohio Valley to the Year 1860* . . . (New York, 1914), 63–65; Grace Pierpont Fuller, *An Introduction to the History of Connecticut As a Manufacturing State* (Northampton, Mass., 1915), 45; James Neal Primm, *Economic Policy in a Development of a Western State, Missouri* (Cam-

the West. As the shrewd Achille Murat noted in the 1830's, the manufacturing interest of the West "is not constituted by the manufactories which exist, but those which they look forward to in prospective."[11] An agrarianism uncompromisingly hostile to industry and urbanization — to what was called "manufacturing as a system" — existed only in the South and can not be separated from the ideological leadership of the slaveholding planters. Even there, those seriously interested in economic progress saw the link between agricultural reform and industrialization and tried to work out proposals for increased manufactures that would be palatable to their fellow slaveholders.[12]

The West was able to import capital because Eastern manufacturers and European creditors were confident of her growth and prosperity. Outside credits at that time had to be accumulated by the importation of commodities and the maintenance of an unfavorable trade balance. The immense internal market guaranteed the West an import surplus until 1850. Its insatiable demand for manufactured articles contributed to the unfavorable trade balance of the United States, but on the whole this was not a serious problem for the country because American importers were strong enough to obtain long-term credits on relatively easy terms; and, during the 1850's, profits from shipping and other invisible gains largely restored the balance.[13] Thus, on the one hand, the national economy was sufficiently strong to overcome the worst effects of a trade deficit, and, on the other hand, the agrarian West was able to obtain the credits required for industrial development. The South did not benefit from this arrangement. It provided an exportable surplus, which, although of great help to the national economy in offsetting the large quantity of imports, was exploited by Northern capital. The invisible gains that were so important to national growth were made partly at the expense of the South.

The population statistics of 1860 offer a clue to the structure of the market. If we exclude Maryland, in which slavery was declining, and Delaware, which was a slave state in name only, the median population per square mile in the slave states was 18, and Kentucky was high with 31. In comparison, Massachusetts had a population of 158 per square mile; Rhode Island, 138; Connecticut, 98; New York, 84; New Jersey, 81; and so forth. In the West, Ohio had 59; Indiana, 40; and Illinois, 31.

These figures do not tell the important part of the story. A country that is sparsely settled, in absolute terms, may have a high population density, in economic terms, if its system of transportation and commodity production are well developed and integrated. For example, the Northern states in 1860 had a much

bridge, Mass., 1954), 56–59; Frank W. Taussig, *The Tariff History of the United States* (7th ed., New York, 1923), 68–108; and Bray Hammond, *Banks and Politics in America, from the Revolution to the Civil War* (Princeton, 1957).

[11] Achille Murat, *America and the Americans* (New York, 1849), 19.

[12] For examples, see the remarks of M. W. Philips and John J. Williams, *Mississippi Planter and Mechanic*, II (May 1858), 157–58; of Thomas J. Lemay, *Arator*, I (November 1855), 237; and of Andrew Johnson, *Congressional Globe*, XXIII, 312.

[13] See Simon S. Kuznets, *Economic Change; Selected Essays in Business Cycles, National Income, and Economic Growth* (New York, 1953), 307 ff; and Charles F. Dunbar, *Economic Essays* (New York, 1904), 268.

higher population density — from an economic point of view — than the thickly populated countries of Asia. When we consider the superiority of Northern transportation and economic integration, relative to those of the South, we must conclude that the difference in the magnitude of the market greatly exceeded that suggested by the population figures.

Historians have long appreciated — at least since the pioneer researches of U. B. Phillips — that the Southern trasportation system tied the staple-producing areas to the ports and that this was the best possible arrangement for the planters. The planters controlled the state legislatures in an era in which state participation was decisive in railroad construction and generally refused to assume the tax burden necessary to open the back country and thereby encourage and strengthen politically suspect farmers. Without a fully developed railroad network tying the South into an economic unit, the absorption of nonstaple producers into the market economy, except in a peripheral way, was impossible. Poor transportation was, for example, one important factor in the retardation of the Southern cotton textile industry.[14]

With good reason alert Southerners spoke of the connection among railroads, markets, diversified agriculture, and manufacturing. James Robb pointedly described improved transportation and greater industry as necessary ingredients in the process of unifying the South. Oscar M. Lieber noted that without an adequate transportation system South Carolina farmers were prevented from entering the market as corn producers. John Bell warmly supported federal land grants to railroads to strengthen the bonds of commodity production.[15] Within the South these men could, at best, expect to be received with an impatient silence. Where their message was sometimes listened to attentively was in the upper South, as for example in what came to be West Virginia; the subsequent construction of road and railroad links to existing markets generally bound parts of the upper South to the free states and helped remove them from the slave-holders' domain.

In the slave South the home market consisted primarily of the plantations, which bought foodstuffs from the West and manufactured goods from the East. The planters needed increased Southern manufacturing but only for certain purposes. They needed cheap slave clothing, cotton gins and a few crude agricultural implements, rope for cotton bagging, and so forth. This narrow market could not compare with the tremendous Western demand for industrial commodities of all kinds, especially for agricultural implements and machinery on the more capital-intensive Western farms. The Northeast had the capital and skilled labor for fairly large-scale production and had established its control over existing markets in the North and West. Southern manufacturers could not

[14] See Milton S. Heath, *Constructive Liberalism: the Role of the State in Economic Development in Georgia to 1860* (Cambridge, Mass., 1954), 290–91, and Seth Hammond, "Location Theory and the Cotton Industry," *Journal of Economic History*, II (1942), Supp., 101–17. The opposition of entrenched landowning classes to the extension of transportation has been general in colonial, underdeveloped countries. See George Wythe, *Industry in Latin America* (New York, 1945), 4.

[15] De Bow (ed.), *Industrial Resources*, II, 154; Oscar M. Lieber, *Report on the Survey of South Carolina . . . 1857* (Columbia, 1858), 106; *Congressional Globe*, XXI, pt. 1, 867–68.

hope to compete with Northern outside the South, and the same conditions that brought about Northern control of the Northern market made possible Northern penetration of the Southern market despite the costs of transportation.

The South was caught in a contradiction similar to that facing many underdeveloped countries today. On the one hand, it provided a market for outside industry. On the other hand, that very market was too small to sustain industry on a scale large enough to compete with outsiders who could draw upon wider markets. Only one fifth of the manufacturing establishments of the United States were in the South, and their average capitalization was well below that of the manufacturing establishments of the free states. Consider the situation in two industries of special importance to the South — cotton textiles and agricultural implements. New England had almost three times as many cotton factories as the entire South in 1860, and yet the average capitalization was almost twice as great. The concentration in this industry had proceeded so far by 1850 that of the more than 1,000 cotton factories in the United States only forty-one had one half the total capital investment. As for the agricultural implement and machinery industry, New York, Pennsylvania, Ohio, and Illinois each had a greater total capital investment than did the entire South, and in three of these the average capitalization was between two and two and a half times as great as the average in the South.[16] This Northern advantage led Edmund Ruffin and T. L. Clingman, among others, to look forward to a Southern confederacy protected by high tariffs against Northern goods.[17]

In view of the nature of the plantation market it is not surprising that data on the cotton textile industry almost invariably reveal that Southern producers concentrated upon the production of the cheapest and coarsest kind of cloth to be used in the making of slave clothing.[18] Even so, local industrialists had to compete for this market with Northerners who sometimes shipped direct and sometimes established Southern branches and who had facilities for the collection and processing of second-hand clothing.[19] Just as New England supplied

[16] U.S. Census Office, *Manufactures of the United States in 1860 . . .* (Washington, 1865), xxi, ccxvii, lxxiii, 729–30; Evelyn H. Knowlton, *Pepperell's Progress; History of a Cotton Textile Company, 1844–1945* (Cambridge, Mass., 1948), 32. The average capitalization of manufacturing establishments was in 1850 more than 25% higher in the free states and territories than in the slave states, and the gap widened in the 1850's when the increase in average capital investment was 68% in the free states and territories and only 51% in the slave states. The lower South (North Carolina, South Carolina, Georgia, Florida, Alabama, Mississippi, Louisiana, and Texas) fell even further behind. The average capitalization here, 38% less than in the free states in 1850, was 47% less by 1860. Furthermore, the rate of increase in the number of establishments during this decade was appreciably greater in the North than in the South.

[17] Edmund Ruffin, Incidents of My Life, 19–20, in Edmund Ruffin Papers (Southern Historical Collection, University of North Carolina); T. L. Clingman's speech to the House of Representatives, January 22, 1850, in *Selections from the Speeches and Writings of Hon. Thomas L. Clingman of North Carolina . . .* (Raleigh, N.C., 1877), 233–54, especially 250.

[18] See Patent Office, *Annual Report, 1857, Agriculture, Senate Exec. Docs.,* 35 Cong., 1 Sess., No. 30, pt. 4 (Serial 928), 308–309, 318; and Richard H. Shryock, "The Early Industrial Revolution in the Empire State," *Georgia Historical Quarterly,* XI (June 1927), 128.

[19] Jesse Eliphalet Pope, *The Clothing Industry in New York* (Columbia, Mo., 1905), 6–7.

much of the South's "Negro cloth," so it supplied much of the boots and shoes. Firms like Batchellor Brothers of Brookfield produced cheap shoes especially for the Southern market and as early as 1837 opened a branch at Mobile to consolidate its Southern market.[20]

Producers of better cotton goods had little hope of making a living in the South. Occasionally, a William Gregg could penetrate Northern markets successfully, but Southern demand for such goods was too small to have much effect on the industry generally. Northern firms like the Pepperell Manufacturing Company or A. A. Lawrence Company did little business in the South. On the other hand a rising demand for textiles in the agrarian West had greatly influenced the New England cotton industry since 1814.[21]

The Southern iron industry, hampered as it was by the restricted railroad development in the slave states, also had a poor time of it. American iron producers generally were handicapped because much of the country's railroad iron was being imported. The small scale of operations and resultant cost schedule, which hurt the industry nationally, hit the Southern manufacturers especially hard. Dependent upon a weak local market, Southern iron manufacturers had great difficulty holding their own even during the prosperous 1850's.

No wonder the Augusta, Georgia, Commercial Convention added to its demand that Southerners buy Southern goods the qualification, unless you can get Northern cheaper. And no wonder the proposal was ridiculed as amounting to "Never kiss the maid if you can kiss the mistress, unless you like the maid better."[22]

We can not measure precisely the extent of the Southern market nor even make a reliable, general, quantitative comparison between the Southern and Western rural markets, but we can glean from various sources some notion of the immense difference. For example, Phelps, Dodge & Co., a prominent cotton shipping firm that also distributed metals, tools, machinery, clothing, and an assortment of other items, reported at the beginning of the Civil War that only five per cent of its sales were to the South and that those were primarily to the non-cotton states. We do not know the extent of the firm's participation in the cotton export trade, but it was considerable. Phelps, Dodge & Co. was in an excellent position to exchange industrial goods for cotton, but the Southern demand for imported goods could not compare in bulk or value with the supply of cotton. In the West, on the other hand, farmers and townsmen provided a growing and lucrative market, and the firm had more customers in Ohio than in any state except New York.[23]

An examination of the 1860 manuscript census returns and other primary sources pertaining to two representative cotton counties in Mississippi and to two in Georgia permits us to judge roughly the extent of the market in the

[20] Blanche Evans Hazard, *The Organization of the Boot and Shoe Industry in Massachusetts Before 1875* (Cambridge, Mass., 1921), 57–58.

[21] Knowlton, *Pepperell's Progress*, 83–84; Caroline F. Ware, *The Early New England Cotton Manufacture; a Study in Industrial Beginnings* (Boston, 1931), 48, 55.

[22] Herbert Wender, *Southern Commercial Conventions, 1837–1859* (Baltimore, 1930), 25.

[23] Richard Lowitt, *A Merchant Prince of the Nineteenth Century, William E. Dodge* (New York, 1954), 31 ff, 37.

cotton belt by estimating the expenditures made by planters and farmers in these counties. (See above, note 8.) The estimates are the most generous possible and exaggerate the extent of the Southern rural market in relation to the Western in two ways: There were far more rural poor with little or no purchasing power in the cotton belt than in the West, and the concentration of landholdings in the South resulted in fewer landowners than could be found in a Western area of comparable size. Thus, even if the estimate of the expenditures made by these Southern planters and farmers had been larger than the expenditures of a similar group of individual proprietors in the West — which was by no means true — the total purchased in each county would still have been far less than in a comparable Western area. Furthermore, as food was a major item in the expenditures of the Southerners, the market for industrial commodities was much smaller than might appear.

The concentration of landholding and slaveholding in the Mississippi counties meant that six per cent of the landowners commanded one third of the gross income and probably a much higher percentage of the net. That is, the majority of landowners were faced with a disproportionately small portion of the total income accruing to the cotton economy as a whole.

Only the largest planters — ten per cent of the landowners — spent more than $1,000 a year for food and supplies, and they rarely spent more. These expenditures include the total purchases for the slaves. The slaveholding farms and plantations in Mississippi annually spent above thirty or thirty-five dollars per person for food and supplies; nonslaveholders spent about twenty-five dollars per person. In Georgia slaveholding farms and plantations spent about twenty-five dollars per person, and nonslaveholders were just about self-sufficient.[24] In contrast, Philip Foner reports that contemporary newspapers and other sources indicate that the small farmers who made up the great majority of the rural population of the West accumulated store bills of from one hundred to six hundred dollars.[25] Even if we allow for considerable exaggeration and assume that the accounts were generally closer to the lower estimate, these figures, which are exclusive of cash purchases, mail orders, payments to drummers, and so forth, are at least a clue to the impressive purchasing power of the Western countryside.

However imprecise the estimates for the South may be, they indicate the lack of purchasing power among the rural population of the cotton belt and demonstrate how greatly the situation there differed from that in the West. With such a home market the slave economy could not sustain more than the lowest level of commodity production apart from that of a few staples. The success of William Gregg as a textile manufacturer in South Carolina and the data produced by Professor John Hebron Moore showing that a cotton textile industry could and did exist in ante bellum Mississippi would seem to contradict this conclusion; but Gregg, who was aware of the modest proportions of the home market, warned Southerners against trying to produce for local needs and suggested that they focus on the wholesale market. His own company at Graniteville, South

[24] In Mississippi a sample of 584 units with 7,289 slaves and an estimated 2,480 whites spent about $316,500; in Georgia a sample of 100 units with 2,354 slaves and an estimated 710 whites spent about $73,300.

[25] Foner, *Business & Slavery*, 143.

Carolina, produced fine cotton goods that sold much better in New York than in the South. Gregg's success in the Northern market could not easily be duplicated by others, and when he discussed the Southern market, he felt compelled, as did Benjamin L. C. Wailes and other astute observers, to advocate production of cheap cotton goods for the plantations.[26] Moore's conclusion that his data prove the adaptability of manufacturing to the lower South requires for substantiation more than evidence of particular successes, no matter how impressive;[27] it requires evidence that Southern producers were strong enough to drive out Northern competition and, more important, that the market was large enough to sustain more than a few firms.

The plantation system did have its small compensations for industry. The planters' taste for luxuries, for example, proved a boon to the Petersburg iron industry, which supplied plantations with cast-iron fences, lawn ornaments, balconies, fancy gates, and other decorative articles.[28] A silk industry emerged briefly but was destroyed by climatic conditions as well as by a shortage of capital.[29] The hemp industry, which supplied rope for cotton baling, depended heavily on the plantation market.

Some Southern industrialists, especially those in the border states, did good business in the North. Louisville tobacco and hemp manufacturers sold much of their output in Ohio. Botts and Burfoot of Richmond, Virginia, reported the sale of $1,000-worth of straw cutters in the North during a six-month period. The more successful Southern iron producers were those of the upper South, who were able to sell outside the slave states. Smith and Perkins of Alexandria, Virginia, began production of locomotives and railroad cars in the 1850's and obtained a good many orders from the North; but the company failed because shipping costs made consolidation of its Northern market difficult and because only a few orders were forthcoming from the South. Similarly, the paper industry in South Carolina did well until the 1850's, when Northern orders dropped and no Southern orders appeared.[30] The political dangers of these links with the free states

[26] William Gregg, *Essays on Domestic Industry; or An Inquiry into the Expediency of Establishing Cotton Manufactures in South-Carolina* (Graniteville, S.C., 1941), 4; Benjamin L. C. Wailes, *Address Delivered in the College Chapel Before the Agricultural, Horticultural and Botanical Society, of Jefferson College* (Natchez, Miss., 1841), 22–23; *De Bow's Review*, XXIX (October 1860), 496–97; Broadus Mitchell, *William Gregg, Factory Master of the Old South* (Chapel Hill, N.C., 1928), 106.

[27] John Hebron Moore, "Mississippi's Ante-Bellum Textile Industry," *Journal of Mississippi History*, XVI (April 1954), 81.

[28] Edward A. Wyatt, IV, "Rise of Industry in Ante-Bellum Petersburg," *William and Mary College Quarterly*, s. 3, XVII (January 1937), 32.

[29] Southerners were very much interested in silk cultivation and manufacture and saw fine market possibilities. See Charles G. Parsons, *Inside View of Slavery; or a Tour Among the Planters* (Boston, 1855), 71 ff; C. O. Cathey, "Sidney Weller: Ante-Bellum Promoter of Agricultural Reform," *North Carolina Historical Review*, XXI (January 1954), 6; Spaulding Trafton, "Silk Culture in Henderson County, Kentucky," *Filson Club History Quarterly*, IV (October 1930), 184–89.

[30] Lippincott, *Manufactures in the Ohio Valley*, 64; *Southern Planter*, III (April 1843), advertisement on back cover; Lester J. Cappon, "Trend of the Southern Iron Industry Under the Plantation System," *Journal of Economic and Business History*, II (February 1930), 361, 371, 376; Carrol H. Quenzel, "The Manufacture of Locomotives and Cars in Alexandria in the 1850's," *Virginia Magazine of History and Biography*, LXII (April 1954),

were widely appreciated. The Virginia Commercial Convention, for example, reported that West Virginia was being cut off from the South in this way.[31] During the Civil War, William Henry Holcombe, a thoughtful doctor from Natchez, listed in his diary various reasons for the adherence of the border states to the Union and placed close commercial ties high on the list.[32] One suspects that there was more than hindsight here, for politically sophisticated Southerners were alert to the danger well before 1861. But what could they have done about it?

The inability of the slave South to generate an adequate rural market inhibited industrialization and urbanization, which in turn limited the market for agricultural produce and undermined attempts at diversification. With the exception of New Orleans and Baltimore, the slave states had no large cities, and few reached the size of 15,000. The urban population of the South could not compare with that of the Northeast, as is generally appreciated; but, more to the point, it could not compare with that of the agrarian West either. The urban population of the lower South in 1860 was only seven per cent of the total population, and in the western part of the lower South, embracing most of the cotton belt, there was a relative decline during the preceding twenty years. In New England, the percentage was thirty-seven; in the Middle Atlantic states, including Ohio, thirty-five; and perhaps most significantly, in Indiana, Illinois, Michigan, and Wisconsin, fourteen.[33]

The urban market in the South was even less developed than these figures suggest. If we except New Orleans, which was a special case, three cities of the lower South had a population of 15,000 or more: Mobile, Charleston, and Savannah, with a combined population of 92,000. Of this number, thirty-seven per cent were slaves and free Negroes, who may be assumed to have represented only minimal purchasing power. In the 1850's American families certainly did not spend less than forty per cent of their incomes on food, and the importance of a large urban market for foodstuffs may be judged accordingly.[34]

Eugene W. Hilgard, state geologist of Mississippi, explained his state's failure to develop a cattle industry largely by the absence of a local market. Similarly, Oscar M. Lieber, state geologist of South Carolina, warned farmers in a state that was never comfortably self-sufficient in corn not to produce more corn than they could consume, for there was no place to market the surplus. Charles Yancey of Buckingham County, Virginia, wrote that planters and farmers would

---

182 ff; Ernest M. Lander, Jr., "Paper Manufacturing in South Carolina Before the Civil War," North Carolina Historical Review, XXIX (April 1952), 225 ff.

[31] De Bow (ed.), Industrial Resources, III, 465.

[32] William Henry Holcombe Diary (Southern Manuscript Collection, University of North Carolina), entry for September 6, 1855, but obviously written in 1861.

[33] Urban area defined as incorporated places of 2,500 or more. See U.S. Bureau of the Census, Urban Population in the U.S. from the First Census (1790) to the Fifteenth Census (1930) . . . (Washington, 1939).

[34] This estimate is from Edgar W. Martin, The Standard of Living in 1860 (Chicago, 1942), 11–12, and may greatly underestimate the situation in urban households. According to Richard O. Cummings, laborers in Massachusetts probably spent about three fourths of their weekly wages on food in 1860. R. O. Cummings, The American and His Food; a History of Food Habits in the United States (Chicago, 1941), 266.

not grow oats because the only possibility of disposing of them lay in person to person barter.[35]

The weakness of the market for agricultural produce had many detrimental consequences for the South, of which we may mention only two. First, those sections of the border states which found markets in the Northern cities were increasingly drawn into the political-economic orbit of the free states at the very moment when the slave states required maximum solidarity to preserve their system. Second, the weakness of the market doomed the hopes of agricultural reformers and transformed their cry for diversification into a cry for a backward step toward natural economy.

When that great antislavery Kentuckian, Cassius M. Clay, finally receives from historians the honor and attention that he deserves, he will surely be recognized as one of the most penetrating commentators on the economics of slavery. Consider his remarks on the problem of markets, with which we are presently concerned:

> Lawyers, merchants, mechanics, laborers, who are your consumers; Robert Wickliffe's two hundred slaves? How many clients do you find, how many goods do you sell, how many hats, coats, saddles, and trunks do you make for these two hundred slaves? Does Mr. Wickliffe lay out as much for himself and his two hundred slaves as two hundred freemen do? . . . All our towns dwindle, and our farmers lose, in consequence, all home markets. Every farmer bought out by the slave system send off the consumers of the manufacturers of the town: when the consumers are gone, the mechanic must go also. . . . A home market cannot exist in a slave state.[36]

Plantation slavery, then, so limited the purchasing power of the South that it could not sustain much industry. That industry which could be raised usually lacked a home market of sufficient scope to permit large-scale operation; the resultant cost of production was often too high for success in competition with Northern firms drawing on much wider markets. Without sufficient industry to support urbanization, a general and extensive diversification of agriculture was unthinkable. Whatever other factors need to be considered in a complete analysis, the low level of demand in this plantation-based slave society was sufficient to retard the economic development of the South.

[35] Eugene W. Hilgard, *Report on the Geology and Agriculture of the State of Mississippi* (Jackson, 1860), 250–51; Lieber, *Report,* 106. See also Patent Office, *Annual Report, 1849, Agriculture, Senate Exec. Docs.,* 31 Cong., 1 Sess., No. 15, pt. 2 (Serial 556), 137.

[36] Horace Greeley (ed.), *The Writings of Cassius Marcellus Clay* . . . (New York, 1848), 179, 227. For a recent biography, see David L. Smiley, *Lion of White Hall: The Life of Cassius M. Clay* (Madison, Wis., 1962).

Resistance to Slavery

GEORGE M. FREDRICKSON AND CHRISTOPHER LASCH

How did the slave view his predicament? The difficulty for the historian is that there is virtually no evidence that can be brought directly to bear on the question, for although there are a number of narratives composed by emancipated slaves, it is virtually impossible to assess the states of mind of the hundreds of thousands of human beings who lived and died within the confines of the peculiar institution. Traditionally, those who have defended the ante-bellum Southern way of life have maintained that slaves were contented with their lot and that they established harmonious relations with their masters. Conversely, historians of an abolitionist bent have argued that the innumerable instances of discontent and the few of outright rebellion indicate that Negroes characteristically resisted their owners. There is evidence for both points of view, and historians' personal attitudes toward the modern race question have generally determined their interpretative stances. A few years ago, however, Stanley Elkins urged that the slaves' apparent acceptance of an intolerable existence could be understood only by analogy to a psychologically comparable modern situation, the behavior of the Jews in German concentration camps. In the following essay George M. Fredrickson and Christopher Lasch concur in Elkins's behaviorist approach, but contend that he used an inappropriate analogy. Comparison with concentration camp inmates explains why Negroes accommodated themselves to slavery, but it does not help us to understand why so many resisted and rebelled. Fredrickson and Lasch propose a "total institution," the modern prison, as an alternative analogy, on the grounds that the behavior of men in prisons displays both the acceptance and resistance manifested by slaves. They draw on the extensive sociological literature of prison life to illustrate the relevant patterns of prisoner-slave behavior, and claim to have discovered a model that very nearly corresponds to the structure of slave society. Are analogy and model-building valid historical methods? What is the corollary, for slavery, of the prisoner's admitted acceptance of the legitimacy of his incarceration?

I

The issues involved in the study of "resistance" to slavery are badly in need of clarification. The problem, one would suppose, is not whether the plantation slave was happy with his lot but whether he actively resisted it. But even this

Reprinted by permission of the publisher from *Civil War History*, 13 (December 1967), pp. 315–329.

initial clarification does not come easily. Too many writers have assumed that the problem of resistance consists mainly of deciding whether slaves were docile or discontented and whether their masters were cruel or kind. In this respect and in others, as Stanley Elkins noted several years ago, the discussion of slavery has locked itself into the terms of an old debate.[1] The pro-slavery stereotype of the contented slave, which was taken over without much conceptual refinement by U. B. Phillips and others, has been attacked by recent historians in language much the same as that employed by the abolitionists more than a hundred years ago, according to which slaves hated bondage and longed to be free. "That they had no understanding of freedom," Kenneth Stampp argues, ". . . is hard to believe." A few pages later, and without any intervening evidence, Stampp progresses from this cautious thought to a fullblown statement of the case for "resistance." "Slave resistance, whether bold and persistent or mild and sporadic, created for all slaveholders a serious problem of discipline." He concludes, in a burst of rhetoric, that "the record of slave resistance forms a chapter in the story of the endless struggle to give dignity to human life."[2]

It should be apparent that the traditional terms of reference, on either side of the dispute, are not sufficiently precise to serve as instruments of analysis. One of the faults of Phillips' work is his consistent failure to distinguish between cruelty and coercion. By compiling instances of the kindness and benevolence of masters, Phillips proved to his own satisfaction that slavery was a mild and permissive institution, the primary function of which was not so much to produce a marketable surplus as to ease the accommodation of the lower race into the culture of the higher. The critics of Phillips have tried to meet him on his own ground. Where he compiled lists of indulgences and benefactions, they have assembled lists of atrocities. Both methods suffer from the same defect: they attempt to solve a conceptual problem — what did slavery do to the slave — by accumulating quantitative evidence. Both methods assert that plantations conformed to one of two patterns, terror or indulgence, and then seek to prove these assertions by accumulating evidence from plantation diaries, manuals of discipline, letters and other traditional sources for the study of slavery. But for every instance of physical cruelty on the one side an enterprising historian can find an instance of indulgence on the other. The only conclusion that one can legitimately draw from this debate is that great variations in treatment existed from plantation to plantation. (But as we shall see, this conclusion, barren in itself, can be made to yield important results if one knows how to use it.)

Even if we could make valid generalizations about the severity of the regime, these statements would not automatically answer the question of whether or not widespread resistance took place. If we are to accept the testimony of Frederick Douglass, resistance was more likely to result from indulgence and rising expectations than from brutalizing severity.[3] A recent study of the geographical distribution of authentic slave revolts shows that most of them occurred in cities

[1] Stanley Elkins, *Slavery: A Problem in American Institutional and Intellectual Life* (Chicago, 1959), Ch. 1.

[2] Kenneth Stampp, *The Peculiar Institution* (New York, 1956), pp. 88, 91.

[3] Frederick Douglass, *The Narrative of the Life of Frederick Douglass, An American Slave* (Cambridge, 1960), pp. 132–133.

and in areas of slavebreeding and diversified agriculture, where, according to all accounts, the regime was more indulgent than in the productive plantation districts of the Cotton Kingdom.[4] Open resistance cannot be inferred from the extreme physical cruelty of the slave system, even if the system's cruelty could be demonstrated statistically.

II

There is the further question of what constitutes resistance. When Kenneth Stampp uses the term he means much more than open and flagrant defiance of the system. To him resistance is all noncooperation on the part of the slaves. And it cannot be denied that the annals of slavery abound in examples of this kind of behavior. Slaves avoided work by pretending to be sick or by inventing a hundred other plausible pretexts. They worked so inefficiently as to give rise to the suspicion that they were deliberately sabotaging the crop. They stole from their masters without compunction, a fact which gave rise to the complaint that slaves had no moral sense, but which is better interpreted as evidence of a double standard — cheating the master while dealing honorably with other slaves. Nor was this all. Their grievances or frustrations led at times to the willful destruction of the master's property by destroying tools, mistreating animals, and setting fire to plantation buildings. Less frequently, they took the ultimate step of violent attack on the master himself. Perhaps the most common form of obvious noncooperation was running away; every large plantation had its share of fugitives.[5]

The question which inevitably arises, as Stampp piles up incident after incident in order to show that slaves were "a troublesome property," is whether this pattern of noncooperation constitutes resistance. Resistance is a political concept. Political activity, in the strictest sense, is organized collective action which aims at affecting the distribution of power in a community; more broadly, it might be said to consist of any activity, either of individuals or of groups, which is designed to create a consciousness of collective interest, such consciousness being the prerequisite for effective action in the realm of power. Organized resistance is of course only one form of political action. Others include interest-group politics; coalitions of interest groups organized as factions or parties; reform movements; or, at an international level, diplomacy and war. In total institutions, however, conventional politics are necessarily nonexistent.[6] Politics, if they exist at all, must take the form of resistance: collective action designed to subvert the system, to facilitate and regularize escape from it; or, at the very least, to force important changes in it.

Among despised and downtrodden people in general, the most rudimentary form of political action is violence; sporadic and usually short-lived outbursts

---

[4] Marion de B. Kilson, "Towards Freedom: An Analysis of Slave Revolts in the United States," *Phylon*, XXV (1964), 179–183.

[5] Stampp, *Peculiar Institution*, Ch. III.

[6] Total institutions are distinguished not by the absolute power of the authorities — a definition which, as will become clear, prejudges an important issue — but by the fact that they are self-contained, so that every detail of life is regulated in accordance with the dominant purpose of the institution. Whether that purpose is defined as healing, punishment, forced labor, or (in the case of the concentration camps) terror, all total institutions are set up in such a way as to preclude any form of politics based on consent.

of destruction, based on a common sense of outrage and sometimes inspired by a millennialistic ideology. Peasant revolts, all over the world, have usually conformed to this type.[7] In total institutions, prison riots are perhaps the nearest equivalent. In American slavery, the few documented slave rebellions fall into the same pattern.[8] What makes these upheavals political at all is that they rest on some sense, however primitive, of collective victimization. They require, moreover, at least a minimum of organization and planning. What makes them rudimentary is that they do not aim so much at changing the balance of power as at giving expression on the one hand to apocalyptic visions of retribution, and on the other to an immediate thirst for vengeance directed more at particular individuals than at larger systems of authority. In the one case, the sense of grievance finds an outlet in indiscriminate violence (as against Jews); in the other, it attaches itself to a particular embodiment of authority (as in prisons, where a specific departure from established routine may set off a strike or riot demanding the authority's dismissal and a return to the previous regime). But in neither case does collective action rest on a realistic perception of the institutional structure as a whole and the collective interest of its victims in subverting it. That explains why such outbreaks of violence tend to subside very quickly, leaving the exploitive structure intact. Underground resistance to the Nazis in western Europe, on the other hand, precisely because it expressed itself in an organized underground instead of in futile outbreaks of indiscriminate violence, had a continuous existence which testifies to the highly political character of its objectives.

It is easy to show that Negro slaves did not always cooperate with the system of slavery. It is another matter to prove that noncooperation amounted to political resistance. Malingering may have reflected no more than a disinclination to work, especially when the rewards were so meager. Likewise, what is taken for sabotage may have originated in apathy and indifference. Acts of violence are subject to varying interpretations. If there is something undeniably political about an organized, premeditated rebellion, an isolated act of violence could arise from a purely personal grievance. Even the motive of flight is obscure: was it an impulse, prompted by some special and immediate affront, or was it desertion, a sort of separate peace? These acts in themselves tell us very little. We begin to understand them only when we understand the conceptual distinction between resistance and noncooperation; and even then, we still feel the need of a more general set of conceptions, derived from recorded experience, to which slavery — an unrecorded experience, except from the masters' point of view — can be compared; some general model which will enable us to grasp imaginatively the system as a whole.

[7] See E. J. Hobsbawm, *Primitive Rebels: Studies in Archaic Forms of Social Movement in the 19th and 20th Centuries* (Manchester, 1959); Norman Cohn, *The Pursuit of the Millennium* (New York, 1957).

[8] Nat Turner's rebellion in 1831, the only significant slave uprising in the period 1820–1860 that got beyond the plotting stage, would seem to be comparable to a millennialist peasants' revolt. Turner was a preacher who according to his own testimony, received the visitation of a spirit commanding him to "fight against the serpent, for the time was fast approaching when the first should be last and the last should be first." Quoted in Herbert Aptheker, *American Negro Slave Revolts* (New York, 1943), p. 296. See also Aptheker, *Nat Turner's Slave Rebellion* (New York, 1966).

III

Only the testimony of the slaves could tell us, once and for all, whether slaves resisted slavery. In the absence of their testimony, it is tempting to resort to analogies. Indeed it is almost impossible to avoid them. Those who condemn analogies, pretending to argue from the documentary evidence alone, delude themselves. Resistance to slavery cannot be established (any more than any other general conception of the institution can be established) without making an implicit analogy between Negro slavery and the struggles of free men, in our own time, "to give dignity to human life" by resisting oppression. The question, in the case of slavery, is not whether historians should argue from analogy but whether they are willing to make their analogies explicit.

Stanley Elkins compares slavery to the Nazi concentration camps and concludes that the effect of slavery was to break down the slave's adult personality and to reduce him to a state of infantile dependence, comparable to the condition observed by survivors of the concentration camps. In evaluating this particular analogy, we are entitled to ask how well it explains what we actually know about slavery. In one respect, it explains too much. It explains the fact that there were no slave rebellions in the United States comparable to those which took place in Latin America, but it also rules out the possibility of non-cooperation. Elkins' analogy suggests a state of internalized dependency that does not fit the facts of widespread intransigence, insubordination, and mischief-making. Stampp may not adequately explain this pattern of behavior, but he convinces us that it existed. Elkins is open to criticism on empirical grounds for failing to take into account a vast amount of evidence that does not fit his theory of slave behavior. Many of Elkins' critics, however, have not concerned themselves with the substance of this analogy. Raising neither empirical nor theoretical objections against it, they have seized on its mere existence as a means of discrediting Elkins' work. He should rather be congratulated for having made the analogy explicit, thereby introducing into the study of slavery the kinds of questions that modern studies of total institutions have dealt with far more systematically than conventional studies of slavery.

Elkins was careful to emphasize the limits of the comparison. He did not argue that the plantation resembled a concentration camp with respect to intentions or motives; "even 'cruelty,'" he added, "was not indispensable as an item in my equation." His "essentially limited purpose" in bringing the two institutions together was to show the psychological effects of closed systems of control; and the objections to the analogy may after all derive not from the analogy itself but from a tendency, among Elkins' critics, to take it too literally. As Elkins observes, the "very vividness and particularity [of analogies] are coercive: they are almost too concrete. One's impulse is thus to reach for extremes. The thing is either taken whole hog . . . ; or it is rejected out of hand on the ground that not all of the parts fit." It is precisely because all the parts don't fit that an analogy is an analogy rather than a literal correspondence, and it ought to be enough, therefore, if just one of the parts demonstrably fits.[9]

The real objection to Elkins' analogy is not that analogies in themselves are pernicious but that there is no compelling theoretical reason, in this case, to

[9] Elkins, *Slavery*, pp. 104, 226.

stop with one. The concentration camp is only one of many total institutions with which slavery might have been compared; a total institution being defined, in Erving Goffman's words, as "a place of residence and work where a large number of like-situated individuals, cut off from the wider society for an appreciable period of time, together lead an enclosed, formally administered round of life."[10] An excellent example — the one, indeed, that springs immediately to mind — is the prison, "providing," Goffman says, that "we appreciate that what is prison-like about prisons is found in institutions whose members have broken no laws."[11] In several respects, prisons, especially penitentiaries, are more analogous to plantation slavery than concentration camps. Prisons are not, like the concentration camps, designed as experiments in deliberate dehumanization, although they often have dehumanizing effects; in this respect the motive behind the system more nearly approximates that of slavery than of the concentration camp. More important, the problem of control is more nearly analogous. The disproportion between the authority of the guards and the impotence of the inmates is not absolute, as it was at Dachau and Buchenwald, but subject, as it seems to have been under slavery, to a number of variables — the temperament of the guard or master, the composition of the prisoners or slaves, the immediate history of the institutions involved.

Prison officials, like slaveowners and overseers, face a constant problem of noncooperation. "Far from being omnipotent rulers who have crushed all signs of rebellion against their regime, the custodians are engaged in a continuous struggle to maintain order — and it is a struggle in which the custodians frequently fail."[12] This situation occurs, according to the sociologist Gresham Sykes, because although the custodians enjoy an absolute monopoly of the means of violence, their enormous power does not rest on authority; that is, on "a rightful or legitimate effort to exercise control," which inspires in the governed an internalized sense of obligation to obey. In the absence of a sense of duty among the prisoners, the guards have to rely on a system of rewards, incentives, punishments, and coercion. But none of these methods can be carried too far without reaching dangerous extremes of laxity or demoralization. As in most total institutions — the concentration camp being a conspicuous exception — rigid standards of discipline tend to give way before the need to keep things running smoothly without undue effort on the part of the custodians. An absolute monopoly of violence can be used to achieve a state of total terror, but it cannot persuade men to work at their jobs or move "more than 1,200 inmates through the mess hall in a routine and orderly fashion."[13] The result, in the maximum-security prison, is a system of compromises, an uneasy give-and-take which gives prisoners a limited leverage within the system. To the extent that this adjustment limits the power of the guards, a corruption of authority takes place.[14]

[10] Erving Goffman, *Asylums: Essays on the Social Situation of Mental Patients and Other Inmates* (Garden City, 1961; Chicago, 1962), p. xiii.

[11] *Ibid.*

[12] Gresham M. Sykes, *The Society of Captives: A Study of a Maximum Security Prison* (Princeton, 1958), p. 42.

[13] *Ibid.*, p. 49.

[14] *Ibid.*, pp. 52–58.

Plantation literature produces numerous parallels. We can read the masters' incessant and heartfelt complaints about the laziness, the inefficiency, and the intractability of slaves; the difficulty of getting them to work; the difficulty of enlisting their cooperation in any activity that had to be sustained over a period of time. We can read about the system of rewards and punishments, spelled out by the master in such detail, the significance of which, we can now see, was that it had had to be resorted to precisely in the degree to which a sense of internalized obedience had failed. We see the same limitation on terror and physical coercion as has been observed in the prison; for even less than the prison authorities could the planter tolerate the demoralization resulting from an excess of violence. We can even see the same "corruption of authority" in the fact that illicit slave behavior, especially minor theft, was often tolerated by the masters in order to avoid unnecessary friction.

One of the most curious features of the "society of captives," as described by Sykes is this: that while most of the prisoners recognize the legitimacy of their imprisonment and the controls to which they are subjected, they lack any internalized sense of obligation to obey them. "The bond between recognition of the legitimacy of control and the sense of duty has been torn apart."[15] This fact about prisons makes it possible to understand a puzzling feature of the contemporary literature on slavery, which neither the model of submission nor that of resistance explains — the curious contradiction between the difficulty of discipline and the slaves' professed devotion to their masters. Those who argue that the slaves resisted slavery have to explain away their devotion as pure hypocrisy. But it is possible to accept it as sincere without endorsing the opposite view — even in the sophisticated form in which it has been cast by Stanley Elkins — that slaves were children. The sociology of total institutions provides a theory with which to reconcile the contradiction. "The custodial institution," Sykes argues, "is valuable for a theory of human behavior because it makes us realize that men need not be motivated to conform to a regime which they define as rightful."[16] It is theoretically possible, in short, that slaves could have accepted the legitimacy of their masters' authority without feeling any sense of obligation to obey it. The evidence of the masters themselves makes this conclusion seem not only possible but highly probable. Logic, moreover, supports this view. For how could a system that rigorously defined the Negro slave not merely as an inferior but as an alien, a separate order of being, inspire him with the sense of belonging on which internalized obedience necessarily has to rest?

IV

It might be argued, however, that slaves developed a sense of obedience by default, having had no taste of life outside slavery which would have made them dissatisfied, by contrast, with their treatment as slaves. It might be argued that the convict's dissatisfaction with prison conditions and the insubordination that results derives from his sense of the outside world and the satisfactions it nor-

[15] *Ibid.*, p. 46.
[16] *Ibid.*, p. 48.

mally provides; and that such a perspective must have been lacking on the plantation. Elkins, in denying the possibility of any sort of accommodation to slavery short of the complete assimilation of the master's authority by the slave, contends that a consciously defensive posture could not exist, given the total authority of the master and the lack of "alternative forces for moral and psychological orientation."[17] This objection loses its force, however, if it can be shown that the slave did in fact have chances to develop independent standards of personal satisfaction and fair treatment within the system of slavery itself. Such standards would have made possible a hedonistic strategy of accommodation, and in cases where such a strategy failed, strong feelings of personal grievance.

It is true that the plantation sealed itself off from the world, depriving the slave of nearly every influence that would have lifted him out of himself into a larger awareness of slavery as an oppressive social system which, by its very nature, denied him normal satisfaction. In order to understand why slaves did not, as Elkins suggests, become totally submissive and ready to accept any form of cruelty and humiliation, it is necessary to focus on an aspect of slavery which has been almost totally ignored in discussion of slave personality. The typical slave, although born into slavery, was not likely to spend his entire life, or indeed any considerable part of it, under a single regime. The slave child could anticipate many changes of situation. It would appear likely, from what we know of the extent of the slave trade, that most slaves changed hands at least once in their lives; slave narratives and recollections suggest that it was not at all uncommon for a single slave to belong to several masters in the course of his lifetime of servitude. In addition, the prevalence of slave-hiring, especially in the upper South, meant that many slaves experienced a temporary change of regime. Even if a slave remained on the same plantation, things could change drastically, as the result of death and the accession of an heir, or from a change of overseer (especially significant in cases of absentee ownership).[18] Given the wide variation in standards of treatment and management techniques — a variation which, we suggested earlier, seems the one inescapable conclusion to be drawn from the traditional scholarship on the management of slaves — we are left with a situation that must have had important psychological implications. An individual slave might — like Harriet Beecher Stowe's Uncle Tom — experience slavery both at its mildest and at its harshest. He might be sold from an indulgent master to a cruel one or vice versa. He might go from a farm where he maintained a close and intimate relationship with his master to a

---

[17] Elkins, *Slavery*, p. 133n.

[18] Frederic Bancroft, in *Slave Trading in the Old South* (New York, 1959), concludes (pp. 382–406) that more than 700,000 slaves were transported from the upper South to the cotton kingdom in the years 1830–1860, and that most went by way of the slave trade. He also estimates (p. 405) that in the decade 1850–1860 an annual average of approximately 140,000 slaves were sold, interstate or *intra-state,* or hired out by their masters. This meant that one slave in twenty-five changed his *de facto* master in a given year. When we add to these regular exchanges the informal transfers that went on within families, we get some idea of the instability which characterized the slave's situation in an expansive and dynamic agricultural economy. The way slaves were sometimes shuttled about is reflected in several of the slave narratives, especially Frederick Douglass, *Narrative; Solomon Northrop, Twelve Years a Slave* (Auburn, Buffalo, and London, 1853); and [Charles Ball] *Fifty Years in Chains: Or the Life of an American Slave* (New York, 1858).

huge impersonal "factory in the fields," where his actual master would be only a dim presence. These changes in situation led many slaves to develop standards of their own about how they ought to be treated and even to diffuse these standards among the stationary slave population. By comparing his less onerous lot under a previous master to his present hard one, a slave could develop a real sense of grievance and communicate it to others.[19] Similarly, slaves were quick to take advantage of any new leniency or laxity in control.[20] Hence it is quite possible to account for widespread noncooperation among slaves as resulting from a rudimentary sense of justice acquired entirely within the system of slavery itself. These standards would have served the same function as the

[19] Positive evidence of this development of internal standards and of the vacillation between contentment and dissatisfaction to which it gave rise is as difficult to find as evidence on any other aspect of slave psychology. As we have indicated, adequate records of personal slave response simply do not exist. There is, however, some indication of this process in the slave narratives and recollections. One of the most revealing of the slave narratives is Charles Ball, *Fifty Years in Chains*. Ball's account seems truer than most to the reality of slavery because, unlike most fugitives, he escaped from servitude at an age when it was difficult for him to acquire new habits of thought from his free status and association with abolitionists. Ball recounts the common experience of being sold from the upper South with its relatively mild and permissive regime into the more rigorous plantation slavery farther south. Upon his arrival on a large South Carolina cotton plantation, Ball, who was from Maryland, makes the acquaintance of a slave from northern Virginia who tells him what he can now expect. "He gave me such an account of the suffering of the slaves, on the cotton and indigo plantations — of whom I now regarded myself as one — that I was unable to sleep this night" (pp. 103–104). Later, he describes himself as "far from the place of my nativity, in a land of strangers, with no one to care for me beyond the care that a master bestows upon his ox . . ." (p. 115). The regime is indeed a harsh one, and he feels very dissatisfied, except on Sunday when he is taken up by the general hilarity that prevails in the slave quarters on the holiday. Eventually, however, he experiences a temporary improvement in his situation when he is given to his master's new son-in-law, who seems kindly and permissive. In a remarkable description of slave hedonism, Ball recalls his state of mind. "I now felt assured that all my troubles in this world were ended, and that, in future, I might look forward to a life of happiness and ease, for I did not consider labor any hardship, if I was well provided with good food and clothes, and my other wants properly regarded" (p. 266). This is too good to last, however; and Ball's new master dies, leaving him in the hands of another man, "of whom, when I considered the part of the country from whence he came, which had always been represented to me as distinguished for the cruelty with which slaves were treated, I had no reason to expect much that was good" (pp. 271–272). His new master turns out to be much less harsh than anticipated, but the master's wife, a woman with sadistic tendencies, takes a positive dislike to Ball and resents her husband's paternal attitude toward him. When the master dies, Ball recognizes his situation as intolerable and resolves upon flight (p. 307). Ball's narrative reveals the way in which a slave could evaluate his changes of condition by standards of comfort and accommodation derived from experience within the system itself. In desperate situations, this evaluation could lead to extreme forms of non-cooperation.

Despite the fact that he was recalling his experience after having escaped from slavery and, presumably, after coming under the influence of northern antislavery sentiment, Ball's general attitude remained remarkably accommodationist, at least in respect to slavery at its best. In a revealing passage, he notes that the typical slave lacks a real sense of identity of interest with his master, is jealous of his prerogatives, and steals from him without qualms. Yet, Ball concludes, there "is in fact, a mutual dependence between the master and his slave. The former could not acquire anything without the labor of the latter, and the latter would always remain in poverty without the judgment of the former in directing labor to a definite and profitable result" (p. 219).

[20] See Stampp, *Peculiar Institution*, pp. 104–108.

standards convicts bring from the outside world into the prison. At the same time it is necessary to insist once again that they give rise to a pattern of intransigence which is hedonistic rather than political, accommodationist rather than revolutionary.

If this picture of slave motivation is less morally sublime than contemporary liberals and radicals would like, it should not be construed as constituting, in any sense, a moral judgment on the Negro slave. Sporadic noncooperation within a broad framework of accommodation was the natural and inevitable response to plantation slavery. It should go without saying that white men born into the same system would have acted in the same way. Indeed, this is the way they have been observed to act in modern situations analogous to slavery. In total institutions, the conditions for sustained resistance are generally wanting —a fact that is insufficiently appreciated by those armchair moralists who like to make judgments at a safe distance about the possibilities of resistance to totalitarianism. Rebellions and mutinies "seem to be the exception," Erving Goffman observes, "not the rule." Group loyalty is very tenuous, even though "the expectation that group loyalty should prevail forms part of the inmate culture and underlies the hostility accorded to those who break inmate solidarity."[21]

Instead of banding together, inmates of total institutions typically pursue various personal strategies of accommodation. Goffman describes four lines of adaptation, but it is important to note that although these are analytically distinguishable, "the same inmate will employ different personal lines of adaptation at different phases in his moral career and may even alternate among different tacks at the same time." "Situational withdrawal," a fatalistic apathy, is the condition into which many inmates of concentration camps rapidly descended, with disastrous psychic consequences to themselves; it undoubtedly took its toll among slaves newly arrived from Africa during the colonial period. "Colonization," which in some cases can be regarded as another type of institutional neurosis, rests on a conscious decision that life in the institution is preferable to life in the outside world. Colonization, in turn, must be distinguished from "conversion," the inmate's internalization of the view of himself held by those in power. In Negro slavery, this is the "Sambo" role and is accompanied, as in the concentration camp, by an infantile sense of dependence. Colonization, on the other hand, would apply to the very small number of slaves who agreed to re-enslavement after a period as free Negroes.[22]

[21] Goffman, *Asylums*, pp. 18–19. Cf. Donald Clemmer, *The Prison Community* (New York, 1958), pp. 297–298: "The prisoner's world is an atomized world. . . . There are no definite communal objectives. There is no consensus for a common goal. The inmates' conflict with officialdom and opposition toward society is only slightly greater in degree than conflict and opposition among themselves. Trickery and dishonesty overshadow sympathy and cooperation. . . . It is a world of 'I,' 'me,' and 'mine,' rather than 'ours,' 'theirs,' and 'his.' " Clemmer adds, p. 293: "Such collective action of protest as does arise, comes out of an immediate situation in which they themselves are involved, and not as protest to an idea."

[22] Colonization, while uncommon among slaves, is frequently encountered in prisons and particularly in mental institutions. The high rate of recidivism among convicts and the frequency with which mental patients are sent back to asylums reflect not simply a relapse into a former sickness which the institution did not cure, but in many cases, a sickness which the

The fourth type of accommodation is "intransigence," which should not be (4 confused with resistance. The latter presupposes a sense of solidarity and an underground organization of inmates. Intransigence is a personal strategy of survival, and although it can sometimes help to sustain a high morale, it can just as easily lead to futile and even self-destructive acts of defiance. In slavery, there was a substantial minority who were written off by their masters as chronic trouble-makers, "bad niggers," and an even larger group who indulged in occasional insubordination. It is precisely the pervasiveness of "intransigence" that made slaves, like convicts, so difficult to manage, leading to the corruption of authority analyzed above. But as we have already tried to show, there is nothing about intransigence that precludes a partial acceptance of the values of the institution. In fact, Goffman observes that the most defiant of inmates are paradoxically those who are most completely caught up in the daily round of institutional life. "Sustained rejection of a total institution often requires sustained orientation to its formal organization, and hence, paradoxically, a deep kind of involvement in the establishment."[23] The same immersion in the institutional routine that makes some inmates so easy to manage makes others peculiarly sensitive to disruptions of the routine, jealous of their "rights" under the system. Indeed, periods of intransigence can alternate, in the same person, with colonization, conversion, and even with periods of withdrawal.

The concentration camp was unique among total institutions in confronting the typical prisoner with a choice between situational withdrawal, which meant death, and conversion, which, in the absence of alternatives, came to dominate the personality as a fully internalized role. In other total institutions, however, all four roles can be played to some extent, and "few inmates seem to pursue any one of them very far. In most total institutions most inmates take the tack of what some of them call 'playing it cool.' This involves a somewhat opportunistic combination of secondary adjustments, conversion, colonization, and loyalty to the inmate group, so that the inmate will have a maximum chance, in the particular circumstances, of eventually getting out physically and psychologically undamaged."[24] The slave had no real prospect of "getting out," but unless he was infantilized — a hypothesis that now seems quite untenable — he had a powerful stake in psychic survival. He had every reason to play it cool; and what is more, slavery gave him plenty of opportunities.

But the most compelling consideration in favor of this interpretation of slavery is that the very ways in which slavery differed from other total institutions would have actually reinforced and stabilized the pattern of opportunistic response that we have described. The most obvious objection to an analogy between slavery and the prison, the mental hospital, or any other institution of this kind is that slaves for the most part were born into slavery rather than coming in from the outside as adults; nor did most of them have any hope of getting out. We have answered these objections in various ways, but before

---

institution itself created — an institutional neurosis which has its own peculiar characteristics, the most outstanding of which is the inability to function outside systems of total control.

[23] Goffman, *Asylums*, p. 62.

[24] *Ibid.*, pp. 64–65.

leaving the matter we should point out that there is, in fact, a class of people in modern asylums — a minority, to be sure — who spend the better part of their lives in institutions of one kind or another. "Lower class mental hospital patients," for instance, "who have lived all their previous lives in orphanages, reformatories, and jails," are people whose experience in this respect approximates the slave's, especially the slave who served a series of masters. As a result of their continuous confinement, such patients have developed a kind of institutional personality. But they are not, as one might expect, Sambos — genuine converts to the institutional view of themselves. Quite the contrary; these people are the master-opportunists, for whom "no particular scheme of adaptation need be carried very far."[25] They have "perfected their adaptive techniques," experience having taught them a supreme versatility; and they are therefore likely to play it cool with more success than those brought in from the outside and incarcerated for the first time. These are the virtuosos of the system, neither docile nor rebellious, who spend their lives in skillful and somewhat cynical attempts to beat the system at its own game.

V

There is a passage in Frederick Douglass' *Narrative* that suggests how difficult it was even for an ex-slave — an unusually perceptive observer, in this case — to understand his former victimization without resorting to categories derived from experiences quite alien to slavery, categories that reflected the consciousness not of the slaves themselves but, in one way or another, the consciousness of the master-class. Douglass described how eagerly the slaves on Colonel Lloyd's Maryland plantations vied for the privilege of running errands to the Great House Farm, the master's residence and home plantation. The slaves "regarded it as evidence of great confidence reposed in them by the overseers; and it was on this account, as well as a constant desire to be out of the field from under the driver's lash, that they esteemed it a high privilege, one worth living for. He was called the smartest and most trusty fellow, who had this honor conferred upon him the most frequently."

Then follows a passage of unusual vividness and poignancy:

> The slaves selected to go to the Great House Farm, for the monthly allowance for themselves and their fellow-slaves, were peculiarly enthusiastic. While on their way, they would make the dense old woods, for miles around, reverberate with their wild songs, revealing at once the highest joy and the deepest sadness. . . . They would sometimes sing the most pathetic sentiment in the most rapturous tone, and the most rapturous sentiment in the most pathetic tone. Into all of their songs they would manage to weave something of the Great House Farm. Especially would they do this, when leaving home. They would then sing most exultingly the following words: —
> "I am going away to the Great House Farm!
> O, yea! O, yea! O!"
> This they would sing, as a chorus, to words which to many would

[25] *Ibid.*, pp. 65–66.

seem unmeaning jargon, but which, nevertheless, were full of meaning to themselves. I have sometimes thought that the mere hearing of those songs would do more to impress some minds with the horrible character of slavery, than the reading of whole volumes of philosophy on the subject could do.

But as these passages so clearly show, the "horrible character of slavery" did not lie, as the abolitionists tended to think, in the deprivations to which the slaves were forcibly subjected — deprivations which, resenting, they resisted with whatever means came to hand — but in the degree to which the slaves (even in their "intransigence") inevitably identified themselves with the system that bound and confined them, lending themselves to their own degradation. In vying for favors they "sought as diligently to please their overseers," Douglass says, "as the office-seekers in the political parties seek to please and deceive the people."[26]

Even more revealing are the reflections that follow. "I did not, when a slave, understand the deep meaning of those rude and apparently incoherent songs. I was myself within the circle; so that I neither saw nor heard as those without might see and hear." It was only from without that the slave songs revealed themselves as "the prayer and complaint of souls boiling over with the bitterest anguish" — anguish, it should be noted, which expressed itself disjointedly, "the most pathetic sentiment" being set to "the most rapturous tone." It was only from without that the "dehumanizing character of slavery" showed itself precisely in the slave's incapacity to resist; but this perception, once gained, immediately distorted the reality to which it was applied. Douglass slides imperceptibly from these unforgettable evocations of slavery to an abolitionist polemic. It is a great mistake, he argued, to listen to slaves' songs "as evidence of their contentment and happiness." On the contrary, "slaves sing most when they are most unhappy." Yet the slaves whose "wild songs" he has just described were those who were "peculiarly enthusiastic," by his own account, to be sent to the Great House Farm, and who sang "exultingly" along the way. The ambiguity of the reality begins to fade when seen through the filter of liberal humanitarianism, and whereas the songs revealed "at once the highest joy and the deepest sadness," in Douglass' own words, as an abolitionist he feels it necessary to insist that "crying for joy, and singing for joy, were alike uncommon to me while in the jaws of slavery."[27]

If the abolitionist lens distorted the "horrible character" of slavery, the picture of the docile and apparently contented bondsman was no more faithful to the reality it purported to depict. But this should not surprise us. It is not often that men understand, or even truly see, those whom in charity they would uplift. How much less often do they understand those they exploit?

[26] Douglass, *Narrative*, pp. 35–37.
[27] *Ibid.*, pp. 37–38.

Classes and Sections

AILEEN KRADITOR

*Today, more than ever before, the abolitionists fascinate students
of American history. They are interpreted as the first national civil
rights movement, the first to confront the American race dilemma
honestly, and the first to combine moral idealism and activism in
a productive way. One of the most serious impediments to a truly
historical understanding of the abolitionists, however, is the very
immediacy of our own differently founded racial concerns. Aileen
Kraditor's essay on the nature of abolitionist propaganda has the
double virtue of dealing with the abolitionists on their own terms
and of trying to distinguish their problems from ours. Her argument is that the abolitionists were fundamentally Christian reformers, concerned not with social classes or economic arrangements but with the redemption of individual souls. The key to
understanding the abolitionists and their tactics lies in accepting
that they believed that structural changes in American society
could be brought about only by convincing individuals that slavery
was evil, that Negroes were equal to whites, and that conscience
demanded that slavery be acted against immediately. Abolitionism's
moralism in action was what made it so difficult for abolitionists
and working-class radicals to understand one another. The workers
believed that they, equally with chattel slaves, were the victims of
an oppressive social system and that their improvement depended
upon basic changes in the system. The abolitionists, however, rejected the environmentalism inherent in the labor outlook (degraded men are the products of an unjust and corrupt society) in
favor of a Christian emphasis on self-improvement. From the abolitionist point of view, therefore, slaves were much worse off than
free laborers since they did not possess the freedom to strive to
help themselves. For both oppressor and oppressed, abolitionists
saw the solution as individual moral acts rather than as the seizure
of power from one class by another. Logic impelled the abolitionists
to strive for the conversion of slaveholders, for they believed that if
they touched the Southern conscience, the masters would cease
their evil ways. When simple propagandizing of the South was impeded by restrictions on the inflow of propaganda, the abolitionists
turned to more striking acts of moral protest, but their aim remained to convince individual Southerners of the immorality of
slavery. And even if the South could not be converted quickly, it
would ultimately respond to a North united in its moral opposition
to slavery. The theme of Kraditor's essay, the dominance of moralism and individualism in abolitionist propaganda, should help to
clarify how thoroughly the abolitionist approach differed from the*

structural and environmental emphasis of current American radi-
calism. It is very important that we understand the abolitionists
in their own terms, for although they represented only a tiny pro-
portion of the Americans of their era (and failed dramatically to
convince Americans of the equality of the races), no other group
played such a direct role in bringing the conflict over slavery to
the boiling point.

The complaints of the modern black-power agitator about the well-meaning white liberal recall the abolitionist's complaint about the average Northerner of his day. The white liberal today favors race equality but "not too fast," and the agitator asks: "How does your passive approval of a theoretical equality diminish actual oppression? Whatever your intentions, is not your abstract support actually an impediment to the sort of action that can bring significant change; is it not a respectable façade to shield the more obviously intransigent?" Most Northerners before the Civil War, and indeed many slaveholders, were "against slavery." But "the Constitution prevented Northerners from doing anything about it," or "the Negroes would not work if free," or "property rights must be respected." Even where opposition to slavery was evidently sincere, there was patently an enormous difference between conviction and commitment, faith and works, theory and practice. The Rev. Orange Scott of Lowell, Massachusetts, speaking at the annual meeting of the Massachusetts Anti-Slavery Society in 1837, addressed a question to those who favored abolition but opposed the abolitionists' measures:

> [In] what do you differ from what has always been the sentiment
> of our whole country? Until very recently, nobody has attempted
> to defend slavery *in the abstract.* But, what has this sentiment
> amounted to? Slavery has grown up under it till it is now become a
> great Oak, which defies the storms of public sentiment — ay, the
> winds of heaven too! . . . Suppose an individual should say, "I am
> benevolent, *except the measures.*" . . . Every body is willing to
> say to the poor, "Be ye warmed, be ye filled;" but when we come
> to the *measures* for feeding and clothing them, the miser starts
> back! Such benevolence does no good. . . . Mr. Jefferson, and
> William Wirt, and many other patriots and philanthropists, have
> been opposed to slavery; but what has their opposition amounted
> to?[1]

The abolitionists recognized also that they must continually reinforce their own commitment to their cause. The frequent meetings and intragroup journals of any movement for change serve an indispensable function even when they

[1] *Fifth Annual Report of the Board of Managers of the Massachusetts Anti-Slavery Society,* p. vii.

repeatedly pass the same resolutions and proclaim familiar truths to the already committed. These activities help to assure members that they are part of a group with a historic mission, are not fighting alone, and have somewhere to go and others to turn to when public opprobrium weakens their dedication.[2]

The twin tasks of refreshing the commitment of abolitionists and of converting outsiders' passive disapproval of slavery into active opposition differed only in emphasis, especially after the movement had grown from a handful of pioneers into a network of societies with thousands of members. In propaganda aimed at both groups, the abolitionists relied heavily on the same arguments: among others, that slavery denied the humanity of the Negro and prevented the slave from having normal family relations and religious life, that the North shared the slaveowners' guilt, that absolute power of one individual over another encourages atrocities, that slavery was responsible for the degraded condition of Northern free Negroes, and that the talent and manliness of Negroes such as Frederick Douglass and Charles Lenox Remond demonstrated the inherent equality of the races. There was, in addition, a somewhat different tactic employed by abolitionists both among themselves and in their public propaganda. It may be illustrated by William Lloyd Garrison's reaction to an experience he had while on a trip to Britain.

One summer day in 1846 in Liverpool, Garrison was accosted by a prostitute. Later he told of how he had imagined that wretched woman as his sister or daughter. Merrill supposes that this fantasy was Garrison's way of "successfully avoiding temptation."[3] Whether or not that is so, there is abundant evidence that his response manifested an attitude consciously cultivated by abolitionists. On other occasions he deliberately pictured himself in the place of the oppressed. For example, in a speech at the Massachusetts State House, he exclaimed, "Who can contemplate the wife of his bosom — the children of his love — subjected to this fearful suffering and indignity, and for one moment entertain the idea" of gradual abolition?[4] On the first anniversary of his marriage, he wrote to his brother-in-law describing his happiness and extolling the institution of marriage; and he added, how horrible it would be if he and Helen were slaves and were

[2] The therapeutic function of conventions is mentioned in Elizur Wright, Jr., to Theodore D. Weld, April 2, 1836, in Barnes and Dumond, eds., Weld-Grimké Letters, I, 291; circular letter from New-Jersey Anti-Slavery Society, July 16, 1841, Weld Papers, Box 7, UM; L. B. C. Wyman and A. Wyman, Elizabeth Buffum Chace, 1806–1899: Her Life and Its Environment (Boston, 1914), I, 137. Elizur Wright, Jr., in a letter to his father, September 20, 1834, Wright Papers, LC, advocated a plan whereby individuals would contribute 12½¢ a month to the cause: "Not the least advantage of this plan is involved in the law of human nature, 'that our sympathy for the suffering is in proportion to what we do for their relief.' Those who give systematically will feel. And their feelings will not grow cold." During the petition campaign, abolitionists sometimes pointed out that a person who could be induced to sign his name would feel committed thereby and become more receptive to further propaganda.
[3] Walter M. Merrill, Against Wind and Tide, p. 192. John L. Thomas, The Liberator: William Lloyd Garrison, pp. 339–40, mentions the incident but offers no comment other than that Garrison was glad he was a Bostonian.
[4] The Liberator, February 14, 1840.

separated by sale. All the more reason, then, to rededicate his life to the abolition of slavery.[5]

This theme, which for convenience will be referred to as "empathy," appears
repeatedly in abolitionists' private discourse and public propaganda, in exhorta-
tions among themselves to increase their zeal and in efforts to induce complacent
whites to imagine themselves in the place of the slaves. Its shorthand expression
was the New Testament verse Hebrews 13:3, seldom placed within quotation
marks, never identified, and always made an integral part of the writers' own
sentences: "Remember them that are in bonds, as bound with them."[6]

If the abolitionist movement had been composed chiefly of its own intended
beneficiaries, one of the two uses of the empathy theme would of course have
been unnecessary. Negroes in the North — those active in the convention movement, the vigilance associations, and other societies — had no need to remind
themselves of their bond with the slaves of the South. But the abolitionist
movement comprised mainly white men and women, most of whom had never
been South. The empathy theme can thus be seen, perhaps, as a substitute for
direct involvement in the suffering that the movement was dedicated to end.

It appeared in other forms as well. When Abby Kelley Foster was asked how
she could leave her baby with others, to travel the abolitionist lecture circuit,
she replied, "For the sake of the mothers who are robbed of all their children."[7]
The abolitionist educator Beriah Green, answering the perennial question asked
by Northerners, "What can we do?" replied in part:

> You can act as if you felt that you were bound with those who are
> in bonds; as if their cause was all your own; as if every blow that

[5] Garrison to George W. Benson, September 4, 1835, Garrison Papers, BPL.

[6] I do not contend that this verse appears more often than any other. In fact, abolitionist
writings prior to 1850 reveal thorough familiarity with the Bible; many essays (by Garrison,
especially) contain dozens of scriptural phrases incorporated integrally in the writers' own
sentences, to such an extent that it is clear that the Bible provided the frame of reference
for much abolitionist thinking in the 1830s and 1840s. But Hebrews 13:3 appears often
enough to have special significance. A few examples are: Wyman and Wyman, *Elizabeth
Buffum Chace*, I, 94 (quoting journal entry by Mrs. Chace in 1842); Garrison, "Repeal of
the Union," *The Liberator*, May 6, 1842; letter to the editor from Noah Jackman, telling
of a circular, adopted at an antislavery meeting in Massachusetts and sent to ministers to be
read to their congregations, *ibid.*, February 16, 1844; Garrison, "Gerrit Smith's Constitutional Argument. No. III," *ibid.*, October 4, 1844; "Annual Report of the Weymouth
Female Anti-Slavery Society," *ibid.*, October 17, 1845; Garrison, in introduction to "Letter
from Another Martyr in the Cause of Freedom," *ibid.*, June 8, 1848; Beriah Green, *Things
for Northern Men to Do* (1836), excerpted in Pease and Pease, eds., *The Antislavery Argument*, p. 186; Nathaniel P. Rogers, "Color-Phobia" (1838), *ibid.*, p. 319; Elizur Wright,
Jr., to Beriah Green, March 29, 1836, Wright Papers, LC; Samuel J. May in *Fourth Annual
Report of the Board of Managers of the Massachusetts Anti-Slavery Society* (Boston, 1836),
pp. 4–5; [Angelina E. Grimké], *An Appeal to the Women of the Nominally Free States*
(New York, 1837), p. 18; James Forten, *An Address Delivered before the Ladies Anti-
Slavery Society of Philadelphia*, on the Evening of the 14th of April 1836 (Philadelphia,
1836), p. 13, as quoted in Keith E. Melder, "The Beginnings of the Women's Rights Movement in the United States, 1800–1840," Ph.D. dissertation, Yale University, 1964, p. 158;
two letters from women's antislavery societies to the Anti-Slavery Convention of American
Women (see *Proceedings of the Anti-Slavery Convention of American Women* [Philadel-
phia, 1838], pp. 17, 18).

[7] Wyman and Wyman, *Elizabeth Buffum Chace*, II, 283.

cuts their flesh, lacerated yours. You can plead their cause with the earnestness, and zeal, and decision, which self-defence demands.[8]

Green's reference to self-defense is significant, for the effort to induce empathy with the slaves in complacent Northerners was more than a heuristic device, although it was that too. Abolitionist propaganda reiterated that Northern whites were in fact indirectly "bound with" the slaves. Paradoxically, the North was not only accessory to the enslavement of Negroes; it was at the same time a secondary victim of the slaveowners. With their strong religious motive for proclaiming the duty of emancipation regardless of consequences, the abolitionists could not in good conscience appeal to the North solely or chiefly on the basis of interest. The empathy theme enabled them in a remarkable way to combine interest with principle, for if a Northern white could be made to feel bound with the slave he would fight the slave power to defend himself, as Beriah Green suggested, as well as to exculpate himself. To free the slave would be to free himself of both guilt and bondage; the two motives would become one. The abolitionists' theory that the North was both accomplice and victim of the slave power, combined with their theory of conversion, suggests a framework for studying certain leading themes in their propaganda approaches to both North and South. We shall examine first their conception of the slave system and how Northerners became its victims and partners in oppressing Negroes in the North as well as in the South; then we shall discuss how the abolitionists' empathy theme and conception of the nature of slavery affected their approach to the Northern working class; then, shifting our attention to the South, we shall investigate the way abolitionists viewed the slaveowners and the possibility of converting them.

Given the radical abolitionist's special theological premises, and his extravagantly simple view of the relation among belief, motivation, and behavior, the conclusions follow like the consecutive clicks of a row of falling dominoes. The special significance of Stephen S. Foster and a handful of other abolitionists whose unconventional behavior has tempted historians to give them disproportionate attention is that they accepted every corollary, and every corollary of every corollary, of a syllogism constructed from those premises. Their tenets and church-disrupting activities demonstrate where this "domino logic" might lead, whereas the more moderate Garrison shrank from following it to its farthest conclusions.[9] If the sin of slavery existed partly by virtue of the aid that Northerners gave it, and if God commanded every person to wage war upon all sin (and of course God would not command an impossibility), then a North-

---

[8] *Things for Northern Men to Do*, in Pease and Pease, eds., *The Antislavery Argument*, p. 186. New York abolitionists, in a fund-raising appeal to children, asked them to act as if "their own fathers and mothers were in chains and bleeding beneath the whip" (*Emancipator Extra*, June 6, 1835, quoted in Bertram Wyatt-Brown, "The Abolitionists' Postal Campaign of 1835," *Journal of Negro History*, L [October 1965], 228).

[9] "I could wish that bro. Foster would exercise more judgment and discretion in the presentation of his views; but it is useless to reason with him . . ." (Garrison to his wife, November 27, 1842, Garrison Papers, BPL). Edmund Quincy also disapproved of Foster's tactic of disturbing church services; see his "Divisions of Abolitionists," *The Liberator*, December 30, 1842.

erner who aided slavery in any way was guilty of heinous sin. Anyone who failed to use an opportunity to fight slavery was at that moment aiding the slave power. Hence a man who was anything but a full-time battler against slavery was as bad as a slaveholder.[10] His guilt was so enormous, and the identification of the average Northern white with the slaveholder so complete, that the Foster mentality could not separate them or mitigate the Northerner's guilt sufficiently to see him as also a victim. Garrison and most of the radical abolitionists, along with the more conservative abolitionists, recognized degrees of guilt. For propaganda purposes they occasionally would picture the Northerner as the greater sinner[11] (having less excuse than the slaveowner), but almost always they distinguished sufficiently between the aggressive slave power and the Northern white to portray the latter as a victim as well as an accomplice of the former. The North, said the annual report of the Massachusetts Anti-Slavery Society in 1849, "has been willing to purchase the delusive benefits of a deceptive Union at the successive cost of these concessions of its own true interest and the interests of humanity."[12] "These concessions" were the splitting off of Kentucky from Virginia, giving the slaveholders another state, the purchase of the Louisiana Territory and admission of the State of Louisiana, the War of 1812, the tariff (presumably that of 1816), the Missouri Compromise, nullification and the tariff compromise, the Florida war, the annexation of Texas, the Mexican War, and the conquest of the Mexican Cession — all

[10] Foster presented a resolution at a meeting in 1845: "Resolved, That as the Constitution of the United States guarantees the support and protection of the slave power, all who acknowledge allegiance to the federal government are, emphatically, slaveholders, and as such, are justly chargeable with all the guilt inherent in the slave system." The motion was tabled (*Twelfth Annual Report Presented to the Massachusetts Anti-Slavery Society, by Its Board of Managers* [Boston, 1844], p. 89). The restraint doubtless shown by Foster because this was a meeting of an antislavery society was absent when James Boyle presented the following resolution passed at a meeting of "New Covenant Believers from various parts of the country" at Hartford in 1843: "Resolved, That no member of the church of Christ has ever held a slave or apologized for slavery, has ever practised or advocated war, physical resistance to evil — has ever practised or advocated intemperance, or manufactured drunkards, has ever practically or theoretically taught the inferiority of woman or the rightfulness of her subordination to man, or has claimed exclusive possession of any thing in heaven or earth or sea." (*The Liberator*, March 31, 1843) See also a Foster resolution, as reported *ibid.*, September 17, 1841. Abby Kelley, whom Foster married a few years later, was the butt of some good-natured chaffing based on a tongue-in-cheek application of domino logic. Miss Kelley of course approved of recent antislavery resolutions condemning most American churches as "brotherhoods of thieves" and "bulwarks of slavery." According to a letter from one Garrisonian to another, Miss Kelley at breakfast one day "was telling us of her going to Mtg. in Deacon somebody's carriage — whereupon J. G. Gibbons pencilled the following 'Whereas Abby Kelly [sic] did by her own confession, ride in a Deacon's carriage, said Deacon being a member of the Bulwarks. — Therefore, — Resolved that she has *not* come out & separated herself from the American Church & is "striking hands" — with living body snatchers — and cat o' nine tail devils.'" (Sarah Pugh to Richard and Hannah Webb, June 17, 1842, Anti-Slavery Letters, BPL)
[11] For example, see editorial "Progress of the Anti-Slavery Movement," *The Liberator*, January 28, 1842, in which Garrison refers to "the still more guilty North."
[12] *Seventeenth Annual Report, Presented to the Massachusetts Anti-Slavery Society, by Its Board of Managers* (Boston, 1849), p. 11.

by means of the federal government acting as the instrument of the slave power.[13]

The most conservative abolitionists concurred with the Garrison-dominated Massachusetts Society on this point. James G. Birney asserted in 1840 that "the North, in relation to the South, is as a conquered province," for in the last six years its rights have been invaded one by one, and since the Missouri Compromise the government has been in the hands of the slave power. The North, he added, is beginning to show signs of alarm and is making efforts to redeem herself;

> but she yet requires a great deal more of agitation to rouse her up to a full perception of the danger into which she has been brought, and to the necessity, *if she would save her own liberty*, either of severing her connections with the South, or of acting incessantly on the South for the abolition of slavery.[14]

Arguments purporting to show that the Constitution prevented Northerners from abolishing slavery were clearly beside the point, for the North, according to this well-developed category of abolitionist propaganda, must fight to defend its own share in federal power and its own freedom of speech, petition, and travel. Slavery could not exist alongside liberty to petition Congress, liberty to discuss slavery in the press and in meetings, liberty of Northerners to travel in the South. The slave power was aggressive by nature, and concessions by the North were self-defeating. Since those concessions helped the slave power and hurt the Northerners who made them, abolitionists could point out the expediency of ceasing to commit this sin. Northerners who were "against slavery" but unwilling to act on their conviction might be roused to defend their own freedom and in the process discover that they were in fact "bound with" the slave.

One important difference between abolitionism and the modern Negro freedom movements is that the latter is an attempt to practice freedom, whereas

---

[13] *Ibid.*, p. 10. Almost every issue of every antislavery newspaper contained these and similar arguments. See Julian P. Bretz, "The Economic Background of the Liberty Party," *American Historical Review*, XXXIV (January 1929), 252–57, for analysis of antislavery propaganda aimed at proving that the depression that began in 1837 was the fault of the slave power. Russel B. Nye, *Fettered Freedom, passim*, describes in great detail the abolitionists' efforts to show the North that its own freedom of speech was doomed if slavery were not abolished. For the portrayal of the North as willing victim of the South, see, for example, Elizur Wright, Jr., to Beriah Green, March 29, 1836, Wright Papers, LC. Wright wrote that abolitionists would "be both *wicked* and *weak*" if they neglected to show the North the danger of a certain legislative action on the part of defenders of slavery (emphasis in original). See also two editorials by Garrison, "Shall Texas Be Annexed to the Union? — No. 1," and "The Texas Question," *The Liberator*, June 30, 1837, in which he wrote that Northerners were not ignorant of their part in upholding slavery but were ignorant of how that complicity threatened their own freedom; racism had blinded them. Hence it was their interest as well as their duty to fight against slavery. In the decade before the Civil War the verse from the Epistle to the Hebrews appears less often than before, partly because the religious motive was less important, but also, one suspects, because events were convincing the North that it *was* a victim of the slave power.

[14] Birney to Myron Holley, Joshua Leavitt, and Elizur Wright, Jr., May 11, 1840, *Birney Letters*, I, 567–71.

the former was not. It was not primarily a movement of Negroes asserting the ‖
rights of free people, but a movement to convert whites to the belief that Ne- ‖
groes ought to have those rights.[15] It was therefore more of a propaganda
movement and essentially directed toward changing the minds of whites rather
than the circumstances of Negroes. Its very existence thus depended on access
to the public ear, and abolitionists were careful to point out that restrictions on
their own freedom to speak and publish were restrictions on the North's freedom to hear and read.[16] That is why the linking of abolitionism with the cause
of free speech for whites was a legitimate tactic, even though it might seem to
start from the racist premise that it was ethical to emphasize their own stake
in the free-speech battle, to rouse whites to anger, rather than to concentrate
on the denial of the Negroes' very humanity.[17] The legitimacy of this tactic
was well expressed by Francis Jackson of Boston at the time he joined the abolitionist movement in 1835:

> Mobs and gag laws . . . betray the essential rottenness of the cause,
> they are meant to strengthen. . . . Happily, one point seems already
> to be gaining universal assent, that slavery cannot long survive free
> discussion. Hence the efforts of the friends and apologists of slavery
> to break down this right. And hence the immense stake, which the
> enemies of slavery hold, in behalf of freedom and mankind, in its
> preservation. The contest is therefore substantially between liberty
> and slavery.[18]

Closely linked with the abolitionist defense of free speech, and presenting the
same ethical problem, was another tactic used somewhat less often but frequently enough to compel our attention. The sometimes sensational articles in
antislavery papers about slaves who were white[19] may be interpreted as evidence
that the abolitionists, despite their protests against race prejudice, felt the

[15] Abolitionists did, of course, help *Northern* Negroes assert those rights, as, for example,
when two of them protested when Frederick Douglass was ejected from a railroad car; they
were thrown out along with him and then tried in vain to ride in the Jim Crow car with
him. That incident and others are described in a letter to the editor from John A. Collins,
The Liberator, October 15, 1841. Another article in the same issue prints protest resolutions
passed at public meetings. Other items of this nature can be found from time to time in
The Liberator. Abolitionists were also active in efforts to repeal the anti-intermarriage law
and the law permitting Jim Crow accommodations on public carriers in Massachusetts and
in efforts to integrate Boston public schools.

[16] A good example of this argument is in *Proceedings of the Rhode-Island Anti-Slavery
Convention* (Providence, 1836), pp. 55–56.

[17] Abolitionists recognized the ethical problem involved. Ellis Gray Loring, for instance,
wrote an essay intended to show the legitimacy of appealing to other interests of Northern
whites as well — the esteem in which labor was held, the prosperity of the Northern
economy, the morals of the young, and the peace of the community. "I would never, even
in argument," he wrote, "subordinate conscience to interest. . . . Nevertheless, I would take
pains to let men see that it is no less a part of God's truth, and, according to the order of
his Providence, that a community will not be the poorer for righteousness, than it is that
it is the duty of a community to be righteous." (*The Liberator*, November 5, 1841.)

[18] Jackson to Samuel J. May, November 25, 1835, in Ruchames, ed., *The Abolitionists*,
p. 120.

[19] *The Liberator* occasionally printed such items in its section reserved for miscellaneous
reprints of news items from other papers.

enslavement of a white person somehow more deplorable than the enslavement of a Negro. Perhaps the accusation has merit in some cases. It should be noted, however, that these news items were sometimes the subject of separate editorial comment to the effect that the white reader must realize that slavery was no distant danger, that he himself could be seized and sold South on the claim of a slave catcher, that slavery knew no bounds of color.[20] It is clear that the purpose of at least some of these articles was to force the reader to put himself imaginatively in the place of the slave. This would be the first step toward his learning that the black man felt the degradation of slavery as he himself would.

When abolitionists attempted to induce empathy with the Negro in Northern whites who opposed slavery only passively, they were consciously trying to meet the greatest challenge to their cause, the widespread fear that unconditional emancipation would bring social equality in its wake. According to one student of Northern public opinion, "The key to the explanation of anti-abolition is race prejudice." Most Northerners, he explains, were opposed at the same time to slavery and to race equality and therefore supported the American Colonization Society.[21] Abolitionists, realizing this, always saw their struggle to discredit colonizationism as part of their fight against racism. In fact, their slogan of immediate and unconditional emancipation ought itself to be understood as, among other things, an assertion of the equality of the races. White-supremacist Northerners at the time understood this better than modern historians who have assumed that the slogan represented a naive call for a revolutionary transformation they thought could come in the near future.[22] Barnes, for example, criticizes the aboli-

[20] See especially Garrison's editorial "The Declaration of American Independence," *The Liberator*, September 5, 1835, in which he mentioned instances of whites having been enslaved and stated that he had been shocked to encounter such cases, "not because I deemed it a more heinous crime in the sight of God to enslave a white than a black man, or to lacerate a white than a black woman, but because it revealed the utter insecurity in which the liberty of all my countrymen was placed, especially those whose skins are less transparent than others." Any of us, he added, including the swarthy Daniel Webster, might be kidnapped and sold; for at what shade could one draw the line? There were thousands of slaves whiter than their masters. See also Gerrit Smith's speech reported in *Third Annual Report of the American Anti-Slavery Society* (New York, 1836), pp. 17–18. Abolitionists were fond of quoting the 1835 message of Governor George McDuffie to the South Carolina legislature in which he defended slavery as the best status for all laborers, "bleached or unbleached." Garrison printed the speech in *The Liberator*, December 12, 1835. Two of many instances of its use in abolitionist propaganda are: *Proceedings of the Rhode-Island Anti-Slavery Convention*, p. 37; and William Goodell, *Slavery and Anti-Slavery*, p. 413. A similar point, in somewhat different context, is made by Jules Zanger, in "The 'Tragic Octoroon' in Pre-Civil War Fiction," *American Quarterly*, XVIII (Spring 1966), 63–70, especially pp. 64–67.

[21] Lorman Ratner, "Northern Opposition to the Anti-Slavery Movement, 1831–1840," Ph.D. dissertation, Cornell University, 1961, pp. 212, 31.

[22] Younger historians are reading the sources with deeper understanding. See Martin Duberman, "The Northern Response to Slavery," in Duberman, ed., *The Antislavery Vanguard*, pp. 402–6; and the brilliant article by Anne C. Loveland, "Evangelicalism and 'Immediate Emancipation' in American Antislavery Thought," *Journal of Southern History*, XXXII (May 1966), 172–88. According to Miss Loveland, "historians have usually misconstrued the immediatist slogan, interpreting it as a temporal rather than a moral and religious requirement. They have read into it a deadline for emancipation that misses the point and purpose of the abolitionist demand." "When abolitionists demanded immediate

tionists for adopting the immediatist slogan, because it repelled those who might otherwise have been converted to antislavery. But the abolitionists' aim was not chiefly to convert masses to *antislavery*; if all the Northerners who already believed slavery to be evil had entered the movement in the 1830s, that movement would have rivaled the Whig party in size — and been no more effective in ending slavery. Abolitionists knew this. Nathaniel P. Rogers, for one, blamed "color-phobia," of which colonizationism was one type, for anti-abolition. Colorphobia, he wrote,

> abhors slavery in the abstract — wishes it might be done away, but denies the right of any body or any thing to devise its overthrow, but slavery itself and slaveholders. It prays for the poor slave, that he might be elevated, while it stands both feet on his breast to keep him down.[23]

The differences between that "antislavery" multitude and the abolitionists were first, that the abolitionists saw slavery as a sin, and second (the relevant point here), that they asserted the equality of the races. Hence much of their propaganda effort, often in the form of the empathy theme, was directed at inducing Northern whites to see the Negro as their brother.[24]

They also proclaimed that Northern racism hurt the interests of white labor; by identifying manual labor with a despised caste, it made labor itself disreputable.[25] Hence abolition of chattel slavery, which produced the caste system, was in the interest of the Northern working class. But the abolitionists, as is well known, made little headway in enlisting the labor movement in their crusade, and part of the explanation for their failure lies in their emphasis on the empathy theme. That theme was no doubt an aid to commitment, but it did not help the

---

emancipation, they were . . . arguing that abolition was fully within man's power and completely dependent upon his initiative," and "since action was the test of belief, true repentance virtually entailed the abolition of slavery" (pp. 173, 184, 185). An excellent formulation of this function of the immediatist slogan, by an abolitionist, is in Samuel J. May to Amos A. Phelps, March 18, 1834, Phelps Papers, BPL. See also James G. Birney to Gerrit Smith, November 14, 1834, in *Birney Letters*, I, 148.

[23] Nathaniel P. Rogers, "Color-Phobia" (1838), in Pease and Pease, eds., *The Antislavery Argument*, p. 319. See also Merton L. Dillon, "The Failure of the American Abolitionists," *Journal of Southern History*, XXV (May 1959), 165–67. Here is one of the few points at which a parallel can be drawn between the abolitionist and black-power movements.

[24] One of many documents that support the abolitionists' approach as well as Ratner's thesis (see note 21 above) is an article in the *Wilmington Loco-Foco* which Garrison appropriately reprinted in his "Refuge of Oppression" column, *The Liberator*, July 23, 1841. The *Loco-Foco* proclaimed its devotion to the principle of universal liberty as formulated in the Declaration of Independence, the U.S. Constitution, the constitution of every state, and the platform of the Democratic party. But, "Phrenology has established the disparity of the different castes of the human race on too firm a foundation for abolitionism to overthrow, a union between which is naturally abhorrent and repugnant to the human heart; . . . and while this natural repugnance exists, the superior caste will bear the palm." Since the *Loco-Foco* felt it would be unjust to continue enslaving Negroes or to expatriate them forcibly, it concluded that the problem "must be left to the inscrutable wisdom of Him, who, in his all-wise providence," would ordain the solution.

[25] For example, [Edmund Quincy], "Chattel Slavery and Wages Slavery," *The Liberator*, October 1, 1847; and Garrison, "Lyman Beecher," *ibid.*, August 6, 1836.

abolitionists' understanding of the nature of the evil they were committed to destroy. It influenced them to regard the slaves as suffering individuals (see their ritual repetition of phrases such as "bleeding humanity"), but it threw no light on the cause of the suffering. In fact, the empathy theme may have impeded that understanding, because it encouraged abolitionists to see the oppressors too as individuals, whose behavior could be explained solely in terms of individual sin and guilt. Despite their repeated use of the term *slave power* and their recognition that the slaveholders were a self-conscious oligarchy that acted as one in defense of its interests, there is little evidence in the abolitionists' writings of insight into the social sources of ideology or the class nature of the slave system. Spokesmen for labor such as George Henry Evans were committed to a social philosophy and program for change that denied the very premises of the abolitionists' crusade. The labor reformers stressed interest where the abolitionists stressed principle, talked of classes where the abolitionists talked of individuals, urged reform of institutions where abolitionists preached repudiation of sin. It is no wonder that the abolitionists failed, so far as the workingmen's movement was concerned, in their effort to combine interest with principle by means of the empathy theme.

It is this conflict in philosophy, rather than the abolitionists' failure to sympathize with Northern labor, that explains why the two movements were not allied. Some abolitionists did in fact sympathize with underpaid American workers, starving Irish peasants, and disfranchised English factory operatives.[26] Garrison, for one, was shocked to learn that British abolitionists did not as a matter of course support the Chartists' demand for electoral reforms, and when he learned the cause of the hostility between the Chartists and the British abolitionists, he sided with the former.

The issue was presented to him for the first time in July 1840 as he entered a hall in Glasgow to attend an antislavery public meeting. Someone handed him a leaflet entitled *Have We No White Slaves?* In his speech at that meeting Garrison answered the question, No! British workers are not slaves, you own your own wages, are permitted to learn to read and write, and can better your condition. The leaflet asked, Are we not grievously oppressed, starving in the midst of abundance? Garrison replied, Yes! And, according to his account of the incident, he "called upon British abolitionists to prove themselves the true friends of suffering humanity abroad, by showing that they were the best friends of suffering humanity at home." He then asked the audience whether British abolitionists were not friends of their own suffering countrymen and was surprised to hear

[26] Anti-Slavery Letters, BPL, include letters by James Mott, Edward M. Davis, and Wendell Phillips written during the potato famine, strongly sympathizing with the Irish and deploring the circumstances that forced so many to emigrate. On the other hand, some abolitionists seem to have been amazingly ignorant of New England workers' conditions. See, for example, John Greenleaf Whittier's pamphlet *Justice and Expediency* (1833), as excerpted in Ruchames, ed., *The Abolitionists*, pp. 46–57; on p. 54 he contrasts the slave system to "the beautiful system of free labor as exhibited in New England, where every young laborer, with health and ordinary prudence, may acquire by his labor on the farms of others, in a few years, a farm of his own." Whittier's automatic identification of free labor with rural employment may perhaps be excused in view of the early date of his pamphlet.

"No! no! no!" from all parts of the hall, whereupon he said, "Then I am very sorry to hear it — I hope that it is not true of all of them — I am sure it is not true of the abolitionists of the United States; for they sympathize with the oppressed, as well as the enslaved, throughout the world."

He went on to advise British workers to help their cause by self-reform; it is at this point that the philosophic chasm separating abolitionists from workers' spokesmen becomes evident. Shortly after that meeting in July, Charles M'Ewan, a Chartist, published a handbill in the form of a letter to Garrison, to whom he sent a copy. Garrison commented on it in *The Liberator*, first paying tribute to its "bold and manly style." M'Ewan objected to Garrison's call for self-reform, and Garrison, in his editorial reply, asked whether self-reform would not help the British worker.

> That "a great amount" of the suffering of the laboring population in England (including Scotland and Ireland, of course), arises from intemperance, it is idle for Mr. M'Ewan to deny; that they are too frequently induced to seek the intoxicating bowl, in consequence of their ignorance, destitution and severe toil, is also doubtless true; that the temperance cause has reclaimed thousands of them from drunkenness, banished from their domestic hearths no small portion of their misery, and qualified them to carry on the cause of political reform, is a delightful fact; and that they are far more ready to adopt the "tee-total pledge" than the more opulent classes, I most cheerfully bear witness.[27]

This incident has been commented on by historians; what has been overlooked is that passage in Garrison's reply in which he blamed the intemperance on the workers' circumstances and not their circumstances on their intemperance, while of course asserting that the intemperance worsened the conditions that caused it. And he suggested that self-reform might improve the laborer's ability to work for political reform, not make political reform unnecessary. M'Ewan's chief complaint seems to have been that Garrison mentioned self-reform at all, for he thereby gave a weapon to the enemy. But American abolitionists chronically thought in terms of appeals to individuals — oppressor and oppressed alike — and in terms of individual reformation rather than of a struggle for power, and it is clear that Garrison simply did not see M'Ewan's point.

The Glasgow rally was addressed by other abolitionists, British and American. One of the latter, Nathaniel P. Rogers of New Hampshire, said during his speech that he had learned that some British newspapers opposed the cause of universal freedom and he hoped that none of the gentlemen on the platform with him supported such papers. M'Ewan's letter attempted to enlighten Rogers and other Americans who shared his ignorance of the British abolitionist movement: "It may be astonishing, but the fact stands uncontrovertible, that none of them read any thing else but papers either directly or indirectly opposed to universal freedom."

Garrison's accompanying editorial mentioned that he had recently read that

[27] *The Liberator*, December 18, 1840.

Chartists and socialists had broken up several British antislavery meetings. He could understand their conduct, he wrote, but he condemned their use of force.

> In their struggle to obtain those rights and privileges which belong to them as men, and of which they are now ruthlessly deprived, I sympathize with all my heart, and wish them a speedy and complete victory! But I cannot approve of any rude behaviour, or any resort to violence, to advance their cause: that cause is just, and can best be promoted by moral and peaceable instrumentalities — by appeals to reason, justice, and the law of God — by an unwavering reliance upon that truth which is mighty to the pulling down of strong holds.[28]

His attitude toward the wage worker was identical, then, to his attitude toward the slave, so far as their mode of redress was concerned.

It is clear that he did not see the free workers as a downtrodden class, but neither did he see the chattel slaves as a downtrodden class. He did see both as aggregations of suffering individuals, and in that light the chattel slaves were certainly more in need of a movement to champion their interests. Given the personal terms in which the abolitionists saw the problem of oppression, the slave deserved priority over the free worker because enslavement was personally more degrading than mere oppression. In their propaganda the abolitionists always stressed the degradation rather than the poverty of the slaves. Their individualistic and religious frame of reference happened to direct their primary attention to precisely that aspect of the slave's status which the free worker did not share, and it caused them to portray as secondary those evils which the slave suffered in common with the free worker. That is, both were poor (the abolitionist was willing to admit that some slaves were better off in a material way than some workers), but the slave's poverty resulted from his status: although the abolitionists differed as to how much the worker was responsible for his own

---

[28] *Ibid.* See also Garrison's editorial "The London Convention," *ibid.*, October 23, 1840, in which he expressed his low opinion of British abolitionism (excepting individuals such as George Thompson, Harriet Martineau, and Charles Stuart) as motivated by "nothing more than the natural humanity of the people." In England, he wrote, "it costs no effort to denounce that which does not exist on her soil at home, to wit, slavery. Her abolitionism 'walks in silver slippers,' is *patronized* by her majesty the Queen, receives the condescending support of Prince Albert. . . . Hence, individuals may be very zealous and devoted there in the anti-slavery cause . . . and yet be as hostile to the spirit of freedom, and as unwilling to encounter odium and persecution by espousing an unpopular and radical reform at home, as is the pro-slavery party in the United States." Chartists who broke up antislavery meetings "have not been actuated by any hostility to the anti-slavery enterprise; but, perceiving that some of those who are most vociferous in denouncing oppression abroad, care nothing for suffering humanity at home, they have been stirred up to acts of violence, in their disgust at such hollow-hearted philanthropy. Their conduct is not to be justified, but it certainly admits of some palliation. The Chartists, in their struggle for emancipation, are the abolitionists of the United States; and they are as much hated and feared by all that is conservative, inhuman or despotic." Edward M. Davis, in a letter to Elizabeth Pease, February 15, 1842, Anti-Slavery Letters, BPL, asked, "Why are not the abolitionists of G. Britain [*sic*], chartists repealers & ultra democrats? If hatred of oppression has taken root in the *soul* not in the *fancy*, will not those who cherish it, favour political as well as personal and I may ask religious liberty? There is no beauty in that love of liberty which sympathises with the American slave and forgets the oppressed at home."

poverty, they agreed that that poverty was at least not a necessary evil which he had no legal right to ameliorate. The slave was a chattel; the worker was a man with some freedom to better his lot. The slave could not plead his own cause. Deprived of legal rights, he could not, except by escape, do much to change his condition; others must agitate in his behalf. The free worker had all the legal prerogatives that the abolitionist had and could use the ballot in his own interest.[29] Hence the criticism of the abolitionist for his selective compassion misses the point; given his frame of reference, his choice is unassailable. Those who, like John A. Collins, did come to see the white workers as an oppressed class left the abolitionist movement.[30] There was no necessary conflict between a movement to abolish wage slavery and another to abolish the more extreme form of class oppression, chattel slavery. But the individualistic terms in which the abolitionists saw their task, their enemy, and the beneficiaries of their efforts made common cause impossible in practice.

When the abolitionists declared that the free worker, unlike the slave, had the legal right to improve his condition, especially in the United States where he possessed the ballot, and hence was partly to blame for his poverty, the latter's spokesmen replied that the worker was as much a slave as the Negro; hunger was as compelling an inducement to forced labor as was the whip and made him the slave of the capitalist class rather than of an individual master. The opposing views became the subject of a heated debate in the columns of *The Liberator* in 1846 and 1847.[31] It began while Garrison was in Britain and Edmund Quincy was editing the paper. In the issue of September 4, 1846, Quincy reprinted a letter Wendell Phillips had addressed to George Henry Evans, editor of *Young America*, explaining that he had for some time subscribed to Evans's paper and agreed with some of its doctrines, especially its advocacy of distribution of public lands. But he now had to protest Evans's tenet that a man robbed of his land was worse off than a man robbed of himself. Evans replied in an editorial, reprinted by Quincy:

> If it be true, as I most firmly believe it is, that wages slavery, in its legitimate results of crowded cities, debasing servitude, rent exactions, disease, crime, and prostitution, as they now appear in England and in our Northern and Eastern States, are even more destructive of life, health, and happiness than chattel slavery, as it exists in our Southern States, then the efforts of those who are

[29] The fact that American workers had the vote and British workers did not helps explain American abolitionists' greater sympathy for the latter and their willingness to agree that British workers were oppressed. See, for instance, speeches by Charles Lenox Remond and John A. Collins, reported in *The Liberator*, July 30 and August 6, 1841.

[30] Collins's letters to Garrison, in Anti-Slavery Letters, BPL, during his British tour in 1840 and 1841, show his gradual change in views and growing interest in communitarian socialism. Wendell Phillips ridiculed those views in a letter to Elizabeth Pease, August 24, 1843, same collection. Collins's departure from the abolitionist movement is mentioned in "Chattel Slavery and Wages Slavery," editorial by [Edmund Quincy] in *The Liberator*, October 1, 1847. His disillusionment with communitarianism is explained in his article "Ourselves," reprinted from his paper, *The Daytonian* (Dayton, Ohio), in *The Liberator*, August 28, 1846.

[31] The March 27, 1846, and July 10, 1846, issues contain minor items on the subject before the real debate began.

endeavoring to substitute wages for chattel slavery are greatly misdirected. . . .

Evans went on to say that "the usurpation of the soil . . . makes the working
classes the slaves of wages" and that "men robbed of their land *are* robbed of
themselves most effectually. The National Reform measures would not merely
substitute one form of slavery for another, but would replace every form of
slavery by entire freedom."

Evans was seconded by another National Reformer, William West of Boston,
in one of many of his letters to *The Liberator*. In the issue of September 25,
West explained that the National Reformers did not condemn wage slavery
solely because it caused poverty.

> They oppose it because it holds the laboring classes in a state of
> abject dependence upon capitalists, not only for the bread it is their
> right to eat and the work it is their duty to do, but for the continua-
> tion of their lives, and the preservation of their morals, begetting
> starvation, pauperism, prostitution, infanticide, patricide, suicide,
> murder and piracy, and rendering necessary governments of violence
> and religions of fraud, with the pauper receptacles for the living and
> the dead, and then, Home Missionary and Tract Societies, their
> vindicative penal codes and their revengeful "eye for eye, tooth
> for tooth" creeds, their turnkeys and hangmen, their soldiers and
> marines, and this condition of the laboring classes they conceive
> to be far worse than that of horses and oxen, which is the worst
> possible condition chattel slaves ever can be reduced to. . . . Their
> rallying cry is, *"Down with all slavery, both chattel and wages,"*
> and their single object is, the "Freedom of the Land."

West added that the progress of slavery could never be arrested and reversed
until monopoly of the soil was abolished. Abolitionists must therefore unite with
the National Reformers to limit the amount of land an individual might own,
exempt it from execution for mortgage and debt, and make it inalienable except
to the landless. Slaveowners would have to free their slaves because enormous
plantations would disappear. Many plantations would become vacant, and the
freedmen would settle on them and become yeomen farmers.

The following March, Garrison, back from Europe, joined the debate. "The
evil in society," he wrote, "is not that labor receives wages, but that the wages
given are not generally in proportion to the value of the labor performed." When
capital draws the lion's share, it makes human interests "antagonistical, instead
of co-operative; and those who can obtain power are disposed to oppress the
weak." Various schemes, he said, had been proposed to cure society's ills — distribution of public lands, voting every man a farm, Fourierism, preaching the
gospel, free trade, abolition of money — and he agreed a social reorganization was
necessary. But "we cannot yet see that it is wrong to give or receive wages; or
that money, which is in itself harmless, is the source of almost every human woe
(though we think that ignorance and selfishness are). . . ."[32]

[32] "Free and Slave Labor," *The Liberator*, March 26, 1847. See also Garrison to his wife,
May 20, 1840, Garrison Papers, BPL, in which he describes extremes of wealth and poverty
he has observed on his trip to New York City and attributes the suffering to selfishness.

A few months later it was Wendell Phillips's turn. "Except in a few crowded cities and a few manufacturing towns," he wrote in *The Liberator* of July 9, "I believe the terms 'wages slavery' and 'white slavery' would be utterly unintelligible to an audience of laboring people, as applied to themselves." Workers as a class were neither wronged nor oppressed, and in any case they possessed ample power to defend themselves.

> Does legislation bear hard upon them? — their votes can alter it. Does capital wrong them? — economy will make them capitalists. Does the crowded competition of cities reduce their wages? — they have only to stay at home, devoted to other pursuits, and soon diminished supply will bring the remedy. . . . A wiser use of public lands, a better system of taxation, disuse of war and of costly military preparation, and more than all, the recognition of the rights of woman, about which we hear next to nothing from these self-styled friends of labor, will help all classes much. But to economy, self-denial, temperance, education, and moral and religious character, the laboring class, and every other class in this country, must owe its elevation and improvement.

And he added an admonition that the condition of the American worker must not be equated with that of the disfranchised European worker.[33]

Three months later Edmund Quincy contributed the last major polemic in the debate (it continued for a while in the form of occasional letters to the editor). Replying to a recent editorial in *Young America*, he denied that the need to work made the laborer as dependent as the slave. Yes, he was dependent on his employer, but no more than the employer was dependent on him. This was true in a slave society too; but there capital owned labor, whereas in free society labor owned itself and was free to make the best possible bargain with capital. Proof of this was the continual fluctuation in wages according to the state of the labor market. Further, the large annual immigration into the United States, wrote Quincy, proved that even the poorest workers could move about freely.

> The very paper, which has furnished the text for this Discourse, is established for the purpose of arousing these very *wages-slaves* to redress their wrongs, and establish a better state of things by POLITICAL ACTION! *Slaves* "voting themselves farms," and altering the laws of the land by their ballots! . . . If the white laboring men in America are *slaves*, whose fault is it? They are Slaves that hold

---

[33] The article is reprinted in John R. Commons and others, eds., *A Documentary History of American Industrial Society*, VII (*Labor Movement: 1840–1860*) (New York, 1958), 219–21. Phillips stressed the difference between working conditions in Britain and the United States more than most of his associates, perhaps because he had traveled more extensively and sojourned longer in Britain and on the Continent and unconsciously emphasized the greater oppression of European labor by exaggerating the opportunities open to American labor. For example, see his letter to Richard Webb, January 13, 1848, Anti-Slavery Letters, BPL, in which he enumerated certain categories of British labor paid so little that such workers could be considered "*unpaid*, uncompensated, in any just sense."

the sceptre of Sovereignty in their own hands. . . . Is it so with the chattel Slaves?

And, as if to dispel any remaining doubt that he had failed completely to grasp the labor spokesmen's essential thesis, he asked the question that repeatedly appears in abolitionist arguments on this subject: If wage slaves are worse oppressed than chattel slaves, why do we not see them clamoring for owners?[34]

That Garrison, Phillips, and Quincy spoke for large numbers of Garrisonian abolitionists was demonstrated when antislavery meetings passed resolutions endorsing their views and defeated others representing the doctrines of the National Reformers.[35] A resolution accurately expressing the Garrisonian attitude toward the Northern working class was approved at a meeting in 1849:

> Whereas, the rights of the laborer at the North are identified with those of the Southern slave, and cannot be obtained as long as chattel slavery rears its hydra head in our land; and whereas, the same arguments which apply to the situation of the crushed slave, are also in force in reference to the condition of the Northern laborer — although in a less degree; therefore
> Resolved, That it is equally incumbent upon the working-man of the North to espouse the cause of the emancipation of the slave and upon Abolitionists to advocate the claims of the free laborer.[36]

When Garrisonian abolitionists favored advocacy of the claims of the free laborer they meant, of course, improvements in his condition, not change in his status.[37] The radical change they looked forward to . . . was of a totally different

---

[34] "Chattel Slavery and Wages Slavery," *The Liberator*, October 1, 1847.

[35] See accounts of the New England Anti-Slavery Convention of 1847, *ibid.*, June 4, 1847; and of the annual meeting of the AASS the following year, *ibid.*, May 19, 1848. Cf. George Bradburn's scorn for "such men as Edmund Quincy and Wendell Phillips, the latter of whom has expressed the opinion, that all the people of this country, excepting the slaves, may easily become 'capitalists' by a little 'piety' and 'economy'; and the former gentleman tells us, in the last Liberator I received, that it is purely the fault of the masses themselves, if every thing is not right with them, in this glorious country of ours!" Bradburn to Gerrit Smith, October 8, 1847, Gerrit Smith Miller Collection, SU.

[36] "Seventeenth Annual Meeting of the Massachusetts A. Slavery Society," *The Liberator*, February 2, 1849. Before the resolution was voted on, a member said most of the workers' problems were due to drinking and that this was especially true of the Irish. The mover, Charles Stearns, defended his resolution with remarks on the sufferings of Northern workers. The incident is reported also in *Seventeenth Annual Report, Presented to the Massachusetts Anti-Slavery Society, by Its Board of Managers*, pp. 85–86. See also Garrison's resolution, reported in *Fifteenth Annual Report, Presented to the Massachusetts Anti-Slavery Society, by Its Board of Managers* (Boston, 1847), p. 91: "*Resolved*, That of all classes in this country, to whom the three millions of our enslaved and chattelized countrymen have a right confidently to look for sympathy, aid, and complete deliverance from their horrible servitude, THE WORKING-MEN of the North constitute that class; and so long as they stand aloof from the Anti-Slavery enterprise, they will not only be guilty of manufacturing yokes for the necks, and fetters for the limbs, of the Southern Slave population, but will fail in all their efforts to remove those burdens and monopolies, under which they themselves are groaning."

[37] For example, Samuel J. May and Garrison believed the laborer had to work too hard and too long, and they wished he had more than one day off each week. Garrison to May, January 10, 1848, Garrison Papers, BPL; and May to Garrison, January 15, 1848, Anti-Slavery Letters, BPL.

sort from that demanded by the secular, class-conscious labor spokesmen, but it was radical for all that. It was an early nineteenth-century analogue of modern Christian anarchism; they both envisioned a fundamental change in the social structure and social values but endeavored to construct the good society not by seizure of power from one class by another, but by acts of individual compassion and individual conversion, acts that were to have an ever widening impact until brotherhood and cooperation had quietly transformed the social system. It is in the light of this vision, and not opposition to labor's objectives, that Garrison's "hostility" to labor must be understood.[38] And labor's "hostility" to abolitionism was likewise due, not to opposition to the abolitionists' objectives, but to its preoccupation with its own grievances and program. The gains the labor movement was fighting for were all ameliorative in nature, would not have affected the power of the slaveholders, and were therefore irrelevant to the needs of the slaves; and hence labor's tactics had little relevance to those the abolitionists had adopted. According to Joseph Rayback, outright hostility to abolition was not typical of labor leaders.

> Really typical was a disinterested attitude which had a deeper motivation. Its roots could be found in an awakened class consciousness, one that suggested the possibility of the emancipation of labor through strong trade unions, ten-hour days, mechanics' lien laws, anti-garnishee legislation, prohibition of child labor, land limitation, free grants of the public domain to actual settlers, abolition of chartered monopolies, and universal education. These matters held far more vital importance to workingmen than the liberation of three or four million black men.[39]

The "awakened class consciousness" to which Rayback refers ought perhaps to be called *partial* class consciousness, for all the demands he lists were reformatory, not radical; they could have been (and have been) realized with a less drastic change in American society than was required by the abolition of slavery. When the more far-seeing labor leaders asserted that black labor could never be completely freed by a movement that did not work for the interests of white labor, they were right.[40] And when abolitionists declared that white labor could not emancipate itself unless it worked also for the emancipation of the chattel slaves, they were right. But neither movement took to heart this admonition by some of its own theorists, and one suspects that the theorists themselves did not grasp the full meaning of the principle they stated; it was a propaganda device of each movement to secure the help of the other.

The philosophic difference between the radical abolitionists and the radical

---

[38] Cf. David Donald's interpretation in "Toward a Reconsideration of Abolitionists," in *Lincoln Reconsidered* (New York, 1956), p. 31, which is different from but compatible with mine.

[39] Joseph Rayback, "The American Workingman and the Anti-slavery Crusade," *Journal of Economic History*, III (November 1943), 152–63; the quotation is on p. 155. The fullest discussion of the relation of abolition to the workingmen's movement is Bernard Mandel, *Labor, Free and Slave: Workingmen and the Anti-Slavery Movement in the United States* (New York, 1955).

[40] See Rayback, p. 159, for a statement to that effect by a utopian socialist paper in 1843.

labor spokesmen suggests an inconsistency in the abolitionists' analysis of the nature of slavery. Utopian socialists argued that the worker's legal freedom was a mockery when circumstances conspired to crush his spirit and destroy his incentive to rise; the profit system fostered competitiveness and selfishness, and that system must be changed if love and cooperation were to characterize human relations. No, thundered Garrison; a theory that makes a man the creature of circumstances denies that he is responsible to God for his actions. Such a theory could absolve the slaveholder of guilt for his free choice to continue holding his slaves.[41] It could absolve Northerners of their guilt of complicity with the slave power.

Yet the abolitionists incessantly denounced the slave system for, among other things, fostering brutality, indolence, and arrogance in the masters[42] and demoralization in the slaves.[43] The system, moreover, by requiring the slaves to be illiterate and ignorant, diminished their chances of hearing the word of God and achieving salvation.[44] Fugitives like Frederick Douglass were considered especially worthy of admiration for their success in overcoming the stultifying effects of slavery; how many potential Douglasses, as well as Shakespeares and Luthers, had wasted away their lives in the cotton fields?

The abolitionists' difficulty on this point can be illustrated by articles written by two Garrisonians in *The Liberator*. In a letter to Garrison, printed in the issue of August 27, 1847, Henry C. Wright told of a conversation he had recently had with Robert Owen and concluded by denouncing as "a self-evident *untruth*" Owen's "fundamental principle that *man is the creature of circumstances,* and the necessary inference from it . . . that he is therefore *irresponsible.*" Five issues later, Edmund Quincy wrote that associationism and Land Reform both erred "in vastly exaggerating the evils that environ the life of the white laborer, while they strangely undervalue those that crush the minds as well as the bodies of the chattel slaves."[45] It might be argued that the abolitionists blamed the sinful slaveowners and not the slave system for these crimes. But a slave doomed to hell (although perhaps not the lowest level of it) because his owner had prevented him from hearing the saving gospel was as damned, through no fault of his own,

[41] See, for example, "The Constitution — Political Action. Number III," *The Liberator,* May 1, 1846, in which Garrison wrote, "There is no necessity imposed on any man to be a villain, or to sanction villany [*sic*]."

[42] Slaveholders' "understandings have become brutish, their consciences seared as with a hot iron, and their hearts harder than adamant" (Garrison to Joseph Pease, August 3, 1840, Garrison Papers, BPL). The tendency of slavery is "adverse to the improvement of master as well as slave. Slavery takes away the spur of intellectual, not less than of physical enterprise. . . ." (*Second Annual Report of the American Anti-Slavery Society* [New York, 1835], p. 58)

[43] "[S]uppose it true what has been asserted, that the vast majority [of slaves] are contented and happy — *this* contentment and happiness should be considered not as the best, but as the very worst and most deplorable effect of slavery." ("Address to the People of the United States," by a committee of the New-England Anti-Slavery Convention, *The Liberator,* September 6, 1834.)

[44] This is one of the most frequently encountered indictments of slavery. One instance of its use is in Theodore S. Wright, "Prejudice against the Colored Man" (1837), in Ruchames, ed., *The Abolitionists,* p. 137.

[45] "Chattel Slavery and Wages Slavery," *The Liberator,* October 1, 1847.

as he would have been had the system prohibited the propagation of Christianity. In either case he was a victim of "circumstances." But Garrison spoke for many abolitionists when he scornfully referred to "Robert Owen's absurd and dangerous dogma, that men are 'the creatures of circumstances' — not sinful, but unfortunate — not inwardly corrupt, but outwardly trammelled."[46]

When an abolitionist discussed specific examples of prejudice he usually explained that prejudice was the result of slavery. But when he discussed the religious duty to abolish slavery, he often characterized prejudice and slavery as twin products of the unregenerate soul, manifested in love of domination and in a perverse rejection of the Christian message of brotherhood. In the former case, it would follow that slavery must be abolished in order that prejudice might be eliminated and brotherly feeling made possible. In the latter case, conversion, generating love of all men as brothers, must create the will to abolish slavery. When the abolitionist debated the labor spokesman, he emphasized the advantage of the free worker over the slave by denying that the former was the victim of circumstances. But when he described the effects of slavery he was forced to recognize the effects of circumstances on the mind and soul of the slave; that is, one of the things he most hated slavery for contradicted his own reason for rejecting the "doctrine of circumstances." We need not wonder at the abolitionists' failure to solve the problem of free will versus determinism that has baffled philosophers. It is doubtful, however, that they were even aware of its existence in their rationale.[47] They were agitators, not systematic thinkers, and although most of their theories did form a coherent whole, especially in Garrison's case, they drew from an arsenal of arguments as the specific incident or the weekly editorial required.[48]

[46] Garrison to Henry C. Wright, April 1, 1843, Garrison Papers, BPL. He was specifically criticizing Owen's doctrine that, as Garrison put it, "it is by association alone, in a distinctive community formed on the basis of equal rights and equal property, that the regeneration of the world is to be effected." Garrison was sympathetic to the Northampton community of which his brother-in-law, George W. Benson, was a member; however, members of that community did not own its property in common (see William Bassett to Elizabeth Pease, July 22, 1844, Anti-Slavery Letters, BPL), and Garrison in any case saw such communities as results rather than causes of individual regeneration. Ten years later Garrison expressed the same conviction: at a Woman's Rights Convention in Cleveland in 1853, he replied thus to Ernestine Rose's statement that "society" was to blame for oppression of women: "Society! I know nothing of society. I know the guilt of individuals. Society is an abstract term: it is made up of individuals, and the responsibility rests with individuals." (Elizabeth Cady Stanton and others, eds., The History of Woman Suffrage [New York, 1881], I, 139.)

[47] The only evidence of such awareness that I have seen is Garrison's letter to Henry C. Wright, December 16, 1843, in Garrisons, Garrison, III, 94n–95n. After criticizing Collins's recent conversion to communitarianism, Garrison wrote: "He holds, with Robert Owen, that man is the creature of circumstances, and therefore not deserving of praise or blame for what he does — a most absurd and demoralizing doctrine, in my opinion, which will make shipwreck of any man or any scheme under its guidance, in due season. Still, it cannot be denied that circumstances are often very unfavorable to the development of man's faculties and moral nature; and if, by a reorganization of society, these can be rendered more favorable, — as doubtless they can, let it take place. But it is an internal rather than an outward reorganization that is needed to put away the evil that is in the world."

[48] The abolitionists' dilemma concerning their rejection of the "doctrine of circumstances" while recognizing the effects of slavery on the slaves finds an interesting parallel with the dilemma of modern liberal historians who recognize the effects of environment on

When we turn from an examination of how the abolitionists saw the problem of converting Northerners, to an examination of how they saw the problem of converting slaveholders, we make a surprising discovery: the two approaches were the same, with minor variations. On second thought, this should occasion no surprise; the reasons have already been made clear. First, they considered Northerners deeply involved in the sin of slavery and saw no essential difference between Northern and Southern attitudes toward the Negro.[49] Second, a number of abolitionists — several of the Lane Rebels, James G. Birney, the Grimké sisters, and others — were reformed slaveholders, and abolitionists understandably believe that many more could be induced to follow their path.[50] Third, the individualistic and evangelical terms in which they defined both their task as agitators and the nature of conversion to abolitionism assured them that the conscience of even the most unregenerate slaveholder could be awakened by the redeeming truth if only the channels of communication were kept open and flooded by unremitting propaganda that permitted the guilty soul no hiding place. Those abolitionists who finally gave up hope of converting the South did so, it appears, not because they had lost faith in the power of their message to work conversions but because Southern leaders prevented the message from reaching its intended audience.[51] Southern postmasters and local leaders who could burn *Liberators*

---

personality, as a general proposition, yet assume (sometimes unconsciously) an inherent love of freedom or an irreducible human dignity impervious to environmental conditioning. See the perceptive critique of Kenneth Stampp's *Peculiar Institution* in Stanley Elkins, *Slavery*, p. 23, for a similar point.

[49] Nathaniel P. Rogers used this common abolitionist proposition to argue against Garrison's disunionist policy: "Why should they [the North and the South] separate? Are they not *agreed*? Are they not alike? Are they disagreed as to *slavery*, — or any other iniquity? . . . They shouldn't separate on the slavery question, for they don't differ on it. The North is a little more servile and pro-slavery than the South, to be sure, but not enough to *warrant any quarrel*." Reprint from *The Herald of Freedom*, of "New-England Convention," *The Liberator*, June 21, 1844.

[50] See Theodore D. Weld to James Hall, May 20, 1834, in Barnes and Dumond, eds., *Weld-Grimké Letters*, I, 138–39. Of the eighteen speakers at the Lane Seminary debates, Weld wrote, eight had been born and lived all their lives in slave states; the other ten had lived in slave states, six from one to six years. The states in which these students had gained their firsthand knowledge of slavery were Virginia, the Carolinas, Alabama, Tennessee, Missouri, Kentucky, Louisiana, Arkansas (territory), Maryland, and Mississippi. The *First Annual Report of the American Anti-Slavery Society*, pp. 49–50, cited the Lane episode as proof that slaveholders could be converted, reported evidence from various parts of the South that abolitionist literature was having an effect, and pointed to recent efforts in Kentucky and Tennessee to abolish slavery gradually (the report argued the fallacy of gradualism but praised the good intentions manifested). *Proceedings of the Rhode-Island Anti-Slavery Convention* (1836), p. 52, cited Birney's conversion as proof that slaveholders' consciences could be reached.

[51] There were exceptions, however. Garrison seems to have vacillated between confidence in the power of the truth — a confidence required by his religious tenets — and pessimism resulting from his realistic appraisal of evidence. One expression of this pessimism is in his letter to Joseph Pease, August 3, 1840, Garrison Papers, BPL, in which he wrote "that there is no instance recorded . . . in which the oppressors and enslavers of mankind, except in individual cases, have been induced, by mere moral suasion, to surrender their despotic power, and let the oppressed go free." West Indian emancipation was no exception, for "it was effected by the colossal power of the mother country, and in opposition to the feelings and wishes of the West India planters." There was, he added, no more chance of convert-

and intimidate subscribers could not stop private correspondence, and individual abolitionists with slaveholding acquaintances continued by letter the efforts they were prevented from exerting in an organized way.[52]

The abolitionists' approach to the South has been the occasion for some rather blatant errors of the "presentist" type among historians. Antiabolitionist scholars, noting the hopelessness of converting the South and the uselessness of converting the North, contemn the whole abolitionist enterprise. Proabolitionist scholars, noting the hopelessness of converting the South, diligently search for and find justifications for agitation confined to the North. Those justifications are, I think, better founded than the motive that led to their discovery.[53] Howard Zinn, for example, argues that "only the hypothesis of common interest for the entire population can justify an appeal to the opponent on the basis of reason, asking him to perceive his interest more accurately"; therefore Garrison was justified in using harsh language, for a radical cannot hope "to please that element of the population which cannot possibly be pleased by anything short of total surrender of principle, whose self-interest in fact dictates rejection of any reform.[54] The fact is that during the period covered in the present study it was not at all clear *to the abolitionists* that large numbers of slaveholders were past

---

ing the mass of American slaveholders by appeals to conscience and reason than of transforming "wolves and hyenas into lambs and doves, by the same process." See also Garrison to Elizabeth Pease, November 6, 1837, in Garrisons, *Garrison*, II, 183–84. Lydia Maria Child early became convinced that slavery would end only by violence. See her letter to Abby Kelley, October 1, 1838, in Stephen S. and Abby Kelley Foster Papers, AAS; and to Angelina G. Weld, October 2, 1838, in *Weld-Grimké Letters*, II, 704. James G. Birney had periods of pessimism and depression in which he lost hope of converting slaveholders. For one such period, see his letters to Gerrit Smith, July 14 and September 13, 1835, in *Birney Letters*, I, 202, 243. Angelina G. Weld wrote to Elizabeth Pease, August 14, 1839 (*Weld-Grimké Letters*, II, 784–85), that she was beginning to fear the slaveholders would not repent and that abolition must come by violence. It should be noted that these doubts were expressed only in private letters. Except for Mrs. Child, the doubters were not fixed in their pessimism, in the period covered by this study.

[52] See, for example, copy of Gerrit Smith to General John H. Cocke, December 11, 1840, Gerrit Smith Miller Collection, SU; and *Correspondence between the Hon. F. H. Elmore, One of the South Carolina Delegation in Congress, and James G. Birney, One of the Secretaries of the American Anti-Slavery Society* (New York, 1838). Betty Fladeland, in *James Gillespie Birney*, pp. 162–63, explains the circumstances surrounding Birney's correspondence with Elmore.

[53] Louis Filler, eager to demonstrate the reasonableness of the abolitionists, states that their problem in the 1830s "was not to persuade the South to emancipate its slaves. Only a few persons were infatuated enough to imagine that Southerners might do so. The problem was to persuade the North to permit the abolitionists to voice their testimony against slavery" ("Nonviolence and Abolition," *University Review*, XXX [March 1964], 172). The reference to conversion of slaveholders is clearly inserted as polemic against antiabolitionist historians, for the two tasks are not mutually exclusive. But Filler may in his eagerness have hurt his cause by stating that those who believed efforts to convert slaveholders might succeed were "infatuated"; there are innumerable statements proving that that is precisely what they believed (see note 58 below). Inability in the 1830s to survey the problem from a twentieth-century perspective is no proof of infatuation.

[54] "Abolitionists, Freedom-Riders, and the Tactics of Agitation," in Duberman, ed., *The Antislavery Vanguard*, pp. 434–35. Elsewhere in the essay Zinn does, in my opinion, convincingly defend Garrison's harsh language; the quoted passage does not, however, strengthen the defense, since it is based on an erroneous assumption.

saving, and it was clear *to the abolitionists* that slaveholders, slaves, and Northerners did have common interests — in salvation and social justice.[55] The *one* question for us to ask," wrote Mrs. Child,

> is, What is our duty? What course will best promote the true interests of the slave and the slaveholder? Whoever looks upon the subject in the light of principle and reason, will see that the interests of those two classes, fearfully as they now clash, would, in a right order of things, be most harmonious.[56]

Further, the harsh language used by Garrison and most other abolitionist propagandists, in denouncing the sin of slavery, was not defended on the ground that the chief sinners would reject all appeals in any case and hence need not be considered so far as tactics were concerned. On the contrary, abolitionists repeatedly explained that the slaveholders' consciences could be reached in no other way than the plain — and therefore harsh — declaration that their relation to their chattels was sinful and must be abandoned if the wrath of God were to be averted.

> You may go to the profligate man [explained Amos A. Phelps], and tell him it is for his interest to reform, and he will be a profligate still. So with the slave-holder. You must reach his conscience, and in order to [do] this, you must tell him the plain truth in regard to the moral character of his conduct.[57]

Added the Rhode-Island Anti-Slavery Society: "We expect not to dissuade men from their sins by concealing from them the fact that their conduct is sinful. . . ."[58] The evangelical cast of most abolitionists' thinking provided the initial

[55] David Brion Davis, in "The Emergence of Immediatism in British and American Antislavery Thought," *Mississippi Valley Historical Review*, XLIX (September 1962), 229, explicitly links the evangelical approach to conversion to abolitionism with the abolitionists' rejection of the "doctrine of circumstances" discussed above: "Whereas the gradualist saw man as at least partially conditioned by historical and social forces, the immediatist saw him as essentially indeterminate and unconditioned. The gradualist, having faith in the certainty of economic and social laws, and fearing the dangers of a sudden collapse of social controls, was content to wait until a legal and rational system of external discipline replaced the arbitrary power of the slaveowner. The immediatist, on the other hand, put his faith in the innate moral capacities of the individual." Although Davis is not here discussing conversion of slaveholders, it is clear that this attitude on the part of abolitionists would cause them to assume that innate moral capacities of slaveholders would permit conversion regardless of economic interest in holding their slaves. On p. 228, Davis explains: "Acceptance of immediatism was the sign of an immediate transformation within the reformer himself; as such, it was seen as an expression of inner freedom, of moral sincerity and earnestness, and of victory over selfish and calculating expediency." Surely, the same process could take place within the slaveholder.

[56] [Lydia Maria Child?], "Dissolution of the Union," reprinted from *The National Anti-Slavery Standard* in *The Liberator*, May 20, 1842.

[57] *First Annual Report of the American Anti-Slavery Society*, p. 4.

[58] *Proceedings of the Rhode-Island Anti-Slavery Convention*, p. 43. This determination to show the slaveholders the sinfulness of their conduct implies an assumption that such efforts were not foredoomed to failure. According to Filler, "few persons" shared that assumption. A quick survey of the 1833–1850 sources shows that these "few" included: Lewis Tappan, 1839 and 1843; Garrison, 1834; the Massachusetts Anti-Slavery Society's board of managers, 1835 and 1838; Newburyport Anti-Slavery Society, 1836; Sarah M.

urge to employ the strong language of the preacher warning his flock of the consequences of their persistence in sin. The preacher saw no incompatibility between the sinner's present intransigence and the possibility of his eventual conversion; in fact, it was the existence of both facts that made the harsh language necessary. Similarly, the abolitionist accepted both the present intransigence of the slaveholder and the phenomenon of conversion; his own harsh language was to be the bridge between the two.

There was more than one path to the slaveholders' consciences, however; interest was one. It is important to understand that when the abolitionists explained to Southerners that slaves were less productive than free workers, that the poverty of the South was due to the slave system,[59] that the civilized world condemned them, and that bloodshed might result from their failure to emancipate their bondsmen, they were not replacing their principled appeals by others that had a better chance of being heeded.[60] On the contrary, if the South, wrote Elizur Wright, Jr., was compelled, solely by considerations of interest, to abolish slavery,

and Angelina E. Grimké, 1837; James S. Gibbons, 1842; Essex County Women's Anti-Slavery Society, 1842; a large group of Unitarian ministers, 1845; Theodore D. Weld, 1834, 1836, and 1838; James G. Birney, 1834 and 1835; John G. Whittier, 1833; Elizur Wright, Jr., 1833; Dr. Charles Follen, 1836; Sereno Streeter, 1836; the American Anti-Slavery Society in its annual reports for 1835 through 1838; and Henry B. Stanton, 1839. See Lewis Tappan, "A Third Political Party" (letter to the editor), The Emancipator, November 14, 1839; Lewis Tappan to John Scoble, March 1, 1843, in Annie. H. Abel and Frank J. Klingberg, eds., A Side-Light on Anglo-American Relations, 1839–1858 (n.p., 1927), pp. 114–15; The Liberator, November 22, 1834, August 22, 1835, October 29, 1836, July 21 and August 25, 1837, August 10, 1838, May 13 and 27, 1842; "Protest" against slavery by Unitarian ministers, 1845, in May Papers, BPL; Weld to Birney, June 19, 1834, and September 10, 1834, in Birney Letters, I, 120–21, 133–35; Introduction to Emancipation in the West Indies (1838), in Ruchames, ed., The Abolitionists, p. 152 (though originally written by others, the book was completely revised and shortened by Weld, who presumably wrote the introduction); Whittier, ibid., pp. 49, 53; Elizur Wright, Jr., ibid., p. 60; Follen, ibid., p. 134; Streeter to Weld, August 9, 1836, in Weld-Grimké Letters, I, 326; Annual Reports of the American Anti-Slavery Society: 1835, p. 64; 1836, pp. 46–47; 1837, p. 55; 1838, pp. 108–9; Stanton in Sixth Annual Report of the American Anti-Slavery Society (New York, 1839), p. 12. See also sources cited elsewhere in this chapter.

[59] Examples of such arguments are too numerous to need citation. One remarkable passage warrants quotation, however, for its modern-sounding analysis of the propensity to consume characteristic of precapitalist landed aristocracies: "The slave labor system is notoriously unfavorable to the accumulation of capital. In the management of resources, every thing is sacrificed to present profit. The habit of despotic control generates one of free expenditure." Slaveowners who deviate from this pattern, added the writer, are usually Northern-born. "But to keep up the value of slaves, it is necessary that employment should be found for them, increasing in the same geometrical ratio as the slaves themselves; and to give this employment, far more capital is required than to employ free labor. Whence is this capital to come? From the free states. But will it go from the free states, after slavery comes to be placed on a moral footing with piracy?" (Fifth Annual Report of the Executive Committee of the American Anti-Slavery Society [New York, 1838], p. 110.)

[60] Wendell Phillips was an exception. See his letter to George Thompson, July (?), [1839], Anti-Slavery Letters, BPL, in which he wrote that those who were deaf to appeals to principle could be forced by economic distress; they might close their ears to the pulpit, but they would listen to the voice of the market place (he was advocating encouragement of cotton-growing in India).

the sin would be unrepented and the reformation only nominal.[61] But appeals to interest could open the door by jarring the slaveholder from his complacency; the abolitionist might then open the door a bit wider by showing the troubled sinner the link between his wordly and his eternal interests.

But how could he reach the slaveholder's ear after the South had imposed its intellectual embargo on antislavery propaganda? By imposing a "moral embargo" on the South, Elizur Wright, Jr., formulated thus the theory concurred in by many of his coworkers:

> It were idle to expect to convert the mass of slaveholders by a diffusion of pamphlets; that can only be done by placing them under a moral embargo — by letting them see the image of their crime thrown back upon them from the moral sentiment of every non-slaveholder they meet. The work lies chiefly at the North.[62]

The work lay partly in Britain as well, according to Frederick Douglass in a speech that he delivered over and over, with variations in wording:

> I am met by the objection, that to do so [organize abolition societies in England] is to excite, irritate, and disturb the slaveholder. Sir, this is just what I want. I wish the slaveholder to be irritated. I want him jealous: I desire to see him alarmed and disturbed. Sir, by thus alarming him, you have the means of blistering his conscience, and it can have no life in it unless it is blistered.[63]

In short, if the slaveholders refused to allow direct appeals to their consciences, the abolitionists must find an indirect route. They must ostracize Southerners at

[61] "On Abstinence from the Products of Slave Labor," *Quarterly Anti-Slavery Magazine*, I (July 1836), 399. James G. Birney expressed the same thought in a letter to Gerrit Smith, November 14, 1834, in *Birney Letters*, I, 148: if emancipation were demanded "as a matter of *policy, worldly policy*, the cause of holiness gains nothing — even if you were to succeed, which I hold to be impossible in the South-West — for you have not put to death, and rendered odious, the *sin* of Slavery by leading those who have committed it to repentance before God." Hence, he added, the failure of all gradualist schemes, for gradualism cannot "lay hold of mens consciences." And hence, he wrote later in that letter (p. 151), the need for denunciation and violent language: "Do you not think it probable, that very gentle and calm measures would not have been sufficient to rouse up from its torpor the public sentiment of this nation, and make it, in spite of itself, look steadfastly at the sin and injustice of Slavery?"

[62] "Advance of the Abolition Cause," *Quarterly Anti-Slavery Magazine*, I (October 1835), 103.

[63] Farewell Speech to the British People, 1847, in Foner, ed., *Life and Writings of Frederick Douglass*, I, 227. See also Douglass's letter to Horace Greeley, April 15, 1846, *ibid.*, pp. 144–49; a speech in Moorfields, England, 1846, *ibid.*, pp. 162–65; another in New York before the AASS, 1847, *ibid.*, p. 237. In his public letter to his former master, 1849, Douglass wrote that "the heart of the slaveholder is still within the reach of the truth" (*ibid.*, p. 404). The letter from Phillips cited in note 60 above suggests another reason why British abolitionism could affect American slavery: Britons could not be accused of selfish motives, as American abolitionists were, although falsely. Slavery, he wrote, was most often defended from the Bible. "If WE construe a text in favor of Liberty — it is set down to partiality and prejudice." But "Your appeals sink deep — they can neither be avoided nor blunted by any such pretence & their final result must be conviction. Distance lends them something of the awful weight of the verdict of posterity."

Northern resorts like Newport, refuse fellowship with them in churches, proclaim their iniquity throughout the world via platform and printing press, demonstrate that slavery was in the long run destructive to the soil of the South as well as the soul of the Southerner, and perhaps make that system unprofitable in the short run by boycotting slave-grown produce. It was hoped that slaveowners, deprived of the friendship, fellowship, and patronage that lulled their consciences, would be forced to see themselves as the civilized world saw them, and examine the morality of their way of life. At that point they would become receptive to appeals to their sense of justice and their fear of God.[64] Interest would yield to principle. It will be noted that this tactic was identical to the one used to convert the North; there too appeals to interest were to plow the ground in which the seed of principle would be planted.

After the South imposed its blockade on abolitionist propaganda, it became clear that the seed of principle must first take root and the crop be harvested in the North to make the same process possible in the South. Hence, the abolitionists' concentration of effort to abolitionize the North did not represent an abandonment of the Southern field; rather, it was seen as a precondition for converting the South.[65] On this tactic all abolitionists concurred. They differed on how an abolitionized North could have an impact on the South, but most of them remained convinced, throughout the period covered by this study, that abolitionist propaganda not only could but did have that impact. Repeatedly they quoted statements by eminent Southerners expressing fears that such propaganda was troubling slaveholders' consciences and damaging their morale. The Annual Report of the AASS in 1836, for example, noted the burning of anti-slavery literature in Charleston and President Jackson's message to Congress in which he recommended passage of a law prohibiting circulation in the South of literature intended to instigate slave revolts. The report commented that Southern leaders knew that abolitionists did not direct their propaganda to the slaves or favor insurrections, but that the literature was intended to appeal to the consciences of the whites. It quoted Duff Green, editor of the *United States Telegraph*, "one of the most authoritative organs of *Southern* opinions," to the effect that the South had nothing to fear from slave revolt and that the abolitionists neither intended to, nor could if they would, incite rebellion. "We believe," it quoted Green as saying, "that we have most to fear from the organized action upon the CONSCIENCES and fears of the slaveholders themselves. . . . It is only

[64] One example of this line of reasoning is in an article by Sarah and Angelina Grimké, 1837, in *Weld-Grimké Letters*, I, 366–72.

[65] One of many expressions of this view is in "Letters to Catherine E. Beecher. No. VIII," by Angelina E. Grimké, *The Liberator*, August 25, 1837: ". . . we know that when public opinion is rectified at the North, it will necessarily throw an anti-slavery light from its millions of reflecting surfaces upon the heart and soul of the South, through a hundred thousand different mediums of influence and communication. Public opinion at the North will be the vehicle by which moral truth will be rolled in upon the South, a blazing shield turning every way and exhibiting to the eye of every slaveholder in our country the unchangeable and imperishable principles of justice and truth." The South, added Miss Grimké, knew full well what the abolitionists were aiming at and feared the moral power of the North and the world. See also *Fifth Annual Report of the Executive Committee of the American Anti-Slavery Society*, pp. 108–9.

by alarming the *consciences* of the weak and feeble, and diffusing among our own people a morbid sensibility on the question of slavery, that the abolitionists can accomplish their object." The report then quoted John C. Calhoun to the same effect. Angelina E. Grimké quoted the same words by Green and Calhoun, in a pamphlet published in 1837, and added similar statements by other Southerners. Two years later a pamphlet by William Jay quoted the editorial which Green may by then have regretted ever having written.[66]

Ralph E. Morrow has drawn attention to a fact that makes abolitionist efforts to convert slaveholders appear reasonable: that white Southerners were not united and thoroughly convinced of the rightness of slavery. True, the abolitionists attributed Southern qualms of conscience to what remained of real Christianity in the South and to their own agitation, whereas Morrow shows that they were largely due to the persistence of Jeffersonian thought.[67] But the qualms were there, and abolitionists were quite correct in inferring that not all slaveholders' minds were abolutely shut to their message. Morrow also quotes a statement by the eminent proslavery theorist George Fitzhugh that suggests another defense of abolitionist tactics against criticism by modern historians. Fitzhugh wrote that since many Southerners suspected slavery to be morally wrong, "we must vindicate [the] institution in the abstract."[68] If Fitzhugh was right, so were the abolitionists in attacking slavery in the abstract, that is, as a moral wrong, for such a tactic struck at the slaveholders' most vulnerable spot.

It is interesting to speculate what the result would have been if a large part of the abolitionist movement had not weakened the moral focus of its propaganda and accepted the compromises dictated by political expediency. I am not arguing that the slaveholders could have been converted en masse by attacks on slavery as a sin; I think Garrison was right when he said that no oppressor class ever had given up its power and the American slaveholders would be no exception. But one cannot help wondering whether the abolitionist movement did not yield too much when the major part of it, during the 1840s, played down the purely agitational sort of tactics in favor of a type of political action that gave increasing emphasis to pragmatic alliances with politicians who would not denounce slavery in the abstract. One wonders whether a perseverance in the tactic of agitation and conversion would not have helped to weaken the slaveholders' will to fight.

[66] *Third Annual Report of the American Anti-Slavery Society*, pp. 46–47; [Angelina E. Grimké], *An Appeal to the Women of the Nominally Free States*, pp. 4–5; William Jay, *A View of the Action of the Federal Government, in Behalf of Slavery*, 2nd ed. (New York, 1839), pp. 220–21.

[67] Ralph E. Morrow, "The Proslavery Argument Revisited," *Mississippi Valley Historical Review*, XLVIII (June 1961), 83–84. See also Charles G. Sellers, Jr., "The Travail of Slavery," in Charles G. Sellers, Jr., ed., *The Southerner as American* (1960; New York, 1966), pp. 40–71; on p. 53 he quotes Duff Green's statement quoted on page 379 above.

[68] Fitzhugh, *Cannibals All! or, Slaves without Masters* (Richmond, Va., 1857), pp. 294–95, as quoted in Morrow, "The Proslavery Argument Revisited," p. 86.

Politics and Prejudice: The Free Soil Party and the Negro, 1849–1852

ERIC FONER

There is little doubt that a great majority of nineteenth-century Americans were prejudiced against Negroes. The race question was, of course, fundamental to the institution of slavery in the South, but it was also a deeply divisive issue in the nonslaveholding states of the North and West, and it was central to the attitudes of the national political parties. Race was a particularly crucial issue for the short-lived Free Soil party, heir to the Liberty party and to most antislavery Whigs. The Free Soilers, in 1848 and again in 1852, succeeded in capturing the bulk of the antislave voters in the North, and for the first time the slavery issue threatened to destroy the national political balance. Ironically, as Eric Foner observes, the Free Soilers were very cautious in their demands for the Negro, since they recognized that their supporters would not accept sweeping assertions of racial equality. Deep down, most ante-bellum Americans envisaged the United States as a white man's country, however much they disliked slavery and opposed its introduction into the territories. The Free Soilers went just as far as they felt political expediency would allow them to go, even in 1852 after many of the faint-hearted had returned to the Democratic party. Foner illustrates his argument by close analysis of Free Soilers in Ohio and Massachusetts, to show how the national party attempted to disguise its more radical egalitarian tendencies in the confusion of state and local politics. More important, he indicates the political problems confronting the antislavery movement in the United States prior to the Civil War. Many Americans were opposed to slavery, but most Americans were infected with race prejudice: What could unite antislavery Negrophobes and Negrophiles? The question assumed even greater importance with the emergence of the Republican party later in the 1850's, and of course it proved one with which the political system could not cope. Foner has analyzed the character of the Republicans in his recent volume, Free Soil, Free Labor, Free Men, *in which he deals more intensively with the problem of Northern political ideology (and somewhat more kindly with the Free Soilers), but the present essay suggests the political dilemma which immobilized the ante-bellum political system.*

The formation of the Free Soil party in 1848 by New York Barnburner Democrats, radical anti-slavery Whigs, and the bulk of the Liberty party, marked a distinct turning point in the development of the American anti-slavery movement. For the first time an anti-slavery candidate and platform won the support of many thousands of Northerners, and both major parties saw their Northern wings sundered by the issue of slavery. At the same time, the Free Soilers were the first major anti-slavery group to avoid the question of Negro rights in their national platform. Abolitionists had always included a demand for equal social and political rights for free Negroes as an essential aspect of their program. The Free Soilers, however, recognized that many Northerners, although opposed to the peculiar institution or its extension into the territories, were alienated by these appeals for equal rights for colored citizens. A majority of the citizens of the free states were convinced, as a British observer put it, "that the colored race is by nature a subordinate race; and in no circumstances can it be considered equal to the white."[1] Yet the successes of the Free Soil party and its successor, the Republican, were to show that most of these Northerners would support an anti-slavery doctrine which did not touch on the demands of free Negroes for political and social equality.

The leading organizers of the Free Soil party in 1848 had been the New York Barnburners, who had bolted the Democratic party of the Empire State when it refused to endorse the Wilmot Proviso. The Barnburners had emphasized that their opposition to the extension of slavery was motivated solely by concern for the interests of free white laborers, who would be "degraded" by association with "the labor of the black race." It was because of the Barnburners' opposition that no call for equal rights for free Negroes of the North had been included in the Free Soil platform of August, 1848.[2]

By 1850, however, the Barnburners had returned to the Democratic party, leaving the Free Soil party in the hands of former Whigs and Liberty men, who viewed more favorably the demand for equal rights by Northern Negroes. But the national Free Soil platform of 1852 continued to avoid this issue. The party's leaders realized that in a society characterized by an all but universal belief in white supremacy, no political party could function effectively which included a call for equal rights in its national platform. In addition, the Free Soilers who favored equal suffrage and opposed racial discrimination, were themselves highly ambiguous in their attitude towards the Negro race. Almost all accepted the prevailing belief in the Negro's intellectual inferiority, and many were uneasy about the prospect of a permanent Negro population in their own states. Even where the Free Soil party fought resolutely for the rights of the free Negro, it always treated this problem as a local issue, irrelevant to the central problem of the extension of slavery. This study will focus on the conflicting tendencies in the

Reprinted by permission of the publisher from *The Journal of Negro History*, 50 (October 1965), pp. 239–256. Copyright © by The Association for the Study of Negro Life and History, Inc.

[1] William Chambers, *Things As They Are in America* (London, 1854), 354–55.

[2] See my article, "Racial Attitudes of the Free Soil Party in New York," *New York History*, XLVI (October, 1965).

party's attitude towards the Negro in the states where it was most successful —
Ohio and Massachusetts, in an attempt to explain why the Free Soilers in 1852
avoided the question of Negro rights in their national platform.[3]

I

Of all the Northern states, Ohio placed the greatest restrictions on its colored
citizens in 1848. Negroes were virtually excluded from the state, barred from
the militia and the public schools, and were prohibited from serving on juries
or testifying in cases involving whites. Anti-slavery men in Ohio had been striving for the repeal of the "Black Laws" for several years, and from the moment
of its formation, the Ohio Free Soil party made this one of its primary
objectives.[4]

The election of 1848 gave the Free Soilers the balance of power between
Whigs and Democrats in the state legislature, and the Free Soil members made
repeal of the Black Laws a *sine qua non* of cooperation with either of the major
parties. The State Free Soil convention, meeting in January, 1849, condemned
the laws as "legalized injustice." At the same time, however, the delegates avowed
their displeasure at the prospect of a permanent Negro population in Ohio. For
they resolved, "we desire a homogenous population for our state and believe that
we shall have it whenever slavery shall cease to force the victims of its tyranny
into the uncongenial North."[5] None the less, the Negroes who were in Ohio
deserved better treatment and after a series of negotiations the Democrats agreed
to the election of Salmon P. Chase to the Senate and to the repeal of the Black
Laws, in exchange for Free Soil support in electing several state officials. The
Black Laws were repealed by large majorities in both houses, although as the
Cleveland *True Democrat* observed, the Democrats favored repeal not from
principle, but "by contract."[6]

The Negro of Ohio was still, however, a second-class citizen. He could neither
vote nor hold office. When a convention was called in 1850 to draft a new state
constitution, Free Soil candidates ran on platforms insisting that the state's
colored citizens be afforded equal political rights. The party elected eleven delegates, but when the question of Negro suffrage came up, the unanimous support of the Free Soilers present could not prevent the measure from being de-

[3] In analyzing the racial attitudes of the Free Soilers, ambiguities and contradictions
will be stressed. Yet it must be remembered that these views, unenlightened by modern
standards, were advanced for their own time.

[4] Frank U. Quillin, *The Color Line in Ohio* (Ann Arbor, 1913), 23; Charles T. Hickock,
The Negro in Ohio, 1802–1870 (Cleveland, 1896), 47; Edgar A. Holt, "Party Politics in
Ohio," *Ohio Archaeological and Historical Quarterly*, XXXIII (1929), 94–5, 130–31.

[5] *National Era*, February 8, 1849.

[6] Hickok, *Negro in Ohio*, 50; *Nile's National Register*, January 24, 1849; Theodore C.
Smith, *The Liberty and Free Soil Parties in the Northwest* (New York, 1897), 162–71;
Holt, "Party Politics," 360–67; Albert G. Riddle, "Recollections of the Forty-Seventh
General Assembly of Ohio, 1847–48 (sic)," and N. S. Townshend, "Comments on Mr.
Riddle's Paper," *Magazine of Western History*, VI (August, 1887), 341–51, and (October,
1887), 623–28; Cleveland *True Democrat*, March 26, 1850.

feated by a large margin. Nevertheless, subsequent Free Soil platforms in Ohio reiterated the demand for Negro suffrage.[7]

The Free Soil Congressmen from Ohio echoed these views in Washington. Joshua Giddings, who since 1840 had served as an anti-slavery Whig in the House of Representatives, was one of the leading national spokesmen for Free Soil. Giddings often expressed the conviction that Negroes, as human beings, had certain inalienable rights, and were capable of intellectual elevation, and on several occasions he defended Negro suffrage on the floor of the House. He and Joseph Root, another Free Soil Congressman, were commended by the 1849 Convention of the Colored Citizens of Ohio, for "advocating our claims in the United States Congress." Like most Free Soilers, however, Giddings would not equivocally state that the Negro was the white man's equal. Indeed, at the party's Buffalo Convention of 1848, he told the delegates that slavery had been established "by force of the physical and intellectual superiority of the whites over the colored race."[8]

Salmon P. Chase was another long-time defender of Negro rights. In the Senate, he made it clear that he opposed the restriction of the suffrage to white citizens, and he also criticized proposals which would prohibit Negroes from entering Ohio, as well as measures for compulsory colonization. Yet Chase also felt that considerations of climate would prevent many Negroes from coming to his state, and he echoed the resolutions of the Ohio Free Soil Convention by saying, "Ohio desires a homogenous population, and does not desire a population of varied character."[9]

Such uneasiness about the presence of the Negro in Ohio was evident throughout the state's Free Soil party. It is true that ten of the eleven Free Soil delegates to the Constitutional Convention refused to add their names to a petition to Congress, signed by two-thirds of the delegates, which urged the establishment of a steamship line to Liberia, to encourage colonization. But a majority of the Free Soilers in the Ohio Senate approved a resolution instructing the state's Congressmen to procure the passage of a law setting aside a portion of the public lands for the exclusive settlement of Negroes. This proposal for "internal

[7] Akron *Free Democratic Standard*, January 10, March 21, May 2, 1850; *Report of the Debates and Proceedings of the Convention for the Revision of the Constitution of the State of Ohio* (Columbus, 1851), II, 554–55; David H. Bradford, "The Background and Formation of the Republican Party in Ohio, 1844–61," (Ph.D. dissertation, University of Chicago, 1947), 114.

[8] *Congressional Globe*, 30 Congress, 1 Session, 1019, 2 Session, 55, 128, 31 Congress, 1 Session, 1090; Richard W. Solberg, "Joshua Giddings, Politician and Idealist," (Ph.D. dissertation, University of Chicago, 1952), chapter 1; *Minutes of the State Convention of the Colored Citizens of Ohio* (Oberlin, 1849), 20; Oliver Dyer, *Phonographic Report of the Proceedings of the National Free Soil Convention* (New York, 1848), 9.

[9] J. W. Schuckers, *The Life and Public Services of Salmon P. Chase* (New York, 1874), 78; Frederick Douglass to Chase, May 30, 1850, Salmon P. Chase papers (Manuscript Division, Library of Congress); *Congressional Globe*, 31 Congress, 1 Session, 136; *National Era*, March 24, 1853. During the 1850's, Chase and Giddings insisted that free Negroes be eligible to receive homestead grants, although Congress invariably limited such measures to whites. Their position, of course, did not contradict the Ohio Free Soil party's reluctance to accept a permanent Negro population *in Ohio*. See *Congressional Globe*, 31 Congress, 1 Session, 1090, 33 Congress, 1 Session, 504, 1071, Appendix, 1121, 1744, 1832.

colonization" also received the support of the state's leading Free Soil organ, the Cleveland *True Democrat*. Arguing that God had intended that the Negro race "remain a separate and distinct people," the journal urged the government to set aside land "in the southern climate," for the Negroes of America.[10]

Proposals for internal colonization aroused the same opposition among Negro leaders as colonization to Liberia. Men like Frederick Douglass realized that the idea of separating the two races was grounded in racial prejudice.[11] It is true that the same *True Democrat* would assert on other occasions that once prejudice and discrimination were eliminated the Negro might elevate himself to a position of equality. But despite their commitment to Negro rights, the Ohio Free Soilers realized that an appeal based on the plight of the Negro race would not gain wide support in a state which denied the Negro the elementary rights of citizenship. And they themselves were often uneasy about the presence of a Negro population in Ohio. Free Soil was therefore presented as a doctrine intended for the benefit of the white man, and the party emphasized not the condition of the slave, but the economic and social plight of the poor white in slave areas. "The slave question," wrote the *True Democrat*, "is no Negro question. It goes far beyond the colored race. It touches to the very quick the life and mind, the hopes and happiness, the prospects and progress, of our kith and kin, of every white man in the South."[12]

II

The Free Soilers of Massachusetts demonstrated the same contradictory attitude towards the Negro as their Ohio counterparts. Colored citizens in the Bay State enjoyed a greater degree of equality before the law than other Northern Negroes. Massachusetts had been the second state to abolish slavery, and had long been dominated by the Federalist and Whig parties, which were more receptive to the idea of equal rights than the Democratic. In addition, a relatively articulate Negro leadership had developed, as well as a militant abolitionist movement, and their appeals for equal rights had found many receptive listeners in a state characterized by an individualistic and libertarian heritage. While other states were imposing legal restrictions on their colored citizens, Massachusetts Negroes had access to all the elective offices of the state, could vote, serve on juries, and testify in court.[13]

None the less, in many phases of their lives, the Negroes of Massachusetts were harassed by segregation, and some communities, one Whig complained, were marked by "inveterate prejudice against the unfortunate race." During the late 1830's and early 1840's, the anti-slavery leaders of Massachusetts, many of whom were to become prominent Free Soilers, endeavoured to ameliorate this

[10] *Thirty-Fourth Annual Report of the American Colonization Society*, (Washington, D.C., 1851), 74; *Ohio Convention*, II, 604; *Journal of the Senate of the State of Ohio*, 47 General Assembly, 1 Session, 690; *Proceedings of the Convention of the Colored Freemen of Ohio* (Cincinnati, 1852), 26; Cleveland *True Democrat*, February 27, 1851.

[11] *Frederick Douglass' Paper*, January 29, February 26, 1851.

[12] Cleveland *True Democrat*, September 23, 1853, December 18, 1850; Lester H. Cook, "Anti-Slavery Sentiment in the Culture of Chicago," (Ph.D. dissertation, University of Chicago, 1952), 82–88, 107.

[13] Leon F. Litwack, *North of Slavery* (Chicago, 1961), 3, 16, 94.

prejudice and eliminate segregation. In the state legislature, Charles Francis Adams was known as "the champion of the Negro," and he, John G. Palfrey and Henry Wilson waged a struggle to end the ban on inter-racial marriages, which resulted in the repeal of the law in 1843. Adams was also instrumental in the successful attack on the segregated seating practices of the state's railways. Charles Sumner, too, opposed racial discrimination before he became a Free Soiler, and refused to speak at the New Bedford lyceum because Negroes were excluded from membership and relegated to the poorest seats.[14]

With this background, it was not surprising that the Free Soil party of Massachusetts was a staunch defender of the rights of the free Negro. Free Soil Congressman Palfrey, for instance, defended the Negro race against a Southerner's charge of inferiority, and attempted to have the restriction of suffrage to whites removed from the Constitution of the Territory of Oregon. He also protested against the treatment of free Negroes of Massachusetts in the South. Palfrey was not the only one concerned with this problem; in 1852 the party's state convention adopted a resolution insisting that the rights "of our colored citizens going to other states must be protected."[15]

Despite the gains made in combatting segregation in the 1840's, two flagrant examples of discrimination still remained in the Bay State: the exclusion of Negroes from the militia and the segregated public schools in Boston and other communities. At the Constitutional Convention of 1853, the Free Soil delegates, led by Henry Wilson and Charles Sumner, tried unsuccessfully to rectify the former. Wilson sponsored a motion providing that no distinction on account of race or color should be made in the organization of the militia, and he emphasized that "wherever and whenever we have the power to do it, I would give to all men, of every clime and race, of every faith and creed, freedom and equality before the law." But in spite of the arguments of the Free Soilers, the motion was tabled.[16]

The segregated public schools of Boston had long been the subject of attack by the anti-slavery forces of the state. When a Negro mother brought suit against the Boston School Board in 1849, she had the almost unanimous support of the leaders of the Massachusetts Free Soil party, and she was represented before the state's Supreme Court by Charles Sumner. Sumner's argument, which in many ways forecast the reasoning of the United States Supreme Court over one hundred years later, was based on the contention that separate facilities were a violation of equality before the law. He insisted that Negro schools were in fact inferior to those reserved for white children, and argued that being separate, they

[14] Zephania W. Pease, ed., *The Diary of Samuel Rodman, 1821–1859* (New Bedford, 1927), 269; Howard Carroll, *Twelve Americans* (New York, 1883), 59–60; Louis Ruchames, "Race, Marriage and Abolition in Massachusetts," *Journal of Negro History*, XL (July, 1955), 268–71; Frank O. Gatell, *John Gorham Palfrey and the New England Conscience* (Cambridge, 1963), 95–96; Litwack, *North of Slavery*, 109.

[15] *Congressional Globe*, 30 Congress, 1 Session, 149, 246, 610, Appendix, 134; John G. Palfrey to S. E. Sewall, January 29, 1847, Norcross Papers (Massachusetts Historical Society); Boston *Commonwealth*, September 16, 1852.

[16] *Official Report of the Debates and Proceedings in the State Convention . . . to Revise and Amend the Constitution of the Commonwealth of Massachusetts* (Boston, 1853), II, 72, 75–81, 92, 98.

were inherently unequal. Although his reasoning was not adopted by the court, and it was not until 1855 that the state legislature outlawed school segregation, the Free Soiler was praised by the judges for his argument and received the thanks of Boston's Negro community.[17]

Sumner's plea for equal treatment of the free Negro was echoed by the Free Soil press of Massachusetts. The party's chief organ, the Boston *Republican*, urged Negroes throughout the North to intensify their efforts for equal rights, and called on all anti-slavery men to aid them. Nevertheless, the Massachusetts Free Soilers were not free from the prejudice which was exhibited by their brethren in other states. Richard Henry Dana, who had no interest in the fight for integrated schools and railways, and who flatly asserted that Negroes were inherently inferior to whites was, to be sure, a rarity in the Massachusetts party. But few of his fellows could completely escape the prejudices of their time. Congressman Orin Fowler, for instance, made the familiar proposal in 1852, that a section of the public land be set aside for free Negroes and emancipated slaves. Such an endorsement of segregation was also made by one Free Soiler at the Constitutional Convention, who emphasized that he would not compel the state's militia "to train in company with Negroes," but would allow the colored citizens to organize a militia of their own.[18]

Even the legislators who had accomplished the repeal of the inter-marriage ban had strong doubts about the equality of the races. As late as 1867, for example, Charles Francis Adams wrote that he found it "almost impossible to resist the conviction" that the Negro race was an innately inferior one. John G. Palfrey was, as his most recent biographer puts it, "acutely conscious of race," and desired no social relations with free Negroes. And even Charles Sumner, Frederick Douglass could complain, refused to recognize "the entire manhood and social equality of the colored people."[19] The noted educator Horace Mann, as a Free Soil member of Congress, declared that prejudice was a "moral disease," spread by the "infection" of slavery, and he often reiterated his conviction that each human being should be afforded the opportunity to "develop and cultivate the facilities which God has bestowed upon him." Yet when Mann served as Secretary of the State Board of Education, he was sharply criticized by abolitionists for his "timidity" regarding the question of segregated schools. He gave no aid to a proposal that the legislature outlaw segregation, and his annual reports avoided the issue. "Mr. Mann," *The Liberator* complained, "has yet to utter his first word against it."[20]

An unusual, but revealing controversy developed in 1852, when Mann addressed a letter to the annual Convention of the Colored Freemen of Ohio. In it

[17] Boston *Chronotype*, October 31, 1849; Charles Sumner, *Works of Charles Sumner* (Boston, 1870), II, 327–76.

[18] Boston *Republican*, December 22, 1848; Samuel Shapiro, *Richard Henry Dana, Jr., 1815–1888* (Lansing, 1961), 33–34, 99, 123–26; *Congressional Globe*, 32 Congress, 1 Session, Appendix, 396; *Massachusetts Convention*, 75.

[19] Charles Francis Adams Diary, January 4, 1867, Adams Papers (Massachusetts Historical Society); *Palfrey*, 155, 228; David Donald, *Charles Sumner and the Coming of the Civil War* (New York, 1960), 235.

[20] *Congressional Globe*, 32 Congress, 1 Session, Appendix, 1072; Horace Mann, *Slavery: Letters and Speeches* (Boston, 1851), 143–45; *The Liberator*, December 24, 1847, February 11, 1848.

he wrote: "In intellect the blacks are inferior to the whites; while in sentiment and affection, the whites are inferior to the blacks." Mann also predicted that the Negro race would eventually migrate to the equatorial regions of the earth. It is understandable that some Negroes were upset by this communication. A short time after the publication of the letter, a Colored Convention in New Bedford, Massachusetts wrote to the Free Soiler, asking that he clarify his statements. In reply, Mann repeated his description of the differences between the races, and his belief that the Negro was suited for warm climates. The New Bedford Negroes then reconvened and adopted a resolution condemning Mann for "expressing sentiments inimical to our much oppressed and downtrodden race," and affirming their determination to remain in this country. But the Free Soiler was undisturbed by the censure. He wrote to Theodore Parker, again reiterating his position:

> You will see that the New Bedford people are in a rage. I have allowed the colored race superiority of the affections and sentiments, — the upper end of man's nature; but they want the intellect too.[21]

As in most Northern states, the Democratic party of Massachusetts had traditionally been less inclined to support Negro rights, and more prejudiced in its racial outlook, than the Whig. But the Free Soil leaders did not let their differences with the Democrats on racial matters dissuade them from forming a coalition which elected a Democratic governor in 1851 and sent Charles Sumner to the Senate. It is true that many Free Soilers, who had always been Whigs, were unenthusiastic about joining with their former enemies, but their opposition stemmed from a distrust of the Democratic leadership and the Democratic style of politics. Only Samuel Gridley Howe among the prominent Free Soilers raised a more fundamental objection. Howe, who was, in the words of his most recent biographer, "far in advance of his time" in his racial views, believed that coalition with racist Democrats might be disastrous for the anti-slavery party. Early in 1851, he wrote to Horace Mann:

> The truth is that though the sentiments of the Democratic masses point in the right direction *when let alone,* they will not be let alone by the leaders, nor by their own prejudices. They would plunge the country in war and go to the death to rescue three hundred white Americans from Indian, Russian, or Algerian bondage — but as for the three million *black* Americans, why *"damn' em! good enough for them!"*

And a few months later, Howe prophesied to Sumner:

> We must fight the Democrats before long. They have not — the masses have not — intelligence enough to overcome their prejudice against color.[22]

It is significant, however, that, as in other states, most Free Soilers of Massachusetts saw no contradiction between racial prejudice and anti-slavery feeling.

---

[21] *National Era*, April 22, 1852; *The Liberator*, October 22, November 20, 1852; Mary Peabody Mann, *Life of Horace Mann* (Washington, D.C., 1937), 383.

[22] Harold Schwartz, *Samuel Gridley Howe, Social Reformer, 1801–1870* (Cambridge, 1956), 260–61; Laura E. Richards, ed., *Letters and Journals of Samuel Gridley Howe* (Boston, 1909), II, 334, 352 (italics in original).

The question of Negro inferiority was, as Palfrey put it, "a great problem," but one which had no "material connection with the main question" — the extension of slavery. They realized that the eradication of prejudice posed enormous difficulties, and insisted that, inferior or not, Negro citizens were entitled to equal rights. Nevertheless, the attitude of most of the state's Free Soilers towards the Negro was beset by the same contradiction as in Ohio. As Henry Wilson said in the Senate a few years later, "the natural equality of all men I believe in, as far as rights are concerned. So far as mental or physical equality is concerned, I believe the African race inferior to the white race."[23]

III

The portion of the Free Soil party drawn from the Liberty party was plagued by these same conflicting tendencies. A good illustration is the treatment of the Negro by the Washington, D. C., journal, the *National Era*. As a Liberty organ for over a year and a half after its founding in 1847, and then as the chief national organ of the Free Soil party, the *Era* consistently opposed all legal distinctions between the races, and termed Black Laws and measures excluding Negroes from certain states "atrocious" and "inhuman." It urged white men to strive for the elimination of prejudice and the elevation of colored citizens, and vigorously opposed any suggestion that free Negroes be forcibly colonized.[24]

But the *National Era* coupled its criticism of compulsory colonization with an acknowledgement that, as many Americans complained, the presence of the Negro race was indeed an "inconvenience," and it felt that citizens should voluntarily emigrate to Africa, or to a separate portion of the public lands. The *Era* emphasized, indeed, that it feared its opposition to colonization had "unintentionally repressed the spirit of voluntary emigration among the colored people." "Were we a colored man," this editorial continued, "we would never rest from our wanderings till we had found a place where our children might grow into the dignity of a noble manhood." On several occasions, the Free Soil journal berated Negroes for their reluctance to leave their homes, and advised them to emulate "that spirit of enterprise which animates the Anglo-Saxon race." In fact, the *Era* complained, the Negro's lack of initiative hindered the efforts of anti-slavery men to secure his emancipation. Though the paper noted that the characteristics it ascribed to the Negro race — "patience, contentment, and fidelity" — could be "admirable" traits, it complained that it was "the real evil of the Negro race that they are so fit for slavery as they are." Such words sound strange indeed emanating from one of the most widely read anti-slavery journals in the country.[25]

IV

In summary then, the Free Soil party approached the election of 1852 with a background of support for the rights of colored citizens in Northern states,

[23] *Congressional Globe*, 30 Congress, 1 Session, Appendix, 134–35, 834, 36 Congress, 1 Session, 1684; Boston *Republican*, December 22, 1848. Cf. *Address of the Committee Appointed by a Public Meeting . . .* (Boston, 1846), Appendix, 10.

[24] *National Era*, February 8, September 13, 1849, November 28, 1850, April 24, May 15, 1851, January 29, 1852, March 10, 17, 1853.

[25] *National Era*, April 19, May 3, 1849, November 28, 1850, March 13, 27, 1851, June 2, October 27, 1853.

coupled with at least a partial acceptance of the prevailing belief in the inferiority of the Negro race. The party which faced the task of selecting a national ticket and platform in 1852 was substantially different from that organized at Buffalo four years earlier. Most of the anti-slavery Democrats had returned to their party, as had many Whig Free Soilers. The committee established by the Cleveland Free Soil Convention of 1851 to call a nominating convention the following year, reflected the shift in leadership which had taken place. There were only a handful of ex-Democrats in the group; a large majority had Whig or Liberty backgrounds. As George Julian later recalled, "all the compromising and trading elements that had drifted into the movement in 1848 had now gravitated back to the old parties, leaving a residuum of permanent adherents of the cause."[26]

Inevitably, the 1852 Pittsburgh platform reflected this change; in many respects it was more radical than the one adopted at Buffalo in 1848. The most significant change was that slavery was termed "a sin against God and a crime against man," and abolition was expressly called for, although the federal government, as in 1848, was enjoined from interfering with the institution in the states. The platform as adopted, in fact, differed from those of the remaining fragment of the Liberty party in only one major respect. While the Liberty platforms always included demands for equal rights for the free Negro, the Pittsburgh Free Soil platform avoided this issue entirely.[27]

Nor was this omission an accidental oversight. The question was forcefully raised at Pittsburgh, in a minority platform submitted by the leader of the surviving Liberty party, Gerrit Smith. Smith's resolutions expressed several of the ideas in the majority platform in stronger language, and introduced two new proposals — that slavery, as a violation of human rights, was incapable of legislation, and that the party would "faithfully endeavour" to secure equal political rights for all persons, regardless of color or sex. Smith's report aroused a heated debate, largely concerning the first of his new proposals. After several compromises had been suggested, the resolution terming slavery a sin, which "no human enactment can make right," was adopted. Smith was not satisfied with this concession, but many of his supporters felt there was no substantial difference between his proposal and the compromise.

Though most of the discussion centered on Smith's first proposal, it was apparent that there was a greater difference of opinion regarding the second — the endorsement of equal rights. Moreover, since most of the delegates did not take the idea of equal rights for women very seriously, the real issue was whether to include an affirmation of the rights of the free Negro in the platform.[28] The private attitude of the majority of the delegates was clear, and it was a much more enlightened one than had prevailed at Buffalo. When a Negro delegate was refused service at a railroad station restaurant en route to the convention, all the delegates present walked out. And at Pittsburgh, Frederick Douglass en-

[26] Samuel Lewis to George Julian, November ?, 1851, Giddings-Julian Papers (Manuscript Division, Library of Congress); George W. Julian, *Political Recollections* (Chicago, 1884), 113.

[27] Kirk H. Porter and Donald B. Johnson, eds., *National Party Platforms* (Urbana, Illinois, 1956), 18–20.

[28] *National Era*, August 19, 1852.

countered none of the difficulties which he had met at Buffalo. The delegates of 1852 "were far more ready to welcome to [their] platform the man of sable hue."[29]

But private attitudes and public political pronouncements were two different things. It may well have been true that, as George Julian later recalled, "an assemblage of purer men never convened for any political purpose," but the realities of politics demanded that some of the purity be sacrificed, and many of the delegates reacted sharply to Smith's proposal. The veteran abolitionist Owen Lovejoy of Illinois, for example, told the convention that he "was not willing to make fools of ourselves" to appease Smith or gain the votes of his small band of followers. Joshua Giddings, speaking for the majority platform, said he did not wish to have the platform "embarrassed by indefensible positions." Giddings, of course, believed in equal rights, and he hastened to point out that the Ohio Free Soilers had achieved the repeal of that state's Black Laws. He insisted, nevertheless, that such a matter should not be in the national platform, but that each Free Soiler should decide the issue for himself. Charles Francis Adams, the vice-presidential nominee of 1848, agreed with Giddings, terming Smith's proposals "not even plausible." And it was apparent that a majority of the convention felt the same. After the compromise on the "legalization" of slavery was adopted, Smith's resolutions were tabled by 197 to 14.[30]

The Free Soil press of the country viewed the Pittsburgh platform enthusiastically, and some newspapers were critical of Smith's resolutions. Some of the party's leaders, however, felt the platform was too radical, even without the equal rights plank. Men like Salmon P. Chase, though they supported the convention's nominee, John P. Hale, privately expressed the conviction that the delegates should have adopted "no extreme resolutions."[31]

Gerrit Smith, however, voiced the opposite complaint. At first, perhaps influenced by his friend Frederick Douglass' swift endorsement of Hale, Smith decided to support the Free Soil candidate, though he felt that the platform was marked by "wariness and timidity." But by September, he had concurred in a call issued by the Liberty party leader, William Goodell, for a new Liberty convention. Frederick Douglass, too, took part, although he acknowledged that "what is morally right is not at all times politically possible." The address of this assembly, which nominated Goodell for president, was written by Smith, and illustrated the essential difference between the Free Soil and Liberty parties. For while conceding that the Pittsburgh platform was "essentially the platform of the Liberty party, . . . if judged of in light of its general principles," the convention adopted as its first resolution;

> The Liberty Party cannot consent to fall below, nor in any degree to qualify, its great central principle, that all persons — black and

[29] *Reunion of the Free-Soilers of 1848, at Downer Landing, Higham, Massachusetts* (Boston, 1877), 43; *Frederick Douglass' Paper*, August 20, 27, 1852; H. M. Addison, "An Episode of Politics," *Magazine of Western History*, IX (January, 1888), 274.

[30] *National Era*, August 19, 1852; New York *Tribune*, August 13, 1852; Julian, *Political Recollections*, 113; Charles Francis Adams Diary, August 11, 12, 1852, Adams to Charles Sumner, August 15, 1852, Adams Papers (Massachusetts Historical Society).

[31] Boston *Commonwealth*, August 16, 1852; Salmon P. Chase to E. S. Hamlin, August 13, 1852, Chase Papers (Library of Congress).

white, male and female — have equal political rights, and are equally entitled to the protection and advantages of the Civil Government.[32]

V

Thus the Free Soilers of 1852 continued the divorce of anti-slavery and the ideal of equality, which the party had begun in 1848. Yet some contended that this separation was a negation of the very basis of the anti-slavery movement. For it, as many abolitionists argued, race prejudice lay at the root of slavery, then only by combatting that prejudice could abolition be achieved.[33] The Free Soilers, however, rejected such assertions. For, as the *National Era* wrote, at the time of the Pittsburgh Convention:

> A patriot may desire to check the progress of the slave system, for reasons which concern the national honor and prosperity, whether the black man is capable of social and political equality with the whites or not, and without being at all responsible for the decision of that question.

The *Era* maintained that an anti-slavery Northerner was not bound "to admit a black man to his table for the sake of consistency." "There are millions of white men in the United States," it wrote, ". . . who are not Abolitionists, [who] would gladly abolish slavery today, if the slaves could be removed to a foreign country."[34] Free Soil was the only anti-slavery position which could gain the support of such men. For the party had no official position on the status of the free Negro. As Giddings suggested at Pittsburgh, each Free Soiler could make up his own mind.

Moreover, the Free Soilers recognized that the charge of "Niggerism" which was raised against them might prove fatal to their chances of success. Their evasion of the question of Negro rights was an attempt to prevent what Henry Wilson complained of in the Senate a few years later:

> Whenever we resist the expansion of slavery into the territories, we have a lecture about the equality of the races. When we propose the homestead policy for the free men of this country, we have lectures about maintaining the equality of the races . . . This is not a question of the equality of the races.[35]

Once the North was convinced that anti-slavery was, in fact, "not a question of equality of the races," but a movement which would benefit the white man, the foes of slavery could gain unprecedented support in the free states . . . Before the emergence of the Free Soil party, the anti-slavery movement had been un-

---

[32] *The Liberator*, August 27, 1852; *Frederick Douglass' Paper*, September 10, October 15, 1852; Gerrit Smith to George Julian, September 2, 1852, Gamaliel Bailey to Julian, September 7, 1852, Giddings-Julian Papers; Ralph V. Harlow, *Gerrit Smith* (New York, 1939), 191; the 1852 Liberty platform is in Works Projects Administration, eds., *Calendar of Gerrit Smith Papers, in the Syracuse University Library* (Albany, 1941), II, between pages 136 and 137.

[33] Cf. Chambers, *Things As They Are in America*, 358.

[34] *National Era*, August 12, 1852.

[35] *Congressional Globe*, 32 Congress, 1 Session, Appendix, 1119, 33 Congress, 1 Session, 275–80, 36 Congress, 1 Session, 1684.

able to enlist the support of a large segment of Northern workers. Many felt the abolitionists were indifferent to the conditions of Northern laborers, and feared that emancipation would precipitate an influx of Negroes, whose competition would depress wages and threaten the jobs of white working men. But the Free Soilers' promise of free land, coupled with the assurance that slavery would be excluded from the territories, and, in many instances, that free Negroes would be restricted to their own portion of the public lands, won many working men to the anti-slavery ranks for the first time. Men who had no sympathy for the plight of the Negro, free or slave, became convinced that the rights of white men were threatened by the spread of the peculiar institution.[36]

"The cry of Free Men," Frederick Douglass' North Star declared in 1849, "was raised, not for the extension of liberty to the black man, but for the protection of the liberty of the white."[37] Douglass was right, but he overstated his case. It was true that the party had originally been organized by New York's Barnburners, who were indeed solely concerned with the future of the white man. But it also numbered among its leaders men who were sincerely committed to the attainment of equal rights by Negro citizens. Even these men, however, realized that the anti-slavery movement had striven for years to ameliorate racial prejudice, with little success. Indeed, astute observers noted that in many areas, the spread of anti-slavery sentiment had been accompanied by an actual increase in anti-Negro feeling. But political expediency was not the only reason for the party's avoidance of the question of Negro rights. Even the Free Soil party's staunchest defenders of the rights of the free Negro — men like Giddings, Chase, and Palfrey — did not, as Gerrit Smith was fond of pointing out, regard the Negro as "fully a man."[38] They were therefore prepared to acquiesce in the elimination of equal rights from the anti-slavery platform in 1848, and bow to considerations of political effectiveness in 1852, by refusing to reinsert that plank. A man like Smith, on the other hand, who had close personal relations with free Negroes, and who completely rejected any notion of white supremacy, could never agree to such an alteration. Yet the platform of the Free Soilers, avoiding as it did the question of Negro rights, was the only anti-slavery position that Northern society was willing to accept and support. Within a few years it would become the most formidable political force in the nation.

[36] Louis Filler, The Crusade Against Slavery (New York, 1960), 90–91; Joseph G. Rayback, "The American Workingman and the Anti-Slavery Crusade," Journal of Economic History, III (November, 1943), 152–63; Williston H. Loften, "Abolition and Labor," Journal of Negro History, XXXIII (July, 1948), 249–83.

[37] North Star, January 12, 1849.

[38] Proceedings of the National Liberty Convention (Utica, 1848), 46–47; New York Herald, August 13, 1852.

Policies and Possibilities

W. R. BROCK

It was more difficult to end the Civil War than to begin it, just as it has seemed easier to understand what was at stake during the war than to analyze the Reconstruction controversy. In some ways, however, Reconstruction is vastly more important to contemporary Americans, since the political and constitutional legacy of the years immediately following April 1865 has never been more keenly questioned than in the years since the Supreme Court's desegregation decisions of 1954. W. R. Brock attempts to set out in a straightforward fashion the problems involved in reestablishing national government as they appeared to Americans in the months from Lincoln's "ten per cent" plan of December 1863 to the adoption of the Thirteenth Amendment two years later. He concentrates his attention especially on the situation in the last half of the year 1865, when the South had surrendered, Andrew Johnson had succeeded Lincoln in the presidency, and the people of both North and South were suddenly thrust into a bitter controversy over how the nation should resume its ordinary affairs. Some of the problems are obvious. There was general agreement in the North that the Southern states had to be reintegrated into the Union, that slavery had to be ended, and that the North should control the formulation of national policy, but there was no consensus as to what exactly these desiderata meant or how they were to be achieved. Perhaps the most general feeling was that the rebellious states ought not to be readmitted without providing at least minimal guarantees of good behavior, but there was a deep division among Unionists as to what kind of equality the free Negro was entitled to. An already difficult situation was rendered even more confused by the authoritarian and unilateral course along which President Johnson hurled himself and the nation. Brock carefully sorts out the elements of the problem as Johnson, the Republicans, and the Southerners saw them, although he makes little effort in this essay to explain the origins or character of their attitudes. Compare his presentation with Eric McKitrick's very different mode of analysis. Consider also the ways in which the constitutional structure and political practice of the United States combined to shape the alternatives open to the statesmen of the era. Then, as now, the actions of politicians were limited in many ways, a point frequently ignored by those displeased with particular results of the American political process.

Three questions lay at the heart of the Reconstruction controversy: who was to control the South, who was to govern the nation, and what was the status of the negro? Like many simple questions they demanded intricate answers and it was an error of Northern opinion to expect easy ones. In May 1865 Sam Wilkinson, of the firm of Jay Cooke, gave a picture of Northern opinion distilled from the reports of some 4,000 loan agents. "The feeling is now general," he wrote, "that the war must be prosecuted until the Rebels lay down their arms and submit to the Government. To the poor deluded soldier in the ranks, pardon — if repentant. To the leaders and their accomplices in Treason, the justice that is due to *Traitors!!* No peace until it can be made a permanent peace — and the feeling is, that peace cannot be permanent with Slavery in the country."[1] This statement was typical of much Northern opinion, and its various elements were to recur again and again with countless variations. Submission and a return to allegiance was the first requisite, and once the Southern armies had laid down their arms this was not difficult to obtain. Indeed the willingness of Southerners to take an oath of allegiance to the United States as the price of amnesty became a source of embarrassment to Northerners who concluded that the formal oath of loyalty was being taken by large numbers who remained at heart enemies of the United States. Allegiance as a legal concept was not enough, but how could it be defined in such a way that it would include those who were loyal at heart and exclude all others? This question was to plague and weaken every Northern plan of Reconstruction. A possible escape from the dilemma seemed to be indicated by Wilkinson's second point, for it might be possible to achieve a workable solution by distinguishing between the mass of the Southern people and their leaders. The North had evolved a convenient theory that the real will of the Southern people had always been in favour of the Union and against secession, but that they had fallen under the selfish domination of their aristocratic leaders. There might be ardent secessionists among the men in the ranks, and there might be true Unionists among the leaders, but they did not form the majorities in their respective classes; though some of the wicked might flourish and some of the innocent might suffer, discrimination by class might be the most equitable way of distinguishing the secessionists goats from the deluded sheep. This argument made it necessary to define a leader and here the difficulties began. Every plan of Reconstruction proposed by the two Presidents and by Congress included some scheme for discriminating against Confederate leaders, but the proposals ranged from a narrow schedule which would penalize only those who had held high executive or military rank and members of legislatures to the exclusion of all who had supported the Confederacy. The more far-reaching the proposal for penalization the more difficult it became to provide for law and order in the South, and the more restricted the discrimination the more likely was the South to fall into "disloyal" hands.

The difficulties in devising a programme for penalizing the leaders of secession did not alter the invincible repugnance of the Northerners to the idea that Con-

Reprinted by permission of the Macmillan Company of Canada Ltd., St. Martin's Press, Inc., and Macmillan London and Basingstoke from *An American Crisis: Congress and Reconstruction, 1865–1867* by W. R. Brock, pp. 15–48.
[1] Library of Congress, *Butler Papers,* 3 May 1865.

federate leaders should resume their places of authority in the nation. This was indeed one of the pivots upon which the crisis of Reconstruction turned, and it was one of the common strands which bound together the diverse elements of the Republican party.

The problem was complicated by the myth of Southern Unionism. The favourite belief that many, perhaps the majority, of those fighting for the Confederacy were "deluded" and not true secessionists was supplemented by a persistent conviction that there were large numbers of faithful Unionists in the South, suppressed and persecuted during the war, but ready to step forward and assume the lead. Again it was a common feature in all plans of Reconstruction that power should be transferred to this hard core of real Unionists. Lincoln's ten-per-cent plan implemented this idea, and so, for that matter, did Andrew Johnson while war governor of Tennessee. This transference of power might be effected in Tennessee and Arkansas, where considerable districts had remained Unionist during the war, and might just work in Louisiana if the Unionists could capture the commercial interests of New Orleans; elsewhere in the South it was unlikely to succeed because the Unionists were scattered and drawn from the least educated portions of the population. And even if the Unionists could be placed in power by the authority of the national government they were unlikely to win from former Confederates that degree of respect and consent without which government would be impossible. Was it better to entrust civil government to a despised minority with the support of Federal troops, or to allow the suspect majority to resume or continue the functions of civil government, or to continue unqualified military rule until loyalty had grown deeper roots in the South? And if the South was held in tutelage was this more likely to lead to reconciliation through a change of heart or to permanent alienation? Again the simple expectation led into a bewildering maze of speculation.

The myth of Southern Unionism was but one aspect of Northern ignorance about Southern society. One way or another Northerners had accumulated a good deal of information about the South but much of it came through partisan channels. The pictures drawn by abolitionists, by wartime propaganda, and by genuine Southern loyalists, were unlikely to present the whole truth about the society or the men whom they condemned. A great many Northerners, including some of the politicians, had been in the South as soldiers, but the impressions gathered by armies of occupation are notoriously unreliable as sources of information about conquered peoples. Northern journalists and writers who went South after the war visited it as alien territory — to discover the facts which reinforced pre-conceived notions about the Southern character — and saw a demoralized and partially ruined society in which it was difficult to distinguish between the effects of war and the consequences of defects in the social system. For most of the time, therefore, Northerners were not only feeling in the dark but in a darkness which they had been taught to despise and attributed to slavery and "aristocracy." Northern congressmen had, however, their own sources of information and during the winter of 1865–6 their desks were being piled high with letters from the South which spoke of secessionism revived, of Unionists ostracized or even persecuted, of negroes denied their rights as free men, and of a bitterness which seemed incompatible with formal professions of allegiance to the United States.

Of all Republican propositions the easiest to state was the obligation to end slavery, and it was not difficult to demonstrate that this was not fulfilled with the formal act of abolition. If the negro was no longer a slave he had still to be made a citizen, and this carried Northern aims into the heart of Southern society. As Carl Schurz observed in his report on the South which President Johnson commissioned and rejected: "The General Government of the republic has, by proclaiming the emancipation of the slaves, commenced a great revolution in the South, but has as yet not completed it. Only the negative part of it is accomplished. The slaves are emancipated in point of form, but free labor has not yet been put in the place of slavery in point of fact. And now, in the midst of this critical period of transition, the power which originated the revolution is expected to turn over its whole future development to another power which from the beginning was hostile to it and has never yet entered into its spirit, leaving the class in whose favor it was made completely without power to protect itself and to take an influential part in that development."[2] In course of time President Johnson was to evolve a theory of Reconstruction by which the whole of congressional policy was the outcome of a Radical conspiracy to force negro suffrage upon the South, and modern writers have added to this a corollary that the motive behind negro suffrage was the wish to fasten the economic domination of the North upon the South. In a sense the Johnson theory was true because abolitionists saw negro suffrage as a necessary element in Reconstruction, but on no point did they find it harder to convince the bulk of the Republican party. Even among the Radicals there was hesitation, and rank and file Republican politicians showed no eagerness to commit themselves. At the close of the war the Republicans could be divided into three main groups: those who carried on with varying degrees of sincerity and enthusiasm the abolitionist quest for racial equality, those who believed in the biological inferiority of the negro and were conscious of the dislike of the negro among their constituents especially in the Midwest, and those who believed in racial equality as an abstract proposition but thought that any attempt to give the negro all the rights of citizens was inexpedient and premature. Most members of the party were, however, able to subscribe to the general proposition that the rights of the negro must be protected against his former masters. Like other simple statements this concealed a multitude of snags and difficulties.

What were the rights which ought to be protected? The majority of Republicans, shirking the difficulties of full equality under the law, attempted to compromise by distinctions between the various kinds of right. There were, ran the theory most popular among moderate Republicans, three kinds of right — civil, political and social. The first ought to be secured to all citizens, the second lay within the discretionary power of State legislatures, and the third — being mainly affected by the private decisions of individuals — was beyond the reach of any law. Civil rights were confined to equal status in courts of law and equal protection outside; political rights included suffrage and the laws for such matters as public transport and public education; social rights were those which individuals could freely accord to or withhold from their fellow citizens when receiv-

[2] F. Bancroft (ed.), *Speeches, Correspondence and Political Papers of Carl Schurz* (New York, 1913), I, 355.

ing them into their homes, giving them equal participation in business or equal status as labour, or welcoming them into private associations or private schools. Some Republicans could make and adhere to these distinctions to their own satisfaction; others were troubled from the start by the illogicality of declaring that a man was an equal citizen while allowing "political" and social discrimination against him; Radicals such as Sumner and Thaddeus Stevens believed from the start that equal right was an indivisible concept though the latter was prepared to temporize in order to gain a point. Behind the theory of equal right, however subdivided, was a further and major difficulty, for the protection of negro rights was an implicit recognition of his inferiority in society. The Radical answer was that this inferiority was an artificial condition imposed by the slavery, and that once the negro was armed with the rights of a citizen he would raise himself to economic and educational equality; others were not so sure. It was an act of faith to believe in the unproven assumptions of racial equality, and circumstances alone could produce the admission that they were worth a trial. Opportunism brought more men to an acceptance of equal rights than faith in the principle, but it would be an error to discredit the cause because some men came to support it because they believed that it was necessary before they believed that it was right. Few great movements of reform would not be open to the same accusation.

The many variations upon the Republican attitude were in sharp contrast to the theory of State rights. The key doctrine was that the States were indestructible and retained under all circumstances rights which were guaranteed to them under the Constitution. These rights could be changed only by an amendment to the Constitution, and an extreme version of the State rights theory could maintain that even an amendment was unconstitutional if it subtracted from the essential reserved rights of States.[3] Paradoxically the upholders of State rights seized avidly upon the equally mystical doctrine that the Union was indissoluble. Secession was void and must be treated as a nullity; individuals had renounced their allegiance to the United States and had gone into rebellion, but the States could not do this as the war had been fought to prove, and it followed that once individuals had ceased their resistance to lawful authority the rights of States, which were a part of that authority, were resumed without alteration or diminution. The only Reconstruction which was necessary and lawful was for the people in the States to choose a new government and this government would then have exactly the same rights in the Union as loyal States and neither the President nor Congress could impose any conditions which were not already in the Constitution. This theory had a superficial logic for a people accustomed to believe that law was superior to events, but a close examination of its arguments will show an even deeper confusion than that which existed on the Republican side. It pretended that events which were legally void had never happened. It confused the State as a geographical entity, as a government, and as a community of people, and assumed that when the government and people had fought the United States there remained some quality inherent in the land of a State which was different from the will of its people. It failed to recognize that the initiative in remaking the States had to come from somewhere, and

[3] Cf. *Congressional Globe*, 38.2.222 [and p. 266 in the book from which this selection is taken].

that in most of the Southern States there was no effective authority save the occupying armies of the national government. It imagined that a legalistic theory could compel a government with the power to act to acquiesce in chaos or in what its supporters believed to be wrong.

There was moreover one entering wedge which weakened the State rights position, and which appeared to have great force. Emancipation had automatically terminated the provision of the Constitution under which slaves counted as three-fifths of a man in making the count upon which congressional representation was based. If the law took its course without amendment the Southern States, when restored, would find themselves with a handsomely increased congressional apportionment. At the same time it was evident that, if left to themselves, no Southern States would give the vote to any negroes. It could be argued that the Northern States counted unnaturalized foreigners for the purpose of apportionment, but there was a difference between counting those who would probably become qualified voters before the next census and counting those who were considered by their States to be permanently debarred from the suffrage. Calculations varied but it seemed that the South might expect between twelve and twenty additional seats in the House of Representatives, and therefore in the electoral colleges, because of abolition. This was a prospect which even sympathetic Northerners were disposed to regard with alarm.

In point of fact no plan of Reconstruction accepted the State rights theory as its starting-point. Lincoln ignored it and attempted to deal with things as they were. Johnson ignored it when he imposed his own conditions on the South, but invoked it to prevent the Republicans from imposing their conditions. Yet in a sense State rights did lie at the end of every Reconstruction road, for sooner or later the Southern States must be back in the Union with the same rights as all other States. Johnson believed that this must come soon; Radicals believed that it must be delayed until a revolution had been consummated in the South; but both accepted the eventual equality of all States in the Union. This gave a particular flavour to the great debate over Reconstruction because everyone knew that the Southerners must return to Congress (and perhaps with Northern Democrats to control the national government) and that even if they remained there as an isolated group they would have the power to resist amendments to the Constitution. If Republicans could see this danger only too clearly, the sad fragment of the once invincible Democratic party looked eagerly to the promised land; the future of both parties was at stake, and this gave an added bitterness and a frantic urgency to the debates over Reconstruction. The constitutional deduction for Republicans was that any programme which they enacted must be enshrined in amendments to the Constitution and not left at the mercy of future congressional majorities, and thus moderates were driven towards constitutional changes which might otherwise have alarmed them. Whatever policy was agreed would also have to be enacted before the Southerners returned, because future Congresses might be unwilling or unable to pass the necessary laws. The main casualty was any programme of staged development which might lead the negroes from their depressed condition towards full citizenship.

This is the background for the various Reconstruction policies from Lincoln to the Reconstruction Acts. In his Proclamation of 8 December 1863 Lincoln offered a full pardon to all who had participated in the rebellion on condition that they would take an oath of allegiance to the United States and undertake to observe all presidential proclamations respecting slaves. This general amnesty was qualified by a long list of exceptions which excluded from its provisions all who had held positions of authority under the Confederacy or left offices under the United States to join the rebellion. When the loyal portion of the State, so defined, amounted to ten per cent of the votes cast in 1860, this minority could then set up a government which would be recognized by the President as the lawful government of the State. The President would not object to laws affecting the freedmen which "shall recognize and declare their permanent freedom, provide for their education, and which may yet be consistent as a temporary arrangement with their present condition as a laboring, landless, and homeless class."[4] Critics noticed in this the lack of any specific requirement that the freedmen should be given civil rights (though it was recognized that it was difficult to be more precise so long as emancipation depended solely upon a proclamation issued under the war power), and they were disturbed by the President's deliberate sanction to the continuance of pre-war State constitutions and legal codes which had included discriminatory treatment of free negroes. The most striking fact about this ten-per-cent plan was, however, its role in war strategy. In the midst of a war it was extremely useful to set up, in secessionist States, governments which could claim to be loyal; puppet Unionist administrations could give a show of legality to Northern rule in occupied areas, might serve to attract waverers back into the Union fold, and would encourage Unionists still under Confederate rule. These arguments were, however, no longer applicable once the South had surrendered. If the ten-per-cent governments acted as magnets to attract the support of lapsed or defeated Confederates their future might be assured, but they were far more likely to be treated as governments dependent upon Federal arms and composed of discreditable men who had abandoned the cause in the hour of need. Thaddeus Stevens made a cogent criticism of the ten-per-cent plan, as a means of Reconstruction, when he said that "the idea that the loyal citizens, though few, *are the State*, and in State municipalities may overrule and govern the disloyal millions, I have not been able to comprehend. . . . When the doctrine that the *quality* and not the *number* of voters is to decide the right to govern, then we no longer have a Republic but the worst form of despotism. The saints are the salt of the earth, but the 'salt of the earth' do not carry elections and make governments and presidents."[5]

The Wade-Davis Bill of July 1864 is usually contrasted sharply with Lincoln's plan, though Lincoln described himself as "fully satisfied with the system for restoration contained in the bill as one very proper plan for the loyal people of any State choosing to adopt it," and was prepared "to give the Executive aid and assistance to any such people. . . ."[6] Lincoln vetoed the bill because he did not

[4] Proclamation of Amnesty and Reconstruction, 8 Dec. 1863. J. D. Richardson (ed.), *Compilations of the Messages and Papers of the Presidents, 1789–1897* (Washington, D.C., 1907), IV, 213 ff.

[5] 22 Jan. 1864. C.G. 38.1.317.

[6] Proclamation of 8 July 1864, Richardson (ed.), *Messages and Papers*, VI, 222. The Wade-Davis Bill was sponsored by Ben Wade (cf. p. 82 [in the book from which this selection was taken]) and by Henry Winter Davis. The text of the bill can be found in Richardson (ed.), *Messages and Papers*, VI, 223 ff.

wish to be committed to any one scheme of Reconstruction and because it included a clause emancipating the slaves in the Confederate States which he thought must be done by constitutional amendment. The Wade-Davis plan operated in three stages. The first required an oath to support the Constitution of the United States, and when a majority of white males in a State had taken this oath the next stage of Reconstruction could begin. In the second stage a convention was to be elected by loyal white male citizens who could take the "iron clad" oath of 2 July 1862 which excluded all who had given any aid or support to the rebellion; this convention was to make a Constitution which would exclude from voting for the State legislature or governor all persons who had held "any office, civil or military, except offices merely ministerial, and military offices below the grade of colonel, state or confederate, under the usurping power," to abolish slavery and to repudiate debt incurred under the Confederacy. This Constitution was then to be ratified by a majority of the legal voters as already defined. The third stage was the recognition by the United States (i.e. by President and Congress) of the State government as republican in form. It was specifically stated that the State should then be re-admitted to representation in Congress, but the right of Congress to accept or reject individual senators or representatives was tacitly assumed. The laws of the State, other than slave codes, in force before the rebellion would remain in force except that "the laws for the trial and punishment of white persons shall extend to all persons" and the qualification for jurors should be the same as that for voters. The bill then emancipated slaves in the rebel States and imposed penalties upon persons who restrained the liberty of freedmen with the intention of reducing them to involuntary servitude or labour. Looked at in reverse this procedure meant that in taking an oath of allegiance to the United States the majority of former Confederates would give assent to the remaking of the State by the Unionists, to the emancipation of the slaves, to civil rights for the freedmen, and to congressional control over the process of Reconstruction. Once the process of Reconstruction was complete all white males, with the exception of the disqualified classes, would be able to vote though nothing would prevent the convention from imposing restrictions beyond those which were mandatory in the bill.

It was expected that the process laid down in the Wade-Davis Bill would be a slow one, and in no Southern State would the white majority surrender constitution-making power to the Unionists so long as a hope of Confederate victory or of a negotiated peace remained. In the eyes of many Republicans this delay was a merit of the bill. "These States," said Wade, "must remain under military dominion, but I hope with all the equities that can be extended to a people thus unfortunate, until such time as they manifest to the people of the United States that they are able to govern themselves properly and subject to the laws of the General Government. . . . The only sensible plan is to leave these communities until in some way we can have at least reasonable evidence to show that a majority of them are loyal, and in a condition to maintain a free republican government of their own."[7] "Reasonable evidence" would be a willingness on the part of the majority to assent to the procedure laid down by the Wade-Davis

[7] C.G. 38.2.560.

Bill. The Bill would have prevented the institution of puppet ten-per-cent governments during the war, but it might not have worked too badly when defeat persuaded a majority of Southerners to agree to any conditions as the price of a return to normal political relations within the Union. It would also have satisfied the Northern demand for the exclusion from public life of the Confederate leaders and for a guarantee of negro civil rights. It did not introduce negro suffrage which was the ultimate abomination in Southern eyes. The least which can be said of the Wade-Davis Bill is that it would have been better than no plan at all which was what the United States had when Lincoln was assassinated and the war ended.

Lincoln was like a good poker player who had kept his hand concealed, and it will never be known whether it contained a straight flush or a single pair. His last public utterance gave little away, and he had confided in none of his cabinet ministers. The last public address was concerned largely with the question of Louisiana, which had established the most stable of the ten-per-cent governments. Lincoln did not give an unequivocal undertaking to support that government; "as to sustaining it," he said, "my promise is out . . . but, as bad promises are better broken than kept, I shall treat this as a bad promise and break it, whenever I shall be convinced that keeping it is adverse to the public interest; but I have not yet been so convinced." This might be taken as a veiled threat to the Louisiana government that it would have to conform to the wishes of the President in order to keep his support. He seemed then to admit that the Louisiana government was not all that might be desired, but argued that it was probably better to keep it in being as the twelve thousand voters who had supported its constitution would be better encouraged than repelled and demoralized. "We encourage the hearts and nerve the arms of twelve thousand to adhere to their work, and argue for it, and proselyte for it, and fight for it, and feed it, and grow it, and ripen it to a complete success." Whatever the present deficiencies of the Louisiana government it was the best which could be obtained, and might prove to be the nucleus around which the State could re-form as a loyal and acceptable member of the Union.[8] Lincoln's advice was therefore purely empirical, devoted largely to the affairs of one problem child which had advanced a small way along the road to Reconstruction, and offered no solution for those States in which even a ten-per-cent government still lay beyond the range of practical politics. It is untrue to say that Lincoln had a "plan" of Reconstruction; he had certainly announced no method of dealing with the new situation created by the collapse of the South.

In this new situation two plans, poles apart, were to emerge. There was a Radical plan, associated particularly with Thaddeus Stevens, and a conservative plan which was put into operation by President Johnson. Stevens wanted to give the former Confederate States Territorial status without any statement of the conditions under which they would be readmitted to the Union.[9] This would

[8] *Writings of Abraham Lincoln*, Constitutional ed., VII, 362 ff.
[9] Thaddeus Stevens tried to steer clear of the complex argument over that status of the States. Cf. C.G. 39.1.697. "It has several times been said in the course of debate that I hold that States that were engaged in the rebellion are dead. Now, I have never said anything of that kind. In my speech on this subject, I argued that, whether they are out

have had some advantages. The status of a Territory was familiar to law and opinion in the United States, it would give to the Territories local self-government with their own legislatures, but with governors and officials appointed by the President with the consent of the Senate, while reserving to Congress power to make general laws affecting them. It provided a procedure by which the Territories would submit their constitutions to Congress when applying for statehood. There is no doubt that Stevens intended the period of Territorial status to be employed to reconstruct Southern society; he intended to destroy the power of the Southern ruling class by imposing political disabilities, by confiscating their estates, and by distributing their land among the freedmen to provide the economic basis for a free negro peasantry. Stevens did not favour immediate negro suffrage because he believed that in their present condition the freedmen would fall under the influence of their former masters, but when they had been made economically secure he expected them to be given the vote and assume a Jeffersonian role as cultivators of the soil and bulwarks of political virtue. "This is not a 'white man's Government,'" he said, "this is a man's Government; the Government of all men alike." He did not expect any but white men to be elected to office for "long ages to come" because "the prejudices engendered by slavery would not soon permit merit to be preferred to color. But suffrage would still be beneficial to the weaker races. In a country where political division will always exist, their power joined with just white men, would greatly modify, if it did not entirely prevent, the injustice of majorities."[10] Reconstruction in the South would thus create a new political interest which would act as a safeguard for the Union and a pillar of support for the party of the Union. The plan proposed by Stevens had the advantage of letting everyone know where they stood; its disadvantage was that it had not the slightest chance of being enacted.

President Johnson succeeded at a moment which could hardly have been more awkward. As the news of the surrender of the remaining Southern forces came in he had to make decisions which would affect the whole future of the United States, and he had to do so with all the handicaps of inexperience in an atmosphere charged with emotion. The first decision was whether to call Congress into special session to consider the problems of the peace. It is known that Lincoln had not intended to anticipate the normal session of Congress in December 1865, but it was probably a mistake for Johnson not to do so. Lincoln had behind him a triumphant re-election, he was closely acquainted with leading men of all shades of opinion in the Union party, and he had spent the whole of his political life in the climate of opinion of the Northern and Midwestern States; he knew from experience and political instinct what was or was not possible and he knew how to defeat ardent friends without making enemies. Johnson was an accidental President; everyone knew that he could not have reached even the Vice-Presi-

---

of the Union, or dead, lying about in the Union, it amounts to practically the same thing. But I have never pretended that those States are dead; I insist that they have never been dead, that they have always lived as States. The only difference in my position from that of some other gentlemen who have spoken is that I affirm that during the war they were States under the Confederate government, and not under the Government of the Union."

[10] C.G. 39.1.74.

dency except on the Lincoln ticket. His personal prestige had suffered from his unfortunate lapse during the inauguration. He was a Southern Unionist and had very little idea of the way in which the Northern mind worked. He was not on familiar terms with leading men in the Republican party. It was therefore urgently necessary for him to establish the kind of relation with Congress which is necessary for a successful President; it was necessary for him to know Congress and for Congress to know him and if he intended to continue the wartime ascendancy of the Presidency the way to do so was by understanding the co-ordinate branch of government and not by appearing to slight it. Failing an early call to Congress Johnson should have made an effort to impress his views upon congressional leaders and to hear their views in return, for these were men who would ultimately come to sit in judgment upon his policy. Yet though several congressional leaders called upon Johnson most of them found the experience singularly unsatisfying and Johnson himself made no overtures towards the men who, whatever their merits or demerits, were the chief movers among the representatives of the people.[11]

At his succession to the Presidency the career of Andrew Johnson formed one of the great success stories of American history. From humble origins in a small country town and handicapped by early illiteracy he had made his way to the supreme position in the United States. His great assets had been honesty, fixity of purpose, and a command of the kind of oratory which was so popular with rural American audiences. Lacking subtlety he met attacks by attacking vigorously himself. He had become the spokesman of the small farmers of Tennessee in their running fight with the large planters who dominated the Mississippi valley in the State, and epitomized the aspirations of Jacksonian democracy in the West. At the outbreak of the Civil War he had earned fame as the only Southern senator to oppose secession (though he was as bitter against abolitionists as against secessionists), and in the war years he became the most distinguished representative of the elusive Southern Unionists and thus a key figure in the nation. This won him the vice-presidential nomination in 1864 at a time when it was particularly important to prevent the slave States in the Union from going sour on the war effort. Before that he had been a severe and successful governor

---

[11] At one time there was a chance that the Radicals might get a representative into the Cabinet, and Ben Butler believed that he was the man. Before Lincoln's death he told Wade that he was willing and thought that the Radicals might succeed if they backed him. (L.C. *Butler Papers*, Butler to Wade, 1 Mar. 1865.) Soon after Lincoln's assassination Butler was told that all but five or six of the Massachusetts State senators had signed a petition in his favour, and Wade took this to the President (ibid., Wade to Butler, 9 May 1865). In July a further petition was stimulated from New Hampshire urging Butler's appointment, and again Wade took it to the President. On this occasion he "did not hesitate to say to him that . . . I believed it to be his bounden duty to call around him the ablest men in the nation and those in whom the public had most confidence." The President seemed responsive, but Wade was no longer hopeful and explained that "were it not for the experience we have both had in regard to the impressions made upon his mind (which the event has shown up to have been entirely mistaken) I should have but little doubt that you would soon be called into the public service" (ibid., Wade to Butler, 19 July 1865). Butler was perhaps the most eligible of the Radicals; he had been chairman of the Breckinridge Democratic Convention in 1860, was then a Union Democrat, and had carried a substantial element of the Massachusetts Democracy with him into Radical Republicanism.

of occupied Tennessee, introducing emancipation, and standing no nonsense from former Confederates. In spite of his Democratic antecedents his war record led him well into the fold of the Union party and it seemed that there was little to distinguish him from many Republicans. Indeed the Radicals rather than the moderates took comfort from the fierceness of his denunciations of Southern traitors. As President he was to prove a good administrator (much better than the somewhat casual Lincoln) and he had a natural dignity which made him a much more impressive figure than such predecessors as Pierce and Buchanan. He earned the respect and loyalty of the majority of those who worked closely with him in the administration, and there can be little doubt that in happier times he would have made a successful President.

Yet with all his qualities Johnson had limitations which were to be disastrous for his own policies. General Richard Taylor, son of the former President, who saw a good deal of him during the period of controversy, found "that he always postponed action, and was of an obstinate, suspicious temper. Like a badger, one had to dig him out of his hole; and he was ever in one except when on the hustings addressing a crowd. . . . He had acquired much knowledge of the principles of government, and made himself a fluent speaker, but could not rise above the level of the class in which he was born and to which he always appealed. He well understood the few subjects laboriously studied, and affected to despise other knowledge, while suspicious that those possessing such would take advantage of him. . . . Compelled to fight his way up from obscurity, he had contracted a dislike of those more favoured of fortune, whom he was in the habit of calling 'the slave aristocracy,' and became incapable of giving his confidence to any one, even to those on whose assistance he relied in a contest . . . with Congress."[12] These comments may be discounted as those of a Southern gentleman and old Whig but the points made are corroborated too frequently to be dismissed: initial indecision, followed by a decision which was then adhered to with great obstinacy, a kind of defensive arrogance towards those who were better endowed by birth or nature, a fear of betraying his thoughts, and a confirmed reluctance to take counsel with those who might give him unwelcome advice, were all characteristics which unfitted him for the delicate tasks which the President was called upon to perform. Men who went to see him on business often found him apparently receptive and went away with the impression that they had made their points; when they discovered, from his later actions, that they might never have spoken, they were apt to conclude that they had been intentionally deceived.

Johnson hoped to surprise the country, and to win over public opinion, by the striking success of his Southern policy. Unable to admit that he had ever been wrong, he treated all criticism as betrayal or as the work of a malignant and frustrated minority. His perseverance in a policy which was obviously running into difficulties has often been described as "courageous"; but his was not a courage illuminated by understanding, and never for one moment would he consider an escape from the lonely rock upon which his own logic had stranded him. This loneliness is perhaps the most evident symptom of Johnson's personal tragedy.

[12] Richard Taylor, *Destruction and Reconstruction* (Edinburgh and London, 1879), 326–7.

With an invalid wife and a drunken son, working enormously long hours at his desk, and seeing the world as a succession of faces which appeared before him for brief interviews, he created the self-portrait of a man of the people who could interpret their wishes without listening to what they were saying. This withdrawal from the real world of politics became disastrous when the people whose wishes would decide policy were those of the Northern and Midwestern States whose opinions Johnson never had understood and never would.

During the five weeks after he became President Johnson reached the decision from which he never afterwards withdrew, and on 29 May 1865 he issued a Proclamation of Amnesty and a Proclamation on North Carolina which was to be the model for others issued to all those Southern States which had not already set up governments under the Lincoln plan. The amnesty promised a pardon to all those who would take an oath of allegiance to the United States and of obedience to the proclamations affecting the emancipation of slaves. A very long list of exceptions to the general amnesty included all those already made by Lincoln and added men with taxable property of over $20,000 who had taken part in the rebellion; but these drastic exclusions from pardon (and thus from public life and a valid title to property) were qualified by a promise that special application could be made for pardon by all members of the excepted classes and "such clemency will be liberally extended as may be consistent with the facts of the case and with the peace and dignity of the United States."[13] The Proclamation on North Carolina laid the constitutional foundations for the President's action by stating his duty to take care that the laws be faithfully executed and inferring that it therefore became necessary and proper for him to carry out and enforce the obligation of the United States to secure to the States a republican government. The claim to act without the participation of Congress was sound in logic but weak in application: the President might be bound to enforce the law but he was operating in a new situation in which the supreme legislature of the United States had been given no opportunity to say what the law should be. The proclamation went on to appoint a provisional governor "whose duty it shall be, at the earliest practicable period, to prescribe such rules and regulations as may be necessary and proper for convening a convention composed of delegates to be chosen by that portion of the people . . . who are loyal to the United States, and no others." Loyalty was defined as willingness to take the oath prescribed in the amnesty proclamation. This convention was to draw up a new Constitution and either it or the new legislature "will prescribe the qualification of electors and the eligibility of persons to hold office under the constitution and laws of the State—a power the several States composing the Federal Union have rightfully exercised from the origin of the Government to the present time."[14]

The Reconstruction proclamations came like a tonic to the demoralized South. The mass of the people were unconditionally pardoned, and their leaders were led to expect a favourable consideration if they made personal application

[13] Richardson (ed.), *Messages and Papers*, VI, 310.
[14] Ibid., 312.

for presidential pardons. All except the unpardoned could take part in Reconstruction if they took a simple oath to the United States, which was no more than a recognition of the situation following Southern defeat. The vital power of fixing the qualifications for office and suffrage was specifically given to the States, and the claim of Congress to exclude leaders of the rebellion from State office or to alter the suffrage was denied. The whole process was unencumbered with conditions, and though Johnson was later to insist upon ratification of the Thirteenth Amendment abolishing slavery and repudiation of the Confederate debt, and to suggest limited negro suffrage, he did so only when Southern hopes of "home rule" had so far revived that they felt able to reject advice or to accept it on conditions. The hope which dawned for the majority of Southerners with Johnson's proclamations was a mortal blow to Southern Unionists. They had enjoyed a brief spell of influence so long as it seemed that they might be given a special role to play in remaking the Southern States and their subsequent plight is epitomized in the frantic plea to Ben Butler of a humble loyalist, who claimed to have broken through the lines at Richmond to bring intelligence to the Northern armies: "I am out of employment and get nothing to do. The rebels won't employ me because I went to the Yankees, and I went to Gen. Terry but he had nothing to give me to do; all the positions he had to fill were filled, and most of them by rebels — young men who served in the rebel army. My most noble Patron, I tell you such treatment is almost enough to make a man curse his Government."[15] At the end of the year, when Johnson had issued pardons in profusion, another reported a conspiracy amongst ex-Confederate soldiers in Louisiana to renew the struggle for secession or at least to prescribe Union men. "All this is nonsense you may say in the North, but it is death or ruin to the Union men of the South. And what is the real cause of all this new Southern movement? In our opinion, it is the too early granted pardons to them. No one is punished as the law directs. The sovereignty of the law is not enforced — no it is made a perfect nullity. The rebels are courted and flattered instead of reproved."[16]

Southern exuberance was the natural consequence of restored hope and unexpected freedom of action, but they used their opportunities with a singular lack of wisdom. They should have realized that the final word on their readmission would lie with Congress, and wisdom would have counselled a cautious respect for Northern opinion. One difficulty was that their only channel of communication with the North was through the President. Few Northern newspapers circulated in the South except the New York World which was emphati-

---

[15] L.C. *Butler Papers*, D. D. Bulmer to Butler, 14 Nov. 1865. There were complaints of this nature as early as May 1865, cf. General J. W. Turner to Butler, *Private and Official Correspondence of Benjamin F. Butler*, (Norwood, Mass., 1917), V, 616, 7 May 1865. "It is not satisfactory to us to see a dozen or more Major Generals of the rebel service headed by General Lee, drawing their rations daily of the Government, and then ostentatiously displaying their uniforms on the streets and in public places. The way matters look now, we don't quite understand what we have been fighting for. A rebel uniform today in Richmond carries a man where a Federal uniform will not. It takes him into all our own public offices and further into society."

[16] L.C. *E. B. Washburn Papers*, anon. to E. B. W., 1 Dec. 1865.

cally pro-Southern, and it was said that even Federal officials found it impossible to obtain newspapers such as *Tribune* and other influential Northern papers.[17] Southerners believed that the President was on their side, and they may have seen him as a new Andrew Jackson come to judgment, who would overawe Congress and force through his policy. They overlooked the fact that while Jackson had stood upon the strong ground of popular support in the North and West Johnson represented nobody. Johnson himself was singularly hesitant in the advice which he offered and did not exploit to the full the enormous influence which he could have exerted upon Southern actions.[18] Even his famous telegram to Governor Sharkey advising the extension of suffrage to negroes on some literacy or property test was offered as a tentative suggestion on grounds of expediency because it "would completely disarm the adversary." His pardons seemed often to follow rather than to anticipate Southern movements and were given not infrequently to those who had already been chosen for office; nor does he seem to have used the pardon as an instrument by which men of influence could be bound to the national government.[19]

Under these circumstances, the people of the South followed their natural preferences and chose for State offices the respected leaders of the Confederacy. More discretion might have been expected in the choice of senators and representatives for Congress, but the delegations which presented themselves at Washington in December — and included several Confederate congressmen and members of State legislatures under the Confederacy, four generals and five colonels of the Confederate army, and Alexander H. Stephens sometime Vice-President of the Confederate States — seemed to epitomize in Northern eyes the unchastened spirit of rebellion. More grievous and provocative was the passage by the new Southern legislatures of "black codes" for the emancipated negroes. That some form of regulation was necessary could hardly be denied though the States might have been justified in leaving responsibility for the time being to the Federal Freedmen's Bureau. The Southern States did give formal recognition to the legal rights acquired with freedom, allowing negroes the right to hold property, to sue and be sued, to make contracts and to marry, but in some States the conferment of these rights was accompanied by apprenticeship and vagrancy laws which made it clear that the negroes were to be treated as a subordinate caste assigned to labour. The code of Mississippi laid down that labour contracts should be in writing and that "every civil officer shall, and every person may, arrest and carry back to his or her legal employer any freedman, free negro or mulatto who shall have quit the service of his or her employer before the expiration of his or her term of service without good cause." Louisiana laid down conditions of labour and added, "Bad work shall not be allowed. Failing to obey reasonable orders, neglect of duty, and leaving home

---

[17] L.C. E. B. *Washburn Papers*, D. Richards to Washburn, 21 May 1866 (from Florida). "I have subscribed for the N. Y. Tribune, Washington Chronicle, and N. Y. World, but they have all stopped coming. They would undoubtedly let the World come through if they could know what paper it is without tearing off the wrapper."

[18] E. L. McKitrick, *Andrew Johnson and Reconstruction* (Chicago, 1960), Ch. 7, section IV passim.

[19] Ibid., 149 ff.

without permission will be deemed disobedience; impudence, swearing, or inde-
cent language to or in the presence of the employer, his family or agent, or
quarreling and fighting with one another will be deemed disobedience. . . . All
difficulties arising between the employers and laborers . . . shall be settled by
the former; if not satisfactory to the laborers, an appeal may be had to the
nearest Justice of the Peace and two freeholders, citizens, one of the said citizens
to be selected by the employer and the other by the laborer." Mississippi had
an elaborate apprenticeship law under which negroes under the age of eighteen
who were orphans or whose parents had not the means or will to support them
were apprenticed to employers; the law laid down conditions for humane treatment and for teaching those under fifteen to read and write, but any apprentice
could be ordered to return to his or her master by any justice of the peace and
severe penalties were provided for not doing so. Negroes over the age of eighteen
without lawful employment or business, and all white persons "usually associ-
ating" with them, were deemed vagrants and subject to heavy fines. It was an
old Southern belief that the negro would not work without compulsion and it
was reasonable to maintain that coercion was necessary to revive the Southern
economy, but a system under which negroes were forced to make labour contracts
under the penalties of the vagrancy laws, then held strictly to the conditions of
service — with grievances determined by employers in the first instance and then
by white officials whose interests were likely to be those of the employing class
— was not free labour as understood in the North.[20] If the codes did not re-enact
slavery they might well make the condition of the negro worse in some respects
than it had been under slavery, for the machinery of the States was now brought
in to enforce obligations which had hitherto been the responsibility of the
master. "This arbitrary and inhuman act," said the Radical Henry Wilson of
the code of Mississippi, "makes the freedmen the slaves of society, and it is far
better to be the slave of one man than to be the slave of arbitrary law."[21]
Exaggeration was to be expected from Radical critics, but no one aware of
the sensitivity of Northern opinion to the negro question could have expected
approval. What was perhaps more shocking than anything else was the assumption that the negro was condemned by nature to a dependent status; as the
compiler of a collection of South Carolina laws remarked, "These two great
classes, then, are distinctly marked by the impress of nature. They are races
separate and distinct: the one the highest and noblest type of humanity, the
other the lowest and most degraded." He believed that to mingle the social and
political existence of the classes more closely "would surely be one of the highest
exhibitions of treason to the race."[22]

President Johnson himself was probably unhappy about the trend of events
in the South, and Gideon Welles, who of all the Cabinet was nearest to him in
temperament and opinion, wrote in his diary on 1 August 1865, "The tone

[20] The Black Codes of Mississippi and Louisiana are given in H. S. Commager (ed.),
Documents of American History (New York, 1949), II.

[21] C.G. 39.1.39.

[22] Quoted by Louis M. Hacker, *The Shaping of the American Tradition* (New York,
1947), 628 ff. from H. Melville Myers, *Stay laws and . . . Freedmen's Code* (Charleston,
1866).

of sentiment and action of people of the South is injudicious and indiscreet in many respects. I know not if there is any remedy, but if not, other and more serious disasters await them, and us also perhaps, for if we are one people, dissension and wrong affect the whole."[23] Johnson, however, regarded the indiscretions of Southerners as irritating but irrelevant to the main issue of Reconstruction. Fundamentally he agreed with them about the place of the negro in society, though sufficiently humane not to close the door of opportunity to those who could deserve it. The strong expressions of gratitude which he was receiving from the South convinced him that he was on the right lines in overcoming as rapidly as possible the feelings of resentment and hatred in the South. Nor was he without support in the North from quarters in which a man of his antecedents was least likely to expect it. Merchants in the Eastern cities tended to favour a policy which would lead to an early resumption of normal commercial relations, and on 20 October Adam Badeau wrote to E. B. Washburn, "Everywhere I hear warm commendation of Mr Johnson's policy; in New York as well as at Washington — just as at Galena, all the sober substantial men seemed to support him. The attempt of foolish impractical men to foist their notions upon the country has met with no success, so far as I can judge."[24] The comment was not without significance for Adam Badeau was secretary to General Grant who was susceptible to the opinions of sober substantial men. By the middle of December Johnson had on his desk a concise report from the General himself on conditions in the South in which he said that "the citizens of the Southern States are anxious to return to self-government, within the Union, as soon as possible; that whilst reconstructing they want and require protection from the government; that they are in earnest in wishing to do what they think is required by the government, not humiliating them as citizens, and that if such a course were pointed out they would pursue it in good faith."[25] Warmed by the gratitude of Southerners, supported by his Cabinet, Johnson believed that his policy of restoration was a success, that its opponents were troublemakers and hollow men, and that Congress would respond to the arguments of the first annual message which he had commissioned George Bancroft to cast in literary form. Beyond Congress were the people of the Northern and Western States, a shadowy entity conceived perhaps as a vastly enlarged audience of Tennessee farmers who had always been so responsive to his oratory.

There were, however, indications of dissent which Johnson might have taken more seriously. There was for instance the report of Carl Schurz which reached him before the meeting of Congress. Schurz was the most distinguished of German Americans; a refugee from Germany inspired by the liberalism of the mid-century he had seen in the Republican party an American version of the universal movement for freedom; he had had much to do with winning Midwestern Germans from their Democratic affiliations, and had gone on to a distinguished career in the army reaching the rank of Major-General. He had made no secret of his Radical leanings, and he was therefore surprised to receive in July a request from the President accompanied "with many flattering assur-

[23] H. K. Beale (ed.), *Diary of Gideon Welles* (New York, 1960), III, 347.
[24] L.C. E. B. *Washburn Papers*, 20 Oct. 1865.
[25] *Senate Executive Documents*, 39th Congress, 1st Session, No. 2, 107 ff.

ances of his confidence in my character and judgment" to undertake a tour in the South and to report upon conditions. By his own account he told the President that "so far as I was then informed, I considered the reconstruction policy ill-advised and fraught with great danger, but that if my observations should show this view to be erroneous, no pride of opinion would prevent me from saying so." The President repeated his expressions of confidence and sent him on his way.[26] Schurz was not a rich man and he was receiving only nominal pay for his mission; with something less than complete discretion he allowed some Northern friends to pay the premium on a life insurance and during his tour contributed anonymous articles to Northern newspapers on conditions in the South. The real cause of his offence to Johnson was, however, a well-meant effort to interfere in a dispute between Governor Sharkey of Mississippi and General Slocum, commanding the Federal troops, in which the latter attempted to stop the arming of the State militia. Johnson sustained Sharkey and rebuked both Slocum and Schurz. It was probably this incident (in which most fair-minded men would admit that the President was wrong) which convinced Johnson that Schurz was intriguing against him.[27] Whatever the explanation Schurz received on his return the coldest possible reception from the President, who informed him that there was no need for him to submit a report.[28] Schurz nevertheless wrote one, though it is doubtful whether Johnson read it and because of its Radical authorship it has been largely ignored by historians. This neglect has been unfortunate for the report was the work of a humane and unusually intelligent man who had immersed himself for six months in the problems of the South.

Schurz was able to appreciate the tragedy of the South and left it "troubled by great anxiety." "No fair-minded man could have had my experiences in the Southern country without conceiving and cherishing a profound and warm sympathetic feeling for the Southern people, white as well as black." He respected the gallantry of the South though lamenting that it had been "wasted upon a hopeless cause — the cause of slavery — which, while held sacred by the white people of the South, was abhorred by the moral sense and enlightened opinion of the century."[29] He wasted no words in pointless accusations of treason, but emphasized the magnitude of the Southern crisis: "Now the South found precipitated upon it a problem of tremendous moment and perplexing difficulty — the problem of abruptly transforming a social organism based upon slave labor into a free labor society." Southerners, true to their traditions, tried to avoid the implications of abolition, and attempted to combine a professed willingness to accept the results of the war with a true purpose which was "to use the power of the State Governments, legislative and executive, to reduce the freedom of the negroes to a minimum and to revive so much of the old slave code as was thought necessary to make the blacks work for the whites." These were the facts of the case as he saw them, and the true remedy was not to indulge in frantic denunciations of the Southerners but to take action if a

---

[26] *The Reminiscences of Carl Schurz* (New York, 1908), III, 157 ff.
[27] McKitrick, op. cit., 163–4, 193–4. *Reminiscences of Carl Schurz*, III, 189 ff.
[28] *Reminiscences of Carl Schurz*, III, 201–2.
[29] Ibid., 199.

different result was desired. On the vital question of Southern loyalty his report was illuminating and his separation of Southern leaders into various groups demonstrated how easy it was to draw different conclusions according to one's Southern company: first there were men, mostly of mature age and experience — planters, merchants and professional men — who "have a clear perception of the irreversible changes produced by the war, and honestly endeavour to accommodate themselves to the new order of things" (these were the men with whom Grant talked on his brief visit, and in this class one might also include some of the Confederate military leaders); then there were those who wanted at all costs to restore their States to influence in the Union and would make any concession which did not threaten their own control at home — these were mainly the professional politicians and all were strong supporters of Johnson and bitter opponents of the Freedmen's Bureau; the third group was composed of the irreconcilables, mainly young men who continued to talk of eventual Southern independence and were actively suppressing negroes and Unionists, but of whom many had taken the oath of allegiance and worked temporarily with the politicians; finally there was the mass of the people "whose intellects are weak, but whose prejudices and impulses are strong."[30] Reviewing the whole problem he believed that there were great dangers in "home rule" without national protection for negroes and Unionists, nor did he believe that danger threatened the blacks alone for there was no knowing what savage impulses might not be released if the promise of negro freedom remained unfulfilled.

Throughout the summer and autumn the storm clouds gathered on the Radical front. A few days after the North Carolina Proclamation Sumner was writing to Ben Wade asking whether he could give him "any comfort with regard to the policy of the President. *He has missed a golden opportunity*, and is entailing upon the country trouble, controversy and expense. *He cannot prevent the triumph of the cause.* This is certain. But he may delay it."[31] In July Ben Butler was telling one correspondent that he still had faith in the President's "integrity and desire to do right" and that he expected him to change his policy when he saw it to be wrong,[32] but was writing to Wade that "all is wrong. We are losing the just results of this four years struggle."[33] Wade told the President frankly that "the policy he was pursuing with regard to reconstruction was filling many of our best friends with alarm" and that he ought to add some Radical representation to his Cabinet, but thought that his advice would be ignored.[34] He then wrote to Sumner that "all appears gloomy. The President is pursuing, and I believe is resolved to pursue a course in regard to reconstruction that can result in nothing but consigning the great Union, or Republican party, bound hand and foot, to the tender mercies of the rebels we have so lately conquered in the field and their copperhead allies in the north. . . . We have in truth already

[30] Bancroft (ed.), *Speeches, Correspondence and Political Papers of Carl Schurz*, I, 285.
[31] L.C. *Wade Papers*, 12 June 1865.
[32] L.C. *Butler Papers*, draft reply to J. Ogden Smith, 1 July 1865.
[33] L.C. *Wade Papers*, 26 July 1865.
[34] L.C. *Butler Papers*, Wade to Butler, 19 July 1865.

lost the whole moral effect of our victories over the rebellion and the golden opportunity for humiliating and destroying the influence of the Southern aristocracy has gone forever."[35] In October the influential though erratic Wendell Phillips was saying the same thing to Butler: "It seems to me that the Administration is handing us over, bound hand and foot, into the power of the rebels."[36] He added that "the Administration needs to be defied or overawed by such an exhibition of popular sentiment as you and Sumner and one or two others could easily start. To be effectual this should be attempted before Congress meets."

To men who believed that Reconstruction must be drastic to be just the future seemed bleak, for the majority of the Republican party might be swayed to an easy acceptance of Johnson's restoration.

Ben Butler wrote to Henry Wilson, with a copy to Thaddeus Stevens, suggesting a preamble to a Reconstruction Act which would declare the negroes entitled to the rights of citizens, and that Congress, acting upon the second section of the Thirteenth Amendment, should declare void all discriminatory State legislation, and adding that "the whole preamble seems to be necessary in order to hold the weak kneed brethren of the Republican party, who are troubled upon the question whether the States are in or out of the Union will be carried by the claim that they ought to vote to admit some States so as to have ratified the Constitutional Amendment by the requisite majority." He hoped to force the wavering majority to commit themselves "to give life and effect to the Constitutional Amendment and in favor of liberty and equal rights not raising however any question of the rights of suffrage."[37] But it is difficult to demonstrate a Radical plot in the rising tide of disquiet in the Northern Press, and the most disturbing influence was emanating not from Radical quarters but from the South itself with its choice of Confederate leaders, its black codes, its reviving arrogance, its open contempt for the moralistic ideas of the North, and its clear determination to rescue as much as possible from the past. Most alarming of all was Johnson's apparent tolerance of these things, and his failure to indicate that the South was not going to have everything its own way.

At the end of November the mild-mannered Schuyler Colfax, speaker designate of the new Congress, came to town and made a little speech which attracted considerable notice. He praised the President warmly, but warned against haste. He did not think that Congress ought to be in a hurry about the admission of Southerners. He was not satisfied with Southern behaviour because the States had quibbled about ratifying the abolition amendment, about repudiating their debts and about nullifying secession, because of their hostility to Unionists and because they had not made proper laws for the freedmen. The government had given the slave his freedom and meant to maintain it. He did not, however, believe that these doubts meant a rupture with the President and thought that "the executive and legislative departments of government, when they compare views together, will cordially co-operate in this great work before us

[35] L.C. *Wade Papers*, Wade to Sumner (draft), 29 July 1865.
[36] L.C. *Butler Papers*, Phillips to Butler, 24 Oct. 1865.
[37] L.C. *Butler Papers*, 20 Nov. 1865.

all, and so act that the foundations of our Union, wisely and patriotically reconstructed, shall be eternal as the ages, with a hearty acceptance by the South
of the new situation."[38] This speech — with its temperate statement of Northern
doubts, its expressed willingness to work with the President and its belief in
harmony with justice — was widely welcomed in the North. The speech did,
however, indicate that Congressional leaders intended to take the initiative
and this was sheer Radicalism to a man who believed that "restoration" was
complete. Johnson did not expect to alter or enlarge his policy to comprehend
Northern anxieties which were, he was convinced, the work of a few trouble-
makers. He was, however, about to meet Northern opinion in the form of a
Congress chosen at the same election as that which had raised him to the
Vice-Presidency, and the meeting was to prove a shock for both.

Some Radicals wished to scrap the whole presidential plan, but a majority
in the party were ready and willing to allow the President credit for his work
in restoring the normal machinery of government and to believe that he would
readily accept the additional "guarantees" proposed by Congress. These guarantees were aimed to protect the Union against its enemies and the negro against
those who would deprive him of civil rights. According to temperament or
interest men stressed one danger or one remedy more than another. Roscoe
Conkling said later that the one binding tie amongst all Republicans was a
conviction "that the destinies of the nation should never be yielded up to men
whose hands and faces are dripping with the blood of murder"[39] and Schuyler
Colfax had written privately to a friend, "I remember very well that last day
I was in Congress, they were fighting us and killing our soldiers, and had their
members in the Rebel Congress. It would be rather pleasant for them to take
their seats the first day of the next session; but I am a little too old fogyish for
that. I want to be very certain that a majority of their voters are — not merely
whipped back into the Union, as they say — but heartily devoted to the Union
and ready to fight with us against all its enemies at home and abroad, now and
in the future."[40] Other Republicans saw negro rights as the dominant and
binding issue. "The Union party are agreed," said Senator Stewart (who wanted
a general amnesty), "that all men are entitled to life, liberty and the pursuit
of happiness, and they will endorse any reasonable means to secure these
inalienable rights to every American citizen. . . . The President's plan of restoration was unsatisfactory because it ignored the rights and excluded from constitutional liberty four million loyal citizens guilty of no offence but fidelity to
the Government . . . because it placed the State government of the South in the
hands of the very men who plunged the country into war for secession, and
the extension of slavery, and because it admitted into Congress an increased
representation of the disloyal elements of the rebellion."[41] Nearly all Republicans
felt the force of one or other of these criticisms, and even Henry J. Raymond,
who clung to the President long after other Republicans had abandoned him,

[38] McKitrick, op. cit., 185–6. Willard H. Smith, *Schuyler Colfax* (Indianapolis, 1952),
222.
[39] C.G. 39.1.4272.
[40] Smith, *Schuyler Colfax*, 221.
[41] C.G. 39.1.2798.

and who wished to accept the restoration of the Southern States as suggested by him, wished also to "provide by law for giving to the freedmen of the South all rights of citizens in courts of law and elsewhere," to exclude from Federal office "the leading actors in the conspiracy which led to the rebellion," to make such amendments to the Constitution as might seem appropriate, and to use troops to prevent the overthrow of Southern governments which were Republican in form.[42]

Public opinion in the North had been bewildered by the course of events, and there was no clear determination as the year 1865 drew to its close upon the policy which should be followed. But in a negative sense there was a growing consensus of opinion that not enough had been done. Anyone could have predicted that Radical attacks would be made, but the new factor in the situation was the response which they aroused. Many moderate Republicans were sincerely anxious for a generous peace and were likely to be extremely cautious of any commitments on the racial problem, but even they felt that further guarantees were necessary. Thaddeus Stevens declared that the Southern States ought "never to be recognised as capable of acting in the Union, or being counted as valid States, until the Constitution shall have been so amended as to make it what its framers intended; and so as to secure perpetual ascendancy to the party of the Union; and so as to render our republican government firm and stable for ever."[43] Though expressed by the sternest of Radicals this assertion united rather than divided the party. Equal rights in the Constitution and perpetual union proved to be the two hinges upon which congressional policy turned, and the doom of Johnson's policy lay in the discovery that the party could be united upon the need for certain "guarantees" which he had failed to provide.

The Republican consensus was as yet limited in scope and it did not extend to any advanced propositions about racial equality. For many Republicans the sticking-point was the question of suffrage. A good many were prepared to see the vote given to negroes with property and education, and even the Democrat Reverdy Johnson was ready to admit that many of the negroes were "capable of as much and as high a civilization as the white race" and that if protected by the paramount authority of the Constitution "they will ere long become valuable citizens of the country."[44] But there was a long gap between this kind of statement and a commitment to immediate and unqualified suffrage. On the one hand many Republicans were aware of the racial prejudice in their own constituencies — several Northern States excluded negroes from the suffrage and were to reaffirm this during the Reconstruction controversy — and on the other some Republicans were alarmed by the idea of indiscriminate suffrage extended to the illiterates of either race. Privately Horace Greeley proposed that the suffrage should be given to all who had voted prior to 1861 and to such others "as shall have read understandingly the Constitution of the United States, and have paid a State tax during the year preceding."[45]

[42] C.G. 39.1.491.
[43] C.G. 39.1.74.
[44] C.G. 39.1.373.
[45] L.C. Butler Papers, 24 Aug. 1865.

Though no agreement on negro suffrage was likely in the immediate future, the case for it was being made. Speaking for the negro to the annual meeting of the Massachusetts Anti-Slavery Society in 1865 in a lecture called "What the Black Man Wants" Frederick Douglass explained that they wanted suffrage "because it is our *right* first of all. No class of men can, without insulting their own nature, be content with any deprivation of their rights. We want it again as a means of educating our race. . . . Again I want the elective franchise, for one, as a colored man, because ours is a peculiar government, based upon a peculiar idea, and that idea is universal suffrage. If I were in a monarchical government, where the few bore rule and the many were subject, there would be no special stigma resting upon me, because I did not exercise the elective franchise." He concluded that if the negro "knows as much when sober as an Irishman knows when he is drunk, he knows enough to vote, on good American principles."[46] The abstract case for negro suffrage was, however, being powerfully reinforced by a purely political argument. In March 1865 Sumner, whose sincerity in the cause of racial equality cannot be doubted, was writing to Bright that without negro votes "we cannot establish stable government in the rebel States . . . without them the enemy will reappear, and under forms of law take possession of the governments, choose magistrates and officers, and in alliance with the Northern democracy, put us all in peril again."[47] It could also be argued that negro suffrage must be the keystone for any policy of guarantees and when Congress met, the Radical George Boutwell argued that restoration without negro suffrage "opens the way to the destruction of this government from which there is no escape" while rights without suffrage were illusory for "with the right of voting everything that a man ought to have or enjoy of civil rights comes to him. Without the right to vote he is secure in nothing."[48] Thus stood the question of negro suffrage at the end of the year 1865: with strong advocates, encountering many doubts, drawing upon the stock of traditional American beliefs, and provided with arguments arising from the political situation and increasing in cogency as men pondered upon the future distribution of power in the United States. For those who believed that negro suffrage in the South would be a disaster the best tactics would have been to settle with the moderate Republican majority before they were forced to choose between the negro vote and the abandonment of what they deemed to be essential. Such would have been the wisdom of political calculation, but in times of stress politicians are, perhaps, no more likely than other men to calculate correctly. Johnson, his supporters, and the South were set upon the surest road to colourblind democracy but they remained oblivious of the direction in which they were heading and adhered instead to their belief that "restoration" could be achieved without "guarantees."

[46] Frederick Douglass. Speech at the Massachusetts Anti-Slavery Society, 1865. Issued as a pamphlet, *What the Black Man Wants*, Boston, 1865.
[47] E. L. Pierce, *Memoirs and Letters of Charles Sumner* (Boston, 1877–94), IV, 229.
[48] C.G. 39.1.309.

A Democratic Society Emerges
from Total War

ERIC L. MC KITRICK

*Why should American society still bear the scars of the Civil War?
For all of the attention that has been lavished upon the conduct of
national politics during the period of postwar Reconstruction, relatively little notice has been paid to the sociology of reconciliation.
In the following chapter from his more general study of Andrew
Johnson and Reconstruction, the Columbia University historian
Eric L. McKitrick launches an imaginative attack upon the problem. He points out that the Civil War and the two world wars
of the twentieth century are the only "total" wars that Americans
have experienced, and he hypothesizes that the end of the Civil
War, like the end of the world wars, left Americans with conflicting feelings of hatred for the enemy and a desire to return to
normal life. The difference, as McKitrick sees it, is that the country
displayed an overwhelming preference for a rapid resumption of
prewar behavior following the wars of this century, whereas it
opted for a policy of revenge within two years after the peace at
Appomattox Courthouse. In explaining this discrepancy, he centers
his interest upon the attitudes of the defeated population, comparing the Japanese of 1945 with the Southerners of 1865. The
roots of uncharitable and uncompromising Reconstruction are to
be found, he thinks, in the fact that Southern comportment after
the end of the fighting denied Northerners the psychic and symbolic rewards of victory. McKitrick thus removes his arguments
from the narrowly political context of traditional historical writing,
borrowing freely from the techniques of political scientists and
social psychologists.*

I. Public Feeling: "War Hatred"
Versus "Back to Normal"

It is part of the post–Civil War legend that the ruthless quality of Southern
reconstruction was the outgrowth of hatreds carried over from wartime and
interminably prolonged. The legend in its gross form is accurate enough; the
Northern people have ultimately acknowledged that they did not really know
how to administer their great victory once they had got it, and that on the

whole they managed it badly. This admission must itself stand as part of the legend; the North, for three generations, has had something on its conscience which will probably never be exorcised. But inasmuch as reconstruction, in the form which it finally took, was not inaugurated until two years after the moment of victory, there remains the question of how fully the case is covered by depending on the notion of "war hatreds" alone to explain it.[1] Was there perhaps a conspiracy, somewhere along the way, to manipulate and aggravate those hatreds? But if so, why did the movement take so long to mature and how could a political society which embraced a population of over twenty million have been "manipulated" so successfully?

If there had been a strong desire in the North, born of the passions of war, to punish the South, then it would seem that the most auspicious time to harness such passions ought to have been the very moment of victory. Yet victory itself, at least for the victor, functions powerfully as a solvent for hatreds, if we may judge from the nation's wars in the twentieth century. How is it, then, that for so many years after the Civil War there was a malignancy of feeling toward the late enemy not experienced in the wake of the two world wars, even while the enemies of the fratricidal conflict partook of a spiritual and cultural rapport not shared with later enemies of the Republic? It is conceivable that this malignancy was not entirely a matter of "war hatreds." There may have been other feelings besides those growing specifically out of war, and it may have been the victory, as much as the war, that engendered them. The nature of that victory would come to seem, as time went on, very different from what it had seemed at the beginning.

The experience of total victory, in a total war which has successfully made the ultimate claim upon the resources, energies, and loyalties of a whole people, is an experience which Americans have actually undergone only three times in all their history. It is the kind of thing that, in the memory of a people, has acute point but not much breadth; memory leaves too little room for it between the war time and the postwar time, between the unrelieved hate of the one and the deepening oblivion of the other. The quality of feeling in that interim time, as one tries now to grasp at it, seems an intense surge of the undefinable — some-

---

[1] The basic study on the resumption of peaceful pursuits after the Civil War — a process which took so extraordinarily long to complete — is Paul H. Buck, *The Road to Reunion, 1865–1900* (Boston: Little, Brown, 1937); see esp. chap. i ("Victory"), pp. 3–25. This work, unique of its kind, is painstaking, thorough, and indispensable for an understanding of the problems of reconciliation. The slow nature of the reunion process (the book covers a thirty-five-year period) is, however, taken more or less for granted, which means that the author has not asked himself whether real alternatives were present at war's end for launching the process in a direction from that which it in fact took. He did not, of course, have the benefit of World War II and its aftermath as a test of what really great differences were possible in achieving an emotional settlement between two former enemies. If, however, one should assume that such alternatives did exist and that the painful slowness of post-Civil-War reunion was not necessarily foreordained and inevitable after all, then the story would have to be organized somewhat differently. Less emphasis would be placed on the "long slow healing" aspect; one would tend instead to shift the emphasis to the conditions of 1865, the very first year after the war, and assign them great critical importance. Part One of the present work represents such an effort.

thing of war, something of peace — so full and yet so transient as to repel any effort to give it limits and a character of its own.

Two notions come to mind as one tries to re-create the sense of an American society moving from war to peace. One of them, to be sure, is "war hatred"; the other is "back to normal." After each of the two world wars of this century, Americans have experienced a "back to normal" urge which has been all but irresistible, even to the point — someone was always there to say — of fatuous imprudence. At the close of our Civil War, however, if such an impulse toward peace and oblivion existed, it was shortly to be submerged in something very like its opposite. Here, then, is a kind of suspended balance: on the one hand, vindictiveness and hate; on the other, magnanimity, forgiveness, and peace. That the latter theme should prevail seems natural and normal, but perhaps not inevitable.

There is still something in the interim moment of consummation and solvency that should not be allowed to slide out of view too soon: a great sea of undifferentiated emotion, long since set in turmoil by all the hopes and fears and agonies of war, and long since having passed the bounds of ordinary guidance and control. This deep emotional submersion of all society appears to be not only an inevitable feature of a democratic war but actually a functional necessity for the full prosecution of such a war.[2] What becomes of it when the war is over? How does the sea of feeling calm itself? What is the principle of prediction? It is not entirely in the power of the victor to settle such a question. Here the conquered, for all the completeness of his subjugation, seems to retain rather more initiative than might at first be imagined.

The people of the North received the news of Lee's surrender much in the way that the Armistice of 1918 and the German and Japanese capitulations of 1945 would be received years later — with spontaneous upheavals of relief, joy, and thanksgiving. "The sun in his course on this blessed tenth of April, 1865, beholds a Union restored, inseparable, indivisible, eternal!" One hundred thousand people were said to have thronged the streets of Chicago on that day, and the *Tribune* reported with awe the tremendous manifestation of feeling. "Nothing

---

[2] Tocqueville, in one of his shrewdest predictions on the behavior of democratic nations, guessed that a democracy, though reluctant to begin a war, and though faltering in the war's initial stages, would ultimately fight it with irresistible determination and energy. "When a war has at length, by its long continuance, roused the whole community from their peaceful occupations, and ruined their minor undertakings, the same passions which made them attach so much importance to the maintenance of peace will be turned to arms. War, after it has destroyed all modes of speculation, becomes itself the great and sole speculation, to which all the ardent and ambitious desires that equality engenders are exclusively directed. Hence it is that the selfsame democratic nations which are so reluctant to engage in hostilities, sometimes perform prodigious achievements when they have taken the field." Alexis de Tocqueville, *Democracy in America,* trans. Henry Reeve (Cambridge: Sever & Francis, 1863), II, 341. Democratic war would tend, by this logic, toward total involvement. The moral as well as the physical resources of the nation would eventually be organized in support of the war effort, and the conflict itself would readily take on the quality of a great crusade, fought by all society for the preservation of its principles. Some of our wars, of course, have not required this total commitment. But for those that have, Tocqueville's predictions retain an essential soundness.

like it has ever been witnessed in our streets. . . . It seemed as if the fountains of the great deep were broken up and poured forth their floods."[3]

This emotion appears to have been directly tied to the energy which had sustained the war effort itself:

> It was like the steam of a giant locomotive, being blown off when it reached the end of its journey. It was that pent-up power that propelled the engine. The tumultuous raptures of yesterday was the sudden letting loose of the feeling which for four years has nerved the heart of the people to fight on and to hold out and when the first born fell, to send to the battle the second and the third born. It was this unconquerable spirit in the common people to save their Union, unconditionally, which won the contest.[4]

Inherent in that first swell of thanksgiving, and held in unsteady suspension, were two distinguishable themes. One was the theme of peace: the binding-up of wounds, the resumption of normal pursuits, and magnanimity toward the beaten enemy. The chord had already been touched by President Lincoln in his Second Inaugural, and echoes were sounded once more with the fall of Richmond and the collapse of the Army of Northern Virginia. "Let us not forget, in our rejoicing," counseled Postmaster-General Dennison amid the tumult of Washington on the tenth, "that, as freely as we have poured out our treasure and copiously as has been shed the blood of our sons and brothers in the defense of the government, they would have availed nothing but for the Divine favor which has enlightened our darkest hours . . . ; and we can well afford to be magnanimous."[5]

There was, however, a second theme, without which the first would not have had much meaning. This was the sterner note of justice and security: ". . . let it be carefully borne in mind," continued the Postmaster-General, "that the only magnanimity we can further exercise must be that which will secure to the nation permanent peace and universal freedom." This motif, emphasizing safeguards for the fruits of victory, assumed a sudden urgency a few days later with the assassination of the President, an event which thousands in their distraction took as a sign that magnanimity and leniency would be inadequate as the sole keynote for a policy toward the vanquished rebels.

And yet the "back to normal" urge, though chastened and qualified, continued to diffuse itself and gain headway. By the first of June, a number of things had happened to nurture this more peaceful sentiment and bring it to some form of initial maturity. There were the continued surrenders of the rebel armies, a process which was complete and final with the capitulation of Kirby Smith on May 26. No guerrilla warfare materialized thereafter. There was the death of Booth and the speedy launching, on May 10, of military trials for the other conspirators. The summary quality of this proceeding was muted by a certain official defensiveness; the sessions of the court were made semi-public, and they were accompanied by daily reporting of the testimony. There was the cap-

[3] Chicago *Tribune*, Apr. 11, 1865.
[4] *Ibid.*
[5] *Ibid.*

ture of Jefferson Davis on May 10, and although Davis was to remain a prisoner for two years, the sentiment for making an example of him was never resolute enough to command wide popular support.[6] Even less determination could be mobilized for the punishment of Robert E. Lee. Moreover, there were the stories of devastation that were beginning to filter up from the stricken South — stories not without their effect upon Northern sympathies, judging from the frequency with which they were being printed by early summer.[7] Finally, there was the grand review of the Armies of the East and West at Washington, where for two days, on May 23 and 24, the great rank and file of the defenders of the Republic paraded in their ultimate and seasoned glory, thence to disperse forever. The catharsis of demobilization was under way. "We want true union and concord in the quickest possible time," announced the Springfield *Republican*, "and by such means as will make these blessings perpetual. Are these ends to be gained by reproaches and invectives; by prolonging the spirit and the evils of war after the war itself has terminated?"[8]

President Johnson meanwhile, through proclamations and the exercise of executive power, was launching his program of reconstruction. For the public this represented, among other things, further progress in clearing the air. It was not so much that it was either a good policy or a bad one; the plan was not ostentatiously punitive; at the same time, there were aspects of it that certainly exceeded in sternness the Lincoln proclamation of eighteen months before. And Johnson's own phrase, "Treason is a crime and must be made odious," still rang in Northern ears. The important thing now was that someone had taken charge of the problem, and a little of the urgency and burden of speculation and debate had been lifted. Reconstruction had at least been set in motion. The result was that by mid-June the two themes — peace, normality, and leniency on the one side, and security, justice, and guarantees for future loyalty on the other — were more or less in a state of balance. The wide range of expectations which together these themes represented could, for the time being, unite in a "trust-Johnson" sentiment which was widespread and generally shared. We tend now to forget the extent of Johnson's initial support. Among the leading journals, such support comprised every shade of Unionist sentiment, from the Midwest's formidable Chicago *Tribune* to the New York *Herald*, and including all three of the great New York Unionist dailies, the *Times*, the *Herald*, and the *Tribune* — not to mention such leading weeklies as *Harper's* and the *Nation*.[9] It is important

---

[6] Thaddeus Stevens, who thought that the punishment of individuals was a waste of time and whose own emphasis was on the reconstruction of governments, actually offered to defend both Davis and Clement C. Clay when it became known that the administration was planning to prosecute them for complicity in the murder of Lincoln. Horace Greeley, in June, 1866, offered to sign a bond for Davis. These stories are in Robert L. McElroy, *Jefferson Davis: The Unreal and the Real* (New York: Harper & Bros., 1937), II, 560–61; and Richard N. Current, *Old Thad Stevens* (Madison: University of Wisconsin Press, 1942), p. 212.

[7] E.g., there is a great deal of material in the *Nation* during this period from correspondents traveling in the South, and destruction forms a major theme in it.

[8] Springfield (Mass.) *Weekly Republican*, June 10, 1865.

[9] Editorially, the most hard-bitten of the great Unionist dailies of the country was probably the Chicago *Tribune*, whose columns were noted for their sentimentality toward the South. Yet even the *Tribune* had been a leading supporter of Lincoln, the man of

in any diagnosis of Johnson's subsequent downfall not to belittle the fact that virtually every Republican paper in the country, including those later to be designated as "radical," was initially on the President's side. Even the most extreme of these journals would remain with him for a number of months, and the majority would not fully sever connections until early in 1866.

Still, returning to the idea of a balance of themes inherent in post-victory feeling and inherent to all intents and purposes in the President's policy, it is well to note that a balance is by nature something uneasy and precarious. So it was with this one. The "back to normal" side was legitimate and real for the great masses of the Northern public. But the qualifications and *caveats* — the other side of the balance — included items so formidable and so complex that no prelude to such a subject as reconstruction would be properly completed without some further consideration of them. Here the implications of "security" and "justice" are not fully covered by the concept of "war hatred" — or, as it was later called, the waving of the bloody shirt.

---

mercy; the *Tribune*, moreover, was only too willing that peaceful pursuits be resumed in return for a change in the rebellious spirit of the South. "If this reaction," it declared in an editorial of April 8, "shall be spontaneous, hearty and in good faith, the path to Union will be cleared of its only formidable obstacle." The New York *Tribune*, however, stigmatized by so many writers of recent years as incorrigibly radical, was anything but that, in the spring and summer of 1865, with regard to the question of clemency and forgiveness. Scarcely a trace of vindictiveness is to be found in its editorial columns throughout all this time, and the paper would not hear of executing Davis or any other Southern leader. "The Southern mind is now open to kindness," it declared on April 14 (a sentiment which it continued to express after the tragedy of Lincoln's assassination), "and may be magnetically affected by generosity. Let assurance at once be given that there is to be a general Amnesty and no general Confiscation. This is none the less the dictate of wisdom because it is also the dictate of mercy." The New York *Times*, on the other hand, whose moderation on all questions, then and now, is legendary, was at first all for hanging Davis and treating the Southern people with stern justice. "So far as their *civil rights* and *franchises* are concerned, they are today practically as much outside the pale of the Federal Constitution as the people of Russia. They are subject to military rule only" (May 5). And yet this notion was counterbalanced elsewhere in the *Times* by the note of magnanimity. "Their courage [it said on June 12] . . . has been our enemy, but hereafter it is to be our friend." And further: "It is not for us to poison the wound we have inflicted on their pride, nor to stab, with insulting blows, the dead body of their ambition." The most interesting case of all is that of the New York *Herald*, whose zeal by midsummer in promoting Southern restoration put that journal well out on the fringes of Unionist opinion. Yet the *Herald*, in the spring of 1865, was full of hot words on rebel punishment and many times expressed itself in favor of Negro suffrage in some form (on the latter point, indeed, all these journals in principle agreed during this early period). Said the *Herald* on April 22: "All the conspirators of the South, responsible as the contrivers or managers of this prostrate rebellion, whether as confederate-rebel rulers or local leaders, would do well to quit the country without delay. This advice is the best that we can now do for them in the way of charity."

The point of this hasty survey is to illustrate the oscillation of sentiment — not always consistent — within the Union ranks, between the themes of mercy and sternness, up to the time of Johnson's launching of presidential reconstruction. It can be said, further, that Johnson's initial promulgations of policy did something to "jell" these diverse feelings and hold them in a temporary state of balance. This seems borne out by the willingness of all these papers, representing every conceivable facet of Unionist opinion, to offer the President their support. It might also be added (though this is somewhat ahead of the story) that all of them ultimately deserted him.

II. "Symbolic Requirements"

By the end of the summer and fall of 1865 an uneasy conviction had spread throughout most of the North that somehow the South had never really surrendered after all. This was hardly a "rational" persuasion in the ordinary sense: the evidence was overwhelming that the Southerners had had their fill of fighting. There was no way in which the military security of the North was in the least threatened; the Southern armies had fully dispersed; no legitimate forum for the expression of Southern sentiment, not one of the agencies of government, state or local, showed the least inclination to rebel further against the authority of the United States. And yet Northern feeling, well before the meeting of Congress could give it any clear leadership, had already become noticeably poisoned with fear and suspicion.

Of course, there were many men in the North of violent radical proclivities who would have been quite willing that sectional bitterness be prolonged until such time as thoroughgoing changes might be effected in Southern society. But it would be difficult, this early, to locate any such group of men sufficiently well organized, and exerting enough general influence and authority throughout the North at large, to have manufactured such asperities themselves. Indeed, these feelings were neither focused nor organized; they were pervasive, they seemed to ooze from everywhere, and they invaded the repose of weary men who would have given much to be rid of them. Charles Sumner, to be sure, wrote letters to his friends all summer long, tirelessly sounding the alarm. But Charles Sumner was hardly the tribune of the Northern people and never had been; if the Northern people had a tribune at this time, it was still Andrew Johnson. Probably this phenomenon of feeling did not have much direct connection with the work of individual Northern or Southern leaders. It may actually have had more to do with the meaning of victory itself, and with the peripheral meanings that hover about the notion of surrender.

Centuries ago, men gave much thought and effort to the problem of bringing a kind of *de jure* sanctity to the *de facto* brutality of conquest in war. They were oppressed by the realization that, right or no right, it was in the nature of war that the conqueror was somehow not to be thwarted from having his will in the end. Many of the things written by the commentators upon the ancient laws of war were therefore based on the implicit question of why, in fact, this had to be. Though the victor ought to use prudence in his exactions and temper his demands with mercy, the arbitrary inequity of "might makes right" flowed from the very nature of conquest. The victor in any war emerges from his conquest preoccupied with a whole set of requirements, and in his hour of triumph he is in the supreme position to insist upon their fulfillment. Both victor and vanquished desire peace and a return to peaceful occupations. But the conqueror's conception of peace is of a far more sweeping character than that of the conquered; the latter expects nothing, the former expects all. He requires a kind of total security; his idea of "peace" is a function of his sense of security.

These barbaric thoughts of a former age are implicit, for example, in the writings of Grotius, who assures the conqueror that he "is entitled to impose ANY terms upon the conquered, who is now placed, by the external laws of war, in a situation to be deprived of every thing, even personal liberty or life, much more then, of all his property, either of a public or private kind." But now that the conqueror knows his rights to be absolute, he should in practice observe limits: ". . . *as far as security allows*, it is always laudable to incline to moderation and clemency. Sometimes even circumstances may require such a line of conduct and the best conclusion of any war is that, which reconciles all contending claims by a fair adjustment, and a general amnesty. The moderation and clemency to which the vanquished appeal, are by no means an abolition but only a mitigation of the conqueror's absolute right."[10]

Such principles have their shortcomings as international jurisprudence.[11] But although they have little to tell us about the right and the good, there has been many a garbled insight into men's psychic needs hidden away in the old categories of political economy, philosophy, and law. Here we seem to have a glimpse of certain "spiritual" requirements with which men have perennially emerged from battle, and of the appropriate behavior which may follow upon their satisfaction. Let the conqueror feel that his victory and dominion — and therefore his security — are absolute, so that the granting of clemency, if it suits his pleasure, may itself be absolute.

This "security" concept has a significance that goes beyond the gross fact of physical conquest and disarming of the enemy. There are deeper requirements: the victor needs to be assured that his triumph has been invested with the fullest spiritual and ceremonial meaning. He must know that his expenditures have gone for something, that his objectives have been accomplished, and that the righteousness of his principles has been given its vindication. The assurances must be accorded him in terms that go well beyond the physical and objective; he must have ritual proofs. The conquered enemy must be prepared to give symbolic satisfactions as well as physical surrender; he must — in some way appropriate to his customs and his culture — "act out" his defeat.[12] This properly done, with satisfying gestures, the conditions are created wherein peace and clemency, if they are to obtain at all, will have their most auspicious setting. The foolish doubts which may still congest the victor's mind regarding the completeness of his vic-

---

[10] Hugo Grotius, "On Good Faith between Enemies," in *The Rights of War and Peace*, trans. A. C. Campbell (London: M. W. Dunne, 1901), p. 399; italics added. Grotius' original treatise was published in 1625. Most of the classical treatises on international law (including the rights of conquest), beginning with the fourteenth-century *De bello, de repraesalis et de duello* of Giovanni da Legnano, have been handsomely republished both in photographic reproductions of the originals and in translation, under the auspices of the Carnegie Endowment for International Peace. The series title is "Classics of International Law," ed. James Brown Scott (Oxford: Clarendon Press, 1911–   ).

[11] They were attacked and discredited by Locke and, following him, by the writers of the Enlightenment. Rousseau quotes the Marquis d'Argenson in support of his own attack on Grotius: "Learned researches upon public right are often only the history of ancient abuses; and it is lost labor to take the trouble to study them too much." See Jean Jacques Rousseau, *The Social Contract*, trans. Rose M. Harrington (New York: G. P. Putnam's Sons, 1893), p. 5. The value of such writings as those of Hobbes and Grotius certainly does not lie in their adequacy as law and right but rather in their refracted descriptions of men's actual behavior in situations where different sets of values (such as clemency and security) appear at loggerheads.

[12] It was thus, for instance, that the victory processions of ancient times would include the enemy chieftains, followed by files of captives loaded with chains, who would at the appropriate moment throw themselves upon the clemency of the conquering sovereign.

tory — and which may cloud his impulses toward mercy, if he has any — could thereby be swept away at the very outset.

War being what it always has been — a species of ritual slaughter — there is much reason to think that the ceremonial requirements of earlier days still find some echo in those of more modern and enlightened warfare. Our war with Japan, judging from the results, affords considerable proof of the point.[13] What is one to think, then, coming upon an instance in which the passions, hatreds, and suspicions of war have not been swept away at all but seem to have been unduly and abnormally prolonged? It may be that in such a case the victor has had his "security" — in this enlarged, symbolic sense — withheld from him. His principles may never have been vindicated at all; he may have wrested the enemy's arms from him, but nothing more: perhaps no rituals of submission were performed to satisfy his deeper needs. Something of this sort seems to have been involved between North and South in 1865. In this case, the psychic fulfillments needed for a proper transition from war to peace were experienced by no martial sovereign but by an entire people. It is here that the quality of total commitment in a modern, democratic war becomes of particular importance.

The Civil War could in a way be called the most democratic of all our wars — conceivably the most democratic war of all time. The *levée en masse* was not the feature which made it so; many another culture has had that. The war was democratic in a kind of total, political sense: it was carried on within an intensely democratic political culture, and its democratic and its political features are impossible to separate. Unlike our foreign wars, this one had to be prosecuted and promoted — "campaigned for," as it were — almost as an expanded political platform. Consequently the sense of a "cause" (vital to any war) was not to be imposed by remote authority. The cause had to be something whose effectiveness, from both without and within the individual citizen, depended to a remarkable degree on its being voluntarily assumed. The moral coercions flowed not from the fiat of the state but from consensus in the community. Such coercions, of course, are the hardest of all to resist, for no one can really personify their source; they emanate, in the ultimate sense, from "the people."[14] The principles

[13] See below, pp. 432–434.

[14] We may imagine a counter-instance in the loyal Austrian peasant of 1914 being conscripted into the imperial army. "The powers above," he might have said, "tell me that I must go and do my duty; therefore, of course, I must." This is in the tradition of authority, acceptance, and obedience. The same tradition can also be one of revolution and mutiny: there is something removed from the community scene, yet something focused and personified in the heads of the state, that can specifically be resisted. Indeed, there have been thousands of cases, among our own European immigrant forebears, where such resistance to military authority has been a matter of great pride. And yet in our own military tradition, such as it is, there are no such themes, either of implicit acquiescence to authority or of revolt. The conviction that our military enterprises are just and righteous does not flow automatically from on high. At the same time, one does not point with pride to an ancestor who evaded duty in any of our wars. Where, then, are the coercions? They emanate, in a special sense, from ourselves. Nobody, for instance, wants very much to be drafted for military service, but the sanctions are hard to "mutiny" against; they come not so much from the President as from "a local board composed of your neighbors." The principle of "conformity," for all its odium, is a democratic concept (the odium is itself symptomatic of the individualistic as well as the mass themes of democracy); "conformity" does not,

that justify such a war must thus strike very deep. They must be strong enough and safe enough to be carried about in the individual's own conscience throughout all vicissitudes, and they must constantly be refreshed, renewed, and re-created by a process essentially political in nature.

The consequences of this democratic quality in our Civil War can be illustrated in a number of ways. There was a very intimate relationship, for instance, between battles and elections. Throughout the war, the political prospects of almost anyone running for major state and federal offices depended upon the military situation. It was more imperative than ever in wartime that the government remain sensitive to public feeling; both state and federal administrations had to carry the population with them in order to prevent being hamstrung, in their conduct of the war, by the elections. Military campaigns had to be "ratified," in effect, at the polls. Conversely, the administration party's success, or lack of it, was one fairly dependable criterion for judging how things were going in the field.[15]

Another feature of the war was that of full and constant communication. There were few aspects of the war's military progress — the location of troops, their disposition, the attributes of their commanders, and so on — which were not most of the time a matter of general knowledge. An extraordinary amount of information was carried simply by men going back and forth on furlough, and since units were made up geographically rather than at random, news of the regiment would be cherished at home by the entire community. Above all, there were the newspapers. One has only to follow for a week or two the reports, the dispatches, and the maps in the wartime files of any leading daily to be convinced that this was the best-reported war in history.[16] Hand in hand with this pitch

---

in any case, mean the same thing as "obedience to authority." It means conformity to standards that one has one's own part in maintaining, if only negatively, and that would collapse if substantial numbers of one's friends and neighbors refused to support them.

[15] This connection between battlefield success and success at the polls may be tested by noting that the two lowest points of the war for the North coincided with ebb tides in the fortunes of the Union party. In 1862, after the abortive Peninsular campaign and Second Bull Run, the Democrats won extensive victories which included the governorships of New York and New Jersey. They made similar inroads in the legislatures and congressional delegations of Ohio, Pennsylvania, Illinois, and Wisconsin. Republican Governor Oliver Morton was faced with an antiwar majority in the Indiana legislature, against which his heroic efforts to maintain his state's troops in the field have become part of the wartime legend. See William B. Hesseltine, Lincoln and the War Governors (New York: Alfred A. Knopf, 1948), pp. 265–71; also Kenneth Stampp, Indiana Politics during the Civil War (Indianapolis: Indiana Historical Commission, 1949), pp. 179–85, and William Dudley Foulke, Life of Oliver P. Morton (Indianapolis: Bowen-Merrill, 1899), I, 203 ff. The second low point for the Union party came in the summer of 1864 with the desperate and apparently fruitless bloodletting of Grant's army in Virginia. Seldom had Lincoln's political future looked so dark. His subsequent success at the polls, and in effect the administration's mandate to continue the war, were directly related, as everyone knows, to Sherman's capture of Atlanta and the victories of Sheridan and Farragut. The people did, of course, have a clear alternative: they could have voted for the "peace plank" of the Democratic party.

[16] For much interesting material on the fiercely competitive efforts of the New York dailies to outdo each other both in the completeness of their war coverage and in the speed with which they got their stories before their readers, see Bernard A. Weisberger, Reporters for the Union (Boston: Little, Brown, 1953); and Louis M. Starr, Bohemian Brigade (New York: Alfred A. Knopf, 1954).

of awareness and sensitivity to every development in the military situation, so fully diffused among the entire population, went the widest latitude for criticism of the war effort.[17] Principles, objectives, and dedication to the cause would have been put to the sternest of tests amid so minute a process of communication. The commitments, to survive such a process and retain their vitality and meaning, would have had to reach great depths in the popular soul.

Even the procurement of troops depended, in a way that would never again be so direct, upon the maintenance of these principles and commitments as justification for re-enlistment. The nucleus of the Union army in 1864 was composed of veterans who had enlisted in 1861 and whose three-year terms were then running out. Only persuasion could keep them in; they could not be conscripted. Yet nearly three-fourths of them did re-enlist; to the end, only about 6 per cent of the Union troops would be brought in by the draft. The 1864 re-enlistment of three-year volunteers was thus in effect a ratification, by the army itself, of the war and its principles.[18]

The most important point of all, in considering the democratic, shared quality of this war and its effect on the sense of dedication necessary to prosecute it, is the aspect of sacrifice. There is no very precise way to measure dedication, but there is a rough way of indicating its ultimate test. The people had to be convinced, and to convince themselves, that the cause for which their sons were fighting was worth sacrifices that would go well beyond the experience of any other generation of Americans, before or since. The Union casualty rate was between six and seven times heavier than the comparable percentage of American losses in the Second World War.[19] It is well and just that war should be pronounced the most depraved and useless of all modes of human enterprise. But

[17] "Despite great provocation there was no Espionage Act and no Sedition Act during the Lincoln administration. During a time when disloyalty was widespread and defiant, the anti-Lincoln and anti-Union organs were, as a rule, left undisturbed; and the continuous stream of abuse which the opposition papers emitted was in itself a standing evidence of the fact that liberty of the press, even to the point of license, did exist." James G. Randall, *Constitutional Problems under Lincoln* (New York: D. Appleton, 1926), p. 508.

[18] "Union armies in the Civil War did not sign up for the duration. They enlisted by regiments, and the top term was three years. This meant — since the hard core of the United States Army was made up of volunteers who had enlisted in 1861 — that as the climactic year of 1864 began, the army was on the verge of falling apart. Of 956 volunteer infantry regiments, as 1863 drew to a close, 455 were about to go out of existence because their time would very soon be up. Of 158 volunteer batteries 81 would presently cease to exist.

"There was no way on earth by which these veterans could be made to remain in the army if they chose not to stay. If they took their discharges and went home — as they were legally and morally entitled to do — the war effort would simply collapse." Bruce Catton, *This Hallowed Ground* (New York: Doubleday, 1956), p. 317. "Astoundingly, 136,000 three year veterans re-enlisted. They were the men who had seen the worst of it — men who had eaten bad food, slept in the mud and the rain, made killing marches, and stood up to Rebel fire in battles like Antietam and Stone's River, Chickamauga and Gettysburg — and they had long since lost the fine flush of innocent enthusiasm that had brought them into the army in the first place." *Ibid.*, p. 318.

[19] In round figures, Union casualties have been estimated at 360,000 deaths from all causes, out of a population of about 20 million. American losses in World War II came to 384,000 deaths from all causes, from a population of 135 million. This is a comparison of 1.8 per cent to 0.28 per cent. A casualty rate in World War II comparable to that of the Civil War would have required nearly 2.5 million deaths.

there are special times when such a judgment is better withheld than uttered. Not much is gained in telling a people that the ordeal from which they have just emerged is without moral meaning; nor does one ever say these things to a Gold Star mother. Once the sacrifice is made, the principles themselves, despite the corrosions and disillusionments of time, become in some way consecrated. They become, like the young man in death, incorruptible.

The meaning of victory, then, would be to declare all the ideals successful. The nation had told itself that, with victory, the war principles would be vindicated, and now, with the collapse of the rebellion, they were presumably vindicated and secured beyond all question. The logic of military events, at least, would appear to have made them so. As for just what these principles were, it was not that easy to say. The fundamental thing about them was not their precision, for they had none; it was rather their pervasiveness and depth. Lincoln, as poet, had given them their fittest expression at Gettysburg. The basic symbol was that of the Union, whose sub-theme was freedom. The poet himself had become a sacrifice, and it was now required of the beaten enemy that he pay some form of homage to the symbol. The thing could not be fully consummated with the surrender of the Confederate army. It was somehow necessary that the South go a little farther in acting out its defeat, though no one had much of a notion as to just when the curtain should be allowed to fall. But among the millions of witnesses there would have to be at least a consensus of sorts that the effort had been made — and that reunion had been accepted with appropriate and satisfying ritual gestures. Peace on the battlefield must be followed by a willingness to bring peace to the Northern mind.

There were no precedents at all for the case of two American communities facing each other in the attitudes of victory and defeat. In the North, men talked of "guarantees," knowing that they did not quite mean guarantees for their homes and firesides. They longed for "reassurances," but knowing the courage of the men who had fought them, they hardly expected abject and groveling servility. On "reconstruction," some form of which was universally anticipated, there were many variations of opinion and much muddled reasoning in matters of both procedure and principle. But they did want something in the way of satisfaction; they wanted a security that was more than military. In the things they said, it is possible to make out at least some pattern of consistency.

For one thing, the fire-eating "secesh" style in Southern manners would have to be repudiated and discredited. There must be some transcendent assurance, willingly given by all of society, not only that the South was "loyal" in the passive sense, but also that the act of secession was somehow wrong. No blood sacrifice was asked. Nothing really overwhelming was demanded — but the notion of "repentance" kept recurring like a leitmotif.[20] Meanwhile those who had been active secessionists should be firmly ostracised "for the time being,"[21] and "ex-

---

[20] "Let them take their own time in coming in to supper. We can stand it as long as they can; and besides, we can rely upon the repentance of men who have been cured of their folly upon empty stomachs and cool reflection." New York *Herald*, May 3, 1865.

[21] Washington *Evening Star*, June 12, 1865.

cluded from all participation in political affairs,"[22] so that they might have leisure to reflect upon their errors.

> We hold that repentance, a repentance not to be repented of, should go before absolution and perfect pardon. We believe in the conversion of sinners, but we are slow to believe in instantaneous conversions. Let fruits meet for repentance be first brought forth, and then let the repentant prodigals be restored to the rights of sonship and brotherhood, and not before.[23]

Directly related to this need for some visible and articulate rejection of secessionism was the requirement that Southern Unionists be given some kind of security for having been Unionists. Not only must they receive protection, but upon them should fall the responsibility of forming the postwar governments.

> The reorganization of the several Southern States' governments must necessarily be exclusively entrusted to men who have played no active parts in the rebellion, who besides being against it originally, have at no time and in no manner given it the countenance of their willing support.[24]

The Unionist position must now in some way be redefined as "right." No doubt practical considerations would render an utter revolution in leadership impossible; perhaps it would sooner or later be realized that there were not so many Southern Unionists as one had initally thought and that the South's best men had been rebels. But at least the new values of postwar Southern society should to some extent be imparted by the men who had been loyal and Unionist throughout; society should accord them some kind of meaningful honor.

In the third place, it was of great symbolic importance that the masses of Southern Negroes, especially the ex-soldiers,[25] be conceded full protection in their newly conferred freedom. Slavery and its appurtenances should be fully repudiated. The new society must be based on a system of free labor which would include the ex-slave's freedom to work where he pleased, physical security in his comings and goings, and fair treatment in all matters pertaining to legal rights. The period of victory's immediate aftermath coincided with the period of least pessimism in Northern minds over this entire question. This was the time when the North's sense of responsibility for the freedmen was at its maximum, and

---

[22] *Illinois State Journal*, May 29, 1865. "But there are, and long will be, bad men in every Southern State, who are filled with the most rancorous hate of the government, and whose whole study hereafter will be how to do it injury. All such men can be shut out of Congress by the very stringent oath of allegiance which is now required before allowing a seat in either body. But they should also be precluded so far as possible, from all eligibility to State offices, and from the elective franchise. A State ruled by such men would become a nest for hatching new treason." New York *Times*, May 5, 1865.

[23] *Nation*, 1 (Oct. 19, 1865), 485.

[24] Washington *Evening Star*, June 12, 1865.

[25] "From first to last there were 178,975 Negroes in the United States Volunteer army, and of this number 36,847 were killed, wounded, and missing. They participated in four hundred and forty-nine battles, and served in nearly every military department of the United States Army. Besides this large military force there were at least one hundred and fifty thousand Negro laborers in the Quartermaster and Engineering departments." George W. Williams, *A History of the Negro Troops* (New York: Harper & Bros., 1888), p. 324.

the question had a moral clarity then that was later to disintegrate when the issue of Negro suffrage became a political football in partisan battles.

This sense of responsibility flowed from two sources, both full of coercion for the Northern conscience. Emancipation had become one of the war principles and was now an accomplished fact whose rightness had been sanctioned by victory. The Negro population, moreover, represented a strong salient of loyalty to the Union. "It is the duty of the government," asserted the *Illinois State Journal* of Springfield, "not only to protect its friends among the white population of the South, but to maintain the rights of the freedmen also, who have been solemnly clothed with the privileges of citizenship."[26] But although the prime responsibility for this protection and security should lie with the federal government, it must somehow be morally certified by the South itself. It was not simply that the Southern constituent assemblies were being asked to ratify the new emancipation amendment. The North was really concerned with how the thing would be done. Northerners wanted to see it acted out, and to judge its style.[27]

Finally, there were expectations, vague but palpable, regarding the reception of Northerners in Southern communities. Such expectations could not be announced in any manifestoes, but they were there. "A reunion of hands and hearts" was a note sounded surprisingly often in the immediate post-victory period. This did not necessarily represent a simple willingness to forgive and forget. It is rather that one may, reading a little between the lines, think of such a sentiment as yet another function of victory. The Northern conquest should be, among other things, a conquest of hands and hearts. "There must be a change of heart": the victor was coming, and he would have to be welcomed. The North had besieged the South with arms and she had submitted; the South, now in her defenseless, "feminine" entity, had no further right to repel the North, should the North now assume the role, as it were, of suitor. The South would henceforth be disarmed in all ways: not only was she to receive armies of occupation, of whose authority there was to be no question, but a new era of

[26] May 29, 1865. This thought (the Negro as a responsibility, implied in both emancipation and the Negro's own loyalty) was elaborately discussed in a New York *Times* editorial of May 5, 1865, entitled "The Points To Be Secured before Reconstruction." "Some security," the *Times* insisted, "must be provided for the freedmen of the South. They have been unswervingly loyal to the government from the beginning of the rebellion, and that alone is enough to entitle them to its special protection. However, the government, for its own purposes, made them what they are, and it therefore is bound to take care that emancipation shall be a blessing to them, and not a curse. The fulfillment of these duties is really the hardest difficulty, the very gordian knot of reconstruction."

[27] "They [the delegates to the Southern state conventions] will signify unconditional submission to the Union — they will surrender slavery, by ratifying the constitutional amendment providing for its abolition, and last, but not least they will adopt such measures toward the freedmen — their recent slaves — as will guarantee them full protection in their persons and the enjoyment, prospectively, if not at once, of all their political rights. If, on the other hand, the Southern people are not yet prepared to accept the position of faithful citizens under a Government, which is not only founded upon common ideas of National sovereignty and unity, but under which all men shall be, in the spirit of the Declaration, free and equal, that fact will doubtless be manifested, not only in a failure to do the things above specified, but in the display of a hostile temper which will betray the treason lurking in their souls." *Bureau County* (Ill.) *Republican*, Oct. 5, 1865.

hospitality to Northern immigrants, Northern enterprise, and Northern ideas was about to be inaugurated.[28]

Before considering how these requirements were responded to, let us experiment briefly with a kind of analogy. In many ways the German and Japanese occupations in 1945 may constitute a bad parallel for the post-surrender situation that followed the Civil War. But in at least one limited respect the parallel, such as it is, can be enlightening. It seems to show that there is such a thing as "symbolic" needs and that their fulfillment does make a great difference in the quality of feeling that will characterize the postwar behavior of former enemies toward each other. The analogy can show nothing specific about which ceremonial affirmations of defeat may be peculiarly proper but simply that the need for them exists. These requirements were fulfilled so automatically and so completely after World War II that they never constituted a problem for us; this in itself may be a good reason for making a point of it, and for suggesting that the point is applicable to more than one war.

Societies with a long tradition of accommodating themselves to power will have acquired, in the course of things, a deep knowledge of power in all its forms and meanings. They will know, for example, how to recognize superior power and how to appreciate and respond to it when they meet it. They will have little need of instruction on the requirements of a conqueror, and even less need of being told that he has them. Such societies, schooled in the ways of power, will know by instinct the cleanest ways of liquidating defeat; they will recognize, as a matter of self-interest, that when the requirements are met, the willingness (whatever its limits) of the conqueror to be merciful, to grant clemency, forgiveness, and oblivion, is at its maximum. So there is a sense in which the ancient law of conquest, to the extent that it makes the matter explicit, need not be thought of as entirely inhumane. It is here that our experience of victory in World War II seems particularly illuminating.

Those who participated in the last stages of the offensive against Germany in 1945, and subsequently in the occupation, will remember their surprise at the total collapse of all forms of resistance, civilian as well as military. The lack of sullenness on the part of the population was most remarkable; respect and deference, bordering on the obsequious, to the occupying power was everywhere in evidence. Before long there was even a willingness by the Germans themselves to try, and to convict, their own "war criminals." In the light of their supposedly arrogant ways, the people at large showed an amazing spirit of accommodation to the presence of our army; and the friendliness of the women was especially notable.[29]

[28] As the *Nation* put it, "They must deal better with . . . the stranger that may be within their gates, than they have ever yet done. . . ." I (Oct. 19, 1865), 485.

[29] Here is one point (among several) at which it is important not to let the analogy get out of hand. It is true that the overpowering and occupying of one country by another has both figuratively and literally all sorts of "sexual" overtones. But on the more literal level, the community morals of nineteenth-century America, even under conditions of fullest hospitality, would not have allowed anything like the freedom that existed between American soldiers and the women of post–World War II Germany. And yet that need not banish the parallel altogether. Allowing for the differences in mores, one can still ask what hap-

And yet all this pales before the tableau that was acted out, in virtually pure form, by the Japanese. The chronology of the first year's occupation of Japan, taken in sequence through the pages of one of the news magazines, will evoke renewed amazement at the week-by-week story of how all the horror and loathing of the Japanese, and all the wartime hatreds, simply melted away. Before the first landings, early in September, 1945, the Americans were filled with misgivings. Perhaps we as a nation had been tricked in our decision to retain the Emperor. We were outnumbered, as General MacArthur later put it, "a thousand to one." There seemed no reason why the Japanese, with an undefeated army of several million — many of whom would shortly be unemployed brigands — could not carry on underground activity indefinitely. The troops were given dire warnings against the women: ". . . they have been taught to hate you. . . . The Geisha girl . . . may entice you only to poison you."[30]

Meanwhile, the peacemaking government decreed the banishment of autocracy and the inauguration of democracy, all of which was legalized by the Diet, while the *Nippon Times* pronounced the death of the old order and called for all haste in the work of building the new. Coming ashore was "like a veteran's dream of victory" for the tautly apprehensive Americans. Advance detachments were smothered with attentions which included turtle soup, roast beef, cold beer, and beds with clean linen sheets. A sign on a factory roof read, "Three cheers for the U.S. Navy and Army." The arrival of the conqueror was as extravagantly heralded in the newspapers as had been the early victories of the imperial forces. Three weeks later in the United States it was being reported, with bated optimism, that "the big news from Japan was what had not happened." Not a single demonstration of enmity had occurred; on the contrary, the people were giving every evidence of sincere accommodation and submission.[31]

Almost immediately, the Japanese repudiated their militarist leadership, and even before the official war criminal lists were prepared, the Japanese themselves were suggesting names for them. They reacted with unfeigned symptoms of guilt to the stories of atrocities to American prisoners, published in their own newspapers, and asked to set up their own courts for the punishment of those responsible.[32]

In October, General MacArthur "decreed revolution," which involved the most sweeping changes in Japanese life: full civil liberties, free speech and free thought, release of political prisoners, abolishment of all totalitarian powers, the inauguration of democratic government, the organization of labor, and the dissolution of the zaibatsu, or great family business combines. "Japanese officialdom bowed low, smiled, and consented," and a new cabinet was formed by Baron

---

pened, in the South of 1865, to the *ad hoc* society that seems to spring up on the spot, in all times and places, whenever there are young people. The fact was that in 1865 not even the normal and accepted gradings in relationship between men and women were sanctioned by Southern society vis-à-vis the Northern occupying force — and here it was the women themselves who made the law.

[30] *Time,* Aug. 27, 1945, pp. 27–29.

[31] *Ibid.,* Sept. 3, 1945, p. 28; Sept. 10, 1945, pp. 28–29; Sept. 24, 1945, p. 21.

[32] *Ibid.,* Sept. 10, 1945, p. 29; Sept. 17, 1945, p. 27; Sept. 24, 1945, p. 22; Nov. 19, 1945, p. 31.

Shidehara, one of the few surviving prewar liberal leaders. New parties sprang into existence, and the general election which was held in the spring brought 27 million voters to the polls. With Olympian understatement, the Supreme Commander pronounced it "satisfactory."[33]

The Japanese eagerness to please was manifested in a hundred ways. The Tokyo theater featured such plays as Drinkwater's *Abraham Lincoln* and Lillian Hellman's anti-Fascist *Watch on the Rhine*. With the decrees of female equality came an influx of women into politics; there was a flood of new business for the divorce courts; and the Emperor himself asked for an American woman tutor for the crown prince. The first contingent of Navy wives was welcomed at the pier by a delegation of Japanese women announcing their desire to learn American ways. The popular songs became heavily American in style; the efforts at Americanization extended even to the underworld.[34] On the anniversary of Hiroshima's destruction a tremendous "Peace and Reconstruction Festival" was joyously staged by the city's boosters.[35] And finally, nothing was half so well suited to softening the asperities of war as the way in which the girls of Japan welcomed their American suitors. It was necessary at one point for General Eichelberger, on the interests of propriety and good military order, to issue a directive against "public displays of affection."[36]

After one year, the progress report on occupation could sum up a great success, from anyone's viewpoint. The Japanese had magnificently acted out all that was required of them;[37] the symbolic satisfactions of occupation had changed everything between the two peoples. With our Oriental enemies of over a generation, there now existed something closer to a "union of hands and hearts"

---

[33] *Ibid.*, Oct. 1, 1945, p. 28; Oct. 15, 1945, p. 29; Apr. 22, 1946, p. 32.

[34] *Ibid.*, Feb. 25, 1946, p. 50; July 1, 1946, p. 50; Apr. 1, 1946, p. 32; May 6, 1946, p. 35; Sept. 9, 1946, pp. 59–60; July 1, 1946, p. 25; Apr. 29, 1946, p. 48; June 24, 1946, p. 35. Giichi Matsuda, boss of the Matsuzakaya gang, tried to get his followers to wear Western-style sack suits and pursue more democratic and progressive business methods. When an outraged henchman assassinated Matsuda, the latter's widow was elected as the first woman gang chief ever known in Japan.

[35] *Ibid.*, Aug. 19, 1946, p. 36. A child whose mother and sister had been killed by the bomb said to a *Time* correspondent: "American soldier good. American number one." *Ibid.*, July 15, 1946, p. 38.

[36] *Ibid.*, Apr. 1, 1946, p. 25. A few months later, however, the military authorities were issuing phrase books with hints on "sweet talk." *Ibid.*, July 15, 1946, p. 38.

[37] "Last September MacArthur came to Japan whose people were imprisoned in feudalism and superstition, whose cities were ashen ruins, whose militarist traditions had no place for such concepts as defeat and war guilt. The Supreme Commander's first job was to destroy what was left of Japan's war potential. But he said: 'I am not concerned with how to keep Japan down but how to get her on her feet again.'

". . . By last week the U.S. imprint was strong on Japan. Japanese girls strolled hand in hand with G.I.'s beside the imperial moat. Children played with toy models of American 'jeepu'; women copied U.S. fashion. In Tokyo a special school taught U.S. slang, and cinema fans queued up to see Hollywood movies (biggest hit: *Tall in the Saddle*, a Western). In geisha houses, the girls gaily crooned *You Are My Sunshine*.

"The Japs, long used to following the leader, followed American democracy in much the same spirit as they accepted U.S. jazz. When MacArthur ordered them to hold an election, 27 million of them trooped to the polls. They organized Western-style political parties and prepared to accept a Western-style constitution. When they were ordered to cease worshiping their Emperor as a god, they willingly obliged." *Ibid.*, Sept. 2, 1946, p. 27.

than any American, in the bitter days of Bataan, Corregidor, and Guadalcanal, could very well have imagined.[38]

To expect from the conquered South any such behavior as that just described would have been grotesque. It would have been not only impossible but probably undesirable; it might conceivably have undermined a more permanent objective, that of remaking two peoples into one. Indeed, neither side had more than the dimmest idea of what was proper under the circumstances: Americans had never been conquered before, and had never really known authority, had had no real experience or appreciation of power, in either the active or the passive sense, and no instinct was sharp enough to warn of the behavior appropriate to any given instance of it. Such things lay outside the realm of anyone's experience. So the South could not in the truest sense submit, not really knowing how, and that was the way things had to be. But there would still have to be a price: the North still realized — dimly, perhaps, but somehow — that something was missing.

As the North waited, first in expectancy and then in deepening mortification, it began to dawn on the people that they were being somehow cheated of all the truly meaningful satisfactions of their victory. The South "accepted the situation," but this, as Northerners came to realize, was an idiomatic phrase brought into being especially for the purpose; it covered, with a special nicety, military defeat and no more.[39] As the reports came in, it began to appear that the deeper

[38] It is being argued that the experience of victory, together with the appropriate tokens of acquiescence, constitutes the most effective — and indeed the indispensable — ritual catharsis for the liquidation of prior hatreds. A final example of its profundity, before leaving the point, might come out of a few comparisons between American attitudes toward wartime "friends" and toward defeated enemies. In 1898, after the close of hostilities in Cuba, our hearts went out to the gallant Spaniards, whose submission was perfect, while we quickly perceived what an unsavory lot our friends, the suffering Cuban rebels, had been. On this point see Walter Millis, *The Martial Spirit* (New York: Literary Guild, 1931), pp. 363–64. (The same thing, of course, happened in the Philippines.) In Europe, our unsteady friendship for the French and Russians in World War II paled beside the real warmth which developed in our feelings for the prostrated Germans. And in Asia our relationship with our wartime friends, the Chinese, has become odious in every way conceivable.

[39] This point was explained by E. O. Dunning to the Joint Committee on Reconstruction. *Report of the Joint Committee on Reconstruction*, 39 Cong., 1 sess., Part II, "Virginia, North Carolina, South Carolina," p. 48.

Of all the groups in society, however, that element closest to the full ritual requirements of war appears perennially to be the military. The ceremonial of surrender made its deepest impression on those who actually participated in it — namely the armies — and those Southerners most convinced of defeat, and of the need for performing the gestures appropriate to it, were the Confederate soldiers. This should be taken mainly, of course, as a matter of degree, since no one class in a democratic society can be expected to remain aloof very long from the moral coercions of the rest of society. But the attitude was still noticeable enough, in the first six months or so following the war, that any number of otherwise critical Northern observers made a point of commenting on it, simply to emphasize the recalcitrance of Southern society at large. "Indeed," wrote Whitelaw Reid, "nothing was more touching, in all that I saw in Savannah, than the almost painful effort of the rebels from Generals down to privates, to conduct themselves so as to evince respect for our soldiers. . . ." *After the War: A Southern Tour* (London: Sampson Low, Son & Marston, 1866), p. 156. Sidney Andrews wrote, "I found it almost everywhere true in Georgia and the Carolinas that the best citizens of to-day are the Confederate soldiers of yesterday." "Three Months among the Reconstructionists," *Atlantic Monthly*, XVII (Feb., 1866),

gratifications, even in their mildest form, could never be accorded by the erstwhile enemy.

Representative James Garfield of Ohio, by the fall and early winter of 1865, was one of the numerous public men receiving letters from the Southern states, with details of the political activities going on there, and it was made clear to him that in none of these states could the late enemy help glorying in his secession. "The 'secesh' ticket in this county was elected throughout," wrote Joseph R. Putnam from Huntsville, Alabama.[40] L. A. Sheldon, a conservative Northern businessman, wrote from New Orleans that "politically the state is in the hands of the men who voted her out of the Union."[41] "In a word," declared James Atkins, writing from Atlanta,

> the control of everything down here is in the hands of the thoroughly disloyal. At a distance I felt a great sympathy for the people here: now that I am here and know how the pulse of the people beat, I have lost a great portion of my sympathy. The people have suffered terribly and are in a pitiable condition for the most part. Nevertheless all their sympathy is with those who distinguished themselves in behalf of the Confederacy. Men are advocated for such virtues openly. . . .[42]

Conversely, Southern Unionists found, even after the South's defeat, that their Unionism not only conferred no moral status whatever in their home communities but actually made their very existence intolerable there. The first test occurred in Virginia, where a large number of local elections, held late in May and early in June, brought solid rebel victories. "There is no security here for such men as me," flatly declared J. E. Brush of Norfolk,[43] and James H. Clements

---

242. Conversely, the Union armies constituted the most conservative class in all Northern society, so far as further exactions on the South were concerned. This is not fully explained simply by saying that the soldiers had had their fill of war and its horrors and now wanted to end it once and for all. The point is rather that the armies had participated in a very profound and compelling experience which was denied the respective civilian populations — the experience of surrender. The ceremony had, of course, opposite meanings for the opposing participants, but for a moment it brought them spiritually very close together. It prepared the Southern soldier for submission, the Northern soldier for magnanimity. But then, the meaning of such an occasion has to be tremendously enlarged and extended for the civilian who could not be there, or for the man whose son was sacrificed in order that it might take place. That is why, for full satisfaction, the gestures of surrender could not end with Appomattox.

[40] Joseph R. Putnam to James Garfield, Nov. 10, 1865, Garfield MSS, Library of Congress. Putnam was a Union soldier whose regiment, stationed at Huntsville, was about to be mustered out.

[41] L. A. Sheldon to Garfield, Nov. 21, 1865, Garfield MSS.

[42] James Atkins to Garfield, Dec. 7, 1865, Garfield MSS. Atkins was a federal officeholder in the Department of Internal Revenue.

[43] J. E. Brush to Sumner, June 9, 1865, Sumner MSS, Harvard College Library. "The undersigned is a Native of this Town, but left immediately after hostilities commenced destined for the City of Memphis with high hopes of being able to reach the Federal lines, but failed, was in Memphis 26 months, was there when the city was captured, absent from my family that length of time, 9 months of which did not hear from them. . . . Was born and reared here, but have bitter enemies because of the decided stand which I took and the liberal opinions which I now entertain. Many things I could tell you about [conditions] here provided I could get a hearing from you or some other influential man in the Congress of the U. States."

assured Charles Sumner that "if the Rebels continue to have the same privileges as now appears to be the policy to give them in this State, God help the
Union men."[44] "The real Union men of this state," lamented G. W. Welker of
North Carolina, "are but few and are so situated that they must look abroad
for aid. . . . We entreet Congress never to place us again under the power of
the men who betrayed us, plundered us & oppressed us."[45] It was observed by
Sidney Andrews that "In Barnwell and Anderson districts, South Carolina,
official records show the murder of over a dozen Union men in the months of
August and September. . . ."[46] And Gillet Watson more imploringly to Thaddeus
Stevens from Richmond: "We represent the loyal people of this section, many
of whom have fought and bled, and lost their all in defence of the stars and
stripes. Are these men to be turned over to an excited and infuriated mob, by
the U.S. Representatives?"[47]

Meanwhile, whatever illusions the North may have cherished regarding the
future of the Southern Negro began to dissolve. The ideals of emancipation and
free labor, as well as the hope of an incorruptible Unionist bulwark (which required at least some form of citizenship), faded before the reports. Even the
most sanguine Northerner became heavy-hearted at what he read and heard. "As
for your niggers," said a Virginia ex-colonel to Whitelaw Reid, "you've got 'em
on your hands. They won't work unless you force them to it, and they'll steal
rather than starve. You even talk about giving them suffrage! There are no words

[44] James H. Clements to Sumner, June 11, 1865, Sumner MSS. Clements, who called
himself "simply a Mechanic," had left Portsmouth, Virginia, at the outbreak of the war
in order to join the Union Forces. "I hope sir," he said to Sumner, "you will excuse the
freedom I take in addressing you, but sir the interest I feel in my future welfare and that
of my family justifies me in calling on the rulers of my country."

[45] G. W. Welker to Thaddeus Stevens, Dec. 2, 1865, Stevens MSS, Library of Congress.
Another North Carolina Unionist, who signed himself only "Union," summarized for
Stevens the result of the recent congressional election in his district:

" 'I cannot take the oath, if I would' & (defiantly) 'I would not, if I could.' Stubbs.
" 'I cannot take the oath.' Speed.
" 'I can honestly and truthfully take the oath, having never done any thing inconsistent
with it except *involuntarily* under military or mobocratic coercion.' Bond.

"The result was — Stubbs 2783, Speed 2013, Bond 450!!! Speed and Stubbs won
simply on the hope, that the oath would be repealed. Let Congress do that, & the seats
from the South will be occupied by the 'Secesh,' the Unionist in the South forever pro-
scribed by them & the Group in constant danger from their plots & intrigues." "Union"
to Stevens, Nov. 27, 1865, Stevens MSS.

[46] Andrews, "Three Months among the Reconstructionists," p. 238. "I spent the months
of September, October, and November, 1865," Andrews wrote, "in the States of North
Carolina, South Carolina, and Georgia. I travelled over more than half the stages and
railway routes therein, visited a considerable number of towns and cities in each State,
attended the so-called reconstruction conventions at Raleigh, Columbia, and Milledgeville,
and had much conversation with many individuals of nearly all classes."

[47] Gillet Watson to Stevens, Dec. 5, 1865, Stevens MSS. Watson was chairman of the
Union League of Virginia. "Sir," wrote a Louisiana correspondent of Nathaniel P. Banks,
"the present Legislature boast on the streets that they intend to *ostracise* all so called loyal
men to the United States Government by giving them no private or public employment, &
thus force them to leave the State for more agreeable quarters." J. P. Henderson to Banks,
Nov. 26, 1865, Banks MSS, Essex Institute.

to express the infamy of such a proposition. This is a white man's government, and must be kept so till the end of time."[48] "Three-fourths of the people," wrote Sidney Andrews,

> assume that the negro will not labor, except on compulsion; and the whole struggle between the whites on the one hand and the blacks on the other hand is a struggle for and against compulsion. The negro insists . . . that he shall be free to come and go as he pleases; the white insists that he shall come and go only at the pleasure of his employer. . . . I did not anywhere find a man who could see that laws should be applicable to all persons alike; and hence even the best men held that each State must have a negro code.[49]

Such a movement, indeed, was well under way by December. The hitherto circumspect *Nation*, confronted with the codes of South Carolina, Alabama, and Mississippi, was appalled at these "disgraceful statutes." "Such are some of the open manifestations of the mood of 'our Southern brethren' in circumstances when they would have been tempted to make a show at least of complete acquiescence in the will of their magnanimous conquerer."[50]

Finally, in receiving her triumphant conqueror, the South was unable to tender even the civilly measured hospitality that accompanies a forced submission.[51] Northerners with plans for emigration were chilled to discover that their arrivals were openly discouraged[52] and that there were no guarantees, except

[48] *After the War*, p. 318.

[49] "Three Months among the Reconstructionists," p. 243.

[50] *Nation*, I (Dec. 28, 1865), 806.

[51] Sidney Andrews, who did more listening than talking and therefore got into less trouble than many Northern travelers, reported that he had much less to complain of than most of his fellow Yankees. Yet there were numerous snubs and humiliations at hotels and boarding houses; "at one house in South Carolina," he noted, "when I sought accommodations for two or three days at a boarding-house, I was asked by the women in charge, 'Are you a Yankee or a Southerner?' and when I answered, 'Oh, a Yankee, of course,' she responded, 'No Yankee stops in this house!' and turned her back upon me and walked off. In another town in the same State I learned that I was the first Yankee who had been allowed to stop at the hotel since the close of the war." "Three Months among the Reconstructionists," p. 237. This was easily the most commonly shared experience of Northern travelers. It even extended to the military. General Grant's aide, Cyrus Comstock, at New Orleans with the General's party, laconically wrote in his diary for February 5, 1866: "Saw Gen. Baird. Says feeling in Nov. & Oct. was very bad, that officers were insulted at St. Charles, that officers wives at St. Charles table were not waited on and that on remonstrances being made were told they were not desired there as it might affect the custom of the house." Diary of Cyrus B. Comstock, Feb. 5, 1866, Library of Congress.

[52] "At the time I am writing, the owners of property in Richmond are holding it at such high rates as to repel Northern purchasers. Letters from the city say, the residents have determined to sell no property to Northern men, when they can possibly avoid it." Thomas W. Knox, *Camp-Fire and Cotton Field: Southern Adventure in Time of War* (New York: Blelock, 1865), p. 497. "One of our firm, Jos. Glenn," wrote Richard Smith (of the Cincinnati *Gazette*) to James Garfield, "has been travelling in Miss. and Louisiana for some time and bought a cotton plantation, which he now regrets. He says that if the troops are withdrawn Northern men could neither live nor travel there. . . ." Smith to Garfield, Jan. 14, 1866, Garfield MSS.

for the presence of federal troops, that they were even safe in their persons.[53] But what really must have struck the Northerner to the heart, in all the flush and pride of his victory, was the implacability of the Southern women. The women, far from performing for their people any of the gentler rites of peace, were the bitterest of all. "A day or two ago," wrote Carl Schurz from Savannah, "a Union officer, yielding to an impulse of politeness, handed a dish of pickles to a Southern lady at the dinner table of a hotel in this city. A look of unspeakable scorn and indignation met him. 'So you think,' said the lady, 'a Southern woman will take a dish of pickles from a hand that is dripping with the blood of her countrymen?' "[54] The Northern and Southern hands were not to join, even over the sour formality of a dish of pickles.

In no case were specific violations of the Confederate surrender involved in any of these stories. It was the protocol of defeat for an entire people that had been violated, a protocol whose spirit and overtones could hardly be specified in any articles of surrender. Under the circumstances, there may have been very little help for it: there were no cues in the national experience to follow in

[53] John Murray Forbes declared that "if you withdraw the army, and give back the local government to the Governors and Mayors and Magistrates and Constables who have been fighting us, any northern man who wishes to emigrate south must either cut out his tongue and his conscience, or provide himself with an India rubber neck and a ball proof jacket!" Forbes to N. M. Beckwith, Aug. 6, 1865, Carl Schurz MSS, Library of Congress. "It follows, of course," wrote Sidney Andrews in milder vein, "that safety of person is not assured. Very likely one might travel through every country of either State without harm; but any Union man must expect to hear insulting words; and any Northern man is sure to find his principles despised, his people contemned, and himself subjected to much disagreeable contumely; while any man holding and openly advocating even moderately radical sentiments on the negro question, stands an excellent chance, in many counties of Georgia and South Carolina, of being found dead some morning, — shot from behind, as is the custom of the country. Of course the war has not taught its full lesson till even Mr. Wendell Phillips can go into Georgia and proclaim 'The South Victorious.' " *The South since the War, As Shown by Fourteen Weeks of Travel and Observation in Georgia and the Carolinas* (Boston: Ticknor & Fields, 1866), p. 385.
[54] Carl Schurz, "Letters from the South, No. 4," July 31, 1865, Schurz MSS. "As we rode through the city," wrote Grant's aide at Charleston, "I saw several who called themselves ladies make faces at the Yankee officers with us. It is useless to say they are only women — they express openly what their husbands & brothers feel but do not show." Diary of Cyrus B. Comstock, Dec. 1, 1865. Even President Johnson's emissary, Benjamin Truman — whose report was specifically designed to present Southern conditions sympathetically — corroborated other witnesses on this point. "There is a prevalent disposition not to associate too freely with northern men," Truman wrote, "or to receive them into the circles of society; but it is far from insurmountable. Over Southern society, as every other, woman reigns supreme, and they are more embittered against those whom they deem the authors of all their calamities than are their brothers, sons and husbands." *Senate Executive Documents*, 39 Cong., 1 sess., No. 43, "Report of Benjamin Truman," p. 6. Here Truman was assuming that with the melting of that insignificant barrier, all would be changed. He little appreciated the formidability of the women: they did *not* melt. Joseph LeConte of Columbia, South Carolina, writing of the later reconstruction period, said that the men of Columbia were very cordial to the officers stationed there, "but the ladies were inexorable." "I became quite friendly with some of the officers," he wrote, "but I could never induce my wife to invite one of the gentlemen to the house for a social meal." *Autobiography of Joseph LeConte*, ed. William D. Armes (New York: D. Appleton, 1903), pp. 236–37.

setting matters to rights once they had gone awry. But whatever the cause, there were poisons in the Northern bosom by December, 1865, that had not been there in May. In one sense they had been carried over from a long, costly, and bitter war. But something had now been added, a new malaise, created not so much by war as by peace. It had been a most irregular peace, very uncertainly managed, a peace whose quality was quite different from anything that had been expected. Many were saying, by early 1866, that the wartime principles were now tarnished, the fruits of victory soured, and the sacrifices rendered meaningless; there seemed little left to show for the overwhelming moral commitment which the war had once represented. The moral victory which the North imagined itself to have won had come to nothing.

Although the above themes may tell us something important about the new turn in sectional feeling that occurred in the latter half of 1865, they still make up only a part of the story. The Southerners in the beginning could hardly have been so blind to their own deepest interests; nor could Northerners have been quite so muddled about what they required of the South. Still other things were involved during that summer of 1865, among them the fact that the most important channels of communication between the North and the South were not really open. The United States government, whose most authoritative agency at this time was the Republican party, was not in full functioning for the settlement of Southern problems, nor would it be until the end of the year. No one, meanwhile, could be expected to know how much difference this made; nor was it clear to what extent President Johnson considered himself the spokesman of that agency. Each of the interested parties had quite different notions on this point. Indeed, the entire period — the summer and fall of 1865 — might be seen from a later viewpoint as a season of self-delusion on nearly all sides. So if Southerners misconceived the accuracy with which the Northern will was being communicated to them, there remains the question of how much of this was properly their responsibility. Other explanations must be sought, more perspectives established, further trial balances struck.

The Effect of the Civil War on American Industrial Development

STEPHEN SALSBURY

The business historian Stephen Salsbury addresses himself to the question of the impact of the Civil War upon American economic development. A number of historians, following Charles Beard, have contended that the Civil War marked the triumph of capitalism over Southern agrarianism. If this had been the case, the war should have proved a stimulus to the economy, and particularly to the industrial sector. Recently, however, Thomas Cochran and historians using statistical measurement have contended that the disruptive character of the war actually retarded American economic growth. Salsbury seems to be taking the position that the war sustained development, and, thus, he cautiously defends the Beard point of view. He points out that growth rates for industrial development were higher in the decade immediately following the war than in the decade immediately preceding it. But he warns us not to place too much reliance upon statistical analysis, for there are always important aspects of economic problems that are difficult if not impossible to quantify. In this category he places the indirect effects of the Civil War such as changes in government and social organization. Salsbury's essay does not propose answers so much as it reveals the opportunities and obstacles inherent in economic history.

Much has been written about the Civil War. Until quite recently, however, historians were concerned mainly with its cause and they largely ignored the economic effects of the War. In the nineteenth century most northerners simply blamed the War on slavery. In the same period southerners merely accused politicians of being irresponsible and claimed that fanatical abolitionists ignited the conflict. But to Charles A. Beard, writing in the 1920's these old statements seemed unconvincing.

Beard viewed America's history as a great movement away from Jefferson's agrarian type of society to the capitalistic, industrial, mechanized, and urban society that we have now. In his view, the forces that moved people were economic ones and not idealistic concerns over states' rights or over the immorality of slavery. Beard's pre–Civil War America consisted of a northern, capitalistic, industrial economy with, opposing it, the southern agricultural system. He saw the economic interest and political power of the South, in the Electoral College, the Senate, House of Representatives, and Supreme Court, as frustrating the economic needs of the rapidly growing industrial north.

Professor Louis Hacker stated the Beard thesis in its most extreme and naked form in his book, *The Triumph of American Capitalism*. "By 1860," he summarized,
1940

> a critical situation had arisen in American affairs. Because the southern planter capitalists were in control of the instrumentalities of the national state and, as a result, were thwarting the advance of the (too slowly) growing northern industrial capitalism, their claims to power had to be challenged. This the newly formed Republican party did. The partial success of the Republican party at the polls in 1860 drove the southern leaders — pushed on by extremists in their

Reprinted by permission of the publisher from *The Economic Impact of the American Civil War*, edited by Ralph Andreano (Cambridge, Mass.: Schenkman Publishing Company, Inc., 1962), pp. 161–68.

midst who were under heavy economic pressures — into secession. The Civil War broke out. The Union government, after the departure of the southern legislators, was now wholly possessed by the Republican party.[1]

In Beard's words, the Civil War was the "social cataclysm in which the capitalists, laborers, and farmers of the North and West drove from power in the national government the planting aristocracy of the South. Viewed under the light of universal history, the fighting was a fleeting incident; the social revolution was the essential portentous outcome."[2]

This explanation of the causes of the Civil War lead Beard and Hacker to the conclusion that the conflict spurred economic growth in the United States:

> The Second American Revolution (Civil War) while destroying the economic foundation of the slave-owning aristocracy, assured the triumph of business enterprise. As if to add irony to defeat, the very war which the planters precipitated in an effort to avoid their doom augmented the fortunes of the capitalist class from whose jurisdiction they had tried to escape. Through financing the federal government and furnishing supplies to its armies, northern leaders in banking and industry reaped profits far greater than they had ever yet gathered during four years of peace. When the long military struggle came to an end they had accumulated huge masses of capital and were ready to march resolutely forward to the conquest of the continent — to the exploitation of the most marvelous natural endowment ever bestowed by fortune on any nation.[3]

Beard

But Beard made no systematic use of statistical evidence in trying to analyze the War's effect.

Prior to 1860 southern planters successfully used their power in the national government to oppose measures such as the tariff, the Homestead Bill, national banking, etc., favored by the northern industrialists and western farmers. Beard, however, made no attempt truly to evaluate the importance of such measures in economic terms and merely assumed that because northern capitalists could not get their way, their plans for expansion and profits were hindered and that economic growth was thus retarded. Starting with this assumption, Beard saw the War as aiding industrialism. He argued that the transference of power from the Democratic to the Republican party (a condition which lasted, with two short exceptions, from the 1860's until 1932) enabled businessmen to shape government policies that were most helpful to their plans for profit and expansion.

Beard cited the policies and legislation which, he claimed, specifically aided economic growth. He considered as most important the direct federal aid to the vast transcontinental railroad projects; it started with the subsidy and land grant to the Union Pacific and Central Pacific railroads in 1862 and included federal land grants in the following years to the Northern Pacific, Kansas Pacific, Santa Fe (Atlantic and Pacific), and Southern Pacific routes. The protective tariff was

---

[1] Louis M. Hacker, *The Triumph of American Capitalism* (New York, 1940), p. 339.
[2] Charles A. Beard and Mary R. Beard, *The Rise of American Civilization* (New York, 1933), vol. II, p. 54.
[3] *Ibid.*, p. 166.

named as specifically aiding economic growth. He named also the acts designed to make easy the removal of land (whether farmland, timberland, or mineral land) from the public domain to private hands, the Immigration Act of 1864 which gave federal blessing to the importation of workingmen under contracts "analogous to the indentured servitude of colonial times," and the national banking laws and many others.[4]

But more important than any specific legislative act, according to Beard's interpretation, was the ascendancy of the Republican party in Washington; this created a climate that tolerated no interference with the private capitalists. Gone were the Jacksonian ideas that opposed the concentration of economic power in the hands of large corporations. After 1860, Leland Stanford, Collis P. Huntington, John D. Rockefeller, John M. Forbes, Jay Gould, and Mark Hanna had almost unlimited freedom to do as they pleased. And when men such as these ran into trouble with labor, their control of the government assured them that federal power would be used to smash opposition.

Charles Beard's main effort was to explain why the United States in the period between 1860 and 1910 became the world's most productive and powerful industrial nation. In giving his explanation, he made only a random use of statistics. But while he was perfectly content to make almost totally undocumented assertions, such as that which attributed the post-Civil War boom to "huge masses of capital made available by war profits greater than . . . [capitalists] had ever yet gathered," Louis Hacker attempted to support this argument by statistical evidence. He used, for instance, an analysis of the census data to substantiate the thesis that "industrial capitalism (more particularly, *heavy* industry) benefited from the Civil War and it continued to make great forward strides (despite a severe depression) after the political victory was firmly secured."[5]

Lately, the role of the Civil War in positively contributing to the American Industrial Revolution has been questioned. Among the most recent and able of these questioning re-evaluations is Thomas C. Cochran's "Did the Civil War Retard Industrialization?"[6] In "reiterations of the effect of the Civil War on industrialism," he writes, giving examples, "statistical series seem to have been largely neglected."[7] Cochran's conclusion, after an examination of statistics (available mainly in the 1949 and 1960 editions of *Historical Statistics of the United States*[8] and in the report of the Conference of Research on Income and Wealth in *Trends in the American Economy in the Nineteenth Century*), strongly suggests that the Civil War slowed industrial growth.

Cochran observes that generally during the two decades preceding the Civil War (1840–1860) and the two decades (1870–1890) following the ten-year census period in which the war occurred, the rate of growth exceeded that of the

[4] Beard and Beard, *Rise of American Civilization*, vol. II, p. 106.
[5] Hacker, *Triumph of American Capitalism*, p. 438.
[6] Thomas C. Cochran, "Did the Civil War Retard Industrialization?", *Mississippi Valley Historical Review*, vol. XLVIII (Sept., 1961), p. 198.
[7] *Ibid.*, p. 198.
[8] Bureau of the Census, *Historical Statistics of the United States 1789–1945* (1949), and Bureau of the Census, *Historical Statistics of the United States Colonial Times to 1957* (1960).

"war decade" (1860–1870). In short, he points to rapid expansion between 1840 and 1860, then actual stagnation in some areas, and but slight increases in most others during the war period (1861–1865), which caused a slower growth rate for the decade 1860–1870, and finally a resumption of rapid growth in the decades between 1870 and 1890.

Behind Cochran's conclusion that the Civil War retarded industrial growth lies the very unstatistical and also partly unsubstantiated assumption that by 1840 all the ingredients favorable to fast industrial growth were overwhelmingly present in the American society. This implies that by the end of the Van Buren administration, the ground was laid for an almost continuous and uninterrupted expansion. This expansion, however, did not occur and the assumption is made that disruptive effects of the Civil War removed vital capital building goods and services for the economy between 1861 and 1865, making the growth after 1865 less rapid than it otherwise would have been.

Now, available statistics do indicate certain American economic reverses during the War. Cotton production almost ended, cotton textile manufacturing in the North fell sharply, and so did the construction of new railroad tracks. Yet, despite this, other segments such as bituminous coal, Pennsylvania anthracite, pig iron, and railroad rails continued to expand, although some at a slightly reduced rate. From this point of view, statistics show that the economy grew less rapidly during the five Civil War years than at other times. We might fairly conclude that war disruption was partially, at least, responsible for this.

Yet the conclusions of Beard, Hacker, and the other historians who claim that the Civil War speeded the Industrial Revolution do not stand or fall on an analysis of the short run, immediate effects which the War had upon the economy. Rather, these conclusions, which see the War as assuring the "triumph of capitalism," and as producing a long term surge of industrial production, rest on longer range analyses.

Professor Cochran's arguments may be met by comparing the post-Civil War growth rate with prewar activity. If one does this, some surprising results present themselves. Let us, for example, instead of comparing the three decades 1850–1860, 1860–1870, 1870–1880, as Cochran does, compare the decade preceding the Civil War (1850–1860), with that immediately following it (1865–1875).[9] Pig iron production in tons, which he considers as "the most significant commodity index of nineteenth century American industrial growth,"[10] increased about 50 per cent between 1850 and 1860, but more than doubled between 1865 and 1873 before it fell, due to the depression which started in 1873. Bituminous coal, "the second most essential commodity series,[11] tells a similar story: here production increased slightly less than 100 per cent during the decade of 1850–1860, while during the years 1865–1875 it increased by about 145 per cent.

[9] Note that many of the series used by Professor Cochran, especially those in *Trends in the American Economy in the Nineteenth Century* (National Bureau of Economic Research Conference on Research in Income and Wealth, Princeton, 1960), are not year-by-year statistics but show changes only every tenth year (usually the census year) and thus it is not possible strictly to compare the decade 1850–1860 with the decade 1865–1875.

[10] Cochran, "Did the Civil War Retard Industrialization?", p. 200.

[11] *Ibid.*

Railroad track construction, which he deems "essential for industrialization," tells an even more striking story: during the period 1850–1860 about 20,000 miles of track were laid down, compared to roughly 40,000 during the decade 1865–1875. Clearly then, in these areas which Cochran considers the most important indicators of nineteenth century economic growth, the postwar decade evidences a substantial boom with growth rates much above those of the pre-Civil War era.

Although this kind of analysis tends to cast doubt on the argument and could be used to support Hacker's assertion that "industrial capitalism (more particularly, heavy industry) benefited from the Civil War," such a conclusion would have the weakness which plagues any attempt to assess the economic effects of the Civil War by reference to growth rates, and industrial or agricultural output. Such statistics tell us only how much was produced, or how much the growth rate declined or increased, but they do not tell us why. This returns us to the non-statistical explanation of Beard which conflicts dramatically with Cochran's underlying assumption that all the ingredients for rapid economic growth dominated the American society by the beginning of William Harrison's administration.

Professor Cochran recognizes that what he calls "indirect effects" may have had some influence upon post-Civil War economic development. For purposes of analysis we can put these "indirect effects" into two categories. First, there were the changes in the political and social system which the War produced; and second there were the stimulants, such as inflation and the creation of a substantial federal debt, which resulted directly from the War itself. Relative to the second category, Cochran admits that "sharp wartime inflation had the usual effect of transferring income from wage, salary, and interest receivers to those making profits, . . . (which) meant concentration of savings in the hands of entrepreneurs who would invest in new activities."[12] He also points out that inflation "eased the burdens of those railroads which had excessive mortgage debts."[13] But Cochran seems willing to dismiss these effects of the War with the casual statement that "a great deal of new research would be needed to establish causal connections between inflationary reallocation of wealth, 1863 to 1865, and the high rate of industrial progress in the late 1870's and 1880's."[14] With this sentiment one can only agree. We add that until such attempts are made one must be careful about characterizing the Civil War as a retarder of industrialization.

Cochran's analysis is similar in his statements about the effect of expanded and superior credit resulting from the establishment of national banks and the increase of the national debt from $64,000,000 in 1860 to over $2,700,000,000 in 1866. He gives no statistics which would indicate the impact of the new banking system and the enormous federal debt, but merely states that "since 1800 a multiplication of banks had made credit relatively easy to obtain in the United States, and in the North this continued to be the situation."[15] Further, he observes that the War destroyed southern banking, and that by 1875 some 40 per cent

[12] *Ibid.*, p. 207.
[13] *Ibid.*
[14] *Ibid.*
[15] *Ibid.*

of the banks were still outside the national banking system. With these statements there can be little disagreement, yet it is difficult to see how they prove or disprove the thesis that the War retarded economic growth. In precise terms, how easy was credit to obtain before 1860? Was there ample credit for large scale ventures? Was there any change in this picture after 1865? If there was, did it result from the War? These questions still remain to be answered. And the fact that some "40 per cent of the banks" in 1875 were outside the national banking system seems almost irrelevant without a great deal of additional analysis which is not supplied.

Finally, Cochran recognizes that he must meet the argument which asserts that the Civil War changed the social structure of the nation. He agrees that there is a "possibility that the northern victory had enhanced the capitalist spirit"; but he maintains that this "highly generalized argument is difficult to evaluate." This is undoubtedly true (and the same statement could be made about most attempts to explain human behavior). But the Beard thesis is not so vague but what it is subject to some trenchant criticism. It is possible to analyze in detail the measures which the Republican Party enacted, and to determine how they affected economic growth. It has already been suggested that it may be feasible to measure the amount of investment capital made available by the creation of the national banking system, and the large national debt. There might also be a thorough quantitative study of government aid to internal improvements. While it is true that "federal and state administrations preceding the Civil War could . . . be regarded as friendly to business," it might be well to compare, as Professor Cochran suggests, federal and state aid during and after the Civil War with that in other periods. This should include an attempt to determine the precise amount in constant dollars made available to transportation enterprises by the various state and local governments and the national Congress. We do have readily available information on federal land granted for such purposes. Some idea of the new Republican attitude can be gained from the fact that, in the single year 1865, the national government granted more land for internal improvements than in all years prior to 1861.

There can be no doubt that the exodus from Washington of southern congressmen speeded by ten years or more the building of our entire transcontinental railroad network. Mr. Cochran suggests that such ventures were "built for speculative purposes uneconomically ahead of demand . . ." and thus concludes without supplying any evidence that they may "for a decade or even two have consumed more capital than their transportation services were then worth to the economy."[16] Although this judgment is not necessarily wrong, it will take much research to prove it one way or the other. Certain it is that the building of our vast transcontinental railway systems, which is partially reflected in 40,000 miles of track laid down between 1865 and 1875, had enormous economic effects both from the point of view of consuming (thus stimulating) the products of heavy industry, and of opening up agricultural land in California, Kansas, Nebraska, Wyoming, Colorado, Utah, Idaho, Montana, Washington, Oregon, Arizona, Nevada, and New Mexico. Here it must be noted that since the first transcon-

[16] *Ibid.*, p. 209.

tinental road was not finished until May 1869, the statistical impact of these roads in agriculture would not be seen until the decade 1870–1880.

Professor Cochran's assertion that the Union Pacific, during its first decade, was a drain on the economy has been sharply challenged by Robert Fogel. Fogel not only analyzes the rate of return on the Union Pacific's cash expenditures; he also presents estimates of the line's "social return," that is, the increased national income due to the railroad but not reflected in the company's earnings. In both respects Professor Fogel finds the Union Pacific a success, returning an average of 11.6 per cent on its cash expenditures for the first decade of its operation, and an average social return of 29.9 per cent for the same period.[17] While it must be conceded that the social return statistics as yet mean little since we have few comparable figures for other railroads or other kinds of investments, it is only by this type of investigation that we will finally be able, through the aid of numbers, to shed light upon the question of the economic effect of the Civil War on the railroads.

Finally, however, we must face the inherent limits of statistics. Cochran's argument that the Civil War's contribution to the "spirit of capitalism" is difficult to measure is all too correct. Such actions as those of the Republican-appointed Supreme Court, which interpreted the Fourteenth Amendment to the Constitution to insure the sanctity of corporate property and to protect it from attacks by hostile state legislatures, are not subject to statistical measurement. Yet they vitally affected industrial development, at least the industrialism which characterized nineteenth-century America.

In summary, historians must not discard or avoid statistics; they can prove invaluable in drawing a clear picture of what happened. Numbers may even answer questions such as, was the Union Pacific a stimulant to economic growth? and if so how? and in what areas of the economy? Yet the broader question — did the Civil War accelerate industrialism by placing in undisputed power men of business? — is only partially susceptible to statistical analysis. We can gain insight into the impact of some measures (tariffs, aid to railroads, land distributed under the Homestead Act, etc.) through numerical data, yet historians must never fail to integrate such information with interpretations based upon nonstatistical social, political, and psychological analysis.

[17] Robert W. Fogel, *The Union Pacific Railroad, A Case in Premature Enterprise,* pp. 95–103.